A
DICTIONARY
OF
SUFFOLK CRESTS

Heraldic Crests of Suffolk Families

A
DICTIONARY
OF
SUFFOLK CRESTS

Heraldic Crests of Suffolk Families

by

JOAN CORDER, FSA

General Editor

JOHN BLATCHLY

The Boydell Press

Suffolk Records Society

VOLUME XL

Issued to subscribing members to celebrate
the Society's 40th year

1998

A Suffolk Records Society publication
First published 1998
The Boydell Press, Woodbridge

ISBN 0 85115 554 5

The Boydell Press is an imprint of Boydell & Brewer Ltd
PO Box 9, Woodbridge, Suffolk IP12 3DF, UK
and of Boydell & Brewer Inc.
PO Box 41026, Rochester NY 14604–4126, USA

A catalogue record for this book is available
from the British Library

This publication is printed on acid-free paper

Printed in Great Britain by
St Edmundsbury Press, Bury St Edmunds, Suffolk

CONTENTS

Wood engraved bookplate of John Gage Rokewood
showing crests of Rookwood and Gage. Designed by
Thomas Willement *c.*1840.

From
Sir Conrad Swan,
K.C.V.O., Ph.D., F.S.A.
Garter Principal King of Arms

College of Arms,
Queen Victoria Street,
London, EC4V, 4BT.,
Telephone: 0171.248.1188.

28th July 1995

One of the many good things about this country is surely the
existence of those cognoscenti who, though it is not part of their
profession or avocation, devote years to the study of a particular
subject without any desire or expectation of reward save the
satisfaction of adding to the explicit knowledge of the subject in
question.

One such scholar is Joan Corder, my – if I may coin such a
phrase – sister-Fellow of the Society of Antiquaries.

To her we are already indebted for the *Dictionary of Suffolk
Arms*, published by the Suffolk Records Society in 1965. This was
followed about a decade later by her Suffolk section in Peter
Summers' *Hatchments in Britain, 2, Norfolk and Suffolk* (1976).

Meanwhile, Miss Corder worked on the definitive edition of
William Hervy's Visitation of Suffolk 1561 which was ultimately
published by the Harleian Society in two volumes, dated 1981 and
1984.

Now we come to a companion volume to her *Dictionary of Suffolk
Arms* which will, I understand, be entitled *A Dictionary of Suffolk
Crests*. Such is, to my knowledge, unique in being an Ordinary of
Crests.

Although rooted in Suffolk, the work exhibits as well many
genealogical and heraldic connections between that county and its
neighbour, Norfolk.

The purpose of this work is to serve as a guide to the
identification of Crests when found alone. As is often the case,
such occur on armorial china, bookplates, signet rings, table
silver and the like. Their frequent incidence on such objects
probably helps to explain why to so many anything heraldic is 'a
Crest'.

A Dictionary of Suffolk Crests is a work of impeccable
scholarship as are all those from the same pen, and I anticipate
its forthcoming publication with something akin to impatience.

Conrad Swan
Garter

INTRODUCTION

An Ordinary is a collection of Arms or Crests arranged in such a manner that they may be readily identified when the name of the holder is unknown. The normal arrangement is alphabetical by name, an Armory; an Ordinary is an arrangement by charge or object, using certain standardised groupings. A combination of both is a Dictionary, hence my title.

WORKING METHOD

I do not know of any Ordinary of Crests, in manuscript or print, and therefore have been obliged to make an arrangement of my own, more difficult than an Ordinary of Arms as having no Rules of Blazon as its framework. The great variety of Crests has meant that each section has required different treatment and therefore the List of Headings varies considerably in arrangement and in the number of sub-sections necessary. I hope that the Headings, which I have tried to keep as simple as possible, will prove to be both understandable and easy to use; for this reason I have included a Glossary of heraldic terms, relating to the Headings only, as a help to those readers not well versed in such terms.

Demi-Beasts and Demi-Monsters always precede the whole creature, as Cubit-Arm precedes Arm.

Beasts and Monsters are placed in the attitude adopted, e.g. Rampant, Passant, Statant, etc., the active action decreasing until Dormant is reached. Within the attitude they may be Crowned, Gorged, Charged or Holding, the first three given alphabetically by name, but in Holding the arrangement depends on the object being held, also in alphabetical order.

It has not been possible to separate Birds by attitude, the position of the wings having proved too difficult to judge from the assorted and sometimes contradictory blazons. Crests may appear in several places, for instance Lion's Head may be given by one source without any further description (Unspecified), by another source as Couped and by a third as Erased, all variations easily traceable by reference to the Index of Names. Another reason for occasional multiple entry is where Crests, varying only slightly or even not at all, will be found more than once in the same section because, in attempting to quote sources in chronological order, I will have noted them possibly several centuries apart.

All spellings of names given in the Ordinary will be found in the Index of Names, however remote from the usual. Figures within round brackets after the name denote the number of entries in the column.

Editorial comment is contained within square brackets.

An asterisk (*) denotes an illustration of the Crest.

SOURCES

I have attempted to give the Sources in chronological order, but the fact that so many manuscripts are undated and un-named meant that precise dating was impossible; an approximate date, giving the average middle of a known compiler's working life has been taken where his dates or, more usually, date of death, are known, otherwise by the style and appearance of the manuscript itself. The earliest Sources I have quoted are *Stall Plates, 1348–1485* and *Wall's Book* and *Banners & Standards,* both of *c.* 1530.

Notes on the Sources

As with my *Dictionary of Suffolk Arms*, the work of David Elisha Davy is paramount, his *Armoury of Suffolk* forming the basis of both my compilations. His *Armoury*, the final copy dated 1848, three years before his death, is Vol. LXXXII of his Suffolk Collections, B.L. Add. MS 19,158. *Grants & Certificates,* reprinted from *The Genealogist* in 1913, proved to be an extremely valuable source of otherwise, to me, unknown official Grants, Confirmations and Exemplifications, some of which I included (although of another part of the Country when the Grant was made) if agreeing in name or arms with those borne in Suffolk at some period.

The published collections of Crests by *Washbourne* (1851) and *Fairbairn* (1905) have been quoted only where the crest is given as 'of Suffolk'; with a few exceptions in the cases of an example given by either corroborating a rare or 'difficult' crest. The illustrations to both these works are intended to serve a number of blazons, some of which approximate only to the engraving; therefore my reference asterisk (*) appears only where blazon and illustration agree.

Burke's Peerage and *Burke's Landed Gentry* have not been exhaustively searched or quoted as copies of the many editions of each work are readily available in reference libraries.

The *Heraldry of Suffolk Churches* (*Her.Suff.Ch.*) comprises a series of fifty booklets of great value in that the heraldry existing at the present time is recorded. It must be borne in mind, however, that many artefacts such as ledger stones, churchyard and also interior monuments are uncoloured, the tinctures given, which I have duly quoted, being taken largely from the work of the Revd Edmund Farrer.

The *Topographers of Suffolk* is a work invaluable for dates, biographies and references relating to many compilers of Suffolk manuscripts and printed sources used in this book and is always worth consulting for further information.

The *Corder Collection* is my gathering, over some fifty years, of Heraldic Manuscripts, Church Notes, Pedigree Rolls, Grants of Arms, Estate Maps, etc., relating to East Anglia. So far gathered, they number 95, and were catalogued by John Blatchly in 1993 (his first task on retiring from the Headmastership of Ipswich School). It is my wish and hope that this Collection will eventually be housed in Suffolk Record Office at Ipswich, where it will be available for study and use by future lovers of the heraldry of Suffolk.

ACKNOWLEDGEMENTS

For almost forty years I received great encouragement, in any work I undertook, from the late Sir Anthony Wagner, Garter Principal King of Arms 1961–78, later Clarenceux King of Arms. Despite his tragic blindness, he liked to be sent occasional reports on the progress of this book, the last one written to Aldeburgh in late December, a few months before his death on 5th May 1995 at the age of 86.

Sir Conrad Swan, Garter King of Arms from 1992–96, also lives in Suffolk and has been most encouraging. I am most grateful to him for the Foreword he wrote when first he learnt of the project.

Robert Yorke, Archivist of the College of Arms kindly assisted my attempts to identify the compiler of the *MS Alphabet of Crests*.

I deeply appreciate the constant encouragement and interest shown by John Blatchly. Since I undertook this task in 1988, his evident wish for another working tool frequently acted as a goad when the end appeared infinitely remote and terminal lassitude threatened to set in.

Just as the Marc Fitch Fund Trustees made a grant in aid of my 1965 *Dictionary*, so their successors on the Council of Management have generously assisted with funds for this companion volume. I am most grateful to them, and to all at The Boydell Press who have worked on the book's production. I realise how very difficult the typesetter must have found the Ordinary and record my admiration for his accuracy.

Joan Corder
November 1997

GLOSSARY OF HERALDIC TERMS RELATING TO THE LIST OF HEADINGS ONLY

At Gaze — Said of a deer statant guardant

Basilisk — A monster resembling a Cockatrice but with a Dragon-like head at the end of the tail

Cabossed — Beast's head full-faced and without any part of the neck showing

Centaur — A creature having the body and legs of a horse but with a man's trunk, arms and head

Charged — Bearing one or more small charges

Cockatrice — A monster with a cock's head, two legs and a Dragon's tail and wings

Couchant — Lying down with the head raised

Couped — Cut off cleanly

Courant — Running

Cubit — An arm and hand couped below the elbow

Demi — The upper half of a beast, bird, monster, etc.

Dormant — Sleeping. Couchant with head down and eyes closed

Dragon — A scaly monster with four legs, bat-like wings and eagle's claws, the tongue and tail barbed

Ducal Coronet — Coronet or Crown of three strawberry leaves, now usually termed a Crest Coronet. No indication of rank

Erased — Torn off roughly leaving a ragged edge

Gorged — Collared

Griffin — A monster with the hind parts of a lion and the head, breast, claws and wings of an eagle; also has ears and sometimes a short beard. When Rampant it is termed Segreant

Guardant — Full-faced

Harpy — A monster with the body of a vulture and the bust and head of a woman

Heraldic Antelope — A monster with the body of an antelope but with an Heraldic Tiger's face, tusks, two serrated horns, tufts down the spine and a lion's tail

Heraldic Tiger — A monster quite unlike the natural tiger, having an unstriped lion's body, tufts, pointed ears, tusks and a beak at the end of the nose

Ibex — A monster drawn like the Heraldic Antelope except that the horns, usually serrated, point forwards rather than curve backwards

Issuant — Emerging or proceeding from

Lion Dragon — A monster having the foreparts of a lion and the hind parts of a Dragon

Lodged — Said of a deer when couchant

Mural Coronet — A Coronet or Crown in the form of an embattled wall

Pantheon — A monster with a body and head like that of a hind, cloven hoofs and a bushy tail, the body powdered with stars or mullets. Somewhat resembles the Theow

Panther — Quite unlike the natural panther, the Heraldic Panther is shown with flames issuing from mouth and ears and is usually spattered with roundels or spots of various tinctures

Passant — Walking with the dexter fore-leg raised

Pegasus — Winged horse

Phoenix — A demi-eagle issuant from flames

Rampant — Beast or Monster standing on one hind leg with the forelegs raised

Reguardant — Looking backwards over the shoulder

Salamander — A lizard-like reptile surrounded by flames

Salient — Beasts or Monsters jumping, leaping or rearing; shown with both hind legs on the ground and the forelegs level with each other

Sea Coney — A monster like a rabbit with a dorsal fin and webbed feet, sometimes scaled

Sea Dog A monster like a Talbot with webbed feet, scales, a dorsal fin and a rudder like an otter

Sea Horse A monster like the fore-part of a horse with a dorsal fin and webbed feet joined to the lower part of a fish the tail nowed

Sea Lion A monster with the upper part of a lion with a dorsal fin and webbed feet joined to the lower part of a fish with tail nowed

Sea Unicorn A monster similar to the Sea Horse but with the long twisted horn of the Unicorn

Segreant Rampant when used of Griffins

Sejant Sitting erect with fore-paws on the ground

Serpent Woman A monster with a woman's head full-faced and the body of a serpent nowed

Sphinx A monster with the bust of a woman, the head in an Egyptian head-dress, and a lion's body couchant

Springing Salient when used of Deer

Statant Standing with all four feet on the ground

Talbot The medieval hunting dog, with a mastiff's body, hound's head and long drooping ears

Theow A monster resembling the Pantheon but with a short-legged wolf-like body, sometimes charged with roundels, a long tail and cloven hoofs. Shown with a collar and chain

Trippant Passant when used of Deer

Triton A monster shown as the bust of a man with a dolphin's tail, usually holding a twisted sea shell

Unicorn A monster drawn as a horse with a single long twisted horn, lion's tail and the legs and cloven hoofs of a stag

Vested Clothed or habited

Volant Flying

Woodwose Wild man of the woods, usually bearded and largely covered in long green hair

Wyvern A monster shown as a Dragon in every respect except that in place of hindquarters it has a barbed serpent's tail

LIST OF HEADINGS

xiv

ACORN see FRUIT

ANCHOR
An anchor.
> EBDEN, of Ipswich, Haughley. *Davy, A.*
> GRAY, Charles W., of Deerbolt Hall, Earl
> Stonham, died 1920; widow died 1925.
> *Her.Suff.Ch., Altar tomb, Earl Stonham*

In the sea Vert an anchor Or.
> UFFORD. *Davy, A.*

In the sea an anchor in pale ensigned by a dove
holding in its beak an olive branch.
> NEWENHAM, of Suffolk. *Davy, A.*

A dolphin Argent entwined round an anchor erect
Sable.
> FRANKLAND, FRANKLYN, FRANCKLYN, of Beccles,
> Suffolk. *Visitation 1664–8. Bokenham. Davy, A.*
> *Washbourne*. Fairbairn**

An anchor and cable Sable and a sword Azure hilted
Or in saltire.
> FITZURSE, FITZOURSE. *Davy, A.*

An anchor Azure between two wings Or.
> HIGGAT, 'Suff.' *Fairbairn**

ANGEL
A demi-angel holding in the dexter hand a griffin's
head erased.
> BLOSS, BLOSSE, of Ipswich, Stowmarket.
> *Davy, A. Washbourne. Fairbairn*. Her.Suff.Ch.,*
> *formerly on Tablet, Stowmarket*

St. Michael the Arch-angel in armour holding a
spear in his dexter hand his face neck arms and legs
bare all Proper the wings Argent and hair auburn.
> MITCHALL-CARRUTHERS, Rev. W., The Rectory,
> Holbrook. *Fairbairn**. [Second crest, first crest
> see CARRUTHERS]

An angel Proper vested Argent holding in the dexter
hand a sword the blade Proper hilt and pommel Or.
> CANDLER, 'Suff., Norf. and Worc.'
> *Washbourne**

ANNULET
An annulet Or interlaced with two cross crosslets
fitchy Sable in saltire.
> RUSTAT, Tobias, Esq., Yeoman of the Robes to
> His Majesty; Grant by W. Dugdale, Norroy,
> 30 December 1676. *Grants & Certificates (Add.*
> *MS 14,830)*

ANNULETS
Three annulets conjoined Or.
> EVERARD, of Hawkedon. *Davy, A. Fairbairn**

Three octangular annulets interlaced Or.
> EVERARD, of Hawkedon. *Bokenham (p.Camden,*
> *1624). Visitation 1664–8*. Davy, A.*

ARM NO COVERING SPECIFIED

CUBIT ARM, holding:
A man's hand and arm couped at the elbow
supporting a hawk.
> RAMSEY, of 'Kenton Hall, Suff.' *Fairbairn*

An arm couped at the wrist and erect holding in the
hand a fish as in the arms [*sic* Or and Gules].
> SOLLEY, Rev. B., Rector of Barsham, died 1714.
> *Her.Suff.Ch., Ledger stone, Barsham*

An arm couped at the elbow the hand holding three
ears of Guinea wheat.
> THOMPSON. *MS Martin's Crests*

An arm erect in the hand a bugle horn.
> FOSTER, Samuel, D.D., died 1680. *E.A.N. & Q.*
> *I. 105, Redgrave Ch. Stone*

A hand and arm erect holding a mullet of six points.
> SCOTTOWE, of Yoxford, Somerleyton. *Davy, A.*

A left hand couped at the elbow holding an oak slip
Proper.
> SMYTHIAS. *Bokenham*

An arm couped at the elbow holding in the hand a
globe or sphere.
> FIELD. *MS Martin's Crests*

A dexter arm erect holding in the hand a sword
Argent hilted Or.
> ENSOR, of Exning, Ipswich. *Davy, A.*

An arm erect holding in the hand Proper a broken
sword Proper hilt and pommel Or.
> REVETT, RYVETT, 'of Cambs. and Crettinge,
> Suff.' *Fairbairn*

A cubit arm Argent holding in the hand Proper a
broken sword blade Argent hilt and pommel Or.
> RICHARDSON, of Hadleigh. *Davy, A.*

ARM
An arm couped at the shoulder Azure.
> GODBOLD, William, died 1687. *Davy, A.*
> *Her.Suff.Ch., Wall tablet, Mendham*

ARM, holding:
'to his crest an Arme sa/ holding an anker or/'
> MALYN. 'to Willm Malyn son of henry Malyn of
> Staplehurst in Kent and M^r of Arts.' *MS*
> *Alphabet of Crests, fo. 84*

An arm embowed couped at the shoulder Sable
holding in the hand an annulet or ring (anchor).
> MALYN, of Occold. John, Clerk, died 1728, Rev.
> Robert, died 1736, Rev. Robert, died 1820.
> *Her.Suff.Ch., Ledger stones, Occold*

An arm embowed holding in the hand an arrow.
> GODBOLD, John, of Terling Hall in Essex, died
> 1737. *Her.Suff.Ch., Slab, All Saints Sudbury*

An arm holding a battle-axe.
> REVETT, RYVETT, of Stowmarket, Cambs. *Davy,*
> *A. Washbourne. Fairbairn*

A dexter arm embowed holding in the hand an oak
branch Proper.
> WEBBE alias WOOD, of Elmswell, Bury. *Davy,*
> *A., Elmswell church and St. Mary's Bury*

Issuing out of a cloud Argent and Azure an arm
fessewise Proper holding in the hand a bunch of
seven feathers alternately Gules and Argent.
> BLACKNELL, BLACKNOLL, BLAKENHALL. *MS*
> *Heraldic Collections, fo. 58*. Washbourne* 'six*
> *feathers Argent and Gules'*

A hand and arm Argent holding a dragon's head
erased Vert.
> SAYER, SAWYER, of co. Essex. *MS Fairfax (Tyl.)*

An arm grasping in the hand a lance.
> WOODROFFE. *Davy, A.*

An arm reflectant the hand holding a peel Sable
thereon three manchets Argent.
> PISTER. *MS Martin's Crests*

A dexter arm issuing from clouds fesseways holding
in the hand a sphere.
> FIELD, of Sutton. *Davy, A.(M^r. B.)*

A dexter arm embowed throwing a dart Proper.
> MONTALT, of Framsden. *Davy, A.*

A sinister arm embowed grasping a dagger.
> SCHREIBER, John, died 1968. *Her.Suff.Ch.,*
> *Window, Marlesford*

An arm from the shoulder holding in the hand a
dagger Proper.
> INNES, Bart. *Davy, A.*

An arm embowed grasping in the hand a falchion.
> JACOB, of Laxfield. *Green Memoir, 63, Ch.slab*

A dexter arm embowed holding in the hand a
scimitar.
> JACOB, of Laxfield. *Davy, A., Church*

ARM ARMOURED

CUBIT ARM, holding: [Objects in alphabetical order]

A cubit arm in armour erect Argent holding in the hand Proper a battle-axe.
    ATWOOD, of Aspal, Mendlesham, Ipswich. *Davy, A. Fairbairn*

From leaves Vert a cubit arm in armour Proper the gauntlet grasping a battleaxe staff Gules headed Argent the arm tied round with a scarf of the second [*sic*].
    WORLICHE, Charles, of Cowling, co. Suffolk; Confirmation by R. Cooke, Clar. *Grants & Certificates (Harl. MS 1,359)*

A cubit arm in armour holding in the hand a branch of oak fructed Proper.
    MORRISON, of Seckford Hall. *Davy, A.*

An armed hand and arm Proper holding a fleur-de-lis Argent.
    BLOYSE, Bart., of Grundisburgh. *Sharpe*

An armed arm couped at the elbow and erect Proper holding in the gauntlet a fleur-de-lis Sable.
    RAMSDEN, John, of Longley, co. Yorks.; Grant by W. Flower, Norroy. *Grants & Certificates (Stowe MS 706).* Ramsden, Rector of Grundisburgh. *Davy, A.*

A cubit arm in armour erect issuing from clouds Proper holding in the gauntlet a marigold, a rose and a pomegranate all Proper and environed with a ducal coronet Or.
    ROCHESTER, of Eriswell. *Davy, A.* Without clouds; 'Sr. Robert Rochester', *MS Knight's Visitations, Essex*. MS Philpot's Visitations, Essex**

A cubit arm in armour Proper charged with two crosses paty fitchy in pale Azure holding in the hand Proper a grenade Sable fired Proper.
    GUTHRIE, Sir Connop, Bart., of Brent Eleigh Hall, died 1945. *Her.Suff.Ch., Wall tablet, Brent Eleigh*

An arm in armour couped at the elbow holding in the hand a fire-ball all Proper.
    BOYCOTT, of Eye. *Davy, A.*

A cubit arm erect mailed Azure tied about the wrist with a riband ends flotant Or [or Or and Gules] holding in the hand Proper a dragon's head erased Vert.
    SAYER, George, of Colchester. *MS Knight's Visitations, Essex*. MS Philpot's Visitations, Essex**

A dexter arm in armour couped above the wrist Proper holding a broken lance and a laurel Proper.
    CHAPMAN. *MS Heraldic Alphabet*

A cubit arm erect in mail in the hand a pistol all Proper.
    WALLE, Thomas, son of Thomas, of Stonepitt, co. Kent; Patent 1591. *Grants & Certificates (Stowe MS 670)*

A cubit arm erect in armour Proper holding in the gauntlet a spear Proper headed Argent embrued Gules.
    JONES, Rector of Huntingfield, lands in Westhall. *Davy, A., Huntingfield church*

A cubit arm in mail garnished Or holding in the gauntlet of plate Argent two halves of a broken tilting spear Sable the spear end erect the butt end in sinister bend.
    GISLINGHAM. 'William Gislingham and Wynfred Chambers his Wiffe'. *MS Knight's Visitations, Suff.* * MS Philpot's Visitations, Norf.**

A cubit arm in armour fesseways issuing from a cloud all Proper the hand grasping by its stand a terrestrial globe Or.
    FIELD, John, Gent., of Ardesloe, co. Yorks.; Confirmation of Arms and Grant of Crest by W. Hervey, Clar., 4 September 1558. *Grants & Certificates (Add. MS 14,295.; Harl. MS 1,359) Bookplate**

An arm in armour couped at the elbow holding in the hand a broken sword Proper.
    CHUTE. *MS Martin's Crests*

A mailed arm couped at the elbow in fesse holding a sword Argent erect transfixing a boar's head couped Or.
    CRADOCK, Sir Edmund Cradock Hartopp, Bart., of Wissett. *Her.Suff.Ch., formerly in window, Wissett*

An arm in armour erect Proper holding a sword Argent hilt Or.
    INNES, Bart., of Ipswich. *Davy, A. Hatchment, St. Matthews. Proc.S.I.A. VII. 203*

A cubit arm erect in armour the gauntlet brandishing a sword all Proper garnished Or.
    MANBY, William, Gent., of London. *Grants & Certificates (Add. MS 4,966)*

A cubit dexter arm in armour erect Sable couped and cuffed Argent grasping in the hand Proper a broken sword Azure hilt and pommel Or.
    REVETT, of Brandeston, 1616–1745. *Her.Suff.Ch., Monument, Tablet, Slabs, carved desk, Plate, Brandeston*

An arm couped at the elbow in armour and holding a sword erect.
    REVETT, Nicholas, died 1804. *Partridge, 128 (Darby, 1825)*

A cubit arm in armour holding in the hand a dagger all Proper the upper arm charged with a cross paty Or.
    WHITE, Nina Emily, died 1940. *Her.Suff.Ch., Glass, Chelmondiston*

A cubit arm in armour erect holding in the gauntlet a dagger.
    VANE. *Bookplate**.

A cubit arm erect in armour Azure the gauntlet Argent holding by the blade Argent a sabre or falchion hilted Or.
    BEDLE, of Wolverstone. *London Visitation 1633–4 (H.S.) I. 61**

A dexter arm in armour erased at the elbow lying fesseways holding in the hand a scimitar erect enfiled with a boar's head couped all Proper.
    HOW, HOWE, Lord Chedworth, of Ipswich. *Proc.S.I.A. VII. 204, Hatchment, St. Matthews*

ARM

An arm in armour couped at the shoulder embowed fesseways the hand bare all Proper.
    ARMSTRONG. *MS Ordinary of Arms, fo. 13**

A dexter arm vambraced in armour the hand Proper.
    ARMSTRONG, of Melton. *Davy, A.*

ARM, holding: [Objects in alphabetical order]

An arm embowed in armour garnished Or holding in the hand an anchor all Proper.
    CROKER, of Battisford. *Davy, A.*

An arm in armour embowed Proper holding in the hand Proper an arrow point downwards Or feathered and barbed Argent.
    CLARKE. *MS Ordinary of Arms, fo. 207**

An arm in armour the hand holding an arrow.
    CLARKE. *MS Martin's Crests*

An arm in armour holding an arrow fesseways Proper.

CUBITT, of Fritton House, Lowestoft, Bucklesham. *Crisp's Visitation, XVII. 26 and XVIII. 33*

A dexter arm in armour embowed Sable garnished Or holding in the hand an arrow Or.

DAWSON, of Gt. Waldingfield. *Davy, A., church*

An arm embowed in chain mail Proper tied about the wrist with a scarf Gules in the hand Proper an arrow Argent head and feathers Or.

DOWNING, Roger, of Lopham, co. Norf.; Grant by R. Cooke, Clar., 14 August 1576. *Grants & Certificates (Stowe 700)*

An arm embowed habited in mail Proper tied round the wrist with a riband Or [or Or and Vert] holding in the hand an arrow Argent barbed and flighted Or.

DONNYNGE, DOWNING, DOWNYNG, of co. Norfolk. 'Arthur donnynge', *MS Knight's Visitations, Norf.*. *Muskett. I. 96*

An arm embowed armed [mantique?] Proper [eschafroned?] towards the sinister Vert holding in the hand a broad arrow Argent plumed and pointed Or.

DOWNING. *MS Heraldic Alphabet*

An arm embowed armed á [beautique?] Proper [eschaped?] towards the sinister Vert holding in the hand a broad arrow Argent plumed and pointed Or.

DOWNING, Bart., of Dunwich. *Davy, A.*

An arm in armour embowed holding in the hand an arrow point downwards.

FOWKE, Sir Sydenham, Kt., died 1743; widow died 1752. *Suff. Green Bks., West Stow.* Fowke, Elizabeth, wife of William F., died 1820. *Her.Suff.Ch., Altar tomb, churchyard, Chelsworth*

An arm in armour Proper [or Argent] wreathed about Or and Azure with the ends flotant holding in the gauntlet an arrow Sable feathered and headed Argent.

GODBOLD, of Mendham, Westhall, Sudbury, Bury. *Visitation 1664–8. Davy, A., Mendham church. Washbourne*, 'Ess. and Suff.' Fairbairn, 'of Westhall, Suff. and Hatfield, Essex'*

A dexter arm in armour embowed holding in the hand Proper an arrow.

SHEPPARD. *Davy, A., Wetheringsett church*

A dexter arm couped at the shoulder embowed in armour grasping in the hand an arrow shaft to the sinister.

SHEPPARD, John, Clerk, died 1689. *Her.Suff.Ch., Ledger stone, Wetheringsett cum Brockford*

A mailed arm embowed Proper the hand grasping an arrow Or.

SMYTH, of Stoke Hall in Sproughton. *E.A.N. & Q. XIII. 140., Monument, Sproughton*

An arm embowed in armour Proper supporting a battle-axe.

ARGALL. *Davy, A.*

An arm in armour embowed holding in the hand a battle-axe Proper.

FERRAND, of Tunstall. *Davy, A.*

An arm in armour embowed Proper holding in the hand Proper a battle-axe Sable.

GIBBS. *MS Ordinary of Arms, fo. 240**

An arm in armour embowed Proper holding a battle-axe Argent.

GIBBS, of Stoke by Nayland. *Bokenham. Davy, A.*

An arm embowed in armour Proper garnished Or the gauntlet grasping a battle-axe the staff Gules bands and knob Or headed Proper.

LEWSON, John, of Wolverhampton, co. Staff.; Confirmation by L. Dalton, Norroy, 26 November 1591; Crest Granted by Sir C. Barker, Garter. *Grants & Certificates (Harl. MS 1,359; Stowe MS 692)*

An arm in armour flecting inwards Proper holding in the hand Proper a battle-axe staff Gules knobbed at the end.

LEVESON. *MS Heraldic Alphabet*

An arm embowed in armour Proper garnished Or holding in the gauntlet a battle-axe handle Gules blade Argent.

LUSON, Samuel, son of Robert L., of Blundeston, died 1766. *Her.Suff.Ch., Wall tablet, Blundeston*

An arm in armour embowed Proper the gauntlet grasping a battle-axe staff Sable headed Argent around the wrist a scarf Or.

QUILTER, William, of Staple, co. Kent., Grant by Sir G. Dethick, Garter. *Grants & Certificates (Add. MS 26, 753)*

An arm in armour embowed the gauntlet grasping a battle-axe all Proper the fore arm tied about with a scarf Argent and Sable.

QUILTER, William, of Staple, co. Kent; Confirmation by Sir G. Dethick, Garter, 12 June 1552. *Grants & Certificates (Harl. MS 1,441; Stowe MS 703)*

An arm in armour embowed Proper garnished Or holding in the hand Proper a battle-axe.

QUILTER. *MS Ordinary of Arms, fos. 168* and 186**

An arm in armour embowed holding a battle-axe all Proper a scarf round the wrist Argent.

QUILTER, of Walton. *Davy, A.*

In front of a dexter arm embowed in armour Proper garnished Or the hand in a gauntlet Proper grasping a battle-axe handle Sable headed Argent around the arm a scarf Argent, a Cornish chough Proper.

QUILTER, Sir William, Bart., died 1911. Son Roger Quilter, composer, died 1953. *Her.Suff.Ch., Altar tomb, churchyard, Bawdsey. Photograph*

A dexter arm embowed and vambraced holding in the hand a battle-axe.

WICKS, George, died 1761; widow Aldez, died 1774. *Her.Suff.Ch., Ledger stone, Thurston*

An arm embowed in armour couped at the shoulder erect from the elbow holding in the hand all Proper a battle-axe Or.

WOLRICH, WORLICH, of Cowlinge. *Visitation 1577. Bokenham*

An arm embowed in armour Argent garnished Or holding in the hand Argent a battle-axe Or.

WORLICH. *MS Knight's Visitations, Suff.** 'Charles woorlyche' *MS Philpot's Visitations, Suff.**

A dexter arm in armour erect Argent garnished Or out of a wreath Vert bound with a ribbon in the centre of the arm Sable holding in the gauntlet a battle-axe Argent handle Gules garnished Or.

WORLICHE, of Cowlinge. *Davy, A.*

An arm embowed in armour Proper erect from the elbow Argent studded Or [*sic*] holding in the hand Proper a battle-axe Or.

WORKLYCH, WORLICHE. *Davy, A. Washbourne*, 'Worklych, Suss. and Suff. Armour and hand Proper'*

A sinister arm in armour embowed Proper garnished Or holding in the hand Proper a baton Or.

BATE, BATES. *MS Ordinary of Arms, fo. 11**

An arm in armour Proper holding a crossbow with

arrows Gules headed Argent.

CUDDON, of Shadingfield, Weston, Dunwich, Wyverstone, Halesworth. *Visitation 1664–8*. Davy, A. Burke L.G. 1952 ed.**

An arm embowed in armour the hand grasping a bow strung and fully bent in fesse the arrow in pale point upwards Proper.

CUDDON. *Fairbairn*, 'Norf. and Suff.'*

An arm embowed in armour Proper garnished Or the gauntlet grasping a branch of palm Vert.

WATSON, Jonathan, of St. James', Westminster; Confirmation by John Anstis, Garter and John Vanbrugh, Clar., 16 December 1720. *Grants & Certificates (Add. MS 14,830)*

An arm embowed in armour Proper garnished Or holding in the gauntlet a palm branch Vert.

WATSON, of Rendlesham, Ringshall, Woodbridge. *Sharpe. Davy, A.* Watson, Christopher, Rector of Melton, died 1870, and others. *Her.Suff.Ch., Wall tablet, Melton*

A dexter arm in armour embowed Argent garnished Or resting the hand Proper on the capital of a pillar Or and grasping a chaplet Vert.

COO, of Groton. *MS Knight's Visitations, Suff.*, the hand in a gauntlet. MS Heraldic Collections, fo. 60**

A dexter arm in armour garnished Or resting the elbow on a pillar Argent capital Or and holding in the hand a chaplet Vert.

COO, of Boxford, Groton. *Davy, A. Coe, 'Supported by a pilaster Or'*

A dexter arm in armour Proper [or Argent] garnished Or holding in the hand Proper a chaplet Vert.

SMITH, of Cratfield; Granted by Richard St. George, Clar., 9 July 1663. *Visitation 1664–8*. Bokenham. Davy, A. Washbourne., 'Suff.' Fairbairn, 'Suff.'* Smith, Penelope, wife of John S., of Cratfield, died 1681. *Her.Suff.Ch., Ledger stone, Mendham*

An arm in armour Proper couped at the shoulder holding a chaplet Vert.

SMITH, of Cratfield. *Davy, A.*

A dexter arm embowed habited in mail holding in the hand all Proper a spiked club Or.

BATHURST, Rector of Hollesley. *Davy, A.*

An arm in armour embowed Proper bound with a shoulder ribbon Gules holding in the hand a club Proper.

COVILL, of Parham. *Davy, A.*

An arm in armour embowed Proper the gauntlet grasping a horseman's mace Or headed Argent.

SINGLETON, Edward, son of Thomas S., of Broughton Tower, co. Lanc.; Grant by L. Dalton, Norroy, 20 May 1560. *Grants & Certificates (Harl. MS 1,359)*

An arm in armour holding in the hand a cross crosslet fitchy.

ALDRED, of North Cove. *Davy, A., church*

A dexter arm embowed in armour Or holding a cross formy fitchy Argent.

MAPLESDEN, 'Joh'es, Archdeacon of Suffolk & Norfolk'. *Kent Visitation 1619 (H.S.), 156*

An arm in armour Proper garnished Or couped at the shoulder lying fesseways on the wreath the hand erect from the elbow Proper holding a covered cup Or.

ODLARD, HODIERNE, of Oulton, Sibton, Yoxford. *Davy, A.*

A dexter arm embowed in armour Sable garnished Or holding in the hand Proper an escallop.

RAW, of Rishangles. *Davy, A.*

An arm in armour holding in the hand a firebrand.

BRAND. *Partridge, 203 (Darby, 1830), Wherstead churchyard*

Two snakes coiled Vert from the centre of them an arm in armour embowed Proper holding in the hand a brand fired at both ends Proper.

BRAND, of Wherstead, Hemingstone, Woodbridge. *Davy, A.*

In front of a dexter arm embowed in armour couped at the shoulder and fessewise Sable holding in the gauntlet a flagstaff Proper therefrom flowing to the sinister a banner Argent charged with a lyre Sable, three escallops fessewise Or.

TACON. 'Charles Tacon, Eye, Suff.' *Fairbairn, 'arm in armour Or gauntletted Sa.' Burke, L.G. 1900 and 1952 eds.,* 'of Red House in Eye, Lowestoft'*

An arm couped at the shoulder embowed armed with mail Proper holding in the hand Proper four ears of wheat Or stalked Vert [or Proper].

RISBY, RYSBY, of Lavenham, Thorpe Morieux. *MS Knight's Visitations, Suff.* 'Wyll Risbye' MS Philpot's Visitations, Suff.* Bokenham. Muskett. I. 66 (Harl. MS 1820)*

An arm couped at the shoulder embowed in armour Proper holding in the hand Proper four ears of wheat Or stalked Vert.

RISBY, of Lavenham, Thorpe Morieux. *Davy, A.*

A dexter arm in armour Proper [or Argent] garnished Or holding in the hand a gauntlet Proper [or Argent].

GROME, GROOM, GROOME, of Ufford, Rattlesden, Bergholt, Bury, Lavenham, Aldeburgh, Earl Soham. *Visitation 1577. MS Knight's Visitations, Suff.*. MS Philpot's Visitations, Suff.*. Visitation 1664–8. Bokenham. Davy, A., Ufford church. Washbourne, 'Suff.' Fairbairn, 'Grome, Suff.'* Groome, Rev. John, Rector of Earl and Monk Soham for 26 years, died 1845. *Her.Suff.Ch., Wall tablet, Earl Soham*

An arm in armour Proper garnished Or holding in the hand Proper a gem ring Or.

VYNER, VYNOR, of Ilketshall St. Lawrence. *Davy, A.*

An arm in armour embowed gauntletted Or holding a leopard's head Or.

PAYNE, of Hengrave, Stoke by Nayland. *Davy, A. Washbourne, 'Suff.' Fairbairn, 'of Stoke Neyland [sic], Suff. All Or.'*

An arm in armour embowed Proper the gauntlet grasping a lion's head erased Or.

PAYNE, John, of Stoke-next-Nayland, co. Suffolk, son and heir of John Payne of the same place; Confirmation of Arms and Grant of Crest by Sir W. Segar, Garter, 23 July, 13 Jas.1. [1615/6]. *Grants & Certificates (Harl. MS 1,172; Add. MS 12,225)*

An arm in armour Proper garnished Or the gauntlet grasping by the hair a man's head couped Proper.

RUSHE, Sir Francis, of Essex; Grant January 1605. *Grants & Certificate (Stowe MSS 706 and 707; Harl. MS 6,059)*

A dexter arm in armour Argent garnished Or holding in the hand by the hair a man's head affronty Proper dropping blood.

RUSH, of Chapman's in Sudbourne. *Davy, A.*

A dexter arm embowed in armour Proper garnished Or entwined by a branch of oak Vert and charged with two Catherine wheels in pale Gules the hand grasping a dragon's head erased Proper.

HARDY, GATHORNE - HARDY, Viscount Cranbrook. *Burke, Peerage, 1891 ed.* Her.Suff.Ch., Wall brass 1915, Great Glemham.* [Second crest see GATHORNE]
A dexter arm in armour embowed Proper garnished Or the hand grasping a griffin's head erased Or.
SAWYER, Mary, widow of John Sawyer, died 1734. *Her.Suff.Ch., Floor slab (now covered by choir stalls), Brent Eleigh*
An arm armed holding a horse-shoe.
SMYTH, of Cratfield. *Bokenham*
'Et pour son Tymbre sur un torce de se couleurs, un bras, et main dextre, armèe, avançant une Lance en charge rompu'.
HILL, James, Commander of Cavalry, from co. Suffolk; Exemplification of Arms and Crest by Sir William Segar, Garter, 2 September 16 James I., 1618. *Miscellaneous Grants (H.S.), I. 108–9 (MS Ashm. 840, 415, in Ashmole's hand)*
An arm flecting inwards armed Proper wreathed about the lower part of the arm and knotted Argent and Sable holding in the gauntlet the lower part of a lance erect and resting on the wreath the top rompu Or.
MICHELL. *MS Heraldic Alphabet*
An arm embowed in armour quarterly Or and Azure the gauntlet Proper holding a broken lance Or.
THOMPSON, of Brandon, Southwold. *Davy, A., Southwold church. Fairbairn*, 'Durham, London, Suff. & Yorks.'* Thompson, George, died 1711. *Her.Suff.Ch., Wall tablet, Hinderclay*
An arm in armour Proper holding in the hand a bunch of burdock leaves Vert.
BURWELL, of Badingham, Rougham. *Davy, A.*
A dexter arm in armour embowed holding in the hand (or gauntlet) a man's leg erased at the middle thigh Proper.
PRIME, of Suffolk *MS Heraldic Alphabet*
An arm in pale armed Sable holding in the gauntlet Argent by the haft a 'malet of the arme'.
GYBSON. *Wall's Book*
'to his Crest an Arme in pale armed sa/ the gauntlet ar/ holding in the hand a mallet of the arme by the haft.'
GYBSON. *MS Alphabet of Crests, fo. 47*
An arm embowed in armour garnished Or holding in the hand Proper a maul or beetle [a mallet] Sable handled Argent.
GIBSON. *Davy, A.*
An arm in armour couped at the shoulder Proper holding in the hand a portcullis Or lined at the top.
FIREBRACE. *MS Martin's Crests*
A dexter arm in armour Proper supporting by the hand a portcullis chained Or.
FIREBRACE, Bart., of Long Melford. *Davy, A.*
A dexter arm in armour embowed Proper garnished Or about the the elbow a wreath of oak Vert and in the hand a roll of paper Proper.
BICKERSTETH, Rector of Acton, 1811–37. *Davy, A.*
An arm in armour flecting inwards holding in the hand Proper a sceptre with a star Or.
SINGLETON. *MS Heraldic Alphabet*
An arm in armour embowed Proper the hand grasping a sceptre Or on the top an entoile Or.
SINGLETON. *Fairbairn *, 'of Lancs. and of Dykelborough and Mendlesham, Norf. [sic]*
A mailed dexter arm couped the hand brandishing a spear.
BRAND. *E.A.N. & Q. XIII. 149, Tomb, Wherstead church*

A dexter arm in armour embowed holding in the hand the lower part of a broken tilting spear.
BROOKS, Francis, MD., St. Felix, Felixstowe. *Fairbairn*
A sinister arm in armour embowed Proper garnished Or holding in the gauntlet a tilting spear Or.
BROWNE, of Benhall, Framlingham, Marlesford. *Davy, A.*
A dexter arm embowed in armour holding a broken tilting spear environed with a chaplet of laurel all Proper.
CHAPMAN, Bart., of Loudham Hall, Horringer, Sibton. *Sharpe. Davy, A.*
An arm embowed habited in mail Proper cuffed Argent holding in the hand Proper a broken tilting spear Or enfiled with a chaplet Vert.
CHAPMAN alias BARKER. 'Sir Edmund Barker, Kt., lord of the Manor of Peasonhall, died 1676.' *Her.Suff.Ch., Monument and Ledger stones, Sibton*
An arm in armour holding in the hand a broken spear Proper. *MS Martin's Crests*
DOWNING.
A dexter arm in armour Proper garnished Or holding in the gauntlet the two parts of a broken spear Sable.
FELTHAM, of Mutford, Halesworth. *Davy, A.*
An arm embowed in armour Proper holding in the hand a broken spear point downwards Argent.
GILBERT, of Bury. *Davy, A.*
An arm in armour embowed Proper holding in the hand Sable two halves of a broken tilting spear Argent the spear end erect and the butt end in sinister bend.
GISLINGHAM, of Stuston. *Visitation 1577*
A dexter arm in armour embowed Argent garnished Or holding in the hand the two parts of a broken spear Sable headed Argent.
GISLINGHAM, of Gislingham, Stuston, Eye. *Davy, A.*
An arm armed grasping a broken spear Proper
KING, of Melford. *Bokenham*
A dexter arm in armour embowed and gauntletted Proper garnished Or holding erect a tilting spear Proper with pennon Gules bearing a cross paty Argent.
LOGIN. *Her.Suff.Ch., Window, Old Felixstowe church*
An arm in armour embowed Proper holding in the gauntlet the butt end of a broken tilting spear Or.
THOMPSON, Robert, of London, Clothworker. *Grants & Certificates (Harl. MS 5,869)*
An arm couped at the shoulder embowed and erect from the elbow in armour garnished Or holding in the gauntlet Argent a spear Or.
WINCOLD, WINCOLE. *MS Knight's Visitations, Suff.* MS Philpot's Visitations, Suff.**
An arm couped at the shoulder embowed and erect from the elbow in armour Argent [or Proper] garnished Or holding in the hand Proper a broken spear Or headed Argent.
WINCOLD, WINCOLL, WYNCOLD, WYNCOLL, of Lt. Waldingfield, Hitcham. *Visitation 1577. MS Philpot's Visitations, Suff.* Bokenham. Davy, A. Washbourne*, 'Wincold, Wincoll, Leic. and Suff.' Fairbairn, 'Wincold, Wincoll, Waldingfield, Suff. and Leics.'*
A dexter arm in armour issuing out of a cloud fesseways Proper and holding in the hand Proper a sphere Or.
FIELD. *Her.Suff.Ch., Stained glass shield in Vestry, 'Presented by H.W. Field'; now in private*

house, 1982. Debach
An arm embowed in armour Or holding in the
gauntlet a spur Argent leathered Sable.
> MAPES. Grant by Camden, Clar., 1587. *Grants &
> Certificates (Harl. MS 1,441). Davy, A., 'of
> Thelnetham'. Washbourne, 'of Norfolk'*

An arm armed reflectant the hand holding a star.
> VYNER. *MS Martin's Crests*

An arm in armour embowed Proper holding in the
hand a sword Argent hilted Or thereon a boar's head
couped Sable the neck issuing blood.
> ACTON, of Baylham, Ipswich, Bramford,
> Hemingstone. *Visitation 1664–8. Bokenham.
> Sharpe. Green Memoir, 80. Davy, A. Proc.S.I.A.
> IX. 154, Flagon, Bramford church. Her.Suff.Ch.,
> Monumemt & Slabs in church, Altar tombs in
> churchyard, Baylham.* Acton, Nathaniel Lee, of
> Livermere Park, died 1836. *Her.Suff.Ch.,
> Hatchment, Stonham Aspal*

A dexter arm in armour embowed holding in the
hand a sword.
> ARCEDECKNE, of Glevering Hall, Hacheston.
> *Davy, A.*

An arm embowed mailed Proper in the hand a
sword pommel and hilt Or.
> ARCEDECKNE, Andrew, of Glevering Hall, died
> 1849. *Her.Suff.Ch., Hatchment, Hacheston*

Out of a tower Or an arm in armour Argent
garnished Or wielding in the gauntlet a dagger
Argent hilt and pommel Or.
> BEESTON. *MS Heraldic Alphabet*

A dexter arm embowed in armour Proper garnished
Or in the hand a scimitar all Proper.
> BLUNDELL, Viscount, of Somerton. *Davy, A.*

A dexter arm embowed in armour Argent holding in
the hand a sword Proper.
> BOTELER. *MS Martin's Crests*

An arm embowed in armour holding a sword
Proper.
> BUTLER, of The Priory in Clare, Owners of
> Newmarket, etc. *Davy, A.*

A dexter arm embowed in armour Proper grasping a
dagger.
> CARTHEW, Rev. Thomas, Minister for 40 years,
> died 1831; Others, c. 1875. *Her.Suff.Ch., Wall
> tablet, Woodbridge*

An arm in armour embowed holding in the gauntlet
a broken sword.
> COLBY, COLBYE, of Beccles. *Visitation 1561
> (MS G.7*).* 'Thomas Colby of Beckles in Com
> Suffolke esquier', *MS Lilly's Visitation of Suffolk**

An arm in armour embowed Proper, or Sable,
garnished Or holding a broken sword Argent hilt
and pommel Or.
> COLBY, COLBYE, of Brundish, Beccles, Waltham.
> *Visitation 1561 (Iveagh Copy*) and (ed. Metcalfe).
> Norfolk Visitation 1563 (Dashwood, 95). Visitation
> 1664–8. Harl.772 *. MS Fairfax*

A sinister arm in armour couped at the shoulder Or
grasping a broken sword Proper.
> COLBY. *MS Heraldic Alphabet*

An arm in armour embowed holding in the hand a
broken sword.
> COLEBYE. *MS ex-Taylor Coll. **

An arm in armour embowed Proper garnished Or
holding in the gauntlet a broken sword Argent hilt and
pommel Or the broken end embrued with blood.
> COLBY, of Brundish, Beccles. *Davy, A., Glemham
> church. Washbourne, 'Middx., Norf. and Suff.'*

An arm in armour Proper garnished Or holding in the
gauntlet a broken sword Argent hilt and pommel

Gules the broken end of the sword embrued with
blood.
> COLBY, John, died 1540; Widow Alice, died
> 1560; Sir John, died 1559. *Her.Suff.Ch., Effigy
> brasses, Brundish*

A dexter arm in armour holding in the hand a sword
Proper.
> ELTON. *MS Martin's Crests*

An arm embowed in armour Proper holding in the
gauntlet a scimitar Argent round the arm a scarf
Vert.
> ELTON, of Bury. *Davy, A.*

An arm in armour embowed holding in the hand a
sword.
> ETOUGH, Rector of Claydon. *Davy, A.*

Issuant from a tower an arm in armour wielding a
scimitar all Proper.
> FITZOURSE, FITZURSE. *Davy, A.*

An arm in armour embowed holding in the hand a
sword.
> FOWLE. *MS Heraldic Collections, fo. 52**

An arm in armour brandishing a sword Proper.
> GISSING, of Eye, Bocking. *Davy, A.*

A dexter arm embowed in armour the gauntlet
grasping a sword Proper hilt and pommel Or
transfixing a leopard's face Sable.
> HEMSWORTH, of Gislingham. *Davy, A.*

An arm in armour embowed holding in the hand a
sword all Proper between two spears erect shafts
Sable.
> HIGHMOOR, HIGHMORE. *MS Ordinary of Arms
> fo. 237**

An arm armed Proper brandishing a falchion Argent
hilt and pommel Or between two leading pikes
Gules headed Or.
> HIGHMOOR. *Davy, A.*

An arm embowed holding in the gauntlet a scimitar
all Proper.
> HOLDITCH, ? of Framlingham. *Davy, A.*

An arm in armour couped and embowed resting the
elbow on a wreath and holding a sword Proper.
> IVE. *Davy, A.*

An arm embowed in armour grasping with the
gauntlet a falchion all Proper garnished Or.
> KIRKE, Captain David; Augmentation to Arms by
> Patent by R. St. George, Clar., 1 December 1631.
> *Grants & Certificates (Stowe MS 677)*

An arm in armour embowed Proper holding in the
hand a sword Proper hilt Or.
> KNAPP. *MS Ordinary of Arms, fo. 233**

An arm embowed in armour holding in the hand a
broken sword fesseways point to the dexter hilted
Or and a bunch of bay leaves Vert.
> KNAPE. *MS Knight's Visitations, Suff. ** 'Edward
> Knape', *MS Philpot's Visitations, Suff.*, 'armour
> Argent garnished Or . . . sword in bend sinister
> point downward'*

An arm embowed in armour Or [or Proper]
garnished Argent holding in the hand Proper by the
blade a broken sword Argent hilt and pommel Or
with a branch of laurel Vert.
> KNAPP, KNAPPE of Ipswich, Tuddenham,
> Needham, Washbrook, Hintlesham, Battisford,
> Westleton. *Visitation 1612. Visitation 1664–8 **
> 'John Knapp, St. Peter's, Ipswich', *Cotman's
> Suffolk, plate 38*. Page. Davy, A. St. Peter's
> church, Ipswich and Monument, Westleton.
> E.A.N. & Q. III. 307 and (N.S.) XII. 117*

An arm in armour embowed garnished Or the hand
of the first [sic] grasping by the blade a broken
sword Argent hilt and pommel Or.

KNAPP. *Washbourne*, 'Suff. and Norf'*
An arm in armour embowed Proper garnished Or the hand Proper grasping by the blade a broken sword Argent hilt and pommel Or with a branch of laurel Vert.

KNAPP. *Fairbairn, 'Needham and Washbrook, Suff. and Tuddenham, Norf.'* Knapp, John, Merchant and Portman of Ipswich, died 1604. *Her.Suff.Ch., Effigy brass, formerly in St. Peter's, now in Ipswich Museum. Book-plate.**

The sun in splendour surmounted of a dexter arm in armour embowed holding in the hand a sword all Proper.

KYNASTON, Bart., of Risby. *Davy, A. (Burke). Washbourne*. Fairbairn**

An arm embowed in armour the gauntlet grasping a sword all Proper garnished Or between two dragon's wings Argent.

LONDON, Robert, of Alby, co. Norfolk, Esq., J.P. *Grants & Certificates (Add. MS 14,294)*

An arm in armour embowed grasping in the hand a scimitar.

MACKY, Sarah, wife of John Macky, died 1698. *Her.Suff.Ch., Hatchment formerly in church recorded by Farrer; Ledger stone, Pakenham*

An arm embowed in armour in the hand a scimitar all Proper.

MAJENDIE, of Hedingham Castle, co. Essex. *Burke, L.G., 1900 ed.*

A dexter arm couped at the shoulder armoured Proper grasping in the hand a sword in bend sinister hilt and point Or blade Argent entwined by a serpent Or.

MORIARTY, Lt. Col. Roland, no date given. *Her.Suff.Ch., Glass, St. Mary's, Bury*

A dexter arm embowed in armour holding in the hand a sword.

NORMAN, Harry, M.D., M.R.C.P., died 1966. *Her.Suff.Ch., Wall tablet St. Gregory, Sudbury*

An arm in armour embowed Proper garnished Or holding in the gauntlet a scimitar Argent hilt and pommel Or.

PHILPOT. *MS Ordinary of Arms, fo. 271**

An arm embowed in armour Argent holding in the gauntlet a sword Argent hilted Or.

PAWLETT, POWLETT. *MS ex- Taylor Coll.**

A dexter arm in armour embowed in the hand a sword.

REILLY, of Westhorpe. *Davy, A.*

Issuing from clouds Proper an arm in armour embowed the gauntlet grasping a falchion all Proper garnished Or.

SALMON, Thomas, of Hackney, co. Middlesex, Alderman and Merchant of London; Confirmation by W. Segar, Clar., and Sir R. St.George, Norroy, 23 February 1621; also Confirmed by W. Segar, as Norroy. *Grants & Certificates (Harl. MS 6,140; Add. MSS 12,225 and 14,295; Stowe MS 714)*

A dexter arm in armour embowed holding in the hand a falchion Proper.

SALMON, of Wickham Market, Saxmundham, Mickfield, Pettistree. *Davy, A. Bildeston, 75*

An arm in armour embowed holding in the hand Proper a sword.

SCAMBLER. *MS Ordinary of Arms, fo. 7**

A dexter arm in armour embowed grasping in the hand a dagger all Proper.

SCHREIBER, of Kelsale, Round Wood in Ipswich, Melton. *Davy, A. Burke, L.G., 1900 ed.*

A dexter arm embowed in armour Proper garnished Or holding in the hand a dagger point to the dexter

all Proper pommel and hilt Or.

SCHREIBER, William Frederick, died 1860. *Her.Suff.Ch., Window, Rushmere*

An arm in armour embowed and erased grasping in the hand a sword.

SKIPPON, Sir Philip, Kt., died 1691. *Her.Suff.Ch., Wall tablet, Kedington, 'sword missing 1988'*

An arm embowed in armour quarterly Gules and Azure holding in the hand Proper a scimitar.

THOMPSON, Rector of Hinderclay. *Davy, A., 'church 1711'*

An arm in armour embowed holding a cutlass all Proper.

TRENCH, LE POER-TRENCH, Earls of Clancarty. Jack le P. Trench, died 1941. *Her.Suff.Ch., Tombstone, churchyard, Tostock*

A dexter arm embowed in armour tied round the wrist with a ribbon and holding in the hand a scimitar embrued.

TUFNELL. *Bookplate**

A dexter arm embowed in armour Proper holding in the gauntlet a cutlass Azure hilt Or.

TUFNELL, of Langleys, co. Essex. *Her.Suff.Ch., Wall tablet, East Bergholt*

A dexter arm in armour embowed holding in the hand a sword entwined with a snake all Or.

WALKER, of Levington. *Davy, A.*

A dexter arm in armour embowed holding in the gauntlet a dagger point upwards to the dexter.

WARNER, Henry. *Bookplate**

An arm in mail couped at the shoulder holding a truncheon.

GRETTON. *Washbourne*, 'Suff.' Fairbairn, 'Suff.'*

A dexter arm embowed in armour holding in the hand a wreath.

MALYN, of Occold. *Davy, A., church*

TWO ARMS, holding:

Two arms in armour embowed holding in the gauntlets a battle-axe all Proper.

ANSTRUTHER, of Hintlesham Hall. *Davy, A. Burke, L.G., 1900 ed. Fairbairn*, 'of Hintlesham, Suff.'*

Two arms in armour counter-embowed Proper supporting a round buckle tongue erect Or.

LUTHER, Anthony, of Kelvedon, co. Essex; Confirmation in July and November 1614. *Grants & Certificates (Harl. MS 6,059; Stowe MSS 706 and 707)*

Two arms embowed in armour Proper holding in the hands a round buckle.

LUTHER, of Bricett. *Davy, A.*

Armed arms the hands supporting an open helmet.

ARMIGER. *MS Martin's Crests*

Two arms in armour Argent garnished Or holding in the gauntlets a short spear fesseways the butt end a trefoil Or the point Or and pointing to the sinister.

CURSON. 'Henry Courson', *MS Philpot's Visitations, Norf.**

Two arms in armour Proper couped at the shoulders garnished Or holding a sword fesseways the hilt in the dexter gauntlet and the point in the sinister.

CURSON, of Sutton. 'Henry Curson of Letheringsett', *MS Knight's Visitations, Norf.* Davy, A.*

ARM NAKED

CUBIT ARM

A naked cubit arm the fist clenched Proper.

POYNTZ, POYNS. *MS ex-Taylor Coll.* *
Over a dexter cubit arm erect Proper a crescent
Argent between two branches of laurel also Proper.
  HARVEY, of Gorleston. *Davy, A.*

CUBIT ARM, holding: [Objects in alphabetical order]

A cubit arm erect holding in the hand Proper an
anchor erect Sable.
  COCKRAM. *Davy, A.*
A cubit arm erect Proper holding in the hand an
anchor Azure flukes and ring Or.
  COURTHOPE, of Parham. *Davy, A.*
A cubit arm erect the hand grasping an arrow all
Proper.
  YOUNG, of Ipswich, Chediston. Vicar of
  Stowmarket, 1655. *Davy, A., St. Nicholas
  church, Ipswich*
A cubit arm erect Proper holding in the hand a
battle-axe upright Argent hafted Sable.
  DRAKE. *MS Ordinary of Arms, fo. 119* *
A cubit arm erect Proper holding in the hand a
battle-axe Argent headed Or.
  STANE, of Wilby, Kenton. *Davy, A.*
A cubit arm erect holding a branch of oak fructed
Proper.
  DALLING, Bart., of Bungay, Earl Soham.
  Davy, A.
A cubit arm holding a branch of acorns all Proper.
  RHODES, Col. Frank, C.B., D.S.O., died 1905. Of
  Dalham. *Her.Suff. Ch., Wall tablet, Dalham*
An arm erect holding an escallop.
  WICHINGHAM, of Yoxford, Theberton. *Davy, A.
  Washbourne*, 'of Wichingham, Witchingham
  [sic], Suff'.*
An arm erect Proper holding in the hand an escallop
Or.
  'WICHINGHAM, WITCHINGHAM [sic], Suff'.
  Fairbairn *
An arm couped at the elbow erect holding in the
hand a cinquefoil slipped.
  HOWCHIN, William, Gent., died 1729. ? DYKES.
  Her.Suff.Ch., Ledger stone, Eye
'On a healme forth of a wreath of their coullers
[Sable and Or] a hand [shown as a cubit arm] Proper
houlding a fuzill of the second'; Grant of Arms and
Crest to William and Thomas Essington, of Cowley,
co. Glos., by Segar, Garter, 28 July 1610.
  ESSINGTON, of Brightwell. *Misc. Gen. et Her.,
  4th S. II. 3* *
A hand couped from the elbow Proper holding a
fusil Or.
  ESSINGTON. *MS Heraldic Alphabet*
A naked arm erect Proper holding in the hand a
lion's gamb erased.
  BROWNE, of Ipswich, Framlingham, Woodbridge.
  Davy, A., Coddenham church
An arm couped at the elbow Proper wound about
with a scarf Gules holding in the hand a dragon's
head erased Vert.
  SAYER. *MS Martin's Crests*
In front of a cornucopia fessewise Or an arm erect
Proper holding in bend sinister a key Or.
  DUNN, Sir William, Bart., The Retreat,
  Lakenheath, Brandon, Suff. *Fairbairn* *
An arm erect holding an eagle's leg erased a la guise
[sic-shld. be á la quise].
  BROWNE. *Green, 150., Slab, Framlingham
  church*
A cubit arm erect Proper the hand grasping a
lozenge Or.

ESSINGTON, William and Thomas; Grant 28 July
1610, by Sir W. Segar, Garter. *Grants &
Certificates (Add. MS 12,225; Harl. MS 6,140)*
A naked arm erect holding in the hand Proper a
mullet Gules.
  ODINGSELS, DODINGSELLS, of Cavendish.
  Davy, A.
'on a wreathe or & azure an Arme from the wrest
charnew [sic- flesh colour] holdinge in his hand a
penn proper'; Grant of Arms and Crest to Ralf
Skryvener of Ipswich by Cooke, Clar.,
30 September 1576.
  SCRIVENOR of Ipswich. *Grant*, East Suffolk
  Records Office, Ipswich*
An arm couped at the elbow and erect holding
between the thumb and finger a pen all Proper.
  SCRIVENER, SCRIVENOR, of Ipswich, Sibton.
  'Raffe Scryvener . . . pen Sable', *MS Philpot's
  Visitations, Suff.* MS Fairfax (Tyl.) Bokenham.
  Davy, A. Washbourne*, 'Screvener, Scrivener,
  Suff.' Fairbairn*, 'Screvener, Scrivener,
  Scrivenor, Ipswich, Suff. and Norf.'*
A cubit arm erect holding in the hand a serpent the
tail enwrapped about the wrist Proper.
  BIGG, BIGGS. *MS Ordinary of Arms, fo. 183* *
A dexter arm erect holding in the hand a staff
surmounted by a cinquefoil.
  HOWCHIN, of Eye. *Davy, A., church*
A naked cubit arm erect holding in the hand a
falchion.
  REVETT. On brass of John Eldred, Merchant
  Venturer, died 1632; placed by son, Revett
  Eldred. *Rubbing of brass, Gt. Saxham church*
An arm couped at the elbow holding in the hand a
broken dagger in bend sinister Gules.
  RICHARDSON. *MS Martin's Crests*
An arm erased below the elbow and erect Proper
holding in the hand a falchion Argent pommel and
hilt Or the blade embrued in three places Gules.
  'GARNYS, Syr Christopher'. *Banners &
  Standards* *
A cubit arm erased Argent crined Or holding in the
hand a scimitar Argent embrued Gules guard and
pommel Or grip Gules.
  GARNEYS, of Kenton. *Visitation 1561 (MS
  G.7*); (Iveagh Copy*), not crined, scimitar hilt
  all Or.*
A cubit arm erased holding in the hand a scimitar
Argent embrued Gules guard and pommel Or grip
Gules, charged with a crescent for difference.
  GARNEYS, of Mendlesham. *Visitation 1561
  (MSS G.7.* and Iveagh Copy*)*
A cubit arm erased grasping a scimitar embrued all
Proper hilt and pommel Or.
  GARNEYS, of Kenton. *Visitation 1561 (ed.
  Metcalfe). 'Garnyshe', MS Knight's Visitations,
  Suff.* Washbourne, 'Garnish, Suff.' Fairbairn,
  'Garneys, Garnish, of Laxfield, Heveningham,
  Kenton, Mickfield, Redesham, Suff. and Norf.'*
An arm erased at the elbow and erect Proper holding
a scimitar Argent hilt and pommel Or the blade
marked with blood in three places.
  GARNISH, GARNEYS, of Mickfield, Redisham,
  Kenton, Mendlesham, Somerleyton. *Harl. 772*.
  Suckling, I. 63. Davy, A. Muskett, I. 189 (Harl.
  MS 1820, fo. 51b.) and II. 259*
Between a branch of oak and another of laurel a
dexter cubit arm erect Proper the hand holding a
trident Or on the staff a flag hoisted Azure thereon
the word 'Rosario' in letters Or.
  HARVEY, Captain Booty Harvey, R.N., of

Wordwell.; Arms and ? Crest Granted by Earl Marshal's warrant, 11 March 1816. *Davy, A., Monument, Wordwell church. Wordwell Register (S.G.B.), 299–303. Washbourne. Her.Suff.Ch., Wall tablet, Wordwell*
A cubit arm erect Proper holding a Civic wreath Vert and three arrows one in fesse and two in saltire points to the dexter Argent.
BRODIE. Bart., of Boxford. *Davy, A. Washbourne. Burke, Peerage, 1891 ed.* Fairbairn*, Dexter arm . . . arrows untinctured*

ARM, holding: [Objects in alphabetical order]

A dexter female arm holding in the hand a balance.
BOWNESS, of Lowestoft. Rev. Francis Bowness, Rector of Corton and Gunton. *Gillingwater, ix, 343. Davy, A., Monument, Gunton church*
A dexter arm embowed holding a baton (?).
BRAND, Rear-Admiral Ellis Brand, died 1759. *Her.Suff.Ch., Altar tomb, churchyard, Wherstead*
A naked arm embowed grasping in the hand a shin bone all Proper.
WOLSEY. *Davy, A., Cretingham church. Washbourne*, 'Woolsey, Suff.' Fairbairn, 'of Cottingham [sic], Suff.'*
An arm holding a drawn bow.
ARROW, Rev. John, Vicar of Lowestoft for 28 years, died 1789. *Gillingwater. Davy, A.*
An arm embowed holding in the hand a branch of laurel all Proper.
BURRELL, Baron Gwydyr, of Stoke Park in Ipswich. *Davy, A., St. Mary Stoke church. Burke, Peerage, 1891 ed.* E.A.N. & Q. IX. 338.*
A naked dexter arm embowed couped at the shoulder holding in the hand an olive branch Proper.
BURRELL, Hon. Lindsey Burrell, of Stoke Park, died 1848. Burrell, Baron Gwydyr, of Stoke Park. *Crisp's Visitation. XII. 134–142*, Pedigree, Bookplate. Her.Suff.Ch., Wall tablet, St.Mary Stoke, Ipswich*
An arm embowed Proper grasping a branch of oak Vert fructed Or.
KNAPP, Henry, of Hintlesham in Suffolk. *Grants & Certificates (Harl. MS 1,359)*
A dexter hand and arm holding a club raguled all Proper.
CLUBB, of Whatfield. *Sharpe*
A naked arm embowed grasping in the hand a club.
CLUBBE, of Whatfield, Earl Soham, Brandeston, Framlingham. *Davy, A.*
An arm embowed holding a club all Proper.
LEAVER. *Davy, A.*
A dexter arm embowed couped below the shoulder and covered with hair Argent charged with five pellets in saltire and holding in the hand a cross botonny fitchy Gules.
'LUCAS, Mayster'. *Banners & Standards**
A dexter arm naked grasping a sole (fish).
SOLLEY, Rector of Barsham, died 1714. *Davy, A.*
A naked dexter arm embowed Proper holding in the hand a rose Gules stalked and leaved Vert.
LE HEUP, LEHEUP. *MS Ordinary of Arms fo. 201**
A naked dexter arm bent at the elbow holding a rose slipped Proper.
LE HEUP, of Hessett, Rougham, Drinkstone, Bacton, Bradfield. *Misc.Gen. et Her. 4th S. II. 114, Pedigree*
A dexter arm couped and embowed holding three wheat stalks Proper.

CRESSENOR. *Davy, A. (Blois MS)*
A dexter arm embowed couped at the shoulder Proper holding in the hand three stalks of wheat Proper.
VESEY, William, died 1699. *Her.Suff.Ch., Wall tablet, Whatfield*
A naked arm holding in the hand a garland or wreath Vert on the upper part of which upon a label the word 'Virtute'.
COOPER, Bart. (of Nova Scotia), of Worlington. *Davy, A.*
A dexter arm couped and embowed holding up in the hand a grenade fired all Proper.
CHAMBERLEN, of Alderton. *Davy, A.*
An arm embowed holding in the hand a swan's head erased.
BAKER. *MS Ordinary of Arms, fo. 151*. Partridge, 17, Stoke by Nayland churchyard (Darby, 1828)*
An arm embowed Proper holding in the hand a swan's head erased Argent beaked Gules.
BAKER, of Fressingfield. *Davy, A.*
A hand and arm Argent holding a dragon's head erased Vert.
SAYER, SAWYER, of co. Essex. *MS Fairfax (Tyl.), Monument, Brent Eleigh church. Misc.Gen. et Her. 2nd S. II. 3**
A naked arm bent Proper round the wrist a wreath Argent and Gules holding in the hand a dragon's head erased Vert.
SAYER, of Thorndon, Bacton. *Davy, A.*
A dexter arm couped grasping a snake Proper.
TODENI, TONNY, TONY, of Mells. *Davy A.*
A dexter arm holding a roll of vellum Proper.
LEW. M.P. for Suffolk, 1343. *Davy, A.*
A dexter arm couped at the shoulder erect holding in the hand a cross-saw.
BARNES, John, M.A., died 1729. Dorothy Barnes, died 1710. *Her.Suff. Ch., Floor slabs, Acton*
An arm embowed Proper round the wrist a ribbon Azure in the hand a broken tilting spear Or.
SMITH, SMYTHE, of Nedging, Hundon. *MS Knight's Visitations, Suff.* 'John Smythe', MS Philpot's Visitations, Suff.*, spear in pale. Davy, A., 'Granted by Cooke, 17 December 1576'.*
A dexter arm holding in the hand a sword.
ARCEDECKNE, of Glevering Hall, Suffolk. *Burke, L.G., 1853 ed.*
A dexter arm embowed holding in the hand a sword.
CARTHEW, of Benacre, Woodbridge. *Davy, A.*
A man's arm erased Argent wielding in the hand a falchion Argent hilted Or.
GARNISH, of Suffolk. *MS Heraldic Alphabet*
A dexter arm embowed Proper brandishing a scimitar Proper hilt and pommel Or.
STRAHAN, of Butley Abbey. *Davy, A.*

ARM VESTED

CUBIT ARM

A cubit arm vested in a shirt sleeve Argent the fist clenched Proper.
POYNTZ. *Davy A.*

CUBIT ARM, holding: [Objects in alphabetical order]

A cubit arm erect vested Gules cuffed Argent holding in the hand an annulet Argent.
CONOLLY, of Friston, Aldeburgh. *Davy, A.*
An arm erect habited to the elbow Gules cuffed Ermine holding in the hand Proper a broad arrow.

CHARLETON. *Davy, A. (Edms.)*
A cubit arm erect habited Azure slashed Argent holding in the hand Proper the attire of a stag Gules.

PARKER. *MS Ordinary of Arms, fo. 112**
A dexter arm erect vested Azure cuffed and purfled, or slashed, Argent holding in the hand Proper an attire of a stag, or piece of coral, Gules.

PARKER, Bart., of Long Melford, Benhall. *Davy, A. Washbourne*. Burke, Peerage, 1891 ed.** Rev. Sir William Hyde Parker, Bart., D.L. of Suff.' *Fairbairn*.* Sir Hyde Parker, Bt., Vice-Admiral of the Blue, lost at sea 1782. Sir William, 7th Bart., died 1830. Sir Hyde, 8th Bart., died 1856. *Her.Suff.Ch., Altar tomb and Hatchments, Long Melford*
A dexter arm couped at the elbow habited Azure cuffed Argent holding in the hand a battle-axe handle Azure blade Or.

BLIGH, Rev. Reginald, D.D., Rector of Cockfield, died 1841. *Her.Suff.Ch., Hatchment recorded by Farrer in 1912 but no longer in church*
A cubit arm vested Vert cuffed Argent in the hand Proper a square banner Or charged with three bars wavy Azure and a canton of St. George.

GOULD, of Dorchester; Grant by Sir W. Segar, Garter. *Grants & Certificates (Add. MS 12,225)*
An arm erect vested Vert holding in the hand Proper a banner Or charged with three bars wavy Azure and on a canton Argent a cross Gules.

GOULD, of Bury, Hoxne. *Davy, A.*
A cubit arm erect vested Gules cuffed Argent the hand Proper grasping a cresset Sable with fire issuing Proper.

PRESCOTT, Alexander, of London; Patent of Confirmation of Arms and Grant of Crest by W. Camden, Clar., 1 March 1611/12. *Grants & Certificates (Stowe MSS 706 and 707; Harl. MS 6,095)*
An arm in pale habited Gules cuffed Ermine holding in the hand Proper a beacon Sable fired Proper.

PRESCOTT, of Hoxne. *Davy, A.*
An arm couped at the elbow per pale Gules and Argent three slashes in fesse and cuffed Argent on the hand Proper a bird Azure collared Argent.

WASTELL. *MS Heraldic Alphabet*
A cubit arm erect vested Gules charged with three gutties Or cuffed Argent holding in the hand Proper a dove Azure collared Argent.

WASTELL, of Risby. *Davy, A.*
A hand couped from the elbow clothed Azure cuffed Argent in the hand Proper [drawn, supposedly a jawbone] Argent.

BAYNES. *MS Heraldic Alphabet*
An arm erect couped vested Argent holding in the hand a jaw bone Argent.

BAINES, Vicar of Acton, died 1729. *Davy, A.*
A cubit arm vested Azure cuffed Erminois the hand holding a jaw bone Argent.

BAYNES. *Her.Suff.Ch., Window, Chelmondiston*
A cubit arm erect vested holding in the hand a book open. Another, the book closed.

APPLETHWAITE, of Huntingfield, Stoke Ash. *Davy, A., Huntingfield and Bramfield churches*
A right arm erect vested Vert cuffed Argent the hand Proper holding an apple branch leaved and slipped Vert.

BLOWER; Grant of Arms and Crest to Peter Blower, son of Robert Blower of Suffolk, by Richard Lee, Clar., 1 June 13 Elizabeth, 1596/7. Of Lavenham. *Essex Visitation 1634 (H.S.) I. 351. Berkshire Visitation 1665–6 (H.S.) I. 175.*

'Patt.[t] to Peeter Blower son to Blower of Suff.A.[o] 15 [sic] Q. Eliz.' *MS ex-Taylor Coll.**
A cubit arm erect vested Vert cuffed Argent holding in the hand Proper a branch of – Vert.

BLOWER, of Suffolk. *Davy, A.*
A cubit arm erect habited Gules holding two bunches of laurel Vert disposed orlewise.

COOPER, Rev. Sir William, Bart., died 1835. *Her.Suff.Ch., Tablet, Worlington*
An arm erect couped at the elbow vested Azure cuffed Argent holding in the hand Proper an acorn branch Vert fructed Proper.

NASH, Joseph, R.I., died 1922. *Her.Suff.Ch., Wall brass, Somerleyton*
'a demy arme azure, and hand proper, holding a Branche of Oke leaves with Akornes Or sett in a wreath of his colours'.

SMITHES, George, of Wike, co. Somerset; Exemplification of Arms and Grant of Crest by Dethick, Garter and Camden, Clarenceux, 9 March 1602. *Misc.Gen. et Her. II. 96**
A cubit arm erect vested Azure cuffed Argent in the hand Proper a branch of oak Vert fructed Or.

SMITHES, George, of London, gent., Sheriff and Alderman; Grant by W. Dethick, Garter (no date). *Grants & Certificates (Stowe MSS 676, 706 and 707)*
An arm in pale habited Azure cuffed Argent holding in the hand Proper three acorn branches Vert fructed Or.

SMYTHIES, of Alpheton. *Davy, A. (Edms.)*
A cubit arm erect habited Sable cuffed Argent holding in the hand Proper an oval buckle Argent.

CASE, of Bury. *Davy, A.*
A cubit dexter arm vested Gules charged with two bends wavy Sable cuffed Argent the hand Proper clenched and holding a round buckle Or.

CASON, Sir Henry, of Payton[sic]Hall in Suffolk, living 1634. *Herts. Visitation 1634 (H.S.) 37*
An arm erect couped at the elbow vested Argent holding in the hand Proper a chaplet of thorns Vert.

CLEAVER, Howard, died 1948. *Her.Suff.Ch., Tomb, churchyard, Wetherden*
An arm couped at the elbow vested Argent charged with two bends wavy Azure cuffed Argent holding in the hand Proper a chaplet Vert.

KEMP, of Cavendish, Barningham. *Visitation 1561 (ed. Howard) II, I, note., (Harl. MS 1650). MS ex-Taylor Coll.* , 'Finchingfeild in Co. Essex'. Davy, A. Washbourne, 'Kemp, Kempe, Ess.& Suff.' Fairbairn, 'Kemp, Kempe, Essex and Suff.'*
An arm couped at the wrist Proper clothed Gules the hand holding a club full of spikes Or

CLENCH. *Bokenham*
Out of the clouds Proper a dexter arm couped at the elbow and erect habited Argent charged with four sinister bends Sable holding in the hand Proper a club Proper over it this motto 'Frappe fort'.

WODEHOUSE, of Ashbocking. *Davy, A.*
A cubit arm erect vested Sable cuffed Or the hand Proper grasping the line from the collar Gules of a greyhound Argent passing behind the arm

LOVELL, Thomas, gent., of Laxfield, co. Suffolk; Confirmation by Sir G. Dethick, Garter, 25 June 1579. *Grants & Certificates (Harl. MS 1,441; Stowe MS 703)*
A cubit arm vested Or cuffed Argent holding in the hand a pair of compasses Or.

SAXTON, SHAXTON, of Suffolk. *Davy, A.*
A cubit arm erect vested Azure cuffed Argent the

hand Proper holding an estoile of eight points Or.
  SCOTTOW, of Norwich; Grant by Sir E. Bysshe,
  Garter, 1647. *Grants & Certificates (Add. MSS
  26 and 758; Stowe MS 677)*
A cubit arm erect habited Or holding in the hand
three ostrich feathers the inner one Sable the outer
ones Or.
  WYNTER. *Fairbairn, 'of Aldeburgh, Suff.'*
A hand couped from the elbow clothed Gules cuffed
Argent in the hand Proper four feathers per pale
Argent and Gules.
  BLACKNALL. *MS Heraldic Alphabet*
A cubit arm erect vested bendy wavy of four Azure
and Gules holding in the hand Proper a fish Argent.
  BRAME, of Suffolk. *Davy, A.*
In front of a cubit arm vested Ermine cuffed Argent
holding in the hand Proper a fleur-de-lis Sable, a
mascle Sable.
  ELEY, Charles, of East Bergholt Place, died 1902.
  Burke, L.G., 1952 ed.. Her.Suff.Ch., Wall tablet,
  East Bergholt*
A cubit arm erect vested Gules cuffed Argent
holding in the hand Proper a fleur-de-lis per pale
Argent and Sable.
  LOSSE, of Copdock; Grant 1633. *Davy, A.
  Washbourne*, 'cubit arm in pale'. Fairbairn, 'of
  Cobdock [sic], Suff. Arm in pale'. Grants &
  Certificates (Add. MS 12,225)*
A cubit am erect habited Azure cuffed Argent
holding in the hand Proper a fleur-de-lis per pale
Argent and Sable.
  NELSON. *MS Ordinary of Arms, fo. 226*
A cubit arm erect vested quarterly Argent and Sable
cuffed Argent the hand Proper holding a fleur-de-lis
per pale Argent and Sable.
  NELSON, Thomas, of Elseth Hall, co. York.; Grant
  by Sir R. St.George, Norroy, 1607. *Grants &
  Certificates (Add. MS 14,295). 'Nelson Robert, of
  Aldeburgh in Suffolk, whose ancestors came from
  Yorkshire'; same Arms, but no Crest given.
  Grants & Certificates (Stowe MS 677)*
A cubit arm erect vested Gules cuffed and charged
with three fleurs-de-lis Argent in the hand Proper a
fleur-de-lis Or.
  THURKELL, Robert, of London. *Grants &
  Certificates (Harl. MS 5,869)*
Issuing out of clouds a cubit arm erect vested Azure
cuffed Argent holding in the hand a bunch of ?
gillyflowers leaved Vert fructed Or.
  CARSEY, 'Thomas, of southbarowe'. *MS Knight's
  Visitations Norf.*
Issuing out of clouds Argent and Azure a cubit arm
vested Azure slashed Argent holding in the hand a
bunch of gillyflowers 'grey' [sic] leaved Vert.
  CARSEY, 'Thomas'. *MS Philpot's Visitations,
  Norf.*
A hand and arm couped at the elbow and erect
vested Azure purfled and cuffed Argent holding in
the hand a bunch of gillyflowers all Proper.
  CARSEY, CARSS, of Bury. *Davy, A.*
A cubit arm erect sleeved Purpure cuffed – in the
hand Proper three ears of rye Or.
  RYE, of Thelnetham, Hepworth. *Davy A.*
A cubit arm erect vested Vert holding in the hand
Proper three rye-stalks Or.
  RYE. *Fairbairn, 'Norf. and Suff.'*
A cubit arm vested and turned up Argent holding in
the hand Proper four, or seven, ears of wheat Or.
  DENNY, Lord, of Mettingham. *Davy, A.,
  Lavenham church*
A cubit arm fessewise vested and cuffed holding in

the hand five wheat ears.
  DENNY *Proc.S.I.A. XIX. 331*
A cubit arm vested and cuff turned up Argent
holding in the hand Proper seven ears of wheat Or.
  DENNY, Thomas, of Lavenham, died 1716.
  Her.Suff.Ch., Floor slab, Lavenham
A dexter arm erect habited Gules cuffed Argent
holding in the hand Proper three ears of wheat Or.
  THOMPSON, of Thetford. *Davy, A., St. Mary's
  church*
An arm erect vested Gules cuffed Argent holding in
the hand Proper five ears of wheat Proper.
  THOMPSON, of Saxmundham, Thorpe Hall near
  Hasketon. *Davy, A., Monument, Thetford
  church. E.A.N. & Q. I. 136*
An arm couped at the elbow vested Or charged with
two bars wavy Azure cuffed Argent holding in the
hand Proper a buck's head cabossed Gules.
  GIFFARD, Earl of Buckingham, of Gt. Blakenham.
  Davy, A.
A cubit arm erect vested per pale embattled Azure
and Or holding in the hand Proper a dragon's head
erased Azure.
  GOOCH, of London. *MS Ordinary of Arms,
  fo. 86**
A dexter arm couped at the elbow erect habited
Gules grasping in the hand Proper a dragon's head
erased Vert.
  SAYER, Elizabeth [née Sayer], wife of Edward
  Freston of Mendham, died 1727. *Her.Suff.Ch.,
  Wall tablet, Mendham*
Issuant from the battlements of a tower Proper a
cubit arm erect vested and cuffed Or the hand
Proper holding an antique lamp Sable fired Proper.
  LUCAS, 'John S., F.S.A., of Blythburgh, Suffolk
  and London'. *Fairbairn**
Issuant from a tower Proper a cubit arm clothed Or
holding a lamp Sable flamed Gules.
  SEYMOUR-LUCAS, John, died 1923. *Her.Suff.Ch.,
  Wall tablet, Blythburgh*
A cubit arm erect paly of four Or and Gules cuffed
Argent holding in the hand Proper by the centre a
tilting lance in bend sinister point downwards Or.
  LEIGH, of Sotterley. *Visitation 1664–8*
A cubit arm erect vested Azure cuffed – charged
with a cross formy Argent holding in the hand
Argent a slip of leaves Vert.
  BINGHAM. *MS Heraldic Collections, fo. 8*,
  'Dorset'. 'Washbourne, 'of Dorset'*
A cubit arm erect vested Or charged with a fesse
between four barrulets – cuffed Argent holding in
the hand Proper a mullet Or.
  ALLOTT, of Lt. Thurlow. *Davy, A.*
An arm couped at the elbow clothed per pale crenelly
Or and Argent holding in the hand a mullet Sable.
  DOUGHTY. *MS Martin's Crests*
A cubit arm erect vested per pale crenelly Or and
Argent cuffed Or holding in the hand Proper a
mullet Sable pierced Or.
  DOUGHTY. Mrs. Mary Ann, died at Wortham
  Rectory 1910. *Her.Suff.Ch., Wooden shield on
  organ, Wortham*
A cubit arm erect habited per pale Or and Azure
cuffed Gules holding in the hand Proper a mullet
Argent [shown as badges, but with wreaths].
  'HAUNSART, Mayster Wyllm . . . co. Lyngcoll'.
  *Banners & Standards**
A cubit arm erect vested Or cuffed Argent holding
in the hand Proper a mullet Argent.
  HANSARD, of Hasketon. *Davy, A., Fressingfield
  church*

An arm couped at the elbow and erect vested Gules cuffed Argent holding in the hand Proper three nails Or all between two wings Argent.

ALEFOUNDER, of East Bergholt. *Davy, A., Bergholt church. Washbourne*, 'of Ess.'*

An arm erect habited bendy holding in the hand a baker's peel thereon three cakes.

PISTER, of Bury. *Davy, A., Claydon church*

A cubit arm with a ruffle round the wrist holding in the hand a quill pen Argent.

SCRIVENOR, of Ipswich. *MS Knight's Visitations, Suff.**

Out of clouds Azure a cubit arm habited per pale Azure and Gules holding in the hand Argent a pheon Sable.

HOLT, of Bury St. Edmunds. *Visitation 1561 (MS G.7.*) and (Iveagh Copy*) and (ed.Howard) II. 45**

An arm erect couped at the elbow habited per pale Azure and Gules in the hand Argent a pheon Sable.

HOLT, of Bury. *Visitation 1561 (ed. Metcalfe and ed. Howard. II. 49). Harl. 772*. Fairbairn, 'Holt, Holte, Suff . . . hand Proper'*

A cubit arm erect habited per pale Azure and Gules charged with a crescent – [for difference] holding in the hand Proper a pheon point downwards Sable garnished Or.

HOLT. *MS Heraldic Collections, fo. 12*, 'co. Oxford'*

An arm erect vested per pale Argent and Sable holding in the hand a pheon Or.

HOLT, of Redgrave. *Visitation 1561 (ed. Howard) II. 52., on Holt monument in Redgrave church*

A cubit arm erect habited per pale Argent and Sable cuffed Argent holding in the hand Proper a pheon point downwards Sable.

HOLT. *MS Ordinary of Arms, fo. 226*. Her.Suff.Ch., Redgrave, 'pheon Argent'*

A hand couped at the elbow Proper clothed per pale Argent and Sable holding a pheon Sable.

HOLT, of Redgrave. *Bokenham.*

An arm erect couped at the elbow habited per pale Azure and Sable in the hand Argent a pheon Sable.

HOLT, Sir John, Lord Chief Justice, died 1709. *Her.Suff.Ch., Effigy monument, Redgrave*

A dexter arm erect couped at the elbow habited barry wavy of six Azure and Or cuffed Argent holding in the hand Proper a parchment roll Proper.

EVANS, of Parham, Hacheston. *Davy, A.*

A cubit arm habited and cuffed holding in the hand a roll of parchment. (habited Sable cuffed Argent, parchment Proper.)

KILLETT, William, died 1731; widow Mary, died 1750. *Her.Suff.Ch., Ledger stone, Gorleston*

Out of park pales Or a cubit arm erect habited Gules lined Ermine holding in the hand Argent a roll of paper Argent and charged on the wrist with a crescent – [for difference].

SCOTT, of Leiston, Essex. *Visitation 1561 (MS G.7.*) and (Iveagh Copy*)*

A cubit arm erect vested Vert cuffed Argent holding in the hand Proper a roundel Vert.

BLOWER. *Davy, A. (Burke)*

A hand couped from the elbow per pale Or and Azure cuffed Argent holding in the hand Proper a scythe Azure staff Or the turn at lower end Gules.

THICKNESSE, 'THICKNIS'. *MS Heraldic Alphabet*

A cubit arm erect vested per pale Azure and Gules cuffed per pale counterchanged holding in the hand a scythe Proper blade downwards.

THICKNESSE, of Felixstowe. *Davy, A.*

An arm reflectant couped at the elbow Vert grasping in the hand a spear Proper.

FOWKE, of Weston. *Bokenham*

A cubit arm erect vested paly of four Or and Gules cuffed Argent the hand Proper holding the parts of a broken tilting spear Or headed Argent.

LEIGH, Richard, of High Leigh, Esq.; Confirmation by Sir G. Dethick, Garter, 3 December 1580 of previous Grant of 20 July 1556. *Grants & Certificates (Harl. MSS 1,359 and 1,441; Stowe MS 703)*

A dexter arm to the elbow habited paly Or and Gules holding in the hand Proper a spear Or.

LEIGH, of Sotterley. *Bokenham. Davy, A.*

'beryth to his crest an arme in pal garnysched cheque silver and vert the hand charnu [flesh colour] holdyng thre dartes gold. Edw. IV.'

SMYTH. *Wall's Book*

'to his crest an Arme in palle garneshed cheque ar/vert/ the hand charnu holding iij Darts or/'

SMYTH, of Essex. *MS Alphabet of Crests, fo. 118.*

A cubit arm erect vested Azure the hand brandishing a falchion Proper hilt and pommel Or.

HERBERT, of co. Glamorgan; Confirmation by W. Dethick, York Herald, 13 November 1574. *Grants & Certificates (Stowe MS 676)*

An arm flectant couped at the elbow clothed Sable garnished Or holding a broken sword Proper adorned with three bay leaves Vert.

KNAP, of Ipswich. *Bokenham*

A cubit arm erect vested Or the hand in mail Argent cuffed Or holding a dagger fesseways Argent hilt and pommel Or.

MANBY, MANSE. *MS Knight's Visitations, Linc.*, 'Manby'*

A hand couped above the wrist erect sleeved Azure cuffed Argent holding a sword Proper pommelled and hilted Or pierced through the jaw of a boar's head couped Sable vulned and distilling drops of blood.

PURCELL 'now FITZGERALD', of Bredfield, Wherstead, Boulge. *Davy A.*

A cubit arm erected vested per pale Argent and Sable holding in the hand a broken sword, or scimitar, Azure hilt and pommel Or.

REVETT, RIVETT, RYVETT, of Bricett, Suffolk. *Visitation 1561 (MSS G.7.* and Iveagh Copy*). MS Rivett Pedigree Roll* (Copy of Visitation 1612); Corder MS 88*

A dexter arm erect couped at the elbow vested per pale Argent and Sable the hand Proper grasping a broken sword Argent hilt Or.

REVETT, RIVETT, of Brandeston, Bildeston, Rishangles. *Visitation 1561 (ed. Metcalfe). London Visitation 1633–4 (H.S.) II. 197*, [charged with a mullet for difference]. Visitation 1664–8. Harl. 772*. Bokenham. Washbourne, 'Ryvett, Suff.' Fairbairn, 'Rivett, Stowmarket, Suff. and Cambs., . . . cuffed counterchanged'*

A cubit arm erect bendy of four Argent and Sable grasping in the hand Proper a broken sword Argent hilt and pommel Or.

REVETT, RIVETT, of Brandeston, Bildeston, Rishangles. *Davy, A. Washbourne, 'Revett, Camb. and Suff.'*

An arm erect couped at the elbow per pale Argent and Sable cuffed per pale Sable and Argent holding in the hand Proper a broken sword the handle [sic-grip] Sable the pommel and hilt Or.

RIVET, Mary, dau. of Thomas R., of Rishangles, married John Eldred. *Her.Suff.Ch., Effigy brass, Gt. Saxham*

A cubit arm erect vested Sable cuffed Argent the hand Proper brandishing a broken falchion Proper.

RICHARDSON, Ferdinando, of co. Glos.; Patent by R. Cooke, Clar., 1588. *Grants & Certificates (Harl. MS 1,359)*

ARM

A dexter arm the hand open Proper in a maunch Or cuffed Gules.

DEBENHAM, of Wenham, Acton, Alpheton. *Davy, A., Capel church. Debenham, 87* (Burke)*

An arm couped at the shoulder in a maunch elbow on a wreath Proper.

FLOWERDEW, of Suffolk. *Davy, A.*

A dexter arm in a maunch Azure cuffed Or the hand clenched Proper.

LORD. *Davy, A. Washbourne*

ARM, holding: [Objects in alphabetical order]

A dexter arm embowed habited Vert cuffed Argent holding in the hand Proper an arrow Or barbed and feathered Azure.

FOWKE, of West Stow. *Davy, A., church*

A dexter arm embowed habited Vert cuffed Argent holding in the hand an arrow Or barbed and flighted Argent point downwards.

FOWKE, Sir Sydenham, Kt., died 1743; widow died 1752. *Her.Suff.Ch., Floor slab, West Stow*

A Moor's arm Proper enfiled with a wreath of the colours [Gules and Or] advancing a pole-axe Or head Argent.

PITMAN, 'Geffry, of Woodbridge, Suffolk, High Sheriff of that county'; Patent by Sir W. Segar, Garter. *Grants & Certificates (Add. MS 12,225)*

A Moor's arm Proper escarroned of the colours [*sic*- checky Gules and Or] advancing a pole-axe handled Or headed Argent.

PITMAN, of Woodbridge. *Davy, A. Fairbairn, 'of Woodbridge, Suff.'*

A Moor's arm Proper habited Sable tied at the elbow Gules and Or advancing a poleaxe handle Or headed Argent.

PITMAN, Jeffrey, sometime High Sheriff, died 1627; Others. *Her.Suff. Ch., Effigy monument Woodbridge*

A dexter arm embowed habited Azure charged on the arm with a plate cuffed Argent holding in the hand Proper a baton Or.

MAJOR, HENNIKER-MAJOR. Baron Henniker, of Thornham Hall, Worlingworth Hall. Major, Sir John, 1st Bart., died 1781; Henniker, John, 2nd Baron, died 1821; Henniker, John Minet, 3rd Baron, died 1832. *Davy, A. 'Washbourne*, 'Suff.' Burke, Peerage, 1891 ed.*. Fairbairn, 'Henniker, Baron, Thornham Hall, Eye'. Her.Suff.Ch., Hatchments, Wall tablets, Gt. Thornham*

A dexter arm embowed habited Gules cuffed Argent charged on the elbow with a plate holding in the hand Proper a baton Or.

MAJOR, called HENNIKER. *Her.Suff.Ch., Window and carved poppy head of choir stall, Gt. Bealings*

A dexter arm embowed habited Sable cuffed Argent holding in the hand Proper a baton Argent.

MAJOR, Sir John, Bart., died 1781. *Her.Suff.Ch., Wall tablet, Worlingworth*

An arm embowed vested Or in the hand Proper an oak branch Vert fructed Or.

WEBB, Thomas, of Gillingham in Kent; Confirmation by R. Lee, Chester Herald. *Grants & Certificates (Stowe MS 670)*

A dexter arm embowed vested bendy of six Or and Azure cuffed Argent holding in the hand Proper a cross crosslet fitchy Sable.

IBGRAVE, of Suffolk. *Davy, A. Washbourne, 'of Herts.'*

A dexter arm embowed habited Or charged with roundels Sable in pale holding in the hand Proper a cross crosslet fitchy Gules.

LUCAS, LYCAS. *MS Ordinary of Arms, fo. 158**

A dexter arm embowed Proper habited Argent on the elbow a quatrefoil Sable holding a cross crosslet fitchy Gules.

LUCAS. *Davy, A.*

A dexter arm embowed Proper vested Or cuffed Gules holding in the hand a covered cup Or.

DREWELL. *Davy, A. Washbourne, 'of Bucks.'*

An arm embowed vested Gules cuffed Argent holding in the hand Proper four feathers per pale Argent and Gules.

BLACKNELL, of Parham, Oulton. *Davy, A.*

A dexter arm embowed quarterly Argent and Sable holding in the hand Proper a fleur-de-lis Or.

HOPKINS, of Yoxford, Harwich. *Davy, A., Harwich church*

A dexter arm sleeved Gules turned down Argent holding in the hand Proper a fleur-de-lis Or.

THIRKLE, of Ipswich. *Sharpe*

A hand and arm clothed Or sleeved [*sic-* ?cuffed] Ermine holding a bunch of flowers.

ROSIAR. *Bokenham*

An arm embowed vested Azure cuffed Argent the hand Proper holding a bunch of grapes pendant Purpure leaved Vert.

BUTLER, John, of Hanley [*sic* ? Henley]; Patent August 1606. *Grants & Certificates (Stowe MS 707)*

An arm embowed habited Azure cuffed Argent holding in the hand a bunch of grapes Proper.

BUTLER, of Ipswich. *Davy, A.*

An arm clothed Azure sleeved and ruffled Argent the hand holding five wheat ears Proper.

DENNY, of Ravingham [*sic*]. *Bokenham*

An arm couped at the shoulder embowed and erect from the elbow habited – holding in the hand Proper four ears of wheat Or.

RISBY, of Thorpe Morieux. *Visitations 1577 and 1664–8*

An arm couped at the shoulder embowed and erect from the elbow vested Azure holding in the hand Proper four ears of wheat Or stalked Vert.

RESBYE, 'Suff.' *Washbourne. Fairbairn, 'Resbye, Suff.'*

A dexter arm embowed habited Ermines cuffed Argent in the hand Proper a buck's head couped Gules.

WOODROFFE, of Bury. *Davy, A.*

A dexter arm embowed vested Ermines cuffed Argent holding in the hand Proper a buck's head Proper.

WOODROFFE. *Washbourne, 'Suff.' Fairbairn, 'of St. Edmundsbury, Suff.'*

A dexter arm Gules holding in the hand a dragon's head erased Vert.

SAYER, SAYERS, of Eye, Sibton, Hopton. *Davy, A., Eye church*

A dexter arm embowed habited Argent holding in the hand the truncheon (missing 1988) of a broken lance Sable.

THOMPSON, George, died 1711. *Her.Suff.Ch.,*

Wall tablet, Hinderclay
An arm embowed erect from the elbow vested Or
cuffed Ermine holding in the hand four leaves Vert.
    ROSER, ROSIER, ROSSER, of Hacheston.
Visitation 1577. 'Roger Roser', *MS Philpot's
Visitations, Suff.* *MS Fairfax (Tyl.) Davy, A.
Washbourne, 'Rosser, Suff.' Fairbairn, 'Rosser,
Suff.'*
An arm embowed and erect from the elbow habited
Or cuffed Ermine holding in the hand a branch of
?seven laurel leaves.
    ROSIER, Edmund, died 1680; sons Edmund and
Simon, died 1690, 1689. *Her.Suff.Ch., Altar
tomb, churchyard, Stowmarket*
An arm embowed and couped at the shoulder erect
from the elbow habited Gules cuffed Ermine
holding in the hand a branch of four leaves Vert.
    VESEY, VESY, VEYSEY, of Hintlesham. *Visitation
1577. MS Knight's Visitations, Suff.* *, 'hand
Argent'. 'Will.Veysye', MS Philpot's Visitations,
Suff.* *MS Fairfax (Tyl.) MS Heraldic Collections,
fo. 53*. Washbourne, 'Vessey, Suff., Norf., etc.
Muskett. I. 56.* Vesey, Charles, died 1657;
Thomas, died 1736. *Her.Suff.Ch., Wall tablet and
Slab under Altar table, Hintlesham*
An arm embowed couped at the shoulder erect from
the elbow habited Gules cuffed Argent holding in
the hand Proper a branch of six leaves Vert.
    VESEY, of Hintlesham. *Visitation 1664–8**
A dexter arm embowed vested Gules cuffed Ermine
holding in the hand a branch of leaves Vert.
    VEASY, VESEY, of Hintlesham, Bradwell,
Blythburgh, Sibton. *Bokenham, 'three bay
leaves Proper.' Davy, A., Hintlesham and
Bradwell churches. Muskett. I. 56, '5 leaves'
(Harl. MS 1820)*
An arm embowed habited Gules holding in the hand
Argent a mallet Or.
    SOME. *MS Knight's Visitations, Suff.* *MS Philpot's
Visitations, Suff.*, 'habited Purpure'*
An arm embowed habited Gules grasping a mallet Or.
    SOAME, of Lt. Bradley, Thurlow. *Davy, A.*
An arm embowed vested Gules grasping a mullet
[*sic* shld. be a mallet] Or.
    SOAME. *Washbourne, 'Lond. and Suff.'*
A dexter arm embowed sleeved per pale Argent and
Sable (or Sable and Gules) cuffed Argent holding in
the hand Proper a pheon Sable.
    HOLT, of Redgrave. *Davy, A.*
A dexter arm embowed vested Gules holding a
plough paddle handled Gules bladed Or the arm
garnished with a wreath of wheat ears Proper.
    FARMBOROUGH, James, 1876–1958; Edith,
1876–1960. *Her.Suff.Ch., on oak panelling,
Mendlesham*
An arm embowed vested couped at the shoulder
holding in the hand a serpent Sable the tail twisted
round the arm.
    BIGG, of Glemsford. *Davy, A., church (Burke)*
A dexter arm embowed sleeved Azure ruffled
Argent on each joint a bar gemelle Or holding in the
hand a roll of paper Argent.
    KILLETT, of Gorleston. *Davy, A.*
A dexter arm embowed habited per pale Vert and
Gules holding in the hand Proper a spear Argent tied
below the head with a ribbon Gules.
    FOWKE, FOLKES. *MS Ordinary of Arms, fo. 223**
An arm couped at the shoulder reflectant per pale
Gules and Vert grasping in the hand a spear Proper.
    FOULKES, of Barton. *Bokenham*
A dexter arm embowed habited per pale Vert and

Gules cuffed Ermine holding in the hand Proper a
spear Proper.
    FOLKES, Bart., of Bury, Gt. Barton. *Davy, A.*
A sleeved arm embowed holding a broken tilting
spear.
    SMYTH, of Layham, Sudbury. *Surrey Visitation
1530 (H.S.} 136*
'his crest an Arme quarterly or/b/ the gauntlet of the
coller of harnes [armour] holding the troncheon of a
Spere or/ to henry Tompson of ? in Yorksh.r'
    THOMPSON, TOMPSON. *MS Alphabet of Crests,
fo. 128b*
A sinister arm habited Or cuffed Sable holding in
the hand Argent a sword Argent thereon a boar's
head Sable couped Gules.
    ACTON. *MS Heraldic Collections, fo. 57**
Out of a tower a dexter arm embowed habited Azure
holding in the hand Proper a sword Azure hilted Or.
    BEESTON, of Sproughton, Ipswich. *Davy, A.,
Sproughton church*
An arm Proper sleeved Vert holding in the hand a
sword in bend sinister hilted and pommelled Or.
    BOOTY. Grant 3 January 1300 [*sic* but ?] Of
Suffolk and Norfolk. *Booty (John Lodge's
Ordinary)*
A dexter arm embowed habited grasping in the hand
a scimitar.
    BRADLAUGHE, BRADLEY, of Laxfield. *E.A.
Misc. 1926, 90, church monuments*
A sinister arm embowed Sable holding in the hand
fessewise a sword, or dagger, Gules.
    CHAPMAN, Mary, wife of Sir William Chapman,
3rd, Bart., died 1760. *Her.Suff.Ch., Hatchment,
Ufford* (recently restored)
A dexter arm vested Argent holding in the hand a
scimitar Argent hilted Or.
    DISCIPLINE. *Davy, A.*
A dexter arm embowed habited and grasping in the
hand a scimitar.
    JACOB, Thomas, son of Nicholas Jacob; no date
given. *Her.Suff.Ch., Ledger stone, Laxfield*
An arm elbowed habited Gules holding a sword by
the blade point downwards Azure hilted Or.
    LEGROSSE, LE GROSSE, of Suffolk. *Davy, A.*
'to his crest an Arme par pale ar/sa/ holding in his
hand a broken sword pomell and hylted or/blade b/
to James Ryvet of Brysset in Suff.'
    'RYVET'. *MS Alphabet of Crests, fo. 111*

TWO ARMS, holding:

A boot Sable spurred Or topped Ermine above it a
human heart Proper held between two arms issuing
from dexter and sinister vested Azure hands Proper.
    HUSSEY. *MS Heraldic Collections, fo. 10*.
Washbourne*
Two arms couped at the shoulders embowed habited
Sable (Ermine) holding in the hands Proper a sheaf
of cumin Or.
    COMYN, Thomas, Clerk, Incumbent of Wantisden,
died 1832, *Her.Suff.Ch., Wall tablet, Wantisden*
Two arms embowed vested Azure holding in the
hands Proper a leopard's head Or.
    FROWICK, Of Lt. Cornard. *MS Ordinary of
Arms, fo. 85*. Davy, A.*
Two arms erect vested Azure holding between the
hands a leopard's head Or.
    FROWICK. *MS Martin's Crests*
Two arms dexter and sinister embowed vested
Argent holding in the hands a scalp Proper the
inside Gules.
    HUDDLESTON, of Boxford. *Davy, A.*

Two arms habited checky the hands holding a star of six points.

STERESACRE, of Baylham. *Davy, A., church*

Two arms embowed and crossed in saltire near the wrist the dexter vested Gules surmounted of the sinister vested Vert cuffs Argent each holding in the hand a falchion pommels and hilts Or the blades to dexter and sinister.

MOODY, of Ipswich. *Visitation 1664–8*

Two arms in saltire Argent and Vert each holding a falchion hilted Or.

MOODY, of Ipswich. *MS Fairfax*

Two arms couped at the shoulder in saltire one Gules the other Vert fighting with two daggers Proper.

MOODY, of Ipswich. *Bokenham*

Two arms embowed in saltire the dexter vested Gules the sinister Vert each holding a cutlass Argent hilt Or.

MOODY, of Ipswich. *Davy, A. Washbourne, 'Moodye, Suff.'*

ARM WOODWOSE (wild man), holding:

A dexter arm embowed habited in leaves Vert in the hand a branch of honeysuckle all Proper.

WOODROFF, WODROFF, David, Sheriff of London 1554; Grant by T. Hawley, Clar., 15 May I Queen Mary [1554/5]. *Grants & Certificates (Harl. MS 1,463; Stowe MS 700)*

A 'wodwous' arm flecked at the elbow and charged with five pellets in saltire holding in the hand a cross crosslet fitchy Gules.

'LUCAS of Suffolk Auditour'. *Wall's Book*

'to his crest a Woodwoes arme ar/ flected at the elbow/ holding a crosse crosselet feche g/ on the Arme 5 0s in X on y^t in pale' [sic]

'LEWCAS of Suff. audytor'. *MS Alphabet of Crests, fo. 73*

An arm embowed vested in leaves Vert holding in the hand Proper a swan's head erased Or beaked Gules.

BAKER. *MS ex-Taylor Coll.* *

A dexter arm embowed habited in leaves Vert holding in the hand Proper a snake enwrapping it Gules.

BIGG. *MS Martin's Crests*

A 'wodwose' arm erased in pale charnu [charnew, flesh colour] holding in the hand a falchion Argent hilt and pommel Or the 'strokes' bleeding Gules.

GARNEYS. *Wall's Book*

'to his crest a Wodwousse Arme in pale charnu rased holdyng a fachon ar/ crosse and molet [sic] or/ the stroks on the ffachon bleeding g/ knight by h 8'.

'GARNES'. *MS Alphabet of Crests, fo. 46b*

TWO ARMS, holding:

'to his crest ij wodhowse armes g/ vert/ in crosse holding in every hand a fachoy ar/ hylted and hafted or/ Edmond Mowdy dat p/ C hawley 32 of henry the 8' [1540/1].

MOODY. *MS Alphabet of Crests, fo. 81b*

'Upon an helme, on a wreath silver gules, two Woodhouse armes gules and vert in cross, holding in every hand a falchion silver, hilted & shafted gould, mantled gules, doubled silver'.

MOODY, Edmund, of Bury St. Edmunds; Grant of Arms and Crest by Hawley, Clarenceux, 6 October 1541. *E.A.N. & Q. (N.S.) II. 39*

ARROW see also PHEON

An arrow Or.

ARROW, of Lowestoft. *Druery*

On an arrow head towards the dexter fesseways Or a cock Or membered Gules.

LITTELL, Geoffry, of Stoke next Nayland, in Suffolk. *Grants & Certificates (Harl. MS 1,105)*

A cock Or combed and wattled Gules standing on an arrow.

LITTELL, LITTLE, of Stutton, Alpheton, Ballingdon Hall in Sudbury. *Davy, A., All Saints church, Sudbury. Badham, 37*

An arrow erect point downward Gules between two wings Or.

UTBER, of Lowestoft. *Gillingwater, 302. Davy, A. Lees, 95*

An arrow in pale Sable headed and feathered Argent attached to the shaft a pair of wings expanded Or the ball of the arrow in base.

UTBER, Captain John, killed 1665, aged 22. *Her.Suff.Ch., Monument and Ledger stone, St. Margaret, Lowestoft*

An arrow erect Argent entwined by a snake Vert.

WHITBY, of Boulge. *Davy, A., church*

An arrow in pale point downwards entwined with a snake all Proper.

WHITBY, William, died 1792. *Her.Suff.Ch., Tablet, Boulge*

TWO OR MORE ARROWS

Two arrows in saltire Gules headed Argent feathered Or tied with a ribbon Argent.

PINNER, PYNER, Francis, of Bury St. Edmunds, Suffolk; Grant by W. Camden, Clar., 2 May 1612. *Grants & Certificates (Stowe MS 700; Harl. MS 1,172)*

Two arrows in saltire points downward Gules feathered and headed Or banded Argent.

PINNER, of Bury. *Davy, A. (by Camden)*

In front of a garb Or three arrows two in saltire and one in pale points downward Sable.

OTTLEY, Rector of Acton. *Davy, A.*

Three arrows one in fesse and two in saltire Gules flighted Proper encircled by a laurel wreath.

WHITE, Herbert, of Freston House, died 1934. *Her.Suff.Ch., Wall tablet, Freston. Fairbairn, as Jervis White Jervis*

Four arrows.

DAWSON. *Davy, A., Groton church*

'And for his Creast a Wreath or & sable five Broad Arrowes sable feathered and Armed Argent interlaced through a Mascle Or'.

CROW, Christopher, of East Bilney, co. Norfolk; Confirmation of Arms and Crest by William Camden, Clar., 27 May 1614. *Misc.Gen. et Her. 5th S. VIII. 261* (Soc. of Ant. MS 378, fos. 523 and 625)*

Five arrows Sable feathered Argent four in saltire and one in pale tied together with a string Gules between the arrows a mascle Or.

CROWE, of Earl Soham, Coddenham, Ipswich, Debenham. *Davy, A.*

Five arrows Or feathered and headed Argent entwined with a snake Proper.

ELWES, Bart., of Stoke by Clare. *Bokenham. Davy, A. Washbourne*, 'Elves, Elwes, Linc., Suff., etc.' Burke, L.G. 1853 ed.*

Five arrows four in saltire and one in pale Or flighted and barbed Argent entwined by a snake Proper.

ELWES, John, of Stoke College, died 1849. *Her.Suff.Ch., Wall tablet and Window, Stoke by Clare*

A serpent Proper entwined round five arrows shafts

Or feathered and barbed Argent one in pale and four saltirewise.

> HALE, HALES, of Bury. *MS Ordinary of Arms, fo. 272*. Davy, A.*

A bundle of five arrows Proper banded Gules buckled Or.

> KETTLE, of Layham. *Davy, A., church*

Five arrows points downward one in pale the others saltirewise Or feathered and barbed Argent banded about with a wreath Argent and Sable.

> SEGRAVE, of Norfolk. *MS Ordinary of Arms, fo. 19**

Six arrows in saltire Or barbed and feathered Argent girt together with a belt Gules buckled and garnished Or, over the arrows a morion cap Proper.

> CECIL, Marquis of Salisbury, of Aldeburgh. *MS Ordinary of Arms, fo. 34*, untinctured. 'Richard Secyll' MS Philpot's Visitations, Norf.*, morion cap Azure. Davy, A., Laxfield church. Fairbairn**

Six arrows in saltire Proper feathered Argent barbed Or tied with a ribbon Sable.

> KEYNE, of Cretingham. *Davy, A. Washbourne, 'Suff.'*

Six arrows in saltire banded.

> SEGRAVE, of Framlingham. *Davy, A., church steeple*

Six broad arrows in saltire three and three encircled with a girdle.

> SHAW. *MS Heraldic Alphabet*

Six arrows interlaced in saltire Or feathered and barbed Argent bound together with a belt Gules the buckle pendent Or.

> SHAW, Bart., of Brightwell. *Davy, A.*

Seven arrows Proper enfiled with a ducal coronet Or.

> ARROWSMITH, of Huntingfield Hall. *Davy, A. Washbourne*, 'of Suff.' Fairbairn, 'Arrowsmyth of Huntingfield Hall, Suff.'*

Seven arrows six in saltire and one in pale Or heads and feathers Argent entwined by a snake Vert.

> HALES, HALLES, of London; Patent February 1605. *Grants & Certificates (Stowe MSS 706 and 707; Harl. MSS 1,115 and 1,422; 5,829; 6,095)*

A sheaf of arrows Or feathered Argent a girdle Gules buckle and pendent Or.

> SHAW, 'SCHAA, of Lancashire, goldsmyth of London' *Wall's Book. MS Ordinary of Arms, fo. 262*, buckles on either side of girdle*

'to his Crest a sheff of Arrowes Or/ ffethered ar/ a gyrdell g/ buckle and pendant or/ Sha of lancashyr goldsmyth of London' *MS Alphabet of Crests, fo. 117*

AXE BATTLE-AXE, HALBERD

A halbert in pale Or sticking on the point a dragon volant without feet Sable bezanty 'casting fyre at her tayle'

> DAWES, 'Daweus, Sheriff of London, temp. H.7' *Wall's Book*

A halberd erect Or on the point a flying dragon, or wyvern, without legs tail nowed Sable bezanty vulned Gules.

> DAWES, of Stowmarket. *Davy, A. Washbourne*, 'Lond., Suff., etc. A wyvern'*

A talbot sejant against a halberd erect in pale and clinging thereon a snake.

> HUNT, John, died 1764. *Her Suff.Ch., Ledger stone, Wherstead*

A battle-axe erect in pale crossed by a branch of laurel and cypress in saltire all Proper.

> MACLEAN, M.D., of Sudbury. *Davy, A.*

A talbot sejant against a battle-axe erect entwined with a serpent.

> SAFFORD, of Bungay, Ipswich, Weybread, Mettingham. *Davy, A.*

TWO OR MORE AXES

Two halberts in saltire tasselled.

> BULBROOKE, of Tostock. *Partridge, 217, churchyard (Darby, 1827)*

Two battle-axes endorsed saltire-wise ensigned by a dove all Proper.

> FLAMVILLE, Head Steward of Bury Abbey. *Davy, A., (Burke). Washbourne, 'of Leic.'*

Three halberts erect staves Sable headed Argent entwined with a ribbon thereon the words 'Vanes foy Mesme'.

> GILPIN, of Bungay. *Visitation 1664–8*, P' R. Cooke 1574 (Harl. MS 1,085, 30). Bokenham, 'words Une Foy Mesme', p.Cooke, Clar., 1574.*

Three halberts two in saltire and one in pale Proper tied with a ribbon thereon the word 'Foy'.

> GILPIN, Richard, of Bungay; Grant 1574. *Davy, A. Washbourne, 'Suff.' Fairbairn, 'Bungay, Suff.'*

Three halberts Gules headed studded and garnished Or one in pale and two in saltire enfiled by a coronet Or.

> MOWSE. 'TYDUR alias MOWSE', Anthony, of Cotton in Suffolk'; Patent from Sir R. St. George, Clar., 6 October 1633. *Grants & Certificates (Harl. MS 1,105)*

BEAST

UNKNOWN

An animal passant.

> BACON, Edmund, died 1625. *Her.Suff.Ch., Monument, Hessett*

An animal sejant.

> PLUMSTED, Thomas, Gent., died 1750. *Her.Suff.Ch., Ledger stone, Beccles*

DEMI-ANTELOPE

A demi-antelope salient Azure collared gemel and armed Or.

> ROCHESTER, of Essex. *MS Heraldic Alphabet*

A demi-antelope Sable crined and attired Argent charged all over with plates and pierced through the chest with a broken spear Or headed Argent vulned Gules.

> SINGLETON, of Mendlesham, Beccles, Wingfield. *Davy, A.*

A demi-antelope quarterly.

> SPRING, SPRYNGE, of Lavenham. *Visitation 1561* (MS G.7). MS Knight's Visitations, Suff.**

A demi-antelope quarterly Argent and Or.

> SPRING, SPRYNGE, of Lavenham. *Visitation 1561* (Iveagh Copy)*

A demi-antelope quarterly Argent and Sable.

> SPRING, SPRINGE, of Lavenham. *Visitation 1561 (ed. Metcalfe)*

A demi-antelope rampant supporting with both feet a branch of flowers and leaves.

> SPRING, SPRYNG. *MS Heraldic Collections, fo. 88**

A demi-antelope quarterly Argent and Or horns counterchanged.

> SPRING, of Cockfield, Lavenham, Pakenham. *Davy, A. Washbourne, 'Suff.' Fairbairn, 'Suff.'*

ANTELOPE

An antelope seiant Or.

BARKER, of Worlingworth. *Surrey Visitation 1662 (H.S.) 7*. Davy, A., Boxted church*
An antelope trippant Proper.
CHITTOCK. *Davy, A.*
An antelope trippant Argent armed Or.
LISLE. *MS Ordinary of Arms, fo. 55**
An antelope.
PRATT, of Ipswich. *MS Fairfax (Tyl.)*
An antelope Proper collared Or.
RAPER, of Clopton. *Davy, A. Washbourne*
An antelope statant Sable bezanty ducally gorged and armed Or.
ROGERS. *MS Heraldic Collections, fo. 50**
An antelope seiant Ermine attired Or resting his dexter hoof on an escutcheon per pale Or and Argent.
TURNER. *MS ex-Taylor Coll.**
An antelope seiant Ermine attired Or reposing the dexter hoof on an escutcheon Or.
TURNER, of Halesworth. *Davy, A.*
An antelope Sable spotted Or.
YAXLEE, of Yaxley. *Bokenham*

APE

A monkey passant guardant Proper environed about the loins and lined Vert.
BERNERS. 'BARNES, William'. *MS Knight's Visitations, Essex*, 'lined Vert or Azure'*
A monkey Proper environed about the loins and lined Or.
BERNERS, Lord, of Icklingham, Woolverstone. *Davy, A. Washbourne*
A monkey Proper environed about the loins and lined Or holding a scroll with the motto Del fuego io avolo [I escape from the fire].
BERNERS, of Woolverstone Park. *Burke, L.G. 1853 and 1900 eds.*
A monkey Proper environed about the loins and lined Or holding a scroll with the motto Del fuego io avolo.
'BERNERS, Charles Hugh, of Woolverstone Park, Suff.' *Fairbairn*
A monkey passant Proper environed about the loins and lined Or.
FITZGERALD, of Bredfield, Wherstead, Boulge. *MS Ordinary of Arms, fo. 271*. Davy, A.*
A monkey passant guardant Sable collared and chained round the body Or.
FITZGERALD. *Washbourne, 'Suff. and Northamp.' Fairbairn, 'Suff. and Northamp.'*
An ape passant, or passant guardant, environed round the loins and with the chain reflexed over the back.
FITZGERALD. *Livery buttons*.*
A monkey stantant [sic] Proper environed about the middle with a plain collar and chained Or.
FITZGERALD. *Her.Suff.Ch., Window, Groton, 'Fitzgerald and Halifax 1807'*
An ape admiring himself in a looking glass Proper.
MARTIN, of Hemingstone. *Davy, A. Burke, L.G. 1853 ed. E.A.N. & Q. V. 356. Fairbairn, 'of Hemingston, Suff.'* William Martin, of Hemingstone Hall, died 1842. *Her.Suff.Ch., Wall tablet, Hemingstone*
A monkey Proper collared Or admiring himself in a mirror Proper.
MARTIN, Richard Bartholomew, of Hemingstone Hall, died 1865. *Her.Suff.Ch., Hatchment, Hemingstone*

ASS

An ass passant Argent.

ASCOUGH. *Davy, A.*
An ass with long ears statant Argent semy of estoiles Or [sic].
BAYNHAM. *MS Heraldic Collections, fo. 59**

BADGER

A brock, or badger, statant Proper.
BROKE, BROOK. *MS Heraldic Alphabet. MS ex-Taylor Coll.**
A brock, or badger, passant Argent or Proper.
BROKE, of Nacton, Capel, Coddenham. *Visitation 1664–8*. Bokenham. Davy, A. (Barrett MS). Washbourne*, 'badger Proper, with augmentation'.* 'Sir Philip Broke, Bart., of Nacton' *Fairbairn*, with augmentation. Bookplate**
A badger.
BROOKE, Charles Berjew Brooke, of Brantham Place, J.P., died 1922. *Her.Suff.Ch., Wall tablet, Brantham*
A brock, or badger, passant Proper.
BROKE-MIDDLETON, Sir George, 3rd Bart., died 1887. *Fairbairn*. Her.Suff.Ch., Wall tablet and Glass, Nacton; Hatchment, Barham; Glass, Coddenham.* [The second crest, for Broke. First crest, for Middleton, q.v. Third crest, of Augmentation – see Out of a coronet naval a naked arm wreathed and holding a trident]
A badger, or brock, Proper.
VERE, Sir Charles Broke. *Davy, A.*

BAT

A bat displayed volant Argent.
BOGGAS, of Brantham. *Davy, A.*
A bat displayed.
MARRIOTT, Rector of Iken, 1844. *Davy, A. (Seal)*

DEMI-BEAR

A demi-bear salient Sable muzzled Or.
BARNARD, BERNARD, of Akenham. *Visitation 1561 (MSS G.7* and Iveagh Copy*). MS Ordinary of Arms, fo. 106*. MS Martin's Crests. MS Heraldic Alphabet. Bookplates**
A demi-bear erect Sable muzzled Or.
BARNARD, of Akenham, Withersfield. *Harl. 772*. Davy, A. Crisp's Visitation, XIX. 160*
A demi-bear couped Sable muzzled and collared and holding between its paws a mascle Or.
BARNARD, Rev. Thomas and son, Rev. Robert Barnard, Rectors of Withersfield. *Crisp's Visitation, XIX. 153**
A demi-bear Sable muzzled Gules.
BARNARD. *Sharpe*
A demi-bear rampant Sable muzzled collared and chained Or.
MILLS, MYLES, MYLL. *Wall's Book, 'Myll'. Davy, A. Washbourne, 'Mills, Suff.' Fairbairn, 'Mills, Suff.'*
A demi-bear couped Sable muzzled and chained Or.
'MILL'. *MS Martin's Crests*

BEAR

Rampant or Salient

A bear rampant supporting a staff in pale Proper.
MOONE. *Davy, A.*
A bear rampant Argent holding in his paws a ragged staff and collared and chained Or.
SIDNEY, Countess of Leicester. *Davy, A., Thwaite church*
A bear salient Sable muzzled Or.
MILLS. *Sharpe*

Passant

A bear passant Azure muzzled and collared Argent.
  BARWICK, of Westhorpe, Bury. *Davy, A.,*
  Fornham All Saints church
A bear passant transpierced with an arrow in bend
sinister.
  CRETING, of Creeting. *Davy, A. Washbourne,*
  'Cretinge, Suff.' Fairbairn, 'Creting, Kent and
  Cretinge, Suff.'
A bear passant Argent gutty Gules muzzled Gules.
  FORBES, Viscount, Earl of Granard, Ireland. Of
  Chilton near Clare. *Davy, A. Washbourne.*
A bear passant Proper muzzled collared and chained
Or on the shoulder a bezant.
  LEE, of Weybread. *Davy, A. Livery button* *

Statant

A bear statant Sable collared and chained Or.
  IVES, of Belton. *Davy, A., church. E.A.N. & Q.*
  II. 326.
A bear statant Proper muzzled Gules collared and
chained Argent charged on the shoulder with a
bezant.
  LEE, George, Esq., died 1861. *Her.Suff.Ch., Wall*
  brass, Thrandeston

Sejant

A bear seiant Proper.
  BARKER, of Grimston Hall. *MS Ordinary of*
  Arms, fo. 196. Davy, A.*
A bear seiant Or collared Sable.
  BARKER, of Grimston Hall in Trimley. *MS*
  Heraldic Alphabet. Washbourne, 'of Ess. and*
  Suff.' Sir John Fytch Barker, 7th Bart., of
  Grimston Hall, died 1766. Her.Suff.Ch.,
  Hatchment, Trimley St. Martin
A bear seiant holding up her chains with the right
paw collared and ringed Sable.
  BARKER, Bart., of Ipswich. *Davy, A.*
A bear seiant Or torteauxy [*sic*] chained Vert.
  RUSHBROKE. Bokenham
A bear seiant Proper.
  STURMYN. *Davy, A.*
A bear sejant muzzled collared and chained.
  TALKARNE, Edward, Esq., died 1597.
  Her.Suff.Ch., Effigy brass, Stoke by Clare

BEAVER

A demi-beaver salient per pale Or and Vert holding
in his paws a branch of three quatrefoils Argent
slipped and leaved Vert.
  EDEN, of Ballington [*sic*] Hall in Sudbury.
  Bokenham
A beaver passant Proper.
  BEEVOR, Vicar of Henley. *Davy, A.*

DEMI-BOAR

A demi-boar erect Argent bristled Or.
  BOLLE, BOLLES *Davy, A.*
A demi-boar supporting a thistle.
  BURLEY. *Her.Suff.Ch., Ledger stone, Eye*

Rampant or Salient

A demi-boar couped rampant Argent maned Or
pierced in the chest with an arrow Argent feathered
Or.
  BOLLES, BOWLES. 'Rychard Bolles of Haugh'
  MS Knight's Visitations, Linc. MS Ordinary of*
  *Arms, fo. 100**
A demi-boar rampant holding a thistle all Proper.
  BURLEY, of Eye. *Davy, A., church*
A demi-boar rampant Gules.

CROTCHERWOOD, CRATCHWODE, of Cavendish.
  MS Fairfax (Tyl.)
A demi-boar rampant reguardant Or vulned Gules
pierced through the body with a spear Sable lined
Or which he holds in his mouth.
  CRACHERODE. 'William Crocharde' *MS Knight's*
  Visitations, Essex. 'William Corwchard'*
  *MS Philpot's Visitations, Essex**
A demi-boar rampant reguardant Or vulned Gules
pierced through the body with a spear Sable point
downward Argent hafted Or.
  CRACHERODE. 'Mathew Crochrad' *MS Philpot's*
  *Visitations, Suff.**
A demi-boar rampant reguardant Gules armed Or
pierced through the body with a broken spear
Argent which he holds in his mouth.
  CRACHERODE, of Cavendish. *Bokenham, 'boar*
  salient'. Davy, A., Rougham church.
  Washbourne, 'Crochrod, Ess. and Suff.'*
  Fairbairn, 'Crochrod, Essex and Suff.'
A demi-boar salient supporting a thistle.
  BURLEY, of Eye. *Bokenham*
A demi-boar salient.
  NORGATE. *Bookplate**

BOAR

A boar Sable armed Or.
  BACON, of Gorleston. *Davy, A., church*
A wild boar sticking between the cleft of an oak tree
fructed all Proper with a lock and chain holding the
cleft together Azure.
  DOUGLAS, of Halesworth. Vicar of Kenton.
  Davy, A.
A boar quarterly Or and Gules.
  GUINNESS, Baron Iveagh. *Her.Suff.Ch., Glass,*
  Elvedon
A boar.
  MERILL. *Her.Suff.Ch., Bench end, Hollesley*
  'to his crest a bore b/ bryseled the pursell[?] Or.
  VERE, Erl of Oxford knight by h 8' *MS*
  Alphabet of Crests, fo. 132b

Passant

A boar passant Ermine tusks Or on its side a
crescent Or.
  BACON, Sir Nicholas, Lord Keeper of the Great
  Seal; Confirmation by Dethick, Garter; Cooke,
  Clarenceux and Flower, Norroy, 27 February
  1568. *Grants & Certificates (Stowe MS 703)*
The same as for Sir Nicholas Bacon, but with a
mullet in place of the crescent.
  BACON, James, Citizen and Alderman of London;
  third son of Robert Bacon of Drinkstone, Co.
  Suffolk, gent.; Confirmation by Dethick, Cooke
  and Flower, 28 February 1568. *Grants &*
  Certificates (Stowe MS 703)
A boar passant Ermine armed Or.
  BACON, BAKON, of Redgrave, Shrubland,
  Herringfleet, Mildenhall. *Harl. 772*. 'S*r*
  Edmond Bacon of Redgrave in Com Suffolk
  Knight and Barronett' *MS Lilly's Visitation of*
  Suffolk. London Visitation 1633 (H.S.) I. 37*.*
  Bokenham. MS Heraldic Alphabet. Page. Davy,
  A. Washbourne, 'of Norf. and Suff.' Fairbairn*,*
  'Barts., of Redgrave and Mildenhall, Suff.' Bacon
  of Redgrave 1616–1755. *Her.Suff.Ch., Altar*
  tomb, Wall tablets and Hatchments, Redgrave.
  Bacon, Penelope, wife of Lyonell Bacon, died
  1628; Helen, wife of Edward Bacon, died 1646.
  Altar tomb and Wall tablet, Barham. Philip, son
  of Edward Bacon of Shrubland, died 1635.
  Tablet, Woolverstone. Sir Butts Bacon, Bart., died

1661. *Ledger stone, Blundeston.* Bacon of
Coddenham 1666–1795. *Tomb, Wall tablet and
Hatchments, Coddenham.* Bacon, Mary, wife of
T. Machin, died 1796. *Tombstone, churchyard,
Pakefield.* Bacon [not identified]. *Hatchment,
Somersham*
A boar passant.
    BORRETT, of Stradbroke. *Green Memoir, 70.
Page, Slab, church*
A tower triple-towered Argent port Sable a boar
issuing therefrom Sable.
    CANTRELL, of Bury. *Davy, A., Hemingstone
church*
A boar Sable treading among weeds Vert.
    CLOSE, of Ipswich, Hitcham. *Davy, A.*
A boar passant Sable armed bristled and hoofed
Argent.
    EUSTON, of Euston. *Davy, A.*
A boar passant Sable.
    GARDEN, of Redisham Hall. *Davy, A., Ringsfield
church*
A boar passant.
    GARDEN, John, of Redishall [*sic* Redisham] Hall,
died 1820. *Her.Suff.Ch., Tomb, Churchyard,
Ringsfield*
A boar passant Sable ducally gorged and armed Or.
    LE GRICE. 'Charles Legrys of Brokdyshe' *MS
Knight's Visitations, Norf.**
A boar passant Sable ducally gorged.
    LE GRICE, Of Bury, Belton. *Davy, A.*
A boar passant ducally gorged and armed Or.
    GRICE, of Norfolk. *Her.Suff.Ch., on panelling,
Mendlesham*
A boar passant Azure armed and bristled Or.
    HOLLES, Earl of Clare. *Davy, A.*
A boar passant Sable collared and chained Or.
    IVES, of Belton, Yarmouth. *Druery, 154. Page,
Monument, Belton church.* John Ives, died 1776,
aged 25 (the antiquary); John Ives, died 1793.
Her.Suff.Ch., Wall tablet, Belton
A boar passant Proper.
    MAGENIS, Richard, of Ireland, died 1863.
Her.Suff.Ch., Wall tablet, Edwardstone
A boar passant Azure armed Or.
    VERE, VEER, of Blakenham, Stradbroke, Henley.
'Veer, Erle of Oxinford' *Wall's Book. Banners &
Standards**, [as badge]. *Bokenham. Page. Davy,
A. Washbourne, 'Vere, Suff.'*

Sejant
A boar sejant Or.
    BARKER. *MS Fairfax (Tyl.)*

BROCK see BADGER

BULL see OX

CAMEL
'to his crest on a wreth ar/sa/ a camell sa/ Langued
g/ a bowt his neck a gemell Indented bugled [*sic*]
or/'
    CARDINAL. 'willm Cardenall of moche bromley
in Essex'. *MS Alphabet of Crests, fo. 23.*
A camel passant Argent its humps Sable.
    CARDINAL. 'William Cardynall of Muche
Bromley' *MS Knight's Visitations, Essex**
A dromedary statant Argent hump Sable.
    CARDINAL. 'William Cardynall' *MS Philpot's
Visitations, Essex**
A dromedary Proper.
    'CARDINALL' *MS Heraldic Alphabet*
A dromedary Proper charged on the side with a
crescent and collared dancetty Or.

CARDINAL, of East Bergholt. *Davy, A., church
(Barrett)*
A camel couchant the hump and tail Or.
    MAW, MAWE, of Rendlesham. *Visitation 1612*
A camel Sable collared Or.
    WEST, WESTON. *Davy, A.*
A camel passant.
    WHITAKER. Vicar of Fressingfield, Rector of
Withersdale. *Partridge, 104 (Darby, 1825),
Fressingfield churchyard*
A camel passant Argent.
    WHITTAKER, of Mendham, Knodishall. *Davy, A.,
Fressingfield church*
'to his crest a camell sa/ bezanty horned [*sic*] tayled
or/ P norrey harvy the 4&5 P & Mary [1557/8] to
ffrancis Yaxley'
    YAXLEY. *MS Alphabet of Crests, fo. 65*

CAMELEOPARD [GIRAFFE]
A cameleopard Argent pellety attired collared and
lined Or.
    CRISPE, of Elden [*sic*], Rougham. *Davy, A.
(Edms.)*
Upon a rock a cameleopard statant Sable semy of
annulets gorged with a collar with chain reflexed
over the back and holding in his mouth a horseshoe
all Or.
    CRISP, of Rendlesham, Melton, Sternfield,
Chillesford, Butley Abbey, Lt. Wenham Hall, Gt.
Bealings, Playford Hall. Frederick Arthur Crisp,
eldest son of Frederick Augustus Crisp, of The
Hall, Playford, Suffolk; Grant of Arms and Crest
by Sir Albert Woods, Garter and Walter Blount,
Clarenceux, 4 November 1884. *Family of Crispe
(N.S.) 1.89–90*. Crisp's Visitation, XIII. 115*.
Fairbairn*, 'of Playford Hall and The Cedars,
Gt. Bealings, Suff.'*
A cameleopard sejant Or gorged with a collar with
chain reflexed over the back Gules supporting with
the dexter foreleg an oar of the Royal State Barge
Proper.
    CRISP, Bart., of Bramfield, Bungay. *Crisp's
Visitation, XVIII. 204**

DEMI-CAT
A demi-cat rampant guardant Proper.
    MUMFORD, of Yoxford. *Davy, A.*
A demi-cat reguardant per pale Argent and Sable
collared counterchanged holding in her dexter paw a
branch of mulberry Vert flowered Argent the sinister
paw resting on the wreath.
    MURIELL. *Wall's Book*
'to his Crest a Demy catte P pale regardant ar/sa/ a
coller count/ the fyrst foote holding up a braunche of
mulbery Vert the flowers ar/ the other foote on the
wreth'
    MURYELL. *MS Alphabet of Crests, fo. 81b*
A demi-cat guardant per pale Argent and Sable
gorged with a fesse counterchanged holding in her
dexter paw a branch of cinquefoils Argent leaved
Vert.
    'MURYELL, Edw: de London' *MS Ordinary of
Arms, fos. 182* and 199**
A demi-cat per pale Argent and Sable gorged with a
fesse counterchanged holding in her claws a branch
of roses Argent leaved Vert.
    MURIELL, of Yoxford, Sibton. *Davy, A.
Washbourne*
A demi-cat rampant per pale Or and Gules gutty
counterchanged.
    WITHIPOLE, 'VIDEPOL of London' *Wall's Book*
'to his Crest a demy Catte rampant Pty par pale or/

g/ gowtey counter colored.   P. C. Benolt'.
> 'WIDEPOLE of London'   *MS Alphabet of Crests, fo. 132*

A demi mountain cat rampant guardant per pale Or and Gules gutty counterchanged.
> WITHIPOLE, WITHYPOL, of Christ Church, Ipswich.   *Visitation 1561 (MSS G.7* and Iveagh Copy*)* and *(ed. Metcalfe). Davy, A. Washbourne, 'Withypoule, Suff.' Fairbairn, 'Withypoule, Suff.' Withypoll, 17 (Thos. Wall's book of Crests, 1530)*

CAT

Passant

A 'Tabby cat' passant guardant.
> BLAKE.   *MS Ordinary of Arms, fo. 271**

A mountain cat passant guardant Proper.
> BLAKE, Bart., of Langham, Bury.   *Davy, A. Fairbairn, 'Suff.'*

Statant

A cat-a-mountain statant guardant quarterly Or and Azure.
> EURE, 'EVERS, Sir Willam'   *Banners & Standards**

Sejant

A cat-a-mountain sejant guardant Proper collared and chained and on the breast a cross Or.
> BURKE, of Auberies in Sudbury.   *Burke, L. G. 1900 ed. Fairbairn, 'of Auberies, Sudbury, Suffolk'*

A cat-a-mountain sejant guardant Proper collared and chained Or.
> BURKE, of Auberies in Bulmer, co. Essex.   *Crisp's Visitation, III. 43–5*, Pedigree.*

Upon the stump of a tree eradicated Proper surmounted by an anchor in bend sinister Or a martin-cat sejant supporting between the paws a mirror Proper and gorged with a naval crown therefrom a chain reflexed over the back Or.
> MARTIN. 'Major-General William G. Martin, of Hemingstone, Ipswich, Suffolk; Col. Sir Richard Martin, of Aldeburgh, Suff.'   *Fairbairn**

Upon the stump of a tree eradicated Proper surmounted by a martin cat sejant supporting between the paws a mirror also Proper and gorged with a naval crown thereon a chain reflexed over the back Or.
> MARTIN, of Hemingstone Hall.   *Burke, L. G. 1900 and 1952 eds.*

A cat seiant reguardant per fesse Or and Gules pelletty and bezanty counterchanged collared Gules.
> RAYMOND.   *Wall's Book*

'to his Crest a catte or/ pelleted syttyng regardant on the necke a fece cotesed g/ the hynder pts count besanted'
> RAYMOND.   *MS Alphabet of Crests, fo. 109*

A cat seiant Argent.
> RAYMOND, of Hopton.   *Davy, A., church*

DEMI-DEER

A demi-stag Proper attired Or.
> CHITTOKE, of Wortham.   *Visitation 1577*

A demi-stag Gules semy of estoiles and attired Or.
> COURTHOPE.   *Washbourne, 'Suff.'*

A demi-hind erased Proper charged with two bars and holding between her hooves a cross crosslet Or.
> CROSSLEY, Bart., of Somerleyton.   *Burke, Peerage 1891 ed.* Fairbairn*, 'of Somerleyton, Lowestoft, Suff.'*

A demi-hind erased Proper charged with two bars Or and holding between the hooves a cross crosslet Or.

CROSSLEY, Savile, Bart., 1st Baron Somerleyton, died 1935.   *Her.Suff.Ch., Wall monument, Glass and Hassock, Somerleyton*

A demi-hind Sable bezanty.
> DIXON, Samuel, died 1739; widow died 1756.   *Her.Suff.Ch., Wall tablet and Floor slab, Gt. Finborough. Crest missing 1980*

A demi-stag collared and lined.
> FISHER. Bishop of Salisbury. Of Sibton.   *Davy, A.*

A demi-stag Proper attired Or supporting with its forelegs an anchor in pale Or.
> HARDING, Robert, Alderman and Sheriff of London; Grant by Sir G. Dethick, Garter; Robert Cooke, Clarenceux and W. Flower, Norroy, 30 August 1568.   *Grants & Certificates (Harl. MS 1359; Stowe MS 703)*

A demi-buck Proper attired Or holding an anchor Or.
> HARDING.   *Davy, A. Her.Suff.Ch., Ledger stone, churchyard, Eye*

A demi-stag Proper
> SPRING, of Pakenham.   *Visitation 1561 (ed. Howard) I. 166, 'Granted 2 January 1600, Camden's Grants.'*

A demi-stag quarterly Argent and Or.
> SPRING, of Lavenham.   *Visitation 1561 (ed. Howard) I. 166*

A hart Proper couped at the buttocks attired Or vulned by a spear run through his belly Or.
> SYNGLETON, of Mendlesham.   *MS Fairfax*

Reguardant

A demi-stag reguardant Proper charged on the shoulder with three roses chevronwise Argent and supporting a Passion cross Or.
> JUMP, James, of Hardwicke House, Bury St. Edmunds, Suff.   *Fairbairn*

A demi-stag reguardant Proper attired Or.
> 'SHEPHARD, Robert, of Kirby Bedon, co. Norfolk'; Grant by W. Camden, Clarenceux, 1598.   *Grants & Certificates (Stowe MSS 706 and 707)*

Springing. Rampant or Salient

A demi-stag rampant Proper attired Or.
> CHITTOCK, of Wortham, Thrandeston. 'Thomas Chittell'   *MS Philpot's Visitations, Suff.* Davy, A.*

A demi-buck salient Proper attired Or.
> CHITTOCK.   *Bokenham*

A demi-stag salient Gules semy of estoiles and attired Or.
> COURTHOPE.   *Fairbairn*, 'Suff.'*

A demi-hart salient Sable attired Or supporting an anchor erect with a ring Or 'nec Stock' [sic].
> HARDING, 'HARDYNGE'.   *MS Heraldic Alphabet*

A demi-stag rampant Proper.
> HARRIS, of Thorndon.   *Bookplate**

A demi-buck salient Argent attired Or.
> LONE, of Worlingham, Ellough.   *Visitation of Kent 1619 (H.S.) 138, note. Visitation 1664–8. Fairbairn*, 'of Kent and Warlingham and Elloure [sic], Suff.'* Thomas Lone, died 1683.   *Her.Suff.Ch., Ledger stone, Beccles*

A demi-stag rampant Gules.
> ROANE, Anne, dau. of Edward Roane, died 1626.   *Her.Suff.Ch., Funeral board, Layham. 'Pinxit 1736'*

A demi-stag rampant Proper holding in his mouth an acorn Proper leaved Vert.
> ROANE, of Layham.   *Davy, A.*

A demi-roebuck rampant quarterly Argent and Or

holding in his mouth a branch of columbines Vert flowered Azure.

> SPRING. *Wall's Book, 'of Laynham in Essex' [sic]. Visitation 1561 (ed. Howard) 1. 166**

'to his crest a demy Roo Bucke rampant quarterly ar/or/ holdyng in his mouth a braunche of columbynes Vt flowers b/'

> 'SPRYNG of Lanam in Essex' *MS Alphabet of Crests, fo. 117*

A demi-stag rampant quarterly Argent and Sable attired Or.

> SPRING. 'Wyll Springe' *MS Philpot's Visitations, Suff.**

A demi-buck rampant quarterly Argent and Or horned Argent.

> SPRING. *MS Fairfax*

A demi-roebuck rampant Proper.

> SPRING, of Pakenham. *Davy, A.*

A demi-stag springing quarterly Argent and Or in the mouth some flowers Argent.

> SPRING, of Lavenham, Pakenham. *Davy, A. Washbourne, 'Suff.' Fairbairn, 'of Cockfield, Suff.'*

A demi-stag springing.

> SPRING, Sir William, Bart., died 1654; Mary, wife of 2nd Bart., died 1662. *Her.Suff.Ch., Ledger stones, Pakenham*

A demi-stag salient in the mouth a slip of honeysuckle all Proper.

> SWIFT, Robert, of Rotherham, co. York.; Confirmation by Sir G. Dethick, Garter, 10 May 1561. *Grants & Certificates (Harl. MS 1,441; Stowe MS 703; Add. MS 26,753)*

A demi-stag salient in his mouth a lily leaved and seeded Proper.

> SWIFT. *MS Martin's Crests*

A demi-buck rampant Proper in his mouth a honeysuckle Proper stalked and leaved Vert.

> SWIFT, of Gt. Blakenham *Davy, A., church*

A demi-buck rampant Sable holding in the mouth a piece of honeysuckle Proper stalked and leaved Vert, an annulet on the shoulder for difference.

> SWIFT, Richard, of London, Merchant, died in Gt. Blakenham, 1645. *Her.Suff.Ch., Monument in tower, Gt. Blakenham*

A demi-hind erased and salient Or.

> SYMMES, SYMES. *MS Ordinary of Arms, fo. 205*. MS Heraldic Alphabet*

DEER

A buck and vine both Proper.

> BRADSHAIGH. *MS Heraldic Alphabet. Fairbairn*

A stag Proper attired ducally gorged and lined Or.

> BROWNE. *Davy, A.*

A stag Argent attired Or ducally gorged chain and ring Or.

> LISLE. 'S. Nycolas Lysle' *Harl. MS 6163*

A stag Gules armed Or.

> MAYNARD, of Ipswich. *MS Fairfax*

A stag Ermine attired Or ducally gorged Gules.

> SCRIVENER, John, son of Randolf Scrivener, of Ipswich, died 1662. *Her.Suff.Ch., Tablet, Sibton*

Reguardant

A stag reguardant Proper.

> BUSK, of East Bergholt. *Davy, A.*

Springing. Rampant or Salient

A stag springing Gules ducally gorged and lined Or attired Vert at the top of each branch [sic, ?tine] a bezant.

> FELTON, Sir Compton Felton, Bart., died 1719.

Her.Suff.Ch., On monument erected 1657; Wall tablet and Ledger stone, Playford

A buck rampant Gules armed Or between two branches Vert.

> HITCHAM, of Levington, Framlingham. *Davy, A., Framlingham church*

A buck salient Proper attired Or among leaves and the trunk of a tree also Proper.

> HITCHAM, of Framlingham. *Loder, 304. Copinger, IV*

A buck springing holding in its mouth a branch.

> SUCKLING, Rev. Maurice, S.T.P., Rector of Barsham and of Wooton, in Norfolk, died 1730. *Her.Suff.Ch., Ledger stone, Barsham*

Courant

A buck in full course.

> ROGERS, Samuel, Rector of Otley, died ?1749. *Her.Suff.Ch., Ledger stone, Otley*

A stag courant Azure armed Or.

> SUCKLING. 'Robert Suckling of norwiche' *MS Knight's Visitations, Norf.* Muskett. II. 177, 'Suckling of Barsham. The original crest– the colour afterwards changed to Gules, and so shown on some of the family monuments. Queen Elizabeth, on a progress through Norfolk, granted to Robert Suckling a stag Or holding in the mouth honeysuckle.'*

A stag courant Or holding in its mouth a bunch of honeysuckle Proper.

> SUCKLING, of Barsham. *Page. Davy, A. Fairbairn, 'a buck'. Muskett. II. 177 (Suckling 1.41), 200. Crisp's Visitation, XIX, 195*. E.A. Misc. 1918, 114. Burke, L.G.1900* and 1952 eds.* Her.Suff.Ch., Barsham*

Trippant. Passant [Alphabetically by name]

A hind passant Ermine.

> ALINGTON. *MS Fairfax (Tyl.)*

A hind trippant Argent collared with two bars gemel Gules.

> AMYS, of Tilbury, co. Essex. *MS Heraldic Alphabet*

A hind passant Argent collared Gules.

> AMYS, of Rickinghall. *Davy, A.*

A stag trippant Or horns and hooves Sable on a collar Sable three cross crosslets Or.

> BUCKERIDGE, John, Bishop of Rochester, Bishop of Ely, 1628. *Grants & Certificates (Stowe MS 707)*

A stag passant Ermine horns and hooves Or, on its side an annulet Gules.

> CAGE. 'Nicholas Gage [sic], Gent.' *Grants & Certificates (Stowe MS 707)*

A stag passant Ermine attired Or charged on the shoulder with an annulet Gules.

> CAGE, of Ipswich, Pakenham. *Davy, A., Burstall church*

A stag trippant Proper.

> CLUTTERBUCK. *MS Ordinary of Arms, fos. 43* and 59**

A hind trippant.

> COLLETT. *Davy, A., Westerfield church*

A hind trippant Argent.

> COLLET, COLLETT. *Washbourne*, 'Lond. and Suff.' Fairbairn*, 'London and Suff.' Henry Collett, Esq., died 1802. Her.Suff.Ch., Ledger stone, Westerfield*

A stag passant Ermine.

> CORNWALLIS, Bart., of Brome Hall, Soham Lodge. *MS Fairfax, Preston church*

A stag trippant.

CORNWALLIS. Rector of Gt. Wenham 1732 and of Chelmondiston 1738. *E.A. Misc. 1933, 60 (Bookplate)*

A hind passant Gules collared and lined Argent crossed over his [*sic*] back and standing [*sic*] in a bush of fern Vert.

FERNELEY, of West Creeting, Sutton. *MS Fairfax (Tyl.)*

A stag trippant.

HAND, of Ousden. *Davy, A.*

A hart passant Proper horned and membered and hurt in the haunch with an arrow Or feathered Argent.

HURT, of Saxmundham. *Davy, A. Bookplate**

A stag trippant Or, charged with a crescent Gules for difference.

MAYNARD, Sir William, Kt., and Bart., created Baron Maynard, of Wicklow in Ireland by K. James; Confirmation of Arms and Grant of Supporters, 26 November 1621. *Grants & Certificates (Add. MS 12,225)*

A buck passant.

MAYNARD. *MS Martin's Crests*

A buck trippant Or.

MAYNARD, of Hoxne. *Davy, A.*

A stag trippant Sable semy of plates attired Or.

MOOR, MOORE, MORE. 'Moore or More, of Ipswich, Patent 1586' *Grants & Certificates (Stowe MSS 670 and 703; Harl. MS 1,359). Davy, A., St. Lawrence church. Bokenham. Washbourne, 'Moore, Suff.' Fairbairn, 'Moore, Ipswich, Suff.'*

A hart, or buck, trippant Sable attired Or.

MOORE. *E.A. Misc. 1919. 5, 'TALMACH Hall in Lt. Bricett'*

A stag trippant.

POWLE, Rector of Gt. Waldingfield, died 1727. *Partridge, 19 (Darby, 1826) churchyard.* William Powle, A.M., Rector for 33 years, died 1727. *Her.Suff.Ch., Altar tomb, churchyard, Gt. Waldingfield*

A hind trippant Proper charged on the body with three crescents interlaced Or.

PRICKETT, of Browston Hall in Suffolk. *Burke, L.G. 1952 ed.**

A buck passant Proper attired Or holding in his mouth a rose Gules stalked and leaved Vert.

RICKTHORNE, of Cransford. *Davy, A.*

A buck trippant Or.

ROBARTSON, of Exning. *Davy, A., church*

A stag trippant.

ROBERTS. Rev. Robert Roberts, M.A., Vicar of Haverhill for 56 years, died 1875. *Her.Suff.Ch., Wall tablet, Haverhill*

A stag trippant Or attired Gules.

ROBERTSON, Francis, Esq., of co. Linc., died 1657. *Her.Suff.Ch., Funeral board, Exning, 'and within a few yards is a stone'*

A roebuck trippant Vert semy of bezants.

ROBINSON, Thomas, of London, merchant taylor to the King 1634. *Grants & Certificates (Harl MS 5,869)*

A buck trippant Or pellety attired Argent.

ROBINSON, of Ipswich. *Visitation 1664–8*

A buck passant Erminois.

ROBINSON, of Kentwell Hall. *Bokenham*

A buck trippant Or.

ROBINSON, Bart., of Kentwell Hall, Denston. *MS Martin's Crests. Davy, A. Washbourne*, 'Suff.' Fairbairn*, 'of Kentwell Hall, Suff.' Her.Suff.Ch., Funeral tabard, Altar tomb, Wall tablet, Ledger stones, Hatchment, Denston*

A buck trippant.

ROBINSON, of Ipswich, Denston, Dunwich. *Davy, A., St. Mary Tower church, Ipswich; Denston church. Bookplates**

A stag trippant Ermine ducally gorged and attired Or.

SCRIVENER, SCRIVENOR, of Sibton. *Bokenham. Sharpe*

A stag passant Proper attired Or.

SCRIVEN, SCRIVENER, of Stradishall. *MS ex-Taylor Coll.*, 'Skriven'. Davy, A.*

A buck trippant Ermine attired Or ducally gorged Gules.

SCRIVENER. *Davy, A. Washbourne, 'Scrivenor, Suff. A stag Ermine . . .' Fairbairn, 'Scrivenor, Sibton, Suff. A stag Ermine . . .'*

A stag trippant Proper gorged with a coronet and attired Or.

STEWARD, Nicholas, of Okhey, who married Ann Ford and was father of James, living in Essex in 1586. *Grants & Certificates (Stowe MS 670)*

A stag passant Proper attired Or ducally gorged Gules.

STEWARD. *Davy, A.*

A stag passant Proper attired Argent ducally gorged Gules.

STEWARD. *Washbourne, 'Camb., Suff. and Norf.' Fairbairn, 'Cambs., Suff. and Norf.'*

A stag passant Proper attired Azure ducally gorged Or.

STEWARD. *Her.Suff.Ch., Floor slab (now under bookstall), Lavenham*

A doe passant Proper

STEWARD, Johanna, dau. of Edward Bestney, Esq., wife of Simon Steward, died 1583. *Her.Suff.Ch., Wall tablet, Lakenheath*

A buck trippant Gules armed Or.

SUCKLING, of Barsham. *Davy, A.*

A stag trippant Argent holding in its mouth a branch of honeysuckle Proper.

SUCKLING, of Barsham. *Her.Suff.Ch., Glass, Barsham*

A buck trippant Proper

TOWNSEND, Viscount. Of Denham. *Davy, A.*

A buck trippant Or, a crescent for difference.

TROLLOPE, of Denham in Suffolk; Confirmation by Sir J. Borough, Garter, May 1639. *Grants & Certificates (Harl. MS 1,441)*

On the stump of a tree Proper a buck trippant Argent collared chained and attired Or.

WIGHTMAN, of Framlingham, Cransford, Saxted, Clare. *Wightman, 19, 106**

At Gaze. Statant

A stag statant.

BOKENHAM, Hugh, died 1669; Hugh, died 1679; Anthony, died 1703. *Her.Suff.Ch., Wall tablet, Helmingham*

A stag at graze.

BRADSHAIGH, Thomas, Rector for 42 years, died 1752. *Her.Suff.Ch., Ledger stone, Stratford St. Mary*

A stag statant Ermine attired Or.

CAGE, of Walsham le Willows, Pakenham. *Surrey Visitation 1530 (H.S.) 203*

A stag statant Proper gorged with a garland of roses Argent and Azure [*sic*].

CAVENDISH, of Cavendish. *Davy, A., church*

A buck statant Argent between two laurel branches Proper.

CLUTTERBUCK, of Yoxford. *Davy, A.*
A hind statant Argent.
COLLETT, of Westerfield. *Davy, A.*
A stag at gaze Proper.
MAYNARD, of Hoxne. *MS Heraldic Collections, fo. 85b.* Bokenham*
A stag statant Or.
MAYNARD, Viscount, of Hoxne. *Davy, A.*
A buck at gaze Or pellety.
ROBINSON. *MS Heraldic Alphabet*
A stag statant Or pellety attired Argent.
ROBINSON, 'of Dullingham, Cambs., and Denston Hall, Suff.' *Fairbairn.* [First crest, for Robinson. Second crest, for Jeaffreson, q.v.]
A stag at gaze Sable bezanty collared Or.
ROGERS, of Walsham le Willows. Rectors of Clopton and Otley. *Davy, A.*
A stag statant.
ROGERS, Samuel, son of Samuel Rogers, Rector, died 1716. *Her.Suff.Ch., Ledger stone, Otley*
A stag statant Ermine ducally gorged and attired Or.
SCRIVENER. *MS Knight's Visitations, Suff.*, 'Scriveno* of Ipswiche'. MS Ordinary of Arms, fo. 83** [no name given for crest, but arms those of Scrivener]. *MS Philpot's Visitations, Suff.*, 'Skryvenor of Ipshiche' [sic]*
A buck statant Ermine ducally gorged –.
SCRIVENER, of Sibton. *Visitation 1664–8**
A stag statant Proper ducally gorged Or.
STEWARD. *Fairbairn, 'of Cambs., Norf. and Suff.'*
An antelope deer statant Proper ducally gorged Gules attired Or, charged on the breast with an annulet Argent.
STEWART, of Barton Mills. *Davy, A.*
A buck statant Or.
TOWNSEND. *MS ex-Taylor Coll.*, 'Towneshend'*
On the stump of a tree a stag statant collared and lined.
WIGHTMAN. *MS Ordinary of Arms, fo. 250**
A stag at gaze Argent attired Sable.
WILLIAMS, of Stoke by Nayland. *Davy, A.*
A stag statant Argent.
WILLIAMS, Reginald, Sarah and Armin, children of Thomas Williams, died 1694–1699.
Her.Suff.Ch., Ledger stone, Stoke by Nayland
A hind statant Argent ducally gorged lined and ringed Or.
WINTER. 'wyll wynter' *MS Philpot's Visitations, Norf.**

Lodged. Couchant

A buck couchant Proper attired Or.
BOKENHAM, of Thornham, Weston. *Bokenham. Davy, A.*
A stag lodged Proper attired Or.
BOKENHAM. *Sharpe*
A stag lodged Or.
BOKENHAM. 'Lady Berners'. Of Market Weston. *Davy, A., church*
A stag lodged.
BOKENHAM, Elizabeth, wife of Richard Bokenham, Gent., died 1692; Richard Bokenham, Esq., died 1721. *Her.Suff.Ch., Ledger stones, Market Weston*
A buck couchant Ermine.
BOIS, BOYS, of Creeting St. Mary. *Davy, A.*
A stag couchant Proper attired Or.
BROCKETT. *MS Martin's Crests, 'stag lodged'. Davy, A. (Barrett MS)*
A ?brocket [a young deer, shown as normally except

for long ears and without attires] couchant or lodged Vert ducally gorged Or.
BROCKETT. *MS ex-Taylor Coll.**
A stag lodged Sable ducally gorged and lined Or.
BROCKETT, of Westleton. *Davy, A.*
A stag couchant reguardant Proper.
COCKS. *MS Heraldic Alphabet. Bookplate**
A stag lodged Sable attired Or.
COGGESHALL, of Melton, Benhall, Carlton, Hundon, Orford. *MS Knight's Visitations, Suff.** John Coggeshall. Stag attired and hooved Or. *MS Philpot's Visitations, Suff.* Davy, A., Brass, Orford church. Washbourne, 'Suff.'* Fairbairn, 'Suff.'* E.A.N. & Q. XIII. 193.* John Coggeshall, thrice Mayor of Orford, died 1640 (new inscription) *Her. Suff. Ch., Effigy brass, Orford.* Thomas Coggeshall, gent, and wife Sarah; he died 1712, she died 1708. *Floor slabs, Carlton*
A stag lodged Argent attired Or.
COGGESHALL, of Melton, Framlingham. *Visitation 1664–8*. Green, 149*
A stag lodged reguardant Argent attired Or gorged with a chaplet of oak leaves Vert and vulned on the shoulder.
CORNWALLIS, of Brome. *'Cornewalleys' Visitation 1561 (MSS G.7.* and Iveagh Copy*).* 'Sr Frederick Cornewallis Broome hall Knight and Barronett' *MS Lilly's Visitation of Suffolk**
A stag lodged reguardant Argent attired and unguled Or gorged with a chaplet of acorns and vulned in the shoulder Proper.
CORNWALLIS, Margaret, married Richard Cornwallis, died 1603. *Her.Suff.Ch., Wall monument, Cretingham*
A stag lodged Proper.
CREEKMAN, of Wisset. *Davy, A.*
A stag lodged Gules ducally gorged lined and ringed Or attired Vert on the tip of each tine a bezant.
FELTON. *MS Ordinary of Arms, fo. 51*. Washbourne*
A stag lodged.
GROOM, Margaret, 1905–1954. *Her.Suff.Ch., Bench end and outside West door, Hollesley*
A stag lodged Proper.
HOLLINGWORTH, HOLLINGSWORTH. Vicar of Stowmarket. *Davy, A.* Samuel Hollingsworth, died 1843; Arthur Hollingsworth, M.A., Vicar of Stowmarket with Stowupland for 25 years, died 1859. *Her.Suff.Ch., Wall tablets, Stowmarket*
A buck lodged in fern all Proper.
KINSMAN, KYNNESMAN. Master of Bury School. *Davy, A.*
A stag couchant.
POORE. Impaled by Timperley. *Her.Suff.Ch., Incised effigy wall slab, Hintlesham*
A doe couchant at the foot of a tree all Proper.
USBORNE, of Branches Hall in Cowlinge. *Davy, A., church*
A hind cumbent.
WARD, of Gorleston. *Bokenham*
A hind lodged.
WARD, Hannah, wife of Neale Ward, died 1766; Neale Ward, died 1775. *Her.Suff.Ch., Ledger stone, St. Mary's, Bury*

DOG

A dog seiant holding up his dexter foot Or collared Gules studded Or.
BARKER, of Ipswich. *Bokenham*
A curly-coated bushy tailed dog sejant Argent.
CROFT, CROFTES, of Saxham. *MS Knight's*

Visitations, Suff., fo. 108*
A ?dog seiant.
PLAISTED, of Beccles. *Davy, A., church*

HOUND

A hound sejant.
BLENERHAYSET. *Proc. S.I.A. IX. 186, Campsea Ash church flagon*
A hound Sable the snout Argent.
DRURY, 'DRUERY' *Wall's Book*
'to his Crest a hound sa/ the Snowte ar.'
'DREWRY' *MS Alphabet of Crests, fo. 29b*
'to his crest a hound g/ coller and Leche ar/ in a Bushe of fferne Vert'
'FFERNELEY, FFERNLEY' *MS Alphabet of Crests, fos. 38 and 40*
A hound standing Sable collared and chained Or.
HEIGHAM. *Bokenham*
'beryth to his crest a hound silver flecked sable standing on a wreath'.
HEYDON. *Wall's Book*
'to his crest a hound ar/ fflected sa/'
HEYDON. *MS Alphabet of Crests, fo. 54*
A hound statant Argent flecked Sable.
HAYDON, HEYDON. *Wall's Book.* 'Sr xpofer heydon' *MS Philpot's Visitations, Norf.**
A pied hound Argent and Sable.
HEYDON. *MS Martin's Crests*
A hound seiant Argent.
HUNGATE. *MS Martin's Crests.* Thomas Hungate, died 1729. *Her.Suff.Ch., Memorial board, Haverhill*
A hound Gules collared and lined Or the line round the dexter foreleg and tied behind the body in a knot.
MORRIS, MORYS, of Helmingham. *MS Knight's Visitations, Suff.* Bokenham, 'the line between his legs shackled and tied behind in a knot'*
A hound passant with a sprig in its mouth.
SYMONS, William, died 1785; widow died 1818. *Her.Suff.Ch., Ledger stone, St. Mary's, Bury*
A hound reguardant lying down against a bay tree Proper.
TOPPESFIELD, of Fressingfield. *Bokenham*

BLOODHOUND

A demi 'bludhonde' Sable legged and eared Or charged on the neck with a fesse chevronny (? indented) Or standing between two branches of fern Vert.
GORGE. *Wall's Book*
'to his crest a Demy blodhound sa/ the leggs [ermine spot drawn] and a fece chevroney on his necke or/ standing bet ij braunches of fferne Vert'
GORGE. *MS Alphabet of Crests, fo. 47b*
'A bloodhound passant ermyns'
ALINGTON, 'ALYNGTON of Suffolke' *Wall's Book*
'knight by h 8/ to his crest a blod hound passant ermyns'
'ALYNGTON of Suff.' *MS Alphabet of Crests, fo. 3b*

DEMI- GREYHOUND

A demi-greyhound Argent collared and lined Sable.
BARRETT. *Washbourne, 'Suff.' Fairbairn, 'Suff.'*
'to his crest a demy grehound sa/ suporting a trefoyle or/ Coller or Stoded g/ To John Churche of Maldon in Essex 1557'
'CHURCHE' *MS Alphabet of Crests, fo. 25*
A demi- greyhound Sable.
DENT, of Ipswich. *Sharpe*
A demi-greyhound.

HAREWELL. *MS Fairfax*
'for his Crest a Demy grehound sa/ langued [? unreadable word] and armed g/ a bowt his neck a gemell or/ p C Hawley the 5 of E 6' [1551/2].
JERMYN. 'Sr thom Jermyn of Suff' *MS Alphabet of Crests, fo. 65*
A demi-greyhound Argent collared and lined Sable the end of the line coiled.
LOVE. Rector of Somerleyton. *Davy, A.* Rev. Barry Love, ob:1722. *Bookplate**
A demi-greyhound Argent collared and lined Sable the end of the tail [sic ?line] coiled.
LOVE, Edward Missenden Love, M.A., Rector of Somerleyton for 49 years, died 1865. *Her.Suff.Ch., Wall monument, Somerleyton*
A demi-greyhound Argent collared and lined Gules the collar charged with three crosses paty formy Argent.
PECK, Thomas, Esq., late Mayor and Alderman of Norwich; Confirmation by Sir G. Dethick, Garter. *Grants & Certificates (Stowe MS 676)*
A demi-greyhound Or collared Gules holding between its paws an escallop Gules.
TASH, of Haverhill. *Davy, A., church*

Rampant or Salient

A demi-greyhound rampant collared.
CHAMBER, of Stoke by Nayland. *Davy, A.*
A demi-greyhound salient Argent collared Or.
FRESTON, of Mendham. *Bokenham*
A demi-greyhound rampant Argent collared Sable.
FRESTON, of Mendham. *Davy, A., church.* Edward Freston, Gent., died 1708; widow Elizabeth died 1727. *Her.Suff.Ch., Wall tablet, Mendham*
A demi-greyhound rampant Sable collared Or.
FRESTON. *Davy, A. Her.Suff.Ch., Mendham*
A demi-greyhound rampant Sable collared Argent rimmed Or.
FRESTON *Washbourne, 'Suff.' Fairbairn*, 'Suff.'*
A demi-greyhound rampant attired [sic] Sable collared Or.
FRESTON, Ann, widow of Rev. Thomas Freston, died 1764. *Her.Suff.Ch., Ledger stone, Cratfield*
A demi-greyhound rampant Or collared and lined the ends knotted Vert.
PRENTICE. 'William Prentys' *MS Knight's Visitations, Norf.** 'Willm Prentys' *MS Philpot's Visitations, Norf.*, the collar and line as above but Sable*
A demi-greyhound salient Argent collared Gules between two wings erect Sable on each a trefoil slipped Argent.
THELLUSSON, Lord Rendlesham. Of Rendlesham. *Davy, A.*
A demi-greyhound salient Argent collared Sable between two wings Sable each charged with a trefoil slipped Or.
THELLUSSON, Baron Rendlesham. Of Rendlesham, Aldeburgh. *Burke's Peerage, 1891 ed.* Crisp's Visitation. XIV. 121*.* Hugh Edmund, son of 5th Baron Rendlesham, died 1926. *Her.Suff.Ch., Wall tablet, Rendlesham*
A greyhound couped with fleur-de-lis in dexter paw.
TYLLOTT, of Westley. *Proc.S.I.A. VIII. 308, church flagon*
A demi-greyhound salient Ermine collared counter-compony Or and Azure.
WARREN, of Newton. *Visitation 1561 (MS G.7*) and (ed. Metcalfe)*
A demi-greyhound salient Ermine collared checky

Or and Azure.

WARREN, of Newton, Newbourne. *Bokenham. Davy, A. Washbourne, 'of Suff.' Proc.S.I.A. XX. 318*

GREYHOUND

A greyhound.

BARKER, of Grimston Hall in Trimley. *MS Fairfax (Tyl., 'in ye Tower Church Ipsw^ch.')*

A greyhound.

BOLDERO, of Bury. *Tymms, Slab, St. Mary's church*

Salient

A greyhound salient Or.

BOURCHIER, of Whepstead. *Davy, A.*

A greyhound salient Proper, 'a dark russet colour', collared and ringed Or.

RAINSFORD, 'RAYNESFORD of Essex'. *MS Heraldic Alphabet*

Courant

A greyhound courant Gules collared Or.

BALDERO, BOLDERO, of Ixworth, Bury, Fornham St. Martin. *MS Knight's Visitations, Suff., fo. 107* 'John Baldero' MS Philpot's Visitations, Suff.* Bokenham. Gage (Thingoe). Page. Davy, A. Washbourne, 'Beldero, Suff.' Muskett. I. 176, 'p. Cooke, Clar: 6 Sept. 1576, 18 Eliz' (Harl. MS 1820, Raven's note-book) Fairbairn, 'Suff.', collared and ringed*

A greyhound courant.

BOLDERO, George, Gent., died 1609. *Martin's Church Notes, Frag.Gen., St. Mary's church, Bury*

A greyhound courant Argent.

BOLDERO. *MS Heraldic Alphabet*

A greyhound in full course.

BOLDERO, John, died 1829. *Her.Suff.Ch., Brass shield, Ixworth, not found 1988*

A greyhound in full course collared.

BOLDERO, William, A.M., Rector of Woodford, Essex. *Bookplate*. George Boldero, died 1635; widow died 1672. Her.Suff.Ch., Ledger stone, Ixworth*

A greyhound courant collared and ringed charged on the shoulder with a crescent, ?for difference.

CAVE. *MS Heraldic Collections, fo. 14**

A greyhound courant Sable carrying a scroll in his mouth on which the word 'Gardez'.

CAVE. *MS Heraldic Alphabet*

A greyhound courant Argent collared and ringed Or.

DRURY, of Rougham, Hawstead. 'Sir Robart Drewrye of Hawstead Kt.' *MS Lilly's Visitation of Suffolk*, charged on the shoulder with a crescent for difference. 'Robart Drury of Rougham Esquier' MS Lilly's Visitation of Suffolk*, untinctured and without crescent. MS Fairfax (Tyl.) Frances Drury, wife of James Hobart, at Loddon. Cotman's Norfolk Brasses, plate 6 Appendix*, Brass of 1615, untinctured. Muskett. I. 345, 350, 357*

A greyhound courant Argent eared Sable collared Or.

DRURY, of Hawstead. *Davy, A., in the house*

A greyhound courant Argent.

DRURY, of Hawstead, Suffolk. *Bokenham. Davy, A. Muskett. I. 360, on Tombstones, Claydon. Robert Drury, died 1625. Her.Suff.Ch., Shield in Tower, Rougham (missing 1981)*

A greyhound courant Sable collared Or.

DRURY, of Rougham, Hawstead. *Davy, A., both churches*

'a Greyhound current Sable'

HENEAGE. *MS Alphabet of Crests, fo. 61 [in much later hand than the MS of 1580]*

A greyhound courant Sable.

HENEAGE, of Mildenhall, Thornham. *Davy, A.*

A greyhound courant Argent ducally gorged Or.

LEWKENOR. 'Henry Lewkenor of Higham hall in Com Suffolke esquier' *MS Lilly's Visitation of Suffolk**

A greyhound coursant Gules gorged with a coronet Or.

LEWKNOR, of Denham. *Bokenham*

A greyhound courant Argent collared Or.

LEWKENOR, of Denham. *Davy, A.*

A greyhound courant Argent collared Gules.

LEWKNOR. *Fairbairn, 'Suff., Sussex and Worcs.'*

A greyhound courant Sable.

PALMER, of Bury. *Davy, A.*

A greyhound courant.

PALMER, Ashley, died at Bury, 1792. *Misc.Gen. et Her. 2nd S. I. 307*, Wall tablet, Hawstead church*

A greyhound courant Proper (dark russet colour) collared and ringed Or.

RAINSFORD, of Alpheton, Acton. *Davy, A., Letheringham church*

A greyhound courant Ermine collared Azure.

SWALE, of Mildenhall. *Davy, A., church*

Passant

A greyhound passant Argent collared Or eared Sable.

JERMYN, of Rushbrook. *Muskett. II. 243 (Harl. MS 1560)*

A greyhound passant Sable collared ringed and lined Or with a cubit arm erect Proper habited Purpure holding the line.

LOVELL, of Laxfield. *Davy, A., 'Granted 25 June 1579.' Washbourne, 'Suff.' Fairbairn, 'of Laxfield, Suff.'*

A greyhound passant Sable collared Or resting the dexter paw on an escutcheon Azure.

MELLER, MELLERS, of Leiston. Perpetual Curate of Woodbridge. *Davy, A., Fairbairn, 'Meller, Mellers. Laiston [sic], Suff.' Washbourne, 'Suff.', escutcheon Sable*

A greyhound passant Gules collared Or.

TILLOTT, TYLLOTT, of Rougham, East Bergholt. *Bokenham. Davy, A. Fairbairn, 'Tylliot, of East Bardsale [sic], Suff, and Yorks.'*

Statant

A greyhound statant.

CARDINALL. *E.A.N. & Q. XII. 333 (Parker monument, East Bergholt church)*

A greyhound statant Argent.

GRIMSBY, of Leiston, Blythburgh, Wenhaston. *Davy, A., Leiston church*

A greyhound statant Sable collared Or resting the dexter paw on an escutcheon Azure.

MELLER, of Withersfield, Leiston, London. *London Visitation 1633 (H.S.) II. 95**

A greyhound statant Gules collared Or.

TILLOTT, of Rougham. *Visitation 1664–8 (Harl. MS 1085)*

Sejant

A greyhound seiant Argent gorged with a collar and ring to the last a line Or the line held from him by his dexter foot.

BARKER. *Davy, A.*

A greyhound sejant Argent gorged with a collar and

ring having attached to the latter a line Or entwined round the body and held to the ground by the dexter hind foot.

> BARKER. *Washbourne*, 'of Suff.'* Fairbairn, *'of Ipswich'*

A greyhound sejant Gules collared Or.

> BOLDERO. *Fairbairn*, 'Rattlesden, Suff.'*

'Some [descendants], about the close of the 18th Century, changed the crest to a greyhound sejant'

> BOLDERO, of Bury, Ixworth. *Muskett. I. 176*

A greyhound sejant (A greyhound sejant Argent collared Sable.

> CUNLIFFE, William Noel, died 1933. *Her.Suff.Ch., Grave with headstone, churchyard, Thurston*

A greyhound sejant Sable bezanty collared and ringed Or.

> EDMOND, EDMONDS. 'Edmonds of Cambridge' *MS Knight's Visitations, Cambs.* MS ex-Taylor Coll.* Washbourne, 'Camb.'*

A greyhound seiant Argent collared Gules ringed Or.

> FRAMPTON. Rector of Ousden, died 1803. *Davy, A.*

A greyhound sejant Argent collared Gules.

> FRAMPTON, Rev. Thomas, D.D., Rector of Ousden, died 1803. *Her.Suff.Ch., Hatchment, Ousden*

A greyhound sejant Ermines collared – thereunto a leash reflexed over the back then brought to the front.

> GOODAY. 'John Gooday of panfeld' *MS Philpot's Visitations, Essex** [In a different hand]

A greyhound seiant Ermines collared – thereunto a leash affixed reflexed over the back and coming tied in a hank Or.

> GOODAY. *MS Martin's Crests*

A greyhound seiant Ermines collared and lined Or.

> GOODAY, GOODDAY, of Kettlebaston, Preston, London. *London Visitation 1633 (H.S.) I. 322* Bokenham. Davy, A.*

A greyhound sejant Ermine collared and lined Or.

> GOODAY. 'Gooddage, Ess. and Suff.' *Washbourne*. Fairbairn**

A greyhound seiant Sable.

> JENOUR, JENNER, of Laxfield. Davy, A.

A greyhound seiant.

> PALMER, of Bury. *Davy, A., Hawstead church*

A greyhound seiant Argent collared and ringed Gules.

> PLUME, PLUMB. *MS Heraldic Collections, fo. 56**

A greyhound seiant ducally gorged Or.

> PLUME, of Hawkedon. *Davy, A., church*

A greyhound seiant Argent collared Azure garnished Or the dexter paw supporting an arrow Or feathered Argent point down.

> WATTS. 'Hugh Wattes, of co. Somerset; Grant by Sir W. Segar, Garter, in 1616.' *Grants & Certificates (Add. MS 12,225; Stowe MS 703)*

A greyhound seiant Argent collared Azure fimbriated and two rings Or supporting with the dexter leg a broad arrow Or feathered and headed Argent the sinister leg resting on the wreath.

> WATTS. *MS Heraldic Alphabet*

A greyhound seiant Argent supporting with the dexter paw an arrow Or headed and barbed Argent.

> WATTS, of Thorington, Orford. *Davy, A.*

Couchant

A greyhound couchant Sable collar and line Or.

HOVEL. 'HOWELL, . . , of Suffolk; Grant by W. Flower, Norroy, 1587' *Grants & Certificates (Stowe MS 706; Harl. MS 6,140; Add. MS 12,225)*

A greyhound couchant Or collared and lined Sable.

> HOVEL. 'Smyth alias Hovell, of Hunston, Ashfield Hall' *Surrey Visitation 1530 (H.S.). 180 (Harl. 1561). Visitation 1664–8, 'p' Wm. Flower, Norroy'. Davy, A. Muskett. II. 1 (Suff.Visit. 1664)*

A greyhound seiant [*sic* couchant] Or his fore-feet laid out collar and line Sable.

> HOVELL alias SMITH, of Walsham le Willows. *Muskett. II. (Candler; Add. MS 15,520)*

A greyhound couchant Or collared and lined Sable.

> HOVEL, of Wyverstone, Ashbocking, Walsham le Willows. *Davy, A.*

A greyhound couchant Or collared and chained Sable.

> SMITH, SMITH alias HOVELL, of Hunston, Badwell Ash, Walsham le Willows, Ashfield, Wetherden, Tannington. *MS Fairfax. Davy, A. Fairbairn*, 'Smith, of Ashfield, Suff.'*

A greyhound couchant Or collared and lined Sable.

> THURLOW, Lord Of Ashfield. *Davy, A.*

'Thurlow, Edward, 2nd Baron, died 1829; Edward Thomas, 3rd Baron, died 1857; Edward, 4th Baron, died 1874. *Her.Suff.Ch., Hatchments, Great Ashfield*

MASTIFF

A ? wolf, but called 'a mastyf' in MS, passant Argent.

> HOLLAND. 'Bryen Holand' *MS Philpot's Visitations, Norf.**

SPANIEL

A spaniel seiant Argent langued Gules his tail straight and erect.

> CROFTS, of Lt. Saxham. 'Thomas Crofte' *MS Philpot's Visitations, Suff.* Lord Crofts, of Lt. Saxham. Davy, A., church*

A water-talbot (? water spaniel) rampant collared and ringed.

> FERMUR. *MS Heraldic Collections, fo. 87a.*, 'of Suff.'*

DEMI-TALBOT

A demi-talbot Gules eared collared and lined Or holding in his paws the line coiled up.

> BRETON, BRETTON. 'Edmund Bretton' *MS Philpot's Visitations, Norf.* Davy, A.*

A demi-talbot Argent tail upwards.

> LAWRENCE, of Henham. *Davy, A. Washbourne, 'Suff., Lanc., etc.'*

A demi-talbot Proper eared Argent.

> SOTHEBY. 'Robert Southby, of Byrdeshall, co. Yorks.'; Grant by W. Flower, Norroy, 5 August 1563. *Grants & Certificates (Stowe MS 706; Harl. MS 13,159)*

A demi-talbot Purpure.

> SOTHEBY of Bury. *Davy, A., Combs church. Washbourne*, 'Southbey, Southby, Suff. and York.' Fairbairn, 'Southbey, Southebye, Suff. and Yorks.'*

A demi-talbot

> SOUTHWELL. John and Margaret Southwell, effigy monument erected by son Sir John, in 1640. *Her.Suff.Ch., Barham*

Rampant or Salient

A demi-talbot rampant Sable armed and langued Gules.

> FAIRCLOUGH, of Heveningham. *Davy, A.*

A demi-talbot (? water spaniel) rampant collared and ringed.

FERMUR. *MS Heraldic Collections, fo. 87a*, 'of Suff.'*
A demi-talbot rampant collared and lined Or.
SNELL, 'Francis [*sic*], wife of John Snell, of Westleton, died 1681/2. *Her.Suff.Ch., Slab, Westleton*
A demi-talbot rampant Gules collared and chained Or.
SNELL, of Westleton. *Davy, A., church*
A demi-talbot salient.
TRIGGE, of Stoke by Clare. *Davy, A.*

TALBOT

A talbot Gules eared collared and lined Argent in a fern bush Vert.
FERNELEY, FERNLY, of West Creeting, Sutton. 'Fernyley' *Wall's Book. Harl. 772*. Visitation 1612. Bokenham. Davy, A.*
A talbot per pale Argent and Sable.
GOOCH, 'Gouch' *MS Heraldic Alphabet*
A talbot Sable collared Or.
GROVE, Rector of Chevington, died 1726. *Gage (Thingoe), Stone, church*
A talbot Sable collared Argent.
GROVE, of Bury, Aspal. *Davy, A., St. Mary's church, Bury*
A talbot collared.
LEE. *E.A. Misc. 1925, 39*
A talbot Ermine.
SECKFORD, Thomas, of Seckford Hall, died 1575. *Her.Suff.Ch., Monument, Poppy head and Glass, Gt. Bealings; Glass, Woodbridge*
A talbot collared and lined.
SMITH alias HOVELL. *Muskett. II., Gt. Ashfield church*

Passant [Alphabetically by name]

A talbot passant Ermine.
ALINGTON, ALLINGTON, of Halesworth, Milden. *MS Knight's Visitations, Cambs.** Lord Allington, of Halesworth. *Davy, A. E.A. Misc. 1909, 106, Monument, Milden church*
A talbot passant Argent billety Sable.
ALLINGTON. *Bokenham*
A talbot passant Proper.
ALINGTON. 'Jeams', of Milden, died 1626. *E.A. Misc. 1920, 6, Monument, Milden church. Her.Suff.Ch., Effigy monument, Milden*
A talbot passant.
ALINGTON, James, Gent. and wife Judith; no date given. *Her.Suff.Ch., Ledger stone, Eye*
A talbot passant charged with roundels and collared and lined.
BARNES, of Bury. *Davy, A.*
A talbot passant.
CROFTS, Charles, Esq., late of Lincolns Inn, died 1737. *Her.Suff.Ch., Altar tomb, churchyard, Lt. Saxham*
A talbot passant.
CROMPTON. Mary, wife of Rev. John Crompton, Dissenting Minister of Walpole, died 1736. *Partridge, 48 (Darby, 1830). E.A. Misc. 1932, 69, Tomb, churchyard, Walpole*
A talbot passant Or holding in the mouth a cross crosslet fitchy Azure and resting the dexter fore-leg on a cross couped Azure.
CROSSFIELD, 'of Stanningfield, Bury St. Edmunds' *Fairbairn*
A talbot passant Argent ducally gorged Or.
DAVERS, 'of Rougham in Suffolk' *MS Heraldic Alphabet*
A talbot tripping [*sic*] Argent ducally gorged Or armed Gules.

DAVERS, Bart., of Rougham. *Sharpe*
A talbot passant Argent.
DAVERS, of Rougham. *Davy, A., (Burke)*
A talbot passant.
DAWSON. *Gage (Thingoe), Tablet, Gt. Saxham church.* William Dawson, Esq., died 1808; widow died 1834. *Her.Suff.Ch., Wall tablet, Gt. Saxham*
A talbot passant Gules collared lined and ringed Argent among ferns Vert.
FERNELEY, of West Creeting. *Visitation 1561 (MSS G.7* and Iveagh Copy*) and (ed. Metcalfe)*
A talbot passant Argent collared and lined Or through fern Vert.
FERNELEY. *Proc.S.I.A. IX. 220, West Creeting church cup.* Edmund Fernley, died 1679. *Her.Suff.Ch., Ledger stone, Creeting St. Peter*
A talbot passant per pale Argent and Sable.
GOOCH, of Mettingham, Benacre, Brundish. *Visitation 1664–8. Davy, A., Mettingham church. Washbourne*, 'Suff.'* James Wyard Gooch, died 1814; Caesar Thomas Gooch, died 1829. *Her.Suff.Ch., Ledger stone, Brundish*
A talbot passant paly of four Argent and Sable.
GOOCH, of Mettingham, Bungay. *Bokenham*
A talbot passant Or.
GROSVENOR, of Westleton. *Davy, A., Westleton church; Burgh Castle churchyard*
A talbot passant.
GROSVENOR, Humphry, died 1677. *Her.Suff.Ch., Slab against north wall, Westleton*
A talbot passant Sable ducally collared Or.
GROVE, of Ipswich. *MS Heraldic Collections, fo. 31*. MS ex-Taylor Coll.*, 'ducally gorged and ringed'. Davy, A.*
A talbot passant Sable collared Or.
GROVE, Edward, Rector and Patron of Chevington, died 1726. *Her.Suff.Ch., Ledger stone, Chevington.* John Grove White, gift of window in memory of mother, c.1940. *Glass, Chelmondiston*
A talbot passant Sable collared and lined Or.
HIGHAM, of Branches in Cowlinge. *Visitation 1561 (ed. Metcalfe). Harl. 772**
A talbot passant Sable collared and lined at the end of the line a coil or knot Or.
HIGHAM. *Washbourne*, 'Suff. and Ess.' Fairbairn, 'Suff. and Ess.'*
A talbot passant reguardant.
HILLS, of Freston. *Davy, A.*
A talbot passant Sable collared and lined Or.
HIRNE, Thomas, of Ingclose; Patent by W. Dethick, Garter, 22 November 1596. *Grants & Certificates (Harl. MS 1,441; Stowe MSS 676 and 703)*
A talbot passant Sable collared and chained Or.
HIRNE, of Lowestoft. *Davy, A., Granted by Dethick*
A talbot passant Or.
HUNT, John, died 1681. *Her.Suff.Ch., Wall tablet, Walsham le Willows*
A talbot passant Argent ducally gorged Or.
JERMIN, JERMYN. Earl of St. Albans. Of Rushbrook. *Bokenham. Davy, A. Proc.S.I.A. VII. 337. Crisp's Visitation. III. 170. Fairbairn, 'Jermyn, Suff.'*
A talbot passant.
JERMYN, Thomas, Lord Jermyn, Baron of Bury, died 1703; Lady Jermyn, died 1713. *Suff. Green Bks, Rushbrook*
A talbot passant Argent.
JERMYN, Henry, Lord Dover, died 1708, buried in

church of the Carmelites in Bruges; widow
(Judith Poley) buried there 1726. *Suff. Green
Bks, Rushbrook, 331–3*
A talbot passant gorged with a coronet.
JERMYN. *Washbourne, 'Suff.'* Earls of St. Albans
and Barons Jermyn. Of Rushbrook 1644–1703.
*Her.Suff.Ch., Monuments, Altar tombs, Tablets
and Ledger stones, Rushbrook*
A talbot passant Sable collared and line Or the line
tied in a hank between its forepaws.
MARRIOT. Thomas Mariett, of Remenham,
Berks.; Confirmation of Arms and Grant of Crest
by R. Cooke, Clar., 16 June 1568. *Grants &
Certificates (Add. MS 14,295; Harl. MSS 1,172
and 1,359 and 6,169; Stowe MS 620)*
A talbot passant Sable collared and line Or the line
coiled at the end.
MARRIOT, MARRIOTT, MARRYOTT, of Bredfield.
*Visitation 1664–8. MS Fairfax. Bokenham. MS
Martin's Crests. Davy, A. Fairbairn, 'Maryet,
Maryot, Breadfield [sic], Suff.'*
A talbot passant Sable collared and lined Or.
MARRIOT. Robert Marryot. No date given.
Her.Suff.Ch., Wall tablet, Bredfield
A talbot passant Gules collared and lined Or.
MORRIS, of Helmingham. *Visitation 1577.
Davy, A.*
A talbot passant Gules eared collared and lined Or
the line passing back through the legs and ringed.
MORRIS. 'Raffe Moryce' *MS Philpot's
Visitations, Suff.**
A talbot passant Sable ducally gorged Argent.
OAKLEY, WEYOKE, of Debenham. *Davy, A.*
A talbot passant Sable the dexter paw resting on a
stag's head caboshed Or.
'PARKER, . . , of ye Willows, co. Suffolk'; Grant
by Sir W. Segar, Garter, in 1609. *Grants &
Certificates (Add. MS 12,225)*
A talbot passant Sable supporting with the dexter
paw a stag's head cabossed Or.
PARKER, of Walsham, Stanton. *Visitation
1664–8*. Bokenham, 'p' Segar, Garter, 1609'.
Davy, A.*
A talbot passant Argent resting the dexter fore-paw
on a buck's head cabossed Or.
PARKER. *Washbourne*, 'Suff.' Fairbairn, 'of
Willows, Suff.'*
A talbot passant Argent eared and collared Sable.
RUGGE, William, of Felmingham, co. Norfolk.
Grants & Certificates (Harl. MS 1,359)
A talbot passant Ermine.
SECKFORD, of Seckford Hall in Gt. Bealings.
*Page. Miscellaneous Grants (H.S.) II. 225–6,
Deed Poll of attempted grant of Arms and Crest
by Charles Seckford to his kinsman Gibbon
Seckford, 3 January 1575*
A talbot passant its ear slit and bleeding.
STAPLETON. *Davy, A.*
A talbot passant Proper.
TALBOT. *MS Martin's Crests*
A talbot passant ? Sable.
TALBOT, of Brampton. *Davy, A., church*
A talbot passant Sable.
TALBOT, Rev. John, late Rector, died 1728;
daughter Margaret, died 1758. *Her.Suff.Ch.,
Ledger stone, Brampton*
A talbot passant.
TALKARNE, TALKANER, of Stoke by Clare. *E.A.
Misc. 1933. 7*
A talbot passant collared and chained.
TORKINGTON, of Brettenham. *Davy, A., church*

A talbot passant on the shoulder three gutties Gules.
UFFORD. *Davy, A.*
A talbot passant Gules collared and chained Argent
in fern bushes.
VERLEY. *Davy, A.*
'On a Wreath of his cullors a Talbott passant Argent
the eares and Flacks of Hayres redd, about his neck
a Collar and a lease gould'
WADE, of Bildeston. Confirmation of Arms and
Grant of Crest to William Wade of Bildeston by
William Camden, Clarenceux, 8 November 1604.
*Miscellaneous Grants (H.S.) II. (Harl. MS 1470,
fo. 49). MS Suffolk Armorial Families**
A talbot passant Argent semy of torteaux eared
Gules collar and line Or.
WADE, William, son of Robert Wade, of Bildeston
in Suffolk; Grant by W. Camden, Clar. *Grants &
Certificates (Stowe MS 706)*
A talbot passant collared lined and ringed the line
reflexed over the back.
'WAD, Willm wad S. of Robt. Wade of Bilston in
Suff.' *MS Heraldic Collections, fo. 81b*, '8 nov
1604 p'w.Cam.cl.'*
A talbot passant Argent spotted and eared Gules
gorged with a collar and the line reflexed over the
back Or.
WADE, of Bildeston, Raydon, Rendham, Orford,
Debenham. *Bildeston 39. Crisp's Visitation. IV.
137–40, Pedigree*
A talbot passant Sable ducally gorged Or.
WREAHOKE. *Washbourne, 'Suff.'*
A talbot passant Sable.
WREAHOKE. *Fairbairn*, 'Suff.'*

Statant

A talbot statant Ermine.
ALINGTON. 'Gyles Allington of Mildenhall in
Com Suffolk esquier' *MS Lilly's Visitation of
Suffolk**
A talbot statant Gules eared Argent collared and
lines Or in fern Vert.
FERNLEY, of Sutton. *Visitation 1664–8**
A talbot statant per pale Argent and Sable.
GOOCH, Bart., of Benacre Hall. *Burke's Peerage,
1891 ed.* Fairbairn, 'Gooch, Bart., of Benacre
Hall, Suff.'*
A talbot statant.
GROSVENOR. *Davy, A.*
A talbot statant Ermine.
HAYDON. 'S. Harry Haydon of Norff.' *Harl.
MS 6163. 'Sr. xophere Haydon of baconsthorp'
MS Knight's Visitations, Norf.* 'Heydon of
Norfolk' MS ex-Taylor Coll.**
A talbot statant Sable langued Gules collared and
lined Or the line forward and tied in a knot.
HIGHAM, of Cowlinge. *Visitation 1561
(MSS G.7* and Iveagh Copy*)*
A talbot statant collared and lined the line reflexed
over the back and the end knotted.
HIGHAM. *MS Heraldic Collections, fo. 54**
A talbot statant Argent collared and lined the line
reflexed over the back Or.
HUSSEY. *MS Heraldic Collections, fo. 59**
A talbot statant Argent ducally collared.
JERMYN. 'Sr Robert Jermyn' *MS Knight's
Visitations, Suff.**
A talbot statant ducally collared.
JERMYN. 'Thomas Jermyn of debden' *MS
Knight's Visitations, Suff.*, charged on the
shoulder with a crescent. Davy, A. Proc. S.I.A.
VII. 339*

A talbot statant Argent collared and chained Sable.
NUTHALL, of Spexhall Hall in Swilland, Framlingham. *Davy, A.*

A talbot statant.
RUGGE, RUGG alias REPPES. Robert Rugge, in St. John's Maddermarket, Norwich. Brass of 1558. *Cotman's Norfolk Brasses, plate 70*

A talbot statant Ermine.
SECKFORD. 'Sr Thomas Sackford of Seckford Knight' *MS Lilly's Visitation of Suffolk*, talbot eared Sable. Seckford of Woodbridge. *MS ex-Taylor Coll.*. *Davy, A.*, Woodbridge church

A talbot statant Proper collared with a chain reflexed over the back Or.
SMITH, Robert, Gent., died 1734; son Robert, died 1733. *Her.Suff.Ch., Ledger stones, Gt. Ashfield*

A talbot statant Argent charged round the neck with two rows of gutties Gules.
STAPLETON. *MS Ordinary of Arms, fo. 18*

A talbot statant reguardant Argent in front of a laurel tree Vert.
TOPESFIELD. 'Symond Toppesfeld' *MS Knight's Visitations, Norf.*

A talbot statant Argent collared and lined Or ears and flecks of hair Gules.
WADE, of Dallinghoo, Rendlesham, Orford, Blaxhall, Debenham, Bildeston. *Davy, A.*

Sejant

A talbot sejant.
BRAMPTON. *Proc.S.I.A. II. 145, Monument, Eye church*

A talbot seiant Ermine.
CLARKE, of Mellis. *Davy, A.*

A talbot sejant.
CLARKE, John, Esq., died 1762; John, son of Thomas Clarke, no date given. *Her.Suff.Ch., Ledger stones, Mellis*

A talbot sejant Argent, with crescent for difference.
CROFTS, Charles, Esq., son and heir of Thomas Crofts, of Bardwell, died 1616. *Her.Suff.Ch., Wall tablet, Ixworth Thorpe*

A lion, ? talbot, sejant holding in the dexter paw a coil of rope. [It is a talbot]
CROMPTON, Thomas, died 1641. *Her.Suff.Ch., Floor slab, Dalham*

A talbot seiant Argent.
HUNGATE, of Haverhill. *Davy, A., church*

A talbot sejant Argent.
HUNT. *MS Ordinary of Arms, fo. 271*

A talbot sejant Or collared Gules.
HUNT, John, Esq., died 1726; daughter Elizabeth, died 1758. *Her.Suff.Ch., Wall tablet, Walsham le Willows*

A talbot sejant against a halberd erect in pale and clinging thereon a snake.
HUNT, John, died 1764. *Her.Suff.Ch., Ledger stone, Wherstead*

A talbot seiant Argent.
HUSTLER. *MS Martin's Crests*

A talbot seiant Argent gorged with a collar Azure charged with three fleurs-de-lis Or.
HUSTLER, of Bury. *Davy, A.(Edms.) Bookplate*

A talbot seiant Proper the dexter paw holding an escutcheon Or.
METCALFE, of Hawstead. *MS ex-Taylor Coll.*, 'Medcalfe . . . Yorks.' Gage (Thingoe). Davy, A. Burke, L.G., 1853 ed.*

A talbot seiant Sable supporting an escutcheon Or.
METCALFE, Henry, of Hawstead House, died 1849. *Her.Suff.Ch., Hatchment, Hawstead*

A talbot seiant brown colour.
MOOTHAM, of Drinkstone. *Bokenham*

A talbot seiant Gules ducally gorged Or.
PLUME, of Hawkedon. *Visitation 1664–8*. Bokenham, 'p' Rich. St. George'. Davy, A.*

A talbot sejant Gules collared Or.
PLUME, Edmund, of Hawkedon Hall, died 1708. *Her.Suff.Ch., Hatchments and Ledger stone in churchyard, Hawkedon*

A talbot sejant collared and chained.
POTT, Edmund, 'of the line of Pott of Potts Chapel in Cheshire', died 1682. *Her.Suff.Ch., Ledger stone, St. Mary's, Bury*

A talbot seiant against a battle-axe erect entwined with a serpent.
SAFFORD, of Bungay, Ipswich, Weybread, Mettingham. *Davy, A.*

A talbot seiant Argent chained Or.
TALKERNE, of Stoke by Clare, Withersfield. *Davy, A., Stoke by Clare church*

Couchant

A talbot couchant Argent collared and lined Azure at the end of the ring a knot.
HICKMAN, of Bury, Long Melford. *Davy, A.*

A talbot couchant reguardant Argent against a laurel tree Vert.
TOPESFIELD. 'Symond Toppsfild' *MS Philpot's Visitations, Suff.* MS Heraldic Alphabet*

A talbot couchant guardant against a tree all Proper.
TOPSFIELD. *Visitation 1577. Fairbairn, 'Suff. and Norf.'*

On a mount a talbot couchant guardant against a tree all Proper.
TOPSFIELD, of Fressingfield, Gislingham. *Davy, A., Fressingfield church. Washbourne, 'Suff. and Norf.'*

A talbot couchant guardant. (A talbot couchant guardant in front of a tree all Proper).
TOPSFIELD, of Gislingham. *Her.Suff.Ch., Shield on Chancel roof, Fressingfield*

ELEPHANT

An elephant Or surmounted by a castle Argent.
BEAUMONT. *MS Ordinary of Arms, fo. 28*

An elephant Argent surmounted by a tower triple-towered Argent garnished Or.
BEAUMONT, of Hadleigh, Ipswich, Sproughton, Hintlesham. *Davy, A.*

An elephant on his back a tower triple-towered Or.
BEAUMONT. *Washbourne*, 'Leic. and Suff.'*

An elephant and castle Proper.
CORBET. *MS Heraldic Alphabet*

An elephant of the Indies Proper.
CORBOULD, of Otley House. *Corbould*

ERMINE

An ermine ? Gules.
STANTON, of Mildenhall, Sibton Park. *Davy, A., Horringer church*

Passant

An ermine passant Proper.
ATY. *Davy, A.*

An ermine passant Proper collared Gules.
LOWE, William, of Salop; Patent 1586. *Grants & Certificates (Harl. MS 1,359)*

An ermine passant Proper collared lined and ringed Gules.
LOWE. Rector of Ingham, died 1727. *Davy, A.*

An ermine passant Gules on its shoulder a mullet [for difference].
STANTON, STAUNTON. *Davy, A.*

Sejant

An ermine sejant Argent collar and line Or.
> FIRMAGE, Edward, of Ashfield, Suffolk; Patent 1587. *Grants & Certificates (Harl. MS 1,359)*

An ermine seiant Proper collared and lined Or.
> FIRMAGE, of Ashfield. *Davy, A. Washbourne*, 'Suff.' Fairbairn, 'Suff.'*

FOX

A fox Proper [*sic*, should be an ape] collared and lined Or admiring himself in a mirror Proper.
> MARTIN, William, of Hemingstone Hall, died 1842. *Her.Suff.Ch., Hatchment, Hemingstone*

Passant

A fox passant.
> BLUNDESTON, BLUNTSTON, of Blundeston, Henstead. *Davy, A.*

A fox passant Proper.
> PIERPONT, of Wrentham. *Davy, A.*

A fox passant Gules on its shoulder a mullet [for difference].
> STANTON, STAUNTON. *Davy, A.*

Statant

A fox statant Gules.
> BLENNERHASSET, Sir Thomas, at Frenze, co. Norfolk. Brass of 1531. *Cotman's Norfolk Brasses, plate 63* [fox statant in plate, but 'sejant' in text]

A fox statant Argent.
> BLUNDESTON. *MS ex-Taylor Coll.* *

A fox per pale Sable and Gules standing between two wings in pale Or.
> DAWTREY. *Wall's Book*

'to his crest a fox pty par pale sa/ g/ standing bet ij wyngs in pale or/'
> DAWTREY. *MS Alphabet of Crests, fo. 29c*

A fox statant collared and tethered.
> STANTON, of Bungay. *Church booklet, Slab, Holy Trinity*

Sejant

A fox seiant Gules.
> BLENNERHASSET, of Ash, Loudham, Barsham, etc. *MS Knight's Visitations Suff.* MS Fairfax.* Mary Bacon [née B'hasset] at Frenze, co. Norf.; brass of 1587. Untinctured. *Cotman's Norfolk Brasses, plate 83*. Davy, A., Preston church. Washbourne*, 'Suff.'*

A fox seiant Gules.
> BRIDGMAN, of Combs. *Bokenham. MS Martin's Crests*

A fox seiant Sable.
> BRIDGEMAN. *MS Heraldic Alphabet*

A fox seiant.
> BRIDGEMAN, of Newmarket St. Mary. *Partridge 124 (Darby, 1828, Churchyard)*

A fox seiant Proper.
> BRIDGEMAN. *Davy, A. Washbourne*

A fox seiant Argent collared and lined Gules.
> MOUNTNEY. *MS Martin's Crests*

A fox seiant Argent gutty Gules collared and lined Or.
> STANTON, of Chediston, Wilby. 'Robart Stanton' *MS Philpot's Visitations, Suff.*, the line ringed and hanging down in front. Bokenham*

DEMI-GOAT

A demi-Indian buck rampant Argent armed and maned Or.
> LONE, of Ellough, Worlingham. *Davy, A.*

A demi-mountain goat Argent eared and horned Gules gorged with a coronet Or.

SOUTHWELL, Richard, of Horsham St. Faiths in Norfolk, gent.; Confirmation by Sir G. Dethick, Garter, 15 December 1568 and again by Robert Cooke, Clar., 30 November 1577. *Grants & Certificates (Stowe MSS 676 and 703; Harl. MS 1,441)*

A demi-Indian goat rampant Argent eared armed and bearded Gules and charged on the body with three annulets in bend.
> SOUTHWELL. *MS Pedigree Roll, c.1557*; Corder MS 85*

A demi-Indian goat rampant Argent armed and eared Gules ducally gorged Or charged on the body with three annulets bendwise Gules and with a crescent on the shoulder – for difference.
> SOUTHWELL, of Barham. *Visitation 1561 (MS G.7.*)*

A demi-Indian goat rampant ducally gorged charged on the body with three annulets and with a crescent for difference.
> SOUTHWELL, SOWTHWELL, of Barham. *Visitation 1561 (Iveagh Copy*)*

A demi-Indian goat rampant Argent eared and ducally gorged Gules charged on its body with three annulets in pale Gules.
> SOUTHWELL, of Barham. *Visitation 1561 (ed. Metcalfe)*

A demi-Indian goat rampant Argent eared and ducally gorged Gules armed Or charged on its side with three annulets Gules.
> SOUTHWELL, of Barham, Saxmundham. Sir Robert Southwell, Kt., 1635–1702, Clerk of the Privy Council, Knighted 1665, President of the Royal Society 1690, buried co. Glouc. *Bookplate (Lee's British Bookplates, 18). Davy, A.*

GOAT

A goat Argent attired Or.
> BRUYN. *Davy, A.*

A goat Argent attired and gorged with a mural crown Or.
> RUSSELL, Bart., of Bury, Freckenham, Mildenhall, Otley, Woodbridge. *Davy, A.*

An Indian goat Proper armed collared lined and ringed Or.
> WARD, of Mendham. 'Edward Warde of poswyke' *MS Knight's Visitations, Norf.* 'John Ward' MS Philpot's Visitations, Norf.*, 'goat grey'. Davy, A.*

An Indian goat Argent pellety attired Or.
> YAXLEY. *Davy, A. (Edms.) Washbourne, 'Suff.' Fairbairn, 'of Yaxley, Suff.' Her.Suff.Ch., Yaxley*

Rampant or Salient

A goat Argent attired Or salient against a mountain Proper.
> GURDON, of Assington. 'Gourdon' *MS Knight's Visitations, Suff.*, 'mountain Vert'. Davy, A. Washbourne*, 'Hants., Suff., Wilts: Mountain Vert. Fairbairn*, 'Hants., Suff. & Wilts.', Mountain Vert.*

A goat rampant Argent attired Or supporting the stump of a tree Proper with a branch sprouting from it Vert.
> GURDON. *Davy, A.*

A goat climbing up a rock all Proper.
> GURDON, of Norfolk, Suffolk. *Washbourne*. Fairbairn*, 'of Norf. and Suff.' and 'Assington Hall, Suff.'*

A goat Argent horned Or climbing a rock Proper with a sprig issuing from the top Vert.
> GURDON, of Assington Hall. *Burke, L.G. 1853, 1900 and 1952 eds.* Muskett. I. 272 (Harl. MS*

1560). Crisp's Visitation. XVII. 121, 'all Proper'
A goat Argent climbing a rock therefrom sprouting sprigs of laurel Proper.
> GURDON, Baron Cranworth. Patron of Culpho. *Crisp's Visitation. X. 90**

A goat climbing a rock with a sprig issuant from the top all Proper.
> GURDON, of Assington. *Her.Suff.Ch., Monuments and Tablets, Assington.*

A goat climbing a rock with a tree issuant therefrom.
> GURDON. Robert Brampton Gurdon, Coldstream Guards, killed in action 1942; son Charles, died 1945, aged 9. *Her.Suff.Ch., Wooden wall tablet, Grundisburgh*

Passant

A goat passant Sable gutty Argent attired barbed and unguled Or.
> BOYNTON. *MS Martin's Crests. MS Heraldic Alphabet*

A goat passant Sable armed Or.
> CARVELL, KARNELL. *MS Ordinary of arms, fo. 85**

A goat passant Argent armed Or.
> GOATE, of Thrandeston. *Davy, A.*

A goat passant Sable horned Or.
> KERVILL, KARVELL. *Grants & Certificates (Add. MS 14,830)*

A goat passant.
> RISBY, John, of Thorpe Hall, died 1687. *Muskett. I. 72, inscription in Felsham church.* Charles Risby, died 1723; Heigham Risby, died 1740. *Her.Suff.Ch., Floor slabs, Felsham*

A goat passant Argent attired Or.
> RUSSELL, of Sproughton. *MS Ordinary of Arms, fo. 43*, hooved Or. Davy, A., church*

A goat passant Argent attired Or holding in its mouth an oak branch Vert fructed Or.
> WORTHINGTON, of Kersey. *Bokenham. MS Martin's Crests. Davy, A. Washbourne, 'Suff., Lanc., Linc.' Fairbairn, 'Suff., Lancs., Linc., Yorks.'*

A goat passant Argent attired Or. To the dexter a bunch of thistles Or.
> WORTHINGTON. With the coat of Wilmer, of Reydon Hall, 1886. *Her.Suff.Ch., Glass, Reydon*

A goat passant Sable bezanty.
> YAXLEY, of Yaxley. *Visitation 1561 (Iveagh Copy*)*

A goat passant.
> YAXLEY, YAXLEE. Phillipa, wife of Edmund Yaxley, died 1706. *Her.Suff.Ch., Ledger stone, Yaxley*

Statant

A goat statant Sable gutty Argent armed Or.
> 'BOYNTON of Sudberry' *Wall's Book*

'to his crest a got sa/ goutey ar/ armed or/ standing on a wreth ar/sa/'
> 'BOYNTON of Sudbury' *MS Alphabet of Crests, fo. 9b*

HARE

A hare sejant Sable holding in his mouth three ears of wheat Proper.
> MILLES. *MS Ordinary of Arms, fo. 110**

A hare seiant Proper in his mouth three ears of wheat Or.
> MILLES, of Cockfield. *Davy, A. Washbourne, 'Suff.' Fairbairn, 'Suff.'*

A hare seiant Gules in grass Vert.
> NORTON, of Halesworth. *Davy, A. Washbourne*, 'Suff.' Fairbairn, 'Suff.'*

A hare courant.
> WINTHROP, Adam, lord of the manor of Groton, died 1623. *Partridge II (Darby, 1828)*

HEDGEHOG

A hedgehog.
> CALAMY. *MS Martin's Crests*

A hedgehog statant Sable on each spine a bezant.
> CLAXTON, of Chediston, Gt. Livermere. *Visitation 1561 (MSS G.7.* and Iveagh Copy*).* 'Francis Claxton of Cheston' *MS Lilly's Visitation of Suffolk**

A hedgehog Sable bezanty.
> CLAXTON, of Livermere, Chediston. *Visitation 1561 (ed. Metcalfe). Visitation 1664–8. Davy, A. Washbourne*, 'Suff.'* Maurice Claxton, Esq. died 1687. *Her.Suff.Ch., Ledger stone, Gt. Livermere*

A hedgehog Sable.
> CLAXTON, of Chediston, Livermere. *MS Fairfax*

A hedgehog Sable semy of crab apples Or.
> CLAXTON, of Chediston. *Bokenham*

A hedgehog passant.
> CLAXTON, of Chediston, Livermere. *Davy, A., Gt. Livermere church*

HIPPOPOTAMUS

A hippopotamus or sea horse the upper part Argent the lower part Azure collared by five fuzils conjoined Azure and crowned with a crest coronet Or.
> KILLINGWORTH, John, of Bradley, co. Suffolk, gent.; Confirmation by W. Dethick, Garter, 25 November 1586. *Grants & Certificates (Stowe MS 677)*

DEMI-HORSE

A demi-horse Sable.
> HOCKMORE, HUCKMORE, of co. Devon. On wall tablet for Richard Keble, of Roydon Hall, 1653. *Her.Suff.Ch., Tuddenham St. Martin*

A demi-horse salient bridled holding between his hooves an Imperial crown.
> LANE. *MS Martin's Crests*

A demi-horse salient Gules maned Or issuing out of a heap of rushes Vert.
> NORTON, of Chediston. *Bokenham*

A demi-horse salient per pale indented Or and Azure crined Argent.
> PAGE. *MS Heraldic Alphabet*

A demi-horse Ermine environed round the body with a ducal coronet Or.
> STODDARD, of Suffolk. *Davy, A. Washbourne, 'Suff.' Fairbairn, 'Suff.'*

A demi-horse salient collared.
> TOOKIE, TOOKY. Rector of Worlington, died 1748. *Davy, A.*

HORSE

A carthorse Sable mane tail and hooves Or.
> EAST, of Gt. Wenham. *Her.Suff.Ch., Wall plaque, Gt. Wenham*

A bridled horse [*sic*. It is a head, and should be of a bear] per pale Argent and Gules.
> ONEBY, Robert, of Loudham Park, died 1753. *Her.Suff.Ch., Hatchment, Ufford. 'Recently restored'*

Courant

A colt at full speed Sable.
> COLT. *MS Heraldic Alphabet*

A horse courant charged with gutties.

JACKSON. *MS Ordinary of Arms, fo. 174**
A horse courant Argent gutty Gules.
    JACKSON, of Ipswich, Lt. Blakenham. *Davy, A.*
A horse at full speed Argent.
    O'MALLEY, Bart., of Ipswich. *Davy, A.*

Passant
A colt trippant Argent.
    'COLETT, S. Harry. Maior of London' *Harl. MS 6163**
A horse or colt passant Or.
    COLT, of Cavendish. *Visitation 1561 (ed. Howard. II. 27*). MS Knight's Visitations, Suff.* Bokenham. Davy, A.*
A colt passant Sable with the upper part of a broken lance in his mouth Or the head downwards the other half between his forelegs.
    COLT. *MS Martin's Crests*
A colt passant Argent.
    COLT. *Washbourne*, 'Suff.' Fairbairn*, 'Suff.'*
A horse passant Sable.
    EAST, Bart., of Gt. Wenham. *Davy, A., church. Proc.S.I.A. XIII. 234–5, photograph**
A horse passant Or.
    WHITACRE, Stephen, of co. Wilts., gent.; Confirmation by Sir G. Dethick, Garter, 17 March 20 Elizabeth [1577/8]. *Grants & Certificates (Harl. MS 1,441; Stowe MS 703)*
A horse passant Or.
    WHITTAKER, of Beccles, Ipswich. *Davy, A., Beccles churchyard; St. Nicholas church in Ipswich. Her.Suff.Ch., Fressingfield*
A horse passant Argent.
    WHITTAKER. *Davy, A.* Charles Whitaker, died 1873; Others. *Her.Suff.Ch., Slab in churchyard, Knodishall*
A horse passant Argent maned and tailed Or.
    WISEMAN, of Brantham, Thornham. *Davy, A.*

Statant
A horse statant Or.
    WHITAKER, Charles, died 1715. *Her.Suff.Ch., Monument, St. Nicholas, Ipswich (missing 1983)*
A horse statant Argent.
    WHITAKER, Ann (Hale), widow of Charles Whitaker (above), she died 1722. *Her.Suff.Ch., Hatchment, now in Christchurch Museum, Ipswich*

DEMI-LEOPARD see also OUNCE
A demi-leopard Proper charged with a rosette Gules and crowned with an Eastern crown Gules holding an asiatic dagger Proper.
    ASSEY, of Beccles. *Fauconberge 43, church monument*
A demi-leopard holding between his paws an increscent Ermine.
    HARVEY. *Visitations of Cambridgeshire 1575 & 1619 (H.S.) 60. Called Crest 1., 'false'*
A demi-leopard Argent an increscent Ermine on mount held by sinister paw the dexter paw on mount.
    HARVEY. *Source as above. Called Crest 2., 'true'*
A demi-leopard Argent pellety holding between his paws an increscent Ermine.
    HARVEY, of Stradbroke, Alderton, Wickham Skeith, Bedingfield. 'Doctor Hervy, docto^r of the cyvill Lawe & m^r of Trynyte coledge' *MS Knight's Visitations, Cambs.* Davy, A., Alderton and Bedingfield churches. Washbourne, 'Camb. and Suff.' Fairbairn, 'Cambs. and Suff.'*

A demi-leopard resting in his dexter paw a crescent Ermine.
    HERVEY, of Wickham Skeith. *Bokenham*
A demi-leopard Argent resting his dexter paw on an increscent Ermine.
    HARVEY, HARVY. *MS Heraldic Collections, fo. 53**
A demi-leopard.
    HARVEY, William, Gent., died 1681. *Her.Suff.Ch., Ledger stone, Bedingfield*
A demi-leopard holding a palm branch all Proper.
    PALMER. *MS Martin's Crests*

Rampant
A demi-leopard reguardant Proper bezanty holding a pheon Or.
    ARNOLD, ? of Suffolk. *Davy, A.*
A demi-leopard, or tiger, rampant Proper crowned with an antique or Eastern crown Gules holding in his paws a sword erect ? Sable.
    ASSEY, of Beccles. *Davy, A., church*
A demi-leopard rampant reguardant collared and chained Or supporting an escutcheon Gules.
    HAYES, of Nowton, Kettleburgh. *Davy, A., 'Granted 1703 to Daniel Hayes, of Nowton and Kettleburgh, 2nd Captain in the Queen's Trained Bands' (Mr. B.) Fairbairn, 'demi-leopard Proper'*
A demi-leopard, or ounce, rampant Sable bezanty langued Gules in his dexter paw a trefoil slipped Or.
    HERVEY, of Oulton. *Visitation 1561 (MSS G.7.* and Iveagh Copy*)*
A demi-leopard rampant Sable spotted Or holding in the dexter paw a trefoil slipped Vert.
    HERVEY, HERVYE, of Oulton. *Visitation 1561 (ed. Metcalfe). Washbourne, 'Harvey, Suff.' Fairbairn, 'Harvey, Suff.'*
A demi-leopard rampant Sable bezanty holding in his paws a trefoil Vert.
    HERVEY, of Westhall, Cookley, Oulton. *Harl. 772*. Davy, A.*
A demi-leopard rampant Proper holding in his dexter paw an ostrich feather Argent.
    POCKLINGTON, of Chelsworth. *Burke. L.G. 1900 ed. Lt. Col. George H. Pocklington, the Barnards, Chelsworth, Bildeston, Suff. Fairbairn*

Passant [sic]
A demi-leopard passant Sable spotted Or in the dexter paw a trefoil slipped Vert.
    HARVEY, HERVYE, of Ickworth. *Visitation 1561 (ed. Metcalfe)*

LEOPARD or OUNCE

Rampant or Salient
A leopard rampant Or spotted Sable.
    BOURCHIER, Sir James; Patent October 1610. *Grants & Certificates (Stowe MS 707)*
A leopard rampant Proper.
    MOYSE. *Davy, A.*
A leopard salient Sable spotted Or ducally gorged ringed and lined Or.
    SAMS. Rev. J.B. Sams, M.A. *Her.Suff.Ch., Glass, St. Mary's, Bury*

Courant
A 'Leopard Current'.
    ALINGTON, William, Esq., died 1678. *Martin's Church notes (Frag.Gen. IX. 70), St. Mary's, Bury*

Passant
A leopard passant Argent spotted Sable collared and lined Or.

BARNES, of Bury. *Davy, A.* Mrs. Elizabeth Barnes, died 1754; Mrs. Sarah Barnes, died 1778. *Her.Suff.Ch., Ledger stone, Stowmarket*

A leopard passant Proper
BLAKE, Bart. *Davy, A. (Burke). Washbourne*, 'Blake, Bart., Suff.'* James Bunbury Blake, of Thurston House, died 1874. *Her.Suff.Ch., Glass, Thurston*

A leopard passant guardant Proper.
BLAKE, Bart., of Langham, Ashfield Lodge in Bury, Bardwell. *Burke, Peerage, 1891 ed.** Sir Patrick Blake, Bart., of Langham, Suff. *Fairbairn*

A leopard passant guardant Ermine.
CROPLEY, of Cambridge. *MS Heraldic Collections, fo. 77b**

A leopard passant guardant Proper
FARMER, of Denham. *Davy, A.*

A leopard passant Or the dexter foot on a shield Vert charged with a leopard's face Or.
FITCH, FITCHE, of Essex. *Grants & Certificates (Add. MS 12,225)*

A leopard passant Argent pellety.
FREELAND, of Melton, Hasketon, Chilton. *Davy, A. Bookplate**

A leopard passant charged with roundels collared and chained holding in his dexter paw a trefoil slipped.
HERVEY, HERVYE, of Ickworth. *Visitation 1561 (MSS G.7* and Iveagh Copy*)*

An ounce, or leopard, passant Sable bezanty collared lined and ringed the line reflexed over the back holding in the dexter paw a trefoil slipped Vert.
HERVEY, of Ickworth. *Visitation 1561 (ed. Howard.II. 133*, 153*, 164*) Washbourne, 'leopard. Suff. and Devon'. Fairbairn, 'leopard. Suff. and Devonsh.'*

A leopard, or ounce, passant Sable bezanty ducally gorged and chained Or holding in his dexter paw a trefoil slipped Vert.
HERVEY. Marquis of Bristol. Of Ickworth, Oulton. *Visitation 1561 (ed. Howard. II. 145*, 150*). Harl. 772*. Davy, A. Burke, Peerage, 1891 ed.* 'chain reflexed over the back'.* Marquess of Bristol, Ickworth Park, Bury St. Edmunds. Leopard. *Fairbairn*

A leopard passant Argent spotted Sable gorged with a ducal coronet and chained holding in his dexter paw a trefoil Vert.
HERVEY, Earl of Bristol. Of Ickworth. *Bokenham*

A leopard passant Argent pellety collared and lined Or in the dexter paw a trefoil slipped Vert.
HARVY. *Washbourne, 'Suff.' Fairbairn,' Harvy, Suff.'*

A leopard passant ducally gorged.
HOWLAND *MS Heraldic Collections, fo. 81a.*, 'p.Ro.Co.Cla. 10 Jun 1584'*

A leopard passant gorged with a ducal coronet Or langued Gules.
HOWLAND, of Haverhill. *Davy, A.*

A leopard passant Proper [should be a lynx].
LYNCH. William Linch, Receiver General for Suffolk, died 1721; Others. *Her.Suff.Ch., Slab, St. Mary Elms, Ipswich (not found 1979).* William Lynch, Esq., died 1852. *Wall tablet, Walton*

A leopard passant Proper holding in the sinister paw a trefoil slipped Vert.
MILDMAY. *MS Ordinary of Arms, fo. 58**

A leopard passant Proper.
SHRIMPTON, of Southwold. *Davy, A.*

A leopard passant Proper holding in his dexter paw a trefoil slipped Or.

SYMON, SYMONS. *MS Ordinary of Arms, fo. 210**

A leopard passant Proper.
TAYLOR, of Gt. Falkenham. *Addit.Suff.Peds. MS Ordinary of Arms, fo. 51*. Davy, A.* Joseph Taylor, Esq., died 1786. *Her.Suff.Ch., Ledger stone, Honington*

Sejant

A leopard seiant collared and chained.
CHEKE, Sir John. *Davy, A., 'Sir John relinquished this and adopted the following: A crescent and issuant from the horns a cross paty fitchy Gules'*

A leopard seiant Ermine collared.
HELMINGHAM, of Helmingham. *Davy, A.*

A leopard sejant Proper holding in the dexter paw a fleur-de-lis Or.
OVERMAN. *Fairbairn, 'Norf. and Suff.'*

A leopard sejant.
PHILLIPS. Rector of Gt. Whelnetham, died 1873. *Suff. Green Bks., Gt. Whelnetham Registers, 181*

A leopard seiant Proper.
PLAYFORD, of Suffolk. *Davy, A. Washbourne*, 'Kent, Norf. & Suff.' Fairbairn, 'Kent, Norf., & Suff.'*

A leopard seiant Proper collared and chained Azure.
POTT, of Bury. *Davy, A.*

A leopard seiant Ermine ducally gorged lined and ringed Or.
WENTWORTH, of Somerleyton, Darsham, Ipswich. *Visitation 1612. Davy, A., Lt. Thurlow church. Washbourne*, 'Suff.' Fairbairn*, 'Suff.' Muskett. III. 17. (Grant, 11 October 1576).* John Wentworth, died 1651. *Her.Suff.Ch., Effigy monument, Somerleyton. Livery button*, untinctured*

DEMI-LION

No attitude given
A demi-lion Or collared Gules.
AYLOFFE, of Sudbury. *Davy, A.*

A demi-lion.
BADBYE. *MS Fairfax*

A demi-lion double queued ?Gules ducally crowned.
BRUNING. Rector of Semer, died 1663. *London Visitation Peds.1664 (H.S.) 31*

A demi-lion double queued Gules gutty Argent ducally crowned Gules [sic].
BRUNING, Rev. John, Rector for 40 years, died 1663. *Her.Suff.Ch., Wall monument, Semer*

A demi-lion Argent gorged with a coronet Or.
HARE. Patent February 1614. *Grants & Certificates (Stowe MS 706)*

A demi-lion Sable charged with three lions [sic should be bezants] in pale.
KILLIGREW, Robert, Esq., of co. Cornwall, killed in action 1707. *Her.Suff.Ch., Wall tablet, Gt. Thornham*

From clouds Proper a demi-lion Gules semy of fleurs-de-lis Or.
LENNARD, Sampson; Allowed by R. Cooke, Clar., and Chester in 1584; Confirmed by Sir W. Segar, Garter, 1626. *Grants & Certificates (Harl. MS 6,140; Stowe MS 670)*

A demi-lion double queued Azure.
LODGE. *Fairbairn*, 'of Nettlested, Suff.'*

A demi-lion Gules collared gobony Or and Azure.
LUKIN, of Ipswich. *Davy, A.*

A demi-lion.

STONE. *Washbourne*, 'Suff.' Fairbairn*, 'of Wavesdon [sic], Suff.'*
A demi-lion Or.
WILSON, of Bildeston. *Bildeston, 47*
A demi-lion issuing from a tower Sable, or Gules.
VERDON, of Martlesham, Brundish. *Davy, A.*

No attitude given, holding: [Objects in alphabetical order]

A demi-lion holding an anchor Proper.
FULCHER. *Davy, A.*
A demi-lion Gules holding in his paws a broad arrow Or feathered and headed Argent.
BROOKE, of Kersey, Bury. *Davy, A. (Edms.), Kersey church*
A demi-lion Or thereon a bend Gules charged with three mullets Argent and holding in his paws a battleaxe Gules.
CAYLEY. Ralph Calley, gent., of co. Wilts.; Patent 23 November 1579. *Grants & Certificates (Stowe MS 703)*
'And for his Creast vppon the healme on a wreathe golde and sables a demi Lion gules holdinge a Daynishe Axe the Stafe golde the head argent'
CUTLER, of Ipswich. Robert Cutler of Ipswich; Exemplification of Arms and Crest by William Camden, Clarenceux, 21st July 1612. *Herald & Genealogist. I. 83. Misc.Gen. et Her. 1st S. I. 228*. Frag.Gen. X. 80*
A demi-lion Gules holding a battle-axe Proper handle Argent.
CUTLER. *Washbourne*, 'Suff.' Fairbairn*, 'of Ipswich, Suff. Danish battle-axe Arg. staff Or.'*
A demi-lion holding an axe between his paws.
CUTLER, of Ipswich, Sproughton. *E.A.N. & Q. XIII. 139*
The upper part of a tower Azure therefrom a demi-lion issuing Or supporting a banner Argent charged with a cross Gules staff Proper.
WEDDALL, John, of Stepney, co. Middx., Captain of the 'Rainbow', R.N.; Grant 3 May 1627. *Grants & Certificates (Add. MS 12,225)*
The battlements of a castle Argent thereon a demi-lion fixing the banner of St. George upon the same.
WEDDALL. Vicar of Darsham. *Davy, A.*
'to his crest a Demy Lyon or/b/ pty p pale a bowt his neck a flat chayne cnterchanged of the same armed and Langed g/ supporting in his pawes an olyef braunche stalked and Leved vert the frute purfled or P.C. hawley'
OFFLEY. 'Thom Offeley thelder' *MS Alphabet of Crests, fo. 94*
A demi-lion Or collared Azure between its paws an olive branch Vert fructed Or.
OFFLEY. Hugh Offeley, of London, an Alderman; Confirmation by R. Cooke, Clar., 1 September 1588. The arms 'Altered in some things, being over much charged.' *Grants & Certificates (Add. MS 14,295; Harl. MS 1,359)*
A demi-lion Sable supporting a column gobony Argent and Gules capital and base Or.
FORSETT, of Milden. *MS Heraldic Alphabet. Davy, A.* Edward Forsett, of Marylebone, co. Middx. *Grants & Certificates (Harl. MS 6,059; Stowe MS 706), 'a pillar'*
A demi-lion Argent holding in his paws a cross crosslet fitchy Sable.
BUCKWORTH, of Spalding, co. Linc. *Sharpe*
A demi-lion holding a cross crosslet fitchy all Gules.

CALDECOTT, of Wilbraham, co. Cambs. *Fiske, 172*, Shimpling church monument*
A demi-lion Or holding in his dexter paw a cross moline Gules.
COLVILE, of Suffolk. *Davy, A.*
A demi-lion Argent holding in his paws a cross crosslet botonny fitchy Gules.
HARE, of Bruisyard, Homersfield. *MS Fairfax (Tyl.) Davy, A.*
A demi-lion Azure gorged with a mural crown Or holding in his dexter paw a cross crosslet fitchy [Or] and resting the sinister on a shield [Sable] charged with a chevron Argent between three cross crosslets fitchy Or.
STRUTT, Lord Raylagh [sic Rayleigh], of Hadleigh. *Davy, A. Fairbairn*, 'Baron Rayleigh, of Terling Place, Essex.'*
A demi-lion Gules holding a covered cup Argent.
ARGENT, ARGENTINE, of Stutton. *Davy, A.*
A demi-lion holding between his paws an escallop.
ISAACSON, of Newmarket, Lidgate, Lt. Bradley. *Davy, A.*
A demi-lion erased charged with a bomb fired Proper supporting a flagstaff encircled with an Eastern crown Or therefrom flowing towards the sinister a banner Gules inscribed 'Baroach' in letters of gold.
NICHOLSON, of Ufford, Bury. *Davy, A.*
A demi-lion per pale Ermine and Ermines gorged with a chain within a collar gemel Or holding in his dexter paw a gillyflower Proper.
FLOWER, Bart. *Davy, A. Washbourne, 'of Oxon.'*
A demi-lion per pale Or and Azure collared and lined – holding a pink Proper stalked and leaved Vert.
OFFLEY, of Metfield, Wilby, Withersdale. *Davy, A.*
A demi-lion Or holding in his dexter paw a trefoil slipped Vert.
WESTERN, Bart., of Tattingstone Place. *Burke, Peerage, 1891 ed.**
On a tower Azure a demi-lion issuant from the battlements Or ducally crowned Gules holding between the paws a grenade fired Proper.
STANHOPE, Sir Michael, P.C. to Queen Elizabeth and King James. *Her.Suff.Ch., Effigy monument, Sudbourne*
A demi-lion Sable collared and chained holding between his paws a leopard's face jessant-de-lis Or.
PHILLIPS, of Ipswich. *Davy, A.* Lt. Col. Henry Phillips, died 1877; widow died 1894. *Her.Suff.Ch., Wall tablet, Sproughton*
A crescent Gules issuant therefrom a demi-lion Proper holding between his paws a horseshoe Gules.
ALLENBY, of Felixstowe House. *Crisp's Visitation. VIII. 17**
A demi-lion Proper gorged with a collar gemel Sable and holding between the paws a lozenge Azure charged with a cross crosslet Or.
MUSGROVE – MUSGROVE, of Raworth, near Hadleigh, Suff.' *Fairbairn*
A demi-lion Gules collared Or holding in the dexter paw a mullet Sable.
LAMBE, Edward, died 1617. *Her.Suff.Ch., Effigy Wall monument, East Bergholt*
A demi-lion Argent holding between his paws a snake Proper.
BERNARD, of Yoxford. *Davy, A. (Burke), Yoxford church. Bookplates**
A demi-lion Azure holding between his paws the rudder of a ship Or.

ALLEYN, of Assington. 'Gyles Aleyn' *MS Knight's Visitations, Essex*.* 'Gyles Alyn' *MS Philpot's Visitations, Essex*. Davy, A.*
A demi-lion Azure holding in his paws a saw erect Or, on his shoulder an ermine spot Or.

SAWBRIDGE, Edward, Rector of Thelnetham, died 1874. *Burke, L.G. 1952 ed.**
A demi-lion Or supporting a three-masted ship sails furled on each mast a flag of St. George.

IPSWICH, Borough of *Visitation 1561 (MSS G.7* and Iveagh Copy*)*
A demi-lion Sable ducally crowned Or holding between his paws a sphere Or.

BEDFORD, of Stradbroke. *Davy, A. (Edms.)*
'On a wreath of the colours a demi Lion ppr. guttee de sang crowned Or holding in the dexter paw a Cuttelax [*sic* cutlass] as in the Arms.'

KEDINGTON, of Rougham manor, 1702 and 1808. *Copinger. VI. 325*
A demi-lion double queued Ermine holding in the dexter paw a sword erect Argent hilt and pommel Or.

PEACHEY, Lord Selsey. Of Kedington. *Davy, A.*
A demi-lion Azure holding in his dexter paw a sword erect Argent hilt and pommel Or.

SAMPSON, of Kersey, Playford. *Davy, A. Washbourne*, 'Suff.' Fairbairn*, 'Suff.'*

Rampant or Salient [Alphabetically by name]
A demi-lion rampant.

ALLOT. *MS Martin's Crests*
A demi-lion rampant bendy of six Argent and Azure.

BADBY. *Bokenham*
A tower Argent issuing therefrom a demi-lion rampant Gules.

BEVERSHAM. *Washbourne*, 'Suff.' Fairbairn*, 'of Holbrook Hall, Suff.'*
A demi-lion rampant per pale indented Argent and Gules langued Azure.

BLADWELL, BLODWELL, BLOVILL, of Gt. Thurlow. *Visitation 1561 (MSS G.7* and Iveagh Copy*) and (ed. Metcalfe). Harl. 772*. Visitation 1577.* 'Wyll Bladwell' *MS Philpot's Visitations, Suff.* Davy, A. (Edms.) Washbourne, 'Suff. and Norf.' Fairbairn, 'Bladewell, Bladwell, Suff., Staffs. and Norf.'*
A demi-lion rampant per pale indented Argent and Gules.

BLOUYLE. *MS Heraldic Collections, fo. 54* Davy, A. Fairbairn, 'Blodwell, Blouyle, Suff.'*
A demi-lion rampant couped Gules.

BOSANQUET, of Ilketshall St. John's, Kelsale. *Davy, A. Washbourne*
A demi-lion rampant Or.

BRAMSTON, John, of Ashton Hall, co. Essex, died 1696. *Her.Suff.Ch., Wall tablet, St. Mary's, Bury*
A demi-lion rampant Or.

'CAPELL, S. Welyem, Maior of London' *Harl. MS 6163**
A demi-lion rampant.

CAPEL, William, died 1685. *Her.Suff.Ch., Ledger stone, Stanton*
A round top Or thereout a demi-lion rampant issuant Sable.

CAREW. 'S. Welye Carow' *Harl. MS 6163. Banners & Standards*. With and without a mullet for difference*
'to his crest/a Demy lyon sa/ comyng owt of the top of a ship or/ '

CAREW. *MS Alphabet of Crests, fo. 19*
The round top of a ship Or issuing therefrom a demi-lion rampant Sable between six spears three in bend and three in bend sinister Or.

CAREW. *MS Ordinary of Arms, fo. 53**
Issuing from the top mast head of a ship Or a demi-lion rampant between six half-pikes bendways dexter and sinister.

CAREW. *MS Martin's Crests*
A mainmast the round top surrounded with spears and a demi-lion issuant from the centre Sable.

CAREW, of Bury. *Davy, A., St. Mary's church*
A demi-lion rampant Or.

CHILTON, of Ufford, Eyke, Mendlesham. *Davy, A., Mendlesham church*
A demi-lion rampant.

CHILTON, Rev. Richard, A.B., Vicar of Mendlesham, died 1816. *Her.Suff.Ch., Wall tablet, Mendlesham*
A demi-lion rampant.

DENT *MS Martin's Crests*
A demi-lion rampant per pale Erminois and Azure.

DICKINSON, DICKENSON. *MS Ordinary of Arms, fo. 54*. Washbourne*
A demi-lion rampant per pale Ermine and Azure.

DICKINSON, of Playford. *MS Heraldic Alphabet. Davy, A. (Burke)*
A demi-lion rampant Argent.

DICKINSON, of Playford. *Davy, A.*
A demi-lion rampant per pale Argent and Azure.

DICKINSON. Incumbent of Playford, died 1887. *Crisp's Visitation. I. 292–6, Pedigree*
A demi-lion rampant.

DUFTON, William, M.R.C.S., died 1859; Rev. John Dufton, M.A., 15 years Vicar of Bredfield with Pettistree, died 1874. *Her.Suff.Ch., Wall tablets, Bredfield*
A demi-lion rampant Gules.

EAMES, EME, ESME. *MS Ordinary of Arms, fos. 50* and 76**
A demi-lion rampant Sable.

EAMES, of Aspal. *Davy, A.*
A demi-lion rampant.

EDGE. *Davy, A.*
A demi-lion rampant.

FAUCONBERG, of Beccles. *Davy, A.* Henry Fauconberg, LL.D., died 1713. *Her.Suff.Ch., Altar tomb, churchyard, Beccles*
A demi-lion rampant Or.

FIELD, of Sutton. *Davy, A.*
A demi-lion rampant.

FREEMAN. *MS Ordinary of Arms, fo. 262**
A demi-lion rampant.

FREEMAN, of Combs. *Crisp's Visitation. II. 48(Seal)*
A demi-lion rampant.

GARDINER, of Elmswell. *Bokenham*
A demi-lion rampant Or.

GATES, of Bury. *Davy, A.*
A demi-lion rampant Sable armed and langued Gules.

GOODRICH. *Davy, A.*
A demi-lion rampant Argent.

GOULD, of Bury. *Davy, A., (Seal, 1826)*
A demi-lion rampant.

GOULD. *Tymms, 195*
A demi-lion rampant Or.

GOULD, William, of Bury, died 1836. *Her.Suff.Ch., Wall tablet, St. Mary's, Bury*
A demi-lion rampant Or.

GOWARD, of Lakenheath. *Davy, A., church*
A demi-lion rampant.
GRYS,LE Thomas, died 1722. *Her.Suff.Ch.,*
Ledger stone, Homersfield
A demi-lion rampant.
HARVEY. *Davy, A.*
A demi-lion rampant Argent.
KEDMARSTON, of Suffolk. *Davy, A. Fairbairn*,*
'Suff.'
A demi-lion rampant Argent.
KERRISON, Bart., of Hoxne. *Davy, A.*
A demi-lion rampant.
LE GRYS, Thomas, died 1722. *Her.Suff.Ch.,*
Ledger stone, Homersfield
A demi-lion rampant.
LEWIS, of Benhall, Bungay. *Davy, A.*
A demi-lion rampant.
LODINGTON. *MS Ordinary of Arms, fo. 71**
A demi-lion rampant per pale indented Argent and
Gules.
LODWELL. *Bokenham*
A demi-lion rampant Or.
MADDOCKS. *Davy, A.*
A demi-lion rampant Argent.
MANT, M.D., of Ipswich. *Davy, A., Vestry, St.*
Nicholas church
A demi-lion rampant Gules.
NEALE, of Ipswich. *Davy, A., St. Margaret's*
church. Thomas Neale, LL.B., J.P., D.L., Col. of
Ipswich Volunteers, died 1839. *Her.Suff.Ch.,*
Hatchment, St. Margaret's
A demi-lion rampant Ermine.
NORFORD, M.D., of Bury. *Davy, A., St. James's*
church. William Norford, M.D., died 1793.
Her.Suff.Ch., Wall tablet, St. James's, Bury
A demi-lion rampant Gules.
NORTON, of Ixworth. *Davy, A., church.*
Fairbairn*, 'of Ixworth, Suff.' John Norton, died
1597. *Her.Suff.Ch., Wall tablet, Ixworth*
A demi-lion rampant.
RUST. *Washbourne*, 'Suff.' Fairbairn*, 'Suff.'*
A demi-lion rampant Sable armed and langued
Gules.
SCHOMBERG. Rector of Belton, died 1837.
Crisp's Visitation. I. 209–10, Pedigree
A demi-lion rampant his tail wreath [*sic*].
SHERMAN, of Yaxley. *Bokenham*
Out of the top of a tower Gules a demi-lion rampant
Or armed and langued of the second [*sic*].
'SKINNER, John, of London, Sheriff of that City;
Confirmation by Sir W. Dethick, Garter, 29
September 1587'. *Grants & Certificates (Stowe*
MS 676)
Out of a castle Gules a demi-lion rampant Or.
SKINNER, of Lavenham. *MS Fairfax (Tyl.)*
A demi-lion rampant.
STOKES, of Boxford. *Davy, A., church*
A demi-lion rampant Or.
TATLOCK, of Bramfield. *Davy, A.*
A demi-lion rampant.
WODDERSPOON, of Ipswich. *Davy, A.*

Rampant. Crowned only

A demi-lion rampant crowned Or.
MODA. *Washbourne*, 'Suff.' Fairbairn*, 'Suff.'*
A demi-lion rampant Argent ducally crowned Or.
PEACHEY. *MS Ordinary of Arms, fo. 26**
A demi-lion rampant ducally crowned Or.
PHILLIPS, PHILIPS, of Ipswich. *Bokenham. Davy,*
A., St. Lawrence church. E.A.N. & Q. IX. 213
A demi-lion rampant ducally crowned.

PHILLIPS, PHILIPS, . . . , died 1682; Others, died
1692–1726. *Her.Suff.Ch., Ledger stone, Lt.*
Bealings
A demi-lion rampant crowned.
PHILIPS, Richard, M.P. for Ipswich, Died 1720.
Her.Suff.Ch., Ledger stone, St. Margaret's

Rampant. Gorged only

A demi-lion rampant ducally gorged lined and
ringed.
ANSELL. *MS ex-Taylor Coll.**
A demi-lion rampant Proper ducally gorged and
lined Or.
ANSELL, of Bury. *Davy, A., St. Mary's church*
A demi-lion rampant couped Or collared Gules.
AYLOFFE. *MS Ordinary of Arms, fo. 26*.*
'William Ayleff of Bretayns' *MS Philpot's*
Visitations, Essex*. MS Martin's Crests
A demi-lion rampant Azure collared Argent.
FAUCONBERG. 'Fauconbridge of Suff.[k]'
MS Heraldic Alphabet, 'on his Coach'
A demi-lion rampant ducally gorged.
GOODWIN *MS ex-Taylor Coll.*
A demi-lion rampant Argent ducally gorged Gules.
HARE, of Bruisyard, Homersfield. *Davy, A.*
A demi-lion rampant Gules collared gobony Or and
Azure.
LUKIN, of Ipswich. *Davy, A. Crisp's Visitation.*
VII. 33–9* (Seal)
A demi-lion rampant Or gorged with a collar Gules
charged with three fleurs-de-lis Or.
MACHET, John, Chaplain to Archbishop Parker,
son of John Machet, of Gimmingham, co.
Norfolk; Confirmation by Sir W. Segar, Garter,
27 January 1626. *Grants & Certificates (Add.*
MS 12,225)
A demi-lion rampant gorged with a collar charged
with three fleur-de-lis.
MACHETT, of Gisleham. *Partridge 106 (Darby,*
1827), churchyard, Hoxne. Davy, A., churchyard,
Hoxne

Rampant. Charged only

A demi-lion rampant Or charged with two bendlets
Argent [*sic* ?Azure] armed and langued Gules.
BADBY, of Bury. *Davy, A., Rushbrook church*
A demi-lion rampant Argent charged with two
bendlets Azure.
BADLEY. *Fairbairn, 'Suff.'*
A demi-lion rampant Gules charged on the shoulder
with a lozenge Argent.
FREEMAN. *MS Martin's Crests*
A demi-lion rampant Gules charged with a lozenge
Or.
FREEMAN, of Combs, Saxmundham. *Davy, A.,*
(Seal)
A demi-lion rampant Sable charged with three
escallops in bend Argent.
GIBBON, of Botesdale, Bury. *London Visitation*
1633 (H.S.) I. 311*
A demi-lion rampant Sable charged with three
bezants in bend (since left out).
KILLIGREW. *Bokenham*
A demi-lion rampant Sable charged with three
bezants.
KILLIGREW, of Thornham. *Davy, A., church.*
Proc.S.I.A. I. 223 (Seal) and VII. 340
A demi-lion rampant Argent gutty Gules between
two wings expanded.
NEWMAN, NEWENAME. *MS Ordinary of Arms,*
fo. 76*
A demi-lion rampant Argent gutty de sang between

two wings expanded Gules.

NEWMAN, of Melford. 'Thomas Newman, citizen and merchant of London' *Grants & Certificates (Stowe MS 677). Davy, A., Acton church*

A demi-lion rampant charged on the shoulder with a cross crosslet Gules.

WALFORD, of Bucklesham, Woodbridge, Dallinghoo, Melton. *Davy, A.*

A demi-lion rampant Proper charged on the shoulder with a cross crosslet Argent.

WALFORD, of Foxburrow Hall in Melton. *Burke, L.G. 1900 ed.*

Rampant, etc.

A demi-lion rampant double queued Gules gutty Or crowned Or.

BRUNNING. Rector of Semer, died 1663. *Davy, A.*

A demi-lion rampant double queued Gules gutty d'eau ducally crowned Argent.

BRUNING, BRUN, BRUINING. *Fairbairn.*

Rampant or Salient, holding:
[Objects in alphabetical order and including previous sub-sections]

A demi-lion rampant crowned Or holding in his paws ?

KING. Rector of St. Matthew's, Ipswich and of Witnesham. *Proc.S.I.A. VII. 182, St. Mary Tower, Ipswich*

A demi-lion rampant holding in his paws ?

LE GRYS. Rector of Homersfield, died 1722. *Davy, A., church*

A demi-lion rampant Purpure holding [torn away].

LODGE. *MS Heraldic Collections, fo. 57**

A demi-lion rampant Vert charged on the shoulder with a fountain and holding between the paws an anchor.

BROOKS, CLOSE – Arthur Close-Brooks, M.C., died of wounds 1917. *Her. Suff.Ch., Brass, Gt.Glemham. Crest for Brooks*

A demi-lion rampant Or supporting with both paws an anchor Sable.

HALLIDAY. *MS Ordinary of Arms, fo. 234**

A demi-lion rampant Azure bezantée collared Ermine supporting with its paws an anchor Or.

PACKE, John, of London, High Sheriff of Suffolk, Esq.; Grant by Sir Thomas St. George, Clar., 20 January 1696/7. *Grants & Certificates (Add. MS 14,831)*

A demi-lion rampant Azure semy of annulets Or collared Erminois holding between his paws an anchor Or.

PACK, of Stoke Ash. *Bokenham*

A demi-lion rampant Azure bezanty collared Ermine holding in his paws an anchor Sable.

PACK, of Stoke Ash. *Davy, A.*

A demi-lion rampant holding a bundle of arrows.

BOWES. Mary, wife of Richard Bowes, died 1714. *Martin's church notes, Frag.Gen. IX. 64, St. James's, Bury*

A demi-lion rampant Gules holding in his paws a bundle of arrows Argent headed Or.

BOWES, of Bury. *Davy, A., St. Mary's church* 'beryth to his crest a demy lion rampant sable armed geules holding in his pawe a darte on his shulder a brod arrow hede gold'

WYATT. 'Wyot' *Wall's Book* 'to his crest a demy lyon rampant sa/ armed g/ holding in his paw a Dart on his shoulder an arrow hed or/'

WYATT. 'Wyat knight by h 8' *MS Alphabet of Crests, fo. 137*

A demi-lion rampant Sable holding an unfeathered arrow point downwards Or charged on the shoulder with a pheon Or.

WYATT. 'Mayster Whyat' *Banners & Standards*. MS Martin's Crests, holding 'a dart'*

A demi-lion rampant Sable gutty Or holding in his dexter paw a broad arrow Or.

WYATT. 'Edwarde Wyett' *MS Knight's Visitations, Essex**. 'Edward Wyett' *MS Philpot's Visitations, Essex**. 'Whyat of Barking in Essex' *MS Heraldic Alphabet*

A demi-lion rampant Sable holding an arrow Or feathered and barbed Argent.

WYATT. Rector of Framlingham, died 1813. *Davy, A.*

A demi-lion rampant Erminois holding upright a battle-axe Argent staff Sable.

CLOUGH, of Sibton, Gislingham, Bury. *London Visitation 1633 (H.S.) I. 174**

A demi-lion rampant Gules holding a Danish axe staff Or head Gules (?Argent).

CUTLER. *Visitation 1664–8, 'of the Chantry next Ipswich', Sproughton*

A demi-lion rampant Gules holding a halberd Gules staff Argent.

CUTLER. *Bokenham*

A demi-lion rampant Gules holding a battle-axe handle Argent head Azure.

CUTLER, of Ipswich. *Davy, A.*

A demi-lion rampant grasping between the paws a battle axe.

CUTLER, Robert, died 1740. *Her.Suff.Ch., Wall tablet, Sproughton*

'On a wreath of the Colours In front of a demi Lion [rampant] Vert charged on the shoulder with two Barrulets dancette Or holding in the dexter paw and resting on the sinister paw a Battle-axe erect [in front] a Club fessewise entwined with a Serpent proper'

EMERSON, Peter Henry, M.R.C.S., of Oulton, co. Suffolk; Grant by Sir Albert Woods, Garter, 24 September 1897. *Emerson, 4th booklet, 2*, photograph of Grant*

A demi-lion rampant Or holding a battle-axe Azure.

INWOOD, of Sproughton. *Davy, A.*

A demi-lion rampant supporting a banner.

BROMLEY. *MS Martin's Crests, 'later Speaker'*

A demi-lion rampant Gules supporting a banner Gules staff and fringe Or charged with a rose Argent.

STURT, Anthony, of Yately, co. Hants.; Grant by Sir T. St. George, Garter and Sir Hen. St. George, Clar., 19 October 1691. *Grants & Certificates (Stowe MS 714)*

A demi-lion rampant Gules holding a banner Gules staff Or charged with a rose Argent.

STURT, of Bury. *Davy, A., St. James's church*

A demi-lion erased and rampant Or supporting a baton Azure headed with a fleur-de-lis.

JENYNS. 'Jenings' *MS ex-Taylor Coll.**

A demi-lion rampant Argent guttée de sang armed and langued Azure the dexter paw grasping a baton Or tipped Sable.

SOME, Thomas, of Wantisden, co. Suffolk; Grant by Sir C. Barker, Garter. *Grants & Certificates (Stowe MS 692)*

A demi-lion rampant Argent gutty Gules holding in his dexter paw a baton Or tipped at the ends Sable.

SOANE, SONE, SOONE, of Wantisden, Halesworth, Ubbeston. *Davy, A. Washbourne, 'Sone, Soone, Derb. & Suff.' Fairbairn, 'Sone, Soone, Derb. & Suff.'*

A demi-lion rampant Or holding in his paws a baton Gules.

SONE, of Ubbeston. *Dade MS, church monument, (Davy, Suff.Coll., Add. MS 19,083)*

A demi-lion rampant Argent gutty de sang holding a baton Sable with gilt tips in the dexter paw.

SONE. *Her.Suff.Ch., Hassocks c.1972, Corton*

A demi-lion rampant Gules holding in the dexter paw a baton bendy Argent and Gules.

VIELL, of co. Glouc.; Confirmation of Arms and Crest by Sir Richard St. George, Clar., 1629. *London Visitation 1634 (H.S.) 311**

A demi-lion rampant Gules holding in the dexter paw a baton Or.

VYELL, Abraham, of London. *Grants & Certificates (C.24, Visit. of London 1634).* Vyall, Vyell, Abraham, of Shotley, c.1650. *Suffolk Green Bks, Shotley*

A demi-lion rampant Argent holding a rose branch flowered Or stalked and leaved Vert.

EVERINGHAM, Barons. Lands in Suffolk temp. Edw. I. *Davy, A.*

A demi-lion rampant Gules holding between his paws a laurel branch Vert.

FISHER. *MS Ordinary of Arms, fo. 76*. Davy, A.*

A demi-lion rampant Or holding in his paws a branch of ? leaved Vert.

HARE, of Bruisyard. *Visitation 1561 (MS G.7*)*

A demi-lion rampant and erased Ermine crowned Or holding a palm branch Vert.

NORWOOD, Thomas, of Astwood, co. Bucks.; Confirmation of Arms and Grant of Crest at the request of Rouge Croix, by R. Cooke, Clar., 1 November 1585. *Grants & Certificates (Stowe MS 670; Add. MS 14,295)*

A demi-lion rampant Or holding in his dexter paw a branch of laurel Argent berried Or.

SHERIFFE, of Uggeshall, Henstead. *Davy, A.*

A demi-lion rampant Ermine holding in the paws a branch of laurel slipped Vert and charged on the shoulder for difference with a mullet Gules.

SMITH-REWSE, Rev. Gilbert, M.A., Rector of St. Margaret's and St. Peter's, South Elmham, Suffolk. *Fairbairn. Crest for Rewse*

A demi-lion rampant Argent on the shoulder three gutties Gules between the paws a laurel slip Proper.

TATLOCK, Thomas, of St. Dunstan's at Stepney, Citizen and Grocer of London; Grant by J. Anstis, Garter, 25 February 1725/6. *Grants & Certificates (Add. MS 14,831)*

A demi-lion rampant holding in his paws a rose branch.

TIMPERLEY, of Hintlesham. *Davy, A., church monuments. Timperley, 141*

A demi-lion rampant Argent in the paws a branch of damask rose flowered all Proper the mouth grasping a snake Vert entwined about the body and wounding the shoulder Gules.

WISE, Henry, of Brompton Park, Middlesex; Master Gardener of all H.M. Gardens; Grant by J. Anstis, Garter and Sir J. Vanburgh, Clar., 4 April 1720. *Grants & Certificates (Add. MS 14,830)*

A demi-lion rampant Argent a snake coiling round him holding in his paws a rose branch Proper.

WISE, of Ipswich, Ramsholt, Chelmondiston. *Davy, A.*

A demi-lion rampant Sable holding in his dexter paw a bridlebit Or.

MILNER, of Ipswich. *Sharpe. Davy, A., Tomb, churchyard, St. Matthew's. Haslewood, 276*

A demi-lion rampant Or holding in his paws a crescent.

BOUGHTON, of Lavenham. *Davy, A., church*

A demi-lion rampant holding between the two paws a crescent.

BOUGHTON, Henry, died 1750; Others. *Her.Suff.Ch., Floor slab, Lavenham*

A demi-lion rampant holding in his dexter paw a crescent.

CRABTREE. *Davy, A. (Seal)*

A demi-lion rampant Or holding in his paws a cross paty fitchy Gules.

CALDECOTT. *Davy, A., Shimpling church*

A demi-lion rampant Or holding in its paws a cross crosslet fitchy Gules.

CALDECOTT, Ellen Susanne, wife of Frederick Caldecott, died 1828. *Her.Suff.Ch., Wall tablet, Shimpling*

A demi-lion rampant holding between his paws a long cross crosslet fitchy.

CAPEL. *MS Ordinary of Arms, fo. 33**

A demi-lion rampant Or holding in his paws a cross crosslet fitchy Gules.

CAPEL, CAPELL. Capell, of Stanton. *Visitation 1664–8*.* Capell, Earl of Essex. *Burke, Peerage, 1891ed.* Her.Suff.Ch., Ledger stones, Stanton.* Henry Capel Lofft, killed in action 1811, aged 28. *Wall tablet, Troston*

A demi-lion rampant holding in his paws a cross crosslet fitchy Or.

CAPEL, Earl of Essex. Of Icklingham, Stonham Aspal. *Davy, A.*

A demi-lion rampant Sable holding between his paws a cross crosslet Or.

GOODRICH, of Haughley. *Bokenham*

A demi-lion rampant holding between his paws a cross crosslet Sable.

GOODRICH. *Sharpe. Partridge, 210 (Darby, 1827). Proc.S.I.A. IX. 70.* John Goodrich, died 1793; widow died 1830. *Her.Suff.Ch., Ledger stone, Hopton*

A demi-lion rampant Argent holding between his paws a cross crosslet Sable.

GOODRICH, of Ipswich, Gt. Ashfield, Hopton. *Davy, A., Felsham church flagon, Wetherden churchyard*

A demi-lion rampant Argent holding in his paws a cross crosslet Or.

GOODRICH, of Gt. Ashfield, Ipswich, Hopton, Felsham. *Davy, A., Wetherden church*

A demi-lion rampant holding in the paws a cross crosslet.

GOODRICH, John, late of Gt. Ashfield, died 1706; John Goodrich, Surgeon of Ipswich, died 1743; William Goodrich, of Hopton, died 1776; Others. *Her.Suff.Ch., Altar tomb, churchyard, Wetherden.* Robert Goodrich, died 1731. *Floor slab, Felsham*

'A son tymbre ung demy lyon saillant dargent armé Et lang dassur tenant en son patee une Crois Crosseley fisshee de geules assis sur une Torse dor et dassur mantelle de geules double dargent botonny dor'

HARE, Nicholas, of Homersfield; Grant by Christopher Barker, Garter, 7 December 1537. *Suff.Arm.Fams.**

'to his crest a Demy lyon salyant ar/ armed and langed b/ tenant en son pawe ung crois botoney crusseley fyche g/'

HARE, 'of Norff.' *MS Alphabet of Crests, fo. 60b*

A demi-lion rampant couped Azure holding between

his paws a cross formy fitchy Gules.

LODGE. *MS Ordinary of Arms, fo. 40**

A demi-lion rampant couped double tailed Or semy of cross crosslets fitchy Sable holding in his paws a long cross crosslet fitchy Gules.

LODGE. *MS ex-Taylor Coll.**

A demi-lion rampant holding in his paws a cross crosslet Or.

LOFFT (CAPEL), of Troston. *Davy, A., church. Crest of Capel, assumed by Capel Lofft*

A demi-lion rampant holding in his paws a cross crosslet fitchy.

LOFFT, Robert Emlyn, of Troston, Bury St. Edmunds, Suff. *Fairbairn*

A demi-lion rampant Or holding in the paws a cross crosslet fitchy Gules.

LOFFT. Henry Capel Lofft, Lieut. 48th Foot, killed in Spain 1811, aged 28. *Her.Suff.Ch., Wall tablet, Troston. The crest of Capel*

A demi-lion rampant holding a cross crosslet fitchy Sable.

MAPLETOFT, of Hitcham, Stanstead. *Davy, A. Washbourne*, 'Spring Hall, Stansted, Suff.' Fairbairn*, 'Spring Hall, Suff.'*

A demi-lion rampant holding in his dexter paw a cross paty fitchy.

UNDERWOOD. *Davy, A., Gt. Cornard church.* Buxton Underwood, gent. *Her.Suff.Ch., Floor slab, Gt. Cornard*

A demi-lion rampant Argent collared studded and fimbriated Azure supporting a cross -.

WOODCOCK, of Essex. *MS Heraldic Alphabet*

A demi-lion rampant Or collared Azure studded Or grasping a cross botonny fitchy of the last [*sic,* ?Azure].

WOODCOCK, of Middleton. *Davy, A., church*

A demi-lion rampant Gules supporting a covered cup Or.

ARGENT, of the Isle of Ely. *MS Heraldic Alphabet*

A demi-lion rampant Or holding between his paws an escallop Sable.

BARRETT. *MS Martin's Crests*

A demi-lion rampant holding between his paws an escallop.

GIBBON. *Livery button**

A demi-lion rampant holding in his paw an escallop Argent.

GIBBON, of Sudbury. *Davy, A., All Saints church*

A demi-lion rampant Sable holding between his paws an escallop Argent.

GIBBONS. *Fairbairn**

A demi-lion rampant holding in both paws an escallop.

NORTON. 'Sʳ Sampson de Norton' *MS Ordinary of Arms, fo. 59**

A demi-lion rampant Or holding in both paws an escallop Sable.

TAYLOR. *MS Ordinary of Arms, fo. 205**

A demi-lion rampant Ermine between its paws an escallop shell Or.

TAYLOR, Roger, grandson of Roger Taylor, of London, Esq.; Confirmation 27 December 1614 and again in 1632. *Grants & Certificates (Add. MS 12,225)*

A demi-lion rampant Gules crowned Or holding in his paws a scutcheon Azure thereon a fleur-de-lis Or.

BASE, of Saxmundham. *Bokenham*

A demi-lion rampant Proper holding between his paws an escutcheon Azure charged with a fesse dancetty Or.

CURTHOIS, of Tuddenham. *Bokenham, 'p.R. St. George, 1632'*

A demi-lion rampant Gules resting his sinister paw on an escutcheon Argent charged with a fesse Gules thereon another fesse nebuly Or.

THORP, of Ipswich. Vicar of St. Mary's church, Bungay. *Crisp's Visitation. XVII. 181**

A demi-lion rampant Sable holding a fleur-de-lis Or.

FAIRCLOUGH, Hugh, of London, citizen and clothworker; Confirmation 2 November 1583. *Grants & Certificates (Stowe MS 703; Harl. MS 1,441; Add. MS 26,753)*

A demi-lion rampant Sable holding in his paws a fleur-de-lis Azure.

FAIRCLOUGH, of Kedington. *MS Heraldic Alphabet. Davy, A.* Rev. Samuel Fairclough, died 1691. *Her.Suff.Ch., Wall tablet, Heveningham. Fleur-de-lis broken off.* Nathaniel Fairclough, died 1753; widow died 1756. *Ledger stone, Stowmarket. No fleur-de-lis shown*

A demi-lion rampant Gules holding a fleur-de-lis Or.

GILLY, William, 'Fined for Sheriff of London and of good birth'; Grant by Sir E. Bysshe, Garter, 1 June 1650. *Grants & Certificates (Harl. MSS 1,441; 1,144 and 1,172)*

A demi-lion rampant holding in his paws a fleur-de-lis.

GILLY. *MS Martin's Crests. Davy, A.*

A demi-lion rampant Ermine holding in the dexter paw a fleur-de-lis Or.

MARKS, . . ., of co. Suffolk. Patent by Sir W. Segar, Garter. *Grants & Certificates (Add. MS 12,225). Davy, A., 'of Old Newton'. Washbourne*, 'Marks, Markes, Suff.'*

A demi-lion rampant Argent collared Vert rimmed and studded Or grasping in the dexter paw a fleur-de-lis Or.

'TILLOTTS, James, of Ipswich in Suffolk, one of the twelve Portmen of that Town, who was descended from Tillotts of Rougham in Suffolk'; Confirmation by Sir W. Segar, Garter. *Grants & Certificates (Stowe MS 677)*

A demi-lion rampant Argent holding between his paws a rose Gules stalked and leaved Vert.

HARE. *MS Philpot's Visitations, Suff.**

A demi-lion rampant holding in the paws three roses stalked and slipped.

TIMPERLEY, Captain John, died 1629. *Her.Suff.Ch., Incised portrait slab, Hintlesham. Photograph**

A demi-lion rampant Gules holding in his dexter paw a trefoil slipped Or.

HERVEY, Eric Sedgwick Hervey, died 1963; son of Valentine Hervey, of Glasgow. *Her.Suff.Ch., Ledger stone, Lt. Bealings. The lion shown here with a trefoil in each paw.*

A demi-lion rampant Or holding in his dexter paw a trefoil slipped Vert.

WESTERN, of Tattingstone. *Davy, A., church monuments. E.A.N. & Q. VIII. 159. Bookplate*, lion untinctured.* Rear Admiral Thomas Western, died 1814; son Sir Thomas Western, Bart., of Tattingstone Place and co. Essex, died 1873; Sir Thomas Western, died 1877. *Her.Suff.Ch., Wall tablets, Tattingstone*

A demi-lion rampant Gules supporting a garb Or.

PLUMMER, . . .; Patent by Sir W. Segar, Garter. *Grants & Certificates (Add. MS 12,225)*

A demi-lion rampant Gules holding between his paws a garb Or.

PLUMER, of Chediston. *Davy, A.*

A demi-lion rampant holding between his paws a garland of roses Or.

BRIDGEMAN, of Combs, Stowmarket, Creeting St. Olave. *Davy, A.*

A demi-lion rampant double tailed Or holding in his dexter paw a gem-ring Or gem Gules.

CROMWELL. *MS Heraldic Collections, fo. 58**

A demi-lion rampant Argent holding in his dexter paw a gem-ring Or.

CROMWELL, of Haverhill, Freckenham. Earl of Essex. *Davy, A.*

A tower Argent with a demi-lion rampant issuing from the battlements Or ducally gorged Gules holding between his paws a grenade fired Proper.

RATCLIFFE. *Davy, A.*

A tower Azure portal Or issuing from the battlements thereof a demi-lion rampant Or ducally crowned Gules holding between his paws a ? [unidentifiable object] Azure.

STANHOPE. 'Sr Mychaell Stanhope of Orfforde Knight of the Bathe' *MS Lilly's Visitation of Suffolk**

A tower Argent issuing from the battlements thereof a demi-lion rampant Or ducally crowned Gules holding between his paws a grenade fired Proper.

STANHOPE, of Sudbourne. *Davy, A., church*

On a tower Azure issuing from the battlements a demi-lion rampant Or ducally crowned Gules holding between his paws a grenade fired Proper.

STANHOPE. *Her.Suff.Ch., Effigy monument, Sudbourne*

A demi-lion rampant tail forked, or double tailed, Argent charged with three gutties Sable on the mane holding between his paws a martel [war hammer] Azure handle Or.

CROMWELL. 'Sir Rychard Cromwell' *Banners & Standards**

A demi-lion rampant Gules holding in his paw a close helmet Proper.

ARMIGER. *MS Martin's Crests. Second crest*

A demi-lion rampant Gules armed and langued Azure holding in the dexter paw a mullet Gules.

EWING. Major William Ewing, of London. *Fairbairn**. Violet Orr Ewing, widow of Major Miles Barne, died 1969. *Her.Suff.Ch., Glass, Sotterley*

A demi-lion rampant Gules collared Or and between the paws a mullet Sable.

LAMBE, Thomas, of Trimby[*sic*], in Thurleston, co. Suffolk; Grant by W. Hervey, Clar., 3 July 1559. *Grants & Certificates (Add. MS 14,295)*

A demi-lion rampant Gules holding in his dexter paw a mullet Sable.

LAMBE, of Barham Hall, Syleham, East Bergholt, Trimley, Troston. *Visitation 1561 (MSS G.7** *and Iveagh Copy**) *and (ed. Metcalfe). Harl. 772**. *Visitation 1664–8, 'p. Harvey, Clar., 1559'. MS Heraldic Collections, fo. 48**. *Davy, A., Syleham and East Bergholt churches, 'Granted July 3 1559'. Fairbairn, 'Kent & Barham, Suff.'* Edward Lambe, died 1617. *Photograph, Effigy wall monument, East Bergholt*

A demi-lion rampant Gules holding between his paws a mullet Sable.

LAMBE. *MS Ordinary of Arms, fo. 219**. *MS Philpot's Visitations, Suff.**

A demi-lion rampant Gules collared Or holding in his dexter paw a mullet Sable.

LAMBE, of Barham, Trimley. *Visitation 1664–8**. *Bokenham, 'p. Harvey, Clar., 1559'. Washbourne, 'Kent and Suff.'*

A demi-lion rampant collared holding between his paws a mullet.

'LAMBE, Thom. of Trimley in Thurleston in Suff.' *MS Heraldic Collections, fo. 81a**, *'p. Wm Har Cla 3 Jul 1559'*

A demi-lion rampant Gules gorged with a collar of the same [*sic*] charged with three torteaux holding in his dexter paw a pheon Purpure.

WEARG, WERGE, of Lt. Livermere. *Davy, A., church*

'A Demi Lion [rampant] Gules holding in the dexter paw an Ivory Rod and charged on the Shoulder with three Crosses patee fitchee chevronwise Or'

RUST, Rev. Edgar, M.A. of Abbot's Hall, Suffolk; Grant of Arms and Crest by Sir William Woods, Garter and Joseph Hawker, Clarenceux, 4th May 1840. [Grant in my possession; *Corder MS 83*] 'Rev. Edgar Rust, of Abbot's Hall, Stowmarket, Rector of Drinkston, Suff.' *Fairbairn*

A demi-lion rampant Gules holding in his dexter paw an ivory rod and charged on the shoulder with two [*sic*] crosses paty fitchy chevron-wise Or.

RUST, of Stowmarket, Drinkstone. *Davy, A.*

A demi-lion rampant Proper holding in his paws a plate.

HARVEY, of Wickham Skeith. *Page*

A demi-lion rampant Gules bezanty holding between his paws a bezant.

LANE, of Ipswich, Campsea Abbey, Rendlesham. *Visitation 1664–8. Davy, A. Misc.Gen. et Her. 5th S. II. 57*

A demi-lion rampant Or torteauxey [*sic*] holding between his paws a bezant.

LANE, of Ipswich. *Bokenham*

A demi-lion rampant Proper between its paws a plate.

PLATT, . . ., of London, brewer, father of Sir Hugh Platt. *Grants & Certificates (Harl. MS 1,359)*. Sir John Platt, Kt., died 1705. *Her.Suff.Ch., Ledger stone under tower, Wickham Skeith*. 'Richard Platt, a brewer of London & Kentish Town, was granted these arms by Wm. Camden, Clarenceux'.

A demi-lion rampant holding between his paws a roundlet.

PLATT, of Wickham Skeith. *Bokenham*

A demi-lion rampant Gules holding in his paws a bezant.

PLATT, of Wickham Skeith. *Davy, A., church*

A demi-lion rampant Azure supporting the rudder of a ship Or.

ALLEYN. *MS Martin's Crests*

A demi-lion rampant Sable holding in his paws a saltire engrailed Argent.

GREENWOOD, of Burgh Castle. *Visitation 1664–8*

A demi-lion rampant holding a saltire.

GREENWOOD, of Burgh Castle. *Davy, A., 'in the Ch.'*

A demi-lion rampant Or holding in the paws a saltire Argent.

GREENWOOD, Thomas, died 1677. *Her.Suff.Ch., Ledger stone, Burgh Castle*

A demi-lion rampant Or holding a shield Argent thereon a cross formy fitchy Sable.

RYLEY, Bart. *E.A.N. & Q. I. 136, Hatchment, Thetford church*

A demi-lion rampant Argent semy of buckles Sable the sinister paw resting on a shield Sable charged with a wolf's head erased Argent.

WOOD, of Sudbourne Hall. *Burke, L.G. 1900 ed.**

'Vppon the healme a demy lyon golde supportinge a shyppe sables on a wreathe argent and sables ma'teled gulz dobled argent'

IPSWICH. 'John Gardener and Jeffery Gylbert at this present baylyffs of the towne of Ypswyche'; Confirmation of Arms and Grant of Crest and Supporters by W. Hervey, Clarenceux, 20 August 1561. *Proc.S.I.A. VI. 456*. Misc.Gen. et Her. 2nd S. II. 343–4*

A demi-lion rampant Or holding a three-masted ship with sails furled Proper.

IPSWICH, Borough of *Scott-Giles, 29*. Ipswich, Town of *Her.Suff.Ch., Glass, St. James's, Bury; Tooley brass, formerly in St. Mary Quay church, now in Ipswich Museum.* [Differing in details of ship]

A demi-lion rampant Argent gorged with a collar Azure charged with three bezants holding in his paws a shuttle Or.

PEEL, of Highlands, East Bergholt, died 1867. *E.A.N. & Q. XII. 344. Her.Suff.Ch., Wall tablet, East Bergholt*

A demi-lion rampant crowned holding between his paws a terrestrial globe [or sphere].

BEDFORD, of Stradbroke. *Bokenham*

A demi-lion rampant supporting a spear Or headed Argent.

JENYNS. 'Jennings' *MS Martin's Crests*

A demi-lion erased and rampant Or supporting with his paws a spear erect Or headed Azure.

JENYNS, of Eye. *Davy, A.*

A demi-lion rampant Argent supporting a broken spear Or.

SOONE, of Ubbeston. *Bokenham*

A demi-lion rampant Proper crowned with an Eastern crown Gules and holding in his paws a sword erect Proper.

ASSEY. *Fairbairn, 'Suff.'*

A demi-lion rampant crowned with an Eastern crown holding a dagger Proper.

ASSEY. Charles Chaston Assey, Esq., Surgeon in H.E.I.Co., died 1821. *Her.Suff.Ch., Monument, Beccles*

A demi-lion rampant holding a scimitar.

KEDINGTON, Ambrose, died 1743; Others. *Partridge, 5 (Darby, 1826), Palisaded tomb, churchyard, Acton*

A demi-lion rampant crowned holding in its paws a falchion.

KEDINGTON. Frances, wife of Robert Kedington, died 1715; he died 1741. *Her.Suff.Ch., Wall tablet, Stansfield*

A demi-lion rampant per pale Azure and Gules holding between his paws a sword point upwards Argent hilt and pommel Or.

MADDOCKS, MADOX. *MS Ordinary of Arms, fo. 54*

A demi-lion rampant per pale Or and Sable holding in the dexter fore-paw a sword erect Sable, arising from a tower Azure.

SIMPSON. Rear Admiral C.H. Simpson, and his wife. Erected 1956. *Her.Suff.Ch., Wall tablet, Stoke-by-Nayland*

A demi-lion rampant Sable holding in his sinister paw a chaplet [or wreath] of laurel Vert.

BRIDGEMAN, BRIDGMAN. *MS Heraldic Alphabet*

A demi-lion rampant holding between his paws a wreath of laurel.

BRIDGEMAN, of Combs. *E.A. Misc. 1933. 3, Coffin-plate in church*

A demi-lion rampant Or holding a wreath of laurel Vert.

WOOD. *Washbourne*, 'Suff.' Fairbairn, 'Suff.'*

Rampant Guardant

A demi-lion rampant guardant Sable.

BALL. 'Robert Balle' *MS Knight's Visitations, Norf.* 'Robart Balle' *MS Philpot's Visitations, Norf.*

A demi-lion rampant guardant Or between two wings elevated ?barry of six Or and Azure.

CATELYN, CATELINE, of Wingfield Castle. *Visitation 1664–8*

A demi-lion rampant guardant between two wings.

CATELYN, CATELINE, of Wingfield Castle, Barham. *Davy, A.*

A demi-lion rampant guardant Or.

GATES. *MS Martin's Crests*

A demi-lion rampant guardant Sable.

GOODRICH. 'Goodrick' *MS Martin's Crests*

A demi-lion rampant guardant Argent collared Gules charged with three mullets Argent.

HOLLAND, of Ipswich. *London Visitation 1633 (H.S.) I. 389*

A demi-lion rampant guardant Argent gorged with a coronet Or.

HUN, Thomas, of Deepdene, co. Essex (?Depden, co. Suffolk); Confirmation 8 September 1572. *Grants & Certificates (Stowe MS 703)*

A demi-lion rampant guardant Argent.

HUNNE, of St. Margaret's Ilketshall. *Visitation 1664–8. Bokenham, untinctured*

A demi-lion rampant guardant Argent ducally gorged Or.

HUNN, of St. Margaret's Ilketshall. *Davy, A.*

A demi-lion rampant guardant ducally gorged.

HUN, HUNNE, Thomas, died 1689. *Her.Suff.Ch., Ledger stone, Ilketshall St. Margaret*

A demi-lion rampant guardant Sable crowned Or.

LEWIS, of Battisford. *MS Ordinary of Arms, fo. 67*, ducally crowned. Davy, A., church*

A demi-lion rampant guardant Proper.

THOMPSON. *MS Martin's Crests*

A demi-lion rampant guardant Or.

THOMPSON, of Lound, Yarmouth. *Davy, A.*

A demi-lion rampant guardant.

THOMPSON. 'Edward Tompson, died 1826' *Partridge, 154 (Darby, 1832), churchyard, Lound.* Edward Thompson, died 1826; widow re-married, died 1861. *Her.Suff.Ch., Tomb, churchyard, Lound*

Rampant Guardant, holding:

A demi-lion rampant guardant Or supporting an anchor Sable.

HALLIDAY, Sir Leonard, Alderman and Lord Mayor of London; Confirmation of Arms and Grant of Crest by W. Camden, Clar., 23 September 1605. *Grants & Certificates (Add. MS 14,295; Stowe MSS 700 and 707; Harl. MSS 1,115; 1,422; 5,839 and 6,169)*

A demi-lion rampant guardant Or supporting an anchor Proper.

HALLIDAY, of Henstead. *Davy, A., 'or anchor Or'*

A demi-lion rampant guardant holding in his paws an arrow point downwards.

BROOKE. *MS Heraldic Collections, fo. 77b.*

A demi-lion rampant guardant Or supporting a sheaf of arrows Or.

BOWES. *Bokenham*

A demi-lion rampant guardant Azure holding between his paws a bundle of arrows saltire wise Or.

BOWES, of Bury. *Bokenham*

A demi-lion rampant guardant Gules holding in his paws a bundle of arrows Argent headed Or.

    BOWES, of Bury. *Davy, A., St. Mary's church*

A demi-lion rampant guardant Or holding between his paws an escallop Argent.

    GIBBON, GYBBON. *MS Ordinary of Arms, fo. 43**

A demi-lion rampant guardant Or holding in its paws an antique shield Gules the scroll bordured Or.

    FISHER, Edward, of co. Glouc.; Confirmation by Sir W. Segar, Garter. *Grants & Certificates (Harl. MS 6,140; Add. MS 12,225)*

A demi-lion rampant guardant Proper holding a Roman shield Or.

    FISHER. *MS Heraldic Alphabet*

A demi-lion rampant guardant Proper gutty de sang ducally crowned Or holding in his dexter paw a scimitar Argent hilted Or.

    KEDINGTON, of Stansfield. *Sharpe. Davy, A., the lion untinctured. Proc.S.I.A. X. 347, Stansfield church monument. The whole untinctured*

A demi-lion rampant guardant crowned holding in the paws a scimitar Proper.

    KEDINGTON, Ambrose, died 1692. *Her.Suff.Ch., Floor slab, Acton*

Rampant Reguardant

A demi-lion rampant reguardant holding between his paws an escutcheon charged with a cross.

    BOTELL, BOOTLE. *MS Ordinary of Arms, fo. 248**

A demi-lion rampant reguardant Or.

    GATE, GATES. *MS Heraldic Alphabet*

'his crest a demy lyon regardant or/ sa/ P pale holding in his pawes a sword ar/ garneshed or/ issant owt of a tower ar/'

    SIMPSON. 'Sympson Under mareshall of Calles' *MS Alphabet of Crests, fo. 122*

A demi-lion rampant reguardant.

    THOMAS, of Lavenham, Thorpe Morieux. *Davy, A., Thorpe church.* Sarah, wife of Samuel Thomas, of Lavenham, died 1768. *Her.Suff.Ch., Floor slab, Lavenham*

Sejant [*sic*]

A demi-lion seiant Gules crowned Or holding in his paws an antique shield Azure thereon a fleur-de-lis Or.

    BASE, of Saxmundham. *Davy, A.*

A demi-lion sejant Proper supporting a column Or.

    CULLUM. *Washbourne, 'Suff.'*

LION

No attitude given

A lion issuing out of the top of a castle Gules.

    BEVERSHAM. *Bokenham*

A lion issuant Argent holding between his paws a garland of laurels Or.

    BRIDGEMAN. *MS Heraldic Alphabet*

A lion holding a cross patonce.

    DICKENS. Lt. Gen. Sir S.T. Dickens, died 1847. *Her.Suff.Ch., Wall tablet, Sts. Peter and Paul, Felixstowe*

On a torse Sable and Or a lion issuant Sable langued Gules.

    FAIRCLOUGH, of Heveningham. *Muskett. III. 43, Tom Martin's church notes, on a portrait seen 1750*

'for his crest or cognizance a lion proper, holding in his dexter paw a Trefoile Vert, fixed on an helmet with Mantles and Tassels'

    HARVEY, George, of Maldon, co. Essex; Confirmation of Arms and Crest by William

Dethick, Garter and William Camden, Clarenceux, 3 December 1603. *Visitation 1561 (ed. Howard) II. 166*

Out of the battlements of a castle a lion holding in his dexter paw a millpick.

    MOSELEY, of Ousden. *MS Fairfax*

Rampant or Salient
[Alphabetically by name]

A lion rampant.

    BELL, of Haughley, Bury, Sotterley. *Partridge 47 (Darby, 1830), churchyard, Uggeshall. Davy, A., Uggeshall churchyard.* James Bell, Rector for 42 years, died 1678. *Her.Suff.Ch., Altar tomb, churchyard, Sotterley*

A lion rampant Gules.

    BOKENHAM, of Thornham, Weston, Wortham. *Bokenham.* Edmund Bokenham, Esq., died 1620; Dorothy Bokenham, died 1654; Wyseman Bokenham, died 1670. *Her.Suff.Ch., Ledger stones, Gt. Thornham.* Sir Henry Bokenham, Kt., died 1648; widow Dorothy, died 1654. *Effigy Wall tablet, Thelnetham.* L'Estrange Bokenham, A.M., of Wortham, died 1719. *Ledger stone, Redgrave*

A lion salient (?sejant) Gules armed Azure.

    BOKENHAM, of Wortham. *Davy, A.*

A lion rampant Gules.

    BOWES, of Bury. *Bokenham*

A lion rampant Or.

    BRAMPTON. *Davy, A.*

A lion rampant Sable.

    BRISE, Shadrach, died 1699 at Cavendish Place; widow died 1724. *Her.Suff.Ch., Wall tablet, Cavendish*

A lion rampant.

    BROWN, of Tostock, Brent Eleigh. *Davy, A., Brent Eleigh church*

A main mast the round top set off with palisadoes Or issuant therefrom a lion rampant Sable.

    CAREW. *MS Heraldic Alphabet*

A lion rampant Or.

    COLMER, COLMORE, of Sibton, Yoxford. *Davy, A.*

A lion rampant.

    EAMES. *Davy, A. (Seal, 1682)*

A lion rampant Sable.

    FAIRCLOUGH, of Kedington, Heveningham, Stowmarket. *Davy, A., Stowmarket church*

A lion rampant.

    FAIRCLOUGH, Nathaniel, Gent., died 1753; widow Elizabeth, died 1756. *E.A.N. & Q. XI. 208, Ledger stone, Stowmarket*

A lion rampant Azure.

    FERRETT, of Ipswich. *Sharpe*

A lion rampant Argent.

    FRENCH, of Groton. *Davy, A., church*

A lion rampant.

    GARNHAM, of Bury, Ashfield. *Davy, A.*

A lion rampant Or.

    GOOD, of co. Linc. *Her.Suff.Ch., Glass, Wilby*

A lion salient.

    GOODWIN, Edmund, M.A., died 1829. *Her.Suff.Ch., Floor slab, Framlingham*

A lion rampant Argent armed and langued Gules.

    GWYN, of Ipswich. *Sharpe*

A lion rampant Or.

    GWYN, of Ipswich. *Davy, A.*

A lion rampant.

    HARBOROUGH, of Redgrave. *Misc.Gen. et Her. 3rd S. III. 116**

Out of a tower Gules a lion rampant issuant Argent.
 HIGGENS, of Bury. *Davy, A.*
A lion rampant Gules.
 JONES, of Lowestoft, Theberton. *Davy, A.*
A lion rampant double queued Proper.
 MARRIOTT, MARRYOTT, of Southwold. *Davy, A.*
A lion rampant Or.
 MILLS, of Gt. Saxham, Stutton. 'Mill' *MS Martin's Crests. Davy, A., Stutton church. Burke, L.G. 1853 and 1900 eds. Fairbairn*, 'of Saxham Hall, Suff.'* Thomas Mills, Rector for 38 years, died 1879; Thomas Mills, of Saxham Hall, died 1834; Others. *Her.Suff.Ch., Modern brass and Ledger stone (?Vault), Stutton.* Thomas Mills, Rector for 57 years, died 1879; Many others. *Wall tablets and Glass, Gt. Saxham*
A lion rampant Argent.
 NEWTON, of Elvedon, Ipswich. *Davy, A., Slab, St. Nicholas, Ipswich*
A lion rampant.
 NEWTON, Richard, Gent., died 1718. *E.A.N. & Q. X. 56, Marble slab, St. Nicholas, Ipswich*
A lion rampant Sable.
 NEWTON, William, Esq., died 1862. *Her.Suff.Ch., Glass, Elvedon*
A lion rampant Or.
 OWEN. *MS Ordinary of Arms, fo. 56*.* Vicar of Beccles, Rector of Heveningham. *Davy, A.*
A lion rampant Gules.
 PASSELEWE, PASLEW, of Suffolk. *Davy, A. Fairbairn*, 'Paslew, Yorks. and Suff.'*
A lion rampant Sable between two wings erect Argent.
 PIERPONT, of Wrentham. *Davy, A. Bookplates**
A lion rampant.
 POLEY, of Badley. *Her.Suff.Ch., Monuments and Floor slabs, church*
A lion rampant Sable.
 POLEY. 'Poley and Halifax 1854.' *Her.Suff.Ch., Glass, Groton*
A lion rampant.
 PRETYMAN, of Bacton. *Davy, A.*
A lion rampant Gules.
 ROOPE, of Ipswich. *Davy, A.*
Out of a tower Gules a lion rampant Or.
 SKINNER. *MS Heraldic Alphabet*
A lion rampant.
 THORNE, Oliver, Rector of Akenham, died 1720, aged 52. *Partridge 55 (Darby, 1828), churchyard, Akenham.* William, son of Oliver Thorne, Rector of Hemingstone, died 1718, aged 80. *Her.Suff.Ch., Stone, churchyard, Hemingstone*
A lion rampant Sable.
 THORNE, of Wherstead, Hemingstone, Akenham, Whepstead. *Visitation 1664–8. Bokenham. Davy, A. E.A.N. & Q. V. 347. Washbourne*, 'Suff. and Devon'. Fairbairn*, 'Suff. and Devonsh.'* Oliver Thorne, Rector of Akenham, died 1720. *Her.Suff.Ch., Ledger stone, Akenham*
A lion rampant.
 WADDINGTON. Rector of Cavendish, died 1808. *Davy, A.*
A lion rampant double queued per fesse Gules and Argent.
 WORTHAM, of Wortham. *Davy, A.*

Rampant. Crowned only
A lion rampant Azure crowned Or.
 FAIRWEATHER. *Bokenham*
A lion rampant Ermine ducally crowned Or.

GERRARD, Earl of Macclesfield. Of Brandon. *Davy, A.*
A lion rampant ducally crowned.
 KING, John, Barrister, died 1815; widow died 1866, aged 86. *Her.Suff.Ch., Wall tablet, Witnesham*
A lion rampant Or ducally crowned.
 PARKER. John Preston Parker, died 1851. *Her.Suff.Ch., Tablet, Bildeston. Note by Rev. Farrer, 'This is the old coat [sic crest] of the Lords Morley'*
A lion rampant Argent ducally crowned Or.
 PLAYTERS, of Sotterley. *Davy, A.*
A tower Argent on the battlements thereof a lion combatant [*sic* ?rampant] Ermine ducally crowned Or.
 SKRINE, of Gt. Finborough. *Davy, A.*
A lion rampant Argent ducally crowned Or.
 VILLIERS, Duke of Buckingham. Of Leiston, Aldringham, Poslingford, Cavendish, Clare. *Davy, A.*

Rampant. Gorged only
A lion rampant Sable collared lined and ringed Or.
 POLEY, of Boxted, Badley. *Visitation 1561 (MS G.7*), (Iveagh Copy*), drawn as above, but written over 'a lyon rampant Sa a coller & Cheyne golde' (ed. Howard) I. 269*; 300* and 301*, sometimes chained, armed and langued Gules. Harl. 772* MS Knight's Visitations, Suff.* MS Ordinary of Arms, fo. 22*'Sr John Poley of Columbynehall in Com Suffolke Knight' MS Lilly's Visitations of Suffolk*, lion mistakenly tricked Or. MS Humfry Pedigree Roll*; Corder MS 91. Visitation 1664–8*. MS Heraldic Collections fo. 54*. Bokenham. Davy, A. Washbourne*, 'of Boxted Hall, Suff.' Burke, L.G. 1853 ed. Misc.Gen. et Her. 4th S. II. 180 (Bookplate*) Proc.S.I.A. XXVII. 152 (Dandy Ped.)*
A lion rampant Sable collared and chained Or.
 POLEY, of Boxted. *Her.Suff.Ch., Wall monument, Ledger stones, Hatchments, Glass, Boxted.* Cecilia Poley, wife of Sir Charles Crofts, Kt., died 1626. *Wall tablet, Bardwell.* Joseph Poley, died 1828. *Monument, St. Margaret's, Ipswich.* John George Poley, M.A., Rector of Stonham Aspal for 37 years, died 1901. *Brass and Wall tablet, Stonham Aspal*
A lion rampant Sable collared and chained Or.
 POLEY, WELLER-POLEY, of Boxted Hall, Suffolk. *Fairbairn*. Crest 1. for Poley; crest 2, for Weller [q.v.]* Rev. William Weller-Poley, M.A., Rector of Santon, co. Norfolk, died 1887. *Her.Suff.Ch., Wall tablet, Hartest*
A lion rampant Gules ducally gorged Or.
 STEWARD. *Davy, A. Washbourne, 'Cambs., Suff. and Norf. Bookplate**

Rampant. Charged only
A lion rampant Or charged with a bend Gules thereon three mullets Argent.
 CAYLEY. *MS Heraldic Alphabet*
A lion rampant Argent gutty Gules.
 PERYN, PERIENT. *Davy, A.*

Rampant or Salient, holding: [Objects in alphabetical order and including previous sub-sections]
A lion rampant Argent armed and langued Gules holding in his fore-paws an arrow point downwards shafted Or feathered and headed Argent.

CANNING, of Colchester, co. Essex. *Sharpe*
A lion rampant Sable holding in his paws a
battle-axe Argent handle Sable.

THORESBY, of Barton Mills. *Davy, A., church*
A lion rampant Sable holding a battle axe Or.

THORESBY, Thomas, Esq., died 1790; widow
Isabella, died 1794. *Her.Suff.Ch., Wall tablet,
Barton Mills*
A lion segreant [*sic* rampant] Gules laying his paw
on a cross paty fitchy Gules.

BALES, BEALES, Francis, died 1734. *Her.Suff.Ch.,
Altar tomb, churchyard, Woolpit*
A lion rampant Proper holding a cross flory Sable.

DICKENS. *Washbourne, 'Ipswich, Suff.', in
Addenda II. Fairbairn, 'Suff.'*
A lion rampant Argent supporting a cross fitchy
Sable.

PASKE, William, of London, D.D.; Grant by Sir
W. Segar, Garter, 1630. *Grants & Certificates
(Stowe MS 703; Add. MS 12,225)*
A lion rampant Argent supporting, or sustaining, a
cross paty fitchy Sable.

PASKE, of Needham Market, Creeting St. Peter.
Davy, A., Barking church. Washbourne. George
Paske, son of George Paske of Needham Market,
died 1822; widow Jane, died 1874. *Her.Suff.Ch.,
Wall tablet, Creeting St. Peter*
A lion rampant Or supporting a long cross Sable.

WALE, WALL, of Risby, Lackford. *Davy, A.,
Lackford church*
A lion rampant Or holding in his paws an escallop
Sable.

BARRETT, of Wickhambrook. *Davy, A., church.*
Nathaniel Barrett, of Badmondesfield Hall in
Wickhambrook, died 1739. *Her.Suff.Ch., Ledger
stone, Wickhambrook*
A lion rampant holding in its paws an escallop.

GIBBON, John, died 1736; son Lawrence Gibbon,
died 1738. *Her.Suff.Ch., Floor slabs, All Saints,
Sudbury. (Not found 1980)*
A lion rampant holding in his sinister paw an
escallop.

NEWMAN, of Ipswich. *Davy, A.*
A lion rampant Proper holding in the paw a
fleur-de-lis Or.

BROWN, Dr. Thomas Brown, M.D., died 1852.
*Her.Suff.Ch., Hatchment and Wall tablet, Brent
Eleigh*
A lion rampant holding a fleur-de-lis.

BROWN. George J.E. Brown, died 1857; Walter T.
Brown, died 1905. *Her.Suff.Ch., Wall tablets,
Tostock*
A lion rampant holding in his dexter paw a
fleur-de-lis Proper.

BROWNRIG, of Ipswich, Willisham. *Davy, A.*
A lion rampant holding a fleur-de-lis in its dexter
paw.

DALLINGHOO. *Her.Suff.Ch., Floor tiles in
chancel, Huntingfield*
A lion rampant holding in his dexter paw a
fleur-de-lis.

HOLLAND. Rector of Huntingfield, 1849. *Davy,
A. Bookplate**
A lion rampant Or holding in his dexter paw a tulip
Gules slipped Vert.

WAKELIN, of Higham. *MS Ordinary of Arms,
fo. 42*. Davy, A., church*
A lion rampant Argent holding between the paws a
garland of roses.

BRIDGEMAN, Orlando, died 1731. *Her.Suff.Ch.,
Coffin plate in church, Combs. (Not found 1980)*

A lion rampant Argent holding in his mouth a
sinister hand erased Proper.

LONG, Bart., of Erwarton. *Davy, A.*
A lion salient Azure holding a lozenge Vair.

GOODWYN, of Framlingham. *Green 145, church*
A lion rampant Or holding in his paws a millrind
Sable.

MILLES, MILLS, of Redisham. *Davy, A.*
A lion rampant in his dexter paw a mullet under his
sinister [paw] a cross paty.

JOHNSON. *Washbourne, 'Suff.'*
A lion rampant Erminois holding in his dexter paw a
mullet pierced Sable and resting his dexter foot on a
cross moline Gules.

JOHNSON. Rector of Lavenham, died 1855.
Crisp's Visitation. XXI. 1*
A lion rampant Or holding between his paws a pillar
[or column] Or.

CULLUM. 'of Hastede in Suffolk' *MS Heraldic
Alphabet*
A lion rampant Sable supporting a pillar Argent
headed and garnished Or.

CULLUM, of Hawstead, Thorndon. *Bokenham*
A lion rampant Proper supporting a decorative pillar
Or.

MONSON. *MS Knight's Visitations, Linc.**
A lion rampant Or supporting a pillar Argent.

MONSON. *MS Martin's Crests*
A lion rampant Or sustained by a pillar Argent.

MONSON, Lord. Of Sweffling, Bury. *Davy, A.*
A lion rampant supporting an Ionic pillar Proper.

STOCKTON, of Ipswich. *Davy, A.*
A lion rampant Sable charged on the shoulder with a
thistle leaved and slipped and supporting a level
with plummet Proper.

OGILVIE, of Sizewell Hall near Leiston. *Burke,
L.G. 1952 ed.**
A lion rampant ducally crowned holding in his paws
a roundel.

KING, of Shelley, Ipswich, Witnesham. *Davy, A.*
A lion rampant holding a saltire.

GAELL, GALE, of Hadleigh. *Davy, A., church*
A lion rampant Gules holding a saltire engrailed Or.

LONG, Robert, of co. Herts.; Grant by Sir W.
Segar, Garter. *Grants & Certificates (Add. MS
12,225; Stowe MS 703)*
A lion rampant Gules holding in his paws a saltire
engrailed Or.

LONGE, of Barrow, Coddenham. *Davy, A.
Washbourne, 'Herts. and Suff.'*
A lion rampant Or holding in his forefeet a boar
spear Argent headed Or.

WARREN, of Hemley, Newbourne. *MS Fairfax
(Tyl.) Bokenham*
A lion rampant Argent ducally gorged Or supporting
a ragged staff Or.

SOTHILL. 'Edward Suthyll of –' *MS Knight's
Visitations, Linc.**
A lion rampant Argent resting his foot on a ragged
staff Or.

SOTHILL, SOUTHWELL. *MS Fairfax (Tyl.)*
A lion rampant Argent supporting in the paws a
dagger Argent hilt and pommel Or.

DE BATHE. Gen. Sir Henry De Bathe, Bart., of
Ireland and co. Devon, died 1907. *Her.Suff.Ch.,
Wall monument, Somerleyton*
A lion rampant brandishing a sword Proper.

SCOTT, of Bungay. *Davy, A.*
A lion rampant ducally gorged charged on the
shoulder with a crescent supporting with both paws
the trunk of a tree raguly.

SOTHILL. *MS Lilly's Visitation of Suffolk, fo. 2*,
'Suthell Badge', but shown on a wreath*
A lion rampant supporting with both paws the trunk
of a tree raguled.
>SOTHILL, SUTHILL. *MS Heraldic Collections,
>fo. 84b**

Rampant or Salient, Guardant or Reguardant
A lion seiant [*sic* should be salient] guardant Sable
holding a lozenge Vairy.
>GOODWIN, of Framlingham. *Davy, A.*

A lion rampant guardant dimidiating three
demi-boats fesseways.
>IPSWICH, Borough of *Livery buttons**

A lion rampant reguardant Sable.
>JENKIN, of Bury. *Davy, A.*

A lion rampant guardant Azure armed and langued
Gules.
>MILDMAY, of Cretingham, Framlingham. *Davy,
>A. Mildmay of Essex. Muskett I. 47. Bookplate**

A lion rampant guardant Or.
>MILLS, of Gt. Saxham. *Gage (Thingoe), church
>monuments. Page*

A lion rampant guardant Argent supporting a
spear erect Sable headed Argent base of the head
Or.
>ROOKWOOD, of Suffolk. *MS ex-Taylor Coll.**

A lion rampant guardant Or supporting with both
paws a long cross Sable.
>WALL, WALLE. *MS Ordinary of Arms, fo. 42*
>Washbourne, 'Suff., Norf., Ess.' Fairbairn*,
>'Wall, Walle, Resby [sic], Suff., Norf., Essex,
>etc.'*

A lion rampant guardant Or supporting a long cross
Sable.
>WALE, of Risby. *Visitation 1664–8*

Passant
A lion passant Or.
>BEAUMONT, of Harkstead. *Visitation 1561 (MSS
>G.7* and Iveagh Copy*) and (ed. Metcalfe).
>Visitation 1664–8, with mullet on shoulder for
>difference. Davy, A. Washbourne*, 'Leic. and
>Suff.' Fairbairn*, 'Leics. and Suff.'*

A lion passant Or langued Gules.
>BEAUMONT, of Dennington, Hadleigh, Ipswich,
>Sproughton, Hintlesham. *Bokenham. Sharpe.
>Davy, A. Muskett. II. 321*

A lion passant Argent.
>BOOTH, of Coddenham, Barham, Hawstead
>House. *MS Ordinary of Arms, fo. 100*. Davy, A.
>Burke, L.G. 1900 ed.*

A lion passant.
>COBBOLD. John Patteson Cobbold, M.P. for
>Ipswich, died 1875. *Her.Suff.Ch., Brass plate,
>St. Mary Tower*

A lion passant to the sinister (?) Argent(?).
>CRABBE. *Davy, A., Seal*

A lion passant.
>CROMPTON. 'Mr. John Crompton' *Her.Suff.Ch.,
>Altar tomb, churchyard, Walpole*

A lion passant Proper.
>JACOB, Bart., of Ubbeston, Withersfield. *Davy, A.*

A lion passant Ermine.
>LE HUNTE, of Bradley. *Davy, A.*

A lion passant between two ?palm branches.
>ST. JOHN. John de St. John, noted soldier temp.
>Edw. I. *Caerlaverock Poem, 248, Seal*

A lion passant.
>TAYLOR, of Honington. *Davy, A.*

A lion passant Argent.

TURNER, of Bradwell, Halesworth, Yarmouth.
Davy, A. Bookplate*

Passant. Crowned only
A lion passant crowned.
>TRUSSON, Gabriel, died 1766. *Her.Suff.Ch.,
>Slab, churchyard, Kelsale*

Passant. Gorged only
A lion passant ducally gorged.
>CASBORNE. *Visitation 1561 (ed. Howard)
>I. 204**

A lion passant Or ducally gorged Gules.
>CASBORNE, of Newhouse, Pakenham. *Fairbairn,
>'Casborne, Newhouse, Pakenham, Suff.' Burke,
>L.G. 1853 ed.*

A lion passant ducally gorged Gules.
>CASBORNE, Rev. John, Incumbent of Drinkstone,
>Old Newton and Pakenham; John Spring
>Casborne, of New House, Pakenham, died 1822.
>*Her.Suff.Ch., Wall monuments, Pakenham*

Passant, holding: [Objects in alphabetical order and including previous sub-sections]
A lion passant holding an annulet Or gorged with a
ducal coronet Gules.
>CASBORNE, of Pakenham, Wortham. *Davy, A.*

A lion passant crowned holding in his paw an
arrow.
>TRUSSON, Gabriel, died 1766. *Partridge, 106
>(Darby, 1826), churchyard, Kelsale*

A lion passant crowned holding in his dexter paw an
arrow.
>TRUSSON, of Kelsale. *Davy, A.*

A lion passant holding an arrow.
>BIGLAND. *Washbourne, 'Suff.'*

A lion passant Gules holding in his dexter paw a
laurel branch Vert.
>TURNER, Bart. Of Wingfield. *Davy, A.*

A lion passant Proper holding in his dexter paw a
crescent Argent.
>CREPPING, CREPING. *Davy, A.*

A lion passant crowned supporting an escutcheon
Gules thereon a cross Argent.
>SINGH. Duleep Singh, Maharajah of Lahore,
>died 1893. *Her.Suff.Ch., Wall tablet, Elvedon*
>[not found 1988, possibly stolen by Sikhs during
>World War II]
'Upon a helm on top of coronet of an Indian
prince . . .' [*sic* rest of crest presumably as above].
>SINGH. Prince Frederick Duleep Singh, second
>son of the Maharajah, died 1926. *Her.Suff.Ch.,
>Wall tablet, Elvedon*

A lion passant Argent resting his dexter paw on a
fleur-de-lis Gules.
>MORDEN, of Thurlow, London. *London
>Visitation Peds., 1664 (H.S.) 100*

A lion passant Argent holding in his dexter paw a
millrind Sable.
>TURNER, TURNOR, of Stoke Ash, Kettleburgh,
>Haverhill, Lt. Wratting. *Visitation 1561
>(MSS G.7* and Iveagh Copy*) and (ed.
>Metcalfe). Harl. 772* MS Knight's Visitations,
>Suff.* 'Richard Tournour of Gt. Thurlowe in
>Com Suffolke Gent:' MS Lilly's Visitation of
>Suffolk* MS Heraldic Collections, fo. 53*
>Davy, A.*

A lion passant Gules holding in his dexter paw a
mill-rind Or.
>TURNOR, of Lt. Worthing [*sic* Wratting].
>*Turner, 46, Pew in Mulbarton church, Norfolk*

A lion passant Argent gutty Sable holding in the

dexter paw a millrind Sable and in the mouth a cross paty fitchy in bend Or.

ROUND-TURNER, 'of Grundisburgh, nr. Woodbridge, Suff.' *Fairbairn. Crest 1. for Turner. Crest 2. for Round [q.v.]*

Passant Guardant or Reguardant

A lion passant guardant Argent.

COBBOLD, of Ipswich. *Davy, A. Burke, L.G. 1900 ed.*

A lion passant guardant Or.

COBBOLD, of Holywells in Ipswich, Felixstowe Lodge. *Fairbairn*, 'of Ipswich'. Crisp's Visitation. XX. 21, Pedigree*

A lion passant guardant Sable armed and langued Or.

FAIRFAX, of Woodbridge, Bury. *Davy, A.*

A lion passant guardant Argent.

LE STRANGE. 'Sr nycollas Strange' *MS Philpot's Visitation, Norf.**

A lion passant guardant Or.

LE STRANGE, of Pakenham, Bury. *Visitation 1664–8* Davy, A. Washbourne*, 'Lestrange. Middx., Norf. and Suff.' Fairbairn*, 'Lestrange, Norf., Suff. & Middx.' Muskett. II. 171*

A lion passant guardant.

PURCAS. Elizabeth, wife of John Purcas, died 1731. *Tymms, 201, St. Mary's church slab, Bury. Her.Suff.Ch., Ledger stone, St. Mary's, Bury*

A lion passant guardant ducally gorged and chained.

RICHMOND, Duke of *Davy, A., buried at Framlingham*

A lion passant guardant.

TURNOR, William, died 1734; widow Maria, died 1751; Henry Turnor, died 1764. *Her.Suff.Ch., Ledger stones, St. Mary's, Bury*

A lion passant reguardant.

YELVERTON. William Yelverton, at Rougham, co. Norfolk. Died 1586. *Cotman's Norfolk Brasses, plate 82**

A lion passant reguardant Gules.

YELVERTON. 'Henry Yelverton of Rowgham' *MS Knight's Visitations, Norf.* MS Ordinary of Arms, fo. 57* 'Robart Yelvarton' MS Philpot's Visitations, Norf.* MS Martin's Crests*

Passant Guardant, holding:

A lion passant guardant per pale indented . . . and Ermine supporting with the dexter paw an escutcheon of the arms. [Croft of Stillington, see Burke, General Armory, 244].

CROFT, John, 'descended from the family of Croft of Shillington [sic], co. Yorks.' *Her.Suff.Ch., Wall tablet, Woodbridge*

A lion passant guardant holding in his dexter paw a trefoil slipped.

HARVEY, William M. *Visitation 1561 (ed. Howard) II. 179, Bookplate**

A lion passant guardant Or in the dexter paw a mill-rind Sable.

TURNER, John, eldest brother of Sir William Turner, of Commons [sic]. *Grants & Certificates (Stowe MS 716)*

A lion passant guardant Argent holding in his dexter paw a millrind Sable.

TURNER, TURNOR, TURNOUR, of Haverhill. *MS Martin's Crests. Berry, Sussex Gen. 368*, 'of Haverhill, temp.Hen.4.' Washbourne, 'Turner, Glouc., Hunts. & Suff.' Tymms, 188, St. Mary's, Bury. Fairbairn*, 'Turner, Lancs., Hunts. & Suff.' Henry Turnor, died 1764; Others, 1775–1780. Her.Suff.Ch., Wall tablet in tower, St. Mary's,*

Bury. Rev. George Thomas Turner, Rector for 32 years, died 1871. *Wall tablet, Kettleburgh (paw and millrind broken off)*

A lion passant guardant Argent holding in his dexter paw a millrind Gules.

TURNER. *MS Martin's Crests*

A lion passant guardant holding in his dexter paw a millrind Sable.

TURNER, of Haverhill, Lt. Wratting. *Bokenham. Davy, A.*

A lion passant guardant Sable in the dexter paw a mill-rind Argent.

TURNER. *Washbourne, 'Hunts. and Suff.' Fairbairn*, 'Hunts. and Suff.'*

A lion passant guardant Argent holding in the dexter paw a fer-de-moulin Sable and charged on the side with a fret Gules.

TURNOR, TURNOR BARNWELL. Granted 1826 to Frederick Henry Barnwell, Esq., of Bury, on his taking the additional name and arms of Turnor; he died 1843. *Her.Suff.Ch., Glass, St. Mary's, Bury. Crest 2. Crest 1. for Barnwell [q.v.] Wall tablet, St. James's, Bury. The fret Sable*

Statant and Statant Guardant

A lion statant guardant per pale Gules and Argent.

BROWNRIGG, Robert, Barrister, J.P., died 1669. *Her.Suff.Ch., Hatchment, Beccles*

'The Creste vppon the Helme A Lion Sable enarmed gold the Taile forked & knytte standing within a wrethe gold & azure'

GYGGES. Robert, Thomas and John Gygges of Norfolk; Grant of Arms and Crest by Thomas Holme, Clarenceux, 26 February 1477. *Misc.Gen. et Her. 3rd S. I. 1**

A lion with two tails Sable standing with his four feet in a wreath Or Azure Sable and Argent.

'GYGGES of Suffolk sqwyer' *Wall's Book*

'to his Crest a lyon w^t ij tayles sa/ standing w^t his fore fete in a wreth or/b/'

'GYGGS of Suff.' *MS Alphabet of Crests, fo. 46b*

A lion statant Sable.

GYGGES. *MS Knight's Visitations, Suff.* 'Gigge, Suff.' Fairbairn*

A lion statant guardant Or.

LE STRANGE. 'Hamond Le Strange of Hunstone' *MS Knight's Visitations, Norf.* Sir Roger Le Strange, of Hunstanton, co. Norfolk. Brass of 1506. Cotman's Norfolk Brasses, plate 47**

A lion statant Argent holding in his paw a fleur-de-lis Gules.

MORDEN, of Suffolk. *Misc.Gen. et Her. 5th S. VI. 106 (Visitation of London 1664, Harl. MS 1086, fo. 9a.)*

Sejant

A lion sejant Gules.

BLITHE, BLYTHE, of Ipswich. *MS Heraldic Collections, fo. 56*. Sharpe. Davy, A., St. Peter's church*

A lion salient (?sejant) Gules armed Azure.

BOKENHAM, of Wortham. *Davy, A.*

A lion seiant.

BOND, of Hengrave. *Gage (Thingoe), 235. Davy, A., church*

A lion sejant Argent.

BOND, of Bury. *Davy, A.*

A lion sejant.

BRAMPTON, BRAMSTON, of Eye, Bury. *Davy, A., Eye church. E.A.N. & Q. I. 312.* Thomas Brampton, son of Edward Brampton of Eye, died 1712. *Her.Suff.Ch., Ledger stone, Eye*

A lion seiant Proper.
GLASCOCK. *Davy, A.*
A lion seiant with tail serpentine.
HOLT. *Davy, A.*
A lion seiant his tail wreathed Ermine.
HOVELL. *Bokenham*
A lion seiant Ermine.
HUNT, HUNT alias LE HUNTE, of Bradley. 'Sr George Le Hunte of Little Bradley Knight' *MS Lilly's Visitation of Suffolk*. Bokenham. 'Hunt' MS Martin's Crests. 'Hunt' MS ex-Taylor Coll.* Fairbairn, 'Hunt. Norf. and Suff.'* Richard Le Hunte, died 1540. *Her.Suff.Ch., Effigy wall monument, Lt. Bradley. Untinctured*
A lion seiant Argent langued Gules.
LE HUNTE, of Bradley, Barton. *Davy, A., Clare church. Proc.S.I.A. VIII. 223*
A lion seiant Argent.
HUNT. 'Sir George Le Hunte, benefactor to this Church 16 . . .' *Her.Suff.Ch., Glass, Clare*
A lion seiant Sable.
PHILLIPS. *MS ex-Taylor Coll.**
A lion seiant Or.
RANT, of Mendham. *Davy, A., church*
A lion seiant.
RAYMOND, Thomas, Esq., died 1680. *Her.Suff.Ch., Wall tablet, Hopton*

Sejant. Gorged only

A lion sejant Or gorged with a collar Sable charged with three plates.
BRAMPTON, BRAMSTON. *Davy, A.* 'Thomas Bramston, Esq.' *Bookplate**
A lion seiant Argent ducally gorged and lined Or.
PLAYTERS. *'Plater' MS Knight's Visitations, Suff.**
A lion seiant gorged with a coronet and chained.
PLAYTERS, of Sotterley. *Bokenham*
A lion seiant ducally gorged and lined.
PLAYTERS, of Sotterley. *Davy, A.*
A lion sejant collared and lined.
PLAYTERS, William, died 1584. *Her.Suff.Ch., Brass achievement, Sotterley*
A lion sejant Ermine collared and line Or.
WENTWORTH, John, of Somerton [*sic*], co. Suffolk; Grant by R. Cooke, Clarenceux, 11 October 1576. *Grants & Certificates (Harl. MS 1,359)*
A lion seiant Ermine collared and chained Or.
WENTWORTH. *MS Knight's Visitations, Suff.** 'Waintworth of Somerleyton' *Bokenham*
A lion seiant Ermine collared lined and ringed Or the line turned round the front legs.
WENTWORTH. 'John Wentworthe' *MS Philpot's Visitations, Suff.**

Sejant, holding: [Objects in alphabetical order and including previous sub-sections]

A lion sejant holding in the dexter paw a bunch of arrows tips downward.
BOWES, Martin, died 1726. *Her.Suff.Ch., Ledger stone, St. Mary's, Bury*
'Vppon the healme on a Wreath, siluer and asur, a Lyon seant siluer with a Crowne on his head, houldinge in his fore foot a battayll Axe gould, manteled gules, dobled siluer'
GALL, of Wenhaston, London. Confirmation of Arms and Grant of Crest to Robert Gall, of London, by Cooke, Clarenceux, 6 June 1576. *Frag.Gen. IV. 18–19*

A lion seiant Or his tail cast between his legs holding or resting his forefoot upon a halbert Or.
REYDON, ROYDON, of Reydon. *MS Fairfax. Bokenham.* 'Robert Reydon, Lord of Reydon, died 1468' *Her.Suff.Ch., formerly in St. Nicholas, Ipswich (Tyl.MS of 1594)*
A lion seiant his foot on a helmet (or halberd) Or.
RAYDON, 'of Raydon in Samford Hundred'. *Davy, A. St. Nicholas church, Ipswich, 1478.* [The halbert is drawn in *Tyllotson's MS*]
A lion seiant Or supporting a column Argent the capital and base Or.
CULLUM, Bart., of Thorndon, Hawstead, Hardwick House. *London Visitation 1633 (H.S.) I. 210* Visitation 1664–8* Gage (Thingoe). Misc. Gen. et Her. 2nd S. I. 181* Muskett. I. 174. Fairbairn, 'of Hawsted and Hardwick House, Suff.' Bookplate*, untinctured.* Thomas Cullum, Bt., died 1664. *Her.Suff.Ch., Wall monument, Hawstead.* William Cullum, died 1700. *Ledger stone, Thorndon.* William Cullum, late of Thorndon, died 1727. *Floor slab, Brent Eleigh*
A lion seiant Proper supporting a column, or pillar, Or.
CULLUM, Bart., of Thorndon, Hawstead, Bury. *Davy, A.*
A lion sejant Proper holding a column Argent base and capital Or.
CULLUM. 'MILNER-GIBSON-CULLUM, George Gery, of Hardwick House, Bury St. Eds., Suff.' *Fairbairn. Crest 1. for Cullum. Crest 2. for Milner-Gibson [q.v]*
A lion sejant holding a column.
CULLUM. Sir Thomas Gery Cullum, Bt. *Her.Suff.Ch., Glass, St. Mary's, Bury*
A lion sejant Argent supporting a column Or.
DAVY, of Suffolk. *Davy, A. Washbourne*, 'Suss., Suff., Wilts.' Fairbairn, 'Sussex, Suff. & Wilts.'*
A lion sejant supporting with his dexter paw a crescent.
HARVEY, of Woodhall in Stoke Ash. *E.A. Misc. 1920. 97*
A lion seiant Gules resting his paw on a cross paty fitchy Or.
BALES, BEALES, of Norton, Woolpit, Hunston. *Visitation 1664–8*, 'p. Segar, Garter, 20 December 3 Jas. I.' [1605]. Davy, A., Woolpit churchyard*
A lion seiant Gules supporting a cross formy fitchy at the foot Or.
BALES, of Norton. *Bokenham*
A lion seiant holding in his paws a cross paty fitchy in the foot.
BEALES, Francis, died 1734. *Partridge, 219 (Darby, 1827), Woolpit churchyard*
A lion seiant Argent holding in his dexter paw a cross flory Sable.
DICKENS, of Branches Park in Cowlinge, Copdock. *Davy, A., Cowlinge and Rendlesham churches*
A lion sejant holding in his dexter paw a rose, or rose branch, all Or.
RUSHBROOKE, of Gt. Fakenham. *Davy, A., Rushbrook church glass. Washbourne, 'Rushbrook, Suff.' Proc.S.I.A. VII. 336*
A lion sejant holding in his mouth a rose all Or.
RUSHBROOKE, of Rushbrook Park. *Burke, L.G. 1853 and 1900 eds. Fairbairn, 'Suff.' Crisp's Visitation. XIX. 9, Pedigree.* Robert Rushbrook, M.P. *Her.Suff.Ch., Glass, St. Mary's, Bury. Rose slipped Sable.*

A lion sejant holding in its mouth a rose slipped and leaved Or.

> RUSHBROOKE, Robert, gent., of Honington, died 1753. *Her.Suff.Ch., Wall tablet, Honington, Untinctured.* Robert Rushbrook, of Rushbrook Park, died 1829. *Hatchment, Rushbrook.* Captain Bartel Davers Rushbrooke, Suffolk Reg., killed in action 1915, aged 22. *Wall tablet, Rushbrook*

A lion seiant Sable holding a saltire Argent.

> GREENWOOD, of Burgh Castle. *MS Heraldic Collections, fo. 34b.* Davy, A., church. Washbourne, 'Suff. and Oxon.' E.A.N. & Q. II. 327. Fairbairn, 'Suff. and Oxon.'* Thomas Raymond, who married a daughter of Greenwood of Burgh Castle; he died 1680. *Her.Suff.Ch., Wall tablet, Hopton*

A lion seiant Sable holding a saltire engrailed Argent.

> GREENWOOD, of Burgh Castle. *Bokenham*

A lion sejant Gules holding in his paws a saltire engrailed Or.

> LONG, LONGE, of Barrow, Coddenham, Sternfield. *Visitation 1664–8* Sharpe. Davy, A. E.A.N. & Q. VI. 35. Burke, L.G. 1900 and 1952 eds.* E.A. Misc. 1932. 78.* Rev. John Longe, Vicar of Coddenham, died 1834; widow died 1863. *Her.Suff.Ch., Hatchment and Wall tablets, Coddenham. Livery button*, untinctured*

A lion sejant Or the dexter paw resting on a saltire Argent.

> THOMPSON, Samuel; Grant by R. Cooke, Clarenceux. *Grants & Certificates (Harl. MSS 1,359 and 6,140)*

A lion seiant Or supporting with both paws a saltire Argent.

> THOMPSON, of Ufford. *Sharpe. Davy, A.*

A lion rampant sejant [*sic*] supporting with both paws a saltire couped Argent.

> THOMPSON, Thomas, died 1758. *Her.Suff.Ch., Ledger stone, Mildenhall (not seen 1988)*

A lion sejant Gules ducally crowned Or supporting with the dexter paw an antique shield Azure charged with a fleur-de-lis Or.

> BASE, of Saxmundham. *Visitation 1664–8, 83 (Harl. MS 1085),* '? borne by another name'

A lion seiant Proper supporting with his dexter paw a shield Azure charged with a fesse dancetty Or.

> CURTOIS, CURTHOIS, CURTIS, of Tuddenham. *Visitation 1664–8**

A lion seiant Proper supporting with his dexter paw a shield Azure charged with a fesse dancetty between three mural crowns Or. (The arms).

> CURTIS, of Tuddenham Hall, Bury. *Davy, A.*

A lion seiant Proper in his dexter paw a shield.

> CURTIS, of Honington. *Davy, A. Washbourne*,* 'Suff.'

A lion seiant Proper supporting an escutcheon [or shield] of the arms [Argent two bars and a canton Azure].

> PIPARD, of Hintlesham. *Davy, A.*

A lion seiant holding in his paws a spear erect.

> ANTHONY. Rector of Framlingham, died 1703. *Loder, 308. Green, 143. Davy, A., church slab*

A lion seiant holding in his mouth a spear.

> HUGHES, Bart., of East Bergholt. *Davy, A.*

A lion seiant supporting a spear erect Argent.

> ROOKWOOD. *Washbourne, 'Suff.' Fairbairn, 'Rockwood, Rookwood, of Eveston [sic Euston], Suff.'*

A lion sejant – holding in his dexter paw a sword point upwards Argent hilt and pommel Or.

> MADDOCKS, MADOKE. *MS Ordinary of Arms, fo. 51**

A lion seiant Or in his dexter paw a sword Argent hilt and pommel Or.

> MADDOCKS, of Troston. *'Maddox' MS Martin's Crests,* 'lion supporting a sword'. *Davy, A., church*

Sejant, Guardant or Reguardant

'to his crest a lyon seant reguardant sa/ armed and langued or/ carrying his tayl upon his back the end thereof or/'

> BARNABY. *MS Alphabet of Crests, fo. 13b*

A lion seiant guardant Or.

> PROBERT, of Bury. *Davy, A.*

A lion seiant guardant Argent supporting a spear erect Or.

> ROOKWOOD, of Euston. *Bokenham. Davy, A.*

Couchant or Dormant

A lion couchant, or dormant, Or between two branches of ?laurel, or olive, Vert.

> CROPLEY, of Shelland. *Visitation 1664–8. Davy, A. (Barrett MS)*

A lion couchant Or between two branches Proper.

> CROPLEY, of Shelland. *Bokenham, 'p.R.St.Geo., 1635'. Proc.S.I.A. V. 39, Aldrich slab, Hessett church,* 'between two branches of a tree'. *Untinctured*

A lion couchant.

> CROPLEY, of Rockells in Shelland. *Davy, A.*

A lion couchant Or.

> DENTON, of Lakenheath. *MS Martin's Crests. Davy, A.*

A lion couchant.

> DICKINS, Francis, Barrister and Lord of the Manors of Cowling and Lt. Bradley, died 1747. *Her.Suff.Ch., Effigy monument, Cowlinge*

A lion couchant Sable.

> HARVEY, of Cockfield. *Bokenham*

A lion couchant Argent.

> HARVEY, of Cockfield. *Davy, A.*

A lion couchant Gules.

> HARVEY, HARVY. *Washbourne, 'Norf. and Suff.' Fairbairn*,* 'Harvy, Norf. and Suff.' James Harvey, of Clare College, Cambridge, died 1723, aged 20. *Her.Suff.Ch., Effigy monument, Cockfield. Untinctured.* Rev. Calthorpe Harvey, died 1767. *Slab in tower (partly covered), Cockfield*

A lion couchant Or.

> HARVEY, of Cockfield. *Davy, A., Lawshall church*

A lion couchant Or.

> HUGHES, Bart., of East Bergholt. *Davy, A. Burke, Peerage, 1891 ed.** 'Sir Collingwood Hughes, Bart., of East Bergholt, Suff.' *Fairbairn*.* Rev. Sir Richard Hughes, Bt., died 1848; Sir Edward Hughes, Bt., died 1871. *Her.Suff.Ch., Glass, East Bergholt*

A lion couchant Or.

> NUNN, of Southwold, Tostock, Pakenham, Badwell Ash. *Davy, A., Southwold church*

A lion couchant Argent.

> ROUND, ROUND-TURNER, of Grundisburgh House. *Burke, L.G. 1900 ed.*

A tower Argent on the battlements a lion couchant Ermine crowned Or.

> SKRINE. 'John Skryne, of Warleigh in the parish of Bathford in Somerset; Grant by Sir W. Dugdale, Garter and Sir Henry St. George,

Clarenceux, 8 November 1682. *Grants & Certificates (Stowe MS 677)*
A lion couchant between two laurel branches in orle.
>THIRKLE, of Ipswich. *Davy, A. Washbourne*

Couchant, holding:
A lion . . . holding a cross patonce (A lion couchant Or holding in the gamb a cross patonce Sable).
>DICKENS. Lt.Gen. Sir S.T. Dickens, died 1847. *Her.Suff.Ch., Wall tablet, Sts. Peter & Paul, Felixstowe*

A lion couchant Argent charged on the body with three annulets interlaced fessewise Sable holding in his mouth a sword in bend point downwards Proper pommel and hilt Or.
>ROUND, ROUND-TURNER, of Woodbridge, Clopton Hall, Lt. Bealings, Grundisburgh House. *Crips's Visitation, XII. 1*, Pedigree. Fairbairn. Burke, L.G. 1952 ed.**

Couchant Guardant
A lion couchant guardant Argent supporting a banner thereon a hand couped Or.
>CHURCHILL, of Dallinghoo. *Bokenham*

A lion couchant guardant Or.
>HUGHES, Bart. *Washbourne*, 'Suff.'*

DEMI-LYNX
A demi-lynx, vel ounce, rampant Or pellety supporting an escallop Ermine.
>HARVY. *MS Heraldic Alphabet*

A demi-lynx rampant per pale Or and Gules on each side drops counterchanged.
>WITHIPOLE, of Ipswich. *Bokenham*

LYNX
A lynx passant guardant Proper.
>CROPLEY. *Davy, A., Hessett church*

A lynx Proper spotted collared lined and ringed Or.
>HARVY. *MS Heraldic Alphabet*

'For his crest and congnysans vpon a wrethe argent & sables a Lynx passant in his proper couller mantelyd gules dou'lyd argent'
>LYNCH, of Staple, co. Kent. Descendant of Ipswich. Confirmation of Arms and Grant of Crest by Cooke, Clarenceux, 10 December 1572. *Misc.Gen. et Her. N.S. IV. 351–2*

A lynx rampant guardant.
>LYNCH, of St. Mary Elms, Ipswich. *Frag.Gen. X. 92 (silver snuff-box*)*

A lynx Proper.
>TAYLOR, LE TAYLOR, of Lidgate. *London Visitation 1568 (H.S.) I. 23*

A lynx.
>WENTWORTH, of Somerleyton. *Davy, A. (Barrett)*

MARTEN
A marten passant Proper.
>MARTIN, MARTYN, Bart., of Long Melford. *Visitation 1561 (ed.Metcalfe). Bokenham. Davy, A. Washbourne*, 'Martin, Bart., Suff.' Fairbairn, 'Martin, Bart., Suff. One of two Martin crests.'*

A marten statant Proper.
>MARTIN, of Long Melford. *Visitation 1561 (ed. Howard) I. 207**

MOLE
A mole passant Sable.
>MITFORD. Vicar of Benhall, Rector of Weston and Stratford. *Davy, A.*

MONKEY see APE

OTTER
An otter passant wounded in the sinister shoulder with an arrow.
>HOMFRAY, of Gt. Yarmouth, co. Norfolk and Stradishall Park. *Perlustration. I. 336–7. Livery button**

An otter dark russet.
>JAY. *MS Heraldic Alphabet*

An otter passant Proper.
>JAY, of Pettistree, Homersfield, Bardwell, South Town, Lowestoft. *Davy, A.*

An otter Sable in its mouth a fish Proper.
>LUTTRELL, of Moulton, Waldingfield, Debenham. *Davy, A., Wetherden church*

DEMI-OUNCE see also LEOPARD, LYNX
A demi-lynx, vel ounce, rampant Or pellety supporting an escallop Ermine.
>HARVY. *MS Heraldic Alphabet*

A demi-leopard, or ounce, rampant Sable bezanty langued Gules in his dexter paw a trefoil slipped Or.
>HERVEY, of Oulton. *Visitation 1561 (MSS G.7* and Iveagh Copy*)*

OUNCE
A leopard, or ounce, passant Sable bezanty ducally gorged and chained Or holding in his dexter paw a trefoil slipped Vert.
>HERVEY. Marquis and Earls of Bristol. Of Ickworth, Oulton. *Visitation 1561 (ed. Howard) II. 145* and 150*. Harl. 772*. Davy, A. Burke, Peerage 1891 ed.*, chain reflexed over the back. Fairbairn, 'Marquess of Bristol, Ickworth Park, Bury St. Edmunds. Leopard'. Her.Suff.Ch., Wall tablets and Ledger stones, Ickworth. Chain reflexed over the back*

An ounce passant Proper bezanty ducally gorged and chained Or holding in the dexter paw a trefoil slipped Proper.
>HERVEY. Hon. Carr, Lord Hervey, died 1723; Many others. *Suff. Green Bks, Ickworth**

An ounce, or leopard, passant Sable bezanty collared lined and ringed the line reflexed over the back holding in the dexter paw a trefoil slipped Vert.
>HERVEY, of Ickworth. *Visitation 1561 (ed. Howard) II. 133*, 153* and 164*. Washbourne, 'leopard. Suff. and Devon'. Line not reflexed. Fairbairn, 'leopard. Suff. and Devonsh. Line not reflexed*

An ounce passant Argent spotted Sable collared and lined the line reflexed over the back Or holding in the dexter paw a trefoil slipped Vert.
>HARVEY, of Bury. *Visitation 1664–8*

An ounce passant Sable spotted Or collared lined and ringed the line reflexed over the back Or holding in the dexter paw an acorn Or.
>HARVEY, HARVY. *MS Heraldic Collections, fo. 53**

An ounce passant Sable ducally gorged Or.
>HOWLAND. Probably for George Howland, Lord of the Manor of Haverhill, 1768– at least 1784 *MS Manor Court book. Her.Suff.Ch., Hatchment, Haverhill*

An ounce seiant spotted Proper tail erect.
>PLAYFORD. *MS Heraldic Alphabet*

'for his Creaste or Cognoisance uppon his healme on a wreath siluer and sables an Ownce standinge in proper cooler manteled gules dowbled siluer'.
>TAYLOR. John le Talor, of London, Esq.; Confirmation of Arms and Grant of Crest by Robert Cooke, Clarenceux, 20 July 1572. *Muskett. I. 241*

DEMI-OX. BULL

A demi-bull Ermine attired Or pierced through with a broken spear Sable headed Argent the bull vulned Gules.

> LAUNCE, of Suffolk. *Davy, A.*

A demi-bull rampant Proper.

> LAYMAN, of Ixworth, Ipswich. *Davy, A.*

A demi-bull Gules gorged with a chaplet of laurel Vert.

> LEETE. *Fairbairn, 'of Bury St. Edmunds, Suff.'*

OX

A bull tasseled [*sic*].

> STEBBING, of Brandeston. *Bokenham*

A bull quarterly Or and Sable armed Sable.

> WINGFIELD. 'Wyngfeld of Suffolk' *Wall's Book* 'to his Crest a bull quarterly or/sa/ armed of the second'
>
> WINGFIELD. 'Wyngfeld of Suff/ knight by h 8' *MS Alphabet of Crests, fo. 137*

Passant and Passant Guardant

A bull passant.

> ALDRICH, ALDRIDGE, of Hessett. *Bokenham. Davy, A., church*

A bull passant Argent.

> ALDRICH. Rev. John Cobbold Aldrich, 40 years Incumbent, died 1874. *E.A.N. & Q. IX. 186. Her.Suff.Ch., Brass tablet, St. Lawrence, Ipswich*

A bull passant Sable armed and hooved Or.

> DACRE. *MS Ordinary of Arms, fo. 205**

A bull passant spotted.

> HOBART, James, Esq., at Loddon, co. Norfolk. Brass of 1615. *Cotman's Norfolk Brasses, Appendix Plate 6.* [Helm and Crest turned to the sinister]

A bull passant Sable spotted of several colours.

> HOBART, of Weybread. *Bokenham*

A bull passant per pale Sable and Gules bezanty in his nose a ring Or.

> HOBART, of Weybread, Lindsey. *Davy, A., Weybread church.* John Hobart, Esq., died 1683; Robert, son of John Hobart, died 1682. *Her.Suff.Ch., Ledger stones, Weybread.* Edward Hobart, son of James Hobart of Mendham, died 1711, aged 60. *Ledger stone, Mendham*

A bull full face [*sic* guardant] passant.

> REYNOLDS, . . ., died 1720; widow Ann, died 1727. *Her.Suff.Ch., Altar tomb, churchyard, Lavenham.* [*Partridge 12* gives a totally different crest for this tomb]

A bull passant.

> STEYNING, of Earl Soham. *Visitation 1561 (MS G.7*)*

A bull passant Gules.

> STEYNING, of Earl Soham. *Bokenham*

A bull passant quarterly Sable and Or.

> WINGFIELD. 'Sr Thomas Wyngfild of Letheringham in Com Suffolke Knight'. *MS Lilly's Visitation of Suffolk**

A bull passant quarterly Or and Sable.

> WINGFIELD, of Letheringham. 'Harbotell Wyngfild of Wantisden in Com Suffolke Esquier'. *MS Lilly's Visitation of Suffolk*. Bokenham*

Statant

A bull statant quarterly Sable and Or horned membered and tailed Or.

> BOVILE, of Letheringham. *Davy, A., (Rous Pedigree)*

A bull statant per pale Or and Purpure hooved and armed Sable.

FITZLEWIS, of Shimpling. *Davy, A.*

A bull with tail erect standing before a leafless tree whose trunk is divided into two branches.

> RIDLEY. Sir Jasper Nicholas Ridley, son of 1st Viscount Ridley, died 1951; son Patrick C.P. Ridley, died 1952; widow Nathalie, died 1968. *Her.Suff.Ch., Tombstone, churchyard, Claydon*

A bull statant quarterly Sable and Or.

> WINGFIELD. *Davy, A.*

PORCUPINE

A porcupine passant.

> CALAMY, of Bury. *Davy, A.*

'to his crest a porcupyne b tusked a coller wᵗ a chayne or/ Sʳ willm Sydney'

> SIDNEY, SYDNEY. *MS Alphabet of Crests, fo. 119*

A porcupine statant Azure quills collar and chain Or.

> SIDNEY, of Yoxford, Brockford. *Davy, A., Yoxford church*

DEMI-RABBIT

A demi-rabbit rampant Sable gutty Or.

> RABETT. 'Reginald Rabbett' *Bramfield Estate Map, 1771*; Corder MS 94. Davy, A. Burke, L.G. 1853 and 1900 eds., 'of Bramfield Hall, Kettleburgh manor in Cretingham'. Fairbairn, 'of Dunwich and Bramfield Hall'.* Reginald Rabett, High Sheriff of Suffolk 1737, died 1763. *Her.Suff.Ch., Hatchment, Bramfield.* Rev. Reginald Rabett, M.A., of Bramfield Hall, Rector in cos. Northants. and Leics., died 1860; widow died 1875. *Monument, Bramfield.* Three gutties

A demi-rabbit rampant Sable.

> RABETT, Reginald, died 1810. *Her.Suff.Ch., Hatchment, Bramfield*

RABBIT

A coney sejant rampant Argent.

> CONINGSBY, CONISBY. *Davy, A.*

RHINOCEROS

A rhinoceros.

> GARDINER, of Elmswell. *MS Fairfax (Tyl.)*

A rhinoceros passant Argent.

> GARDINER, of Elmswell, Chadacre. *Davy, A.* Sir Robert Gardiner, Kt., Chief Justice and Viceroy of Ireland, died 1619. *Her.Suff.Ch., Effigy monument, Elmswell. Photograph**

A rhinoceros passant.

> WEBB, of Gt. Bealings. *Davy, A., church.* Henry Webb, died 1700; son Thomas Webb, died 1700, aged 19. *Her.Suff.Ch., Ledger stone, Gt. Bealings. Carved on poppy head of choir stall, Gt. Bealings. Photograph**

A rhinoceros Proper.

> WEBB alias WOOD, of Ufford. *Bokenham*

DEMI-SHEEP

A demi-ram salient Sable collared and armed Or.

> VINCENT. *MS Heraldic Alphabet*

SHEEP

A lamb statant Sable semy of estoiles Or ears and legs from the knees downwards Gules.

> BAYNHAM. 'Syr Xpoffer Baynham' *Banners & Standards*, 'Remainder imperfect'*

A ram passant Argent armed and unguled Or.

> GAGE, Bart., of Hengrave Hall. *Visitation 1664–8*. Bokenham. Gage (Thingoe). Davy, A. Washbourne*, 'Gage, Bart., Suff.' Fairbairn*, 'Gage, Bart., Suff.' Bookplate*.* Gage, Rookwood-Gage. 3rd, 5th, 6th, 8th and 9th Baronets, of Hengrave, died 1741–1872. *Her.Suff.Ch., Five Hatchments, Hengrave.* John

Gage, died 1728; widow died 1759. *Slab and Hatchment, Stanningfield.* Sir William Hall Gage, Bt., Admiral of the Fleet, died 1864. *Wall tablet, Thurston.* Sir Thomas Gage. *Glass, St. Mary's, Bury*

A lamb passant Sable charged on the body with a bezant thereon a trefoil slipped Vert.

LAMB, of Ixworth Thorpe. *Davy, A.*

A lamb supporting a banner Argent.

MALMAYNES, of Cowlinge. *Davy, A.*

Within an arch of laurel a ram statant armed Or.

SHEPHEARD. 'Shepard' *MS Heraldic Collections, fo. 23**

Between two laurel branches Vert a ram passant Argent armed and membered Or.

SHEPHEARD, of Exning. *Davy, A., Exning and Edwardstone churches*

A ram passant Proper.

SHEPHEARD, of Exning. *Washbourne*, 'Suff.' E.A.N. & Q. (N.S.) II. 288. Fairbairn*, 'of Ixning [sic], Suff.'* William Shepherd, died 1815. *Her.Suff.Ch., Wall tablet, Edwardstone*

A ram statant guardant.

SHEPHEARD. *Her.Suff.Ch., Wall tablet, Exning. No name or date given*

A ram passant Gules attired Or.

STEYNINGE, STAYNING. *Davy, A. Washbourne, 'Stenynge, Somers. and Suff.' Fairbairn*, 'Stenynge, Somers. and Suff.'*

SQUIRREL, SQUIRRELS

A branch of a tree barways Vert thereon a squirrel Gules cracking a nut Or between two sprigs of hazel nuts Vert fructed Or.

CRESWELL. *Davy, A. Washbourne*, 'of Northants.'*

A squirrel rampant Azure collared Argent charged on the body with three bezants in pale holding in both paws a hazel branch Vert fructed Or.

HASELWOOD. *MS Ordinary of Arms, fo. 202**

A nut tree Proper the trunk raguly on either side a squirrel salient Gules.

LITTLER. *Davy, A.*

A squirrel Proper.

LOVEDAY, of Chediston. *Davy, A. Washbourne*, 'Norf. and Suff.' Fairbairn*, 'Suff. and Norf.'*

A squirrel standing on his hind legs with a nut in his mouth Gules.

PRETTY, of Eye. *Davy, A.*

Sejant

A squirrel seiant.

BARROW, Dr. Isaac *MS Martin's Crests*

A squirrel sitting per pale Argent and Azure against a 'branche of couldre Vert the noisetes and her tayle gold'

BELHOUSE. 'Belhows' *Wall's Book*

'to his crest a Squyrrell syttyng p pale ar/b/ a gaynst a branche of couldrey Vert the nousets and her tayle or/'

BELHOUSE. 'Belhowsse' *MS Alphabet of Crests, fo. 12*

A squirrel sejant.

COLLINSON, of Sproughton. *Davy, A.* Collinson, of the Chantry in Sproughton; three sons in the Army, died or killed in China, India and Jamaica, 1840–1842. *Her.Suff.Ch., Wall monument, Sproughton*

A squirrel sejant.

HINGESTON, of Ipswich. *E.A.N. & Q. XII. 118, Slab, St. Peter's.* Peter Hingeston, gent., 55 years organist, of Ipswich, died 1743. *Her.Suff.Ch., Ledger stone, St. Peter's*

Sejant, holding: [Objects in alphabetical order]

A squirrel sejant Azure collared Or and charged with three bezants in pale holding in its paws a branch of hazel Vert the nuts Or.

HASELWOOD, Edward, of Northampton, gent.; Grant by Sir C. Barker, Garter. *Grants & Certificates (Stowe MS 692)*

A squirrel sejant Azure collared Or charged with three bezants in pale holding a hazel branch Proper fructed Or.

HASELWOOD, HASLEWOOD. Rector of St. Matthew's, Ipswich. *Misc.Gen. et Her. N.S. II. 128*. Crisp's Visitation. VII. 133, Pedigree*

A squirrel sejant Azure bezanty collared Or holding in his paws a spray of oak fructed Proper.

HASLEWOOD. Rector of St. Matthew's, Ipswich, 1875. *Proc.S.I.A. VII. 189*, church glass*

A squirrel sejant Or holding a slip of oak Vert acorned of the first [sic Or].

SMITHSON, Hugh, of London; Certified by W. Riley, Lancaster, 1646. *Grants & Certificates (Harl. MS 1,172)*

A squirrel sejant Or holding in his paws a sprig of oak fructed.

SMITHSON. *MS ex-Taylor Coll.**

A squirrel sejant holding a branch.

SMITHSON, Sarah, wife of James Smithson, died 1720; Elizabeth, died 1754. *Partridge 155 (Darby, 1832), churchyard, Lowestoft*

A squirrel sejant holding in his paws a sprig of oak Proper.

SMITHSON. *E.A.N. & Q. II. 283, Monument, Yarmouth church*

A squirrel seiant holding a branch of nuts (or cracking a nut Proper)

SMITHSON, of Lowestoft. *Davy, A., churchyard*

A squirrel Gules sejant supporting by its paw a cross similar to a Celtic cross.

DONNAN. *Her.Suff.Ch., List of Rectors, Worlingworth*

A squirrel seiant cracking nuts Gules charged with a chevron Or.

BARROW, of co. Cambs. *MS Heraldic Alphabet*

A squirrel seiant erect cracking nuts Or.

BLUNDELL. *MS Heraldic Alphabet*

A squirrel sejant collared Proper holding a nut.

BLUNDELL, of East Bergholt. *Davy, A., church*

A squirrel sejant eating a nut.

BLUNDELL, of East Bergholt. *E.A.N. & Q. XII. 336, Slab, church*

A squirrel sejant Gules collared holding a nut Or.

BLUNDELL, Shadrach, died 1753. *Her.Suff.Ch., Slab, East Bergholt*

A squirrel sejant breaking a nut Gules.

BROUGHTON, 'of Stantford' *Wall's Book*

'to his crest a squyrrell syttyng brekyng a nutt g/'

BROUGHTON. 'of Staff' *MS Alphabet of Crests, fo. 7b*

'beryth to his crest a squyrel sittyng gold krakking a nutte silver'

CORBET. *Wall's Book*

'to his Crest a Squrrell sytyng gold crakyng a nutte ar/'

CORBET. *MS Alphabet of Crests, fo. 20*

A squirrel sejant Or cracking a nut Argent.

CORBET, John, Esq., of Sprouston, co. Norfolk. Brass of 1559. *Cotman's Norfolk Brasses, plate 71*. Untinctured, charged with a mullet for difference.* 'Myles Corbett of Sprowston' *MS Knight's Visitations, Norf.** 'Myles Corbet'

MS Philpot's Visitations, Norf*. Washbourne*, Norf. and Suff.'

A squirrel sitting on the stump of a nut-tree Proper eating a nut Or between two branches Vert fructed of the second [*sic* Or].

> CRESSWELL, Robert, of Pursland, co. Northampton, gent.; Exemplification by W. Dethick, Garter, 20 February 1590. *Grants & Certificates (Stowe MS 676)*

A squirrel sejant eating a nut Proper.

> CRESSWELL. *Washbourne*, 'Suff.' Fairbairn*, 'Suff. . . . cracking a nut'*

A squirrel seiant cracking a nut Proper.

> DOWSING, of Laxfield. *Davy, A., church*

A squirrel seiant cracking a nut.

> LOVELL, of Knettishall, Newton. *Davy, A.*

A squirrel seiant eating a nut.

> REEVE, of Ipswich, Bungay. *Davy, A.*

A squirrel sejant Proper collared Or holding a nut in his paws.

> REEVE, of Bury, Ipswich, Bungay. *Davy, A. Muskett. III. 1. (Harl. MS 1560, fo. 29b)*

A squirrel sejant supporting a ragged staff Or.

> BURLEY. *Washbourne, 'Suff.' Fairbairn, 'Burley, Burly, Suff.'*

A squirrel seiant supporting a ragged staff Or.

> BURLZ, of Depden. *Visitation 1664–8*. Bokenham, 'p.Lee, Clar. 1594' Davy, A.*

DEMI-TIGER see also MONSTER, HERALDIC

TIGER

A demi-tiger Or pelletty.

> ARNOLD. *MS Martin's Crests*

A demi-tiger ducally gorged and lined Proper.

> DACRE. Lord Dacre of the North. of Wrentham. *Davy, A.*

A demi-Royal tiger Proper.

> WOLRICH. *Fairbairn, 'of Cowling [sic], Suff.'*

Rampant

A demi-tiger rampant Gules bezanty tail erect.

> APPLEYARD. *Davy, A.*

A demi-leopard, or tiger, rampant Proper crowned with an antique or Eastern crown Gules holding in his paws a sword erect ?Sable.

> ASSEY, of Beccles. *Davy, A., church*

A demi-tiger rampant ?Azure holding in his paws a broken sword.

> BLOMFIELD, of Bury. Bishop of London. *Davy, A.*

A demi-tiger rampant.

> NORGATE, Thomas, M.D., of Ashfield House, died 1818; widow died 1834. *Her.Suff.Ch., Wall tablet, Badwell Ash*

TIGER

On a tiger Argent a naked man astride Proper wreathed about the temples Argent and Gules.

> BRAMPTON, of Brampton, co. Norfolk. *Davy, A.*

A tiger reguardant Proper laying hold of an arrow shot through his back Gules.

> SIDAY, SYDAY, of Bures. *MS Fairfax. Davy, A., church*

Passant and Passant Reguardant

A tiger passant Argent.

> CHICHELY, CHICHELEY, of Clare. *Davy, A.*

A tiger passant reguardant Argent.

> DANIEL, of Acton. *Bokenham. Davy, A., church. Washbourne, 'Somers., Chesh., Suff.' Fairbairn, 'Daniell, Somers., Chesh. & Suff.'*

A tiger passant reguardant Or vulned in the shoulder Gules.

FLEETWOOD. *MS Martin's Crests*

A tiger passant Proper.

> JACOB, Sir John, Bart., of West Wratting, died 1740. *Her.Suff.Ch., Ledger stone, Withersfield*

A tiger passant Gules chained Or.

> TOTHILL. *MS Martin's Crests*

Statant

A tiger statant.

> TAYLOR, of Gorleston. *Davy, A.*

Sejant

A tiger sejant Ermine.

> JOHNSON, of Lavenham. *MS Fairfax (Tyl.)*

A tiger sejant.

> LAYTON, of Ipswich. *Davy, A., churchyard, St. Matthew's.* Andrew Layton, A.M., died 1772; William Layton, A.M., died 1831, Rectors of St. Matthew's. *Haslewood, 47–8, Stone altar tomb, church*

A tiger seiant.

> STILL. *Davy, A.*

Couchant

A tiger couchant

> PAWSEY, PASSEY, of Lidgate. *Davy, A.*

DEMI-WOLF

A demi-wolf holding in his paws a sprig of oak fructed with an acorn.

> BURLEY, of Eye. *Proc.S.I.A. II. 144, church monument*

A demi-wolf Ermine holding a halbert Argent tasselled Or.

> CHARLES, of Kettleburgh. *Davy, A.*

A demi-wolf Or the sinister paw resting on a pellet charged with a fleur-de-lis Or.

> WILSON, of Stowlangtoft. *Davy, A. Burke, L.G. 1853 and 1900 eds. Fairbairn, 'of Stowlangtoft Hall, Suff.'*

Rampant or Salient

A demi-wolf rampant Vert holding in his paws a sprig of three roses slipped Vert.

> EDEN, of Hanfield, co. Essex. *MS Heraldic Alphabet*

A demi-wolf rampant Argent holding between his paws a lozenge Or.

> FREEMAN. *MS Ordinary of Arms, fo. 262** Broken, but was probably a demi-wolf salient reguardant vulned in the breast Gules (for Lawton of Cheshire. E. Farrer).

> LAWTON, Rev. Joseph, Rector for 54 years, died 1863. *Her.Suff.Ch., Wall tablet, Elmswell*

A demi-wolf rampant.

> NORGATE. *Davy, A., Badwell Ash church.* Thomas Norgate, M.D., of Ashfield House, died 1818; widow died 1834; Others. *Her.Suff.Ch., Wall tablet, Badwell Ash*

A demi-wolf rampant Or.

> WILSON. *MS Ordinary of Arms, fo. 8*.* Richard Percy Wilson, of Bildeston House, died 1837. *Her.Suff.Ch., Tablet, Bildeston. Bookplate*, ?wolf Proper*

A demi-wolf sejant [*sic* rampant] Or langued Gules with the sinister paw resting on a pellet charged with a fleur-de-lis Or.

> WILSON, Henry. *Her.Suff.Ch., Glass, St.Mary's, Bury.* Joseph Wilson, of Stowlangtoft Hall, died 1851. *Hatchment and Glass, Stowlangtoft*

WOLF

A wolf.

> BLENNERHASSET, of Loudham, Barsham, etc.

Davy, A. (Barrett MS)
A wolf Proper between its paws St. Edmunds's head crowned Or.
  BURY ST. EDMUNDS. Borough of *Her.Suff.Ch., Glass, St.Mary's and St. James's, Bury*
A wolf collared and lined holding in the dexter paw a trefoil Proper.
  CLOUN, CLUN, of Tunstall. *Davy, A.*
'to his crest on a torce or/b/ a wolff pty p pale or/g/ open mouthed langed g/'
  GAWDY. 'Gawdy of gawdy hall in Norff.' *MS Alphabet of Crests, fo. 47b*
Leaning against a tree a wolf Or.
  WOLVERSTON. 'Wolverton'. *MS Heraldic Alphabet*

Rampant or Salient

A wolf rampant langued and collared Gules.
  GORE. Paul Alexander Gore, killed in action 1898, aged 20. *Her.Suff.Ch., Wall brass, Copdock*
A wolf salient Or.
  WILSON, of Tannington, Peasenhall, Yoxford. *Davy, A.*

Courant

A wolf courant Proper.
  BOHUN, Earl of Hereford and Essex. Constable of England. *Davy, A.*

Passant and Passant Reguardant

A wolf passant Argent in his mouth an arrow Sable embrued Gules.
  CARWARDINE. Vicar of Cavenham. *Davy, A.*
A wolf passant reguardant Proper.
  FLEETWOOD. *MS Ordinary of Arms, fo. 179**
A wolf passant reguardant Argent vulned in the breast Gules.
  FLEETWOOD, of Chediston. *Davy, A., church*
A wolf passant Argent maned and flecked on the chest Gules.
  FORTESCUE. *MS ex-Taylor Coll.**
A wolf passant per pale Argent and Gules.
  GAWDY, Thomas, of Gawdy Hall, co. Norfolk; Confirmation of Arms and Grant of Crest by Sir G. Dethick, Garter, 25 November 2 Eliz. [1559/60]. *Grants & Certificates (Harl. MS 1,359)*
A wolf passant per pale Argent and Gules, a crescent for difference.
  GAWDY, GAWDYE, of Mendham. *Visitation 1561 (ed. Metcalfe), 'crest I.'* 'Thomas Gadey' *MS Philpot's Visitations, Norf.**
A wolf passant Erminois armed Gules.
  HAYES, Sir Thomas, of London; Confirmation by W. Camden, Clarenceux, in 1613. *Grants & Certificates (Stowe MSS 700, 706 and 707; Harl. MS 6,059)*
A wolf passant Erminois.
  HAYES, of Ubbeston, Cratfield. *Davy, A.* Thomas Hayes, son of Thomas Hayes, gent., late of Cratfield, died 1726. *Her.Suff.Ch., Ledger stone, Cratfield. Untinctured, but 'Grant 1613: a wolf passant Erminois'*
A wolf [but called 'a mastyf' in MS] passant Argent.
  HOLLAND. 'Bryen Holand' *MS Philpot's Visitations, Norf.**
A wolf passant Sable charged on the breast with a mullet for difference.
  HOLLAND, Earl of Kent. Of Framlingham, Bury. *Davy, A.*

A wolf passant Gules.
  ODINGSELS, DODINGSELLS. *Davy, A., Badingham church*
A wolf passant Azure holding in the mouth the body of a woman Proper.
  STRANGE, LE STRANGE. *MS Ordinary of Arms, fo. 51**
Against a tree leaved Vert fructed Or, or Proper, a wolf passant Or.
  WOLVERSTON, WOLFERSTON, WOLVESTON, of Wolverston, Culpho. *Harl. 772* Davy, A. Washbourne, 'Wolverstone, Suff. and Staff. Tree Proper'*
A wolf passant tied to a tree [sic].
  WOLVERSTON, 'Wolferston' *MS Martin's Crests*
A wolf passant Or.
  WOLVERSTONE. *Fairbairn*, 'Suff. and Staffs.'*

Statant and Statant Reguardant

A wolf statant reguardant Sable, charged on the shoulder with a crescent [for difference].
  DANIELL. *Visitation 1561 (ed. Howard) I. 231**
A wolf statant reguardant.
  DANIEL, DANYELL. *MS Heraldic Collections, fo. 54**
A wolf statant Argent langued Gules.
  FORTESCUE. *Harl. MS 6163*
A wolf statant per pale Argent and Gules, charged on the breast with a crescent [for difference].
  GAWDY, GAWDYE, of Mendham, Norfolk. *Visitation 1561 (MS G.7*)*
A wolf statant Argent collared Sable.
  GAWDY. 'Thomas gawdy of gawdy halle'. *MS Knight's Visitations, Norf.**

Sejant

A wolf sejant Gules.
  BLENNERHASSET, BLENNERHASSETT, BLEYNERHAYSET, of Barsham, Norfolk. *Visitation 1561 (MSS G.7* and Iveagh Copy*) and (ed. Metcalfe).* 'William Blannerhassett of Norwyche' *MS Knight's Visitations, Norf.*.* 'Rafe Blanerhasset' *MS Philpot's Visitations, Norf.**
A wolf sejant Gules his tail flected over his back langued Azure.
  BLENERHASSETT. *Washbourne, 'Suff.' Fairbairn, 'Suff.'*
A wolf seiant Or.
  CUDDON. *Davy, A.*
A wolf seiant Proper.
  TODD, of Newton, Norton. *Davy, A.*

Sejant. Gorged

A wolf seiant collared and lined.
  FIENNES, of Wrentham, Ixworth, Hitcham. *Davy, A.*
A wolf seiant Argent gorged with a radiant collar and chain Or.
  FIENNES, Viscount Say and Sele. *Davy, A.* 'Hon. Richard Fiennes, son of William, Visct.Say & Steele [sic], died 1674' *Her.Suff.Ch., Ledger stone, Ixworth*
A wolf seiant Argent collared and lined Gules.
  MOUNTNEY, of Old Newton. 'Rychard Monteny' *MS Knight's Visitations, Norf.** 'Richard Mollntony' *MS Philpot's Visitations, Norf.*, . . . lined and ringed Gules. Davy, A.*
A wolf seiant Argent gutty Gules collared and lined Or.
  STANTON, STAUNTON, of Southwold, Wilby, Chediston. *MS Knight's Visitations, Suff.* Davy, A., Chediston church. Washbourne*,*

'Stanton, Staunton, Suff., Norf. & Warw.'
Fairbairn, 'Stanton, Norf., Warw. and Suff.'
A wolf sejant collared and lined.
STANTON, Captain Thomas, Commander of the
'Returne', died 1691. *Her.Suff.Ch., Ledger
stone, Holy Trinity, Bungay*

Sejant, holding:
A wolf sejant Proper holding a head couped Proper
crowned Or.
BURY ST. EDMUNDS, Benedictine Abbey. *Taylor,
78* (Blomef., Tanner). E.A.N. & Q. IV. 166*
A wolf sitting and holding between its forepaws the
crowned head of St. Edmund all Proper.
BURY ST. EDMUNDS, Borough Council.
Scott-Giles, 345, 'Granted 1609' [sic The Grant
was made by William Camden, Clarenceux, 29
November 1606]*

BEEHIVE
A mount Vert thereon a beehive Or charged with a
chaplet of roses, in chief alighting on the hive a bee
Proper and in base around the hive three bees
Proper.
BULLOUGH, Sir George, Bart. *Her.Suff.Ch., Wall
brass, Moulton. No date*
In front of an oak tree Proper a beehive Or.
NUNN, of Bury. *Davy, A.*

BEZANT see ROUNDEL OR

BIRD

UNKNOWN
A bird rising.
ALDHOUS, ALDOUS, ALDUS, of Moulton,
Akenham. Edward Aldus, of Akenham, died
1711; son Fenn Aldus, died 1762. *Partridge 55
(Darby, 1828), churchyard, Akenham. 'Aldis'
Bookplate*. Edward Aldus, 1711; son Fynn,
1762. Her.Suff.Ch., Altar tombs, churchyard,
Akenham*
A bird rising Gules.
ALDHOUS, ALDOUS, ALDUS, of Moulton,
Akenham. *Visitation 1664–8, '? falcon'.
Bokenham. Davy, A., Akenham church. Muskett.
I. 388*
A bird rising Argent beaked and legged Gules.
ALLEN, ALEYNE. *MS Knight's Visitations, Suff.,
fo. 107b*. 'Thomas Alyne' MS Philpot's
Visitations, Suff.* *
A bird.
ALLEYN, of Fornham. *MS Fairfax (Tyl.)*
A bird with wings addorsed Argent legged and
beaked Or.
ALLEN, ALLEYNE, of Icklingham, Fornham All
Saints. *Davy, A. (Barrett MS)*
A bird Proper between two branches Vert.
DANDYE, DAWNDYE, of Combs Hall. *MS
Fairfax ('Dawndye Pedigree at Combes Hall';
Leverland)*
A bird Argent beaked Gules.
DAUNDY, DANDY. *Davy, A.*
A bird with wings displayed.
FRAMLINGHAM. 'Johannes', died 1425; Sir
Charles Framlingham, died 1595. *Her.Suff.Ch.,
Formerly on a brass; Effigy monument,
Debenham*
A bird with wings extended.
GIRLING, Robert, died 1790; wife Mary, died
1771. *Suff. Green Books, Lt. Whelnetham*
A bird close Sable armed Argent.
GOLDSMITH, of Newton. *Davy, A.*

A bird wings expanded.
HURTON, William, died 1723. *Her.Suff.Ch.,
Ledger stone, Long Melford*
A bird.
IRELAND, Thomas James, of Ousden Hall, died
1863; widow died 1888. *Her.Suff.Ch., Wall
tablet, Ousden*
A bird with wings expanded Azure beaked and
legged Or.
LUDKIN, of Ipswich. *Visitation 1664–8. Davy, A.
Washbourne*, 'Suff.' Fairbairn, 'Suff.'*
A bird close Argent ducally gorged Or.
REYNOLDS. *Her.Suff.Ch., Glass, Ampton*
A bird.
SYMONDS, of Botesdale. *E.A.N. & Q. I. 106,
Tomb, churchyard, Redgrave. Robert Symonds,
of Botesdale, died 1760. Her.Suff.Ch., Altar tomb,
churchyard, Redgrave*
A bird wings expanded Proper.
THOMAS. Rebecca, wife of George Thomas, died
1770. *Hatchment, Kesgrave* [Seen and recorded
in 1952, since disappeared. In my photograph of
*c.*1955 the bird is Azure and seems to be gorged
Or, the spears on either side are very faded].
Photograph. Her.Suff.Ch., Hatchment, Kesgrave*
A bird wings expanded Azure beaked Gules legged
Or between two spearheads points upward tasselled
Or.
THOMAS, George, of Kesgrave and Brockley,
High Sheriff of Suffolk 1820, died 1853.
Photograph. Her.Suff.Ch., Hatchment, Kesgrave*
A bird Sable on the top of a wheatsheaf Or.
WHETCROFT, of Ipswich. *Bokenham*

UNKNOWN BIRD, holding:
A bird (? turtle dove) volant Azure holding in its
beak a laurel, or oak, branch Vert fructed Or.
ANDREWES, ANDREWS, of Bury. *Harl. 772*
MS Fairfax. Bokenham. Davy, A.*
A bird wings expanded Azure holding in the beak a
laurel branch Vert.
ANDREWS *Fairbairn*, 'Suff.'*
A bird holding a ring in its beak.
DAVERS, Bart. *Proc.S.I.A. IX. 74, Rougham
church cup. Sir Charles Davers, Bt., of Rushbrook
Hall, died 1806. Suff. Green Bks, Rushbrook*
A bird Sable wings displayed beaked Or holding in
the beak a spray of ?oak Vert.
FASTOLF, of Badingham, Pettaugh. *MS Humfry
Pedigree Roll*; Corder MS 91*
A bird wings extended holding in its beak a jewelled
ring.
FIENNES. Hon. Richard Fiennes, son of William
Fiennes, Viscount Say & Steele [sic Sele], died
1674. *Her.Suff.Ch., Ledger stone, Ixworth*
A bird holding in the beak a sprig. (A martlet . . .
sprig Vert).
OLIVER. Thomas Hacheson Oliver, died 1865.
*Her.Suff.Ch., churchyard, Gorleston. Not found
1980*
A bird close holding in the dexter claw a sprig.
PERIENT, PERYENT. *Visitation 1561 (ed.
Howard), I. 123* *
A bird with wings expanded holding in its beak an
olive branch all Proper.
WENYEVE. *Fairbairn*, 'of Brettenham, Suff.'*

AUK see also MURR
Upon a rock an auk Proper holding in the beak a
bezant.
CARTHEW. *Fairbairn*, 'Woodbridge Abbey,
Suffolk and London'*

BITTERN

A bittern Or standing among bulrushes Proper.
> BARNARDISTON, of Kedington, Brightwell. 'Sr
> Nathaniell Barnardeston Knight' *MS Lilly's
> Visitation of Suffolk*. First of two crests drawn.
> MS Heraldic Alphabet. Crisp's Visitation. VIII.
> 41; of The Ryes in Sudbury, Pedigree. Fairbairn,
> 'of The Ryes, Sudbury, Suffolk'. Her.Suff.Ch.,
> Monuments, Tablets and Hatchments, Kedington;
> Vault, Funeral helm and Hatchments, Brightwell*

A bittern Or in bulrushes legged and beaked Gules.
> BARNARDISTON. *Proc.S.I.A. VIII. 224, Clare
> church glass*

A bittern Proper beaked and legged Or holding in
the dexter claw a bunch of lilies Argent stalked and
leaved.
> LITTON. 'S. Roberd Lytton', of Knebworth, co.
> Herts. *Harl. MS 6163**

A bittern statant Proper among bulrushes Sable
leaved Vert.
> LITTON. 'Robert Lytton, of Feltham [*sic* Felsham]
> in Suffolk, married – Dade'. *Surrey Visitation
> 1662 (H.S.) 75**

A bittern within a heap of reeds.
> LITTON. *MS Martin's Crests*

A bittern among flags seeded all Proper.
> LYTTON, of Shrubland Hall. *Davy, A.*

A bittern wings elevated Argent collared Gules
holding in its beak a pansy Or.
> SCUTT, of Mickfield. *Visitation 1664–8.
> Bokenham, 'holding a flower'*

CORNISH CHOUGH

A Cornish chough rising Sable beaked and legged
Gules.
> ALLEN. 'John Allein de Suff.' *MS Ordinary of
> Arms, fo. 188**

A Cornish chough.
> ATWOOD, Rev. Thomas, B.A., Rector for 35
> years, died 1905. *Her.Suff.Ch., Brass tablet,
> Bromeswell*

A ?Cornish chough wings displayed Sable legged
Gules.
> CORNWALL. *MS Ordinary of Arms, fo. 38**

A Cornish chough Sable beaked and membered
Gules.
> CORNWALL, CORNWELL, of Haverhill. *MS
> Heraldic Alphabet. Bookplate**

A Cornish chough wings displayed Sable resting its
dexter foot on a leopard's head Or.
> CORRANCE, of Rougham. *Bokenham*

A Cornish chough Sable beaked and legged Gules.
> FORSTER, of co. Lincs. *MS Ordinary of Arms,
> fo. 243**

A chough, or falcon, with wings displayed Or.
> FRAMLINGHAM. *Davy, A.*

A Cornish chough volant Sable beak and legs
Gules.
> FRAMLINGHAM, of Crow's Hall in Debenham.
> *Copinger. VII. E.A. Misc. 1922. 43*

A Cornish chough proper.
> JONES, Perpetual Curate of Nayland, died 1799.
> *Davy, A.* Rev. William Jones, A.M., Perpetual
> Curate of Nayland, died 1800; wife died 1799.
> *Her.Suff.Ch., Wall tablet, Nayland*

A Cornish chough close.
> LANGLEY, of Ipswich. *Sharpe*

A Cornish chough Proper gutty Or.
> MOORE. *Washbourne*, 'Suff.'*

In front of a dexter arm embowed in armour Proper
garnished Or the hand in a gauntlet Proper grasping
a battle axe handle Sable headed Argent around the
arm a scarf Argent, a Cornish chough Proper.
> QUILTER, Sir William, Bt., died 1911; son Roger
> Quilter, composer, died 1953. *Her.Suff.Ch.,
> Altar tomb, churchyard, Bawdsey. Photograph*,
> untinctured*

A chough with wings erect between two rice plants
all Proper
> READE, of Holbrook House. *E.A.N. & Q. VIII.
> 118, Monument and Hatchment, Holbrook church*

Five lozenges conjoined fessewise Or thereon a
Cornish chough Proper
> TAUNTON, George E., of Coldham Hall near Bury,
> died 1894. *Crisp's Visitation. IV. 167*, Pedigree*

A Cornish chough rising Proper between two spears
erect Or.
> THOMAS, of Kesgrave, Brockley, Woodbridge.
> *Gage (Thingoe). Davy, A., Kesgrave church*

A Cornish chough wings expanded Proper between
two spears erect Or headed Argent.
> THOMAS. *Her.Suff.Ch., Hatchment recorded by
> Rev. Edmund Farrer in 1900, Kesgrave. [Gone
> before c.1955.]*

A Cornish chough volant Proper.
> TOMS, of Hadleigh, Framlingham. *Davy, A.*

DEMI-COCK

A demi-cock couped Sable wings displayed beaked
and wattled Argent holding in the beak a sprig of
trefoils.
> COCK. 'John Cooke' *MS Philpot's Visitations,
> Essex**

A demi-?cock with wings expanded.
> DOVER, of Ipswich. *Davy, A.*

A demi-cock couped Gules combed Azure wattled
Or.
> PARKER. 'Nycholas parker' *MS Philpot's
> Visitations, Norf.**

A demi-cock with wings endorsed Gules combed
and wattled Argent.
> PARKER, of Walsham le Willows. *Davy, A.
> (Edms.)*

COCK [Alphabetically by name]

A cock Gules.
> ALCOCK, of Badley, Shottisham. *Davy, A.*

A cock Argent wings elevated and addorsed combed
legged and langued Gules.
> BARRET, Francis Henry, Rector, and wife. He, or
> she, died 1730. *Her.Suff.Ch., Wall monument,
> Boxted*

A cock crowing Or combed wattled and armed
Gules.
> BOLLES. *Washbourne*, 'Suff.' Fairbairn*,
> 'Bolles, Bolls, Suff. . . . and legged Gules'*

A cock holding in the beak a sprig of green.
> COCK, of Ipswich. *E.A.N. & Q. IX. 361,
> Monument, St. Matthew's church.* Richard Cock,
> Portman of Ipswich, died 1629. *Her.Suff.Ch.,
> Effigy monument, St. Matthew's, Ipswich*

A cock Proper.
> COCKBURN. Admiral James Cockburn,
> Commander in Chief of Naval Forces in India,
> died 1872. *Her.Suff.Ch., Glass, Bildeston*

A cock.
> COCKSEDGE, of Bury, Elmswell. Henry
> Cocksedge, Recorder of Thetford, died 1762.
> *Thetford (T.M.) 85, Monument, St. Cuthbert's
> church. Partridge 28, 213 (Darby, 1827),
> Stowlangtoft and Drinkstone churchyards.
> Davy, A., Stowlangtoft and Drinkstone
> churchyards. Misc.Gen. et Her. 4th S. II. 117,*

Pedigree. E.A. Misc. 1918. 10, 19. Thomas
Cocksedge, died 1727; son Thomas, died 1739.
*Her.Suff.Ch., Altar tomb, churchyard,
Stowlangtoft.* Thomas Cocksedge; son Simon, of
Elswell [*sic* Elmswell], Suff., died 1751. *Tablets
on outside wall of church, Drinkstone*
A cock ? Sable.
    COCKSEDGE, of Woolpit, Elmswell, Drinkstone.
*Davy, A., Drinkstone and Fornham All Saints
churches*
'Upon his Healme on a Torse Silver and Geules, a
Cock Rowsand, or otherwise a Cock in his pride,
with his wings spread silver, beaked Geules'.
    CORDELL, of Long Melford. William Cordell, of
Long Melford; Grant of Arms and Crest by
Thomas Hawley, Clarenceux; Ratified by Robert
Cooke, Clarenceux, 3 Edward VI [1549/50].
Visitation 1561 (ed. Howard), I. 246
A cock Proper charged with a crescent Gules.
    CORRY. Hon. Henry W. Lowry-Corry, of
Edwardstone Hall, Boxford, Suffolk.
Fairbairn, First crest for Corry, second crest for
Lowry [q.v.]*
A cock Proper.
    CORRY, LOWRY-CORRY. Earl of Belmore, died
1845; widow died 1904. *Her.Suff.Ch., Brass
tablet, Edwardstone.* Henry William Lowry
Corry, of Edwardstone Hall, died 1927. *Glass,
Edwardstone*
A cock Gules.
    COX, COXE. *MS Ordinary of Arms, fo. 157**
A cock Gules ducally crowned Or.
    COX. Rector of Risby. *Davy, A.*
A cock Gules combed and wattled Sable.
    ERRINGTON, of Westerfield, Sibton. *MS Heraldic
Collections, fo. 29*. Davy, A.*
A cock Argent.
    GOLDSMYTH. *Bokenham*
A cock Azure combed and wattled Or.
    GUYON, of Cornard. *Davy, A.*
A cock Argent combed legged and wattled Gules.
    LANGLEY, of Eye. *Visitation 1664–8. Bokenham.
Davy, A. Washbourne*, 'of Lanc., Suff. and York.'
Fairbairn*, 'York, Lancs. and Suff.'*
A cock.
    LEEDS, LEEDES, Samuel, M.A., Rector for 30 years,
died 1750. *Gage (Thingoe). Suff. Green Bks,
Lt. Saxham, 95, 143. Her.Suff.Ch., Ledger stone,
Lt. Saxham*
A cock, over it on a label 'Amima'
    LYALL. Rector of Hadleigh. *Davy, A.* [Label,
?Anima. Motto of Lyall, An I may]
A cock.
    MACKWORTH, Bart. Of Cavendish. *Davy, A.*
A cock Gules beaked legged combed and wattled
Or.
    MACKWORTH, MACKWORTH PRAED. B.J.
Mackworth Praed, of Ousden Hall, died 1876;
Algernon Mackworth Praed, died 1952.
Her.Suff.Ch., Glass and Tablet, Ousden
A cock.
    MATHEW, of Ixworth. *Davy, A.*
A cock with wings endorsed.
    THEOBALD. *Davy, A. Washbourne, 'Suff.'*
A cock with wings endorsed Gules.
    THEOBALD. *Fairbairn, 'of Barking Hall, Suff.'*
Francis Theobald, late of the Middle Temple,
London, died 1750. *Her.Suff.Ch., Floor slab,
Kersey*
A cock rising Sable beaked combed and wattled
Gules.

THWAYTES, of Essex. *MS Heraldic Alphabet*

COCK, upon:
A cock Gules standing on a trumpet Proper.
    ACHESON. Earl of Gosford, Viscount Acheson of
Worlingham. *Davy, A.*
A cock Gules standing on a trumpet Or.
    ACHESON, Earl of Gosford, Baron Worlingham,
of Beccles, co. Suffolk. *Burke's Peerage, 1891
ed.**
A garb lying along thereon a cock Or.
    ALEXANDER. *MS Martin's Crests*
A cockerel Gules wattled and standing on a garb
fessewise Or.
    COVENTRY. Hon. Henry Thomas Coventry, died
1934. *Her.Suff.Ch., Wall tablet, Stoke-by-Nayland*
On an arrow head towards the dexter fesseways Or a
cock Or membered Gules.
    'LITTELL, Geoffry, of Stoke next Nayland, in
Suffolk'. *Grants & Certificates (Harl. MS
1,105)*
A cock Or combed and wattled Gules standing on
an arrow.
    LITTELL, LITTLE, of Stutton, Alpheton,
Ballingdon Hall in Sudbury. *Davy, A., (Seal).*
John Little, Esq., son of Geoffrey Little, Esq., of
Halstead. Of Ballingdon Hall, High Sheriff of
Essex 1694, died 1720. *Badham 37, All Saints
church, Sudbury*

CRANE see also HERON, STORK
A crane Proper beaked Or.
    CRANE, of Chilton, Stonham, Stowmarket,
Higham. *Visitation 1561 (MSS G.7* and Iveagh
Copy*) and (eds. Howard* and Metcalfe). Harl.
772** 'Sr Robart Crane of Chilton Knight
Barronett' *MS Lilly's Visitation of Suffolk*.
Visitation 1664–8. MS Fairfax. Bokenham. MS
Heraldic Collections, fo. 54*. MS ex-Taylor
Coll.* Davy, A. Washbourne*, 'Suff.' Fairbairn*,
'Suff.'* Probably for William Crane, of Beccles,
c.1650. *Her.Suff.Ch., Hatchment, Beccles*
A crane close Argent.
    CRANEWELL. *Davy, A. (Edms.)*
A ?crane wings elevated Sable beaked and legged
Gules.
    ELRINGTON. 'Edrington' *MS ex-Taylor Coll.**
A stork, or crane, Argent legged Azure.
    THURSTON, THRUSTON, of Hoxne, Ipswich.
Visitation 1664–8. Bokenham. Davy, A.,
Holbrook church. Washbourne*, 'Thurston, Suff.'*

CRANE, holding:
'On a torse argent and azure a crane azure, beak and
legs or, in the mouth an ear of barley or'
    BROWNE. 'A Patent confirmed unto Thomas
Browne of St. Edmondsbury in com' Suffolke
esquyre by Willm Harvey als Clarencyeulx in A⁰
1561'. After the pedigree the date 'The 24 of
June'. *London Visitation 1568 (H.S. 1963), 46,
notes 4 & 5*
A crane holding in its beak an ear of bearded wheat
all Or.
    BROWNE, of Bury. *Davy, A.*
A crane holding in its beak a rose stalked and leaved
Proper.
    GAMBLE, of Bungay. *Davy, A.*
A crane holding in one claw a stone.
    HALL, of Onehouse. *E.A. Misc. 1926, 88,
churchyard*
A crane, or heron, holding in its beak an eel, or
snake.

RAY, of Bury, Tostock. *Davy, A., St. James's church, Bury*
A crane rising Azure beaked and legged Gules gorged with an annulet Argent in the beak a cinquefoil slipped Vert.
> SCUTT, 'John Skutt, of Taunton, co. Somerset'; Grant by Sir C. Barker, Garter. *Grants & Certificates (Stowe MS 692)*

A crane Argent collared Gules holding in the beak a pansy, or rose, Or.
> SCUTT, of Mickfield. *Davy, A.*

A crane Proper holding in its dexter claw a pellet.
> SHORE. Later Lord Teignmouth. Lands in Withersdale. *Davy, A.*

CROW
On a tun a crow Proper holding in its beak a rose branch Proper.
> BRAMPTON, BRAMSTON. *Davy, A.*

A crow Sable.
> 'CROMER of Yarmouth' *Wall's Book*
> 'to his Crest a Croo sa/'
> 'CROMER of Yermouth' *MS Alphabet of Crests, fo. 20*

A crow rising Sable between two javelins erected Argent tasselled Or hilted Proper.
> THOMAS, of Kesgrave. *Sharpe*

CURLEW
A curlew Proper
> EWEN, of Raydon Hall, Sibton, Peasenhall, Southwold, etc. *Crisp's Visitation. I. 127–8, Pedigree.* 'John Norris Ewen, of Reydon Hall, Wangford, Suff.' *Fairbairn*

A curlew statant Proper.
> EWEN. Thomas Glover Ewen, of Ellough and Norwich, died 1813. *Ewen, 228–9 (Seal), Pedigree**

DEMI-DOVE
A demi 'palumb' [dove, or wood pigeon] volant Argent fretty and membered Gules in its beak a branch Vert fructed Gules.
> BRADBURY. 'Bradbery of –' *Wall's Book*
> 'to his crest a demy palombe ar/ volant ffreted membred g/ in his beke a braunche of – Vert the beryes g/'
> BRADBURY. 'Bradbery' *MS Alphabet of Crests, fo. 12b*

A demi-dove volant Argent fretty Gules holding in its beak a slip of barberry bush Vert fructed Gules.
> BRADBURY, of Mildenhall. *Davy, A.*

A demi-dove.
> CLARKE. *Davy, A.*

A demi-?dove wings displayed Proper, or grey, holding in the beak a cinquefoil, or rose, stalked and leaved.
> THWAYTES. *MS ex-Taylor Coll.**

DOVE
A dove rising Argent membered Gules.
> ALLEN, of Fornham All Saints. *Visitation 1577*

A turtle-dove Proper.
> BALL, BALLS, of Newmarket. 'Ball of Cambridge' *MS Knight's Visitations, Cambs.*, 'turtill pro'. Davy, A.*

A dove rising Proper beaked and legged Or.
> BREWSE. 'Thomas Brewse of Wenham in Com Suffolk esquier' *MS Lilly's Visitation of Suffolk*. A second crest drawn*

A dove close Argent beaked and legged Gules standing between branches Vert.
> DANDY, of Ipswich, Cretingham. *MS Humfry*

Pedigree Roll*; Corder MS 91
In front of an olive branch Proper a dove Argent beaked and membered Gules.
> DANDY, DAUNDY. *Proc.S.I.A. XXVII. 152 (Dandy Pedigree)*

A dove Proper.
> DOWSON, of South Town. *Davy, A. Washbourne*, 'Suff.' Fairbairn*, 'Suff.'*

A dove rising.
> FRAMLINGHAM, of Debenham. *Davy, A.*

A dove.
> LENG, John. Bishop of Norwich, 1723–7. *Bedford, 82* (Grant 1723. Blomef.) Bedford, 2nd.ed., 95*

A dove.
> SYMONDS. *Davy, A.*

DOVE, upon:
A garb Or on the sinister side a dove close Argent picking the wheat.
> DANDY, DAUNDY, of Combs, St. Lawrence Ipswich, Sapiston. *Davy, A.*

On a garb Or a dove close Argent.
> DANDY. *Washbourne*, 'Suff.'*

A garb Or on the sinister side a dove Argent beaked and legged Gules.
> DANDY. *Fairbairn, 'of Sapiston, Suff., . . . dove close Argent' Proc.S.I.A. XXVII. 149 (Dandy Pedigree)*

On a tower Argent a dove rising Proper.
> DOVE, of East Bergholt, Ipswich, Gosbeck, Scole, Stradbroke, Dallinghoo. *Visitation 1664–8. Davy, A.*

'A dove rising from ye top of a Castle triple towered'
> DOVE, of East Bergholt. *Bokenham*

On a tower Argent a dove with wings expanded Proper.
> DOVE, of Gosbeck. *Washbourne*, 'Suff.' E.A.N. & Q. V. 313.* John Dove, died 1753; Others. *Her.Suff.Ch., Ledger stone, Gosbeck.*

DOVE, holding: [Alphabetically by name]
A dove holding in the beak an ear of wheat.
> ALSOP, Rev. Thomas, B.D., Incumbent for 37 years, died 1845. *Her.Suff.Ch., Wall tablet, Fressingfield*

A dove rising Azure holding in the beak an olive branch Vert fructed Or.
> ANDREWS, of Bury St. Edmunds. *Visitation 1561 (MSS G.7* and Iveagh Copy*)*

A dove Azure holding in the beak a branch Vert fructed Or.
> ANDREWES, of Bury St. Edmunds. *Visitation 1561 (ed. Metcalfe)*

'to his crest on a wreath ar/b/ a turtell volant in her proper couller holding in her beke a branch of olyfe vert fruite or/ to thoms Andrewes of Bury St. Edmond/'
> 'ANDROWES'. *MS Alphabet of Crests, fo. 1b*

A turtle dove Proper holding in its beak an olive branch Vert fructed Or.
> ANDREWS, of Bury. 'Thomas Andrew' *MS Philpot's Visitations, Suff.* Davy, A. Muskett. III. 24*

A bird (turtle dove) volant Azure holding in the beak a laurel, or oak, branch Vert fructed Or.
> ANDREWES, ANDREWS, of Bury. *Harl. 772*. MS Fairfax. Bokenham. Davy, A. Muskett. III. 24 (Harl. MS 1103), 'a dove'*

A turtle dove Proper beaked legged and collared Gules in the beak an olive branch Vert.

BALL, Thomas, of Newcastle-upon-Tyne. Arms confirmed by Sir William Segar, Garter, 17 January 1602, on proof of a patent from Robert Cooke, Clarencieux, 8 July 1575, for Edward Ball of Cambridge, gent., being the ancient coat and crest of that family, from whom Thomas Ball is descended. This crest confirmed to Tho. Ball, 24 October 1633. *Grants & Certificates (Stowe MS 677), Pedigree*
A dove volant with an olive branch in its beak Proper.

BEVILLE, of Suffolk. *Davy, A. Washbourne, 'of Suff.' Fairbairn*, 'Bevil, Bevile, Suff.'*
On a tun Or a dove Proper holding in its beak a branch Vert fructed Gules.

BRAMPTON, BRAMSTON. *Davy, A.* Thomas Brampton, gent., died 1712. *Her. Suff. Ch., Ledger stone, Eye*
A bird (?dove) Gules wings expanded Or holding in its beak a ?columbine flower Or slipped and leaved Vert.

CLARKE. 'Sr John Clerke' *MS Ordinary of Arms, fo. 154**
A bird (?dove) Gules wings expanded Or holding in its beak an ear of wheat Or.

CLARKE. *MS Heraldic Collections, fo. 57* [drawn more like a teasel]*
A dove wings expanded Argent, or Or, in the beak an ear of wheat Proper.

CLARK, Robert, died 1832; Henry Clark, died 1874; Others. *Her.Suff.Ch., Wall tablet and Glass, Stuston*
A dove rising with a branch in its mouth.

FRAMINGHAM, of Crows Hall in Debenham. *Bokenham*
A dove Argent beaked and membered Gules holding in its beak by the stalk a flower gentle [*sic*] stalked Vert.

GONVILL, GONWELL, of Hemingstone, Gorleston. *Davy, A. Washbourne, 'Gonvill, Norf.' Fairbairn*
A dove Argent beak and legs Gules supporting with the dexter claw a pastoral staff Argent head and knobs Or.

GUNNING. The Right Reverend Peter Gunning, Bishop of Chichester; Grant by Sir E. Walker, Garter, 9 May 1670. *Grants & Certificates (Add MSS 14,293 and 14,294; Harl. MS 1,172)*
A dove holding in its dexter claw a branch of olive Proper.

HIGGS. Rector of Grundisburgh, died 1818. *Davy, A., church monument*
A dove Argent holding in the beak a sprig of laurel Vert.

IRELAND, of Ousden. *Davy, A.*
A dove holding in the beak an olive branch all Proper.

IRELAND, of Ousden Hall near Newmarket. *Fairbairn*, 'of Owsden [sic] Hall, Suff.' Burke, L.G. 1853 ed.* Thomas James Ireland, of Ousden Hall, died 1863. *Her.Suff.Ch., Hatchment, Ousden. The dove close*
A dove close Proper in the beak an olive branch, on the breast a torteau.

JACKSON, of Shelland. *Davy, A.*
A bundle of sugar canes Proper thereon a dove Argent winged Or holding in the beak an olive branch Proper.

KERRISON. Roger Allday Kerrison. *Bookplate*. Fairbairn, 'of Birkfield Lodge, Ipswich, Suffolk'*
A dove rising Proper holding in its beak an olive branch.

LENG, John. Bishop of Norwich, 1723–7. *Heylyn. Davy, A.*
A dove Pean holding in the beak an olive branch Proper.

MOOR. *MS Martin's Crests*
A dove with an olive branch in its beak all Proper, on a label above the words 'Tending to Peace'

MUSSENDEN, MUSSENDEN-LEATHES, of Herringfleet. *Davy, A.* Henry Mussenden-Leathes, Lord of the manor of Haverhill, died 1864; 2nd. Lt. Robert Mussenden Leathes, killed in action 1917; his sister Dulcibel, died 1920, both aged 18. *Her.Suff.Ch., Monument and Wall tablet, Herringfleet*
A dove Azure winged Or and Gules holding in the beak a branch Vert.

REVETT. *Fairbairn*, 'Suff.'*
A dove rising Argent beaked and legged Gules in the beak an olive branch Vert fructed Or.

TAVERNER, Francis, of Hexton, co. Herts., Ancestor of North Elmham, co. Norfolk. Patent February 1514. *Grants & Certificates (Harl. MS 6,059; Stowe MSS 706 and 707)*
A dove with wings expanded Argent beaked and legged Gules holding in the beak a laurel branch Vert.

TAVERNER, of Hawkedon, Dunwich. *Davy, A.*
A dove with a holly branch in its beak Proper.

WARREN, of Long Melford. *Bokenham*
A bird (?dove) with wings expanded holding in its beak an ?olive Branch.

WENYEVE, of Brettenham. *Davy, A., church*

DUCK

A drake Proper beaked and legged Gules in its beak an escallop Argent.

RAWLINSON, Sir Walter. Of Stowlangtoft. *Davy, A.*
A sheldrake Proper in the beak an escallop Argent.

RAWLINSON. Dorothea, wife of Thomas Rawlinson, died 1743; he died 1769. *Her.Suff.Ch., Ledger stone, Haughley.* Sir Walter Rawlinson, Lord of the manor, died 1805; Mary, widow of Sir William Rawlinson, died 1895. *Wall tablet, Stowlangtoft. Untinctured*
A shoveller Sable beaked Or.

READ, of Stoke by Ipswich. *Visitation 1664–8*
A sheldrake Sable.

READ, of Stoke by Ipswich. *Bokenham*
A shoveller Argent armed Gules.

READ, of Stutton, Holbrook. *Davy, A., Stutton church*
A shoveller close Sable.

READ, READE, of Bardwell. *Davy, A.* Thomas Read, died 1678; Sir Charles Crofts Read, Kt., died 1690; Charles Crofts Reade, died 1720. *Her.Suff.Ch., Altar tomb, Tablet and Hatchment, Bardwell. 'beaked and legged Gules'*
A duck Sable.

READ. *Proc.S.I.A. IX. 280, 286, Flagon in Bardwell church and Cup in Thorpe-by-Ixworth church*

DEMI-EAGLE [Alphabetically by name]

A demi spread eagle Or.

ASHMORE. *E.A.N. & Q. IX. 338, Monument, St. Mary Stoke church, Ipswich*
A demi-eagle with wings expanded Or.

BEDINGFIELD, of Bedingfield, Redlingfield. *Visitation 1664–8. Davy, A.*
A demi-eagle wings displayed Gules.

BEDINGFELD, BEDINGFIELD, of Redlingfield.
MS Heraldic Alphabet. Sharpe. Fairbairn,
'Bedingfield House, Eye, Suffolk'.* Sir Thomas
Bedingfield, Judge of the Common Pleas, died
1660. *Her.Suff.Ch., Wall monument, Darsham.*
John Bedingfield, son of Francis Bedingfield of
Redlingfield, died 1720. *Ledger stone, Sibton.*
Dorothy, married Francis Bedingfield of
Redlingfield, she died 1728. *Ledger stone,
Fressingfield.* Henry Bedingfield, Esq., died 1738.
Ledger stone, churchyard, Denham. William
Bedingfield, of Swattishaugh Hall, died 1754;
Nicholas Bedingfield, no date given. *Ledger
stones, Gislingham.* Robert Bedingfield, of co.
Norfolk, died 1714; John James Bedingfield, died
1853. *Ledger stone, Glass and Hatchment,
Bedingfield*
A demi-eagle displayed.
CLARKE. *MS Martin's Crests*
A demi-eagle displayed.
FISHER, William, late of Burgh Castle and
Yarmouth, died 1835. *Her.Suff.Ch., Tablet,
Burgh Castle*
An eagle displayed couped below the wings Argent.
HARBOTTLE, of Crowfield. *Davy, A.*
A demi-eagle displayed Argent.
KEBLE, of Roydon Hall, Stowmarket, Newton.
*Davy, A. E.A.N & Q. II. 167, Monument,
Tuddenham church. Washbourne*, 'Suff.'
Her.Suff.Ch., Tuddenham*
A demi-eagle displayed Azure.
MOXON. *Davy, A.*
A demi-eagle displayed.
NEWMAN, of Kessingland, Sudbury. *Davy, A.*
A demi-eagle displayed Argent.
OLDFIELD, of Brome. *Bokenham*
A demi ?eagle with wings erect, erased.
PAYNELL, of Otley. *Davy, A.*
An eagle couped at the thigh wings displayed Or.
ROUS, ROWSSE. *MS Heraldic Collections,
fo. 59**
A demi-eagle displayed Argent.
SPARKE, James, Churchwarden, 1844.
Her.Suff.Ch., Glass, St. Mary's, Bury
A demi-eagle displayed Or.
STEPHENS. *MS Martin's Crests*
A demi-eagle displayed Or wings Sable.
'STEPHENS, Mr Richard, at the Saracen's Head by
the Mercer's Chapel (1634)' *Grants &
Certificates (Harl. MS 5,869)*
A demi-falcon, or eagle, displayed Or beaked and
winged Sable.
STEPHENS, of Sudbury. *Davy, A.*
A demi-eagle displayed Sable.
UFFORD, Earl of Suffolk. Of Ufford. *Davy, A.*
A demi-eagle displayed Argent winged Or.
WINGFIELD. *Bokenham*

Crowned
'On a wreath of the colours, a Demy Eagle
displayed Erminois, beaked gules and crowned with
a Ducal Coronet Vert'
PAKE. Dr. Samuel Pake, M.D., of Bury St.
Edmunds; Grant of Arms and Crest by John
Anstis, Garter, 21st. November 1723. *Misc.Gen
et Her. 5th S. III. 1–2**
A demi-eagle displayed crowned.
PAKE, PEAKE, of Bury. *Davy, A., St. James's
Bury and Rushbrook churches.* Penelope, wife of
Samuel Pake, M.D., of Bury, died 1724.
Her.Suff.Ch., Ledger stone, Rushbrook

A demi-eagle displayed Argent crowned Or charged
with an ogress.
WEBB, Henry, of Harrow on the Hill, co. Middx.,
1587. *Grants & Certificates (Harl. MS 1,359)*

Gorged
A demi-eagle gorged with a collar.
BARLOW, George, M.A., Rector for 30 years, died
1850. *Her.Suff.Ch., Wall tablet, Burgh*
A demi-eagle displayed Sable beaked and ducally
gorged Or, charged on the breast with a cross
crosslet Argent.
BOUVERIE. 'Desbouverie' *MS Heraldic
Alphabet*
A demi-eagle wings elevated Vert ducally gorged
Or.
QUARLES. *MS Heraldic Alphabet*
A demi-eagle Vert beaked and collared Or.
QUARLES. *E.A.N. & Q. III. 159*
A demi-eagle with wings expanded Or pellety
ducally gorged Gules.
WEBB, of Cavenham. *Davy, A., church, (Edms.)
'Granted 1587'*
A demi-eagle displayed Or gorged with a coronet
Ermine.
WINN, George Esq., late servant and draper to Q.
Eliz.; Exemplification. *Grants & Certificates
(Add. MS 12,225). Fairbairn, 'Winn, of
Aldeburgh, Suff.'*
A demi-eagle displayed Or collared Ermine.
WINNE, WYNNE. *MS Heraldic Collections,
fo. 61**

Charged
A demi-eagle displayed Or gutty de sang.
HOUGHTON, of Buxhall, Friston, Snape. *Davy, A.*
A demi-eagle displayed Argent charged on the
breast with a bar nebuly.
KEBLE, of Stowmarket, Newton. *Visitation
1664–8. Davy, A.*
A demi-eagle displayed Argent charged on the
breast with a bar nebuly Gules.
KEBLE, of Stowmarket. *Muskett. II. 269 (Harl.
MS 1085), 'some say a bar gemel'*
A demi-eagle displayed Or charged on the breast
with a bar nebuly Sable.
KEBLE. *Bokenham. Davy, A. Misc.Gen. et Her.
N.S. III.205.* 'Richard Keble, Roydon Hall 1653'
Her.Suff.Ch., Wall tablet, Tuddenham
A demi-eagle displayed Or charged on the breast
with a fesse wavy Sable.
MORGAN, Hugh, of London, apothecary to Queen
Elizabeth; Grant by Sir W. Dethick, Garter,
2 March 30 Eliz. [1587/8]; Confirmed to Robert
Morgan, of Lt. Hallingbury, co. Essex in 1673.
Grants & Certificates (Stowe MS 676)
A demi-eagle displayed Or charged on the body
with a fesse wavy Sable.
MORGAN, of East Bergholdt. *Davy, A.*

DEMI-EAGLE, holding: [Including previous sub-sections]
A demi-eagle displayed Argent holding in its beak
an arrow paleways Gules headed and feathered
Argent.
LACEY, of Spelman's Hall. *Bokenham*
A demi-eagle Ermine wings addorsed and erect
Azure bezanty charged on the breast with a martlet
Gules and holding in its beak an escallop Gules.
LYNN, of Woodbridge. *Davy, A.*
A demi-eagle Ermine wings addorsed and erect
Azure bezanty charged on the breast with a martlet

Gules and holding in the beak an annulet Gules.

LYNN. *Fairbairn, 'of Woodbridge, Suff.'*

In front of a demi-eagle wings displayed Sable holding in the beak a mascle Argent three like mascles fesseways and interlaced also Argent.

POWNEY, of Milden Hall, Lavenham. *Burke, L.G. 1900 ed.**

A demi-eagle displayed Or on the breast three gutties de sang and in the beak an oak leaf Vert.

STANNOW, of Bedingfield, Beccles. *Davy, A. (Barrett MS)*

A demi-eagle displayed Ermine on the breast three gutties de sang and in the beak a holly leaf Vert.

STANNOW, of Bedingfield, Beccles. *Davy, A.*

A demi-eagle displayed holding in its beak a snake all Proper.

STEEL, of Southwold. *Davy, A., church*

With two heads

A crowned double headed demi-eagle displayed Or.

ASHMORE, William, Esq., died 1815; widow died 1837. *Her.Suff.Ch., Monument, St. Mary Stoke, Ipswich*

A demi-eagle with two heads displayed Sable ducally gorged Or on the breast a cross crosslet Argent.

BOUVERIE, of Parham, Hasketon, Rougham. *Davy, A.*

A demi-eagle with two heads displayed.

SPARKE, of Rougham, Walsham. *Davy, A., Rougham church*

A demi-eagle with two heads per pale Ermine and Gules crowned Or.

STONE, Thomas, died 1752; widow died 1755. *Her.Suff.Ch., Ledger stone, Beccles*

EAGLE

[Alphabetically by name]

An eagle displayed.

ALDERMAN, of Belstead, Peasenhall. *Partridge 41 (Darby, 1825), churchyard, Peasenhall; 192 (Darby, 1828), churchyard, Belstead. E.A. Misc. 1932. 66*

An eagle displayed.

ASHBY, of Lowestoft. *Lees, 106, Monument and Slab, St. Margaret's church.* Sir John Ashby, Kt., died 1693. *Her.Suff.Ch., Monument, Lowestoft.* [Crest gone, but given as above in *Gillingwater, 303*]

An eagle wings expanded Argent beaked and legged Gules.

ATKINSON, of Seckford Hall. *Davy, A.*

An eagle looking at the sun.

BALDOCK, of Brandeston. Rector of Redgrave and Hinderclay, died 1709. *Davy, A.*

An eagle displayed Sable.

BARNE, of Sotterley, Dunwich. *Davy, A. Washbourne*, 'Suff.' Burke, L.G. 1853 ed.*

An eagle wings elevated and displayed Sable.

BARNE, Miles, of Sotterley, M.P. for Dunwich, died 1780. *Her.Suff.Ch., Tablet, Sotterley*

An eagle displayed Or armed Gules.

BEDINGFIELD. 'Bedyngfeld of Suffoulk'. *Wall's Book*

'to his crest an egle or/ dysplayd armed g/'

BEDINGFIELD. 'Bedyngfeld of Suff.' *MS Alphabet of Crests, fo. 7b*

An eagle displayed Or.

BEDINGFIELD. 'S. Edmonde Bedyngfelde, Norff.' *Harl. MS 6163. Davy, A. Bookplate**

An eagle displayed Gules armed Or.

BEDINGFELD, BEDINGFIELD, of Coulsey Wood,

Redlingfield Hall, Swattishall Hall. *Bokenham*

An eagle displayed Or armed Gules.

BIGSBY, of Stowmarket, Carlton, Chilton, Combs, Finborough. *Davy, A. Burke, L.G. 1853 ed. Burke, Ill.Her.Illust.* Fairbairn*, 'of Stowmarket, Suff. and co. Notts.'*

An eagle rising.

BONELL, of Copdock. *Davy, A., church*

An eagle displayed Vert.

BROWNE. *MS Heraldic Alphabet. Davy, A.*

An eagle wings endorsed.

BROWNE, John, Gent., died 1716. *Her.Suff.Ch., Ledger stone, Rickinghall Superior*

An eagle displayed ?Or.

BROWNE, Rev. William, 'many years rector', died 1755. *Her.Suff.Ch., Monumental tablet, Hawkedon. Dexter wing missing*

An eagle with wings endorsed Argent standing on a laurel branch Vert fructed Or.

BUNGAY. *Davy, A.*

Out of a bush of feathers Argent an eagle flying –.

BUTLER. 'Therle of Ormond' *Wall's Book*

'to his crest an Egle fflying owt of a bushe of ffethers Ar/ Erl'

BUTLER. 'Ormond' *MS Alphabet of Crests, fo. 94*

An eagle rising reguardant Proper.

CANDLER. *Washbourne, 'Suff.' Fairbairn*, 'Candler, Suff.'*

An eagle displayed.

COOKE, of Rougham. *Davy, A., Rougham and Oakley churches*

An eagle displayed Proper.

COYTE, of Ipswich. *Sharpe*

An eagle displayed.

COYTE, of Ipswich. *Davy, A.*

An eagle rising.

CURZON. Viscount, later Earl Howe. Of Acton, Charsfield. *Davy, A.*

An eagle with wings expanded looking at the sun Proper.

DAW, of Wrentham, Woodbridge. *Davy, A.*

An eagle displayed Gules.

DRAKE. *MS Heraldic Alphabet*

An eagle displayed Argent armed Or.

EDWARDS, of Bradfield Combust. *Davy, A., church*

An eagle displayed.

EDWARDS. John Bidwell Edwards, of Bradfield, died 1824; widow died 1845. *Her.Suff.Ch., Tablet, Bradfield Combust. Not now visible*

An eagle displayed.

FISHER. *E.A.N. & Q. II. 327, Monument, Burgh church*

An eagle displayed Azure.

GILBERT, of Somerson [*sic*]. *London Visitation 1568 (H.S.) I. 39*

An eagle displayed Ermine beaked and legged Gules.

GLOVER, of Frostenden. *Bokenham. Davy, A.* Glover of Frostenden, 1600–1742. *Her.Suff.Ch., Wall tablets and Ledger stones, Frostenden*

An eagle displayed Or.

HAMBY, of Ipswich. *E.A.N. & Q. IX. 266, Monuments, St. Mary Elms church. E.A. Misc. 1907. 99, Monuments, St. Mary Elms*

An eagle displayed.

HAMBY, Robert, Attorney at Law, died 1735. *Her.Suff.Ch., Wall tablet, St. Mary Elms*

An eagle displayed Gules.

HERRING, of Mendham. *Bokenham*

On a garb an eagle rising all Or.
KEMP. 'Kempe' *Wall's Book*
'to his Crest an Egle the Wyngs rysyng/ on a shef or'
KEMP. 'kemp' *MS Alphabet of Crests, fo. 68*
On a garb lying fessewise an eagle standing with wings endorsed all Or.
KEMP, KEMPE, of Beccles. *Muskett. II. 225*
An eagle volant over a ruined castle Proper.
MINIETT, of Bramford, Henham, Stonham. *Davy, A.*
An eagle displayed Ermine.
MOSELEY, Nicholas, Alderman of London. Patent by R. Cooke, Clarenceux, 1592. *Grants & Certificates (Harl. MS 1,359)*
An eagle displayed Ermine.
MOSELEY. *Davy, A.*
An eagle wings elevated Sable.
NORRIS. *Bookplate**
An eagle displayed Or, or Proper.
PATTLE, of Elmswell. *Davy, A.*
An eagle displayed Or.
PHELIP, Sir William, K.G., Lord Bardolph in right of wife, died 1441. *Photographs**. [At feet of his effigy in Dennington church, his head resting on his great helm with the crest of Bardolph, a bush of feathers issuing from a coronet]
An eagle displayed looking at the sun.
POWERSCOURT (WINGFIELD). 'Lord Viscount Powerscourt' *Bookplates**
An eagle displayed Sable beaked and legged Or.
READ, READE. 'Master Rede of Kynte' *Harl. MS 6163. Crest I.* [Arms given as for Read of Halesworth]
'to his crest a negle halff ffased [side faced] dyspled ar/'
ROUS. 'Rowsse of Suff.' *MS Alphabet of Crests, fo. 109*
An eagle displayed Or.
ROUS. 'Thomas Rous of denyngton' *MS Knight's Visitations, Suff.**
Out of a crescent Argent an eagle displayed Or.
ROUS. *Davy, A., 'The crest, or badge, of Rous before assumption of the crest of Phelip, Lord Bardolph'*
An eagle displayed.
ROUS. Elizabeth, daughter of John Rouse, of Henham, married Francis Warner, died 1649. *Her.Suff.Ch., Ledger stone, Parham*
An eagle displayed Or, or Gules.
SALTONSTALL. *MS Ordinary of Arms, fo. 143**
An eagle perched.
SEARS, David, of Boston, married in 1786, Anne Winthrop. *Her.Suff.Ch., Glass, Groton*
An eagle rising Argent.
SMALLPEECE, Robert, of Hockering, co. Norfolk; Confirmation by R. Cooke, Clarenceux, 20 August 1590. *Grants & Certificates (Harl. MS 1,359; Stowe MS 677)*
An eagle rising Argent.
SMALLPEECE, of Metfield, Worlingham. *Davy, A., Metfield church.* Francis Smallpiece, son and heir of Thomas Smallpiece, died 1652. *Her.Suff.Ch., Ledger stone, Metfield*
? An eagle rising Or.
SOAME. 'Sir Stevens Somes Kt. and Alderman of London, benefactor to this church' *Her.Suff.Ch., Glass, Clare. Part of crest missing*
An eagle displayed.
SPARKE, Rev. Ezekiel, M.A., Incumbent 1852–death 1900. *Her.Suff.Ch., Wall tablet, Tuddenham*

An eagle displayed.
STANHAW. Margaret, wife of John Stanhaw, Gent., of Pulham Market, died 1704. *Her.Suff.Ch., Ledger stone, Wingfield*
An eagle displayed Azure winged Argent armed Or.
SULYARD, SULIARD, SYLLIARD. *MS Heraldic Collections, fo. 44**
An eagle displayed.
SULYARD, SEYLIARD, of Mildenhall. *Davy, A., Mildenhall and Moulton churches*
An eagle.
TALBOT, John, Rector, died 1689. *Her.Suff.Ch., Wall tablet, Icklingham*
An eagle rising Proper.
TRIVETT. Rector of Bradwell. *Davy, A. Fairbairn*, 'Bradwell, Suff.'*
An eagle displayed Gules.
WAHULL, ODELL, ODEHULL. *Davy, A.*
An eagle reguardant wings displayed Sable beaked and legged Or.
WESTON. *Sharpe. Davy, A.*
An eagle displayed looking at the sun.
WINGFIELD, as POWERSCOURT. 'Lord Viscount Powerscourt' *Bookplates**

Crowned

An eagle displayed Sable ducally crowned Or charged on the breast with a cinquefoil Or.
LE BLANC, of Cavenham. *Davy, A. Bookplate*, untinctured*
An eagle displayed and crowned.
PAKE. Penelope, wife of Samuel Pake, M.D., of Bury, died 1724. *Suff. Green Bks, Rushbrook, 89*

Gorged

An eagle Sable ducally gorged Or.
BARNE, Miles, died 1825. *Her.Suff.Ch., Hatchment, Sotterley*
An eagle wings addorsed Argent beaked and collared with a coronet Or.
BARNE. Violet, widow of Major Miles Barne, died 1969. *Her.Suff.Ch., Glass Sotterley*
An eagle [*sic* falcon] with wings expanded Ermine ducally gorged belled and jessed Or.
BOROUGH. *Davy, A.*
An eagle displayed Argent ducally gorged Or.
BROWNE, of Spexhall, Cavendish, Lavenham, Leiston. *Davy, A., Cavendish church*
An eagle displayed Argent beaked and legged Or gorged with laurel Vert.
GOODALL, Thomas, of Earl Stonham, co. Suff., gent.; Grant of Arms and Crest by Sir W. Segar, Garter, 1 March 1612. *Grants & Certificates (Add. MS 12,225; Harl. MS 6,140)*
An eagle displayed Argent gorged with a chaplet of laurel leaves.
GOODALL, of Earl Stonham. *Visitation 1664–8**
An eagle displayed Argent beaked and membered Or gorged with a chaplet of grass Vert.
GOODALL, of Earl Stonham. *Bokenham. Davy, A. Washbourne*, 'Suff.' Fairbairn, 'Suff.'*
An eagle close Argent ducally gorged and lined Or.
REYNOLDS, of Bury. *Davy, A. (Edms.), St. James's church, Bury*
An eagle lodged gorged with a ducal coronet.
REYNOLDS, James, died 1738. *Her.Suff.Ch., Effigy Monument, St. James's, Bury. Photograph**

Charged

An eagle rising Argent charged on the breast with a crescent Gules for difference.
COTTON, of Badingham, Langham. *Davy, A.,*

Badingham church. Proc.S.I.A. X. 390
An eagle displayed Argent armed Gules with a crescent for difference.

COTTON, William, Bachelor of the Civil Law, died 1616. *Her.Suff.Ch., Effigy monument, Badingham. Photograph**

An eagle displayed Azure bezanty.

GILBERT, of Finborough. *Bokenham. 'Gilbartt' MS ex-Taylor Coll.**

An eagle displayed Argent on the body an ermine spot Gules.

GLOVER, . . . , of Norfolk. Patent February 1611. *Grants & Certificates (Stowe MS 706)*

An eagle rising Argent on its breast a crescent Gules.

RIDWARE, of Kettlebaston. *Davy, A.*

EAGLE, holding: [Alphabetically by name]
An eagle displayed Vert in its claws a serpent Or.

BACKHOUSE. Brigadier Edward H.W. Backhouse. No date given. *Her.Suff.Ch., Glass, St. Mary's, Bury*

An eagle rising Proper in its beak a sprig Vert.

CLARKE, of Stuston Hall. *E.A.N. & Q. I. 257, Monument, church*

A falcon, or eagle, with wings expanded Sable preying on a fish Or.

COLE, of Sudbury, Pettistree, Yoxford. *Davy, A.*

An eagle rising Or resting the dexter claw on a book Sanguine garnished Or.

GARDENER, George, of co. Northumberland; father of Dr. Gardener, Dean of Norwich, living 1585. Confirmation of Arms and Grant of Crest by Sir Gilbert Dethick, Garter, 24 April 1577. *Grants & Certificates (Add. MS 14,295; Stowe MS 677; Harl. MS 1,441)*

An eagle displayed holding in its foot a sceptre Or.

HUMPHRIES. *Bokenham*

'beryth to his crest an egle in his nest gold flyeng gryping a child swadeled geules lined ermyns the swadelbond gold'

LATHAM. 'Lathom' *Wall's Book*

'to his Crest a egle in his nest or/ flying gryping a Chyld swadeled g/ Lyned [ermine spot drawn] the swadel bands or'

LATHAM. 'Lathom' *MS Alphabet of Crests, fo. 72*

An eagle Argent preying upon a hare Sable.

MORE, of Needham. *Davy, A.*

An eagle wings elevated Or preying on a fish Argent.

POLE. 'S. Rychard Pooll' *Harl. MS 6163*

On a broken tower Proper an eagle reguardant wings expanded Sable holding a millrind Sable.

TURNER, of Ipswich. *Sharpe*

On a tower Argent broken in the battlements an eagle reguardant with wings expanded Sable grasping in the dexter claw a millrind Sable.

TURNER, of Stoke by Ipswich. *Sharpe, Stonham Aspal church*

With two heads
An eagle with two heads displayed.

ASHBY, of Lowestoft. *Davy, A., church*

A double headed eagle.

ASHBY, Thomas, brother of Sir John Ashby, died 1713. *Her.Suff.Ch., Ledger stone, Lowestoft*

An eagle with two heads displayed charged on the breast with a saltire.

BADHAM, of Waldingfield, Sudbury. *Davy, A. Washbourne*, 'Badham'*

An eagle with two heads displayed Sable armed and

membered Or charged on the breast with the paternal coat – Argent on a fesse Azure three lozenges Or.

FIELDING, Earl of Desmond. Of Euston. *Davy, A.*

TWO EAGLES
A peacock's tail displayed Proper between two eagles Or.

LEAKE, LEEKE, of Yaxley Hall, Hadleigh, Willisham. *MS ex-Taylor Coll.*, 'of Lincolnsh.ʳ' Davy, A., Yaxley church. E.A.N. & Q. I. 313. Proc.S.I.A. XVI. 151*.* Rev. Seymour Leeke, of Yaxley Hall, died 1786; Francis Gilbert Yaxley Leeke, died 1836. *Her.Suff.Ch., Hatchments, Yaxley*

DEMI-FALCON see also HAWK
[Alphabetically by name]
A demi-falcon displayed Argent fretty Gules in its beak a branch Vert.

BRADBURY, of Mildenhall. *Bokenham*

A demi-falcon rising Proper holding in its beak a cinquefoil slipped Argent.

DISCIPLINE, of Bury. *Davy, A., Pakenham church*

A demi-falcon rising Proper holding in the beak a cinquefoil slipped Proper.

DISCIPLINE. Thomas, son of Robert Discipline, of Burnham Overy, co. Norfolk; Arms and Crest granted 23 June 1731. *Misc.Gen. et Her. 4th S. II. 116*

A demi-falcon, or hawk, displayed Proper holding in the beak a cinquefoil slipped Argent.

DISCIPLINE, Thomas, of Bury and Pakenham Hall, died 1752. *Her.Suff.Ch., Hatchment and Ledger stone, Pakenham*

A demi-falcon Or langued Gules wings expanded barry wavy of eight Argent and Azure.

HARBOTTLE, HERBOTTLE, of Crowfield. *Visitation 1561 (MS G.7*)*

A demi-falcon wings expanded.

HARBOTELL, of Crowfield. *Harl. 772**

A demi-falcon Or with wings expanded barry wavy of six, or eight, Argent and Azure.

HARBOTTLE, of Crowfield. *Visitation 1561 (ed. Metcalfe). Davy, A. Fairbairn, 'Suff. . . . barry wavy of six'*

A demi-falcon wings displayed Argent.

HARBOTTLE. *Bokenham*

A demi-falcon rising Azure charged with three bars gemel Or wings elevated Gules the outer feathers Or.

JERNINGHAM. 'Edward Jernyngham de somerleton In suffolke' *Banners & Standards*.* 'Jernyngham of Norffolk' *Wall's Book.* 'Sr Henry Jernyngham' *MS Knight's Visitations, Norf.**

'to his crest a demy ffacon rysyng on the body b/ iij gemelles or/ the Insydes of the Wyngs g/ the owt syde or/'

JERNINGHAM. 'Jernynghm of Norff/' *MS Alphabet of Crests, fo. 64*

A demi-falcon, or eagle, displayed Or beaked and winged Sable.

STEPHENS, of Sudbury. *Davy, A.*

FALCON see also HAWK
[Alphabetically by name]
A bird, ?falcon, rising Gules.

ALDHOUS, ALDOUS, ALDUS, of Moulton, Akenham. *Visitation 1664–8. Bokenham. Davy, A., Akenham church. Muskett I. 388. Partridge 55 (Darby, 1828), Akenham churchyard, 'a bird'. 'Aldis' Bookplate**

A falcon reguardant jessed and belled.
  BARKER. *MS Martin's Crests*
A falcon rising Or.
  BARKER, of Bildeston. *E.A. Misc. 1916. 63*
A falcon with wings expanded Proper belled Or.
  BELL, of Mutford. *Davy, A.*
A falcon with wings expanded Sable belled Or.
  BELL, of Mutford. *Davy, A.*
'And for his Creast or Cognizance On a wreath of
his Colours a falcon Argent wth like difference [a
trefoil Vert] mantled Gules doubled argent'
  BOLTON. 'Thomas Bolton of Woodbridge in the
  Countie of Suffolke, Esquier'; Confirmation of
  Arms and Crest by William Camden, Clarenceux,
  25 August 1610, the VIII of King James.
  [Original Confirmation in my possession, the
  falcon close beaked legged and belled Or. *Corder
  MS 81*]
A falcon Argent belled Or.
  BOLTON, of Ipswich, Coddenham. *Sharpe*
A falcon close Argent on its breast a trefoil Vert.
  BOLTON, of Woodbridge, *Davy, A. Muskett. II,
  220. Fairbairn, 'of Woodbridge, Suff.'*
A falcon rising Or.
  BOWYER. *MS Heraldic Alphabet*
A falcon.
  BROWNE, of Lavenham. *Bokenham*
A falcon with wings expanded Argent beaked
legged and belled Or.
  CULPEPER, of Bures. 'John Coulpeper of
  Yngham' *MS Knight's Visitations, Norf.*
  Davy, A.
A falcon with wings expanded Or beaked and
legged Argent.
  CULPEPER. 'nycholas Colpepor' *MS Philpot's
  Visitations, Norf.*
A falcon rousant Argent belled Or.
  CULPEPER. *MS Heraldic Alphabet*
A chough, or falcon, with wings displayed Or.
  FRAMLINGHAM. *Davy, A.*
On the trunk of a tree raguly Or a falcon close
Gules.
  FRANK. 'Thomas Francke of hatfeild Bodoke'
  MS Philpot's Visitations, Essex
A falcon.
  FRANK. 'Frankes' *MS Martin's Crests*
A falcon belled all Proper.
  FRANK, of Alderton. *Sharpe*
'A son tymbre ung Esprivier ellena't barre de six
pieces dargent & vert la primier else [wing] du
primier, loutre de second, les sonnettes et membre
dor estant sur une torsse dargent et gules, Mantle de
gules double dargent'
  HACON, John, of Norfolk; Grant of Arms and
  Crest by Thomas Wall, Garter, 2 June 1536.
  *Misc.Gen. et Her. 5th S. VIII. 314 (Soc. of Ant.
  MS 378, fo. 603)*
A falcon barry of six Argent and Vair.
  HACON. *Fairbairn, 'Suff. and Norf.'*
A falcon rising Or belled.
  HAMBY, of Ipswich, Dallinghoo. *Sharpe. Davy, A.,
  St. Mary Elms church, Ipswich*
A falcon displayed and belled Or.
  HAMBY, Robert, died 1774/5; his first wife, died
  1758. *Her.Suff.Ch., Hatchments, St. Mary Elms,
  Ipswich*
A falcon wings expanded Azure outer feathers
Gules beaked and legged Or.
  HANSARD. 'Mayster Wyllm. Haunsart . . . co.
  Lyngcoll.' *Banners & Standards*
A falcon Proper belled Or.

HAY, of Ipswich. *Sharpe*
On a ragged staff fesseways Argent a falcon close
and belled Or, on the breast a mullet Gules for
difference.
  HEWETT, Sir Thomas, of co. Notts.; Confirmation
  by R. St. George, Norroy, 12 June 1618. *Grants
  & Certificates (Add. MS 5,524)*
A falcon.
  HEWETT. 'Hewitt' *MS Martin's Crests*
A falcon close Argent beaked legged and belled Or
standing on the branch of a tree couped and raguly
Or.
  HEWETT, Bart., of Brightwell Hall. *Davy, A.*
A falcon rising Or.
  JEGON, John, Bishop of Norwich, died 1618.
  *Blomefield's Norfolk, III. 563, 'Grant by Cooke,
  Clar.' Davy, A. Bedford, 2nd. ed. 94*
On a dexter glove edged and tasselled Or a falcon
wings expanded Or between two branches leaved
Vert fructed Sable.
  JENNEY, JENNY, of Knodishall. *Visitation 1561
  (MS G.7*)*
On a glove in fesse Argent a falcon belled Proper.
  JENNEY, of Knodishall, Herringfleet. *Visitation
  1561 (ed. Metcalfe)*
On a glove in fesse Argent a falcon close belled Or.
  JENNY, Arthur, died 1667. *Her.Suff.Ch., Slab,
  Knodishall*
On a glove in fesse a falcon close armed Or.
  JENNEY, Edmund, of Hasketon and Bredfield,
  died 1852; sister Anne, died 1857. *Her.Suff.Ch.,
  Glass, Hasketon*
A falcon volant Or.
  KNOX. *MS Heraldic Alphabet*
A falcon perched Proper.
  KNOX, Rector of Hadleigh. *Davy, A. Bookplate*,
  falcon belled*
A falcon Proper beaked and belled Or.
  LACON, of Yarmouth, Gorleston. 'Myles Lakinge
  or Lacon' *MS Philpot's Visitations, Essex*
  Davy, A.*
A falcon rising reguardant Azure beaked and legged
Or.
  LEYBOURNE, Sr. William. Temp.E.I. *MS
  Ordinary of Arms, fo. 57**
A falcon volant Azure.
  LUDKIN. *Bokenham*
On a rest a falcon Proper beaked and belled Or.
  MORRICE, of Brampton Hall. *Crisp's Visitation,
  XIV. 55*
A falcon Argent armed beaked and membered Or.
  PLAYTERS. *Washbourne*, 'Platers, Suff.'*
On a staff raguly fessewise Vert a falcon rising
Proper beak and bells Or.
  READE. Thomas Reade, of Barton, co. Berks.
  Grants & Certificates (Harl. MS 1,359)
A falcon rising Proper belled Or standing on a reed
lying fessewise Vert.
  READE, of East Bergholt. *Davy, A., church.
  Fairbairn, 'Read, of East Bergholt, Suff.'*
A falcon displayed Proper.
  SAUMAREZ, Baron de Of Shrubland Park, Broke
  Hall, Livermere Park. *Burke's Peerage, 1891
  ed.**
A falcon volant.
  SHAWE, of Kesgrave. *Davy, A. Washbourne*,
  'Shawe-Newton, of Kesgrave Hall, Suff.' Burke,
  L.G. 1853 ed.*
A falcon volant Proper.
  SHAWE. *Fairbairn*, 'of Kesgrave Hall, Suff.'*
On a lure feathers Argent cap and line Gules ring Or

a falcon belled Or.

SOAME, Sir Stephen, of London. *Grants & Certificates (Harl. MS 5,869).* Thomas Soame, of Brent Eleigh, co. Suffolk. *(Harl. MS 1,359)*

A falcon close Or standing upon a lure Argent stringed Gules.

SOAME, of Little Thurlow. *Her.Suff.Ch., Effigy monument, Wall tablets, Glass and Hatchments, Lt. Thurlow*

A falcon rising.

STEIGER, of West Stow. *Suffolk Green Bks, West Stow Register, 78*, church stone*

A falcon wings extended and belled.

STEIGER, John George, died 1672. *Her.Suff.Ch., Floor slab in tower, West Stow*

A falcon rising Proper.

STERLIE. *Davy, A.*

A falcon volant Proper.

STIMSON, of Aldeburgh, Saxmundham. *Davy, A.*

A falcon rising.

THROGMORTON. *MS Heraldic Collections, fo. 15**

On the stump of a tree raguly and branched Proper a falcon volant Or.

THURSTON, of Wenham. *Bokenham*

A falcon rising belled Or.

THURSTON, of Little Wenham. *Davy, A., church*

A falcon standing on the stump of a tree with a branch growing from the dexter side all Proper,

WHITMORE, of Wiston. *Davy, A. church.* 'Whitmore, –'. *Her.Suff.Ch., Hatchment, Wissington. Falcon sejant*

Gorged

A falcon Or ducally gorged belled and jessed Azure.

ATHILL. *Davy, A.*

A falcon close ducally gorged Or.

BARNE. *Davy, A.*

A falcon rising Ermine ducally gorged and beaked Or.

BOROUGH. 'S. Edward Aborow, of Gainsborough, Linc.' *Harl. MS 6163.*

A falcon wings elevated Ermine ducally gorged and belled Or, charged with a label of three points [for difference].

BOROUGH. 'Thomas Bourght, of Gaynsbourght Lyngcol'. *Banners & Standards**

'A faucon rising ermyns membred beked sonettes and a crowne about her necke gold'

BOROUGH. *Wall's Book*

'to his Crest a facon/ rysing [ermine spot drawn] membred/ beked/ sonetts and a crowne abowt her neck or/'

'BOROUGH knyght by h 8/' *MS Alphabet of Crests, fo. 9*

A falcon rising Ermine ducally gorged Or belled –.

BOROUGH, BURROWS, BURGH. K.G. *MS Ordinary of Arms, fos. 223* and 225**

A falcon rising Ermine ducally gorged Gules.

BOROUGH, of Bury. *Bokenham*

A falcon rising Ermine beaked Or ducally gorged Or.

BOROUGH, Lord *Davy, A.*

An eagle [sic falcon] with wings expanded Ermine ducally gorged belled and jessed Or.

BOROUGH. *Davy, A. Washbourne, 'falcon'*

A falcon collared and belled wings addorsed and inverted.

BURROUGH, Rev. Thomas, Rector of Alpheton and Reader of Bury, died 1726. *Her.Suff.Ch., Ledger stone, St. Mary's, Bury*

A falcon rising ducally gorged and belled Proper.

CARTHEW, of Woodbridge Abbey. *Crisp's Visitation. VIII. 6., Pedigree. 'Crest 2'*

A falcon with wings expanded and inverted Proper ducally gorged Or.

GOSSE. *Davy, A.*

A falcon rising belled and ducally gorged.

POWLETT. *MS Ordinary of Arms, fo. 229**

A falcon rising Or belled Or gorged with a ducal coronet Gules.

POWLETT, of Clare, Athelington. *Davy, A.*

FALCON, holding: [Alphabetically by name and including previous sub-sections]

A falcon Proper beaked and belled Or seizing on a fowl's jamb [leg] erased at the top of the thigh the feathers alternately Or and Gules.

BROWNE. 'William Browne' *MS Knight's Visitations, Essex*.* 'William Browne' *MS Philpot's Visitations, Essex**

A falcon Proper beaked and belled Or seizing on a fowl's jamb erased at the top of the thigh Or.

BROWNE, of Higham. *Davy, A.*

A falcon, or eagle, with wings expanded Sable preying on a fish Or.

COLE, of Sudbury, Pettistree, Yoxford. *Davy, A.*

A falcon Argent belled Or holding in the dexter claw a belt Sable buckled Or.

COTTON, of Earl Soham, Easton, Higham, Beccles, Marlesford. *Visitation 1664–8*. Bokenham, 'or a stirrup Or leathered Sable'. Davy, A., Easton church*

A falcon close Proper belled Or holding in its dexter claw a garter.

COTTON. *MS Heraldic Alphabet*

A falcon Or holding in the dexter claw a belt Sable buckled Or.

COTTON. Probably for Dr. Ralph Cotton, M.D., of Yarmouth, died 1705. *Her.Suff.Ch., Hatchment, Easton*

A rock Proper thereon a falcon belled Or wings displayed Azure on the insides supporting with the dexter claw a banner Azure charged with a garb Or.

EAST SUFFOLK County Council. *Scott-Giles, 343**

A falcon rising Argent belled gutty Gules resting the dexter claw on an antique shield Argent charged with a cinquefoil Gules.

EDGELL. Rector of Uggeshall and Nacton. *Davy, A.* Henry James Edgell, Captain, N. British Fusiliers, died 1874. *Her.Suff.Ch., Brass, Nacton*

A falcon holding in its beak a buckle.

HADLEY, Arthur, O.B.E., died 1954. *Her.Suff.Ch., Gravestone, churchyard, Darsham*

A falcon close in its beak a padlock all Or.

LOCK, Michael; Grant by Sir Gilbert Dethick, Garter. 5 July 1 & 2 Phil. & Mary [1554/5]. *Grants & Certificates (Harl. MS 1,359). Miscellaneous Grants (H.S.) II. 139–40 (Harl. MS 1,116, fo. 45b.)*

A falcon rising belled and holding in its beak a padlock all Or.

LOCK, LOCKE. *MS Ordinary of Arms, fos. 166* and 168**

A falcon rising Or ducally crowned Argent holding in the beak a padlock pendent Sable.

LOCK, of Mildenhall. *Davy, A. Washbourne, 'Suff.' Fairbairn, 'Mildenhall, Suff.'* John Lock, Gent., died 1802. *Her.Suff.Ch., Ledger stone, Mildenhall*

A falcon Proper legged and belled Or preying on a partridge Proper.

ONSLOW, of Norton, Theberton. *MS Ordinary of Arms, fo. 155*. Davy, A. Bookplate**

A falcon Proper beaked legged and belled Or preying on a partridge Or.

ONSLOW. *MS Heraldic Alphabet*

A falcon close Or belled Or preying upon a mallard Proper.

'YERBURGH, Rev. Edmond, Wrentham Rectory, Wangford, Suff.' *Fairbairn**

GOOSE

A goose Sable billed Or.

READE, of Stoke by Ipswich. *Davy, A.*

HAWK see also FALCON
[Alphabetically by name]

A hawk Proper legged and beaked Or.

ATHERTON, of Cretingham. *Davy, A.*

A hawk close belled Or.

BELL. Vicar of Wickham Market, 1831. *Davy, A.*

A hawk close reguardant Argent beaked and legged Or.

BOCLAND. *Davy, A.*

A hawk Proper.

BOLTON. *MS Martin's Crests*

A hawk close Argent belled Or.

BOLTON. Probably for James Richard Bolton. No date. *Her.Suff.Ch., Hatchment, Gt. Ashfield*

A mewed hawk Proper armed Azure belled and jessed Or.

BRABOURNE, BRABON, BRABANT, of Rumburgh. *Davy, A.*

A goshawk.

BROWNE, of Bungay, Rickinghall, Lavenham, Cavendish, Hawkedon, etc. *Davy, A.*

A hawk rising Proper belled Or.

BROWNE. *Davy, A.*

A goshawk rising Or.

BROWNE, John, Gent., died 1716. *E.A.N. & Q. I. 106, Stone, Rickinghall Superior church*

A hawk close.

BURROUGH. Margaret, wife of Samuel Burrough, died 1707. *Martin's Church Notes, Frag.Gen. IX. 92, Stone, All Saints Newmarket. Drawn, not blazoned, beside it 'a Hawk'*

A game hawk Proper hooded and belled Or.

CRAWFURD, of Higham House. *Crisp's Visitation, II. 8*, Pedigree*

A hawk with wings expanded Proper.

DONOVAN, of Thorpe Hall, Horham. *Davy, A.*

A hawk close belled Or.

FRANK, of Alderton. *Davy, A. Fairbairn*, 'Suff.'*

A hawk with wings expanded Argent beaked and belled Or.

GLEMHAM, of Glemham. *Visitation 1561 (MSS G.7* and Iveagh Copy*) 'Sr Thomas Glemham of Glemham Knight' MS Lilly's Visitation of Suffolk*. First of two crests shown*

A hawk with wings expanded Argent beaked and legged Gules belled Or.

GLEMHAM, GLENHAM, of Glemham, Benhall. *Harl. 772*. Davy, A. Washbourne*, 'Glenham, Suff.' Fairbairn*, 'Glenham, Suff.'*

A hawk preparing to fly Argent belled, etc. Or.

GLEMHAM, of Glemham. *Bokenham*

A hawk with wings expanded belled.

GLEMHAM, Thomas, died 1583. *Effigy brass, Brundish. Photograph**

A hawk volant Proper beaked legged and inside of the wings Or.

HAMBY, of Ipswich. *Davy, A.*

A hawk volant Argent belled Or.

HANSARD. *MS Heraldic Collections, fo. 59**

A hawk volant Azure the wings tipped with Gules.

HANSARD. *MS Martin's Crests*

A hawk rising belled.

HURTON, of Long Melford. *Davy, A., church*

On a glove lying fessewise a hawk all Proper.

JENNEY, Arthur, died 1729; Arthur Jenney, of Rendlesham, died 1742. *Her.Suff.Ch., Hatchments, Bredfield*

A hawk close Proper hooded Gules.

KEMPE. 'Robert Kempe of Weston' *MS Knight's Visitations, Norf.** 'Allene Kempe' *MS Philpot's Visitations, Norf.*, hawk 'grey' and belled Or*

A hawk close Proper hooded Gules belled Or.

KEMPE. 'John Kempe of Beckles in Com Suffolke Esquier' *MS Lilly's Visitation of Suffolk**

A hawk close hooded.

KEMPE, of Bricett. *Bokenham*

Standing on a spur leathered 'lyng' [?lying in fesse] Or a hawk volant per fesse Azure and Argent wings Or membered Gules.

KNIGHT. 'Knyght' *Wall's Book. Washbourne, 'Salop'*

'to his crest a hawke Volant b/ ar/ p fece membred g/ standing on a Spurre Lethered lying and her wyngs or/'

KNIGHT. 'Knyght' *MS Alphabet of Crests, fo. 68b*

A hawk reguardant Argent winged Azure belled Or.

PLAYTER, PLATER, of Sotterley. *Visitation 1561 (MSS G.7* and Iveagh Copy*, 'legged Gules' and (ed. Metcalfe)*

A hawk reguardant wings expanded Argent belled Or.

PLAYTERS, of Sotterley. *Harl. 772*. Bokenham. Davy, A. Washbourne, 'Plater, Suff. 'hawk or vulture'*

A hawk reguardant Or winged Azure belled Or.

PLAYTERS, of Sotterley. *Davy, A. (Edms.) Washbourne, 'Suff.' Her.Suff.Ch., Brass shield, Sotterley.* Dame Elizabeth, wife of Sir John Playters, Bt., died 1718. *Altar tomb, churchyard, Worlingham*

A hawk standing on a perch.

READE, of East Bergholt. *E.A.N. & Q. XII. 337, Tomb, church*

On a lure Argent garnished and lined Gules a hawk close Or.

SOAME, Bart., of Lt. Bradley, Kedington, Haughley, Thurlow, Hundon, etc. *London Visitation 1633 (H.S.) II. 250*. Bokenham. Davy, A. Washbourne*, 'Lond. and Suff.' Fairbairn*, 'London and Suff.' Misc.Gen. et Her. 5th S. VIII. 343*

A hawk close belled Proper.

SPARHAWK, of Leiston. *Davy, A., Framlingham church*

A hawk belled and jessed Proper.

STRATTON, STRETTON, of Shotley, Weston. *Davy, A., Shotley church. Washbourne*, 'Stratton, Suff.' Fairbairn*, 'Stratton, Suff.'*

A hawk close Proper bells Or.

YARMOUTH, of Henstead. *Visitation 1577. 'yarmouthe' MS Philpot's Visitations, Suff.*, 'beaked Or'. MS Fairfax (Tyl.) Bokenham. Davy, A.*

A goshawk close Proper legged and belled Or.

YARMOUTH, of Blundeston. *Davy, A.*

A hawk Proper belled Or.

YARWORTH. *Fairbairn*, 'Suff.'*

Crowned
A hawk rising belled and crowned.
LOCK, of Mildenhall. *Misc.Gen. et Her. 3rd S. IV. 149, church monument*

Charged
A hawk closed Argent beak and bells Or on the breast a trefoil Vert [for difference].
BOLTON, Thomas, of Woodbridge, Suffolk, descended from Bolton of Bolton, co. Lanc. Patent 25 August 1615 [*sic* 1610]. *Grants & Certificates (Stowe MS 707)*

HAWK, holding:
A hawk Argent on its breast a star Gules holding in its beak a piece of a garter Azure buckled Or.
COTTON, of Marlesford. *Bokenham*
A hawk wings expanded Sable beaked and legged Or holding in the beak an oak branch Vert fructed Or.
FASTOLF, of Pettaugh. *Visitation 1561 (MSS G.7* and Iveagh Copy*)*
A hawk Sable with wings expanded holding in the beak an oak branch Vert fructed Or.
FASTOLF, of Pettaugh. *Davy, A. Washbourne, 'Falstoffe, Norf. and Suff.' Fairbairn, 'Falstoffe, Norf. and Suff.'*
A hawk feeding on a fish Proper.
GRANDFORD. *Davy, A.*

HERON see also CRANE
A heron within a heap of bulrushes Proper.
BARNARDISTON, of Kedington, Brightwell. *Bokenham*
A heron Proper standing among bulrushes Or and Argent.
BARNARDISTON. Lt. Col. Samuel John Barnardiston. No date. *Her.Suff.Ch., Glass, St. Mary's, Bury*
A heron rising Proper beak and legs Or.
HAYNES, William, of London, gent.; Confirmation of Arms and Crest by R. Cooke, Clarenceux, 10 June 1578. *Grants & Certificates (Add. MS 14,295)*
A heron rising Proper beaked and legged Or.
HAYNES. *MS Heraldic Collections, fo. 41*
A heron Argent.
HERON, HERNE, of Ipswich. *Visitation 1664–8. MS ex-Taylor Coll.* Davy, A.*
A heron Argent beaked and legged Or.
PITT, William, of Steepleton, co. Dorset; Patent by W. Camden, Clarenceux, 13 August 1604. *Grants & Certificates (Stowe MSS 706 and 707; Harl. MS 1,422)*
A crane, or heron, holding in its beak an eel, or snake.
RAY, of Bury, Tostock. *Davy, A., St. James's church, Bury*
A heron Argent.
THRUSTON. *E.A.N. & Q. I. 136, Hatchment, Market Weston church 1861, 'stowed away in the tower'.* Nathaniel Thruston, died ante 1692; Clement Thruston, Gent., died 1692; Elizabeth, wife of John Thruston, Esq., died 1694. *Her.Suff.Ch., Ledger stones, Hoxne*
'his crest a herne in proper couller his beking [beak in] a whelke or/ Confyrmed by C Cowke [Cooke] 1551 [*sic*] 14 of quenne Elizabeth' [1571/2]
WALTER. *MS Alphabet of Crests, fo. 141b*

JAY
A jay Proper holding in its beak a key Or.
DAVERS, Bart., of Rushbrook. *Davy, A., Glass,*

church. *Proc.S.I.A. VII. 337, 'On the roof, church.'*
A jay Proper in its beak an annulet Or.
DAVERS. *Washbourne, 'Suff.'*
A jay in its beak an annulet.
DAVERS, Sir Robert, Bart., died 1721/2; Sir Charles Davers, Bart., last hereditary owner of Rushbrook Hall, died 1806. *Suff. Green Bks, Rushbrook, 90–91*. Her.Suff.Ch., Wall tablets, Rushbrook. Crests missing 1981*

KINGFISHER
A kingfisher Proper ducally gorged and chained Or holding in its beak a fish Argent.
BATTIE. 'Battye' *MS ex-Taylor Coll.* *

LARK
A lark wings addorsed Proper in the beak a pansy flower Proper slipped and leaved Vert.
LARKIN. 'Thomas Larking, Doctor of Physick'. *Grants & Certificates (Add. MS 4,966)*
A lark wings expanded downwards Proper holding in the beak a ?pansy Azure slipped and leaved Vert.
LARKIN. 'Mr Doctor Larkin of the civill lawe' *MS Knight's Visitations, Cambs.*, 'a larke'*
A lark wings expanded downwards Proper holding in the beak a trefoil slipped Azure.
LARKIN, of Cambridge. *MS Heraldic Alphabet*

MAGPIE
A magpie Proper
ECCLESTON, of Crowfield. *Davy, A.*

MARTLET
[Alphabetically by name]
A martlet Argent winged and holding in the beak an acorn Or leaved Vert.
ALLEN, ALLEYNE. *Davy, A. (G.B.J.) Fairbairn, 'Allen, Alleyn. Chesh., Suff. and Wilts.'*
A martlet Sable.
ARGENTINE, of Halesworth. *Davy, A.*
A martlet Proper.
BIDWELL, of Thetford. *Davy, A., church monuments.* Thomas Bidwell, Esq., died 1817; Shelford Bidwell, Esq., died 1823. *E.A.N. & Q. I. 136, Monuments, Thetford church*
A martlet Sable.
BIGOD, Earl of Norfolk. *Davy, A.*
A martlet Sable.
CAMAC, of Brettenham. *Davy, A.*
A martlet Or.
CORNWELL, of Ipswich. *Sharpe*
A martlet.
DAVERS, of Rushbrook. *Bokenham*
A martlet.
EDWARDS. John Proger Herbert Edwards, Esq., died 1758; John Edwards, Esq., died 1775. *Suff. Green Bks, West Stow, 77*, Wall tablets. Untinctured*
A martlet Sable.
EDWARDS, John P.H., died 1758; John, died 1775. *Her.Suff.Ch., Tablets, West Stow*
A martlet.
FYNNE, of Barham, Akenham, Dennington. *Davy, A.* Thomas Fynne, clerk, Rector of Dennington, died 1740; widow died 1767. *Her.Suff.Ch., Slab, Dennington*
A martlet Vert.
GRIMES, of Bury. *Davy, A., 'Granted 1575'*
A martlet rising Gules charged on the breast with a mullet Or [? for difference].
HYDE. *MS Heraldic Collections, fo. 9*
A martlet Argent.

JERVIS. Herbert J. White Jervis, of Freston House, died 1934. *Her.Suff.Ch., Wall tablet, Freston.* *First crest*

On the stump of a tree erased Proper a martlet Sable.
LOCKWOOD. Vicar of Lowestoft. *Druery, 269, Glass in church*

A martlet sitting on the stump of a tree between two branches all Proper.
LOCKWOOD. Vicar of Yoxford and Lowestoft. *Davy, A.*

A martlet.
ROCKLEY, ROKELEY. *Davy, A.*

On a rock Proper a martlet rising Or.
TONG, of Haverhill, Tuddenham. *Davy, A.*

A martlet Gules.
WADDINGTON, of Cavenham. *Davy, A.* Spencer Waddington. *Her.Suff.Ch., Glass, St. Mary's, Bury*

A martlet.
WORSLEY, of Boxted, Eye, Woodbridge. *Davy, A.*

MOOR-COCK

A moorcock with wings expanded per bend sinister Sable and Gules gorged with a ducal coronet Or and charged on the breast with a cross crosslet Or.
HALLIFAX, of Cavendish, Chadacre Hall. *Davy, A.* Thomas Hallifax, of Chadacre House in Shimpling, died 1850. *Her.Suff.Ch., Hatchment, Hartest;* daughter Diana, married J.G. Weller-Poley, died 1884, *Glass, Boxted;* son John Savile Halifax, of Edwardstone House, *Glass, Groton*

A moor-cock with wings expanded combed and wattled Proper ducally gorged and charged on the breast with a cross crosslet Or.
HALLIFAX, of Chadacre Hall. *Burke, L.G. 1853 ed.*

A moor cock Proper.
HIGHMOOR, of Ufford. *Sharpe. Davy, A.*

A moor-cock rising Sable gutty Or combed and wattled Gules in the beak a rose Gules slipped and leaved Vert.
MOORE. Sir John More, Alderman and late Lord Mayor of London; Grant, 28 September 1683. *Grants & Certificates (Stowe MS 714)*

A moor-cock Sable gutty Or beaked combed wattled and legged Gules wings open and holding in the beak a branch of heath Proper.
MOORE, of Kentwell Hall in Melford. *Davy, A.*

A moorcock wings expanded downwards Azure holding in the beak a rose Or slipped Vert.
SCUTT. *MS Heraldic Alphabet*

MURR see also AUK

A murr Proper.
CARTHEW, of Benacre, Woodbridge. *Davy, A.*

A murr Proper ducally gorged Or.
CARTHEW, of Woodbridge. *Sharpe. Burke, L.G. 1853 ed. Crisp's Visitation, VIII. 6, of Woodbridge Abbey, Pedigree. Carthew MS, Bookplate*.* Mary, wife of Rev. Thomas Carthew, died 1771; Rear-Admiral William Carthew, R.N., died 1827. *Her.Suff.Ch., Wall tablet, Hatchments, Woodbridge*

NUTHATCH

A nut hatch feeding on a branch of hazel fructed all Proper.
FIELDING, Earl of Desmond. Of Euston. *Davy, A., 'original crest'. Washbourne, 'Earl of Denbigh, Viscount Fielding'*

OSPREY

An osprey Argent holding in its beak a horse-shoe Sable.

DIGBY. *Wall's Book*
'to his crest an Ospery ar/ holdyng an horsse shewe Sa.'
DIGBY. 'Dygby' *MS Alphabet of Crests, fo. 29*
An osprey Or taking a fish Argent.
POLE. 'Poole of . . . Southsex' *Wall's Book*

DEMI-OSTRICH
[Alphabetically by name]

A demi-ostrich with wings expanded holding in its beak a horseshoe.
BAKER. *Davy, A. Fairbairn, 'of Wattisfield and Wrentham, Suff.'*

A demi-ostrich Argent with wings expanded in its beak a nail Or.
CLOVILE. *Davy, A.*

A demi-ostrich bendy of four Or and Azure in the beak Gules a horseshoe of the first [Or].
EDGAR, William, of Great Glemham, Suffolk, gent. 'Whose ancestors have long borne arms, but he is uncertain how to use them'. Granted to him and his descendants by Sir Christopher Barker, Garter, 6 September 1545. *Grants & Certificates (Stowe MSS 677 and 692)*
'vpon his Crest a demy Osteriche bendy of 4 peces golde and azure, beked goule therein a horseshoo silver, Bottonett golde'
EDGAR, William, of Great Glemham; Grant of Arms and Crest by Christopher Barker, Garter. *MS Suffolk Armorial Families*. Unfinished copy, no date*
'his crest a demy Oysteyche bendey of 4 or/ b/ beked g their in a horsewe ar/ Willm Edgare of grete glemham in Suff.'
'EDGARE'. *MS Alphabet of Crests, fo. 34b*

A demi-ostrich wings displayed bendy Or and Azure holding in the beak a horse-shoe Argent.
EDGAR, of Eye, Gt. Glemham, Ipswich, Norton. *Visitation 1664–8*, 'p Barker, Garter, 16 Sept. 1545'. Bokenham, 'Granted 18 Sept. 1545, 38 Hen. 8' [sic 1546/7]. Robert Edgar, died 1594. Her.Suff.Ch., Brass shield, Sotterley.* Temperance (Sparrow), married Capt. Devereux Edgar, her brother died 1690. *Ledger stone, Wickhambrook.* Robert Edgar, died 1778. *Hatchment, St. Stephen's, Ipswich.* Rev. Mileson Gery Edgar, of Red House, 41 years Incumbent of St. Nicholas, Ipswich, died 1853; Others. *Wall tablets and Hatchments, St. Margaret's, Ipswich.*

A demi-ostrich displayed holding in the beak a key all Proper.
STUBBIN, STUBBING, of Higham, Naughton, Raydon. *Davy, A. Muskett. II. 337 and 406, 'the ancient spelling was Stubbing'*

A demi-ostrich displayed Argent gorged by a crest coronet Gules.
TALBOT, Thomas, of Wyndham in Norfolk; Grant by R. Cooke, Clarenceux, 1584. *Grants & Certificates (Add. MS 14,295; Stowe MS 670; Harl. MS 1,359)*

A demi-ostrich Argent wings expanded Gules ducally gorged Gules.
TALBOT. *Davy, A. '?Granted 1584'. Washbourne, 'Suff. and Devon'. Fairbairn, 'Devonsh. and Suff.'*

A demi-ostrich wings displayed Argent ducally gorged Gules holding in its beak a horse-shoe Azure.
WELLES, WELLS. *MS Ordinary of Arms, fo. 33**

A demi-ostrich displayed Argent wings Sable ducally gorged Or holding in the beak a horse-shoe Azure.

WELLES. *MS Heraldic Alphabet*
A demi-ostrich with wings displayed Argent ducally
gorged and chained holding in its beak a horse-shoe.
WELLES, Lord. Of Exning. *Davy, A.*

OSTRICH
An ostrich.
LAWES, Peter, died 1720. *Her.Suff.Ch., Floor slab, Saxmundham*
An ostrich Or.
RAY, of Bury. *Ray, 5*
An ostrich etc. [*sic*].
TALBOT, John, Rector of Icklingham St. James, died 1689. *Martin's Church Notes, Frag.Gen. IX.98*
An ostrich Proper.
THRUSTON, of Hoxne, Ipswich. *Davy, A.*
An ostrich Or.
WRAY, Bart., of Hawstead. *MS Martin's Crests, 'Linc.' Davy, A.*

OSTRICH, holding: [Alphabetically by name]
An ostrich Argent holding in its beak a key Or.
BAYNING, Viscount Of Sudbury. *Bokenham*
An ostrich sans feet wings expanded holding in its
beak a Passion nail Or.
CLOVILE. 'Clovill' *MS Heraldic Alphabet*
An ostrich Argent in its beak a scroll with this motto
'All is in God'.
CLOVILE. *Davy, A.*
An ?ostrich Gules ducally gorged and holding in its
beak a key Or.
COCK, of Ipswich. *Davy, A., St. Matthew's church. Proc.S.I.A. VII. 206*
An ostrich holding in its beak a horse-shoe Argent.
COCKE, of Barsham, St. Margaret's Ilketshall.
Davy, A.
An ostrich Argent with a horse-shoe.
COKE. *MS Heraldic Alphabet*
An ostrich Argent holding in its beak a horse-shoe
Azure.
DIGBY. 'Dyggeby' *Wall's Book*
An ostrich passant Argent holding in the beak a
horse-shoe.
DIGBY. *MS Ordinary of Arms, fo. 223**
An ostrich Argent holding in its beak a horse-shoe
Or.
DIGBY. 'Thomas Dygby' *MS Philpot's Visitations, Norf.* Davy, A., 'of Finborough'. Bookplate**
An ostrich Proper holding in its beak a horse-shoe
Sable.
DIGBY. 'Digbye' *MS ex-Taylor Coll.**
An ostrich Argent holding in its beak a key Or.
EACHARD. 'Echard of Bucklesham'. *Bokenham*
An ostrich with wings expanded holding in its beak
a key.
EACHARD, of Barsham, Yoxford, Rendlesham,
Cransford. *Davy, A., Barsham and Rendlesham churches. Washbourne, 'Echard, Suff'. Fairbairn, 'Echard, Suff.'* Rev. Christopher Eachard, Vicar
of Cransford for 48 years, died 1743. *Proc.S.I.A. XXV. 306, 'an ostrich wings elevated . . .'* Rev.
Christopher Eachard, A.M., Rector of
Somerleyton, died 1706. *Her.Suff.Ch., Glass, Somerleyton.* John Eachard, Gent., died . . .; his
niece, Elizabeth Eachard, died 1827. *Ledger stone, churchyard, Barsham*
An ostrich holding in its beak an annulet.
EACHARD. Vicar of Cransford, died 1743. *E.A. Misc. 1910. 57, 'on a flat stone within the Communion rails'*

'On a Wreath of the Colours, an ostrich Or, in the
beak a Horse Shoe Azure'.
RAY, Richard, of Haughley; Confirmation of
Arms and Crest by Stephen Martin Leake, Garter,
8 March 1770. *MS Suffolk Armorial Families**
An ostrich Or holding in its beak a horse-shoe
Azure.
RAY, of Haughley, Shelland. *Davy, A., Granted 8 March 1770, in Haughley church. Washbourne*, 'Suff.' Ray, 5, Grant 1770. Fairbairn*, 'of Howleigh [sic], Suff.'* Ray, of
Plashwood in Haughley, 1758–1811.
Her.Suff.Ch., Ledger stones and Hatchments, Haughley
An ostrich holding a horse-shoe in its beak Proper.
SPARHAM. *Bokenham*
An ostrich with wings endorsed holding in the beak
a horse-shoe Proper.
VALENTINE. *Davy, A. Washbourne, 'Suff.' Fairbairn, 'Suff.'*
An ostrich holding a horse-shoe in its beak.
WRAY. *MS Martin's Crests*

OWL
An owl Argent ducally crowned Or sitting in a holly
bush Vert.
BOYS. *MS Knight's Visitations, Norf.** 'John
Boys' *MS Philpot's Visitations, Norf.* Davy, A.*
An owl.
CASTLEY. Mary Gertrude, wife of Thomas
Castley, died at Cavendish Rectory, 1850.
Her.Suff.Ch., Ledger stone, Cavendish
An owl statant guardant Argent.
HORNE. *MS Ordinary of Arms, fo. 272**
An owl Proper gorged with a collar charged with
two mullets issuing from the beak a scroll with the
words 'Nil invita Minerva'.
PRIME, of Thwaite, Bury, Gt. Saxham, Ringsfield.
Davy, A. Washbourne, 'of Suss.'
An owl Proper.
SAVILE. Quartered by Hallifax. Thomas Hallifax,
of Chadacre Hall, died 1850. *Her.Suff.Ch., Hatchment, Hartest*

PARROT or POPINJAY
A parrot rising Gules charged on the dexter wing
with an annulet Or.
ALDOUS, of Fressingfield, Wingfield, Stradbroke,
Brandeston, Gedding Hall, etc. *Burke, L.G. 1952 ed.**
A popinjay wings expanded Or collared –.
CURSON. *MS Ordinary of Arms, fo. 155**
A popinjay volant Or beaked legged and collared
Gules.
CURZON. *MS Heraldic Alphabet*
A popinjay wings expanded Or collared beaked and
legged Gules.
CURSON. *MS Heraldic Collections, fo. 12*. Washbourne, 'co. Derby'*
A popinjay with wings expanded – beaked legged
and collared Gules.
CURZON, of Ipswich. *Davy, A., St. Matthew's church*
A popinjay Vert winged Gules holding in the beak a
gem-ring Or.
DANVERS, DAVERS. *MS Heraldic Collections, fo. 13**
A parrot Vert beaked and legged Gules.
TARBOCK. *Fairbairn*, 'Suff.'*
A bird, ?parrot, close Proper legged and beaked Or.
YARMOUTHE. *MS Knight's Visitations, Suff.**

PARTRIDGE
A partridge rising Or in the beak an ear of wheat Vert.
> PARTRIDGE, Hugh, gent., born in the North parts; Grant by Sir G. Dethick, Norroy, 5 February 2 Edw. VI. [1548/9]. *Grants & Certificates (Harl. MS. 1,359; Stowe MS 676)*

A partridge with wings displayed Or.
> PARTRIDGE, of Hockham Hall, co. Norfolk and Bury. *Crisp's Visitation. VII, 161*, Pedigree. Fairbairn, 'of Hockham Hall, nr. Thetford, Norfolk, also of Bury St. Edmunds'*

DEMI-PEACOCK
A demi-peacock Azure.
> BURMAN. *Davy, A.*

PEACOCK
A peacock in his pride Proper.
> BECK, of Worlingworth. *Bokenham. MS Martin's Crests, 'of Devon'*

A peacock Proper.
> BECK. *Washbourne, 'Suff.' Fairbairn*, 'Suff.'*

A peacock in pride Proper.
> CHAFY, of Bury. *Davy, A.*

A peacock close Or.
> CHARNEL. *Davy, A.*

A peacock Argent.
> EYRE, of Burnham. *MS Heraldic Alphabet*

A peacock in his pride Argent.
> PELHAM, of Bures. *Davy, A.* Herbert Pelham, late of Bures hamlet. No date given. *Her.Suff.Ch., Ledger stone, Bures*

PEEWIT
A peewit Argent gorged with a coronet Or.
> REYNOLDS. *MS Heraldic Alphabet*

DEMI-PELICAN
A demi-pelican Argent vulning herself.
> KENDALL. Rector of Norton, died 1796. *Davy, A.*

A demi-pelican with wings extended Argent vulned Gules.
> KENDALL, Rev. Richard, Rector for 2 years, died 1796. *Her.Suff.Ch., Wall tablet, Norton*

A demi-pelican Argent vulning herself Gules.
> PETT. *MS Heraldic Collections, fo. 53**

PELICAN
[Alphabetically by name]
A pelican vulning herself Proper.
> AGUILLON. *Davy, A.*

A dragon and on its back a pelican vulning herself all Proper.
> ATKINS. *MS Heraldic Alphabet*

A pelican wings displayed Argent vulning herself Gules.
> BAXTER, of Forncett, co. Norfolk. *MS Humfry Pedigree Roll*; Corder MS. 91*

A pelican vulning herself Argent.
> BAXTER, of Mendham. *Visitation 1664–8. Davy, A., church*

A pelican in her piety.
> BOILEAU, John Peter, died 1826. *Partridge 16 (Darby, 1831), Tablet, churchyard, Somerton*

A pelican in her piety Proper charged on the breast with a saltire couped Gules the neck resting on a foreign coronet.
> BOILEAU, John Peter, died 1816. *Her.Suff.Ch., Tablet on outside wall of church, Somerton*

On the stump of a tree a pelican Or vulning herself Gules, or Proper.

> BRIGGES, BRYGGES, of Euston. *MS Heraldic Alphabet. Davy, A.*

A pelican Sable.
> BRIGGS, of Corton. *Davy, A.*

A pelican vulning itself.
> BRIGGS, Robert, died 1718. *Her.Suff.Ch., Slab, Corton. Now covered by carpet*

In front of a pelican in her piety Proper five bezants fesseways.
> GATAKER, of Mildenhall. *Burke, L.G. 1952 ed.**

On the top of a wheat sheaf Proper a pelican Or vulning herself Proper.
> KEMPE, of Ubbeston. *Bokenham. MS ex-Taylor Coll.*, 'a garb Or'*

On a garb lying fesseways Or a pelican vulning her breast Proper.
> KEMP, Bart., of Ubbeston. *MS ex-Taylor Coll.* Davy, A.*

A lemon tree Vert fructed Or therein a pelican Argent on its nest of the last [Argent].
> LEMAN, John, of London, Alderman; Patent 25 January 1615. *Grants & Certificates (Harl. MS 6,059; Stowe MS 706)*

In a lemon tree Proper a pelican in her nest Or feeding her young Proper.
> LEMAN, of Wenhaston, Brampton, Bury. *Visitation 1664–8. Davy, A., St. Stephen's church, Ipswich. Fairbairn, 'Brampton Hall, Suff.'* Robert Leman, died 1637. *Her.Suff.Ch., Effigy monument, St. Stephen's, Ipswich*

A tree Vert in the midst of its branches a pelican Or.
> LEMAN, of Charsfield, Wenhaston. *Bokenham*

A pelican in her piety Or under a tree Vert fructed Or.
> LEMAN, of Ipswich. *E.A.N. & Q. XII. 130, Monument, St. Stephen's church, Ipswich*

In a lemon tree a pelican in her piety.
> LEMAN, of Wenhaston, 1672–1735. *Her.Suff.Ch., Ledger stones, Wenhaston.* N.T.O. Leman, Clerk. *Glass, Wrentham. Recorded by Farrer. All Proper*

In a lemon tree a pelican in her nest feeding her young all Proper.
> LEMAN, of Brampton, 1640–1837. *Her.Suff.Ch., Wall monument and Ledger stones, Brampton.* Matthew Leman, died 1678; Charles Leman, died 1687; Matthew Leman, died 1692. *Ledger stones, Beccles.* William Leman, died 1730. *Wall tablet, Charsfield*

In a lemon tree leaved and fructed Proper a pelican Argent feeding her young in a nest Proper.
> LEMAN. Rev. Naunton T. Orgill, later Leman, died 1837. *Her.Suff.Ch., Hatchment, Charsfield*

A pelican in her piety.
> LEMAN. Rev. Thomas Leman, of Wenhaston Hall, died 1826. 'The last male descendant of his ancient name'. *Her.Suff.Ch., Altar tomb and Ledger stone, Wenhaston*

A pelican vulning herself Proper.
> MEADOWS, of Witnesham, Botesdale, Gt. Bealings. *Page. Davy, A., Burke's Heraldic Register. Washbourne*, 'Berghersh House, Suff.' Burke, L.G. 1853 ed. Fairbairn*, 'Witnesham Hall, Gt. Bealings and Burgersh House, Suff.' E.A. Misc. 1916. 85*

A pelican vulning herself Argent beaked and membered Gules.
> MEADOWS, of Witnesham. *Davy, A., church*

A pelican in her piety.
> MEADOWS, Rev. Philip, Rector of Gt. Bealings for 34 years, died 1837; Others. *E.A.N. & Q. XIII. 263. Her.Suff.Ch., Wall tablet, Ledger stone,*

*Glass and carved poppy head of choir stall,
Gt. Bealings.* William Meadowe, died 1637;
Philip Meadows of Burghersh House in
Witnesham, died 1824. *Wall tablet, Ledger stone,
Witnesham*

A pelican in her nest close vulning herself Proper.
PATTESON, of Coney Weston, Drinkstone,
Hopton. *Davy, A.*

A pelican in her nest feeding her young all Proper.
PATTESON, PATERSON. Rev. Henry Patteson,
Rector of Drinkstone for 20 years, died 1824.
*Her.Suff.Ch., Hatchment, Drinkstone.
Photograph*.* John Paterson, died 1858; son Rev.
George Paterson, M.A., 40 years Rector of Brome
with Oakley, died 1887. *Tomb, or Vault,
churchyard, Brome and Glass, Oakley.* Thomas
William F. Paterson, 1910–1983. *Tombstone,
churchyard, Hoxne*

A pelican in her nest all Or.
PULLEYN, of Halesworth. *Davy, A.*

A pelican wings endorsed Or.
STANNOW. 'William Stannow of Beddingham
[sic] in Com Suffolke Gentleman'. *MS Lilly's
Visitation of Suffolk**

A pelican in her nest feeding her young Or.
TYLDESLEY, of Fornham St. Genevieve. *Davy,
A., church monuments*

A pelican in the nest.
TYLDESLEY. Family memorials in church of
Fornham St. Genevieve, 1727–1733. *E.A. Misc.
1910. 67.*

Gorged

A pelican vulning herself gorged with a ducal
coronet.
PEARCE, PEARSE. Hammond Pearse, died 1762.
Her.Suff.Ch., Tomb, churchyard, Carlton Colville

PELICAN, holding:

A swan, or pelican, Argent preying on a dragon sans
wings –.
ATKINS, ATKYNS. *MS Heraldic Collections,
fo. 77b.**

PHEASANT

A cock pheasant Proper crested membered and
jelloped Or.
ATWOOD, of Aspal. *Davy, A.*

'to his Crest a ffesant Cocke in his proper couller'
'BROMLEY chef Justyce of England'. *MS
Alphabet of Crests, fo. II*

A cock pheasant Proper.
BROMLEY. *MS Martin's Crests, 'temp.Qu: Eliz.'*

A cock pheasant sitting Proper.
BROMLEY, of Wickhambrook. *Davy, A.*

A cock pheasant Proper.
ECCLESTON. *Davy, A.*

A pheasant close Proper.
YARMOUTH, of Blundeston. *Davy, A.
Washbourne*, 'Norf. and Suff.' Fairbairn*,
'Norf. and Suff.'*

POPINJAY see PARROT

QUAIL

A quail.
QUAYLE, of Bury, Barton Mills. *Davy, A.*

RAVEN

A raven volant Proper.
FRAMLINGHAM. *Davy, A.*

A raven Proper.
GATACRE, GATAKER, of Mildenhall. *Davy, A.*

A raven close Sable perched on a torteau.

RAVEN, John, Richmond Herald; Grant by W.
Camden, Clarenceux. *Grants & Certificates
(Add. MS 12,225; Stowe MS 677)*

Gorged

Upon a heart Or a raven Sable gorged with a collar
gemel Argent.
JONES, of Pakenham, Barton Mere. *Crisp's
Visitation. I. 286–7*, Pedigree. Fairbairn*, 'of
Barton Mere, Pakenham, Suff.'*

A raven Proper a portcullis hanging round the neck
by a chain Or.
THURLOW. *Fairbairn, 'Suff.'*

A raven close Proper with a portcullis hung round
its neck Argent.
THURLOW, Lord Of Ashfield. *Davy, A.
Washbourne, 'Suff.'*

RAVEN, holding:

A raven Proper holding in the dexter claw an
escallop Or.
BRIGSTOCKE. *Fairbairn*, 'of Brent Eleigh Hall,
Lavenham, Suff.'*

A raven Sable holding in its dexter claw an
escutcheon Sable charged with a leopard's face Or.
CORRANCE, of Rougham, Orford, Parham Hall,
Loudham Hall. *Davy, A. Washbourne,
'White-Corrance, Parham and Loudham Hall,
Suff.' Burke, L.G. 1853 ed.*

A raven supporting with the dexter claw an
escutcheon Sable charged with a leopard's face Or.
CORRANCE-WHITE, of Parham and Loudham Hall,
Suff.' *Fairbairn*. Second crest, for Corrance*

A raven Proper beaked and peded Or holding an oak
branch Vert fructed Or.
FASTOLFE, of Pettaugh. *MS Fairfax*

A raven rising wings displayed armed and
membered Or holding in the beak a spray of oak
Vert fructed Or.
FASTOLF, *Proc.S.I.A. XXVII. 150 (Dandy
pedigree)*

From the wreath a raven issuing reguardant holding
in the dexter talon a sword in pale.
MURDOCK. Vicar of Pettistree, Rector of
Stradishall. *Davy, A. Washbourne**

ROOK

A rook upon a wheat sheaf pecant [pecking] all
Proper.
ROOKE, of Nacton. *Sharpe*

SEA-MEW [SEAGULL]

A sea-mew resting its foot on an escallop Or.
NEGUS, of Dallinghoo, Melton, Bungay.
Davy, A.

SEA-PIE [OYSTER CATCHER]

A sea-pie Argent beaked and legged Gules.
BURMAN, of Stradbroke. *Davy, A.*

STARLING

A cock starling Proper.
STERLIE, of Suffolk. *Davy, A.*

DEMI-STORK

A demi-stork with wings expanded the neck
'bulbous'.
BROWNE, John, Esq. Brass of c.1597 in St. John's
Berstreet, Norwich. *Cotman's Norfolk Brasses,
plate 86*.* [The stork's neck not nowed, but oddly
drawn]

A demi-stork with wings expanded Proper the neck
nowed.
BROWNE, of Leiston. *Davy, A. Washbourne,*

'Browne, Suff.' Fairbairn, *'Suff.'*
A demi-stork with wings expanded and neck nowed
Azure charged on the dexter wing with a crescent –
[for difference].
> BROWNE, of Leiston. *Visitation 1561 (MS G.7*)*
A demi-stork with wings expanded Azure the neck
nowed.
> BROWNE, of Leiston. *Addit.Suff.Peds*

STORK see also CRANE
[Alphabetically by name]
On the stump of a tree couped a stork close all
Proper.
> BANKS, of Metfield. *MS Ordinary of Arms, fo.
226* Davy, A., church*
A stork among bulrushes all Proper.
> BARHAM. *Davy, A.*
A stork Or amid rushes Proper.
> BARNARDISTON, of Kedington, Clare, Brightwell.
> *Davy, A., Brightwell church, Wyverstone church
> flagon. Proc.S.I.A. VIII. 323. E.A.N. & Q. XIII.
> 327, 'a crane'.* 'Sir . . . Barnardiston Kt.
> Benefactor of this . . .' *Her.Suff.Ch., Glass, Clare*
A stork Proper.
> DALE, of Dale Hall, Ipswich. *Davy, A.*
A stork rising Proper.
> GIBSON. *MS Ordinary of Arms, fo. 160**
A stork rising Argent beaked and legged Or.
> HARRISON, of Thorpe Morieux. *Davy, A. Fiske,
> 206**
A stork wings expanded Argent beaked and legged
Or.
> HARRISON. John Haynes Harrison, of Copford
> Hall, co. Essex, died 1839. *Her.Suff.Ch.,
> Hatchment, Thorpe Morieux*
A stork rising Proper.
> HAYNES, of Stutton. *Davy, A.*
A stork Argent, or Proper.
> PITT, of Debenham, Gt. Bealings. *Davy, A.,
> Thorpe church*
A stork Argent.
> STEEL. *Fairbairn*, 'of Somers. and Suff.'*
A stork Argent.
> STILL, of Hadleigh, Suffolk. *Davy, A.
> Washbourne*, 'Wilts., Somers. and Suff.'
> Fairbairn*, 'Wilts., Somers. and Suff.'*
A stork Argent legged Azure.
> THRUSTON, John, of Hoxne, Suffolk, gent., being
> descended from Thruston of Anderson, in the
> parish of Adlington, co. Lancs.; Confirmation by
> W. Dethick, Garter, 10 February 1586/7. *Grants
> & Certificates (Stowe MS 676, fo. 68)*
A stork, or crane, Argent legged Azure.
> THRUSTON, THURSTON, of Hoxne, Ipswich.
> *Visitation 1664–8*. Bokenham. Davy, A.,
> Holbrook church. Washbourne*, 'Thurston, Suff.'
> Fairbairn*, 'Thurston, Suff.'*
A stork Proper.
> TORLESSE, of Ipswich, Stoke by Nayland.
> *Davy, A.*
A stork Proper.
> UPJOHN. Vicar of Gorleston. *Davy, A.*
A stork drinking out of a whelk shell erect.
> WALTER. Lt. Col. Francis E. Walter, D.S.O., died
> 1960; widow died 1972. *Her.Suff.Ch.,
> Tombstone, churchyard, Hopton*

Gorged
A stork Argent beaked legged and ducally gorged
Or.
> DALE, of Bury. *Davy, A., (Burke)*
À stork Proper gorged with a coronet Gules.

GIBSON, Robert; son Thomas Gibson of
Beckenhall, co. Norfolk, gent.; Confirmation by
W. Dethick, Garter, 6 May 1591. *Grants &
Certificates (Stowe MS 676)*

Charged
A stork Sable bezanty.
> GOLDSMITH, of Wilby. *Davy, A.*

STORK, holding: [Alphabetically by name]
A stork holding in its dexter claw a stone between
two elephant's trunks all Proper.
> ANGERSTEIN. *Davy, A.* 'John Angerstein'
> *Bookplate**
A stork Argent preying on a dragon Vert.
> ATKINS. *MS Martin's Crests*
A stork Argent wings and tail Sable beaked and
legged Gules preying on a dragon ?Vert.
> ATKINS. *Davy, A.*
A stork close Argent holding in its beak a branch of
laurel Proper and resting its dexter claw on a bridle
bit Or.
> MILNER-GIBSON, of Theberton House, Hardwick
> House, Hawstead. *Crisp's Visitation. I. 150*.
> Misc.Gen. et Her. 2nd S. V. 192, Bookplate*.
> Muskett. I. 175. Burke, L.G. 1900 ed. Bookplate*,
> untinctured*
A stork with claws resting on a snaffle-bit holding in
the beak a branch of laurel.
> MILNER-GIBSON. Susan, wife of the Rt. Hon. T.
> Milner-Gibson, died 1885; Others. *Her.Suff.Ch.,
> Wall tablet, Tomb in churchyard for family
> 1806–1889, Theberton. Not found 1980*
A stork holding in its beak a branch of laurel Proper
and resting the dexter claw upon a bridle-bit Or.
> 'MILNER-GIBSON-CULLUM, George Gery, of
> Hardwick House, Bury St. Eds., Suff.' *Fairbairn.
> Second crest, first crest for Cullum [q.v.]*
A stork Proper its leg supporting an anchor Azure.
> TAYLOR, of Alderton Hall, Hinton Hall. *Davy, A.*
A stork Argent winged Sable membered Gules
holding in its beak a snake Vert winding about its
body.
> WIGHTMAN, of Framlingham, Clare. *Davy, A.,
> (Bookplate*). Wightman, 25**

SWALLOW
A swallow Ermine wings expanded downwards
Argent.
> NEWMAN. *MS Heraldic Alphabet*

DEMI-SWAN
A demi-swan Argent ducally gorged Or.
> ATHERTON, of Cretingham. *Davy, A.*
A demi-swan wings expanded Argent beaked Gules
within two halberts erect headed Vert.
> PETIT, PETYT, of Shipmeadow. *Visitation 1561
> (MSS G.7* and Iveagh Copy*)*
A demi-swan displayed Argent beaked Gules
between two battle-axes erect Vert.
> PETIT, PETITT, PETYT, PETYTT, of Shipmeadow.
> *Visitation 1561 (ed. Metcalfe 'An untrue
> informacon', Harl. MS 1177). Harl. 772*.
> Bokenham. Davy, A. Washbourne*, 'Petytt, Suff.'
> Fairbairn, 'Petytt, of Shep Meadow [sic], Suff.'*
A demi-swan with wings endorsed Argent holding
in the bill Or a trefoil Azure.
> SYMONDS. 'Gyles Symonds'. *MS Philpot's
> Visitations, Norf.**

SWAN
A swan couchant Argent with wings expanded and
endorsed.

BARTLET. *Davy, A. Washbourne, 'Suff. and Suss.'*
A swan Argent wings endorsed beaked and legged Sable.
CAREY. *MS Ordinary of Arms, fo. 222**
A swan Argent wings indorsed.
CAREY, Earl of Monmouth. Of Stowmarket, Woodbridge, Halesworth. *Visitation 1664–8. Davy, A.*
A swan.
CLARKE, of Bungay, Henstead, Hulvers [sic], Beccles. *Davy, A., St. Mary's church, Bungay.* Robert Clarke, Gent., late of Bungay, died 1748. *Her.Suff.Ch., Ledger stone, St. Mary's, Bungay*
A swan Proper.
CLARKE, of Woodbridge. *Davy, A.*
A swan Argent.
DALE, of Rowley House, Aldeburgh. *Crisp's Visitation. XIV. 41, Pedigree*
In water a swan swimming wings elevated Proper.
GOBION, GABYON, GUBION, of ?Mildenhall. *Davy, A.*
A swan among bulrushes.
HEARD, Thomas, Churchwarden c.1834. Heard, of Seckford Hall for 60 years. *Church booklet, carved on bench end, Gt. Bealings. Photograph**
On a trumpet Or a swan wings expanded Argent.
LYTE, of Gt. Yarmouth, Bradwell. *Crisp's Visitation. V. 153, Pedigree*
A swan Proper.
PLAMPIN, of Chadacre Hall, Shimpling. *Sharpe. Davy, A.*
A swan.
PLAMPIN, John, died 1730; Rev. John Plampin, M.A., of Chadacre Hall, Rector of Whatfield and Stanstead, died 1825. *Her.Suff.Ch., Wall tablets, Shimpling*
A swan Proper.
PYKARELL, of Burgate. *Davy, A., church*
A swan passant wings endorsed.
POCKLINGTON, of Chelsworth. *Davy, A.*
A swan close Proper.
POCKLINGTON, Robert, Sergeant at Law, died 1767; Pleasance Pocklington, died 1774; Sir Robert Pocklington, died 1840. *Her.Suff.Ch., Hatchments, Chelsworth*
A swan Proper.
WHITE. Rev. John White, M.A., Rector of Chevington 1853–1908. *Her.Suff.Ch., Wall tablet, Chevington*
A swan Argent membered Gules.
WYBORNE, of Flixton. *Davy, A., church*

Charged

A swan Ermine swimming in water Proper wings expanded Or fretty raguly Azure, charged on the breast with an estoile Sable [?for difference]
BROADHURST. Vicar of Brandeston. *Davy, A. Washbourne. The swan Proper*

SWAN, holding:

A swan, or pelican, Argent preying on a dragon sans wings –.
ATKINS, ATKYNS. *MS Heraldic Collections, fo. 77b**
A swan rising – holding in its beak a key –.
EACHARD, of Barsham. *Visitation 1664–8*
A swan devouring a fish Proper.
HILDERSHAM, of Suffolk. *Davy, A. (Burke)*
A swan with wings addorsed devouring a fish Proper [a perch].
LOCH. Edward Douglas, 2nd Baron Loch of

Drylaw, lord of the manor of Stoke, etc., died 1942. *Her.Suff.Ch., Glass, Stoke by Clare*
A swan Argent charged on the wing with an escallop Gules and resting the dexter foot on a water bouget.
SKEELS, of Kirkley. *Crisp's Visitation. V. 19*, Pedigree*
A swan reguardant Argent beaked membered and wings elevated Sable murally crowned Gules reposing the dexter foot on an escallop Or.
SWABEY, of Kedington. *Davy, A. 'Before 22 August 1819, when another crest granted in lieu of this one'*

VULTURE

A vulture Sable wings expanded gutty Argent preying on a fish.
COLE, of Pettistree. *Sharpe*

WOODPECKER

A woodpecker.
THRUSTON, of Hoxne, Ipswich. *Davy, A.*

WREN

On a chess-rook Argent a wren Proper.
SMALL, of Hadleigh, Ipswich. *Davy, A.*

BONE

'to his crest a ded man's hed in the fasshon of Deth/ holding in his mouth a candell or/ at ether end the fflaminge fyer issuing'
'BOLNEY of Sussex'. *MS Alphabet of Crests, fo. II*
A skeleton's head couped at the shoulders Proper holding in the mouth a firebrand Or flamant at both ends Proper.
BOLNEY, of Suffolk. *Davy, A.*
A death's head with a firebrand in the mouth Proper.
BOLNEY, of Wetheringsett. *Davy, A. (Barrett)*
A shank bone and palm branch in saltire Proper.
GALL, of Wyverstone. *Davy, A.*

BOOK

On a Bible open a hand couped close holding a sword erect.
ALLIN, Bart., of Lowestoft, Somerleyton. *Davy, A.*

BOOT

A boot Sable spurred Or topped Ermine above it a human heart Proper held between two arms issuing from dexter and sinister vested Azure hands Proper.
HUSSEY. *MS Heraldic Collections, fo. 10*. Washbourne**
A boot Sable spurred Or topped Ermine.
HUSSEY, of Suffolk, Essex. *MS Martin's Crests. Davy, A. Washbourne, 'Wilts., Essex, Dors. and Salop'*

BOWL

Out of a bowl Or five quills in pale Argent.
LORING, of Hawkedon. *Davy, A.*

BRANCH see also BUSH, FAGGOT

HOLLY

'to his crest a ffagot of holly Vert wᵗ the Beryes g/ alibi blased [blazoned] a bush of holly'
STRICKLAND. 'Stryckland'. *MS Alphabet of Crests, fo. 116*
A holly bush fructed Proper.
STRICKLAND, of Reydon near Southwold. *Davy, A.*
A branch of holly in pale Proper.
WALKFARE, of Barton. *Davy, A.*

LAUREL
Two laurel branches forming a chaplet Vert.
LAWRENCE. *Davy, A. Washbourne**
A battle-axe erect in pale crossed by a branch of laurel and cypress in saltire all Proper.
MACLEAN, M.D., of Sudbury. *Davy, A.*

OLIVE
A sword Proper hilted and pommelled Or and an olive branch also Proper in saltire.
FRASER, of co. Inverness. *Her.Suff.Ch., enamelled shield on post in Cemetery, Ufford*

PALM
A shank bone and palm branch in saltire Proper.
GALL, of Wyverstone. *Davy, A.*
A palm branch in bend sinister Vert in front of a griffin's head erased Or charged with a gemel Gules holding in the beak a hawk's lure Argent lined and ringed Or.
HALL. Rector of Glemsford c.1875. *Crisp's Visitation. IV. 29**. 'Rev. H. Hall, The Rectory, Glemsford, Suff.' *Fairbairn*
An ear of wheat and a palm branch in saltire Proper.
INGELOUS. *Davy, A.*
An ear of wheat Or bladed Vert and a palm branch Vert in saltire.
TINLING, of Bury. *Davy, A.*
A palm branch and a laurel branch in saltire Vert.
TWEEDIE. Rector of –. *Davy, A.*

ROSE
A musk rose branch with buds all Proper.
BAKER, of Stutton. *Davy, A.*
A rose branch Proper.
LE HEUP, of Hessett, Bury. *Davy, A.*

BULRUSHES see REEDS

CALTRAP
A caltrap Or between two wings Argent.
COLMAN, of St. John's Ilketshall, Brent Eleigh. *Visitation 1664–8. Bokenham. Davy, A., Brent Eleigh church monuments. Misc.Gen. et Her. 2nd S. I. 373–6*, untinctured. Bookplate*, untinctured*
A caltrap Or between two wings erect Argent.
COLMAN, Edward, died 1739. *Her.Suff.Ch., Effigy monument, Brent Eleigh. Also two floor slabs, covered by choir stalls, dated 1653 and 1695 and a Hatchment, formerly in the church but missing in 1979*
On a mount a caltrap.
KERRICH. *MS Ordinary of Arms, fo. 204**
On a mount, or hill, Proper a caltrap Sable.
KERRICH, KERRIDGE, of Bury, Shelley Hall, Geldeston Hall near Beccles. *Bokenham, 'p. R. St. Geo., Clar. to Capt. Tho. Kerridge for service in the Gt. Mogul's Country, 1620'. Sharpe. Davy, A., Monuments and Hatchment, Shelley church. Burke, L.G. 1853 ed. E.A.N. & Q. VI. 91. Fairbairn, 'Kerrich, of Geldeston Hall, Suff.' The mount Vert.*
On a mount Proper a caltrap Or.
KERRICH, of Geldeston Hall near Beccles. *Burke, L.G. 1900 ed.*
On a mount Vert a caltrap Sable.
KERRIDGE, of Shelley Hall. Lords of the manor of Shelley 1657–1743. *Her.Suff.Ch., Ledger stones and Hatchment, Shelley*
On a mount Vert a caltrap Or.
RAVEN, John, M.D., Fellow of the College of Physicians of London, sworn physician to the late Queen Anne and King Charles, eldest son of John

Raven, late Richmond Herald. Grant to the father by W. Camden, Clar. of Crest; A raven close Sable perched on a torteau [q.v.] This altered for the son to On a mount Vert a caltrap Or. *Grants & Certificates (Add. MS 12,225; Stowe MS 677)*
On a mount Vert a caltrap Or.
RAVEN, John, Richmond Herald. Of Creeting St. Mary. *London Visitation 1633 (H.S.) II. 187*, 'Vnder the hand of Will. Camden, Clarenceux King of Armes the Creast'. Of Hadleigh. Davy, A.*
On a hill a steel gad erect Or.
RAVEN, of Creeting in Suffolk. *MS Heraldic Alphabet, 'P. Wm. Camden, Clar.'*
A caltrap Or between two wings erect Argent.
YALLOP, of Beccles, North Cove. *Davy, A., Barsham church*
A caltrap.
YALLOP, William, Attorney at Law, died 1764. *Her.Suff.Ch., Ledger stone, churchyard, Barsham. Not found 1985*

CAP
A skull-cap Argent.
BAMBOROUGH, of Rendlesham. *Davy, A. Washbourne*, 'Bambury, of York. and Suff.' Fairbairn, 'Bambrough, Rendlesham, Suff.'*
A Mercury's cap Or wings Argent thereon an eagle's head erased Proper gorged with a collar Ermine.
BARLOW, of Lowestoft, Burgh, Rushmere Hall, Edwardstone, Sotterley. *Davy, A. Crisp's Visitation. II. 62, Pedigree. Barlow, 4*, Photograph*
On a cap with upturned brim two wings.
GLOVER. *MS Heraldic Collections, fo. 83a**
A tall cap per pale Ermines and Argent banded Gules inserted in the band two wings expanded dexter Argent sinister Ermines.
WINGFIELD, WYNGFELD, of Wingfield, Letheringham. *Visitation 1561 (MSS G.7.* and Iveagh Copy*)*
A cap per pale Ermines and Argent charged with a fesse Gules between two wings expanded the dexter Argent the sinister Ermines.
WINGFIELD, of Letheringham, Brantham. *Visitation 1561 (ed. Metcalfe). 'Sr John Wynfeld' MS Philpot's Visitations, Norf.* Visitation 1664–8. Fairbairn, 'Wingfield, Bart. (extinct), of Letheringham, Suff.' Her.Suff.Ch., Tablet, Easton*
A tall cap per pale Ermine and Ermines encircled by a belt with round buckle – and between two wings the dexter Ermines the sinister Ermine.
WINGFIELD. 'Harbotell Wyngfild of Wantisden in Com Suffolke Esquier' *MS Lilly's Visitation of Suffolk**
A bull [*sic* mistake for cap] parted per pale Sable and Argent in the Sable five gouts Argent over all a bar Gules between two wings one Argent the other Sable gutty d'eau.
WINGFIELD. *Davy, A.*
A high bonnet or cap per pale Sable and Argent banded Gules between two wings displayed all gutty counterchanged on the cap a fesse Gules.
WINGFIELD. *Washbourne, 'Salop. and Suff.'*
A cap per pale Ermine and Argent between two wings expanded the dexter Argent the sinister Ermine.
WINGFIELD, of Letheringham, Brantham, Stoneham, Easton. *Davy, A., Letheringham church*
A cap per pale Ermine and Argent charged with a

fesse Gules between two wings expanded the dexter Argent the sinister Ermine.

WINGFIELD, Thomas, died 1652. *Her.Suff.Ch., Wall tablet and Slab, Nettlestead.* Anthony Wingfield, died 1714. *Effigy monument, churchyard, Stonham Aspal, untinctured*

CASTLE see also TOWER

A castle Argent masoned Sable.

ATHELL. *Washbourne*, 'of Suff. and Sco.'*

A castle triple-towered.

BENCE. *Fairbairn*, 'of Thorington, Suff.'*

A castle Argent.

CANTRELL, of Bury. *Bokenham.* 'Sr. – Cantrell of Chesh. & Suff.' *MS. ex-Taylor Coll.**

A castle Argent port Sable.

CANTRELL. *Washbourne*, 'Cantrill, Suff.'*

A castle Argent.

HARDCASTLE. *Fairbairn*, 'of Netherhall, Suff. and of Holt, Norf.'*

An eagle volant over a ruined castle Proper.

MINIETT, of Bramford, Henham, Stonham. *Davy, A.*

A castle Or transfixed with four darts in saltire and inflamed Proper.

RUGGLES, of Clare. *Davy, A., church*

A castle Gules fired Proper in front of three arrows one in fesse the pheon [head] towards the dexter and two in saltire the pheons downwards Or.

SWABEY, of Kedington. *Davy, A., 'Granted 22nd August 1819, in lieu of former crest' [q.v.]*

ISSUANT FROM CASTLE
[Objects in alphabetical order]

Out of the top of a tower Gules a demi-lion rampant Or armed and langued of the second [*sic* Or]

SKINNER, John, of London, Sheriff of that City; Confirmation by Sir W. Dethick, Garter, 29 September 1587. *Grants & Certificates (Stowe MS 676)*

Out of a castle Gules a demi-lion rampant Or.

SKINNER, of Lavenham. *MS Fairfax (Tyl.)*

The battlements of a castle Argent thereon a demi-lion fixing the banner of St. George upon the same.

WEDDALL. Vicar of Darsham. *Davy, A.*

A lion issuing out of the top of a castle Gules.

BEVERSHAM. *Bokenham*

Out of the battlements of a castle a lion holding in his dexter paw a mill-pick.

MOSELEY, of Ousden. *MS Fairfax*

On a tower, or castle, triple-towered Argent a dove rising Proper.

DOVE, of East Bergholt, Ipswich, Gosbeck, Scole, Stradbroke, Dallinghoo. *Visitation 1664–8. Bokenham, 'castle triple-towered'. Davy, A.*

A castle triple-towered Argent issuing out of the port a boar's head Sable, and the words 'Pectus fidele et opertium'

CANTRELL, of Hemingstone. *E.A. Misc. 1916, 21 (Conder MS 43–4)*

Out of a castle Argent charged with three cross crosslets Sable a Saracen's head affronty Proper wreathed Argent and Gules.

CATON. Rev. Redmond Caton and Rev. Thomas Caton, Rectors of Gt. Fakenham and Denham. *Burke, L.G. 1900 and 1952 eds.*

Issuant from a castle with two towers Argent charged with three crosses crosslet fitchy in fesse Sable a Saracen's head affronty Proper wreathed round the temples Or and Gules.

'CATON, Rev. R.B., Great Fakenham Rectory,

Suff.' *Fairbairn*

On the top of a castle Argent a demi-man bareheaded and in mail Proper holding in his right hand an arrow point downwards Sable headed Or and on his left arm a round Shield Or.

WISEMAN. 'Thomas Wiseman son of John Wiseman of Canfield in Suff.' *MS Philpot's Visitations, Suff.** [In a different hand]

On the top of a castle Argent the portcullis shut down Gules a Moor Proper wreathed about the temples Argent and Gules clothed in mail in his right hand a broad arrow Argent in his left a shield Or.

WISEMAN, of Thornham. *Bokenham*

A castle Sable issuing therefrom a demi-griffin segreant Argent holding in the dexter claw a sword Argent hilted Or.

HIGGINS, of Bury. *Davy, A.*

Out of a castle a griffin.

REDE. *Her.Suff.Ch., Bench end, Hollesley*

CHAPEAU or CAP OF MAINTENANCE

A cap of maintenance Ermine.

STUTVILLE, of Dalham. *Bokenham*

ON A CHAPEAU

BEAST [In alphabetical order]

On a chapeau Purpure turned up Ermine a wild boar passant Or.

ARDEN. *Washbourne*, 'of Norf. and Suff.'* Dame Elizabeth (Arden) married Sir William Poley, died 1632. *Her.Suff.Ch., Ledger stone, Boxted*

On a chapeau Gules turned up Ermine a boar passant Or.

DAVIE, of Debenham. *Davy, A.*

On a chapeau Gules turned up Ermine a boar Azure crined and tusked Or.

VERE, DE VERE. 'Lord of Oxynford' *Harl. MS 6163*

On a chapeau Gules turned up Ermine a boar passant Argent [*sic* mistake for Azure].

VERE, DE Earl of Oxford. Of Lavenham. *Davy, A.*

On a chapeau Gules turned up Ermine a stag Sable.

THORPE. *Davy, A. Washbourne*, 'Suff.' Fairbairn*, 'Sussex, Suff. and Norf.'*

On a chapeau Proper a greyhound seiant Argent.

COTTINGHAM, of Laxfield. *Davy, A. Her.Suff.Ch., Laxfield*

On a chapeau Gules turned up Ermine a greyhound trippant [*sic* passant] Sable collar and ring Or.

WENHAM, of Wenham Hall. *Sussex Visitations 1530 & 1633–4 (H.S.) 91*

On a chapeau Gules turned up Ermine a greyhound statant Sable collared Or.

WENHAM, of Wenham Hall. *Berry's Sussex Genealogies, 257*. Davy, A.*

On a chapeau a talbot Gules eared collared and lined Argent in a fern bush Vert.

FERNELEY, FERNLEY, of West Creeting, Sutton. *Davy, A., West Creeting church*

On a cap of maintenance Gules turned up Ermine an ermine passant Argent with an ermine spot on the tail.

ATY. 'ETTYE (or ATHY)', Arthur; Confirmation 1583. *Grants & Certificates (Stowe MS 670)*

On a cap of maintenance Azure turned up Ermine a fox segreant [*sic* should be sejant] Or.

FOX. Rev. Robert Stoke Fox, Rector of Nowton, died 1888. *Her.Suff.Ch., Wall brass, Nowton*

On a chapeau a goat passant Argent.

RISBY, of Thorpe Morieux. *Davy, A., Thorpe Morieux and Felsham churches*
On a chapeau, or cap of maintenance, a goat passant.
RISBY, of Thorpe Morieux. John Risby, late of this Parish, died 1727. *Muskett. I. 72, Inscription, church.* John Risby, died 1727. *Her.Suff.Ch., Headstone outside North wall of chancel, Thorpe Morieux*
On a cap of maintenance a goat statant guardant.
RISBY, John, of Thorpe Hall in Suffolk, died 1687. *Her.Suff.Ch., Floor slab, Felsham*
On a cap of estate Gules turned up Ermine a leopard (or lion statant affronty) tail raised Or ducally crowned Or gorged with a collar gobony Ermine and Azure.
BEAUFORT, Sir Thomas. Earl of Dorset, Duke of Exeter, K.G., died 1426. *Stall Plates, plate XLV*, 'Buried in the abbey church of St. Edmund at Bury'*
On a chapeau Gules turned up Ermine a leopard passant Proper.
BOCKING, of Ashbocking. *Davy, A., Ashbocking and Framsden churches. Washbourne*, 'Suff.' Fairbairn*, 'Suff.'*
On a cap of estate Gules turned up Ermine a leopard (or lion statant affronty) tail extended Or ducally crowned Gules.
BOHUN, Sir Humphrey de Earl of Hereford and Essex K.G., died 1372/3. *Stall Plates, plate XL*
On a chapeau Gules turned up Ermine a leopard Argent ducally gorged Or.
BOWET, of Thorington, Wrentham. *Davy, A. Washbourne, 'York.'*
On a chapeau Azure turned up Ermine a leopard statant Argent spotted Sable.
CATCHPOLE. 'Knatchbull, Richard, of Mersham, co. Kent; Patent by R. Cooke, Clarenceux, 1574. *Grants & Certificates (Harl. MS 1,359; Add. MS 4,966)*
On a chapeau Azure turned up Ermine a leopard statant Argent spotted Sable.
CATCHPOLE, of Mickfield, Letheringham. *Davy, A.*
On a cap of estate Gules turned up Ermine a leopard (or lion statant affronty) tail extended Or ducally crowned Argent.
MOWBRAY, Sir John Duke of Norfolk, Earl Marshal, K.G., died 1432. *Stall Plates, plate XXX*
On a cap of estate Gules turned up Ermine a leopard (or lion statant affronty) tail raised crowned Argent and gorged with a label of three points Argent.
MOWBRAY, Sir John Duke of Norfolk, Earl Marshal, K.G., died 1475/6. *Stall Plates, plate LXXVI*
On a chapeau Gules turned up Ermine a demi-lion rampant.
GILMAN. *MS Ordinary of Arms, fo. 14*
On a chapeau Gules turned up Ermine a demi-lion rampant Or.
GILMAN. *MS ex-Taylor Coll.*
On a chapeau Gules turned up Ermine a demi-lion passant [*sic*] Or between two dragon's wings expanded Gules each charged with two bars Ermine.
HILL, of Buxhall. *Davy, A. 'Rev. Henry Copinger Hill, Buxhall Rectory, Stowmarket.' Fairbairn*
On a cap of maintenance Gules trimmed Ermine a demi-lion statant Or between two wings Gules charged with two bars Ermine.

HILL, Thomas, Lord of the manor of Buxhall, died 1746. *Her.Suff.Ch., Wall tablet and Bench end, Buxhall*
On a cap of estate Azure charged with fleurs-de-lis Or turned up Ermine a lion passant Or langued Gules.
BEAUMONT, Sir John, K.G., died 1396. *MS Heraldic Alphabet. Stall Plates, plate XV*
On a chapeau Azure charged with fleurs-de-lis Or and turned up Ermine a lion passant Or
BEAUMONT, of Haverhill. *MS Martin's Crests. Davy, A.*
On a chapeau Gules turned up Ermine a lion statant guardant collared and ducally crowned.
BOCKINGHAM, of Suffolk. *Washbourne*, 'Bockingham, Suff.' Bokenham Family, 68 (Berry). Fairbairn, 'Bockingham, Suff.'*
On a chapeau – turned up Ermine a lion statant guardant collared and ducally crowned tail extended.
BOCKINGHAM, BOKENHAM. Rev. Joseph Bokenham, Rector of Stoke Ash, 1718. *Bokenham Family*
On a chapeau Gules turned up Ermine a lion statant guardant to the sinister tail extended Or gorged with a ducal coronet Argent.
BROTHERTON, Thomas de Earl of Norfolk. *Davy, A., 'now the crest of Howard'*
On a chapeau Ermine and Gules a lion passant Argent armed and langued Gules.
COLVILE, of Hemingstone. *Sharpe*
On a chapeau Gules turned up Ermine a lion rampant Argent.
COLVILE, of Hemingstone, Lawshall. *Davy, A.*
On a chapeau Gules turned up Argent a lion statant tail extended Argent gorged with a label of three points Gules.
COLVILE, of Carlton Colvile. *Colvile*
On a chapeau Gules turned up Ermine a lion statant Or.
COLVILLE, Robert, of Newton Hall in the Isle of Ely and Hemingstone Hall, died 1799. *Her.Suff.Ch., Wall tablet, Hemingstone*
On a chapeau a lion statant tail extended.
COLVILLE. *Her.Suff.Ch., Tablet on side of South door, Hawstead*
On a chapeau Gules turned up Ermine a lion passant Argent gorged with a file of three lambeaux each charged with three bezants.
COVILL, of Parham. *Davy, A. (Edms.)*
On a chapeau Azure turned up Ermine a lion passant Gules.
ELLIS, of Orford. *Davy, A.*
On a chapeau Gules turned up Ermine a lion statant guardant crowned Or.
ENGLAND, King of *MS Ordinary of Arms, fo. 73*
On a chapeau Gules turned up Ermine a lion statant guardant Or crowned with a ducal coronet Azure and gorged with a collar counter-compony Argent and Azure.
FITZROY, Duke of Grafton. Of Euston. *Warren's map*. Kirby's map*. Davy, A. Burke's Peerage, 1891 ed.*
On a cap of maintenance Gules turned up Ermine a lion passant Argent the dexter foot on a cinquefoil Or.
GURNEY. 'Sir Thomas Gorney, of Stifford, co. Essex, High Sheriff in 1622; Confirmation of Arms and Crest by Camden, 1621. *Grants & Certificates (Stowe MS 706; Harl. MS 5,839)*

On a chapeau turned up Ermine a lion passant supporting his dexter paw on a cinquefoil.

> GURNEY, of Essex. *MS Heraldic Collections, fo. 86**

On a chapeau Gules turned up Ermine a lion seiant guardant Argent.

> HANMER, Bart., of Mildenhall. *Bokenham. Davy, A. Proc.S.I.A. IX. 114, Lt. Waldingfield church.* 'Sir Thomas Hanmer of Hanmer in Com. Flint, Baronet 1707' *Bookplates**

On a chapeau Azure turned up Ermine a lion seiant guardant Argent armed Gules.

> HANMER. *MS Martin's Crests.* Lt. Col. Lambert Hanmer, D.S.O., son of Admiral Hanmer of The Priory, Lt. Waldingfield, killed in action 1918. *Her.Suff.Ch., Brass tablet, Lt. Waldingfield*

On a cap of maintenance Gules turned up Ermine a lion statant Or between two wings Gules each wing charged with two bars Ermine.

> HILL, . . . , of London. Customer of Yarmouth. *Grants & Certificates (Stowe MS 707)*

On a chapeau Gules turned up Ermine a lion Purpure crowned Or.

> HOWARD. 'Lord of Sorrey [*sic* Surrey], Duke of Norfolk' *Harl. MS 6163*

On a chapeau Gules turned up Ermine a lion statant guardant his tail extended Or gorged with a ducal coronet Argent.

> HOWARD. Dukes of Norfolk and Earls of Suffolk. Of Framlingham, Bungay. *Sharpe. Davy, A.* Bernard Howard, 12th Duke of Norfolk, died 1842. *Her.Suff.Ch., Hatchment, Fornham St. Martin. Second crest for Thomas de Brotherton*

On a cap of maintenance Azure turned up Ermine a lion passant guardant Ermine crowned Or the dexter foot resting on a lozenge Gules.

> HULL, Joseph, of Stoke-next-Nayland, co. Suffolk, J.P. and an Utter Barrister at-Law of Lincoln's Inn; Confirmation of Arms with difference and Grant of Crest by Sir W. Dugdale, Garter and Sir H. St. George, Clarenceux, 7 February 1680. *Grants & Certificates (Stowe MS 714)*

'On a Chapeau azure turned up Ermin a Lyon passant guardant of the same crounnedd with a Ducall coronet Or, resting his dexter Paw upon a Lozenge Gules'

> HULL, of Stoke by Nayland. Grant of Arms and Crest to Joseph Hull of Stoke by Nayland, Barrister of Lincoln's Inn, by Sir William Dugdale, Garter, 7 February 1680. *Misc.Gen. et Her. 5th S. X. 93–4 (Stowe MS 714, fo. 98b)*

On a chapeau Gules turned up Ermine a lion passant Argent.

> LOVE. *MS ex-Taylor Coll.**

On a chapeau – turned up Ermine a lion statant tail extended between the attires of a stag.

> MOWBRAY. *MS Ordinary of Arms, fo. 18**

On a chapeau a lion between a pair of dragon's wings.

> MOWBRAY. Dukes of Norfolk. Of Framlingham, Bungay. *Davy, A.*

On a chapeau Gules turned up Argent a lion Azure.

> PERCY. 'Therle of Northehumberland'. *Harl. MS 6163*

On a chapeau Gules turned up Ermine a lion statant tail extended Azure.

> PERCY. *MS Ordinary of Arms, fo. 18**. Percy, Earl of Northumberland. Bishop of Norwich, 1355. Of Cratfield. *Davy, A.*

On a cap of estate Gules turned up Ermine a lion statant tail extended Or.

> TALBOT, Sir Gilbert, K.G., died 1419. *Stall Plates, plate XXIV**

On a chapeau Gules turned up Ermine a lion statant Or tail extended.

> TALBOT, Earl of Shrewsbury. Of Hintlesham, Walsham le Willows. *MS Ordinary of Arms, fo. 35**. *Davy, A.*

ON A CHAPEAU

BIRD [In alphabetical order]

On a chapeau Gules turned up Ermine a cock with wings elevated Gules beaked Or legged Sable.

> THEOBALD, of Barking. *Visitation 1664–8**. *Sharpe*

On a chapeau a cock with wings displayed Gules.

> THEOBALD, of Barking, Henley. *Bokenham. Davy, A., Henley church Hatchment. Washbourne*, 'Suff.' E.A.N. & Q. VI. 12*

On a chapeau Gules and Ermine a cock Gules.

> THEOBALD, John Meadows Theobald, of Claydon Hall; first wife, died 1809. *Her.Suff.Ch., Hatchment, Henley*

On a chapeau an eagle with wings expanded and invected all Proper.

> CODINGTON, of Ixworth. *Davy, A., church*

On a chapeau Proper a falcon rising Or.

> BROOK, of Ash. *Bokenham*

On a chapeau Proper a falcon volant Proper with bells, wings, legs and beak Or.

> BROOKE, of Ash. *Davy, A.*

On a chapeau Gules a martlet Argent.

> ARUNDEL, of Peyton Hall. *Davy, A.*

On a chapeau Gules turned up Ermine a martlet Sable.

> BLAGUE. *Davy, A.*

On a chapeau Azure turned up Ermine an ostrich close Argent holding in its beak a horseshoe Or.

> COOKE, COKE. 'Arthure Cooke of Thurington [*sic* Thorington] in Com Suffolke esquier 2ᵈ sonne to Sr Edward Cooke of Norffolke Kᵗ. *MS Lilly's Visitation of Suffolk**. Coke, of Huntingfield. *Davy, A.*

On a chapeau Sable turned up Ermine an ostrich close Argent holding in its beak a horseshoe Argent.

> COOKE, of Mendham. *Davy, A. Washbourne, 'Suff.' Fairbairn*, 'Suff.'*

On a chapeau Gules turned up Ermine an owl Gules sitting in holly leaves Vert.

> INGHAM, of Weybread, Theberton, Yoxford. *Davy, A., Letheringham church*

On a chapeau Gules turned up Ermine an owl Argent.

> INGHAM, Thomas, Gentleman, late of this Parish, died 1720. *Proc.S.I.A. VII. 231, Wall monument, Theberton*

On a chapeau Gules turned up Ermine a demi-peacock displayed Argent.

> MAWLE, of Bury. *Davy, A. Fairbairn, 'Suff.'*

On a chapeau Gules turned up Ermine a peacock in his pride Proper.

> MANNERS, Duke of Rutland. Of Moulton, Lidgate, Newmarket. *Davy, A. Fairbairn*, 'George E.J. Manners, of Fornham Park, Bury St. Edmunds'*

On a chapeau Gules turned up Ermine a peacock in his pride.

> MANNERS, Lord Of Fornham. *Davy, A.*

On a chapeau Gules turned up Ermine a peacock in his pride Proper.

> ROOS, of Mildenhall. *Banners & Standards*. Davy, A.*

On a cap of maintenance Gules turned up Argent a pelican vulning herself Proper.

PLAYFAIR. Hon. Lyon Playfair, Captain R.F.A., killed in action 1915 aged 26. *Her.Suff.Ch., Glass, Redgrave*

ON A CHAPEAU

HEAD. BEAST

On a chapeau turned up Ermine a boar's head couped Argent.

THIRWALL, of Norfolk. *MS Ordinary of Arms, fo. 102**

On a chapeau Gules turned up Argent a boar's head couped at the neck Argent.

THIRWALL. *MS Heraldic Alphabet. Davy, A.*

On a chapeau Azure turned up Ermine a stag's head cabossed Or.

BAKER, of Wrentham, Wattisfield. 'Thomas Baker' *MS Knight's Visitations, Norf.*, attires Sable.* 'Thomas Baker' *MS Philpot's Visitations, Norf.*, attires Sable. Davy, A., Wattisfield church*

On a chapeau Azure turned up Ermine a buck's head Argent attired Sable.

BAKER. *MS Heraldic Alphabet*

On a chapeau Sable turned up Ermine a lion's head couped Or pellety.

COLBECK, COLBECKE. *MS Heraldic Collections, fo. 56**

On a chapeau Sable turned up Ermine a lion's head erased Sable bezanty.

COLBECK. *MS ex-Taylor Coll.**

On a chapeau Gules turned up Ermine a lion's head erased Or pellety.

COLBECK. Vicar of Fressingfield. *Davy, A.*

HEAD. BIRD

On a chapeau Azure turned up Ermine an eagle's head Argent ducally crowned Or charged on the neck with a cross Gules.

PARSONS. Rector of Hadleigh. *Davy, A.*

HEAD. HUMAN

On a chapeau Gules turned up Ermine a head in profile couped at the shoulders Proper.

HESELRIGE, Bart., of Hoxne. *Davy, A.*

On a chapeau Gules lined Ermine a Scot's head Proper.

HESELRIGE. Sir Thomas Heselrige, Bart., formerly Maynard, of Hoxne manor, died 1817. *Betham's Baronetage. I. 264. Copinger. IV. 52*

ON A CHAPEAU

MONSTER

On a chapeau – turned up Ermine a panther statant guardant Argent spotted Gules and Azure vulning herself [for difference].

SOMERSET, of Wickhambrook. *Visitation 1561 (MSS G.7* and Iveagh Copy*)*

On a cap of maintenance Gules turned up Ermine a panther statant guardant Argent spotted Gules and Azure fire issuing from his mouth and ears Proper.

SOMERSET, of Badmondsfield [Hall] in Wickhambrook. *Visitation 1561 (ed. Metcalfe). Harl. 772**

On a chapeau Gules and Ermine a salamander in flames Proper.

DOUGLAS. *Her.Suff.Ch., Hatchments, Easton. The crest for Dukes of Hamilton*

Out of a coronet placed on a chapeau Proper a tiger

seiant Ermine gorged with a coronet Or on his head two horns 'forthright like an Ibeck' [Ibex].

JOHNSON, of Lavenham. *Bokenham*

On a chapeau Gules turned up Ermine a wyvern disclosed Vert winged Or.

AUDELEY. 'Audeley' *MS Knight's Visitations, Essex**

On a chapeau Gules turned up Ermine a wyvern disclosed Azure winged Or.

'AUDLEY'. *MS Philpot's Visitations, Essex**

On a chapeau Gules turned up Argent a wyvern disclosed quarterly Or and Azure.

AUDLEY, AWDLEY, of Barton. *Visitation 1664–8*. Davy, A.*

On a chapeau a wyvern.

CATCHPOLE, of Ipswich. *Davy, A.*

On a chapeau Gules turned up Ermine a wyvern sans legs wings expanded Argent.

FITZHUGH, Lord *Davy, A.*

On a chapeau Gules turned up Argent a wyvern wings elevated Or.

PIRTON, PYRTON, of Essex. *MS Ordinary of Arms, fo. 87**

On a chapeau Azure turned up Ermine a wyvern with wings elevated Vert.

PYRTON, of Essex. *MS Heraldic Alphabet*

On a chapeau Azure turned up Ermine a wyvern with wings expanded Vert.

PIRTON, PYRTON, of Ipswich. *Davy, A.*

On a chapeau a wyvern Argent tail nowed wings expanded checky Or and Azure.

WARREN, Earl of Surrey. Of Gt. Falkenham. *Davy, A.*

ON A CHAPEAU

VARIOUS [In alphabetical order]

On a chapeau Gules turned up Ermine a cross moline in a wreath.

KIRBY, of Ipswich. *Davy, A.*

On a chapeau Gules an escallop between two wings Proper.

HUGGEN, HUGGENS. *Davy, A. Washbourne*, 'Hogan'. Fairbairn*, 'Hogan'*

A chapeau Gules turned up Ermine therefrom two ostrich feathers Or.

PEDE. 'Richard Peade, of Bury St. Edmond's in Suffolk, son of Thomas of the same place, Registrar to the Bishop of Norwich; Grant by Sir R. St. George, Clarenceux, 28 February 1624. *Grants & Certificates (Harl. MS 1,105)*

A chapeau Gules turned up Ermine with two ostrich feathers one on each side dexter Or sinister Azure.

PEDE, of Bury. *Davy, A. Washbourne*, 'Suff.' Fairbairn*, 'of Bury, Suff.'*

A chapeau Azure turned up Ermine on each side an ostrich feather erect Gules.

UVEDALE, UNYDALL. *MS Heraldic Collections, fo. 59**

A chapeau Azure turned up Ermine on each side stuck in the turn-up an ostrich feather erect Argent.

UVEDALE. *Davy, A.*

On a chapeau Gules turned up Ermine a plume of ostrich feathers Argent out of a ducal coronet Or.

ASHLEY. *Washbourne*, five feathers.* Thomas Ashley, ? of Groton. *E.A.N. & Q. (N.S.) II. 410, Seal*

A cap of estate surmounted by an escutcheon of the arms [A fesse between two chevrons] above which issuant a panache of feathers.

TENDRING, of Stoke by Nayland. 'William

Tendrynge, 14 Ric. II.' [1390/1]. *Visitation 1561 (ed. Howard) I. 42*, Seal.* Sir William Tendring, Brass of 1408 in Stoke by Nayland church. *Cotman's Suffolk Brasses, plate 8*.* [The feathers of crest only showing]
On a chapeau – turned up Ermine a fish in pale head downwards.
    GURNEY, of Norfolk. *MS Heraldic Collections, fo. 81b*. Washbourne*, 'Norf.'*
On a chapeau a quatrefoil pierced Ermine in the centre a bezant.
    BOHUN, BOHAM, of Fressingfield, Westhall, Beccles, Chelmondiston. *Harl. 772*. Davy, A. Washbourne, 'Suff.' Fairbairn, 'Bohun of Tressingfield [sic], Suff.' Her.Suff.Ch., Westhall.* William Bohun, M.D., died 1743; widow Prudence, died 1771. *Ledger stone, Beccles*
On a chapeau Proper a quatrefoil Ermine voided.
    BOHUN, of Westhall. *Bokenham*
On a chapeau a quatrefoil pierced.
    BOHUN, Edmund, Esq., died 1734. *Her.Suff.Ch., Ledger stone, Westhall.*
On a chapeau Gules turned up Ermine a gauntlet Proper grasping a cutlass Argent hilt and pommel Or.
    CRESPIGNY, of Hintlesham, Aldeburgh. *Davy, A.*
On a 'thin Velamen or kind of Bonnet' Gules turned up Ermine the attire of a bull [*sic* horn] Argent pointed Or tipped Sable.
    ASTON. *MS Martin's Crests, 'ye ancient Crest'. Fairbairn, 'a chapeau'.*
On a cap of estate Gules turned up Ermine a bugle horn Sable garnished Or.
    BRYAN. 'Sir Guy de Bryen', K.G., died 1390. *Stall Plates, plate IX**
On a chapeau Gules turned up Ermine a bugle horn Or sans strings tipped and garnished Sable.
    BRYAN. *Davy, A.*
On a chapeau Gules turned up Ermine a bezant within four crescents points inward Ermine.
    BOHUN, of Fressingfield, Chelmondiston, Westhall. *Visitation 1561 (MSS G.7* and Iveagh Copy*)*
On a chapeau Gules turned up Ermine a bezant in the centre of four crescents Ermine.
    BOHUN, of Fressingfield, Chelmondiston, Westhall Hall, Beccles. 'Sr de Bohun de Suff.' *MS Ordinary of Arms, fo. 194*. Bohun*, drawn*
On a chapeau a bezant between four half moons Ermine.
    BOHUN. *Davy, A. (Barrett MS)*
On a chapeau Gules turned up Ermine two sceptres in saltire Or.
    MALLOW, MALLOWS, of Wattisfield, Bury, Eye. *Davy, A.*
On a chapeau – turned up Ermine two swords erect.
    GAWDY, GAWDYE, of Mendham, Norfolk. *Visitation 1561 (MS G.7*)*
On a chapeau Gules turned up Ermine two swords erect on their hilts Argent hilts and pommels Or.
    GAWDY, GAWDYE, of Crow's Hall in Debenham, Mendham, Ipswich. *Visitation 1561 (Iveagh Copy*) and (ed. Metcalfe).* 'Thomas Gawdy of Halneston' [*sic*] *MS Knight's Visitations, Norf.* Davy, A. Washbourne, 'Gawdy, Norf. and Suff.' Fairbairn, 'Gawdy, Norf. and Suff.' Gawdy*
A chapeau turned up Or on which two daggers in pale Argent hilted Or.
    GAWDY. *Wyncoll, 22*
On a chapeau Gules and Ermine two swords palewise Proper.

GAWDY, Sir Charles, died 1650. *Her.Suff.Ch., Hatchment, Debenham*
From a cap of maintenance two swords palewise hilts in base.
    GAWDY, Sir Charles, died 1650. *Her.Suff.Ch., Brass coffin plate on south wall of chancel, Debenham*
On a chapeau a tower Proper.
    ELMY, of Nettlestead, Rumburgh. *Davy, A. Muskett. I. 196 (Davy, Barrett MS)*
On a chapeau Gules turned up Ermine a wing Gules charged with a chevron Argent thereon a lion rampant Sable crowned Or.
    BROOK, BROOKE, of Aspal, Athelington, Woodbridge, Ufford Place. 'George Brooke of Aspall Esquier' *MS Lilly's Visitation of Suffolk*. Green Memoir, 67. Gage (Thingoe). Davy, A. Washbourne*, 'Brooke, Suff.' Burke, L.G. 1853 and 1900 eds. Fairbairn*, 'Brooke, of Ufford Place, Suff.'* Robert Brooke, soldier, died 1646. *Her.Suff.Ch., Wall tablet, Yoxford.* Francis Brooke, of Woodbridge, died 1799; Others. *Hatchments, Ufford.* Arthur John Brooke, of Horringer, died 1818. *Votive tablet in tower, Horringer*
On a chapeau a wing charged with a chevron and thereon a lion rampant crowned.
    BROOKE, George, Gent., died 1752; son George Green Brooke, died 1764. *Her.Suff.Ch., Altar tomb, churchyard, Athelington*
On a chapeau turned up Ermine a wing Ermine charged with a chevron Argent thereon a lion rampant Sable crowned Or.
    BROOKS, William, Gent., late of Horringer, died 1795; Isaac Brooks, died 1812. *Her.Suff.Ch., Ledger stone (partly hatched), Westley*
On a chapeau a wing Argent charged with a Catherine wheel Azure.
    JOYCE, of Helmingham. *Davy, A., Sotterley church*
On a chapeau Sable turned up Ermine a wing Argent.
    MARNAY, MARNEY. *MS Ordinary of Arms, fo. 67**
On a chapeau Gules turned up Ermine a wing per fesse Or and Vair.
    TICHBORNE, of Withersfield. *Davy, A.*
On a chapeau Azure lined Ermine two wings erect and addorsed Or.
    D'EYE, of Eye, Thrandeston. *Davy, A.*
On a cap of maintenance Azure turned up Ermine two wings displayed and elevated.
    D'EYE, of Eye. 'N. D'Eye, Eye' *Misc.Gen. et Her. 2nd S. IV. 24, bookplate**
On a chapeau two wings displayed.
    D'EYE, Nathaniel, died 1718; Francis D'Eye, died 1772; Lorina D'Eye, died 1777. *Her.Suff.Ch., Ledger stones, Eye.* Thomas D'Eye, clerk, late Rector of Palgrave, died 1766. *Ledger stone, churchyard, Oakley. Not found 1988.* Rev. Nathaniel D'Eye, M.A., Rector of Thrandeston, died 1844. *Wall tablet, Thrandeston*
On a chapeau Gules turned up Ermine two wings displayed Argent.
    HENGRAVE. 'Herngrave of Norfolk.' *MS Heraldic Alphabet (Vincent No. 153, fo. 72)*
Out of a chapeau Sable turned up Argent a pair of wings Argent.
    MARNEY. 'S. Herry Marney' *Harl. MS 6163*
On a Duke's hat Sable turned up Ermine about it a lace Or two wings in pale rased.

MARNEY. 'Marny of Lyre Marney in Essex'
Wall's Book
'to his Crest ij Wyngs ar in pale rased standing on a
Duks hat sa/ Dobled [ermine spot drawn] a bowt the
hat a lace or/'
MARNEY. 'Marny of lyre Marny in Essex'
MS Alphabet of Crests, fo. 80
A chapeau Sable lined Ermine winged on the top
Argent.
MARNEY, of Nedging. *Davy, A.*
On a chapeau Gules turned up Ermine two wings
Or.
SEYMOUR. *MS Heraldic Alphabet, 'wings
elevated'. Davy, A.*
On a chapeau Gules turned up Ermine two wings
Azure each charged with a bend Ermine between six
billets Or.
SMITH, John, of Halesworth, co. Suffolk. *Grants
& Certificates (Harl. MS 1,359).*
On a chapeau Gules turned up Ermine two wings
Azure billety Or and on each a bend Ermine.
SMITH, SMYTHE, of Halesworth, Holton. *Soc. of
Ant. MS 378, 'Grant p' Cooke, Clar., 1588'.
Davy, A. Washbourne, 'Suff.' Fairbairn, 'Smith,
Smyth, of Halesworth, Suff.'*
On a chapeau turned up Ermine two wings billety
each charged with a bend Ermine.
SMITH. 'Jo Smith of hallesworth in Suff.'
MS Heraldic Collections, fo. 90*

CHAPLET or GARLAND see also WREATH
On a laurel garland Vert a lion statant Argent.
BOOTH. *MS Ordinary of Arms, fo. 105**
On a laurel garland Proper a lion passant Argent.
BOOTH. *MS Martin's Crests*
In a chaplet of flowers a dove Proper.
DOVE, of Suffolk. *MS Fairfax*
A garland between two laurel branches all Proper.
LOWRY. The Hon. Henry W. Lowry-Corry, of
Edwardstone Hall, Boxford, Suffolk.
Fairbairn*, second crest – for Lowry. Armar
Lowry-Corry, 3rd Earl of Belmore, died 1845;
widow died 1904. *Her.Suff.Ch., Brass tablet,
Edwardstone.* Henry William Lowry Corry, of
Edwardstone Hall, died 1927. *Glass,
Edwardstone*
On a chaplet Vert flowered Or a pelican Or vulned
Gules.
PELL, . . . , of Dembleby, co. Linc.; Grant by R.
Lee, Clarenceux, 19 October 1594. *Grants &
Certificates (Add. MS 14,295; Harl. MS 6,169)*
On a chaplet Vert flowered Or a pelican Or vulned
Gules.
PELL, of Bungay, Henstead, Kettleburgh. *Davy,
A., Henstead church*
Within a garland of leaves Vert with a rose in each
quarter Gules a bee volant Sable.
SEWELL, SEWAYL. *MS Ordinary of Arms, fo. 201**
Within a chaplet or garland of flowers and leaves
Proper a moth or butterfly volant Argent.
SEWELL, of Stutton. *Sharpe*
In a chaplet of roses Argent leaved Vert a bee volant
Argent.
SEWELL, of Alton Hall in Stutton. *Davy, A.*
Issuant from a chaplet of roses Gules a horse's head
couped Argent maned Or and holding in the mouth
a broken spear in bend Or.
WOODS, Thomas, Rose Cottage, Lowestoft,
Suffolk. *Fairbairn*

CHESS-ROOK
A chess rook Sable between two wings Argent.

ROOKWOOD, of Euston. *Bokenham. Davy, A.* Sir
Edward Rookwood-Gage, 9th Bart., died 1872.
*Her.Suff.Ch., Hatchment, Hengrave. Second crest,
the first for Gage [q.v.]*
A chess-rook Argent.
ROOKWOOD. 'Thomas Rokewode, of Coldham
Hall, died 1726' *Her.Suff.Ch., Hatchment*
[recorded by Edmund Farrer in 1901 and by
Harold Hawes in 1953 as one of three in poor
condition then in the Rectory coach-house,
Stanningfield. Since disappeared.]
A chess-rook Or between two wings erect Argent.
ROOKWOOD. Thomas Rookwood, died 1726;
Elizabeth, wife of Robert Gage Rookwood, died
1827; he died 1838. *Her.Suff.Ch., Slabs inside
altar rails, Stanningfield*
On a chess-rook Argent a wren Proper.
SMALL, of Hadleigh, Ipswich. *Davy, A.*

CLAW
An eagle's claw erased.
ARNOLD. August Walter Arnold, of London, died
at Gifford's Hall, 1889. *Her.Suff.Ch., Tomb,
churchyard, Shelley*

CLOUD
[Associated objects in alphabetical order]
Issuing out of a cloud Argent and Azure an arm
fessewise Proper holding in the hand a bunch of
seven feathers alternately Gules and Argent.
BLACKNELL, BLAKENHALL. *MS Heraldic
Collections, fo. 58*. Washbourne*, 'Blacknoll'.
Six feathers*
Issuing out of clouds a cubit arm erect vested Azure
cuffed Argent holding in the hand a bunch of
? gillyflowers leaved Vert fructed Or.
CARSEY. 'Thomas Carsey of southbarowe'.
MS Knight's Visitations, Norf.*
Issuing out of clouds Argent and Azure a cubit arm
erect vested Azure slashed Argent holding in the
hand a bunch of gillyflowers 'grey' [sic] leaved
Vert.
CARSEY. 'Thomas Carsey'. *MS Philpot's
Visitations, Norf.**
A cubit arm in armour fesseways issuing from a
cloud all Proper the hand grasping by its stand a
terrestrial globe Or.
FIELD, John, of Ardesloe, co. York, gent.;
Confirmation of Arms and Grant of Crest by W.
Hervey, Clarenceux, 4 September 1558. *Grants
& Certificates (Add. MS 14,295; Harl. MS 1,359).*
Frederick Field, A.M., Rector of Gt. Saxham and
of Reepham, co. Norf. *Bookplate*, note attached*
A dexter arm issuing from clouds fesseways holding
in the hand a sphere.
FIELD, of Sutton. *Davy, A. (Mr. B.)*
A dexter arm in armour issuing out of clouds
fesseways Proper and holding in the hand also
Proper a sphere Or.
FIELD. *Her.Suff.Ch., Stained glass shield in
vestry 'Presented by H.W. Field', Debach. Now a
private house, so not seen 1982*
Out of clouds Azure a cubit arm habited per pale
Azure and Gules holding in the hand Argent a
pheon Sable.
HOLT, of Bury St. Edmunds. *Visitation 1561
(MSS G.7* and Iveagh Copy*) and (ed. Howard.
II. 45*. Clouds untinctured.)*
A cubit arm in armour erect issuing from clouds
Proper holding in the gauntlet a marigold a rose and
a pomegranate all Proper and environed with a ducal
coronet Or.

ROCHESTER, of Eriswell. *Davy, A.*
Issuing from clouds Proper an arm in armour embowed the gauntlet grasping a falchion all Proper garnished Or.

SALMON, Thomas, of Hackney, co. Middx., an Alderman and merchant of London; Confirmation by W. Segar, Clarenceux and Sir R. St. George, Norroy, 23 February 1621. Also Confirmation by W. Segar, as Norroy. *Grants & Certificates (Harl. MS 6,140; Add. MSS 12,225 and 14,295; Stowe MS 714)*

Out of the clouds Proper a dexter arm couped at the elbow and erect habited Argent charged with four sinister bends Sable holding in the hand Proper a club Proper, over it this motto 'Frappe fort'.

WODEHOUSE, of Ashbocking. *Davy, A.*
From clouds Proper a demi-lion Gules semy of fleurs-de-lis Or.

LENNARD, Sampson; Grant by R. Cooke, Clarenceux, and Chester, in 1584. Confirmation by Sir. W. Segar, Garter, 1626. *Grants & Certificates (Harl. MS 6,140; Stowe MS 670)*

Upon a cloud Proper a crescent Gules issuing fire.

WILSON, of Redgrave. *Davy, A.*
On a cloud Proper a crescent Gules flaming Or.

WILSON, George, Admiral of the Red, died 1826; George St. Vincent Wilson, died 1852; George Holt Wilson, High Sheriff, died 1924; G.R. Holt Wilson, died 1929. *Her.Suff.Ch., Hatchments, Redgrave.* [Crescent of the last hatchment is Argent, against the black background]

Issuing from a cloud Proper a fleur-de-lis Argent.

HART, of Orford. *Davy, A.*
A hand issuing from a cloud fessewise reaching to a garland of laurel Proper.

BUCTON, of Brome, Oakley. *Davy, A. Washbourne**

Out of a cloud a dexter hand erect pointing to a star all Proper.

BUMSTED, of Sotterley. *Davy, A., church. Washbourne**, 'Bumstead or Bumsted, Suff.'

Out of a cloud a dexter hand brandishing a scimitar Proper.

CHARTRES. Elizabeth, widow of Rev. James Chartres, M.A., Vicar of Godmanchester and West Haddon, died 1840. *Her.Suff.Ch., Monument, Mettingham*

Out of a cloud in the sinister a dexter hand fesseways Proper holding a cross paty fitchy Azure.

CORNELIUS, of Ipswich, Nacton. *Davy, A.*
A hand issuing from a cloud fesseways lifting a garb Proper.

LARK. *Davy, A.*
Issuant out of a cloud Proper a star of six points waved Argent.

STODARD, STODART, of Layham. *Davy, A.*
The sun in splendour rising from clouds all Proper, above 'Clarior e Tenebris'.

PURVIS, of Darsham. *Sharpe. Davy, A. Burke, L.G. 1853 ed.*

The sun breaking from behind a cloud Proper.

PURVIS, of Darsham House, Suff. *Washbourne**, *with motto as above.* Charles Purvis, of Darsham House, died 1808. *Her.Suff.Ch., Wall tablet and Hatchment, Darsham*

CLUB

'On a Wreath of the Colours In front of a demi Lion [rampant] Vert charged on the shoulder with two Barrulets dancette Or holding in the dexter paw and resting on the sinister paw a Battle-axe erect [in front]

a Club fessewise entwined with a Serpent proper'.

EMERSON, Peter Henry, M.R.C.S., of Oulton, co. Suffolk; Grant by Sir Albert Woods, Garter, 24 September 1897. *Emerson, 4th booklet, 2, Photograph**

Three clubs one erect and two in saltire Or knotted Gules enfiled with a ducal coronet Or.

COOKE, of Langham, Badwell Ash. *Davy, A.*

COLUMN or PILLAR

On a pedestal a pillar erected Gules crowned and garnished Or.

EDGAR, of Eye. *Bokenham*
A pillar between two wings Or.

EDGAR. *E.A.N. & Q. I. 312, Stone, Eye church*
On two tiers a pillar Gules crowned Or between two wings in lure Or.

EDGAR, of Eye. *Proc.S.I.A. II. 145, Monument, Eye church*

Between two wings expanded a column on the summit thereof a ducal coronet.

EDGAR, of Eye. *E.A. Misc. 1917, 7, church*
A column on the summit thereof a ducal coronet between two wings expanded.

EDGAR, Miles, Gent., of Eye [no date given]; Henry Edgar, Esq., of Eye [no date given]; daughter Susan, married Robert Yaxley, died 1734. *Her.Suff.Ch., Ledger stones, Eye*

A 'piller' fesseways Argent and seated thereon an ounce Proper.

GALL, of Wenhaston, London. *London Visitation 1568 (H.S.), 142*

A snake Proper entwined round a broken column Argent.

HARRISON, of Martlesham. *Davy, A.*
A Corinthian column broken Argent entwined with a snake Proper.

HARRISON, of Palgrave. *Davy, A.*
A Doric pillar Argent entwined with a laurel branch Vert on the top a flame Proper.

LAMPET, of Brightwell, Thorndon. *Davy, A.*
On a pillar enfiled with a ducal coronet an eagle Argent beaked and armed Or.

LEE. Quartered by Guinness, for Viscount Iveagh. *Her.Suff.Ch., Glass, Eleveden*

A crescent Argent in front of a column Or.

MAYDSTON, of Akenham. *Visitation 1664–8*
A pillar crowned between two wings expanded.

MINTER, of Tuddenham. *E.A.N. & Q. XI. 167, Slab and Tomb, churchyard, Tuddenham*

A column Sable in the sea Proper.

PAGANEL. *Davy, A.*
An architectural pillar Azure crowned Or and winged at the base Or.

PELLSE, Robert, of Cransford in Suffolk, son and heir of John Pellse of the same. *Grants & Certificates (Harl MS 1,105)*

A pillar compony Or and Gules supported by two lion's gambs erased and embowed the dexter Ermine the sinister Ermines.

SCARLETT. Confirmation of Arms and Grant of Crest, February 1611. *Grants & Certificates (Harl. MS 6,059; Stowe MS 706)*

ON OR OUT OF CORONET or CROWN
[MURAL CORONET see following section]

BEAST. BEAR

Out of a ducal coronet a bear Proper muzzled Or.

BRERETON, of Hoxne, Framsden. *Davy, A.*

DOG

On a ducal coronet a ? dog passant.

GLEANE, John, Gent., died 1664. *Her.Suff.Ch., Ledger stone, South Elmham St. Cross or St. George*

Out of a ducal coronet Or a demi-greyhound Sable.
  ROBERTS, of Whatfield, Hadleigh. *MS Heraldic Alphabet, 'salient'. Davy, A.*

On a ducal coronet a talbot passant Proper collared and lined Or.
  GROSS. *Davy, A.*

On a ducal coronet a talbot passant all Argent.
  MARCH. 'Thomas March' *MS Knight's Visitations, Cambs.**

On a ducal coronet Or a water 'spaniell' passant Argent.
  MARCH. *Cambs. Visits. (H.S.) 82*

From a crest coronet Argent a demi-talbot Or.
  MORLEY, John, of Barnes, co. Southampton [*sic*]; Grant by R. Cooke, Clar., in 1575. *Grants & Certificates (Harl. MS 6,140)*

Out of a ducal coronet Argent a demi-talbot rampant Or.
  MORLEY, of Saxham. *Davy, A.*

ERMINE

On a crest coronet Or an ermine passant Argent on the tail an Ermine spot Sable.
  LAWES. Thomas Lawse, D.C.L., late of Norfolk, now of Kent; Grant by R. Cooke, Clarenceux, 1584. *Grants & Certificates (Stowe MS 670; Add. MS 14,359; Harl. MS 1,359)*

On a ducal coronet Or an ermine passant Proper.
  LAWES, LAWS, of Rickinghall Superior. *Davy, A., churchyard tomb. Partridge, 93 (Darby, 1828), untinctured.* Elizabeth Lawes, died 1727. *Her.Suff.Ch., Altar tomb, churchyard, Rickinghall Superior*

GOAT

Out of a coronet Sable a demi-goat salient Or.
  MUSKET, of Harleston. *Visitation 1612*

HORSE

Out of a coronet Or a demi-horse Ermine.
  STODDARD. *MS Fairfax (Tyl.)*

Out of a coronet Proper a demi-horse salient Ermine.
  STODARD, of Layham. *Bokenham*

LEOPARD

On a ducal coronet Or a leopard Argent spotted Sable.
  BENTALL, Alice, married Charles W. Grey, of Deerbolt Hall, died 1925. *Her.Suff.Ch., Altar tomb, churchyard, Earl Stonham*

Out of a ducal coronet Or a demi-leopard Argent.
  BUCKLE, of Wrentham, Worlingworth. *Davy, A.*

Out of a ducal coronet Or a demi-leopard rampant guardant Argent pellety.
  COBBES, of Bury. *Visitation 1664–8**

Out of a coronet a demi-leopard salient Argent spotted Sable.
  COBBS, of Bury. *Bokenham*

Out of a coronet a demi-leopard rampant guardant Azure pellety [*sic*].
  COBBES, of Bury, Gt. Saxham. *Davy, A., Gt. Saxham church*

DEMI-LION

On a coronet a demi-lion holding in the sinister paw a sword palewise.
  ALDOUS, Richard, died 1739; widow Mary, died 1753. *Her.Suff.Ch., Ledger stone, Huntingfield*

Out of a ducal coronet a demi-lion rampant Sable supporting a banner, or pennon, Gules charged with a lion passant Or the staff Proper.
  BROMLEY. *MS Heraldic Collections, fo. 54**

Out of a ducal coronet Proper a demi-lion rampant Argent supporting a cross crosslet fitchy Or.
  CAPELL, of Stanton. *Bokenham*

Out of a ducal coronet Or a demi-lion rampant Argent.
  CHURCHILL, of Dallinghoo. *MS Ordinary of Arms, fo. 39*. Davy, A.*

Out of a coronet a demi-lion rampant.
  CHURCHILL. *MS Martin's Crests*

Out of a ducal coronet Or a demi-lion issuant Azure.
  CLAVERING. *MS Heraldic Alphabet*

From a crest coronet Argent a demi-lion rampant guardant Sable armed and langued Gules.
  GOODRICH. 'Thomas Gooderich, of Hardwick, co. Suffolk, gent., son of Thomas Gooderich, of Bury S. Edmonds'; Granted by W. Dethick, Garter, 20 April 1594. *Grants & Certificates (Stowe MS 676, 'Conf. not Granted')*

Out of a ducal coronet Or a demi-lion rampant Argent holding between his paws a battle-axe Argent hafted Or.
  GOODRICH. 'Goderike' *MS Ordinary of Arms, fo. 45**

Out of a coronet a demi-lion rampant Sable supporting a halbert.
  GOODRICH. 'Sr. Henry Goodrick' *MS Martin's Crests*

Out of a ducal coronet Or a demi-lion rampant Argent langued Gules.
  HOLLOND, of Benhall. *Davy, A., Hatchment, church. Burke, L.G. 1853 ed. Fairbairn*, 'Holland, Benhall Lodge, Suff.' E.A. Misc. 1911, 19.* Edward Hollond, of Benhall Lodge, died 1829. *Her.Suff.Ch., Wall tablet, Benhall. Not langued*

Out of a ducal coronet Or a demi-lion rampant Argent.
  LONG. *MS Ordinary of Arms, fo. 30**

Out of a ducal coronet a demi-lion rampant holding in the paws a millpick.
  MOSELEY, Maurice, 'Rector of this parish', died 1705. *Her.Suff.Ch., Ledger stone, Market Weston*

Out of a crown Gules a demi-lion Ermine.
  NICHOLSON, of Ipswich. *MS Fairfax ('Visit. Book for Essex 1634')*

Out of a ducal coronet Or a demi-lion Argent holding a spear Gules headed Or.
  PETTUS, Bart. *Davy, A.*

Out of a ducal coronet Or a demi-lion Ermine vulned and holding erect a piece of a broken tilting spear Proper.
  PETTUS, Bart. *Davy, A.*

LION

A lion passant Sable maned and tufted Or out of a ducal coronet.
  EDWARDS. Master of Bury Grammer School. *Davy, A.*

Out of a coronet Proper a lion seiant Ermine.
  LACEY, of Spelman's Hall. *Bokenham*

Within a ducal coronet Or a lion erased [*sic*] Argent armed Gules.
  MAYHEW, of Colchester, co. Essex. *Sharpe*

On a ducal coronet a lion seiant Proper.
  MUMBEE. *Davy, A., Horringer church*

'In a crowne silver a Lyon seant golde'.
  RANT, John, Of Nowich; Confirmation of Arms

161   162

and Crest by Robert Cooke, Clarenceux, 1 June 1583. *Misc.Gen. et Her. 5th S. IX. 43*
On a ducal coronet Argent a lion sejant Or.
    RANT, of Ipswich. 'Humfray Rant of norwiche' *MS Knight's Visitations, Norf.* Sharpe.*
    Theophila (Freston), wife of Jacob Rant, Esq., died 1721. *Her.Suff.Ch., Ledger stone, Mendham*
On a ducal coronet Or a lion sejant Argent.
    RANT. *MS ex-Taylor Coll.**
On a crown vallary a lion rampant.
    STEWARD, Charles, Esq., of Blundeston. *Bookplate*, book presented May 1845*
A lion rampant Gules ducally gorged Or in a crown vallery Or.
    STEWART, of Ipswich. *Davy, A.*
On a mount Vert within a crown vallery Or a lion rampant Gules.
    STEWARD, STEWART, of Ipswich, Blundeston. *Davy, A. Fairbairn, 'Steward, Stoke Park, Suff.' and 'Stewart, Blundeston, Suff.'* Thomas Fowler Steward, of Gt. Yarmouth, died 1880. *Her.Suff.Ch., Wall brass, Gunton*

LYNX

On a ducal coronet Or a lynx passant guardant Argent.
    LYNCH, of Ipswich. *Davy, A.*

OTTER

Out of a ducal coronet Or an otter Vert.
    GLEANE, of South Elmham St. Cross. *Davy, A., church*

OX

Out of a naval coronet Argent a demi-bull rampant. Gules armed and hoofed Or.
    SAUNDERS, of Gunton. *Davy, A., 'Granted 3 May 1761'*

WOLF

On a ducal coronet Or a wolf passant Argent.
    MARCH, of Wordwell, Icklingham. *Davy, A.*
On a coronet a wolf passant.
    NORGATE, of Ashfield. *Davy, A.*

ON OR OUT OF MURAL CORONET or CROWN

BEAST. DOG

From a mural coronet Or a demi-greyhound Sable.
    ROBERTS, Thomas, of Lt. Braxted, Essex, gent.; Confirmation by Sir W. Segar, Garter, in 1626. *Grants & Certificates (Harl. MS 6,140; Add. MSS 12,225 and 14,293)*

DEMI-LION

Out of a mural crown a demi-lion rampant reguardant holding a sphere.
    ALDERSON. *Proc.S.I.A. IX. 224, Pewter dishes, Stowmarket church*
Out of a mural coronet Argent a demi-lion rampant guardant per pale Or and Sable holding in his dexter paw a sword erect Argent hilted Or.
    ALDHOUSE, of Huntingfield. *Davy, A.*
Out of a mural coronet a demi-lion rampant supporting a pennon Vert charged with a dragon, or griffin, passant.
    BROMLEY. *Bookplate**
In a mural coronet Gules a demi-lion double queued Argent.
    BURGHWASH, of Witnesham. *Davy, A.*
Out of a mural crown a demi-lion rampant Gules holding between his fore-gambs a key Or.
    CRIAL alias DE CROW, of Sole [sic] in Suffolk.

Misc.Gen. et Her. 5th S. III. 256
Out of a mural crown a demi-lion charged with three mullets Gules.
    GRIGBY, Joseph, died 1771. *Her.Suff.Ch., Wall tablet in the tower, St. Mary's, Bury*
From a mural coronet Sable a demi-lion rampant Or holding in its paws a battle axe staff Sable headed Or.
    HANBURY, Thomas, of East Mapledurham, co. Hants., Esq.; Arms and Crest confirmed at the Visitation of Hampshire in 1634 by John Philpot, Somerset Herald. Patents produced at Petersfield 9 August 1686 before Sir H. St. George, Clarenceux. *Grants & Certificates (Add. MS 14,297)*
Out of a mural coronet Sable a demi-lion rampant Or holding in his dexter paw a battle-axe Sable.
    HANBURY, of Bures, Assington, Wiston, Hacheston. *Davy, A., Seal*
Out of a mural coronet a demi-lion rampant holding up a palm branch all Proper.
    HEPWORTH, of Hepworth. *Davy, A.*
Out of a mural coronet Gules a demi-lion Or and Sable.
    KETTERIDGE, of Lowestoft. *Gillingwater, 423, 'demi lion couped'. Davy, A.*
Out of a mural coronet a demi-lion rampant.
    KITTREDGE, John, surgeon, died 1757. Of Gt. Yarmouth. *E.A.N. & Q. II. 284, Monument, church*
From a mural coronet Argent a demi-lion Sable holding in the dexter paw a pick axe Argent.
    MOSELEY, Maurice, of London, merchant; Confirmation of Arms and Grant of Crest by Sir W. Segar, Garter. *Grants & Certificates (Add. MS 12,225; Harl. MS 6,140)*
Out of a mural crown chequy Argent and Sable a demi-lion rampant Or holding in his dexter paw a millpick Proper headed Azure.
    MOSELEY, of Ousden. *London Visitation 1633 (H.S.) II. 114**
Out of a mural crown chequy Argent and Sable a demi-lion – holding in his dexter paw a mill pick Argent.
    MOSELEY, of Ousden, Gt. Glemham. *Davy, A. Fairbairn, 'Moseley, Mosley. Of Owsden [sic], Suff.'* John Moseley, late of Richmond, Surrey, died 1775. *Her.Suff.Ch., Wall tablet, Ousden. Millpick missing.* William Moseley, died 1785. *Slab, Fornham All Saints*
Out of a mural crown a demi-lion rampant.
    MOSELEY, of Gt. Glemham House near Saxmundham *Burke, L.G. 1853 ed.*
Out of a mural coronet chequy Argent and Sable a demi-lion Or holding in the dexter paw a pickaxe Proper.
    MOSELEY-LOFFT, Henry Capell, of Glemham House, Suff. *Fairbairn, first crest – for Moseley*
Out of a mural crown Or a demi-lion rampant Azure holding a fleur-de-lis Or.
    SANDWITH, of Bury. *Lincs. Visitation Notes (Gibbons), 139*
Out of a mural coronet Argent a demi-lion rampant guardant Or sans tail supporting a broad sword hilt and pommel Or.
    SIMPSON. 'Symson' *MS Heraldic Alphabet*
Out of a mural coronet a demi-lion rampant holding in the dexter paw a sword in pale.
    SIMPSON. 'Admiral C.H. Simpson, of Rhydian, Stoke-by-Nayland, Suff.' *Fairbairn*
Out of a mural coronet Proper a demi-lion Or holding between the paws a spur erect Argent winged Gules.

STONEY. 'Francis Goold Stoney, Esq., of Ipswich' *Fairbairn*

Out of a mural crown Or a demi-lion rampant Gules, within a collar gemel Or three bezants [*sic*].

WILLIS, of Fressingfield. *Davy, A.*

LION

Out of a mural crown Or a lion passant Proper charged on the shoulder with a portcullis Or and holding in the dexter paw a cross potent within a wreath Or.

CASTLE, Nicholas Edward, only child of Malcolm Castle, of The Grange, Burgh Castle, drowned in 1938 aged 15. *Her.Suff.Ch., Wall tablet, Burgh Castle*

On a mural coronet Sable a lion passant reguardant Or.

JENKIN, of Bury. 'Jenkins' *MS Martin's Crests, 'out of mural coronet'. Davy, A., Seal*

Out of a mural crown a lion rampant issuant holding a hammer.

MOSELEY. *Gage (Thingoe), Fornham All Saints church*

Out of a mural crown a lion holding in his dexter paw a millpick.

MOSELEY. *Proc.S.I.A. IX. 288, 296, Flagon, Market Weston church*

ON OR OUT OF CORONET or CROWN
[MURAL CORONET see following section]

BIRD. CHOUGH

Out of a ducal coronet Or a demi-Cornish chough Sable beaked Gules winged Or.

AYLMER, of Claydon and co. Essex. *London Visitation 1633 (H.S.) I. 35*. MS ex-Taylor Coll.**

COCK

On a coronet a cock.

ALCOCK, John, Bishop of Ely 1486–1500. *Bedford, 2nd ed., 'Crest or Device'*

Out of a coronet Or a demi-cock Gules wings displayed combed and wattled Or.

BALAM, of Barton. 'Alexander Balam of Beawforde' *MS Knight's Visitations, Norf.* * *Davy, A. Washbourne*, 'Norf. & Suff.' Fairbairn*, 'of Barton, Suff.'*

Out of a crest coronet Or a cock of the same [*sic* Or]

COPPIN. 'Sir George Coppen, Clerk of the Crown'; Patent October, 1608. *Grants & Certificates (Stowe MS 707)*

Out of a ducal coronet a cock Or.

COPPIN, of Dunwich. *MS Heraldic Alphabet. Davy, A.*

Out of a ducal coronet Or a cock wings expanded Sable combed beaked and wattled Gules.

WILLAT. 'Willet of Essex' *MS Heraldic Alphabet*

DOVE

Out of an Eastern crown Or a dove rising Proper.

BYATT. *Fairbairn, 'Suff.'*

DEMI-EAGLE [Alphabetically by name]

Out of a ducal coronet a demi-eagle displayed.

BARKER, John, gent., died 1725. *Her.Suff.Ch., Ledger stone, Wickham Market.* Rev. William Bell Barker, Rector of Frostenden for 34 years, died 1791; Others, of Lowestoft and Wickham Market. *Ledger stone, Frostenden*

Out of a ducal coronet Or a demi-eagle displayed.

CHARNEL, of Carlton, Bruisyard. *Davy, A.*

Out of a ducal coronet a demi-eagle displayed Argent beaked and membered Gules.

COTTON. *MS Heraldic Alphabet*

Out of a ducal coronet a demi-eagle displayed Proper.

CRESSY. *Fairbairn, 'of Hill House, Walton, Ipswich'*

Out of a ducal coronet Or a demi-eagle displayed Ermine.

DAY, of Lt. Bradley. *Davy, A., Brass in church. Proc.S.I.A. XXIV. 198*.* John Daye, of Lt. Bradley, died 1584. *Her.Suff.Ch., Effigy brass, Lt. Bradley*

Out of a ducal coronet Proper a demi-eagle displayed Argent.

DELVES. *MS Martin's Crests. MS Heraldic Alphabet*

Out of a ducal coronet Or a demi-eagle between two wings Sable.

DELVES, of Stoke. *Davy, A.*

'to his Creast upon his heaulme on a wreath Gold and Sable issuante owte of a Crowne Silver a demi Egle displayed Ermyne'

GENT, Thomas, of Bumstead at the Tower, co. Essex, Esq.; Confirmation of Arms and Crest by Robert Cooke, Clarenceux, 12 November 1566. *Miscellaneous Grants (H.S.) I.88–9 (Harl. MS 1432, fo. 163b)*

On a coronet Argent a demi-eagle displayed Sable.

GENT. 'Thomas Gent of bumpstead' *MS Knight's Visitations, Essex**

On a coronet Argent a demi-eagle Sable wings displayed Argent.

GENT, 'Thomas Gent.' *MS Philpot's Visitations, Essex**

On a coronet a demi-eagle displayed.

GENT. *Davy, A.*

Out of a ducal coronet a demi-eagle wings displayed all Or.

HAMMOND, Francis, of London and Hawstead, died 1727/8. *Her.Suff.Ch., Hatchment, Hawstead*

Out of a ducal coronet a demi-eagle, or pelican, rising wings addorsed Argent.

HARTOPP. *Davy, A.*

From a coronet Azure a demi-eagle displayed Or.

HOUGHTON. 'John Haughton, co. Norfolk'. *Grants & Certificates (Harl. MS 6,059)*

From a crest coronet Gules a demi-eagle displayed Or in its beak an arrow of the coronet [*sic* Gules] headed and feathered Argent.

LACY, Thomas, John and William, of Spilmanhall [*sic*], in Suffolk; Grant by Sir G. Dethick, Garter. *Grants & Certificates (Harl. MS 1,441; Stowe MS 703)*

Out of a ducal coronet Gules a demi-eagle with wings expanded Or in its beak an arrow Gules headed and feathered Argent.

LACY, of Walsham-le-Willows. *Davy, A., 'Arms confirmed and crest Granted by Dethick, Garter'. Washbourne, 'Suff. and Norf.' Fairbairn, 'Walsham-in-the-Willows, Norf. and Suff.'*

Out of a crown Sable a demi-eagle displayed Or.

LINDFIELD. *MS Fairfax*

Out of a ducal coronet a demi-eagle rising Or.

MORTON, of Bildeston, Chelsworth. *Bokenham. Davy, A.*

Out of a ducal coronet a demi-eagle displayed.

NEWMAN, John, A.M., late Rector of Lt. Cornard, died 1814. *Her.Suff.Ch., Wall tablet, St. Gregory's, Sudbury*

Out of a ducal coronet Or a demi-eagle displayed Vert.

QUARLES, of Denham, Risby, Newton. *Davy, A.*

Out of a ducal coronet Or a demi-eagle wings displayed Or.

SLATER, SLAUGHTER. *MS Ordinary of Arms, fo. 271**

Issuing out of a ducal coronet Or a demi-eagle.

SLATER, of Nayland, Bury. *Davy, A.*

Out of a coronet a demi-eagle displayed.

STONE. *MS Martin's Crests, 'Oxf.'*

A demi-eagle displayed issuing out of a ducal coronet Or.

WEBB, of Farlingaye Hall in Woodbridge, 1810–14. *Davy, A.*

EAGLE

Out of a ducal coronet Or an eagle displayed Argent beaked and legged Gules.

BARKER, of Lowestoft, Tannington, Parham, Bildeston, Wickham Market. *Addit. Suff. Peds. Bokenham. Davy, A., Tannington church. Bildeston, 48, beak and legs untinctured*

On a coronet an eagle displayed.

BARKER, of Lowestoft. *Partridge, 154 (Darby, 1832). Proc.S.I.A. IX. 43, Paten in St. Margaret's church*

Out of a ducal coronet Or an eagle displayed Sable beaked and legged Gules.

BARKER, John, died 1732/3; widow Jane, died 1754. *Her.Suff.Ch., West end of churchyard, St. Margaret's, Lowestoft. Not found 1979.* Rev. Samuel Barker, A.M., died 1836. *Wall tablet, Tannington*

On a crown vallery an eagle reguardant wings addorsed holding in the dexter claw a fleur-de-lis.

BOWEN, of East Bergholt. *Davy, A., (Bookplate)*

Out of a ducal coronet a falcon, or eagle, with wings displayed.

CLISSOLD, of Wrentham, Chelmondiston. *Davy, A.*

Out of a ducal crown Or an eagle Sable enfiled with a rose Proper.

HAMMOND, of Hawstead, Whepstead. *Muskett, I. 264*

Out of a ducal coronet Or an eagle with wings expanded Sable charged on the breast with a rose Gules.

HAMMOND. *Fairbairn*

'for his Creast An eagle with wings expanded Or, Armed & membered Gules standing upon a Coronet advanceing a spear Or, headed Azure, tasled Gules'.

HUMPHREY. 'This is the Coate Armour & Creast of Charles Humphrey of Rishangles in the County of Suffolk the sonne of Richard Humphrey the sonne & heire of Stephen Humphrey of Drenkston in the County aforesaid Ratified & approved by me. Willm Cambden, Clarenceux King of Armes, etc.' Seen and attested by Thomas Preston, Ulster King of Arms, 1638. *Misc.Gen. et Her. 5th S. VIII. 339 (Soc. of Ant. MS 378, fo. 483)*

On a coronet Or an eagle wings elevated of the same [*sic* Or] beak and legs Gules grasping a lance the staff Or tasselled Gules head Proper.

HUMPHREY, Charles, of Rishangles in Suffolk; Confirmation by W. Camden, Clar., and after to his son Thomas Humphrey of Dublin, 26 January 1638. *Grants & Certificates (Harl. MS 1,105)*

On a coronet an eagle wings elevated Or beaked and legged Gules.

HUMFREY, of Rishangles, Drinkstone. *MS Humfry Pedigree Roll*, at head of Roll; Corder MS 91. MS Fairfax (Leverland, Humfrey Ped.)*

On a coronet Or an eagle standing wings addorsed Or beaked and legged Gules advancing in the dexter claw a sceptre Or.

HUMFREY, of Drinkstone, Occold, Rishangles. *MS Humfry Pedigree Roll*, at end of Roll; Corder MS 91*

On a ducal coronet an eagle with wings endorsed holding in the dexter claw a spear all Or.

HUMFREY, of Holbrook. *Visitation 1664–8*

An eagle (or falcon) wings expanded Or armed and membered Gules standing upon a coronet and advancing a spear Or headed Azure tasselled Gules.

HUMFREY, HUMPHREY, of Occold, Drinkstone, Rishangles, Thorpe Morieux. *Davy, A., Occold church*

On a crest coronet Or an eagle displayed per pale Argent and Sable.

WOOD. Thomas Wood, of co. Suffolk, Doctor of Physick; Grant by R. Cooke, Clarenceux, 1592. *Grants & Certificates (Stowe MS 700)*

On a ducal coronet with cap an eagle wings displayed.

WOOD. 'Thomas Wood of Suff. Doctor of phisyke' *MS Philpot's Visitations, Suff.*.* [In a different hand]

On a ducal coronet Or an eagle with wings expanded per pale Or and Sable.

WOOD, WOODS, of Darsham, Westleton. *Davy, A. Washbourne, 'Wood, Suff.' Fairbairn*, 'Wood, Suff.'*

FALCON

Out of a ducal coronet a falcon, or eagle, with wings displayed.

CLISSOLD, of Wrentham, Chelmondiston. *Davy, A.*

Out of a ducal coronet Or a demi-falcon wings displayed Argent.

JERNINGHAM, JERNEGAN, of Somerleyton. *Visitation 1561 (MSS G.7.* and Iveagh Copy*) and (ed. Metcalfe).* 'Sr John Jernegan of Somerletowne in the Island of Lovingland in Com Suffolke Knight' *MS Lilly's Visitation of Suffolk*. Davy, A. Washbourne*, 'Jermingham. Norf. & Suff.' Fairbairn*, 'Jerningham, Norf. & Suff.' Bookplate**

Out of a crown Proper a demi-falcon displayed Argent.

JERNINGHAM. *Visitation 1561 (ed. Howard) I. 141*

Out of a ducal coronet Or a falcon Proper.

JERNINGHAM, JERNEGAN, of Somerleyton. *Druery, 192*

Out of a ducal coronet a falcon close Proper belled and jessed.

WILLYAMS. Vicar of Exning, died 1816. *Davy, A.*

HEATHCOCK or MOORCOCK

On a ducal coronet Or a heath cock Sable combed and wattled Gules.

WILLAT, WILLETT. *MS Ordinary of Arms, fo. 58**

On a coronet Or a moorcock wings expanded Sable membered Gules.

WILLETT, Thomas, of Walthamstowe; Patent by R. Cooke, Clarenceux. *Grants & Certificates (Harl. MS 1,172)*

MARTLET

On a ducal coronet a martlet Or.

TEMPLE, of Mutford. *Davy, A.*

PEACOCK

Out of a ducal coronet a demi-peacock wings displayed per pale.

CLIFTON. *MS Ordinary of Arms, fo. 216**
Out of a ducal coronet Or a demi-peacock per pale
Argent and Sable wings expanded counter-
changed.

CLIFTON, of Shelley. *MS Martin's Crests. MS
Heraldic Alphabet. Davy, A. (Edms.)*
Out of a ducal coronet a peacock with wings
displayed Proper.

CRESSY. *Bokenham*
On a ducal coronet a peacock all Proper.

SORRELL. *Fairbairn*, 'of Ipswich, Suff. and
Essex'*
From a coronet Or a demi-peacock Proper.

STONE, John, of London; Patent by R. Cooke,
Clarenceux. *Grants & Certificates (Harl. MS
1,172)*
Out of a ducal coronet a demi-peacock with wings
expanded Or.

STONE, of Cliff, [*sic*] Suff. *Davy, A.
Washbourne*, 'Suff. and London'*

PELICAN
From a crest coronet a pelican Or vulning herself
Gules.

HARTOPP, Thomas, of co. Leic.; Confirmation of
Arms and Grant of Crest by R. Lee, Clarenceux,
18 May 1596. *Grants & Certificates (Add. MSS
14,293 and 14,295; Harl. MSS 1,359; 1,438;
5,815 and 6,169)*
From a crest coronet Or a demi-pelican Argent
vulned Gules.

HARTOPP, Sir Edward, of Buckminster, co. Leic.,
Bart.; Confirmation by Sir W. Segar, Garter.
Grants & Certificates (Add. MS 12,225)
Out of a ducal coronet a pelican vulning herself.

HARTOP, of Cambridge. *MS Heraldic
Collections, fos. 86a and 87a**
Out of a coronet Or a demi-pelican Argent vulning
herself Proper.

HARTOP. *MS Martin's Crests*
Out of a ducal coronet a demi-eagle, or pelican,
rising wings addorsed Argent.

HARTOPP. *Davy, A.*
Out of a ducal coronet Or a demi-pelican with wings
endorsed Argent vulning herself Gules.

HARTOPP, Bart., of Wissett. *Davy, A.*
Out of a ducal coronet Or a pelican Argent vulning
herself Proper.

HARTOPP. Sir Edmund Cradock Hartopp, Bt.,
'owned Wissett in 1900' (Edmund Farrer).
*Her.Suff.Ch., Glass formerly in East window,
Wissett*
In a ducal coronet Or a pelican vulning herself.

MEADOWS. *Davy, A.*
In a ducal coronet Or a pelican rising Sable.

MEADOWS, of Benacre, Middleton, Tuddenham,
Chattisham. *Davy, A., Middleton church*
Out of a ducal coronet a pelican rousant with wings
elevated and addorsed Or vulned Gules.

PERN. Rev. Andrew Pern, B.D., Rector for 31
years, died 1772. *Her.Suff.Ch., Wall tablet,
Norton*
Out of a ducal coronet Or a demi-pelican wings
expanded Argent.

PETT. *Davy, A.*

RAVEN
Out of a ducal coronet Or a demi-? raven wings
displayed Sable.

AYLMER. *MS Ordinary of Arms, fo. 168**
On a coronet Or a raven rising Sable.

MEADOWS, Sir Philip; Grant by Sir E. Walker,

Garter, of an Augmentation of Arms. *Grants &
Certificates (Harl. MS 1,172)*

SWAN
Out of a coronet a demi-swan wings expanded Proper.

JAMES. Sir Pane James, of Bury. *Bokenham.
MS Martin's Crests, 'ducal cor.'*
Out of a ducal coronet Or a demi-swan wings
expanded Argent beaked Gules.

JAMES, of Bury. *Davy, A.*
Out of a ducal coronet Or a white swan couchant or
swimming [*sic*].

JOHNSON. Eleanor, daughter of John Johnson, of
West Broyle, co. Sussex, married Thomas
Weller-Poley, died 1945. *Her.Suff.Ch., Glass,
Boxted*
In a ducal coronet Or a demi-swan close Proper.

KEPPEL, Viscount. Of Elvedon. *Davy, A.*
Frederick Keppel. *Bookplate**
Out of a ducal coronet per pale Sable and Gules a
swan rising Argent beaked Gules.

STAFFORD, Duke of Buckingham. Of Offton.
Davy, A.

ON OR OUT OF MURAL CORONET or CROWN

BIRD. COCK
Out of a mural coronet a demi-cock issuing wings
expanded down Azure beaked combed and wattled
Or holding in his beak an ear of barley Or.

ELCOCK. *MS Heraldic Alphabet*
Out of a mural coronet Or a demi-cock Azure
combed beaked and wattled Or holding in his beak
an ear of wheat Or.

ELCOCK. Rector of Westhorpe, died 1638.
Davy, A.

DOVE
Out of a mural crown Or a dove volant Azure.

PITMAN, of Saxmundham. *Misc.Gen. et Her. 5th
S. VI. 78*

DEMI-EAGLE
Out of a mural coronet Or a demi-eagle displayed
Sable.

BALLETT, of Ufford, Coddenham. *Davy, A.*
From a mural coronet Azure a demi-eagle displayed
Ermine beak Or.

HALSTED, Lawrence, Esq., of Sonning, co.
Berks., Keeper of the Records in the Tower of
London, of the family of Halsted, co. Lanc.;
Confirmation of Arms and Grant of Crest by Sir
W. Segar, Garter, 20 November 1628. *Grants &
Certificates (Add. MSS 12,225 and 14,295; Harl.
MS 6,140; Stowe MS 716)*
Out of a mural coronet chequy Or and Azure a
demi-eagle issuant Ermine beaked Or.

HALSTEAD. Rector of Stansfield, died 1728.
Davy, A.
From a mural crown Or a demi-eagle rising Argent.

HASTED, of Hawstead. Henry Hasted.
Her.Suff.Ch., Glass, St. Mary's, Bury
Out of a mural coronet Or a demi-eagle Gules armed
Or.

PAGENHAM, PAKENHAM. *Davy, A., Debenham
church*
Out of a mural coronet Or a demi-eagle displayed
Sable on its breast a bezant charged with a
fleur-de-lis Azure in its beak an arrow Or headed
and feathered Argent.

REBOW, of Bramford, Helmingham, Otley,
Gipping. *Davy, A. Gurdon-Rebow. Crisp's*

Visitation. X. 42*, Pedigree. 'John Gurdon
Rebow' *Bookplate**

MARTLET
On a mural coronet a martlet Argent holding in its
beak an oak branch Vert fructed Or.
TOMLINE, George, M.P., High Sheriff of Suffolk
1832, of Riby Hall, co. Linc. and Orwell Park,
Suffolk, died 1889. *Livery button*, untinctured.
Washbourne. Muskett. II. 308, Pedigree only*

DEMI-PELICAN
Out of a mural coronet Or a demi-pelican vulning
herself Ermine.
CANHAM, of Milden. *Kirby's map. Davy, A.,
church*

**ON OR OUT OF CORONET or CROWN
[MURAL CORONET see following section]**

HEAD. BEAST, ANTELOPE
Out of a ducal coronet Gules an antelope's head
couped Argent armed Gules.
FRERE. *MS Ordinary of Arms, fo. 91**
Out of a ducal coronet Or an antelope's head Or
attired Gules.
FRERE, of Sweffling, Occold. *MS Humfry
Pedigree Roll*; Corder MS 91*
Out of a ducal coronet Gules an antelope's head
erased Argent armed Or.
FRERE, of Finningham, Sweffling, Occold,
Wickham Skeith. *Bokenham. Davy, A. Burke,
L.G. 1900 ed. Bookplates*, untinctured*
Out of a ducal coronet an antelope's head Argent
armed Or.
FRERE, of Roydon Hall in co. Norfolk. *Burke,
L.G. 1853 ed.*
Out of a ducal coronet Gules an antelope's head
Argent armed Or.
FRERE, Edward, Rector of Finningham, died
1841. *Her.Suff.Ch., Wall tablet, Finningham*
Out of a ducal coronet Or an antelope's head Argent
armed and crined Or.
FRYER, of Clare. *MS Heraldic Alphabet.
Davy, A.*
Out of a ducal coronet Or an antelope's, or goat's,
head Argent armed Or run through with a
demi-spear Or headed Argent.
HATLEY. 'Hattley' *MS Heraldic Alphabet, 'on
his Coach'*
Out of a ducal coronet an antelope's head couped
Or.
RANDALL, of Orford, Aldeburgh. *Crisp's
Visitation. III. 174, Pedigree*

ASS
Out of a ducal coronet Or an ass's head Proper.
CHAMBERLAIN. 'John Chamberly' *MS Philpot's
Visitations, Norf.*. 'Chamberlayne'
MS Heraldic Alphabet*
Out of a ducal coronet Or an ass's head Argent.
CHAMBERLAIN, of Bury. *Davy, A., St. Mary's
church*

BEAR
Out of the coronet of a Marquess a bear's head
muzzled and chained.
EVERITT, of Oulton Broad, Suffolk. *Fairbairn*
Out of a naval coronet a bear's head Sable muzzled
Gules [*sic*].
FORD. *Green Memoir*, untinctured. Davy, A.
Washbourne, 'Glouc., Kent and Suff.' Muzzle
untinctured. Fairbairn, 'Glouc., Kent and Suff.'
Muzzle untinctured*

Out of a ducal coronet a bear's head muzzled.
PARKER. Nathaniel Parker, of Gt. Wenham, died
1684. *Partridge, 202 (Darby 1828), churchyard*
Out of a ducal coronet Or a bear's head Sable
muzzled Or.
PARKER, of Erwarton. 'Sr Calthrope Parker of
Arwarton Kt.' *MS Lilly's Visitation of Suffolk*.
Bokenham.* Parker, Lord Morley, of Erwarton.
Davy, A. Nathaniel Parker. Lord of the Manor,
died 1684. *Her.Suff.Ch., Slab outside church,
Gt. Wenham. Too worn to distinguish.*
Henry Parker, Lord of the Manor of Old Hall and
the Commandre, died 1701. *Altar tomb in north
chapel, East Bergholt.* Parker of Erwarton. *Tablet,
Ledger stones, Brass, Erwarton*
Out of a coronet a bear's head Argent.
VINCENT. *MS Martin's Crests*
Out of a ducal coronet Proper a bear's head Argent
muzzles Gules.
VINCENT, Charles, died 1700. *Her.Suff.Ch., Wall
tablet, Polstead.*
Out of a ducal coronet Or a bear's head Argent.
VINCENT. *Her.Suff.Ch., Hatchment, Wortham.
'Probably used for both Philip Vincent of
Marlingford, died 1724 and his second wife,
Elizabeth, died 1728.'*
Issuing from a coronet a bear's head muzzled.
WALPOOLE, of Beccles. *E.A. Misc. 1922, 29*

BOAR
Out of a coronet Or a boar's head couped Sable
between two wings Gules billety Or.
BOLLE. 'Boles' *MS Martin's Crests*
Out of a ducal coronet a boar's head couped close
lying fesseways.
EVANS, of Bury, Eriswell. *Davy, A., St. James's
church, Bury*
On a ducal coronet a boar's head couped fesseways.
EVANS, EVANS-LOMBE, of Norfolk and Suffolk.
Livery button. Evans-Lombe. *Crisp's Visitation.
XIX. 85–90, Pedigree. Arms and Crest of Lombe
only given*
Out of a ducal coronet Gules a boar's head Ermine
tusked Or between two wings Sable billety Or.
LUCY, LUSEY. *Banners & Standards*. Wall's Book*
Out of a coronet a boar's head couped Ermines
tusked and crined Or between two wings Vert.
LUCY. *MS Martin's Crests*
Out of a ducal coronet Gules a boar's head erect
Argent gutty Sable between a pair of wings Sable
billety Or.
LUCY, of Old Newton. *Davy, A.*
Out of a ducal coronet a boar's head and neck all Or.
NORTHWOOD, of about Stonham Aspal. *MS
Heraldic Collections, fo. 52*. Davy A.*
Out of a ducal coronet Or a boar's head couped
Argent.
RAND. *MS ex-Taylor Coll.**

CAMEL
Out of a ducal coronet a camel's head all Or.
SAXTON, SEXTON. *MS Ordinary of Arms, fo. 200**

DEER
Out of a ducal crown Or a stag's head Ermine attired
Or a wreath Argent and Sable round the neck tied
behind with two bows.
BASPOOLE. Baspole, of Beeston, co. Norfolk.
*Misc.Gen. et Her. 5th S. VIII. 223, 'Grant by
Cooke, Clarenceux, 10 August 1576'.* 'Raffe
Baspolle' *MS Philpot's Visitations, Norf.* Wreath
ends flotant*

Out of a ducal coronet Or a buck's head Ermine attired Or.

> BASPOOLE. 'John Baspole of Beston' *MS Knight's Visitations, Norf.* *

Out of a ducal coronet a buck's head couped Ermine attired Or gorged with a wreath Argent and Sable.

> BASPOOLE, of St. Margts. [*sic*]. *Davy, A.*

Out of a ducal coronet Or a stag's head Ermine attired Or wreathed about the neck Argent and Sable tied with two bows.

> BASPOOLE, of St. Margts. [*sic*]. *Davy, A., Marlesford church*

Out of a ducal coronet Or a stag's head Gules attired Or.

> BETTS, of Wortham. *Burke, L.G. 1853 ed. E.A.N. & Q. I. 257. Fairbairn*, 'of Wortham Hall, Suff.' Buck's head.* Sarah, wife of Edmund Betts, gent., of Wortham, died 1745; he died 1788. *Her.Suff.Ch., Ledger stone in churchyard, Oakley.* Rev. George Betts, Rector of Overstrand in Norfolk, died 1822. *Hatchment, Wortham*

Out of a coronet a stag's head

> BETTS, of Wortham. *Betts, embossed on cover of book.* 'George Betts, of Wortham in Suffolk' *Bookplate**

Out of a ducal coronet Or a buck's head Gules attired Or gorged with a collar Argent charged with three cinquefoils Gules.

> BETTS, of Wortham. *Bokenham. Davy, A., Wortham and Yoxford churches.* William Betts, died 1709; widow died 1732. *Her.Suff.Ch., Wall tablet, Yoxford.* Thomas Betts, of Yoxford, died 1739. *Hatchment, Yoxford.*

Out of a ducal coronet a stag's head Argent.

> COLBORNE, of Bramford. *Davy, A.*

From a crest coronet Or a hart's head Ermines attired Or.

> GILBERT, Thomas; Grant by R. Cooke, Clarenceux, 7 August 1576. *Grants & Certificates (Add. MS 14,293)*

Out of a ducal coronet Or a stag's head Ermine attired Or.

> GILBERT, of Mutford Hall. 'Thomas gilbert' *MS Knight's Visitations, Norf.*, Coronet and attires untinctured. E.A. Misc. 1929, 26*

Out of a ducal coronet Or a stag's head Ermine attired Or tied about the neck with a ribbon knotted –.

> GOOCH. *MS Ordinary of Arms, fo. 86**

Out of a coronet a stag's head Ermine attired Or bearing a hawthorn bush with berries Proper.

> HARLESTON. *MS Martin's Crests*

Out of a ducal coronet Or a hind's head Ermine.

> HAWKINS. *Sharpe*

From a crown vallary Or a roebuck's head Proper.

> PARKHURST, . . . , Sheriff of London in 1621; Grant by Sir Richard St. George, Clarenceux, I Chas. I. [1625/6]. *Grants & Certificates (Harl. MS 1,441)*

Out of a ducal coronet a stag's head.

> PERFECT, Emanuel, died 1865. *Her.Suff.Ch., at east end of churchyard, Gorleston*

From a coronet a stag's head all Or.

> ROTHWELL, Stephen, of Ewerby, co. Lincoln; Confirmation by W. Flower, Norroy, 1 April 1585. *Grants & Certificates (Harl. MS 1,359)*

DOG. GREYHOUND

Out of a ducal coronet Argent a greyhound's head Argent collared Or.

> ALABASTER. *Davy, A.*

Out of a ducal coronet Or a greyhound's head Sable gorged with a collar Gules.

> 'BARINGTON, Thomas, of Chester, gent., married Elizabeth daughter of William Hobart, of Revenshall, died 1651' *E.A. Misc. 1913, 35, Hatchment [sic], Lindsey church.* This Funeral Board [not Hatchment], wrongly tinctured in *Her.Suff.Ch.*, was not traced in 1978, apparently stolen two or three years previously. See my *MS Hatchments in Suffolk. II., Addenda, Funeral Boards.* Photograph*

In a crown Argent a greyhound's head couped Or.

> BIRD, BYRDE, of Denston. *Davy, A., Brass in church. Proc.S.I.A. VI, 449*

Out of a ducal coronet Argent a greyhound's head couped Or.

> BIRD. *Fairbairn*, 'of Denston, Suff.'*

Out of a ducal coronet a greyhound's head.

> COLMAN, of Pakefield. Nathaniel Colman, died 1726; daughter Mary Colman, died 1772. *Partridge, 163 (Darby, 1832), churchyard, Pakefield. Her.Suff.Ch., Altar tomb, churchyard*

Out of a ducal coronet Or a greyhound's head Argent erased Gules eared Or [eared like a talbot, but 'greyhownd' in MS] collared ringed and lined Or the end knotted.

> GOTTES. 'Robert gottes' *MS Knight's Visitations, Cambs.**

Out of a ducal coronet Or a greyhound's head erased Argent collared ringed and lined folded up like a hank of cotton Or.

> GOTTES. *MS Heraldic Alphabet*

Out of a ducal coronet Or a greyhound's head Proper collared Or.

> JERMYN. *Washbourne, 'Suff.' Fairbairn, 'Suff.'*

Out of a ducal coronet Or a greyhound's head couped Argent collared Sable.

> WALKER, ? of Troston. *Davy, A.*

TALBOT

Out of a ducal coronet a talbot's head all Or.

> BENDISH. *MS Knight's Visitations, Essex**

Out of an Earl's coronet Or a talbot's head couped Or langued Gules.

> BENDISH. *MS Martin's Crests*

Out of an Earl's coronet a talbot's head Or.

> BENDISH, of South Town, Stowmarket. *Davy, A.*

Out of a coronet a talbot's head.

> CAMPION. *MS Martin's Crests, 'Witham, Essex'*

Out of a ducal coronet Or a talbot's head Argent eared Sable.

> DEVEREUX, Sir John, K.G., died 1392/3. *Stall Plates, plate XIII**

Out of a ducal coronet Or a talbot's head Argent eared Gules.

> DEVEREUX, Sir Walter, K.G., died 1485. *Stall Plates, plate LXXVII**

Out of a ducal coronet Or a talbot's head Argent eared Gules.

> DEVEREUX, Viscount Hereford, Earl of Essex. Of Sudbourne. *Davy, A., Orford Church.* Devereux, Viscount Hereford. *Her.Suff.Ch., Shield on small oak panel. Not found 1981.* [Stolen *c.*1980. J.C.]. Price Devereux, 10th Viscount, died 1748. *Hatchment, Sudbourne*

Out of a ducal coronet a talbot's head.

> EDWARDS, of Framlingham. *Davy, A., Seal*

Out of a ducal coronet a talbot's head Ermine.

> GOOCH. *Davy, A.*

Out of a ducal coronet Gules a talbot's head Azure langued Gules eared and collared Or.

SHAXTON. 'Leonard Saxton' *MS Knight's Visitations, Norf.* * 'Lenerd Shatston' *MS Philpot's Visitations, Norf.* *, ducal coronet Or.*
Out of a ducal coronet Gules a talbot's head Sable collared ringed and eared Or.

SHAXTON. *Davy, A.*

Out of a ducal coronet Or a talbot's head erased Proper.

WOLSELEY, WOLVESLEY. *Davy, A. Washbourne*, 'Wolseley, Bart., Suff.'*

WOLFHOUND

Out of a ducal coronet Or an Irish wolfhound's head per fesse Argent and Ermine charged with an escallop barways nebuly Gules and Sable.

LENNARD-BARRETT, Bart. *Davy, A. Washbourne, 'Essex'. Fairbairn, 'of Belhus, Aveley, Essex. Escallop shell per fesse nebuly'*

ELEPHANT

'to his Crest on a crowne ar/b/ a olyfants hed coupey quartered g/or/ tusked of ye Last. Edward Clarke'

CLARKE 'of ketelbyston in Suff' *MS Alphabet of Crests, fo. 22b*

Out of a ducal coronet Or an elephant's head Sable armed Argent in the front of the coronet a ring Or thereto a line turned over the trunk.

DAVY, of Hoxne, Yoxford. 'Rychard Davy' *MS Philpot's Visitations, Norf.* * Visitation 1664–8. Davy, A.* David Davy, Gent., of Rumburgh, died 1764. *Her.Suff.Ch., Ledger stone, Rumburgh and Stone carving, South Elmham All Saints.* Eleazar Davy, of The Grove, died 1803; David Elisha Davy, died 1851; Lucy Elizabeth Davy, widow of Rev. William Barlee, died 1863. *Wall tablets, Yoxford*

Out of a coronet an elephant's head.

DAVY, of Rumburgh, Yoxford. 'David E. Davy' *Bookplate*. Proc.S.I.A. XXII. 165**

Out of a ducal coronet Or an elephant's head Proper.

DAVY, of South Elmham All Saints, Rumburgh, Yoxford. *Davy, A., S. Elmham All Saints church*

Out of a ducal coronet Or an elephant's head Sable armed Argent.

DAVY. *Washbourne, 'Devon, Norf. and Suff.'*

Out of a ducal coronet Or an elephant's head Argent tusked and eared Or.

HAMMOND, of Ellingham by Bungay, Ubbeston, Walpole, Cookley. *Muskett. I. 257 (Harl. MS 1449 and 1552)*

'upon a helme on a torse ar g An Olyvante hed or issuinge out of a crowne g manteled g dob: argent'

KNOWLES. 'Rychard Knowlys of Cold Ashby, co. Northants.' (Grandfather of Robert Knowles of Walton); Confirmation of Arms and Crest by Sir Gilbert Dethick, Garter, 1580. *Frag.Gen. VII. 70–1**

From a crest coronet Gules an elephant's head Or.

KNOWLES, Richard, of Cold Ashby, co. Northampton, son of Roger, of the same place; Confirmation by Sir G. Dethick, Garter, 8 November 1580. *Grants & Certificates (Harl. MS 1,441; Stowe MS 703)*

Out of a ducal coronet Gules an elephant's head Or.

KNOWLES, of Walton. 'Knowells' *MS Heraldic Alphabet. Visitation 1664–8*. Bokenham. Davy, A., (Barrett MS)*

Out of a ducal coronet Gules an elephant's head Argent.

KNOWLES, of Walton. *Davy, A. Washbourne*, 'Suff., Northamp. and Sco.' Fairbairn*, 'Walton, Suff. and Northamp.'*

GOAT

Out of a ducal coronet Argent a goat's head – armed Or.

BAGGAT, of Harwich. *Sharpe*

Out of a ducal coronet Or an antelope's, or goat's, head Argent armed Or run through with a demi-spear Or headed Argent.

HATLEY. 'Hattley' *MS Heraldic Alphabet, 'on his Coach'*

'his crest a gots hede of Indya or/ pelety eared horned and Berded in a crowne g/ to John Ive atorney in the kings benche'

IVE. *MS Alphabet of Crests, fo. 65*

Out of a crown a goat's head Or attired and barbed Gules.

IVE, of Stoke by Nayland. *MS Fairfax*

Out of a ducal coronet Gules an Indian goat's head Argent gutty Gules attired Or.

IVES, of Stoke by Nayland. *Davy, A.*

Out of a ducal coronet a goat's head Or.

SEDLEY, *Davy, A.*

HORSE

Out of a ducal coronet a horse's head Argent mane and tongue Or.

ALLEN, of Mesner Hall, Essex. *Her.Suff.Ch., Glass, Whepstead*

Out of a ducal coronet a horse's head.

CARBONEL, of Badingham. *Davy, A., West Creeting church*

Out of a ducal coronet Or a unicorn's, or horse's, head Argent bridled Or reined Gules feathered Gules.

DEBDEN, of Depden, Brampton, Brandeston. *Davy, A.*

Out of a ducal coronet Azure a horse's head couped Or maned and bridled Argent.

GOODWIN, of Lt. Stonham. 'Goodwin' *MS Knight's Visitations, Cambs.* * Bokenham. Muskett. I. 235 (Harl. MS. 1043)*

Out of a ducal coronet Azure a horse's head Or bridled Vert.

GOODWIN. 'Goodwyn' *MS Heraldic Alphabet*

A horse's head couped Or maned and bridled Argent out of a ducal coronet Argent.

GOODWIN, of Mendlesham, Stonham. *Davy, A., Mendlesham church*

Out of a ducal coronet Or a horse's head Sable collared Gules [*sic*].

PARTRIDGE, of Finborough. *Davy, A.*

Issuing from a ducal coronet Or a horse's head Sable.

PARTRIDGE. *Washbourne*, 'Glouc. and Suff.'*

Out of a ducal coronet Gules a horse's head Argent.

REDMAN. *Davy, A.*

Out of a coronet Proper a horse's head Argent between two wings Gules.

SEXTON, of Lavenham. *Bokenham*

Out of a ducal coronet Or a horse's head Argent between two wings expanded Sable.

SEXTON, of Lavenham. *Muskett. I. 293 (Norfolk Visit., Harl. MS 1552)*

LEOPARD

Out of a ducal coronet Or a leopard's face Argent pellety.

BRAND, of Gt. Bradley, Edwardstone. *Visitation 1664–8*. Davy, A.*

Out of a ducal coronet Or a leopard's head Argent semy of roundels of the colours [*sic*].

BRAND. *Washbourne*, 'Suff. and London'*

Out of a ducal coronet Or a leopard's head guardant
Argent semy of roundles of various colours.

BRAND. *Fairbairn, 'Suff. and London'*

Out of a ducal coronet a leopard's head spotted.

BRAND, John, Gent., of Edwardstone, died 1642.
Her.Suff.Ch., Brass, Edwardstone

Out of a ducal coronet Or a leopard's head spotted
of various colours.

BRAND. *Her.Suff.Ch., Slab, Raydon*

Out of a ducal crown Or a leopard's head Proper.

BRAND, Joseph, of Grays Inn and Suffolk 1616,
died 1674. *Her.Suff.Ch., Wall tablet,
Edwardstone*

Out of a ducal coronet Or a leopard's face Proper.

BUGG, of Mildenhall. *Davy, A.*

Out of a ducal coronet Or a leopard's head Gules
bezanty.

MAY, of Eyke, Ramsholt. *Davy, A., Eyke
churchyard*

Out of a ducal coronet a leopard's head.

MAY, Robert, Esq., late of Ramsholt, High Sheriff
for Suffolk 1758, died 1761. *Partridge, 132
(Darby, 1828)*

LION [Alphabetically by name]

Out of a ducal coronet Or a lion's head Argent
charged on the neck with a bezant.

BENNET. *MS Ordinary of Arms, fo. 76**

Out of a ducal coronet Or a lion's head Argent.

BLAND, of Gisleham, Eye. *Bokenham.
MS Heraldic Alphabet. Davy, A.*

Out of a ducal coronet a lion's head Proper.

BLAND, of Melton. *Davy, A. Bookplate**

Out of a coronet a lion's head Argent pelletty.

BRAND, of Edwardstone. *Bokenham*

Out of a ducal coronet Or a lion's head per bend
embattled Argent and Gules.

BYLES, of Ipswich. *Davy, A.*

Out of a ducal coronet, a lion's head.

CADOGAN. Charles Sloane, Earl Cadogan, died
1807. *Her.Suff.Ch., Wall tablet, Santon
Downham*

Out of a ducal coronet Gules a lion's head Argent.

FULLER, of Bradwell. *MS Ordinary of Arms,
fo. 78*. Davy, A.*

Out of a ducal coronet Gules a lion's head couped
Argent on his neck an Agross [sic ?] armed Gules.

FULLER, of Ipswich. *Sharpe*

On a ducal coronet a lion's head Ermine collared
Gules and Argent.

GOOCH. *E.A. Misc. 1916, 41, Monument,
Mettingham church.* William Gooch, died 1685.
Her.Suff.Ch., Monument, Mettingham

Out of a ducal coronet Or a lion's head Argent gutty
de sang.

LONG, of Saxmundham. *Sharpe. Davy, A.,
church. Burke, L.G. 1900 and 1952 eds.*
Fairbairn, 'of Hurts Hall, Saxmundham'.*
William Long, of Hurts Hall, died 1875.
Her.Suff.Ch., Shield under window, Saxmundham

Out of a ducal coronet Or a lion's head Gules.

MAY, of Boxted. *Davy, A., church. 'Granted
1573'.* Robert May, late of Ramsholt, High
Sheriff 1758, died 1761. *Her.Suff.Ch., Altar tomb
in churchyard, Eyke*

From a crest coronet Gules a lion's head Ermine
langued Gules.

NICHOLSON. Thomas Nicholson, of London, one
of the examiners in the Court of Chancery,
younger son of Thomas Nicholson, of co.
Lincoln; Confirmation by Sir W. Dethick, Garter,

7 September 1596. *Grants & Certificates
(Add. MS 14,293)*

Out of a ducal coronet Gules a lion's head Ermine.

NICHOLSON. 'Nichelson' *MS Heraldic Alphabet*

Out of a ducal coronet Or a lion's head erased
Gules.

NICHOLSON, of Ipswich. *Davy, A. Bookplates*,
untinctured*

Out of a ducal coronet Or a lion's head and neck
Sable.

POLSTEAD, of Polstead. *Davy, A.*

'on a torce or and purper a Cronet of the first, Lyons
head Argent, Langued erased gules, mantled gules,
doubled Argent'

SHANKE. Thomas Shanke of Rollesby, co.
Norfolk; Confirmation of Arms and Grant of
Crest by Sir Gilbert Dethick, Garter, 15 August
1561. *Misc.Gen. et Her. 5th S. IX. 106 (Soc. of
Ant. MS 378, fo. 457)*

From a coronet Or a lion's head per fesse Argent
and Gules.

SHANKE, Thomas, of Rollesby, co. Norfolk, gent.;
Confirmation by Sir G. Dethick, Garter,
15 August 1562. *Grants & Certificates (Harl.
MS 1,441; Stowe MS 703)*

Out of a ducal coronet Or a lion's head Argent
erased Gules (or per fesse Argent and Gules).

SHANKE, of Beccles. *Davy, A.*

MULE

Out of a coronet a mule's head.

CHAMBERLAIN. *MS Martin's Crests*

OX

Out of a ducal coronet Gules a bull's head Argent
horned Or.

BARBER, BARBOR, of Bury. *Visitation 1577.*
'Roger Barber of Bury' *MS Knight's Visitations,
Suff.** 'Roger Barber of Bury' *MS Philpot's
Visitations, Suff.* Bokenham. Davy, A.
Washbourne*. Misc.Gen. et Her. I.58*,
untinctured. Fairbairn*, 'Barber, Suff.'*

Out of a ducal coronet Or a bull's head Gules
ducally crowned Or.

BASSINGBOURNE. *Davy, A.*

Out of a ducal coronet per pale Argent and Sable a
bull's head Sable attired Or.

BRAGE, BRAGG, BRAGGES, of Roydon. *Davy, A.,
Slab, Stratford St. Mary church*

Out of a ducal coronet per pale Argent and Or a
bull's head Sable attired Or.

BRAGE, of Roydon. *E.A.N. & Q. XII. 147, Slab,
Stratford St. Mary church*

Out of a ducal coronet a bull's head.

BRAGE, Nicholas, late of Roydon, died 1698.
Her.Suff.Ch., Ledger stone, Stratford St. Mary

Issuant out of a ducal coronet an ox's head.

CHAMBERLAIN. *Tymms, 200, Slab in St. Mary's
church, Bury*

From a ducal coronet a calve's head couped.

CHAMBERLAIN, John, died 1726; widow Frances,
died 1735. *Her.Suff.Ch., Ledger stone, St.
Mary's, Bury*

Out of a ducal coronet Or a bull's head Argent
armed Or charged on the neck with a rose Gules
barbed Vert seeded Or.

FANE, VANE. *MS Ordinary of Arms, fo. 231**

Out of a ducal coronet Or a bull's head pied Proper
attired Or charged on the neck with a rose Gules
barbed and seeded Proper.

NEVILLE, Baron Bergavenny, Earl of
Abergavenny. Of Otley. Neville, Baron

Braybrook. Of Shadingfield. *Davy, A.*
Out of a coronet a bull's head Or armed Azure.
> OGLE. *MS Martin's Crests*

A bull's head Argent armed chained and lined Or
out of a ducal coronet Or.
> RATCLIFFE, Earl of Sussex. Lord Fitzwalter. Of
> Framsden. *Davy, A., church*

TIGER see MONSTER, HERALDIC TIGER

WOLF

Out of a ducal coronet a wolf's head all Or.
> CLOPTON. *Visitation 1561 (ed. Howard) I. 20.*
> *Usually borne without a coronet but 'on the*
> *monument of Poley Clopton, the last heir male, in*
> *Lyston Church, Essex, in painted glass Clare*
> *Church (1617) and on the monument of Sir*
> *William Clopton, in the Clopton chapel, Melford*
> *church 1615. [sic, 1618] the wolf's head is*
> *represented issuing out of a ducal coronet Or.*
> *There is no record of a grant of this crest so*
> *differenced.' 'Clopton of Kentwell' MS Lilly's*
> *Visitation of Suffolk*. First of four crests shown.*

Out of a ducal coronet a wolf's head.
> CLOPTON, Sir William, Kt., of Kentwell Hall,
> died 1618. *Her.Suff.Ch., Tomb in Clopton*
> *chapel, Long Melford*

Out of a ducal coronet Or a wolf's head per pale or
and Azure.
> 'CLOPTON, . . . , Kt., a good benefactor to this
> church 1617'. *Her.Suff.Ch., Glass, Clare*

ON OR OUT OF MURAL CORONET or CROWN

HEAD. BEAST, ANTELOPE

Out of a mural crown an antelope's head Proper
attired Or.
> FOWELL, of Coney Weston. *Davy, A.*

BOAR

Out of a mural coronet Gules a boar's head Argent
armed and bristled Or.
> BOTELER. 'Botelar' *MS Heraldic Alphabet*

From a mural coronet Gules a boar's head and neck
Argent bristled and armed Or.
> 'WHITE, Stephen, of London, merchant, since
> knighted'; Certified by W. Riley, Lancaster
> Herald, in 1646. *Grants & Certificates (Harl.*
> *MS 5,869; Stow MS 703)*

Out of a mural coronet Gules a boar's head Argent
crined Or.
> WHITE, of Stoke by Nayland, Bury, Halesworth,
> Orford. *MS Martin's Crests. Davy, A.*

Out of a mural crown Or a boar's head and neck
Argent and Or [*sic*].
> WHITE, of Tattingstone. *Sharpe*

Out of a mural coronet Gules a boar's head Argent.
> WHITE, of Tattingstone. *Davy, A., church*

DEER

From a mural coronet chequy Argent and Sable a
stag's head Proper attired Or wounded through the
neck by an arrow Argent.
> FORSTER. 'George Foster, son of James in the
> Island of Barbados, a J.P. there'; Grant by Sir H.
> St. George, Garter, 3 May 1703. *Grants &*
> *Certificates (Add. MS 14,831)*

Out of a mural coronet chequy Argent and Sable a
stag's head Proper attired Or holding in the mouth
an arrow Argent.
> FORSTER, of Halesworth, Yoxford, Shotley.
> *Davy, A. Fairbairn*, 'Suff.'*

Out of a mural crown Gules a buck's head erased at
the neck Proper gorged with a collar embattled
counter-embattled Or.
> OAKES, of Withersfield, Long Melford. *Davy, A.*

Issuant from a mural crown Or a stag's head Proper
charged on the neck with a well and holding in the
mouth a rose Gules slipped and leaved Proper.
> RODWELL. Sir Cecil Hunter Rodwell, G.C.M.G.,
> of Woodlands, Holbrook, Governor of Fiji, etc.,
> died 1953. *Her.Suff.Ch., Wall tablet, Holbrook.*
> *First crest*

DOG. GREYHOUND, TALBOT

From a mural coronet Argent a greyhound's head
Sable collared Gules rimmed and studded Or.
> HEMPSON. 'Sir Robert Hampson, Alderman, of
> London'; Patent 10 October 1602. *Grants &*
> *Certificates (Harl. MSS 1,115; 1,422; 5,839 and*
> *6,059; Stowe MSS 706 and 707)*

Out of a mural coronet Argent a greyhound's head
Sable gorged with a collar Argent rimmed ringed
and studded Or.
> HEMPSON, of Haughley. *Davy, A.*

Out of a mural crown Or a talbot's head Azure.
> AMORI. 'Amory' *MS Martin's Crests*

Out of a mural coronet Or a talbot's head Azure
eared Or.
> AMORI, DAMORY, of Depden. *Davy, A.*

Out of a mural coronet a talbot's head Gules eared
Argent.
> BRAMPTON, of Kenton, Letton in Norfolk.
> *Davy, A.*

From a mural coronet Argent a talbot's head couped
Azure eared and gutty Or.
> REYNOLDS (or REANALDES) . . . , one of the
> Clerks of the Privy Seal; Patent Granted in April
> 1607. *Grants & Certificates (Stowe MSS 706*
> *and 707; Harl. MS 6,095)*

Out of a mural coronet, or crown, a talbot's head.
> ROUTH, George, M.A., Rector of St. Clements,
> Ipswich and Holbrook, died 1821. *Davy, A., St.*
> *Clements church monument. E.A.N. & Q. IX. 68.*
> *Her.Suff.Ch., Wall tablet, St. Clements, Ipswich*

ELEPHANT

Out of a mural coronet Or an elephant's head Proper
tusks Or.
> KIRBY. KERBY. 'Jefferie Kerby of Ipswich and
> London'; Grant of Arms and Crest by Camden,
> Clarenceux. *London Visitation 1633 (H.S.)*
> *II.29*. Misc.Gen. et Her. 5th S. III. 60–2*,*
> *Pedigree; Kirby died 1632/3*

Issuant from a mural crown Or an elephant's head
supporting with the trunk a sword erect Proper
pommel and hilt Or.
> KITCHENER. Earl Kitchener of Khartoum.
> *Crisp's Visitation. VII. I*. Crest of Augmentation*

GOAT

Out of a mural coronet Or a goat's head Argent.
> COLMAN, of Ipswich. *Sharpe*

Out of a mural crown Sable a goat's head Argent
attired Sable.
> GARFOOT, GARFOOTE, of Farnham. *Visitation*
> *1664–8*. Bokenham*

Out of a mural crown Sable a goat's head Argent
attired Or.
> GARFOOT, GARFOOTE, of Farnham. *MS. Heraldic*
> *Alphabet, '& bearded Or'. Davy, A. Washbourne*,*
> *'Ess. and Suff.' Fairbairn, 'Garfoot, Essex & Suff.'*

HORSE

Out of a mural crown Or a horse's head Ermine

gorged with a wreath of laurel Vert.
FLETCHER, of Ipswich. *Davy, A.*
From a mural coronet Or a horse's head Argent
mane Gules.
REDMAN, William, D.D., Bishop of Norwich;
Confirmation of Arms and Grant of Crest by R.
Lee, Clarenceux, 1 May 1595. *Grants &
Certificates (Add. MS 14,295; Harl. MS 1,359)*
Out of a mural coronet Or a horse's head couped
Argent maned Gules.
REDMAN, William, Bishop of Norwich
1595–1602. Lord of Hoxne. *Blomefield, III. 561,
'Grant by Lee, Clarenceux, 1st May 1595'.
Davy, A. Bedford, 2nd ed., 93*

LEOPARD
Out of a mural coronet Argent a leopard's head
Gules billety Or.
MAY, of Stoke. *Davy, A. Washbourne*, 'Suff.'
Fairbairn, 'Stoke, Suff.'*
Out of a mural coronet a leopard's head ducally gorged.
ST. PHILIBERT, of Chelsworth. *Davy, A.*

LION
Out of a mural crown a lion's face affronty. [*sic*
Leopard]
ASHBY, George, Rector of Stansfield and Barrow.
Davy, A., Stone in Barrow church
From a mural coronet Argent a lion's head Gules
charged with a bezant.
BENNETT, Sir Thomas, Lord Mayor of London.
Grants & Certificates (Stowe MS 707)
Out of a mural coronet a lion's head charged on the
neck with a roundel.
BENNET, BENETT. *MS Heraldic Collections,
fo. 89a**
Out of a mural coronet Or a lion's head Argent [*sic*]
charged with a bezant.
BENNET, of Rougham. *Davy, A.*
Out of a mural coronet Or a lion's head Gules
charged on the neck with a bezant.
BENNETT. *Washbourne*, 'Surr. and Berks.'
Fairbairn*, 'Bennet of Rougham Hall, Suff. and
Tollesbury, Essex'*
Out of a mural coronet Azure a lion's head Or.
HAWES, of Walsham le Willows, Weston, Ipswich,
Belstead, Framlingham, Akenham. *London
Visitation 1633 (H.S.) I. 366 and 368*. Davy, A.
Washbourne*, 'Suff., Surrey and Lond.'
Fairbairn*, 'Suff., Surrey and London'*
Out of a mural coronet a lion's head Or.
HAWES. *Misc.Gen. et Her. 5th S. V. 208–12,
Pedigree. Bookplate**
From a mural coronet Or a lion's head Argent.
KETTERIDGE. 'Richard Keterich, Ketridge or
Ceterich, of London'; Confirmation of Arms and
Grant of Crest by R. Cooke, Clarenceux, in 1593.
*Grants & Certificates (Harl. MS 1,359; Stowe
MS 670; Add. MS 4,966)*
Out of a mural coronet a lion's head all Or.
KETTERIDGE, KETTRICK. 'Rich. Kekridge of
London by R. Cooke Clarenc. Aº 1593' *MS
Ordinary of Arms, fo. 28**
Out of a mural coronet a lion's head.
MARDESTON, DE *Washbourne*, 'Suff.'
Fairbairn*, 'Suff.'*
Out of a mural coronet Or a lion's head Argent semy
of mullets Sable.
VYSE, of Friston, Snape. *Davy, A.*

OTTER
From a mural coronet an otter's head all Or.

SMITH. Thomas Smith, of Bacton, co. Suffolk, in
1572. *Grants & Certificates (Harl. MS 1,359)*

OX
Out of a mural coronet Argent a bull's head Sable
gorged with a collar Argent charged with two bends
Gules.
HOLGATE. *Davy, A., Hawkedon church*
Out of a mural coronet Argent a bull's head Sable
collared bendy of six Gules and Agent.
HOLGATE. *Davy, A.*

TIGER
Out of a mural coronet Gules a tiger's head Or
ducally gorged Azure.
WALSINGHAM. *Washbourne. Fairbairn*.* The
heiress of Walsingham, of Scadbury, co. Kent
married Randolf Scrivenor. *Her.Suff.Ch.,
Monumental tablet, Sibton.* Dorothy Walsingham,
married Sir Henry Bokenham, died 1654. *Effigy
monument, Thelnetham*

ON OR OUT OF CORONET or CROWN
[MURAL CORONET see following section]

HEAD. BIRD, CHOUGH
From a crest coronet Or a chough's head Sable beak
Gules between two wings displayed Gold.
AYLMER. Sir John and Samuel Aylmer, of
Mogelinghall [*sic*], co. Essex. By Patent June
1607. *Grants & Certificates (Stowe MS 707)*
Out of a ducal coronet a sea aylet's [chough's] head
Sable.
AYLMER, of Claydon. *Visitation 1664–8*
Out of a ducal coronet a chough's head Proper.
AYLMER. *Davy, A. (Barrett MS)*

COCK
Out of a ducal coronet Or a cock's head Azure
combed Gules holding a branch Vert.
BRAUNCH. *Davy, A., Raydon church*
Out of a ducal coronet a cock's head Proper.
CHARLESWORTH, of Ipswich. *Davy, A.*
Out of a ducal coronet Or a cock's head Gules
crested [combed] and wattled Or.
FARMER, of Denham. *Davy, A. (Edms.)*
Out of a ducal coronet Or a cock's head Proper.
GOLDINGTON. *Davy, A.*

EAGLE
Out of a ducal coronet an eagle's head and wings
Sable enfiled with a rose Gules issuing rays Or.
HAMMOND, of Whepstead, Hawstead. *Davy, A.
Fairbairn, the eagle charged with the rose.* Gen.
Sir Francis Hammond, of Plumpton and Lord of
the Manor of Whepstead, died 1850. *Her.Suff.Ch.,
Wall tablet, Whepstead*
From a coronet Or an eagle's head Sable beaked Or
between two ostrich feathers Argent.
MANNING, . . ., of Kent; Confirmation by Sir W.
Segar, Garter. *Grants & Certificates (Add. MS
12,225)*
Out of a ducal coronet Or an eagle's head Sable
beaked Or between two ostrich feathers Argent.
MANNING, of Diss, co. Norfolk, Bungay,
Thetford. Rector of Barnardiston, 1714–33.
Davy, A. Crisp's Visitation. II. 121–4, Pedigree
Out of a ducal coronet an eagle's head between two
ostrich feathers.
MANNING. *MS Martin's Crests. Bookplates**.
Rev. John Manning, Rector of Barnardiston, died
1733. *Her.Suff.Ch., Ledger stone, Barnardiston*
Out of a ducal coronet Or an eagle's head Azure
armed Or.

MARTYN. *MS Heraldic Collections, fo. 38**
Out of a ducal coronet an eagle's head.

MARTYN, MARTIN, of Gorleston. *Davy, A.,
church. E.A.N. & Q. II. 325.* Henry Martyn, died
1775. *Her.Suff.Ch., Ledger stone, Gorleston*
Out of a ducal coronet Or an eagle's head between
two wings.

MARTYN. 'Morton, of Bildeston, Chelsworth'
Davy, A. (Barrett MS) 'Marten' *Fairbairn*, 'of
Bildeston, Suff.'*
Out of a ducal coronet an eagle's head erased
between two wings displayed Or.

STONE. *MS Heraldic Alphabet*
Out of a ducal coronet Or a griffin's, or eagle's, head
Argent.

UMFREVILLE, of Stoke by Nayland. *Davy, A.,
church. Proc.S.I.A. IV. 198, 'eagle's head'*
Out of a coronet an eagle's head between two wings
Or.

WINN, Arthur, M.A., F.S.A., Barrister, died 1927.
Her.Suff.Ch., Wall tablet, Aldeburgh
Out of a coronet Gules two eagle's heads crossing
each other Argent.

KNIGHTON. *MS Martin's Crests*

FALCON or HAWK

Out of a coronet a falcon's head erased.

AYLMER, of Claydon. *Bokenham*
On a five-leaved coronet a hawk's head erased
charged with a cross paty fitchy Or.

JACKSON. *Bookplate**
Out of a ducal coronet Or a falcon's head Azure
armed Or.

MARTYN. *Her.Suff.Ch., Ledger stone, Gorleston*

PEACOCK

'beryth to his crest a pecokes hede in his kinde in a
crowne gold'

CLIFTON. 'Clyfton' *Wall's Book*
'to his Crest a pecocks hede in his kynd in a Crowne
or/'

CLIFTON. 'Clyfton' *MS Alphabet of Crests,
fo. 19b*

PELICAN

From a coronet Argent a pelican's head Or vulned
Gules.

PERNE, Andrew, D.D., Dean of Ely and Master of
S. Peter's Coll., Cambridge; Grant by R. Cooke,
Clarenceux, 15 June 1574. *Grants & Certificates
(Stowe MSS 676, 699 and 703)*
Out of a ducal coronet Argent a pelican's head Or
beaked and vulned Gules.

PERNE. 'Doctor perne deane of Ely' *MS Knight's
Visitations, Cambs.** Rev. Andrew Pern, B.D.,
late Fellow of St. Peter's College, Cambridge and
Rector of this Parish for 31 years, died 1772 aged
64. *Her.Suff.Ch., Wall tablet, Norton*
Out of a coronet a pelican's head erased.

PERNE. *Bokenham*
Out of a ducal coronet Or a pelican's head Or
vulning herself Gules.

SALMON. *MS Heraldic Alphabet*
Out of a ducal coronet Gules a pelican's head Or
beaked and vulning herself Gules.

SALMON. *MS Heraldic Alphabet*
From a coronet Or a pelican's head Sable vulned
Gules.

SALTONSTALL, Richard, of London, 1588.
Grants & Certificates (Harl. MS 1,359)
Out of an Earl's coronet Proper a pelican's head
erased Argent vulning herself Gules.

SALTONSTALL. *MS Ordinary of Arms, fo. 143**
Out of a ducal coronet Or a pelican's head Azure
vulning its breast Gules.

SALTONSTALL, of Somerleyton. *Davy, A., church*

PHEASANT

Out of a ducal coronet Or a pheasant's head Proper
charged on the neck with an escallop Argent.

THIRLBY, THORLBY, THORLY. *MS Ordinary of
Arms, fo. 206**

SWAN

Out of a crown Or a swan's head between two
wings Argent.

ATHERTON. *Wall's Book*
'to his crest a swannes hed bet ij wungs ar/ in a
croune or'

ATHERTON. *MS Alphabet of Crests, fo. 3*
Out of a ducal coronet Gules a swan's head
feathered Argent beaked and langued Gules.

BEAUCHAMP, Sir Thomas, K.G., Earl of Warwick,
died 1401. *Stall Plates, plate XLI**
Out of a ducal coronet Gules a swan's head feathered
Argent quilled Or beaked Purpure langued Gules.

BEAUCHAMP, Sir Richard, K.G., Earl of Warwick,
died 1439. *Stall Plates, plate XXXIV**
In a coronet Gules a swan's neck Argent billed
Gules.

BEAUCHAMP, Earl of Warwick. Of Chillesford.
Earl of Worcester. Of Otley. *Davy, A.*
Out of a ducal coronet Or a swan's head and neck
Argent beaked Sable.

KEPPEL. *MS Ordinary of Arms, fo. 206**

VULTURE

Out of an ancient coronet a vulture's head Proper.

AYLMER, of Claydon. *Davy, A.*

ON OR OUT OF MURAL CORONET or CROWN

HEAD. BIRD, OSTRICH

Out of a mural coronet Or an ostrich's head Proper.

SMYTH, of Cavendish. *Visitation 1561 (ed.
Howard) II. 206**
Out of a mural crown Or an ostrich's head Proper
holding in the beak a horse-shoe Or.

SMYTH, of Thrandeston, Haughley. *Bokenham.
MS Martin's Crests*
Out of a mural coronet, or crown, an ostrich's head
Or.

SMYTH, SMITH, of Thorndon. *Davy, A.
Washbourne*, 'Suff.' Fairbairn, 'Smith, Smyth,
Sussex and Suff.'* John Smyth, died 1691; son
John Smyth, died 1723; Sarah, wife of John
Smyth, died 1743/4. *Her.Suff.Ch., Wall tablets,
Haughley.* Thomas Smyth, Gent., died 1702;
widow Dorothy, died 1728. *Shield painted on
wall behind pulpit, Bacton*
Out of a mural crown Gules an ostrich's head Proper
holding in the beak a horse-shoe Or.

SMYTH, SMITH, of Cavendish, Long Melford, Gt.
Barton, Bacton, Haughley, Thrandeston,
Marlesford. *Davy, A.*

PARROT

From a mural coronet chequy Argent and Azure a
parrot's head Vert beaked Gules.

PEARSON. Grant April, 1616. *Grants &
Certificates (Harl. MS 6,059)*

PELICAN

Out of a mural crown Or a pelican's head between
two wings expanded Ermine.

CANHAM, of Milden Hall, Abbot's Hall in Brent Eleigh. *Sharpe. E.A. Misc. 1920, 10*
Out of a mural coronet Or a pelican's head Ermine.
CANHAM. Canham Family, 1699–1731. *Her.Suff.Ch., Floor slab, Milden.* John Canham, of Milden, died 1772. *Wall tablet, Milden*

ON OR OUT OF CORONET or CROWN
[MURAL CORONET see following section]

HEAD. HUMAN, MAN
Out of a Viscount's coronet a hermit's bust in profile vested and having on the head a cowl paly of six Argent and Gules.
BARRINGTON. *Her.Suff.Ch., Bench end, Hollesley*
Out of a coronet Or a man's head couped at the shoulders Proper on his head a fool's cap Gules with a cock's comb and bells.
BOURCHIER *MS Martin's Crests*
Out of a ducal coronet Or a Moor's head in profile Sable wreathed Or and Azure.
BUGG, of Barsham. 'Anthony Bugg' *MS Knight's Visitations, Essex**. 'Bugge' [in a later hand] *MS Philpot's Visitations, Essex*. Davy, A.*
Out of a ducal coronet Or a Saracen's head Argent in his ear a ring Or wreathed about his head Argent tied in a knot the ends flotant above which a fretted cap Argent and Or.
'DARELL, S. Edward' *Harl. MS 6163**
Out of a ducal coronet Or a man's head bearded Proper wreathed about the temples and knotted Argent and Azure.
DARELL. *MS Ordinary of Arms, fo. 19**
Out of a ducal coronet a man's head in profile Proper on his head a round cap Azure with a pom-pom Or.
DARELL, DARRELL. *MS Ordinary of Arms, fo. 24**
Out of a ducal coronet Or an old man's head couped below the shoulders Proper vested Gules turned back Ermine on his head a cap Gules tasselled Or.
FREVILE, of Swilland. *Davy, A.*

WOMAN
Out of a ducal coronet Or a woman's head and neck couped below the breast Proper crined Or.
ELMES, ELMY, of Beccles. *Davy, A.*
Out of a ducal coronet Or a lady's head and shoulders in profile Proper crined Or.
HEBER, of Hadleigh. *Davy, A.*

ON OR OUT OF MURAL CORONET or CROWN

HEAD. HUMAN
On a mural crown a Saracen's head Proper.
CHENERY, Henry, gent., died 1827. *Her.Suff.Ch., Glass, Cretingham*

ON OR OUT OF CORONET or CROWN
[MURAL CORONET see following section]

HEAD. MONSTER, HERALDIC ANTELOPE
Out of a ducal coronet an antelope's head Or tufted and maned Sable.
HATLEY, of Ipswich. *Davy, A.*

COCKATRICE
Out of a ducal coronet Argent a cockatrice's head between two dragon's wings expanded Argent combed and wattled Gules.
THORNTON, of Snailwell in co. Cambs., Denston, Lt. Wratting. *Davy, A.*

DRAGON
Out of a coronet a dragon's head Or.

BARDOLF. 'Bardolph' *MS Martin's Crests*
Out of a ducal coronet Or a dragon's head wings expanded Or.
BARDOLF, of Clopton, Ilketshall, etc. *Davy, A.*
Out of a ducal coronet Or a dragon's head Or with wings expanded Gules.
BARDOLF. *Her.Suff.Ch., under feet of Lord Bardolf's effigy, Tomb, Dennington*
Out of a ducal coronet Or a dragon's head Vert.
CADOGAN, Earl of Of Downham. *Davy, A. Fairbairn*, 'Culford Hall, Bury St. Edmunds'.* Charles Sloane, Earl Cadogan, died 1807. *Her.Suff.Ch., Wall tablet, Santon Downham.* 'Lord Cadogan' *Bookplate**
Out of a coronet a dragon's head.
CARVER, of Halesworth. *Bokenham*
From a crest coronet Or a dragon's head the back part Azure the front Argent.
GLASCOCK. William and John Glascock, gents., brothers, of Much Dunmow and Roxwell, co. Essex; Grant by R. Cooke, Clar., 14 July 1571. *Grants & Certificates (Add. MS 14,295; Harl. MS 6,169)*
Out of a ducal coronet Or a dragon's head per pale Argent and Vert.
GLASCOCK. *Davy, A., 'Granted 1571'*
Out of a ducal coronet Or a dragon's head Gules.
LUCAS, of Bury, Saxham. *Visitation 1561 (MSS G.7* and Iveagh Copy*; ed. Metcalfe; ed. Howard. II. 9*).* 'Thomas fitzlukas' *MS Knight's Visitations, Essex**. 'Thomas Fithelukas' *MS Philpot's Visitations, Essex**. 'William Lucas of Hornesherth' *MS Lilly's Visitation of Suffolk*. MS Heraldic Collections, fo. 53*. Washbourne*, 'Ess. and Suff.' Tymms, 187. Fairbairn*, 'Essex and Suff.'*
Out of a ducal coronet a dragon's head.
LUCAS. *MS Philpot's Visitations, Norf.**
'Fitz-Lucas, of Suffolk' *MS ex-Taylor Coll.**
Out of a coronet Gules a dragon's head.
LUCAS, of Saxham. *MS Fairfax, 'I saw it on his Seale'*
In a ducal coronet a dragon's head Gules scaled Or crowned with a cronel [the head of a jousting lance].
LUCAS, of Bury, Horringer, Lt. Saxham. *Davy, A.*
Out of a ducal coronet Or a dragon's head (or demi-griffin) Or wings addorsed Argent and each charged with three bars Gules.
VAN HEYTHUYSEN, of Oulten. *Davy, A.*
From a coronet Or a dragon's head of the same armed Gules.
WRIGHT, John, of Wright's Bridge in Hornchurch, in the Liberty of Havering at Bower, co. Essex, gent.; Grant by R. Cooke, Clarenceux, 20 June 1590. *Grants & Certificates (Add. MS 14,295; Harl. MS 6,169)*

TWO DRAGON'S HEADS
Out of a ducal coronet Gules two dragon's heads and necks in saltire Argent.
KNIGHTON, KNYGHTON, of Lt. Bradley. *Visitation 1561 (MS G.7*),* [tinctures added in a later hand]
Out of a ducal coronet two dragon's heads and necks in saltire.
KNIGHTON, KNYGHTON, of Lt. Bradley. *Visitation 1561 (MS Iveagh Copy*). Harl. 772*. MS Heraldic Collections, fo. 54**
Out of a ducal coronet Gules two dragon's heads per saltire endorsed 1. Argent 2. Azure.
KNIGHTON, of Lt. Bradley. *Bokenham*

Out of a ducal coronet Or two dragon's heads and necks in saltire Proper.

KNIGHTON, KNYGHTON, of Lt. Bradley. *Davy, A., Gt. Thurlow church. Washbourne*, 'Herts. and Suff.' Fairbairn, 'Herts. and Suff.'* Ann Knighton, married Richard Le Hunte. *Her.Suff.Ch., Effigy monument, Lt. Bradley*

Out of a ducal coronet Or two dragon's heads and necks in saltire Vert.

KNIGHTON. *Her.Suff.Ch., Glass, Lt. Thurlow*

GRIFFIN [Alphabetically by name]

From a crest coronet Or a griffin's head Gules between two wings Or semy of estoiles Gules.

CORY, John, of London, gent.; Patent February 1612. *Grants & Certificates (Stowe MS 707)*

Out of a ducal coronet a griffin's head between two wings Argent each charged with three estoiles in pale Gules.

CORY, of Burgh Castle, Yarmouth. *Davy, A.*

Out of a ducal coronet a griffin's head Or.

FOXWELL. Rector of Rattlesden, died 1731. *Davy, A.*

Out of a ducal coronet a griffin's head wings extended.

MORLEY, of Monk Soham House near Framlingham. *Burke, L.G. 1952 ed.**

Out of a ducal coronet Or a griffin's head Proper.

PINKNEY, of Cavendish. *Davy, A. (Burke)*

Out of a ducal coronet Or a griffin's head Proper.

PLESTOW. Rector of Harkstead, Westerfield. *Davy, A.*

From a coronet Sable a griffin's head Argent beaked Or.

PLOMSTED, PLUMSTED. Bartholomew Plumsted, of Calthorpe, co. Norfolk; Grant by R. Cooke, Clarenceux, 30 August 18 Eliz. [1575/6]. *Grants & Certificates (Harl. MS 1,359)*

Out of a coronet Sable a griffin's head Argent eared and beaked Sable, sometimes charged on the neck with a crescent for difference.

PLOMSTED, PLUMSTED, of Cockfield, Beccles. 'Bartilmew Plomsted' *MS Knight's Visitation, Norf.** 'Bartholme Plomsted' *MS Philpot's Visitations, Norf.* Visitation 1664–8*. Davy, A.*

Out of a ducal coronet a griffin's head.

PLUMSTEAD, Thomas, Gent., of Beccles, died 1679; widow Rebecca, died 1709. *Her.Suff.Ch., Ledger stone, Beccles*

Out of a ducal coronet Or a griffin's head wings displayed Argent.

POLE. 'Poole' *MS ex-Taylor Coll.**

From a coronet per pale Gules and Or a griffin's head Argent beaked Gules collared chequy Or and Gules between two wings Argent each charged with a mullet Sable.

SPENCER, John, of Worstead, co. Norfolk, gent.; Grant by Sir G. Dethick, Garter, 10 September I Queen Mary [1553–4]. *Grants & Certificates (Harl. MS 1,359)*

Out of a ducal coronet per pale Or and Gules a griffin's head Argent gorged with a collar per pale Argent and Gules between two wings expanded the dexter Gules the sinister Or.

SPENCER. 'Leonard Spencer of Worsted' *MS Knight's Visitations, Norf.* 'John Spenser' *MS Philpot's Visitations, Norf.**

Out of a ducal coronet per pale Or and Argent a griffin's head between two wings expanded Argent collared Gules.

SPENCER, of Rendlesham. *Visitation 1664–8.*

Bokenham, coronet untinctured. *Davy, A., church. Washbourne*, 'Beds., Oxon. and Suff.'*

Out of a ducal coronet Or a griffin's head Argent collared Gules between two wings expanded Argent each charged with a fleur-de-lis Sable.

SPENCER. *MS ex-Taylor Coll.*, 'of Bedford^re.'*

Out of a ducal coronet per pale Or and Gules a griffin's head Argent eared and beaked Gules gorged with a collar per pale Gules and Or between two wings expanded the dexter Gules the sinister Argent on each a mullet –.

SPENCER. *Davy, A. Washbourne, 'Suff. and Norf.' Fairbairn, 'of Bradfield, Norf. and Suff.'*

Out of a ducal coronet a griffin's head erased between two wings expanded gorged with a bar gemel.

SPENCER, John, died 1709; son Edward Spencer, died 1727. *Her.Suff.Ch., Ledger stones, Rendlesham*

From a coronet Or a griffin's head Ermine beaked Or between two wings Or.

STONE, William, of London, son of Simon Stone; Grant by R. Cooke, Clarenceux, 10 November 1583. *Grants & Certificates (Stowe MS 700; Harl. MS 1,359; Add. MS 12,225)*

Out of a ducal coronet Or a griffin's head Argent between two wings Or.

STONE. *MS Ordinary of Arms, fo. 215**

Out of a ducal coronet Or a griffin's head between two wings expanded Gules bezanty.

STONE. *Davy, A.*

Out of a ducal coronet a griffin's head between a pair of wings Or.

STONE, Anne, daughter of William Stone, of co. Beds., married Sir Stephen Soame, Kt., Lord Mayor of London, etc. She died 1622. *Her.Suff.Ch., Effigy monument and Glass, Lt. Thurlow*

Out of a ducal coronet Or a griffin's head Gules between two wings displayed Or.

THORNTON. 'John Thornton' *MS Knight's Visitations, Cambs.* MS Heraldic Alphabet*

Out of a ducal coronet Or a griffin's head erased Gules armed Or.

TILNEY, TYLNEY, of Shelley. *Davy, A., church. Washbourne*, 'Tylney, Suff. and Norf.' Fairbairn*, 'Tylney, Suff. and Norf.' Her.Suff.Ch., Wall monument, Shelley*

Out of a ducal coronet Or a griffin's, or eagle's, head Argent.

UMFREVILLE, of Stoke by Nayland. *Davy, A., church. Proc.S.I.A. IV. 198*

From a Baron's coronet a griffin's head erased charged with a rose.

VAUX, Lord Harroden [*sic* Harrowden], died 1663. *Proc.S.I.A. II. 144, Eye church monument*

Out of a ducal coronet a griffin's head all Or.

WEST, of Bury. *Wall's Book, Davy, A.*

'to his Crest a gryffyns hede in a crowne or/'

WEST. *MS Alphabet of Crests, fo. 136b*

Out of a ducal coronet Or a griffin's head Azure beaked and eared Or.

WEST, Lord Delaware Of Fakenham Aspes [Gt. Fakenham]. *Davy, A.*

Out of a ducal coronet per pale Azure and Or two griffin's heads addorsed counterchanged.

POPE. *MS Heraldic Collections, fo. 14**

PHOENIX

On a ducal coronet a phoenix's head in flames in the beak an olive branch.

ONLEY. *Washbourne*, 'Suff.'*
Out of a ducal coronet Or a phoenix's head in flames
Proper holding in the beak a sprig Vert.
ONLEY. *Fairbairn, 'Northamp. and Suff.'*

HERALDIC TIGER

Out of a ducal coronet a tiger's head Argent maned
and tufted Sable.
ARCHDALE, of Suffolk. *MS Heraldic
Collections, fo. 82b*, untinctured. Davy, A.
(Edms.)*
Out of a ducal coronet a tiger's head tufted.
LENNARD. *MS Ordinary of Arms, fo. 225**
Out of an Eastern coronet Or a tiger's head Sable
collared and lined Or.
MILESON, MELLISENT. *Davy, A. (Barrett MS)*
From a coronet Or a tiger's head Sable mane and
tusks [*sic*] Or
OSBORNE, John, 'next door to ye Lord Maiors'.
Grants & Certificates (Harl. MS 5,869)
Out of a ducal coronet Or a tiger's head Sable
maned Or.
OSBORNE. 'Thomas Osborne' *MS Philpot's
Visitations, Norf.**
Out of a ducal coronet a tiger's head Argent maned
Azure.
TEY, TAY. 'Tyee, of Essex' *MS Heraldic Alphabet*

UNICORN

'to his crest a Unycorne hed sa/ issuing owt of a
Crowne or/ horned mayned and berded ar/. Antony
Carleton of baldwyn bryghtwell in oxfordsh^r'
CARLETON, CARLTON. *MS Alphabet of Crests,
fo. 25*
Out of a ducal coronet a unicorn's head the horn
twisted Or and Sable.
CARLETON. *MS Heraldic Collections, fo. 23**
Out of a ducal coronet Or a unicorn's head Sable the
horn twisted Or and Sable.
CARLETON. *Davy, A. (Edms.)*
Out of a ducal coronet Or a unicorn's head Sable
armed and maned Or.
CARRINGTON. *MS Ordinary of Arms, fo. 262*.
Bookplate*, untinctured*
Out of a ducal coronet Or a unicorn's head Argent
horned Or bridled reined and feathered Gules.
DEBDEN. 'John Dybden of est . . .' *MS Knight's
Visitations, Norf.**
Out of a ducal coronet Or a unicorn's, or horse's,
head Argent bridled Or reined Gules feathered
Gules.
DEBDEN, of Depden, Brampton, Brandeston.
Davy, A.
Out of a ducal coronet Gules a unicorn's head Or.
ELLIS, of Cotton, Redisham. *Davy, A., Cotton
church*
Out of a ducal coronet a unicorn's head.
ELLIS, Thomas, M.D., died 1724; John Ellis, Esq.,
died 1739. *Her.Suff.Ch., Ledger stone and Altar
tomb in churchyard, Cotton*
Out of a ducal coronet Or a unicorn's head Gules
attired and crined Or.
HOW, of Stowmarket. *Davy, A., '? Grant by
Cooke, Clar., March 1576'. Washbourne*, 'How,
Howe. Ess. and Suff.' Fairbairn*, 'How, Essex
and Suff.'*
Out of a five-leaved ducal coronet Or a unicorn's
head Azure maned and horned Or.
PRAED. B.J. Mackworth Praed, of Ousden Hall,
died 1876; Algernon Mackworth Praed, died
1952. *Her.Suff.Ch., Tablet and Glass, Ousden*
Out of a ducal coronet Or a unicorn's head Argent

maned Purpure armed Or.
SPARROW, of Wickhambrook. *Visitation
1664–8**
Out of a coronet a unicorn's head erased.
SPARROW, of Wickhambrook. *Bokenham.*
Benjamin Sparrow, died 1725; son Samuel
Sparrow, died 1713; widow Theodosia, died
1750. *Partridge, 81 (Darby, 1826), Table tomb in
churchyard, Hitcham*
Out of a ducal coronet a unicorn's head.
SPARROW, Robert, late of Kettleburgh, died 1761.
Her.Suff.Ch., Ledger stone, Kettleburgh
Out of a ducal coronet Gules a unicorn's head
issuing Argent attired Or charged on the neck with
three hurts.
TRUSTON. *MS Knight's Visitations, Suff.** 'John
Truston' *MS Philpot's Visitations, Suff.* Davy, A.*
Out of a coronet a unicorn's head erased Argent
attired Or.
WENTWORTH, of Gosfield. *MS Martin's Crests*
Out of a ducal coronet Gules two unicorn's heads
endorsed Argent attired Gules.
CASTON, CAUSTON, of Ipswich. *Davy, A. (Mr.
Barnwell), St. Mary Tower church*

WYVERN

Out of a ducal coronet Or a wyvern's head between
two wings displayed Argent.
THORNTON. *MS Heraldic Alphabet*

ON OR OUT OF MURAL CORONET or
CROWN

HEAD. MONSTER, DRAGON

Out of a mural crown Or a dragon's head Sable
gorged with two bars Or.
DAINES, DEYNES, of Coddenham. *Visitation
1664–8*
Out of a mural crown Or a dragon's head Sable
gorged with two bars of the second [*sic*].
DAINES, DEYNES, of Coddenham. *Davy, A.,
'? Blois MS'*
Out of a mural coronet Or a dragon's head Sable
gorged with two bars Or.
DEYNES. *Washbourne, 'Suff.' Fairbairn, 'Suff.'*
Out of a mural coronet a dragon's head erased
Proper.
REEVES, of Thwaite. *Bokenham*
Out of a mural crown Vert a dragon's head erased
Argent.
REEVE, WRIGHT alias REEVE, of Thwaite.
Davy, A.
Issuant from a mural coronet Vert a dragon's head
Argent.
WRIGHT. *Washbourne*, 'Suff.'*

GRIFFIN

From a mural coronet Or a griffin's head Ermine
beaked Or charged on the neck with a cross paty
Sable.
MOSSE, Clement, Chamberlain of London.
Entered 8 February 1634. *Grants & Certificates
(Harl. MSS 1,484 and 5,869)*
Out of a mural coronet Gules a griffin's head issuant
Ermine.
UMFREVILLE. *Washbourne*, 'Lond., Essex,
Suff., etc.'*

SEA HORSE

Out of a mural crown Or a sea horse's head Argent.
CROMPTON, of Coddenham. *Davy, A. (Edms.)*

UNICORN

From a mural coronet Or a unicorn's head Argent

horn Or mane Purpure.

SPARROW. 'Robert Sparowe, of Ipswich, son of John, of Somersham, co. Suffolk'; Grant of Arms by R. Cooke, Clarenceux; Confirmation and Crest granted by R. Lee, Clarenceux, June 1594. *Grants & Certificates (Add. MS 14,295; Harl. MSS 1,359 and 6,169)*

'Out of a Crown Mural and embattled Or Masoned Sable an Unicorn's Head Argent, Exalting his Trunk Or, langued Gules, with the ends of the Hairs upon the Mane Crimson'.

'SPARROW, Thomas, 1419, of Somersham, Ipswich' *Sparrow Pedigree Roll**

Out of a mural crown Or a unicorn's head Argent armed and crined Or.

SPARROW, of Long Melford, Depden, Somersham, Ipswich. *MS Fairfax. Sharpe. Davy, A., Depden church. Fairbairn, 'of Worlingham Hall, Suff.'*

Out of a mural coronet Or a unicorn's head Argent maned Purpure armed Or.

SPARROW, Of Ipswich, Kettleburgh, Worlingham. *Davy, A., St. Lawrence church, Ipswich. Washbourne, 'Sparow, Suff.' E.A.N. & Q. IX. 150. Fairbairn, 'Sparow, of Somersham & Ipswich, Suff.'* Capt. Robert Sparrow, Died 1690. *Her.Suff.Ch., Ledger stone, Wickhambrook.* John Sparrow, M.A., of Stowlangtoft, Rector, died 1722; Rev. Joseph Sparrow, 'Rector of the Parish', died 1748. *Ledger Stone, Westley.* 'Attired Argent'

Out of a mural coronet Gules a unicorn's head Argent.

WILKINSON, of Middleton. *Davy, A.*

Out of a mural crown Gules a unicorn's head Erminois armed and crined Or.

WILKINSON, of Walsham-le-Willows. *Davy, A.*

WYVERN

Out of a mural crown Or a wyvern's head.

DAINES, DEYNES, of Coddenham. *Davy, A. (Barrett MS)*

ON OR OUT OF CORONET or CROWN

MONSTER, HERALDIC ANTELOPE

An antelope Gules horned Or seiant on a crown Or.

ARMIGER, of Tannington, Dagworth. *Davy, A., 'Per Cooke, Clar., 1576'*

'Vpon the heaulme, on a wreathe siluer 't gules, out of a crowne wth a chayne sables, a demy Antelopp gould, mantled gules, dubbed siluer'

MUSKETT, Henry, of Harleston; Confirmation of Arms and Crest by Robert Cooke, Clar., 13 September 1576. *Muskett. II. 363 (Harl. MS 2,146, fo. 120)*

Out of a ducal coronet with a chain and ring attached to the dexter side Sable a demi-antelope rampant Or.

MUSKETT, Henry, of Harleston. *MS Knight's Visitations, Suff., fo. 107b** 'Henry Muskett' *MS Philpot's Visitations, Suff.**

Out of a coronet Or a demi-antelope Or attired Argent armed Or.

MUSKETT. 'Muskete, Muskite of Hawley' *MS Humfry Pedigree Roll*; Corder MS 91*

Out of a ducal coronet Sable a demi-antelope Or chained and ringed Sable.

MUSKETT. *Washbourne, 'Suff. and Norf.'*

Out of a ducal coronet Or a demi-antelope Sable chained and ringed Or.

MUSKETT. *Fairbairn, 'Suff. and Norf.'*

COCKATRICE

Out of a ducal coronet a demi-cockatrice rising.

HUTCHINSON. *MS Heraldic Collections, fo. 87b**

Out of a coronet a cockatrice Sable crested Gules.

WILLAT. *Bokenham*

DRAGON

Out of an Eastern crown a demi-dragon rampant Sable holding between its paws a stave raguly Argent.

FANCOURT. Brigadier General St. John Fancourt, C.B., died 1917. *Her.Suff.Ch., Brass tablet, Stowmarket*

Out of a crown Or a dragon volant Azure.

'FITZHUGH, Baron' *Wall's Book*

'to his Crest a Dragon volant b/ syttyng in a crowne or/'

'FFYTZHUGH, Baron' *MS Alphabet of Crests, fo. 38b*

Out of a coronet a demi-dragon issuant its tail wreathed Azure.

FITZHUGH. *MS Martin's Crests*

From a ducal coronet a demi-dragon rising.

LUCAS. Henry and Edmund, sons of Thomas Lucas, Secretary to Jasper Tudor. *Her.Suff.Ch., Brass removed from ledger stone, St. Mary's, Bury*

Out of a ducal coronet a demi-dragon with wings erect.

LUCAS, of Horringer. *Her.Suff.Ch., Family memorial slab on vestry floor, Horringer*

GRIFFIN

On a ducal coronet Or a griffin segreant Murrey.

ARMIGER, of Bury. *Davy, A.*

Out of a ducal coronet Or a demi-griffin Azure beaked and legged Or.

COPPING, of Stanningfield, Cockfield, Bury, Herringswell, Bramfield. 'Stevyn Coppyng' *MS Knight's Visitations, Norf.** 'Stevne Coppinge' *MS Philpot's Visitations, Norf.** *Davy, A.*

Issuing out of a crown Proper a demi-griffin.

HOWES, HOWSE, of Ashfield, Thorndon. *Davy, A.*

From a ducal coronet Or a demi-griffin wings expanded Gules.

LUCAS. *Washbourne*, 'Northumb., Ess. and Suff.'*

From a coronet per pale Gules and Or a demi-griffin per pale Or and Gules beak Gules.

PAGE, Sir Richard; Confirmation of Arms and Grant of Crest by Thomas Benolt, Clarenceux, 1 February 1530. *Grants & Certificates (Add. MS 14,295; Harl. MS 6,169)*

Out of a ducal coronet per pale Gules and Or a demi-griffin segreant counterchanged beaked Gules.

PAGE. *MS Ordinary of Arms, fo. 163**

Out of a ducal coronet Or a dragon's head, or demi-griffin, Or wings addorsed Argent and each charged with three bars Gules.

VAN HEYTHUYSEN, of Oulton. *Davy, A.*

MERMAID

Out of a naval coronet Or a demi-mermaid Proper.

CHEEKE, of Suffolk. *Davy, A. Washbourne*, 'Suff.' Fairbairn*, 'Suff., holding comb and mirror Proper'*

Out of a ducal coronet Or a mermaid Proper crined Or conjoined to a dolphin hauriant Or devouring her sinister hand.

THORNE. *Washbourne, 'Suff.' Fairbairn, 'Suff. and Shropsh.'*

PANTHER

From a crest coronet Or a demi-panther Argent enflamed at the mouth and ears Proper and spotted various.

SPARKE, . . . , of London; Confirmation by R. Cooke, Clar., 10 August 1571. *Grants & Certificates (Stowe MS 700; Harl. MS 6,140)*

Out of a coronet a demi-panther Argent spotted various tinctures fire issuing from his mouth and ears Proper.

SPARKE, of Glemham. *Davy, A.*

Out of a ducal coronet Or a demi-panther rampant guardant Argent spotted of various tinctures fire issuing from his mouth and ears Proper.

SPARK, SPARKES, of Aldeburgh, Glemham. 'Spark of London' *MS ex-Taylor Coll.* * *Davy, A., Aldeburgh church. Her.Suff.Ch., Glass, Whepstead.* William Sparke, died 1797. *Wall tablet, Aldeburgh. Charged with a crescent Gules for difference*

PHOENIX

Out of a ducal coronet Or a phoenix Or issuing from flames Proper.

SEYMOUR, Duke of Somerset. Of Lidgate, Moulton, Newmarket, Withersfield, Gazeley. *MS Martin's Crests. Davy, A.*

From a ducal coronet Or a phoenix in flames Proper.

SEYMOUR. Francis Charles Seymour-Conway, 3rd Marquess of Hertford, died 1842. *Her.Suff.Ch., Hatchment, Sudbourne*

SEA HORSE

Out of a naval crown a demi-seahorse rampant charged with a cross paty Or.

PAGE, Philip Henry and others of the family, Rectors of Woolpit, 1837–1941. *Her.Suff.Ch., Glass, Woolpit*

HERALDIC TIGER

On a ducal coronet Or a tiger sejant Gules tufted Or.

ARMIGER. *MS Ordinary of Arms, fo. 234*.* 'Thomas Armyger' *MS Philpot's Visitations, Suff.* *

On a coronet a tiger sejant Gules armed and tufted Or.

ARMIGER, of Tannington. *Visitation 1612*

On a crown Or a tiger sejant Ermine maned Or.

ARMIGER. *MS Fairfax*

Out of a ducal coronet Or a tiger seiant Proper.

ARMIGER, of Tannington. *Davy, A.*

Out of a ducal coronet Or an heraldic tiger seiant Argent.

BOWYER, Bart., of Dunwich. *Davy, A.*

Out of a coronet a tiger passant Or maned Sable.

EDWARDS. *MS Martin's Crests*

On a ducal coronet Argent a tiger passant Or.

EDWARDS. *Davy, A. (Edms.)*

UNICORN

Out of a ducal coronet Or a demi-unicorn Gules armed and maned Or.

HOWE, of Stowmarket. *Visitation 1577*

Out of a coronet a demi-unicorn salient Gules armed Or.

HOW, of Stowmarket. *Bokenham*

Issuing out of a crown Proper a unicorn.

HOWES, HOWSE, of Ashfield, Thorndon. *Davy, A.*

WYVERN

Out of a ducal coronet Or a wyvern Gules.

CARVELL. *Davy, A.*

ON OR OUT OF CORONET or CROWN
[MURAL CORONET see following section]

VARIOUS [Objects in alphabetical order]

From a coronet of three fleurs-de-lis a demi-angel affronty Proper winged and crowned Or holding in his dexter hand a sword erect Or, or Argent.

ENGLEHEART, Henry, died 1934; Lt. Col. E.L. Engleheart, died 1943. *Her.Suff.Ch., Wall tablets, Stoke-by-Nayland*

Issuant from a crest coronet of fleurs-de-lis Argent a demi-figure representing an angel Proper vested and with wings erect Azure crined and holding with both hands a mullet Or.

KERR, of Brendhall in Clopton, 1909. *Copinger VI*

ARM [Holding objects in alphabetical order]

Out of a ducal coronet Or a dexter arm embowed in armour holding in the gauntlet a battle-axe Gules.

COVE, of Cove, Cratfield. *Davy, A.*

From a crest coronet Or a dexter arm embowed in armour Proper in the gauntlet a poleaxe erect staff Gules headed Argent all garnished Or.

MADDOCKS. 'John Madox or Madocks, gent., of Middlesex'; Confirmation by Sir W. Dethick, Garter, 26 March 1592. *Grants & Certificates (Stowe MS 676)*

Out of a ducal coronet Or a cubit arm erect vested Gules cuffed Argent holding in the hand a club Sable spiked Or.

CLENCH, of Burgh, Ipswich. *Visitation 1664–8* *

Out of a Saxon crown Or an arm erect couped in the elbow vested Gules cuffed Argent holding in the hand Proper a club Vert spiked Or.

CLENCH, of Holbrook, Bealings. *Davy, A., 'on the verge of the Crown, Tien le droit'. Washbourne* *, 'Suff.' Fairbairn* *, 'Suff.' Her.Suff.Ch., Gt. Bealings*

Out of a crown an arm erect couped at the elbow vested Gules cuffed Or holding in the hand a club Vert spiked Gules.

CLENCH, John, died 1607. *Her.Suff.Ch., Effigy monument, Holbrook*

Out of a crown an arm erect couped at the elbow holding in the hand a club (broken).

CLENCH, John, died 1628. *Her.Suff.Ch., Effigy monument, Gt. Bealings*

Out of a ducal coronet a cubit arm erect habited Or holding in the hand Proper three ostrich feathers the middle one Sable the others Or.

WYNTER, of Aldeburgh. *Davy, A.*

Out of a ducal coronet an arm issuing bendy of six Azure and Or engrailed Ermine at the wrist holding in the hand Proper a buck's frontlet Gules. [*sic*, a buck's head cabossed in Washbourne and Fairbairn].

GIFFARD. 'Gifford' *MS Heraldic Alphabet*

Out of an Eastern crown between two pennons a mailed arm embowed holding a lance.

COMBE, COMBES. Edward Combe, J.P., died 1920. *Her.Suff.Ch., Wall tablet, Gorleston*

Out of a palisaded coronet a dexter arm erect vested Gules cuffed Ermine holding in the hand a roll of parchment Argent.

SCOTT, of Leiston and co. Essex. *Harl. 772*. Davy, A. (Barrett MS)*

Out of a coronet a hand couped at the elbow clothed Or grasping a broken spear Proper.

JETTER, of Beyton, Ellough. *Bokenham*

Out of a ducal coronet a naked arm embowed holding a stick.

MINCHIN. Charles Owen Minchin, died 1930;

Aline Emilie Minchin, died 1938. *Her.Suff.Ch., Tombstone in churchyard, Gunton*
In a ducal coronet Or a cubit arm in armour Argent brandishing a sword Argent hilted Or.
BOYLAND. *Davy, A.*
From a Baron's coronet a dexter arm in armour grasping in the hand a scimitar.
BLUNDELL, William, died 1700; Montague, Viscount Blundell, died 1733. *Her.Suff.Ch., Wall tablet, Somerton*
Out of a ducal coronet Or an arm in armour Proper holding in the gauntlet a dagger Argent hilt and pommel Or.
FENTON. *MS Heraldic Alphabet*
Out of a ducal coronet Or a cubit arm in mail Proper holding in the hand also Proper the blade of a broken sword Argent.
JETTER, of Ellough, Lowestoft, Beyton. *Visitation 1664–8*. Davy, A. Washbourne, 'Suff.' Fairbairn, 'of Bayton, Ellowe [sic] and Lowestoft, Suff.'*
On a Marquess's coronet a dexter arm in armour couped at the elbow and lying fesseways in the gauntlet a sword erect enfiled with a chaplet all Proper.
RICHARDSON. *Davy, A., Melford church*
Out of a ducal coronet Or a mailed arm lying fesseways holding a sword erect on the blade a wreath tied all Proper.
RICHARDSON, Thomas, died 1818. *Her.Suff.Ch., Hatchment, Long Melford*
Out of a naval coronet Or a dexter arm embowed encircled by a wreath of laurel Proper the hand holding a trident erect Or.
BROKE, Bart., of Nacton. Sir Philip Broke, Bart. *Davy, A. Washbourne*. Fairbairn, 'Sir Philip Broke, Bart. of Nacton'.* Lt. Gen. Horatio Broke, died 1860. *Her.Suff.Ch., Wall tablets and Glass, Nacton.* [Family crest blazoned as a beaver, but should be a badger or brock. Sir George Broke-Middleton, 3rd Bart., died 1887.] *Hatchment, Barham; Glass, Coddenham. Two Crests, Broke and this Crest of Augmentation*
Out of a naval crown Or an arm embowed charged with an escarbuncle Or and encircled by a laurel wreath Proper the hand grasping a trident Or.
LORAINE. Rear Admiral Sir Lambton Loraine, Bart., married a co-heiress of Broke of Nacton; Sir Percy Loraine, 12th Bart., died 1961; widow died 1970. *Her.Suff.Ch., Wall tablets, Bramford*
Out of a palisaded coronet a dexter arm erect vested Gules cuffed Ermine a line affixed to the wrist and grasping in the hand a truncheon.
SCOTT, of Leiston. *Davy, A.*
Out of a ducal coronet Or two arms embowed habited Gules holding in the hands Proper a cake of bread Argent.
WALWORTH, of Ipswich. *Davy, A., St. Mary Tower church*
Out of a ducal coronet two arms vested and embowed each holding an ostrich feather.
BARKESWORTH, Rob. de Temp. Edw. I. *Davy, A.*

ARROWS, etc.
Out of a ducal coronet three arrows one in pale and two in saltire points downward Or entwined with a snake Proper.
PONSONBY, of Stutton. *MS Ordinary of Arms, fo. 248*, untinctured. Crisp's Visitation. XII. 105*, Earls of Bessborough. Pedigree*
In a coronet composed of fleurs-de-lis and

strawberry leaves Or two single attires of a stag Gules.
NASSAU, Earl of Rochford. Of Easton. *Warren's map*. Davy, A. Livery button**
A stag's attire Gules issuing from a ducal coronet Or.
NASSAU. ?Hon. Henry Nassau, died 1741; William Nassau, 5th Earl of Rochford, died 1830. *Her.Suff.Ch., Hatchments, Easton.* George Richard Savage Nassau, died 1823. *Hatchment, Trimley St. Martin*
Out of a ducal coronet Or a pointed cap Argent between two elephant tusks Gules.
BOHUN. *MS Ordinary of Arms, fo. 57**
Out of a ducal coronet a chaplet of laurel.
NEALE. *MS Heraldic Collections, fo. 83b*.* Thomas Neale, of Bramfield, died 1704. *Her.Suff.Ch., Slab, Blythburgh*
Out of a ducal coronet Or a chaplet of laurel Vert.
NEALE, of Bramfield. *Davy, A., church*
Out of a ducal coronet a chaplet.
PHILLIPS, of Halesworth, Ipswich. *Davy, A.*
Issuing out of a coronet a crab.
SCROPE. Owners in Nayland, etc. *Davy, A.*
A crest coronet thereon a crescent Sable.
HODGES, ..., of London. Patent October 1610. *Grants & Certificates (Stowe MS 706)*
On a ducal coronet Or a crescent Sable.
HODGES, of Woodbridge, Layham. *Davy, A., St. Matthew's church, Ipswich. Proc.S.I.A. VII. 204*

FEATHERS [Alphabetically by name]
Out of a ducal coronet Or a plume of feathers Argent.
ASTLEY, of Weybread. *MS Heraldic Alphabet. Davy, A., church*
Out of a ducal coronet Or a plume of five feathers.
ASTLEY. Briget, wife of Hobart Astley, died 1714; he died 1718. *Her.Suff.Ch., Ledger stone, Weybread*
A high plume of feathers issuing from a ducal coronet.
BARDOLF. William, Lord Bardolf, died 1441. *Her.Suff.Ch., Beneath head of male effigy, Tomb, Dennington*
Out of a ducal coronet a plume of ostrich feathers Argent and Azure.
BERNEY, of Parkhall in Reedham, co. Norfolk. *MS Heraldic Alphabet*
Out of a ducal coronet Or a plume of feathers Sable.
BRAHAM, of Brantham, Ash, Wickham Skeith. *Davy, A.*
Out of a ducal coronet Or a plume of five ostrich feathers Argent issuant therefrom a falcon rising Argent.
BUTLER, Earl of Wiltshire and Ormond. *Davy, A.*
Out of a ducal coronet Or a plume of feathers Argent.
CLERE. 'S. Roberd Clere, Norff.' *Harl. MS 6163* 'beryth to his crest a bushe of fethers oon monting above an other silver in a crowne of gold'
CLERE. *Wall's Book*
'to his crest a bush of ffethers or [sic] mountynge a bove an other ar/ in a Crowne or/'
CLERE. 'Clere of Norff.' *MS Alphabet of Crests, fo. 19b*
Out of a coronet Or a plume of feathers Argent.
CLERE. 'Cleer' *MS Martin's Crests*
Out of a ducal coronet Or a pyramid of feathers Argent.
CLERE, CLEERE, of Norfolk. *MS Ordinary of Arms, fo. 136*.* 'Sr. John Clere of Ormsby' *MS*

Knight's Visitations, Norf. * 'Wyll Clere' *MS Philpot's Visitations, Norf.* *

Out of a ducal coronet Or a plume of ostrich feathers Argent.

> CLERE, of Thetford. *Davy, A., Yoxford church*

Out of a ducal coronet Gules a plume of ostrich feathers Argent tied with a band Azure.

> CLINTON, Earl of Huntingdon. Of Otley, etc. *Davy, A.*

Out of a ducal coronet Or a bush of feathers Argent.

> COURTENAY, Sir Hugh, Founder K.G., died 1349. *Stall Plates, plate XXXI*. 'Lord of Devenschyre' *Harl. MS 6163*

Out of a ducal coronet Or a plume of seven ostrich feathers Argent.

> COURTENAY, of Leiston. *Davy, A., church*

Out of a ducal coronet Or a plume of ostrich feathers Azure and Or out of the top thereof a dagger Sable pommelled and hilted Or.

> DUKE, of Benhall in Suffolk. *MS Heraldic Alphabet*

Out of a ducal coronet Or a plume of five ostrich feathers alternately Azure and Or enfiled from above by a sword Argent hilt and pommel Or.

> DUKE, Edward, Kt. and Bart. [*sic*], died 1598; Others. *Her.Suff.Ch., Wall tablet, Benhall*

Out of a ducal coronet jewelled Or a bush of feathers Argent.

> ERPINGHAM, Sir Thomas, K.G., died 1428. *Stall Plates, plate XLII* *

Out of a ducal coronet Or a pyramid of feathers the lower half Vert the upper half Sable.

> ERPINGHAM, of Norfolk. *MS Ordinary of Arms, fo. 194* *

Out of a ?ducal crown Gules a plume of feathers Argent.

> ERPINGHAM, of Thornham. *Davy, A.*

Out of a ducal coronet Gules a bush of feathers Ermine.

> FELBRIGGE, Sir Simon, K.G., died 1442. *Stall Plates, plate XVIII* *

Out of a crown Or a 'bushe' of ostrich feathers the one Argent the other Sable.

> 'FIZTLEWES of Essex' *Wall's Book*

'to his Crest a bush of Oystryche ffethers the on ar/ the other sa/ in a crowne or/'

> 'FFYTZLEWES of Essex' *MS Alphabet of Crests, fo. 38*

From a crest coronet Or a plume of ostrich feathers Argent quills Azure.

> HOLLAND, John; Confirmation 19 May 1601 by Sir W. Segar, Garter and W. Camden, Clarenceux, of a Grant by Glover in 1583. *Grants & Certificates (Add. MS 12,225)*

Out of a crown Or a bush of feathers Azure.

> MORTIMER. *Wall's Book*

'to his crest a bush of Blew ffethers in a Crowne Or/'

> MORTIMER. 'Mortymer' *MS Alphabet of Crests, fo. 80*

Out of a ducal crown Azure jewelled Gules and Or a bush of white feathers.

> PHELIP, Sir William, Lord Bardolf, K.G., died 1441. Buried at Dennington. *Stall Plates, plate XLVIII* *

On a crown Vert adumbrated [shadowed] Argent a tuft of sundry feathers Gules.

> PHELIPS. *Visitation 1561 (ed. Howard), I. 141*

Out of a crown, or coronet, Vert garnished Argent a bunch of feathers Gules shadowed Or.

> PHELIPS PHILIPS, Lord Bardolfe. Of Dennington.

MS Fairfax, 'at Mr. Rouses at Henham Hall'. *Bokenham*

Out of a ducal coronet Azure three ostrich feathers Argent.

> PHILIP, PHILIPS, of Suffolk. *Davy, A. Washbourne*, 'Philip, Philips. Lond. and Suff.' *Fairbairn, 'Philip, Suff. and London'*

From a coronet Or a plume of four ostrich feathers Argent quills Or between two wings Or.

> REPPS. 'Reepes (or Reppes), Henry, son and heir of John, second son of Henry Reepes'; Confirmation by L. Dalton, Norroy, 30 November 1560. *Grants & Certificates (Harl. MS 1,359)*

'his crest a plom of Oysteryche fethers ermyns the pennes or/ issuing owt of a Crowne bet ij wyngs or/ henry Reppes'

> REPPS. 'Reppes' *MS Alphabet of Crests, fo. 110b*

Out of a ducal coronet a plume of five ostrich feathers Ermine between two wings Or.

> REPPS. 'Henry Reppes of West Walton' *MS Knight's Visitations, Norf.* *

Out of a ducal coronet a plume of feathers Argent quills Or between two wings Or.

> REPPS, RUGG. *Davy, A.*

Out of a ducal coronet Or two plumes of feathers three and three in a row Purpure.

> REYMES, of Wherstead. 'Richard Reymes of Hempton' *MS Knight's Visitations, Norf.* * *Davy, A. (Barrett MS)*

Out of a ducal coronet Or a cone of ostrich feathers Purpure.

> REYMES. 'Olyver Raynes' and 'John Raynes' *MS Philpot's Visitations, Norf* *

Out of a ducal coronet Or a plume of ostrich feathers Argent.

> SCALES, of Wetherden. *Davy, A.*

Out of a ducal coronet Or a bush of feathers Azure.

> SCROPE, Sir John le Scrope, K.G., Lord Scrope of Bolton, died 1498. *Stall Plates, plate LXX*. 'Lord Scropp of Bolton' *Harl. MS 6163*. 'Scrop, Baron' *Wall's Book*

'beryth to his crest a bushe of Oysteryche fethers b/ in a Crowne or/'

> SCROPE. 'Scrop baron made knight by henry 8' *MS Alphabet of Crests, fo. 117b*

Out of a coronet Or a plume of feathers Azure.

> SCROPE, SCROOP, of Knettishall, Bentley, Bolton, Wherstead. *Davy, A.*

From a coronet Or a plume of feathers alternately Argent and Azure issuing therefrom a griffin's head Gules beak Or, and charged with a mullet Or as borne by his ancestors Tilney, of East Tuddenham.

> TILNEY, Richard, of Rotherwick, co. Hants., Esq., son of Robert Tilney, late of East Tuddenham, co. Norfolk, gent. Descended from a younger brother of the ancestor of Philip Tilney, Esq., of Shelley in Suffolk, who on 20 November 1630 testified that Emery Tilney, his grandfather, and Thomas Tilney, his father, acknowledged the above Robert Tilney and his sons Robert and Richard to be cousins, and further that the said Philip Tilney being then aged 30 years, was at the funeral of the last –named Robert, who ob.S.P., when divers escutcheons were used [the arms of Tilney with a mullet for difference]. Upon which testimony the said arms were confirmed by Sir R. St. George, Clarenceux, 14 May 1632. *Grants & Certificates (Add. MS 14,295)*

Out of a ducal coronet Or a plume of feathers alternately Azure and Argent issuing therefrom a griffin's head Gules beaked and eared Or.

TILNEY, TILLNEYE, TYLNEY, of Shelley. *Visitation 1561 (MSS G.7* and Iveagh Copy*) Harl. 772*
'Phillip Tilney of Shelley esquier' *MS Lilly's Visitation of Suffolk* Davy, A.*
Out of a ducal coronet a plume of feathers and issuing therefrom a griffin's head.

TILNEY, of Shelley. *E.A. Misc. 1925, 17. Her.Suff.Ch., Wall tablet in vestry, Shelley*
Out of a ducal coronet Or a garb Ermine [*sic* shown to be far more like a bush of feathers banded].

TINDALL. 'S. Welye Tyndall. Norff.' *Harl. MS 6163*
From a crest coronet Or five ostrich feathers Ermine banded Gules.

TINDALL. 'Thomas Tyndall, of co. Sussex, son and heir of Thomas Tyndall, one of the Gentlemen Sewers to Queen Elizabeth'. Grant dated 13 Queen Elizabeth [1570/1]. *Grants & Certificates (Stowe MS 670; Harl. MS 1,359)*
Out of a crown Or a bush of ostrich feathers bound Ermine.

TINDALL. 'Tyndale' *Wall's Book*
'to his Crest a bush of Oysteryche ffethers bound ermyne in a Crowne or/'

TINDALL. 'Tyndale' *MS Alphabet of Crests, fo. 126b*
Out of a ducal coronet Or a plume of five feathers Argent.

TINDALL. *Davy, A. Washbourne*, 'Suff. and Norf.' Fairbairn*, 'Tindall, Tindale, Suff. and Norf.' Ostrich feathers*
Out of a ducal coronet Or a plume of feathers Ermine within a basket Gules.

TINDALL, TYNDAL. *Muskett. I. 152 (Harl. MSS 1,411 and 1,542)*
Out of a crown Or a bush of ostrich feathers per pale Argent and Gules.

WALDEGRAVE. 'Walgrave of Suffolk' *Wall's Book*
Out of a ducal coronet Or five ostrich feathers alternately Argent and Gules environed by a looped riband held up by a ring Or.

WALDEGRAVE. 'William Waldegrave of Smallbridge in Com. Suffolke esquier' *MS Lilly's Visitation of Suffolk*
Out of a ducal coronet Or a double plume of ostrich feathers per pale Argent and Gules.

WALDEGRAVE, WALDGRAVE, of Smallbridge in Bures, Hitcham. *MS Fairfax. Bokenham. Davy, A. Washbourne, 'Waldegrave, Walgrave, Suff., Norf., Essex & Northamp.' Badham, 53, 'five feathers' Fairbairn*, 'Waldegrave, Smallbridge, Suff., Norf., Essex & Northamp.'*
Out of a ducal coronet Or a plume of seven feathers per pale Argent and Gules.

WALDEGRAVE, Edward, died 1585. *Her.Suff.Ch., Ledger stone, Stoke by Nayland, 'six ostrich feathers'.* Sir William Waldegrave, died 1613. *Effigy tomb, Bures*
Out of a ducal coronet Or a plume of ostrich feathers Argent issuing therefrom an eagle's leg claws upward Or.

WARREN. *MS ex-Taylor Coll.*, 'of Cheshire'*

FISH, etc.

Out of a coronet Gules a dolphin embowed Or.
ALBANY. 'Albeny' *MS Martin's Crests*
Out of a ducal coronet Or a demi-lucy erect Or.
GASCOYNE, of Barking. *Davy, A., church*
On a ducal coronet a dolphin naiant.
MAXFIELD. *Davy, A.*
On a ducal coronet a dolphin naiant Proper.

STANNARD, of Laxfield. *Davy, A.*
Out of a ducal coronet a fleur-de-lis.
BELGRAVE. Rector of Cockfield. *Davy, A. Fairbairn, 'of Cockfield, Suff.'*
Out of a ducal coronet Or a gilly flower [July flower, carnation or pink] – stalked and leaved Argent.
LE NEVE. *MS Ordinary of Arms, fo. 225*
From a ducal coronet Or a lily Argent stalked and leaved Vert.

LE NEVE. 'William Le Neve, Esq., York Herald, afterwards knighted and made Clarenceux. Descended from an ancient family, owners of 'Le Neves' before and in the reign of K. Edw. III., which from late possessors thereof is since called Spencers, Goodwins and Greses, in Tivetshall, co. Norfolk, with lands in Suffolk; Confirmation of Arms by Sir W. Segar, 5 May 1627. *Grants & Certificates (Add. MS 12,225)*
Out of a ducal coronet a lily flowered and seeded Or stalked and leaved Vert.

NEAVE, of Framlingham. *Davy, A., Framlingham churchyard; St. Mary Tower church, Ipswich*
Out of a ducal coronet Or a lily Argent stalked and leaved Vert bladed and seeded Or.

NEAVE. *Davy, A.*
Out of a ducal coronet Or three pine apples [pine cones] Vert their tops purfled Or.

APPLETON. 'Sr Isaacke Appulton of gᵗ Waldingfilde in Com Suffolke Knight' *MS Lilly's Visitation of Suffolk* Fairbairn, 'Suff'.* Appleton of Waldingfield. *Muskett. I. 322 (Harl. MSS 1196 and 1560)*
Out of a ducal coronet Proper a pine apple Or.

APPLETON. *MS Martin's Crests*
Out of a ducal coronet Sable three pine apples Argent.

APPLETON. *Davy, A., Lt. Waldingfield church, funeral helm seen 1827. Proc.S.I.A. IX. 114*
Out of a ducal coronet Or seven leeks roots upward Proper.

LINGEN-BURTON, 'of Four Sisters, East Bergholt, Suff.' *Fairbairn*, second crest, for Lingen*
Out of a ducal coronet Or a lion's gamb erect Argent.

CREWE, Bart., of Yoxford, Tattingstone. *Davy, A. (Edms.)*
From a coronet a lion's paw [gamb] Or grasping a snake Proper.

DONNE. 'Daniel Dunn, Doctor of Laws, now of Essex, and his brother William Dunn, M.D., now of Bristol'. Patent 8 August 1588. *Grants & Certificates (Harl. MS 1,359)*
Out of a ducal coronet Or a lion's gamb Proper.

GIBSON, of Ipswich, Lt. Stonham, etc. *Davy, A. E.A.N. & Q. (N.S.) IV. 216. Proc.S.I.A. VIII. 322*
Out of a ducal coronet Or a lion's gamb Proper grasping a club Gules spiked Or.

GIBSON, of Ipswich, Lt. Stonham, Theberton, etc. *Davy, A. Bildeston, 85.* Charles Gibson, Clerk, Vicar of Mendlesham, died 1700; William Gibson, died 1737. *Her.Suff.Ch., Ledger stone, Mendlesham.* Rev. Edgar Gibson, died 1714. *Ledger stone, Wetheringsett cum Brockford. The gamb untinctured.* Barnaby Gibson, died 1758. *Ledger stone, Lt. Stonham*
Issuant from a coronet a lion's paw [gamb].

MAYHEW. *MS Martin's Crests*
Out of a ducal coronet Or a lion's gamb erect Sable armed Gules.

SAVAGE, Earl Rivers Of Long Melford. *MS Ordinary of Arms, fos. 41* and 57*. Davy, A. Proc.S.I.A. XXVI. 216.* Thomas, 1st Viscount

Savage, died 1635. *Her.Suff.Ch., Hatchment, Long Melford. Photographs**
Out of a ducal coronet Or a lion's gamb Sable armed Gules.
SCUDAMORE, of Ipswich. 'Scudmore' *MS ex-Taylor Coll.* Davy, A.*
From a coronet Or a garb Argent.
KEMPTON, Edward, of London. Patent by R. Cooke, Clarenceux, 1587. *Grants & Certificates (Harl. MS 1,359)*
Out of a ducal coronet Or a garb Argent.
KEMPTON, of Hitcham. *Davy, A.*
Out of a ducal coronet Or a garb Azure.
MORTYMER. *Harl. MS 6163*
A garb Or enfiled by a coronet Gules.
SCAMBLER, Edward, D.D., Bishop of Norwich; Grant by R. Cooke, Clar., 20 December 1585. *Grants & Certificates (Harl. MSS 1,359 and 6,169; Stowe MS 670; Add. MS 14,295)*
A garb Or within a ducal coronet Gules.
SCAMBLER. Bishop of Norwich, 1584–94. *Heylyn. Blomefield. III. 560, 'Grant by Cooke, 20th Dec. 1585'*
Out of a ducal coronet a hand holding a sheaf of arrows Proper.
CRANBER. *Washbourne, 'Suff.' Fairbairn*, 'Suff.'*
Out of a ducal coronet a dexter hand holding up a swan's head all Proper.
GRIGG, of Lt. Bealings, Snape. *Davy, A. Muskett. I. 200 (Harl. MS 1085)*
Out of a five-leaved ducal coronet Or a dexter hand erect the third and fourth fingers turned down Proper.
KING. Rector of Bromeswell. *Davy, A.*
Out of a Baron's coronet Or the pearls Argent a dexter hand holding a cutlass all Proper.
LE HUNT. *Fairbairn, 'Little Bradley, Suff. and Huntshall, Essex'*
'on the helme a Septer hand proper out of a Crowne golde'
MIDDLETON. 'Sir Hugh Midleton of London, Baronet'; Grant of new Arms and Crest by William Camden, Clarenceux, 1st November 1622. *Miscellaneous Grants (H.S.) II. 147–9 (Harl. MS 1507, fo. 382)*
From a coronet Or a sinister hand appaumée [open, showing the palm] Proper.
MIDDLETON. 'Sir William Midleton'. Allowed 1634. *Grants & Certificates (Harl. MS 5,869)*
Out of a ducal coronet an esquire's helmet Proper.
HALSHAM, of Woodbridge. *Davy, A.*
Out of a coronet two horns one Or the other Sable.
CLOPTON. *MS Knight's Visitations, Suff.**
Two horns one Or the other Gules out of a coronet Or.
CLOPTON, of Clopton. 'Clopton of Kentwell' *MS Lilly's Visitation of Suffolk* Fourth of four crests shown. Davy, A.*
Out of a ducal coronet a horse-shoe inverted Sable between two wings.
FARRER. 'Rev. Edmund Farrer, F.S.A., 1889' *Bookplate**
Out of a ducal coronet Or a demi-archer habited Gules facings brown turban and waist sash Argent drawing a bow to the dexter Proper.
CURSON. *Banners & Standards**
Out of a ducal coronet a demi-woman her hair dishevelled Proper holding in her dexter hand a gem-ring.
WITHAM, of Hasketon. *MS Ordinary of Arms, fo. 172* Davy, A.*

From a coronet Or a lamp of three branches Or lighted Proper.
LETE, . . . , of co. Suffolk. Patent by Sir W. Segar, Garter. *Grants & Certificates (Add. MS 12,225)*
Out of a ducal coronet Or a lamp of three branches Or fired Proper.
LETE, LIGHT, of Bury. *Davy, A., 'Granted by Segar'*
On a ducal coronet an antique lamp Or fired Proper.
LEET, LETE. *Washbourne*, 'Camb., Hunts. and Suff.'*
Out of a ducal coronet two bunches of laurel in orle.
CASEY. *Davy, A.*
Out of a crown Gules a bunch of 'flegges' or water reed leaves Sable.
CLINTON, Baron *Wall's Book*
Out of a ducal coronet Or a cone of bay leaves Vert.
ROUS, of Badingham. *Visitation 1664–8**
Out of a ducal coronet Gules a pyramid of leaves Argent.
WARREN, of Burgh Castle. *Visitation 1664–8. Fairbairn, 'of Burgh Castle, Suff.'*
Out of a coronet Gules ten bay leaves Argent 4.3.2.1.
WARREN. *Bokenham*
Out of a ducal coronet Gules a pyramid of leaves Argent and Gules.
WARREN, of Burgh Castle, Mildenhall. *Davy, A. Washbourne*, 'Suff'. Leaves Argent*
Out of a ducal coronet an armed leg with spur affixed the foot uppermost.
CREETING, CRETING. 'Edm' de Creting' *Caerlaverock Poem, 362 note x. Davy, A.*
Out of a ducal coronet Proper a bear's paw erected Sable armed Gules.
GIBSON, of Stonham. *Bokenham*
Out of a ducal coronet Or a bear's paw in pale Sable armed Gules.
SCUDAMORE. 'Lt. Col. Frederick W. Scudamore, of Chelsworth Hall, Suff.' *Fairbairn**
Out of a ducal coronet Or two pennons dexter Or sinister Sable staves Gules.
CALVERT. Rector of Whatfield. *Davy, A.*
On a naval crown Or the Plume of Triumph, or Chelengk, presented to him by the Grand Seignior.
NELSON, Horatio. Lord Nelson. Of Round Wood in Ipswich, 1798. *Davy, A. Wagner's Historic Heraldry, 91*. The first of two crests*
On a ducal coronet Or a lizard Vert.
GLEANE. 'Thomas Glyne of norwiche' *MS Knight's Visitations, Norf.* 'A lizard'*
On an Imperial crown Gules and Or a star of sixteen points Or in the centre an eye.
EYE, Borough of Grant by William Dethick, Garter, 5th April 1592. *Proc.S.I.A. VII. 33–50, Article and photograph of Grant** [in Latin]
Above an Imperial crown a golden star charged with an eye.
EYE, Borough Council *Scott-Giles, 346**
Out of a ducal coronet a sword erect Argent hilt Or in a plume of five feathers three Azure and two Argent.
DUKE, Bart., of Benhall, Brampton. *Davy, A.*
Out of a ducal coronet Or an ash tree fructed Proper.
ASHBURNHAM, Earl of Of Barking. *MS Heraldic Alphabet. Davy, A. Washbourne*, 'of Suff.'*
From a ducal coronet Or an ash tree Proper.
ASHBURNHAM, Bertram, 4th Earl, of Barking Hall, died 1878. *Her.Suff.Ch., Hatchment, Barking.* Hon. Rev. Richard Ashburnham, son of 4th Earl, Rector of Combs, died 1882. *Wall tablet, Combs*
Out of a ducal coronet Or an oak tree fructed and

penetrated transversly in the main stem by a frame saw Proper the frame Or.

> HAMILTON. Duke of Hamilton and Brandon. Of Rendlesham, Easton. *Davy, A.*

From a ducal coronet Or a frame saw Or cutting an oak tree Proper.

> HAMILTON, Alexander, 10th Duke of Hamilton, died 1852; William, 11th Duke, died 1863. *Her.Suff.Ch., Hatchments, Easton.* Dukes of Hamilton. *On woodwork, Worlingworth*

Out of a ducal coronet Or an oak tree Proper.

> HAMILTON, Sir Collingwood, Bart., of Cransford Hall, died 1947. *Her.Suff.Ch., Wall tablet, Cransford*

Out of a ducal coronet a tree fructed.

> THREEL, Lawrence, of Lewisham [*sic*] co. Sussex. Married Frances Daniel, he died 1700. *Her.Suff.Ch., Slab, Acton*

Issuant from a crown vallary Or an oak tree Proper fructed Or.

> WOOD, Sir John, 1st Bart., died 1951; Gertrude, Lady Wood, died 1927. *Her.Suff.Ch., Glass, Flempton*

WINGS [Alphabetically by name]

Out of a ducal coronet two wings Or.

> BARROW, of Westhorpe, Barningham. *Bokenham, 'Wings extended sideways' Davy, A., Westhorpe church*

Out of a ducal coronet two wings the dexter Or the sinister Sable.

> BARROW. Impaling Smyth. *Her.Suff.Ch., Hatchment formerly in Barningham church. Recorded by Farrer from Davy MS 19,070 – now lost*

Out of a ducal coronet two wings erect all Or.

> BARROW, Maurice, Esq., son of William Barrow, Esq., Patron of the living. No date given. *Her.Suff.Ch., Effigy monument, Westhorpe*

'Out of a crown proper, two angels' wings displayed and opposed and perpendicularly erected Argent, charged each with a cross crosslet botonnée fitché Gules, by the name of Crane'

> CRANE. *Visitation 1561 (ed. Howard) 1.141, 'Reyce's Breviary of Suffolk, quoted by Cole, Vol. 28, p. 207'*

Out of a crown two eagle's wings endorsed perpendicularly Sable bezanty.

> D'OYLEY, Bart. Pond Hall, Ipswich. *Davy, A.*

Out of a ducal coronet Or a pair of wings erect Gules.

> FELTON. Sir Thomas Felton, K.G., died 1381. *Stall Plates, plate XII**

Out of a ducal coronet a pair of wings erect and endorsed all Or.

> FELTON. *MS Ordinary of Arms, fo. 51**

Out of a coronet Or a pair of wings displayed Gules.

> FELTON. 'Sr Henry Felton of Playford Knight Barronett' *MS Lilly's Visitation of Suffolk*. MS Martin's Crests*

Out of a ducal coronet a pair of wings erect Argent.

> FELTON, of Playford, Sudbury. *Davy, A.*

Out of a ducal coronet a pair of wings erect Gules.

> FELTON. *Bokenham. Davy, A.*

Out of a ducal coronet Or a pair of wings Or and Argent.

> FELTON, of Playford; Sir Thomas Felton, Bart., died 1708. *Her.Suff.Ch., Wall tablet and Ledger stone, Playford.* Dame Elizabeth Felton, wife of Sir John Playters, Bart., died 1718. *Altar tomb in churchyard, Worlingham*

Out of a ducal coronet Or a pair of wings Azure

each charged with three estoiles Or.

> GIPPS, of Gt. Whelnetham, Horringer. *Visitation 1664–8. Gage (Thingoe). Davy, A., Horringer church. E.A.N. & Q. (N.S.) III. 318**

Out of a ducal coronet Or two wings expanded Azure (should be semy of estoiles).

> GIPPS, Richard, of Gt. Whelnetham, died 1660. *Her.Suff.Ch., Wall tablet, Gt. Whelnetham. Missing 1978*

Out of a ducal coronet a pair of wings displayed each charged with three estoiles.

> GIPPS, Sir Richard, Kt., of Gt. Whelnetham, 1659–1708. *Suff. Green Bks, Gt. Whelnetham. Ticket for masque, 1683*. Full biography given*

Out of a ducal coronet Or two wings expanded Azure semy of estoiles Or.

> GIPPS. *Washbourne*, 'Suff.' Fairbairn, 'Gipp, Suff.'* Sir Richard Gipps, of Lt. Horringer, died 1681. *Her.Suff.Ch., Slab, Horringer*

Out of a ducal coronet Or two wings erect and addorsed Argent.

> GURDON. Brampton Gurdon, of Assington, died 1650. *Muskett. I. 274 (Harl. MS 1560). Effigy Monument, Assington, photograph c.1955*

Out of a ducal coronet Or two wings displayed Argent.

> GURDON, Brampton, of Assington, died 1650. *Her.Suff.Ch., Effigy monument, Assington. Crest missing 1980*

In a crown Or two wings Gules in pale on each the arms of Howard.

> HOWARD. 'Haward Duke of Norfolk' *Wall's Book* 'Crest p haward/ ij Wyngs g/ in pale on eche of them the armes of haward in a Crowne/ or/'
> HOWARD. 'Haward Duke of Norff' *MS Alphabet of Crests, fo. 54b*

From a ducal coronet Or a pair of wings Gules each charged with a bend between six cross crosslets fitchy Argent [the Arms of Howard].

> HOWARD, Bernard, 12th Duke of Norfolk, died 1842. *Her.Suff.Ch., Hatchment, Fornham St. Martin. First crest*

Out of a ducal coronet per pale Argent and Azure two wings expanded counterchanged.

> JOHNSON, Bart., of Aldeburgh, Friston. *Middlesex Visitation 1663 (ed. Foster), 67. Davy, A.*

Out of a ducal coronet Proper two raven's wings Sable.

> JOHNSON, of Friston, Blundeston Lodge. *Bokenham. Sharpe*

Out of a ducal coronet a pair of raven's wings elevated.

> JOHNSON. *MS Martin's Crests*

A pair of wings issuing from a ducal coronet Proper.

> JOHNSON, of Blundeston Lodge and co. Linc. *Burke, Peerage, 1900 ed.*

ON OR OUT OF MURAL CORONET or CROWN

VARIOUS [Objects in alphabetical order]

Out of a mural coronet –.

> BIGGS, of Glemsford. *Davy, A.*

From a mural coronet Gules a cubit arm vested Or cuffed Argent in the hand Proper a mullet Or.

> ELTON, Nicholas, of London, merchant tailor, son of Richard Elton of Kingston Lisle, co. Berks. *Grants & Certificates (Add. MS 12,225)*

From a mural coronet Argent on a wreath Argent and Gules an arm embowed vested Vert in the hand Proper a bugle horn Sable stringed Argent.

FOSTER, Samuel, of Redgrave, Suffolk, B.D.; Grant by Sir William Dugdale, Garter and Sir Henry St. George, Norroy. *Grants & Certificates (Stowe MS 714)*

Out of a mural crown an arm erect cuffed and sleeved holding in the hand a bugle horn.

FOSTER, Samuel, Rector of Redgrave, died 1680. *Her.Suff.Ch., Ledger stone, Redgrave*

A dexter cubit arm erect Proper issuant from a mural crown Or a crescent Argent between two branches of laurel Proper.

HARVEY. Emma, wife of Edward Kerrison Harvey, died 1886. *Fairbairn, 'Harvey, of Norfolk. The crescent and laurel above the arm.' Her.Suff.Ch., Brass in chancel, Kirkley. Not found 1979*

Out of a mural crown Or a dexter arm embowed in armour entwined by a branch of laurel holding in the hand a flagstaff Proper therefrom flowing a banner forked Gules fringed Or inscribed 'Peninsula' in letters Or.

KERRISON, Bart., of Oakley Park, Brome Hall. *Davy, A., 'Crest of Augmentation'. Fairbairn, 'of Hoxne and Brome, Suff. Honourable augmentation.'* Edward Clarence Kerrison, Bt., died 1886. *Her.Suff.Ch., Glass, Oakley*

Out of a mural coronet Or a cubit arm habited Vert cuffed Argent holding in the hand a spear-headed staff depending therefrom a banner Vert fringed Or charged with a billet Argent.

TURTON. *MS Ordinary of Arms, fo. 210**

Out of a mural coronet Azure two arms embowed in armour Proper holding in the hands a flag Gules flotant to the sinister staff Or.

MAPLESDEN, of Fordley, Middleton. *Davy, A.*

Out of a mural crown Or two arms erect sleeved Gules hands and cuffs Proper supporting a shield Argent.

RUDGE. Vicar of Stoven, 1866–77. *Crisp's Visitation. XV. 145, Pedigree*

Out of a mural crown two arms embowed in armour the hands in gauntlets holding a tilting spear in fesse head to the sinister the staff encircled by a chaplet of oak all Proper.

STUDD, of Ipswich. *Davy, A. Fairbairn, 'of Ipswich'*

On a mural coronet Azure three broad arrows one in pale and two in saltire Or feathered Argent tied together with a scroll Azure.

SIMONS. 'Symons' *MS Heraldic Alphabet*

On a mural coronet Gules three arrows Or feathered Argent two in saltire and one in pale tied in the middle with a ribbon Azure.

SIMONS. Vicar of Bramfield, 1846. *Davy, A.*

Out of a mural coronet seven Lochaber axes Proper.

BIGG. *Davy, A. Washbourne*

Out of a mural coronet Argent a branch of coral between two wings erect.

ZINCKE. Vicar of Wherstead. *Davy, A.*

On a mural coronet Gules an estoile Or charged on the centre with a human heart Gules.

FOX, of Stradbroke, co. Suffolk; Certified by William Croane [sic Crowne], Rouge Dragon and R. Browne, Bluemantle. *Grants & Certificates (Stowe MS 677)*

On a mural crown Or an estoile Or charged with a human heart Gules.

FOX, Simon, of . . ., co. Suffolk; Certified by Robert Browne, Bluemantle. *Grants & Certificates (Stowe MS 703; Harl. MS 1,441)*

Out of a mural crown a dexter hand holding a ?bugle horn.

FOSTER. Rector of Redgrave, died before 1688. *Davy, A.*

Out of a mural crown Or a heart Gules thrust through with arrows one in pale and two in saltire Or feathered and barbed Argent.

ARNEY, of Ixworth. *Visitation 1664–8. Bokenham. MS Heraldic Alphabet, 'heart Proper' Davy, A.*

Out of a mural coronet Or a demi-griffin issuant Argent holding in its claws a mullet Sable pierced Argent.

WOLLASTON, of Finborough, Bury. *Sharpe. Davy, A., Finborough church. Burke, L.G. 1900 ed.* Crisp's Visitation. XII. 73* and XVIII. 121*.* 'Rear Admiral Wollaston, Bury, Suffolk' *Bookplate*, untinctured*

Out of a mural crown a demi-griffin segreant holding a pierced mullet Sable.

WOLLASTON, of Gt. Finborough, 1729–74. *Her.Suff.Ch., Wall tablets and Floor slabs, Gt. Finborough*

On a mural crown Or an ibex Argent horned maned and tufted Or gorged with a wreath of laurel Vert.

NIGHTINGALE, of Brome. *Davy, A. Fairbairn, 'Nightingall, Brome Hall, Norf.' [sic]*

Out of a mural coronet Sable a demi-unicorn Or.

SMYTHIER, of Ipswich. *Bokenham*

On a mural coronet Or a roundel Vert charged with a cross Or and between two wings Argent.

HEATHCOTE, HETHCOTE. *MS Ordinary of Arms, fo. 267**

Out of a mural crown a spear in pale and two palm branches in saltire.

COOPER, of Bungay, Saxmundham, Yoxford, Woodbridge. *Davy, A.* 'Robert Cooper of Woodbridge, gent., son of Nathan Cooper of Saxmundham', died 1804. *Partridge, 53 (Darby, 1825), Yoxford churchyard*

A mural crown Argent thereout issuing the upper part of a spear erect Proper fringed [sic] Or pointed Argent surmounted of two palm branches in saltire Vert also issuing from the coronet, or crown.

COOPER, Nathan, died 1800. *Her.Suff.Ch., Altar tomb, churchyard, Saxmundham.* Robert Cooper, son of the former, of Woodbridge, died 1804. *Altar tomb, churchyard, Yoxford.* Robert Henry Cooper, of Yoxford, died 1851. *Wall tablet, Yoxford*

From a mural coronet Or the upper part of a spear Sable headed and studded Argent.

FOOTE. 'Thomas Footes, gent., of Michelham, co. Sussex' *Grants & Certificates (Harl. MS 1,441)*

Out of a mural coronet six spears in saltire Proper.

BOTETOURT, of Mendlesham. *Davy, A.*

A mural crown thereon a trunk of a tree Proper sprouting Vert surmounted by a pelican of the third [sic] vulning herself of the fourth [sic] ducally crowned Azure.

LIDGBIRD, of Rougham. *Davy, A.*

A mural coronet therein the trunk of a tree Proper sprouting Vert surmounted by a pelican Or vulning Proper ducally crowned Azure.

LIDGBIRD. *Washbourne, 'Lidgbind, Kent and Suff.' Fairbairn, 'Lidgbird, of Rougham, Suff. and Plumstead, Kent.' Crown untinctured*

Out of a mural crown Or two wings expanded each per pale Or and Sable.

COOKE, of Brome Hall. *Visitation 1664–8*

Out of a mural coronet two wings displayed.

COOKE, of Livermere, Suffolk. *MS Martin's Crests*

Out of a mural crown Gules two wings endorsed per pale Or and Sable.
 COOKE, of Bury, Ashfield, Brome Hall. *Davy, A., St. James's church in Bury, Ampton church*
Out of a mural coronet Or two wings expanded per pale Or and Sable.
 COOKE, Roger, Physician and Surgeon, died 1783. *Her.Suff.Ch., Ledger stone, Gt. Ashfield*
Out of a mural coronet two wings displayed Or.
 COKE, of Livermere. *Bokenham*
Out of a mural crown a pair of wings dexter Or sinister Sable.
 COKE, of Lt. Livermere. *Davy, A., church*
Out of a mural coronet Or a pair of wings Azure each charged with three estoiles Or.
 GIPPS. 'Gippes. Cheape Ward. Thomas Gipps of St Edmonds Bury in com.Suffolke' Under the hand of Sir Richard St. George Clarenceux. *London Visitation 1633 (H.S.) I. 315**
Out of a mural coronet two wings displayed each charged with a cross crosslet fitchy Sable.
 LAYTON. 'Gull.Edu.Layton' *Bookplate**

CRESCENT [Alphabetically by name]
A crescent Argent.
 ALDERTON, of Ipswich. *Davy, A. (Burke). Washbourne*, 'of Suff.' Fairbairn*, 'Suff.'*
A crescent Gules issuant therefrom a demi-lion Proper holding between his paws a horse-shoe Gules.
 ALLENBY, of Felixstowe House. *Crisp's Visitation. VIII. 17*, Pedigree*
On a crescent Argent an estoile Or.
 ALSTON, of Marlesford, Newton, Assington, Boxford. *London Visitation 1633 (H.S.) I. 16*. Davy, A. Washbourne*, 'of Suff.' Bright, 73. Fairbairn*, 'Alstone of Newton, Suff., Assington and Marleford [sic] Out of a crescent'*
Within the horns of a crescent an estoile Or.
 ALSTON, of Newton. *Visitation 1664–8*
A crescent surmounted by a star Or.
 ALSTON, of Edwardstone. *Bokenham*
A half moon Argent charged with a star Or.
 ALSTON. *MS Heraldic Alphabet*
A crescent issuing from it an estoile.
 ALSTON, Joseph, late of Washbrook, died 1687. *Her.Suff.Ch., Slab, Bramford*
A crescent.
 ALSTON. Rev. Edward Alston, B.D., late of East Bergholt in Suffolk, Rector of Newton, died 1722. *Her.Suff.Ch., Floor slab, Newton*
A crescent and issuant from the horns a cross paty fitchy Gules.
 CHEKE. *Davy, A., 'Sir John Cheke relinquished this [earlier crest, q.v.] and adopted the following:' [above]*
In a crescent Argent a bundle of five arrows Or headed and barbed Argent tied with a ribbon Gules.
 CREKE, CRICK, of Cockfield, Lt. Thurlow. *Davy, A.*
Two eagle's heads erased and addorsed beaked Or each holding an annulet Gules arising from a crescent Argent.
 CROOKE. Lt. Col. Charles Parry Crooke. No date given. *Her.Suff.Ch., Glass, St. Mary's, Bury*
In a crescent Gules an escallop Or.
 ELSE, ELLIS, of Ilketshall St. Andrew, Blythburgh. *Davy, A. Washbourne, 'of co. Lincs.'*
A crescent charged with an estoile of six points.
 ETHERIDGE, of Fressingfield. *Davy, A., church, 1776*
An estoile issuing from a crescent the crescent

charged with a crescent.
 FROST, of Lavenham. *Davy, A., church*
A crescent charged with a crescent and above it an estoile.
 FROST. Mary, wife of Thomas Frost, surgeon, of Lavenham, died 1741. *Her.Suff.Ch., Floor slab in south chapel (under carpet), Lavenham*
A crescent Or.
 HAINS, of Ipswich. *Sharpe*
On a crescent Or a lion's head erased Sable gutty Argent.
 LONG. *MS Heraldic Collections, fo. 34a*, 'langued Gules'. MS Heraldic Alphabet*
A crescent Argent in front of a column Or.
 MAYDSTON, of Akenham. *Visitation 1664–8*
A crescent Or.
 MONNINGS. 'Monyns' *MS Martin's Crests*
An increscent Or.
 MONNINGS. 'Monins'. Rector of Glemham, 1848. *Davy, A.*
A crescent Argent.
 PAPILLON, PAPYLLON. *MS Ordinary of Arms, fo. 201**
A butterfly within a crescent Argent.
 PAPILLON. Major Philip W.G. Papillon. No date given. *Her.Suff.Ch., Glass, St. Mary's, Bury*
A crescent Or.
 PRESTON, of Suffolk. *Bokenham. Davy, A., Monument, Yarmouth church. Washbourne*, 'Suff. and Iri.'*
? A crescent.
 PRESTON. Mary, wife of Isaac Preston, died 1860. *E.A.N. & Q. II. 309, Wall tablet, Yarmouth church*
A crescent Or between two wings Azure.
 PRESTON. *Washbourne*, 'Suff. and Iri.' Fairbairn, 'Suff. and Ireland'*
Out of a crescent Argent an eagle displayed Or.
 ROUS. *Davy, A., 'The crest, or badge, of Rous before assumption of the crest of Phelip, Lord Bardolph'*
A crescent.
 VENTRIS, of Ipswich. *E.A.N. & Q. X. 56, Slab, St. Nicholas church.* Sir Peyton Ventris, died 1691. *Her.Suff.Ch., Ledger stone, St. Nicholas, Ipswich*
A crescent between two wings.
 WILKINS. Rector of Hadleigh, died 1745. *Davy, A.*
A crescent Or with fire Proper from between the horns.
 WILSON, Thomas (or John), of Kendal, co. Westmorland; Confirmation 1586. *Grants & Certificates (Stowe MS 670; Harl. MS 1,359)*
A crescent Or issuing fire Proper.
 WILSON, of Redgrave. *Misc.Gen. et Her. 2nd S. IV. 252. Burke, L.G. 1853 and 1952 eds.* Bookplate**
Upon a cloud Proper a crescent Gules issuing Fire.
 WILSON, of Redgrave. *Davy, A.*
On a cloud Proper a crescent Gules flaming Or.
 WILSON, George, Admiral of the Red, died 1826; George St. Vincent Wilson, died 1852; George Holt Wilson, D.L., High Sheriff, died 1924; George Rowland Holt Wilson, died 1929. *Her.Suff.Ch., Hatchments, Redgrave.* [Crescent of the last hatchment is Argent, against the black background]
Within a crescent Argent a caltrap Gules.
 YELLOLY. *Fairbairn*, 'of Bracklyn, Clare, Suff.'*

CRESCENTS
A decrescent and an increscent Argent.

BALIOL, of Lothingland House. *Davy, A. Washbourne*, 'of Sco.'*

An increscent and a decrescent interlaced Or.
LACY, of Spelman's Hall. *Davy, A.*

A crescent increscent and decrescent interwoven Or.
MONNINGS, MUNNINGS, of Monks Eleigh, Bury, Nedging. 'Robart Moonings of Monekesellighe' *MS Lilly's Visitation of Suffolk*. MS Fairfax (Tyl.) Gage (Thingoe). Chitting MS. Davy, A. Washbourne*, 'Monnyngs'*

An increscent and a decrescent Argent interlaced within a ducal coronet Or.
WENYEVE, of Brettenham. *Davy, A.*

CRESSET see BEACON

CROSS [Alphabetically by name]

A cross crosslet fitchy Gules.
ADAMSON, of Bury, Horringer. *Davy, A.* Rev. Vere Timothy Adamson, died 1716. *Her.Suff.Ch., Headstone in churchyard, Horringer*

A cross crosslet fitchy Or.
LOVAIN, of Bildeston, Drinkstone. *Davy, A.*

A cross formy Or entwined with a snake Proper.
MEDDOWES, of Wenhaston, Stoke by Nayland. *Davy, A., Wenhaston, Stoke and Bardwell churches*

A cross formy Or entwined with a serpent Proper.
MEDDOWES, Samuel, died 1773. *Her.Suff.Ch., Wall tablet, Stoke by Nayland*

A cross paty fitched.
NOTTAGE. *Washbourne, 'of Halstead [sic], Suff.' Fairbairn*, 'Suff.'*

A cross as in the arms – [Argent on a cross raguly Sable five estoiles Argent].
PETTIWARD, John, of London, merchant, son of Roger, son of John Pettiward, of Bury St. Edmunds, Suffolk, for long a sufferer for the Royal cause; Grant by Sir E. Walker, Garter, 16 July 1660. *Grants & Certificates (Add. MS 14,294; Stowe MS 677; Harl. MS 1,172)*

A cross raguly Sable charged with five estoiles Argent.
PETTIWARD, of Finborough Hall, Onehouse, Bury. *Surrey Visitation 1662 (H.S.) 90*. Davy, A. Burke, L.G. 1900 ed. Fairbairn, 'of Finborough Hall, Suff.'*

A cross raguly Sable charged with four estoiles Argent.
PETTIWARD, Charles, died 1933; widow died 1952; son Roger Pettiward, killed in action 1942. *Her.Suff.Ch., Wall tablets, Gt. Finborough*

A cross raguly Sable charged with four mullets Argent.
[PETTIWARD]. 'Finborough Library' *Bookplate**

A cross crosslet.
WOMACK, of Mettingham. *Misc.Gen. et Her. 5th S. VIII. 317–20, Pedigree*

[Three] cross crosslets fitchy Sable one in [pale] and two saltire-wise encircled with an annulet at their intersection.
RUSTON, of Stutton. *Sharpe*

CROSS-BOW

A cross-bow erect Azure between two wings Or.
GLOVER. Sir Thomas Glover, Esquire of the Body to King James, Knighted 17 August 1606. Patent 11 April 1604. *Grants & Certificates (Stowe MSS 706 and 707)*

A crossbow Or.
LATTON, of Sutton, Helmingham, Rendlesham, Eyke. *Davy, A.*

CRUSTACEAN

CRAB

A crab Proper.
BURKIN. *Washbourne*, 'Suff.' Fairbairn*, 'Suff.'*

A crab Argent.
CRABBE, of Aldeburgh. *Davy, A.*

CUP

A standing cup uncovered Or.
BOTELER. 'Boteler of Kerkelond' *Wall's Book*

A standing cup covered Or.
BOTELER. 'Boteler of Warynton' *Wall's Book*

'to his crest a standing cuppe coverd or'
BOTELER. 'Boteler of Warenton' *MS Alphabet of Crests, fo. 7*

A cup covered.
BUTLER. *MS Martin's Crests*

A standing cup and cover Or.
CROKER. *MS Ordinary of Arms, fo. 170**

A covered cup.
FLACK, of Chattisham. *Davy, A.*

A covered cup Or.
FOLKARD. *Sharpe*

CUSHION

A woolpack, or a cushion, tasselled.
STEBBING, George, died 1733; Others. *Her.Suff.Ch., Ledger stone, Framsden*

On a cushion wreathed Argent and Azure a garb Or.
WAYTH, of Gt. Glemham. *Davy, A., church monuments.* Daniel Wayth, Gent., died 1734; Daniel Wayth, Gent., died 1752; widow Mary, died 1799; Others. *E.A. Misc. 1911, 50*

CUTLASS see SWORD

DAGGER see SWORD

DART see SPEAR

ESCALLOP [Alphabetically by name]

An escallop shell.
CLARKE, of East Bergholt, Stratford, Bentley, Layham. *Davy, A., East Bergholt church*

An escallop Argent charged with a cross patonce Sable between two wings elevated Argent.
FLUDYER, Bart., of Felixstowe. *Davy, A.*

An escallop charged with a cross crosslet fitchy between two wings elevated Argent.
FLUDYER, Sir Samuel Brudenall Fludger [sic], Bart., died 1833. *Her.Suff.Ch., Wall tablet, Old Felixstowe*

An escallop erect Or.
FULLER, of Bradwell, St. Nicholas Ipswich, ?Nettlestead. *Davy, A.*

An escallop.
FULLER, John, died 1716. *Her.Suff.Ch., Ledger stone, St. Nicholas, Ipswich*

An escallop Or.
GLOSSOP. Major Bertram Glossop, died 1941; widow died 1950. *Her.Suff.Ch., Wooden tablet, Waldringfield*

An escallop Or charged with an estoile Gules.
HENNIKER. Lord Henniker, of Thornham Hall. *Sharpe. Davy, A. Torlesse, 29. Bookplates*.* Henniker, Henniker-Major, of Gt. Thornham, 1781–1832. *Her.Suff.Ch., Wall tablets and Hatchments, Gt. Thornham.* Henniker, Lords of Gt. Bealings manor from 1781. *Carved bench end, Gt. Bealings*

An escallop Or charged with a mullet Gules.

HENNIKER. Dame Ann (Major), wife of Sir John Henniker, Bart., died 1792. *Her.Suff.Ch., Tablet, Worlingworth. Mullet shown also on list of Rectors*

Between two palm branches an escallop all Proper.
LOWDHAM. *Fairbairn*, 'Suff.'*

In front of a dexter arm embowed in armour couped at the shoulder and fessewise Sable holding in the gauntlet a flagstaff Proper therefrom flowing to the sinister a banner Argent charged with a lyre Sable, three escallops fessewise Or.
TACON, of Red House in Eye, Lowestoft. *Burke, L.G. 1900 and 1952 eds* Fairbairn, 'Charles Tacon, Eye, Suff.' The arm in armour Or gauntlet Sable*

ESCARBUNCLE
An escarbuncle pometty floretty Argent.
BARWICK. *MS Heraldic Alphabet*

ESCUTCHEON or SHIELD
An escutcheon gyronny of twelve Argent and Gules in the centre point an inescutcheon Or, between two dove's wings Proper.
ELERS, of Rishangles, Monks Eleigh. *Davy, A. Burke, L.G. 1853 ed.*

An escutcheon Sable thereon a cross couped Argent between two wings Argent each charged with a fesse engrailed Sable.
MELLER, of Rushmere. *Crisp's Visitation. VII. 153*, Pedigree*

An escutcheon of the arms [Barry of six Argent and Erminois] between two wings elevated Argent.
PALLANT, of Redgrave. *Davy, A. Washbourne, 'Suff. Wings Proper'. Fairbairn, 'Redgrave, Suff. Wings erect Proper'*

A shield quarterly Or and Sable.
TONG. *Davy, A.*

ESTOILE or STAR
An estoile Or between two wings displayed Azure.
CLERE, of Ormsby in Norfolk. *MS Knight's Visitations, Norf.**

An estoile of eight points.
DE LANDE, of Sudbury, Ipswich. *E.A.N. & Q. (N.S.) I. 81.*

An estoile Gules.
HENNIKER [called MAJOR]. *Her.Suff.Ch., Glass, Gt. Bealings*

From a demi-estoile of six points Or a unicorn's head Sable maned and armed Or.
KITSON. *Davy, A.*

An estoile Argent between two oak branches Proper.
LANGDALE, of Long Melford. *Davy, A.*

An estoile of six points Or.
MARTIN. 'Martyn' *MS Martin's Crests.* Rev. Charles Martin, Rector of Palgrave, died 1864. *Her.Suff.Ch., Hatchment, Palgrave*

An estoile of six points pierced Or.
MARTIN, of Whatfield. *Proc.S.I.A. IX. 202* and 216*

An estoile of eight points Argent.
MOTT, Mark, of Braintree, co. Essex, son of Thomas Mott, of Bocking; Exemplification 10 November 1613. *Grants & Certificates (Add. MS 12,225)*
'On a halme forth of a wreath of his Cullours a starre of eight points Argent'
MOTT. 'Marke Mott of Brayntree in the County of Essex, the sonne of Thomas Mott, sometymes of Bockinge in the said county gent.'; Confirmation of Arms and Grant of Crest by William Segar,

Garter, 10th November 1615 [*sic* see above]. *Misc.Gen. et Her. 5th S. IX. 17 (Soc. of Ant. MS 378, fo. 455)*

An estoile of eight points Argent.
MOTT, of Kedington, Stoke by Nayland, Carlton, Marlesford, Yaxley, Market Weston, Brent Eleigh. *Visitation 1664–8*. Davy, A., Brent Eleigh church slab. Burke, L.G. 1853 ed. Misc.Gen. et Her. 2nd S. II. 4*. Fairbairn, 'Suff. and Essex'*

A star Argent.
MOTT, of Chattisham, Stoke by Nayland. *Bokenham*

An estoile Argent over it on a label 'Nautae fida'.
SIRR. Vicar of Yoxford, 1844. *Davy, A.*

Issuant out of a cloud Proper a star of six points waved Argent.
STODARD, STOTART, of Layham. *Davy, A.*

FAGGOT
A faggot of ling Proper fired and smoking.
BRANDLING, of Ipswich. *Bokenham*

FALCHION see SWORD

FASCES
The Roman fasces in pale Proper.
ELRINGTON, of Withersfield. *Davy, A.*

FEATHER [Alphabetically by name]
A feather in pale enfiled with a ducal coronet.
ALABASTER. *Davy, A.*

A plume of ostrich feathers Argent issuing therefrom a demi-griffin segreant Gules.
ALDERSON, of Lowestoft, Badingham. *Davy, A.*

A bush of ostrich feathers Argent.
ARDERN. 'Ardern' *Wall's Book*
'to his crest/ a Bushe of oysteyche ffethers ar/'
ARDERN. 'Arderne' *MS Alphabet of Crests, fo. 3*

A bush of five ostrich feathers alternately Argent and Azure.
ARDERNE. *MS ex-Taylor Coll.**

A plume of ostrich feathers Argent Gules and Azure.
BERNEY. *MS Martin's Crests*

Three feathers on a cushion.
BLOFELD. Curate of Risby, 1862; Curate of Woolpit, 1863–4. *Crisp's Visitation. XX. 193*

Three ostrich feathers erect encircled with a ducal coronet.
BRAHAM. *MS Heraldic Collections, fo. 41**

Four ostrich feathers erect Sable encircled with a ducal coronet Or.
BRAHAM. *MS Heraldic Alphabet*

Out of a bush of feathers Argent an eagle flying –.
BUTLER. 'Therle of Ormond' *Wall's Book*
'to his crest an Egle fflying owt of a bushe of ffethers Ar/ Erl'
BUTLER. 'Ormond' *MS Alphabet of Crests, fo. 94*

A plume of turkey feathers.
CAMOIS. *Davy, A.*

Two pheasant's feathers bound Azure.
CHEYNEY. *Wall's Book*
'to his Crest ii fesant ffethers bound/ b.'
CHEYNEY. 'Cheney' *MS Alphabet of Crests, fo. 19b*

A plume of feathers.
CLIFTON, of Battisford, Wachesham. *Davy, A.*

A plume of five feathers Argent the middle one enfiling a sword hilt pommel and blade Or.
DRURY, DREWRY, of Brampton. *Davy, A.*

A sword Argent hilted Or stuck pommel upwards in a panache of nine ostrich plumes in two heights of four and five blue and white alternately the midmost feather being blue.

DUKE, of Brampton, Worlingham, Shadingfield. *Surrey Visitation 1530 (H.S.) 70. Surrey Visitation 1662 (H.S.) 37**

A sword Argent hilted Or thrust into a plume of five ostrich feathers alternately Azure and Argent.

DUKE, of Brampton, Shadingfield. *Visitation 1561 (MSS G.7* and Iveagh Copy*)*

A sword thrust into a plume of five ostrich feathers.

DUKE, of Worlingham. *Visitation 1561 (MS Iveagh Copy*)*

A sword Argent hilt Or stuck in a plume of five feathers three Azure two Argent.

DUKE, of Brampton, Worlingham. *Visitation 1561 (ed. Metcalfe). Harl. 772**. 'Duke of Suffolk' *MS Philpot's Visitations, Suff.*,* [in a different hand]. *Washbourne, 'Suff.' Fairbairn, 'Suff. On a plume . . .' Her.Suff.Ch., Benhall, Worlingham*

A sword point downwards Proper behind a plume of feathers Argent.

DUKE, of Benhall, Bentley. *Bokenham*

A sword Argent hilted Or stuck into a plume of five feathers Sable.

DUKE. 'Mrs. Parnell Rous alias Duke, wife of John Duke, of Wallingham. Epitaph made 1658.' *Her.Suff.Ch., Memorial board, Worlingham. Photograph**

A sword Argent hilt Or stuck into a plume of five feathers three Gules and two Argent.

DUKE, Tollemache, died 1713 aged 23. *Her.Suff.Ch., Slab in chancel, Bentley*

A plume of feathers Argent.

EDEN, EDON, of Suffolk. *Davy, A. Washbourne*, 'Kent and Suff.' Fairbairn*, 'Eden, Kent and Suff.'*

A plume of five ostrich feathers, or oak leaves.

FARR, John, Gent., Attorney at Law, died 1727; widow Martha, died 1733. *Her.Suff.Ch., Altar tomb in churchyard, Beccles*

A plume of peacock, or ostrich, feathers Ermine.

FELBRIGGE, of Playford. *Davy, A.*

Three feathers Argent.

FENN. 'Norff.' *MS Martin's Crests*

A plume of three ostrich feathers Argent.

FENN. *Davy, A.*

A plume of ostrich feathers Argent.

GRENTMESNELL. *Davy, A.*

An ostrich wing of six feathers alternately Argent and Gules charged with a bend as in the arms [. . . on a bend Sable three plates].

GULSTON, John, of Gray's Inn, Councellor at Law, etc. [see note on family]. A patent. *Grants & Certificates (Harl. MS 6,059; Stowe MSS 706 and 707). Bookplate*, untinctured*

A wing of five ostrich feathers alternately Argent and Gules surmounted by a bend as in the arms [. . . bend Sable charged with three plates].

GULSTON, of Bardwell, Kesgrave. *Davy, A.*

An ostrich feather in pale Argent.

HAREBRED, of Suffolk. *Davy, A.*

A plume of turkey feathers.

HARSICK. 'The father of Sir John Harsyk, also Sir John, allowed to wear this crest by Grant in the 30th of Edward III [1356/7] from Sir John Camoys' *Cotman's Norfolk Brasses, p. 9.* Harsick of Suffolk. *Davy, A.*

A plume of turkey feathers in a hoop Or.

HARSICK. Sir John Harsyk, Southacre co. Norfolk. Brass of 1384. *Cotman's Norfolk Brasses, plate*

10*, p. 9. Harsick, of Brampton (Camois, granted to Harsick) *Davy, A.*

A plume of three peacock's feathers erect.

LEAKE, of Hadleigh. *Proc.S.I.A. IX. 207, Church paten. E.A. Misc. 1934, 23*

Three feathers.

LOMAX, of Redlingfield. *Davy, A., church*

From five ostrich feathers Azure the head and neck of an ostrich Or.

PAYNE. 'Thomas Paine, of Dunham, co. Norfolk; Patent by R. Cooke, Clarenceux. *Grants & Certificates (Stowe MS 670; Harl. MS 1,359; Add. MS 4,966)*

A plume of feathers Vert.

ROUS, of Cransford. *Davy, A.*

A plume of feathers Argent.

SHARDELOW, SHARDELOWE, of Flempton, Barton Mills, Kessingland, Bungay. *Gage (Thingoe). Page. Davy, A., Barton Mills and Sproughton churches. Fairbairn*, 'of Shardelow [sic], Suff.'*

A plume of five feathers.

SOTTERLEY, of Sotterley. *Davy, A., church*

Paly of six Ermine and Ermines shaped like a plume of feathers.

STUTEVILLE, STOTEVILL, of Dalham. *Visitation 1561 (ed. Metcalfe). Visitation 1577.* Sir Martin Stuteville, died 1631. *Effigy monument, Dalham. Photograph*, c.1950*

Paly of five shaped like feathers Ermines.

STUTEVILLE. 'Stotavyll' *Harl. 772**

A plume of feathers alternately Ermine and Ermines.

STUTEVILLE, of Dalham. *Davy, A., church*

A plume of six feathers Ermine and Ermines.

STUTEVILLE. *Davy, A.*

Three ostrich feathers Argent.

TASBOROUGH, of Flixton. *Bokenham*

A plume of five or six feathers Argent.

TASBURGH, of Flixton. *Davy, A.*

A plume of five feathers.

TASBURGH, Charles, died 1657. *Her.Suff.Ch., Ledger stone, Flixton*

A plume of three feathers.

TASBURGH. Margaret (Heneage), wife of Richard Tasburgh, died 1705. *Her.Suff.Ch., Monument, Flixton*

A unicorn's head ducally gorged in a tuft of five ostrich feathers.

UPCHER, of Sudbury, Willisham, Gt. Yarmouth. *Davy, A., Misc.Gen. et Her. 3rd S. III. 80*, Bookplate for 'Peter Upcher Esq.' Of Gt. Yarmouth*

A plume of five ostrich feathers alternately Argent and Or before them a unicorn's head couped Azure gorged with a ducal coronet Or.

UPCHER. Rector of Halesworth. *Crisp's Visitation. III. 25*, Pedigree*

A double plume of ostrich feathers five in each row per pale Argent and Gules.

WALDEGRAVE. 'Wallgrave' *MS ex-Taylor Coll.**

A plume of seven ostrich feathers three Argent two Sable and two Vert.

WANTON. Simon de Wanton, Bishop of Norwich, 1253. Of Stonham. *Davy, A.*

A plume of feathers.

WARNER. Sir Edward Warner, of Lt. Plumstead, co. Norfolk. Brass of 1565. *Cotman's Norfolk Brasses, plate 76**

A plume of eighteen feathers six in a row the six above reflectant Or.

WARNER, of Mildenhall. *Bokenham*

A double plume of feathers Or.

WARNER, of Mildenhall. *Davy, A.*

A demi-griffin segreant Azure in front of a plume of five feathers alternately Or and Argent.

WYE, of Ipswich. *Visitation 1664–8.*

A demi-griffin segreant Azure in front of a plume of five feathers alternately Or and Azure.

WYE, of Ipswich. *Bokenham. Davy, A.*

A griffin's head wings indorsed Azure issuing from a plume of ostrich feathers two Argent and three Or.

WYE. *Washbourne*, 'Glouc. and Suff.' Fairbairn, 'of Ipswich, Suff. and co. Glouc. Wings addorsed'*

FER-DE-MOLINE see MILLRIND

FIR CONE or PINEAPPLE see FRUIT

FIRE, FLAMES

A phoenix's head issuing from flames.

ADAIR. Theodosia (Meade), wife of Sir Robert Alexander Shafto Adair, 2nd Bt., later Baron Waveney; she died 1871. *Her.Suff.Ch., Statue, Flixton. Two crests, this for Shafto [q.v. But should be a salamander]*

A mountain in flames Proper.

CREVEQUER. *Davy, A.*

Issuing out of a fire Or a tiger's head Sable collared and lined Or.

MILESON, MELLISENT, of Bury, Ipswich, Norton. *Visitation 1664–8*, 'p Ric. St. George, Norroy, 1612'. Davy, A., St. Mary Tower church, Ipswich. 'armed Or'*

A phoenix in flames Proper.

NEEDHAM, of Barking. *Davy, A.*

A salamander Vert in flames Proper.

SHAFTO, of Framlingham. *Davy, A. (Edms.)*

FIRE-BALL or GRENADE

A fire-ball Proper.

STEBBING. *Davy, A., Brandeston and Framsden churches*

FISH

BARBEL

Two barbels interposed frettways one Or the other Sable.

BENNETT. *Bokenham*

DOLPHIN

A dolphin embowed Argent.

ARNOLD, of Lowestoft, Dunwich, Battisford. *Visitation 1664–8. Bokenham. Gillingwater, 305. Druery, 273. Davy, A., Lowestoft church. Fauconberge, 79. Washbourne*, 'of Norf. and Suff.' Muskett. I. 388 (Harl. MS 1085); 392, Monument, St. Margaret's, Lowestoft. Fairbairn*, 'Cromer, Norf., Bellesford [sic], Suff.'* Joseph Arnold, M.D., Surgeon in the Royal Navy, died 1818. *Her.Suff.Ch., Monument, Beccles*

A dolphin naiant embowed Argent.

ARNOLD, of Lowestoft, Ellough. *Davy, A.*

A dolphin embowed.

ARNOLD, Aldous, merchant, died 1792. *Her.Suff.Ch., Monument, Lowestoft*

A dolphin embowed Proper in front of a demi-dragon Azure armed and langued Gules.

BUNN. 'Albert Edward Bunn, 1887–1959.' *Her.Suff.Ch., Wooden shield on chair, Beccles*

A dolphin embowed Or.

CARMINAL. *Davy, A.*

A dolphin embowed Argent.

COURTENAY, COURTNEY. *MS Ordinary of Arms, fo. 267* Bookplates**

A dolphin naiant Proper.

COURTENAY, of Badmondisfield Hall in Wickhambrook. *Davy, A.*

A dolphin embowed Argent.

FISHER, of Bury. *Davy, A., Slab, St. Mary's church*

A dolphin embowed.

FISHER, of Bury. *Tymms, 196.* Samuel Fisher, died 172?; Samuel Fisher, died 1738; widow Ann, died 1766. *Her.Suff.Ch., Ledger stones, St. Mary's, Bury*

A dolphin Argent entwined round an anchor erect Sable.

FRANKLAND, FRANKLYN, FRANCKLYN, of Beccles. *Visitation 1664–8. Bokenham. Davy, A. Washbourne*, 'Franklyn, Frankland, Suff. Anchor Proper'. Fairbairn*, 'Franklyn, Suff. Dolphin hauriant.'*

A dolphin embowed Proper.

SYMONDS, of Belton. *Davy, A., Belton churchyard and Slab, Yarmouth church.* John Symonds, D.D., died 1757. *Her.Suff.Ch., Ledger stone, Pakenham*

A dolphin embowed.

SYMONDS. James Symonds, gent., died 1688. *E.A.N. & Q. II. 309, Slab, St. Nicholas's church, Yarmouth.* Dolphin naiant embowed. Nathaniel Symonds, late of Gt. Yarmouth, died 1754; widow died 1764. *Her.Suff.Ch., Ledger stone, Belton*

A dolphin naiant embowed holding in its mouth a fish Argent.

SYMONDS, of Botesdale, Bury, Belton. *Davy, A., Redgrave churchyard.* Thomas Symonds, A.M., Rector, died 1748. *Her.Suff.Ch., Ledger stone, Ellough.* John Symonds, LL.D., Barrister, Recorder of Bury St. Edmunds, died 1807. *Monument on chancel wall, Pakenham. 'ingulphant of a fish'*

TWO DOLPHINS

Two dolphins entwined erect on their tails saltirewise one Or the other Sable.

BENNET. 'Henry Bennett of Henesbye' *MS Knight's Visitations, Norf.** 'Peter Benett' *MS Philpot's Visitations, Norf.* 'finned Or'*

Two dolphins entwined erect on their tails saltirewise one Or the other Argent, or Sable.

BENNET, of Washbrook, Westhall. *Davy, A.*

Two dolphins addorsed the one superimposed upon the other [sic in saltire] Sable finned Or.

BUMSTED. *MS Heraldic Alphabet**

Two dolphins hauriant and embowed Azure and Or enfiled with a ducal coronet per pale all counterchanged.

ELLERKER, of Frostenden. *Davy, A.*

PIKE

A ged, or pike.

GEDGE, of Bury. *Davy, A.*

A ged hauriant Argent.

GEDGE, of Bury. *Bildeston, 13*

STURGEON

A sturgeon naiant Or fretty Gules, charged with a mullet Sable for difference.

STURGEON, Roger of Whepstead, co. Suffolk; Confirmation by W. Camden, Clarenceux, to him and his brothers. *Grants & Certificates (Harl. MS 6,059; Stowe MS 707)*

A sturgeon naiant Or fretty Gules, sometimes charged on the back with a mullet for difference.

STURGEON, of Whepstead, Bury. *Visitation 1664–8*. Bokenham. Gage (Thingoe). Davy, A. Washbourne, 'Suff.' Fairbairn, 'of Whipstead [sic], Suff.'*
A sturgeon charged fretty Gules.
    STURGEON. Margaret, wife of James Sturgeon, died 1729; James sturgeon, died 1763. *Her.Suff.Ch., Ledger stones, St. Mary's, Bury*

FLAGS see REEDS

FLEUR-DE-LIS [Alphabetically by name]
A fleur-de-lis Or the central petal Argent.
    ASHFIELD, ASHEFELDE. *MS Knight's Visitations, Suff., fo. 106b.** 'Ashley' *MS Philpot's Visitations, Suff.**
A fleur-de-lis per pale Argent and Or.
    ASHFIELD, of Stowlangtoft, Pakenham, Netherhall in Harkstead. 'Sr Robart Ashfild of Stowlangtoft Knight' *MS Lilly's Visitation of Suffolk*. Davy, A.*
A fleur-de-lis Argent banded Or.
    ASHLEY. *MS Heraldic Alphabet*
On the trunk of a tree lying fessewise Or a fleur-de-lis Azure between two sprigs Vert.
    ATWOOD, of Suffolk. *Davy, A. Washbourne*, 'Essex and Middx.'*
A fleur-de-lis Argent.
    BARNWELL. *Davy, A.*
A fleur-de-lis Argent entwined by a snake Proper.
    BIRCH, of Brandon. *MS Ordinary of Arms, fo. 226*. Davy, A., church. E.A.N. & Q. I. 135, Hatchments, Brandon church.* 'Thomas Birch' *Bookplate**
A demi fleur-de-lis per fesse Or and Argent issuant out of the middle leaf a dragon's head Gules langued Argent.
    COPE. 'Coope of Essex' *Wall's Book*
'to his Crest a Demy ffleurdelyce or/ar/ pty p fece/a Dragons hed g/ issuing owt of the mydell leffe langed ar/'
    COPE. 'Cope of Essex' *Alphabet of Crests, fo. 20*
A fleur-de-lis Or issuing from its top a lion's head couped Gules.
    COPE. *MS Martin's Crests*
A fleur-de-lis Or a dragon's head issuing from the top thereof Gules.
    COPE, of Bury. *MS Heraldic Alphabet. Davy, A.*
A fleur-de-lis Or the stem wrapped about with a snake Vert the head issuing from the middle of the fleur-de-lis.
    CROOKE. *Davy, A. (Edms.)*
A fleur-de-lis Azure.
    DIGBY, John, son of William, son of William Digby, of Coggeshall, co. Essex, whose ancestors came out of Leicestershire; Certificate from Robert Browne, Bluemantle. *Grants & Certificates (Stowe MS 677)*
A fleur-de-lis Or.
    EWEN. *Ewen, 277*
A fleur-de-lis Argent enfiled by a crest coronet Or.
    FENTON, Thomas, Anthony and Christopher, sons of Christopher Fenton; Patent from W. Flower, Norroy, 28 February 1575. *Grants & Certificates (Stowe MS 706)*
A fleur-de-lis enfiled by a ducal coronet.
    FENTON. *MS Heraldic Collections, fo. 88b**
A fleur-de-lis Sable enfiled by a ducal coronet Or.
    FENTON. *Davy, A. (Edms.)*
A fleur-de-lis Gules between two wings Sable.
    GLOVER, Anthony. *Grants & Certificates (Stowe MSS 706 and 707)*

A fleur-de-lis between two wings.
    GLOVER. *MS Heraldic Collections, fo. 83a**
Issuing from a cloud Proper a fleur-de-lis Argent.
    HART, of Orford. *Davy, A.*
A fleur-de-lis Gules.
    MUNDEFORD, 'Osbart Mondeforde of fletwell' *MS Knight's Visitations, Norf.* Bokenham*
A fleur-de-lis.
    NEAVE, of Ipswich. 'Capt. William Neave, Portman & Thrice Bayliffe of this Town', died 1703. *E.A.N. & Q. X. 40, Slab, ?in the churchyard, St. Mary Tower. Her.Suff.Ch., Slab, St. Mary Tower. Not found 1979*
A fleur-de-lis Argent.
    NEWDIGATE. *MS Ordinary of Arms, fo. 94*. Washbourne*
A fleur-de-lis per pale Or and Argent.
    'RETHE of Crodmour [sic] in Suffolk Marchant of London' *Wall's Book*
'to his Crest a fleurdelyce pty p pale or/ar/'
    'RETHE of Crodmore [sic] in Suff Marchant of London' *MS Alphabet of Crests, fo. 108b*
'to his crest [fleur-de-lis drawn] p pale ar/sa/ [? unreadable] w^t ij dolphyns there heds metyng thon sa the other ar John Robyns of netherhall in wostersh^r'
    ROBYNS. *MS Alphabet of Crests, fo. 109b*
A fleur-de-lis per pale Argent and Sable between two dolphins hauriant regardant counter changed.
    ROBYNS. 'John Robins, of Netherhall, in Stoketon, co. Worcester; Grant by Sir C. Barker, Garter. *Grants & Certificates (Stowe MS 692)*
A fleur-de-lis per pale Argent and Sable between two dolphins embowed the first Sable the second Argent.
    ROBYNS, of Thorndon. *Bokenham*
A fleur-de-lis Or.
    SPARKES. *Fairbairn*, 'of Glenham [sic], Suff.'*
A leopard's face Or on a fleur-de-lis.
    TIMMS, of Stoke by Clare. *Davy, A., 'jessant de lis'*

FLOWER
A vase containing four flowers. (Out of a well Or a vine and two columbine branches Proper)
    GOLDWELL. *Washbourne**. Henry Goldwell, Esq., Burgess of Bury St. Edmunds, died 1693; widow Frances, died 1712. *Her.Suff.Ch., Ledger stones, Tuddenham*
Six flowers Gules stalked Vert.
    PARR. 'Parre' *Wall's Book*
'to his Crest vj flowers g/ stalked Vert'
    PARR. 'Parre knight by h 8/' *MS Alphabet of Crests, fo. 99*

BROOM
Broom Vert with 'coddes' Gules.
    BROME. 'Brome of Kent' *Wall's Book*
A bunch of broom Vert flowered Or.
    BROME, of Brome Hall, Woodbridge. *Davy, A.*

MARIGOLD
A marigold Proper.
    BOTELL, of Suffolk. *Davy, A.*
A marigold in pale one leaf Argent one other Purpure stalked and leaved Vert issuing therefrom a greyhound's head per pale Argent and Sable on the neck three gutties counter changed.
    CAVE. *Wall's Book*
'to his crest a mary gold in pale the on leve ar/ the other purpur stalked and Leved vert/ owt of the mary gold doth issu a grehounds hede p pale ar/sa/

on the neck iij Dropes count i ij'
CAVE. *MS Alphabet of Crests, fo. 21b*

ROSE

A rose Gules barbed and seeded Proper.
AYTON, of Earl Soham, Knodishall. *MS Ordinary of Arms, fo. 222*. Davy, A.*
A rose Gules.
AYTON, John, Esq., of Scole Lodge in Norfolk, died 1836. *Her.Suff.Ch., Wall tablet, Weybread*
An ilex's (? ibex's) head Or issuing out of the centre of a rose Gules barbed Vert.
BEWLEY, of Suffolk. *Davy, A. Washbourne*, 'Suff. ibex's head'. Fairbairn, 'Suff. ibex's head'*
Out of a pot Or five roses parted per . . . Argent and Gules stalked Vert.
MAC-WILLIAM. *MS Fairfax*
Out of a flower pot Or a branch of five roses per bend Argent and Gules.
MACKWILLIAMS. *MS Martin's Crests*
A rose between two wings conjoined and elevated Argent.
MEREST, of Bury, Wortham. *Davy, A.*
A rose Or.
RUSHBROOKE, of Rushbrook. *Davy, A. (Berry)*
A rose.
SMITH, SMYTH, of Laxfield. *Davy, A., church*
A rose barbed and seeded.
SMITH, SMYTH, of Parkfield in Laxfield. *E.A. Misc. 1926, 85.* Smith, . . ., died 1739. *Her.Suff.Ch., Ledger stone in nave, Laxfield. Not found 1981*
A Saracen's head affronty couped at the shoulders Proper vested Gules on the head a cap checky Argent and Gules in front thereof of the bust three roses Argent.
WARNER. Lt. Cornwallis J. Warner, killed in action 1915. *Her.Suff.Ch., Bronze tablets, Brettenham and Thorpe Morieux.* Col. Sir Thomas Warner, Bart., died 1934; widow died 1947 [parents of Lt. Warner]. *Glass, Brettenham and Hatchment, Thorpe Morieux*

THISTLE

A thistle erect Proper.
PERCEVAL. *Crisp's Visitation. VI. 89*, Pedigree*

FOIL

TREFOIL

A trefoil slipped Vert.
BALDREY, of Ipswich, Stowmarket. *Davy, A.*
A trefoil slipped Proper.
CONYERS, of Cotton, Barton. *MS Heraldic Alphabet. Davy, A.*
A trefoil slipped between two wings erect.
FROST, of Hunston Hall, Whepstead. *Davy, A.*
A trefoil between two wings.
FROST, Mary, wife of John Frost the elder, of Whepstead, died 1703. *Her.Suff.Ch., in churchyard, Whepstead. Given by Gage, but not found 1978*
A trefoil slipped erect.
NEDEN. Rev. Gerard Neden, D.D., Rector of Rougham and Rushbrook, died 1768. *Davy, A., Monument, Rougham church. Proc.S.I.A. VII. 343. Suff. Green Bks, Rushbrook, Biography 115–6*
A trefoil slipped.
NEDEN. Gerard Neden, Rector of Rougham and Rushbrook, Prebendary of Lincoln, died 1768. *Her.Suff.Ch., Ledger stone, Rougham*
A trefoil slipped.

QUINCE, of Honington. *Davy, A.*
A trefoil Sable surmounted of another trefoil Argent.
WANTON. 'Gilbert Wanton of Yermouthe' *MS Knight's Visitations, Norf.** 'John Wanton' *MS Philpot's Visitations, Norf.**

QUATREFOIL

A quatrefoil pierced Ermine in the centre a bezant.
BOHUN, of Westhall. *Visitation 1664–8*
A quatrefoil.
D'EWES. *MS Fairfax (Tyl.)*
A quatrefoil Gules between two wolf's heads erased and addorsed Or.
D'EWES, Bart., of Stowlangtoft. *Davy, A.*
A tiger's head erased per pale indented Argent and Sable tusked Or langued Gules issuing out of a quatrefoil Or.
EYRE. Robert Eyer, of Eye, co. Suffolk. Descended paternally of the house of Hope, co. Derby, and of Eyers, by his mother; Confirmation by Barker. *Grants & Certificates (Stowe MS 692)*
On a quatrefoil quarterly Gules and Vert a lion's head erased Argent.
HUNINGES, HUNYNGE. *MS Ordinary of Arms, fo. 19**

CINQUEFOIL

A cinquefoil Ermine between two wings expanded one Argent the other Gules.
KENT, of Suffolk. *Davy, A.*
A cinquefoil Or.
SEVERNE. Samuel Amy Severne, of Poslingford Park, died 1865. *Her.Suff.Ch., Hatchment and Glass, Poslingford. Photograph**
Out of a cinquefoil Gules a dragon's head Sable bezanty langued Gules holding in the mouth a 'dartes ende' erased Or head upwards Argent embrued Gules.
WHITTINGTON. 'Whitingdon' *Wall's Book* 'to his crest a Dragons hed sa/ bezanted comyng owt of a cynckfoil g/ holding in his mouth a Darts end rased or/ the hed upward ar/ the poynt & the Dragons tong g/'
WHITTINGTON. 'Whytingdon' *MS Alphabet of Crests, fo. 137b*

FOOT

An armed foot in the sun.
BLOUNT. *MS Heraldic Alphabet*

FRUIT

ACORN

An acorn Vert.
ANDREWS. *Davy, A. Fairbairn*, 'Suff.'*

PINEAPPLE or FIR CONE

A pineapple Proper branch Vert.
PARKYNS, of Chediston. *Davy, A.*
A pineapple leaved Proper.
PERRING, Bart., of Southwold. *Davy, A.*

RYE

An ear of rye Or.
AFFLECK, of Dalham. *Davy, A.*

WHEAT

An ear of Guinea wheat Proper.
AFFLECK, of Dalham. *Bokenham*
An ear of wheat bearded Proper.
AFFLECK, of Dalham. *Davy, A. Burke, Peerage, 1891 ed.**
An ear of wheat between two fern branches Proper.
AFFLECK, Sir James, Bart., died 1833.

Her.Suff.Ch., Wall tablet, Dalham
An ear of wheat and a palm branch in saltire Proper.
INGELOUS. *Davy, A.*
A sword and an ear of wheat in saltire Proper.
SOMERI, SOMERY, of Gt. Bradley. *Davy, A.*
An ear of wheat Or bladed Vert and a palm branch
Vert in saltire.
TINLING, of Bury. *Davy, A.*

FUSIL

Between two wings erect a fusil.
BLOMFIELD. Barnabas Blomfield, A.M.,
Incumbent for 47 years, died 1727, son of
Stephen Blomfield, of Mownys in Stonham
Aspal. His widow, Elizabeth, died 1748, aged 90.
Her.Suff.Ch., Ledger stones, Badingham

GAMB or PAW
[Bear's gamb see under PAW]

LION

A lion's paw erased and erect Or.
BOOTHBY, Bart. *MS Heraldic Alphabet.
Davy, A.*
A lion's gamb erased and erect.
GOLDINGHAM, of Belstead. *Visitation 1561
(MSS G.7* and Iveagh Copy*) Harl. 772*
Bokenham. Davy, A.*
A lion's gamb erased and erect Or.
GOLDINGHAM, of Belstead. *Visitation 1561 (ed.
Metcalfe). Washbourne*, 'Norf. and Suff.'
Fairbairn*, 'Norf. and Suff.'*
A lion's gamb erased Or the foot on the torse
[wreath].
GOLDINGHAM, of Belstead. *Davy, A.*
A lion's gamb erased Or.
LEGATT. *MS Ordinary of Arms, fo. 23**
A lion's paw erect and erased Or armed Gules.
NEWCOME. 'Charles Newcomen, of London, and
to John, of co. Linc.' *Grants & Certificates
(Stowe MS 670)*
A lion's gamb erased and erect.
NEWCOME. 'Peter Newcombe, Esq., M.A., F.R.S.,
died 1779. *Partridge, 82 (Darby, 1825), Layham
churchyard. Bookplate**
A lion's gamb erased and erect Sable.
NEWCOME, NEWCOMEN, of Layham, Marlesford.
MS Ordinary of Arms, fo. 75 Davy, A., Layham
churchyard.* Peter Newcombe, died 1779.
Her.Suff.Ch., Altar tomb in churchyard, Layham
A lion's paw Ermine armed Or.
NORWICH, of Mettingham. *MS Fairfax (Tyl. 2.)
Davy, A.*
A lion's gamb erased Argent.
WALTER, of Ipswich. *Davy, A.*

LION'S GAMB, holding: [Objects in
alphabetical order]

A lion's gamb holding a battle-axe Proper.
EMLY, of Aldeburgh. *Davy, A.*
A lion's gamb erased Sable holding a laurel branch
Vert.
BADLESMERE. *Davy, A.*
A lion's leg in pale couped Sable armed Gules
holding a branch of borage leaves and flowers
Proper.
BURNEL, BURNELL. 'Burnell of London' *Wall's
Book*
'to his crest a lyons legge in pale copey sa/ armed g/
holding a branche of lovaigne [?] leves and flowers
in there kynd'
BURNEL, BURNELL. 'Burnell of London.' *MS
Alphabet of Crests, fo. 12*

A lion's gamb erased and erect Or holding a branch
Vert fructed Or.
COUPER. *Davy, A. (Edms.)*
A lion's gamb erased and erect Or holding a vine
branch Vert fructed Gules.
COUPER, COWPER. *MS ex-Taylor Coll.**
A lion's gamb couped and erect grasping a branch of
oak Vert fructed Or.
MONTALT, MONHALT. *MS Ordinary of Arms,
fo. 18**
A lion's paw erased holding an olive branch all
Proper.
OLIVER, of Hawkedon. *Davy, A., church*
A lion's gamb erased holding an olive branch
fructed all Proper.
OLIVER, John. *Her.Suff.Ch., Hatchment,
Hawkedon*
A lion's paw erased and erect Or grasping a branch
of olives Or their cods Argent slipped and leaved
Vert.
SHERIFFE, Lawrence, of Rugeley, co. Warwicks.;
Confirmation by W. Harvey, Clarenceux, 1559.
Grants & Certificates (Harl. MS 1,359)
A lion's paw erased Or holding a branch of dates the
fruits Or in pods Argent stalk and leaves Vert.
SHERIFFE, of Uggeshall, Henstead. *Davy, A.
(Edms.)* Rev. Thomas Sheriffe, of Henstead Hall,
Rector of Henstead, died 1861. *Her.Suff.Ch.,
Hatchment, Henstead*
A lion's paw holding up a cross paty fitchy Sable.
ELINGTON, of Wrentham. *Davy, A.*
A lion's gamb erased Gules holding a cross formy
fitchy Or.
GIBBONS. *MS Heraldic Collections, fo. 15*,
'co. Warw.'*
A lion's gamb Proper holding a cross crosslet Sable.
MATHEW, of Bury. *Davy, A.*
A lion's gamb Sable holding a cross fitchy also
Sable.
MATHEWS. *Washbourne*, 'Pentlow Hall, Suff.'
[sic Essex]*
A lion's gamb holding a cross paty fitchy all Sable.
MATHEWS. *Fairbairn*, 'Suff.'*
A lion's gamb couped supporting five mascles
conjoined in cross.
PAMAN, Bartholomew, died 1721; son
Bartholomew, Gent., of the Middle Temple, died
1725, aged 25. *Her.Suff.Ch., Ledger stone, Hopton*
A lion's gamb Proper bearing a cross moline per
bend Gules and Or.
SPURDENS, of Hoxne. *Davy, A.*
A lion's paw couped and erect Or holding a cross of
five mascles Gules.
TINDALL. John Tindall, of Dickleburgh, co.
Norfolk, son of John of Banham, son of John
Tindall, of New Buckenham, co. Norfolk. Patent
July 1611. *Grants & Certificates (Stowe MSS
706 and 707; Harl. MS 6,059)*
A lion's gamb Proper holding a cross of five mascles
Gules.
TINDALL. *Davy, A.*
A lion's gamb erect holding a cross crosslet fitchy
Vert.
WOODTHORPE, of Walton. *Davy, A., church*
A lion's gamb erased and erect Proper holding an
escallop Sable.
SPURGEON, of Clopton. *Sharpe. Davy, A.*
A lion's paw erased per fesse indented Argent and
Gules holding a fleur-de-lis Or.
CHIPPINGDALE, CHIPPENDALE, of Blakenham.
Davy, A.

A lion's gamb erased and erect Argent holding a fleur-de-lis Or.

DAWE. *MS Heraldic Alphabet*

A lion's gamb erased and erect Gules holding a fleur-de-lis Or.

GOSLING. *MS Ordinary of Arms, fo. 269**

A lion's paw holding a thistle Proper.

FARROW. *Davy, A.* ? William Farrow, late of the City of London, goldsmith, died 1748; widow died 1763. *Her.Suff.Ch., Altar tomb in churchyard, Monks Eleigh*

A lion's paw holding a thistle Proper.

GERBRIDGE. *Davy, A.*

A lion's gamb erect Or grasping three roses Or stalked and leaved Vert.

SKEPPER, of Bradwell. *Davy, A.*

A lion's gamb erased and erect holding a trefoil slipped.

PHIPPS. *MS Martin's Crests*

A lion's gamb erased and erect Sable holding a trefoil slipped Argent.

PHIPPS. Rector of Halesworth and Boxford. *MS Ordinary of Arms, fo. 210*. Davy, A.*

A lion's gamb couped and erect Ermine holding a cow's foot erased Sable hoofed Or.

EDWARDS. *MS Heraldic Alphabet*

'Uppon his helme on a torse silver and Azur a Lyons Arme silver armed azure purfluid gold griping a lyons paw raise gules armed azure Mantled gules doubled silver'.

HUGON, HOUGON. Robert Hougon, of East Bradenham, co. Norfolk; Grant of Arms and Crest by Hawley, Clarenceux, 20 May 1546. *Misc.Gen. et Her. 5th S. VIII. 338 (Soc. of Ant. MS 378, fo. 533)*

A lion's gamb couped and erect Argent holding another erased Gules sans claws.

HUGON. 'Huggon of Norfolk.' *MS Heraldic Alphabet*

A lion's gamb holding a gem-ring Or stone Gules.

CROMWELL, Earl of Essex. *Davy, A.*

A lion's gamb couped and erect Argent grasping an eagle's head erased Gules.

MILTON. Mylton alias Mytton, of co. Oxford; Patent of Confirmation of Arms and Grant of Crest by Sir W. Segar, Garter. *Grants & Certificates (Add. MS 12,225)*

A lion's gamb erect Argent grasping an eagle's head erased Gules.

MILTON, of Ipswich. *Davy, A.*

A lion's gamb holding up a human heart Proper.

HOTOFT, of Stowmarket. *Davy, A., church*

A lion's gamb erased and erect Or grasping three oak, or bur, leaves Vert.

BURWELL, of Woodbridge, Sutton. *Visitation 1664–8*, 'oak leaves'. Davy, A. Washbourne, 'Suff., bur leaves'. E.A. Misc. 1921. 40, bur leaves. Fairbairn, 'Suff. burr leaves'. Her.Suff.Ch., Shottisham and Sutton, bur leaves*

A lion's gamb erect and erased Or grasping an eagle's leg erased at the thigh Gules.

EAGLE, of Lakenheath, Bury. *Davy, A. Washbourne*, 'Suff.' Fairbairn*, 'Suff.'*

A lion's paw Ermine holding a hawk's lure Or.

GERRARD. 'Gerarde' *Wall's Book*

A lion's gamb erased Ermine holding a hawk's lure Or.

GERRARD. *MS Martin's Crests*

A lion's gamb erased Ermine holding a lure Gules garnished and lined Or tasselled Argent.

GERRARD, Earl of Macclesfield Of Brandon. *Davy, A.*

A lion's paw erased and erect Proper grasping a pheon Or.

EARLE, Erasmus, of Salle, co. Norfolk, Esq., son of Thomas, son of John Earle of Salle, where for many generations the family had resided; Confirmation by Sir R. St. George, Clarenceux, 12 April 1635. This true copy made 19 April 1695, B. Fountayne; J. Hare. *Grants & Certificates (Add. MS 14,295)*

A lion's paw erased Proper holding a pheon Or.

EARLE, ERLE. c.1350. Of Willingham, Sotterley. *Davy, A.*

A lion's paw erased Argent holding a saltire Or.

BALDRY. *Bokenham*

A lion's gamb erased Or grasping a saltire Azure.

BOLDERO, of Bury. *Gage (Thingoe). Muskett. I. 176 (Harl. MS 1820, Raven's notebook)*

A lion's gamb erased Argent grasping a saltire Azure.

BOLDERO, of Suffolk. *Davy, A. (Barrett MS). Washbourne, 'Boldrowe, Suff.' Fairbairn, 'Boldrowe, Suff.'*

A lion's gamb erased Gules grasping a sceptre Or.

POWYS, of Hintlesham. *Davy, A., church*

A lion's paw erased holding a spear tasselled Proper.

ROTHINGS, of Bramfield. *Davy, A.*

A lion's paw erased holding up the hilt of a broken sword Proper.

DAGNALL, of Wetheringsett. *Davy, A.*

A lion's paw erased Sable holding *the hilt of a broken sword in pale* Proper.

UFFLET, of Somerleyton. *Davy, A.*

A lion's paw erased armed Gules holding an eagle's wing Sable.

'BROWNE of – in Essex' *Wall's Book*

'knyght by h 8/ to his crest a lyons/ paw rased armed g/ holding the wyng of An Egle sa/'

'BROWNE of – in Essex' *MS Alphabet of Crests, fo. 9*

A lion's gamb erased and erect Argent holding a wing Sable.

BROWNE, of Essex. *MS Ordinary of Arms, fo. 95*. 'Weston Browne' MS Knight's Visitations, Essex*. 'Browne' MS Philpot's Visitations, Essex**

A lion's gamb erased and erect Gules holding a wing Argent.

BROWNE. *MS Ordinary of Arms, fo. 132*. Davy, A.*

A lion's paw erect Argent holding a wing Sable.

BROWN. *MS Martin's Crests*

TWO GAMBS or PAWS [Alphabetically by name]

Two lion's paws in saltire Sable.

BIRMINGHAM. Rector of Redgrave, 1686. *Davy, A.*

Two lion's gambs erased and erect in saltire Or the dexter uppermost between them two demi-spears Or.

BLOBOLD, of Mendham. *Davy, A.*

Two lion's paws erased in saltire the dexter surmounted by the sinister Or.

DOBSON, of Ipswich. *Sharpe*

Two lion's gambs couped and erect Argent in front of two cones Gules and holding between them a bezant.

KERVILL, CARVELL. 'Thomas Karvill' *MS Philpot's Visitations, Norf.**

Two lion's gambs erased the dexter Sable gutty Argent the sinister Argent gutty Sable holding a wolf's head erased –.

KINWELLMARSH. 'Kymelmarche' *MS Ordinary of Arms, fo. 26**
Two lion's gambs united at the bottom gutty Argent and Sable counterchanged holding a wolf's head erased.

KINWELLMARSH. 'Kynnelmarch' *Washbourne*
Two lion's gambs erect Gules supporting a mitre Or.

LEGETT, LEGAT, of Sibton, Bedfield. Rector of Bedfield. *Davy, A., Seal*
Two lion's gambs supporting a regal crown all Or.

LEGETT, LEGAT. *Davy, A.*
Two lion's gambs erased Or in saltire in each a battleaxe palewise Gules.

MARKANT. 'Merkaund, ?Markaunt, John, of Colchester'; Confirmation of Arms and Grant of Crest by W. Camden, Clarenceux, 17th May 1612. *Grants & Certificates (Harl. MS 1,172)*
Two lion's gambs erased in saltire Or each holding a battle-axe Argent handle Gules.

MARKANT, MERCAUNT, of Semer. *Visitation 1664–8*. Bokenham, 'p. Camden, 1612'. Davy, A., church. Washbourne*, 'Mercaunt'. Fairbairn*, 'of Seamur [sic], Suff.'*
Two lion's paws Gules supporting a crescent Argent.

MINSHULL. *Davy, A., 'the original crest'*
Two lion's paws erect and erased supporting a mullet Or.

PRETTYMAN, Sir John, of Boughton, in Norfolk, Knt., son and heir of William Prettyman; Grant by W. Segar, Somerset Herald, 28 July 1599, after Confirmed by W. Camden, Clarenceux, in 1607. *Grants & Certificates (Add. MS 12,225; Harl. MS 6,095; Stowe MS 707)*
Two lion's gambs erased holding a mullet all Or.

PRETTYMAN, PRETYMAN, of Bacton, Bury, Laxfield, Thorndon. *Addit.Suff.Peds. Bokenham. Davy, A. Washbourne, 'Prettyman, Suff.' Burke, L.G. 1900* and 1952. Muskett. II. 281*, '? Grant 1607'. Sir George Pretyman, Kt., died 1732. Her.Suff.Ch., Wall tablet and Ledger stone, Bacton. Nunn Pretyman, late of Laxfield, died 1746. Ledger stone in sanctuary, Laxfield. Waldegrave Pretyman, died 1772; sister Mary, died 1775; Rev. Nunn Pretyman, late Rector, died 1793. Ledger stones, Cotton*
A pillar compony Or and Gules supported by two lion's gambs erased and embowed the dexter Ermine the sinister Ermines.

SCARLETT. Confirmation of Arms and Grant of Crest, February 1611. *Grants & Certificates (Harl. MS 6,059; Stowe MS 706)*
Two lion's paws erased Ermine and Ermines supporting a pillar barry Or and Gules.

SCARLETT, of Hadleigh. *Bokenham*
Two lion's gambs Ermine supporting a pillar barry of six.

SCARLETT. *MS Heraldic Collections, fo. 90**
Two lion's gambs erased dexter Argent sinister Sable holding a pillar Gules the capital Or.

SKARLETT, of Hadleigh. *Davy, A.*
Two lion's gambs erased dexter Ermine sinister Ermines supporting a pillar barry of six Gules and Or the capital Or.

SCARLETT, of Nayland. *Misc.Gen. et Her. 2nd S. I. 224* (Essex Visitation 1664)*
Two lion's gambs erased and erect dexter Argent sinister Gules holding an escutcheon per fesse Argent and Or.

WILLIS. *MS Ordinary of Arms, fo. 55**
Two lion's paws erased and erect dexter Gules

sinister Argent holding an escutcheon Or.

WILLIS, of Bury. *Davy, A.*
Two lion's gambs erased and erect dexter Argent sinister Gules supporting an escutcheon Or.

WILLIS, of co. Cambs. *Muskett. II. 102 (Add. MS 5822)*

GARB [Alphabetically by name]

A garb Or.

BAYLEY. *Bokenham*
A garb Or.

BELL. 'Walter Bell, M.D., 123 London Road, Lowestoft, Suff.' *Fairbairn*
A garb Argent.

BERNEY. 'Martyn Barney' *MS Knight's Visitations, Norf.** 'Barney' *MS Philpot's Visitations, Norf.**
A garb Gules.

BOGGIS, of Ipswich. *Davy, A., St. Nicholas church vestry*
A garb Gules.

BRIDGES, of Ipswich. *Sharpe*
A garb.

BROOKE, John, of Ashbocking Manor, died 1959; widow Ada Mary, died 1979. *Her.Suff.Ch., Headstone in churchyard, Ashbocking*
A garb.

BURKITT, of Sudbury. Myles Burkitt, gent., died 1690; widow Mary, died 1699; Miles Burkitt, M.A., died 1744; Others. *Partridge, 18 (Darby, 1827), churchyard, St. Gregory's, Sudbury*
A garb Argent.

BURKITT, of Hitcham, Sudbury. *Davy, A., St. Gregory's church, Sudbury*
A garb Or.

BURKITT, of Hitcham, Sudbury. *Davy, A., St. Gregory's, Sudbury.* Miles Burkitt died 1699; Thomas Burkitt, died 1793; Others. *Her.Suff.Ch., Altar tomb in churchyard, St. Gregory's, Sudbury. Not found 1980*
A garb Or.

CLOSE, of Ipswich, Hitcham, etc. *Davy, A.*
A garb Or pierced transversely by an arrow, or spear, headed Argent.

CLOSE-BROOKS, Arthur, M.C., died of wounds, 1917. *Her.Suff.Ch., Brass, Gt. Glemham*
A cockerel Gules wattled and standing on a garb fessewise Or.

COVENTRY. Hon. Henry Thomas Coventry, died 1934. *Her.Suff.Ch., Wall tablet, Stoke by Nayland*
A garb Or encircled by a ducal coronet per pale Gules and Azure.

DADE, of Tannington. *MS Knight's Visitations, Norf.* Visitation 1664–8* Bokenham. Dade (MS). Dade*
A garb enfiled with a ducal coronet.

DADE, of Norfolk. *MS Heraldic Collections, fo. 82* Partridge, 59 (Darby, 1828)*
A garb Or enfiled with a ducal coronet per pale Azure and Gules.

DADE, of Shadingfield, Tannington. *Davy, A. Washbourne, 'Norf. and Suff.' Fairbairn*, 'of Woodton, Norf. and Tannington, Suff.'* Thomas Dade, Esq., died 1619; John Dade, died 1732; William Dade, died 1755. *Her.Suff.Ch., Ledger stones and Tablet, Tannington*
A garb Or enfiled with a ducal coronet per pale Gules and Or.

DADE, of Shadingfield. *Davy, A. (Barrett MS)*
A garb.

DADE, Henry, died 1653. *Her.Suff.Ch., Altar tomb in churchyard, Dallinghoo*
A garb encircled with a coronet.
DADE, Rev. Francis, A.M., son of Thomas Dade of Tannington, died 1722. *Her.Suff.Ch., Altar tomb in churchyard, Bramford*
A garb ensigned with a crown.
DADE, Jane, wife of John Dade, of Ipswich, died 1724. *Her.Suff.Ch., Slab, St. Matthew's*
A garb Or on the sinister side a dove close Argent picking the wheat.
DANDY, DAUNDY, of Combs, Sapiston, St. Lawrence, Ipswich. *Davy, A.*
On a garb Or a dove close Argent.
DANDY. *Washbourne, 'Suff.'*
A garb Or on the sinister side a dove Argent beaked and legged Gules.
DANDY, of Suffolk. *Fairbairn, 'of Sapiston, Suff. dove close Argent'. Proc.S.I.A. XXVII. 149 (Dandy Pedigree)*
A garb Argent banded Or.
DARBY. 'Charles Darby of St. edmonds bury' *MS Knight's Visitations, Suff.* Washbourne*, 'Suff.' Fairbairn*, 'Suff.'*
A garb Argent banded Or on it a mullet Gules.
DARBY, of Tuddenham. *Davy, A., '? the mullet for difference'*
A garb Vert charged with three bezants in pale.
ELLIS. Thomas Ellis, of Swyneshed, co. Linc., gent.; Grant by Barker. *Grants & Certificates (Stowe MS 692)*
A garb banded and charged with three roundels in pale.
ELLIS. *MS Heraldic Collections, fo. 85**
A garb Argent banded Ermine in [within] a coronet Or.
FELBRIGGE, of Playford. *Davy, A.*
A garb Or.
GOLDING. *Davy, A. Washbourne, 'Ess. and Suff.' Fairbairn*, 'Essex and Suff.'*
A garb Or.
KELSO, of Bungay. *Davy, A.*
On a garb an eagle rising all Or.
KEMP. 'Kempe' *Wall's Book*
'to his Crest an Egle the Wyngs rysyng/ on a shef Or'
KEMP. 'Kemp' *MS Alphabet of Crests, fo. 68*
On the top of a wheat sheaf Proper a pelican Or vulning herself Proper.
KEMPE, of Ubbeston. *Bokenham. MS ex-Taylor Coll.*, the garb Or.*
On a garb lying fessewise Or a pelican vulning her breast Proper.
KEMP, Bart., of Ubbeston. *MS ex-Taylor Coll.* Davy, A.*
On a garb lying fessewise an eagle standing with wings endorsed all Or.
KEMPE, of Beccles. *Muskett. II. 225*
A garb with a bird on either side.
LEAKE, John, Commander of H.M.S. Grafton, died 1772. *Her.Suff.Ch., Ledger stone in churchyard, Beccles. Not seen 1985*
A garb Vert charged with a fleece Or.
MADDY. Rector of Somerton, Stansfield, Hartest. *Davy, A. Bookplate**, [fleece larger than garb]
A garb Or banded Sable.
MALTBY, . . . , of Maltby, in Cleveland, co. York.; Patent by Sir W. Segar, Garter. *Grants & Certificates (Add. MS 12,225)*
A garb Or banded Gules.
MALTBY, of Stonham Aspal. *Davy, A.*

'And for the Crest on a Wreath of the Colours A Garb Erminois, banded Vert, between two Wings elevated Sable'
MIDDLETON, William, of Cronfield [*sic*] Hall and Shrubland Hall. Grant by Isaac Heard, Garter and George Harrison, Clarenceux, 9 May 1804. *Photo-copy**
A garb Or between two wings Sable.
MIDDLETON, of Crowfield Hall. *Sharpe*
A garb Or banded Vert between two wings Sable.
MIDDLETON, Bart., of Crowfield and Shrubland Halls. *Davy, A. Washbourne**, 'Middleton-Fowle, Bart., Suff.' Fairbairn*, 'Middleton, Bart., Crowfield Hall and Shrubland Hall, Suff.'* Middleton, Baronets, of Crowfield and Shrubland Park, 1829–1887. *Her.Suff.Ch., Wall tablet, Hatchments and Glass, Barham.* Middleton. *Glass, Nacton.* Sir William Fowle Middleton, died 1860; widow died 1867. *Glass, Coddenham, Hatchment, Crowfield. Livery button**, untinctured*
A garb Or banded Sable.
MOLINEUX, MOLINER, of Ipswich. *Bokenham. Davy, A.*
A garb.
MULLINER, of Holbrook. *Visitation 1664–8*
In front of a garb Or three arrows two in saltire and one in pale points downward Sable.
OTTLEY. Rector of Acton. *Davy, A.*
A garb Or banded Gules.
READ. 'Master Rede of Kynte' *Harl. MS 6163.* [Second crest, arms given as for Read, Reade, of Halesworth]
A garb Or banded –.
READ. 'Rede, Reede' *MS Ordinary of Arms, fo. 117**
A rook upon a wheat sheaf pecant [pecking] all Proper.
ROOKE, of Nacton. *Sharpe*
A garb Or banded Gules.
SCAMBLER. Mary, daughter of Joseph Brand and widow of James Scamler [*sic*], died 1714. *Her.Suff.Ch., Slab, Edwardstone*
A garb Or banded with a strap Gules.
SICKLEMORE, of Ipswich. *Visitation 1664–8*
A garb Or with a sickle, the former within a girdle Sable the buckle Or.
SICKLEMORE, of Ipswich. *MS Fairfax*
A garb surrounded by a sickle.
SICKLEMORE, of Ipswich. *Bokenham*
A wheat sheaf.
SICKLEMORE, of Wetheringsett, Debenham. *Page. Burke, L.G. 1853 ed.*
A garb banded.
SICKLEMORE, of Ipswich. *Davy, A., Brandeston church. Washbourne**, 'Suff.'*
A garb Or banded Gules.
SICKLEMORE. *Fairbairn*, 'Suff.'*
Out of a ducal coronet Or a garb Ermine.
TINDALL. 'S. Welye Tyndall, Norff.' *Harl. MS 6163**, [shown to be far more like a bush of feathers banded]
'On a healme forth of a wreath of his Cullers a Garbe gold bound vp wth a Band Argent and Azure beteene two Ostridge Fethers proper'
TROTMAN, Edward, of Cam, co. Gloucester; Grant of Arms and Crest by Wm. Segar, Garter, 27th November 14 James I. [1616/17]. *Misc.Gen. et Her. N.S. IV.188*
A garb Or banded Azure between two ostrich feathers Argent quills Or.

TROTMAN, Edward, of Cam, co. Gloucester, son of Richard Trotman, of the same place; Grant [?Confirmation] by Sir John Borough, Garter (by Sir W. Segar, Garter, 14 King James). *Grants & Certificates (Harl. MSS 1,441 and 6,140)*
A garb Or banded Argent and Azure between two ostrich feathers Argent.
  TROTMAN. *Sharpe. Her.Suff.Ch., St. Peter's, Ipswich*
A garb erect Or banded Argent and Gules between two ostrich feathers Argent quilled Or.
  TROTMAN, of Ipswich. *Davy, A., St. Peter's church*
A garb Or.
  TROTMAN, Robert, Esq., High Sheriff in 1783, died 1813. Of Ipswich. *E.A.N. & Q. XII. 119. Her.Suff.Ch., Wall tablet, St. Peter's. Not found 1983*
A wheat sheaf or gail [sic] Or.
  WAITE, WHAITE, of Glemham. *Sharpe*
A garb Or.
  WAYTH, of Gt. Glemham. *E.A. Misc. 1928, 33 (Darby, 1825)*
On a cushion wreathed Argent and Azure a garb Or.
  WAYTH, of Gt. Glemham. *Davy, A., church monuments.* Daniel Wayth, Gent., died 1734; Daniel Wayth, Gent., died 1752; widow Mary, died 1799; Others. *E.A. Misc. 1911, 50*
A bird Sable on the top of a wheatsheaf Or.
  WHETCROFT, of Ipswich. *Bokenham*
A garb Or charged with a martlet Sable.
  WHETCROFT, WHETCROFTE, of Blaxhall, Ipswich, Witnesham, Eye. *Davy, A. Proc.S.I.A. VI. 104. Fairbairn, 'Whetcroft, Suff.'*

GARLAND see CHAPLET, WREATH

GAUNTLET see also HAND, armoured
A dexter gauntlet couped at the wrist Azure.
  BURTON, LINGEN-BURTON, 'of Four Sisters, East Bergholt, Suff.' *Fairbairn*, First crest, second crest for Lingen [q.v.]*
A dexter gauntlet Or.
  GRUDGEFIELD, GRUDGFIELD, GRUGFIELD, of Fressingfield. *Visitation 1664–8*. Washbourne*, 'Grudgfield, Suff.' Untinctured. Fairbairn*, 'Grudgfield, Suff.'*
A gauntlet Or.
  GRUDGEFIELD, GRUDGFIELD, GRUGFIELD, of Fressingfield. *Bokenham. Davy, A.*
A dexter gauntlet clenched erect Proper garnished Or.
  WIGGES. Richard Wigges or Wigg, son of Thomas, of Grub Street, London, gent.; Entered by H. St. George, Richmond, in 1634. *Grants & Certificates (Harl. MS 5,869 and 6,140)*
A gauntlet.
  WIGGES. *Proc.S.I.A. IX.7, Flagons, Stradishall church*

GAUNTLET, holding: [Objects in alphabetical order]
A dexter gauntlet Proper holding a fleur-de-lis Argent.
  BLOIS, BLOYS, BLOYSE, of Grundisburgh, Yoxford. *Visitation 1664–8*. Bokenham. Washbourne*, 'Bart., Suff.' Burke, Peerage, 1891 ed.* Fairbairn*, 'Sir Ralph Blois, Bart., of Cockfield Hall, Yoxford, Suff.' E.A.N. & Q. XIII. 245.* Blois, Baronets, of Cockfield Hall, 1760–1916. *Her.Suff.Ch., Tablets and Hatchments, Yoxford.* William Blois, died 1621;

William Blois, died 1734; Sir Charles Blois, died 1738. *Ledger stones and Tablet, Grundisburgh*
A dexter gauntlet Proper purfled Or holding a fleur-de-lis Or.
  BLOIS, BLOYS. *Davy, A. Fairbairn, 'Bloys of Ipswich, Suff.'*
'and to his Creast on a Torse or and sable a Gauntlett argent holding a Launce or headed argent'
  LAUNCE, John, of Halesworth; Grant of Arms and Crest by Gilbert Dethick, Garter, 8th November 1580. *Misc.Gen. et Her. N.S. IV. 209–10**
A gauntlet fesseways supporting a lance erect all Proper.
  LAUNCE, John, of Halesworth, in Suffolk, son of John Launce of the same; Confirmation by Sir G. Dethick, Garter, 8 November 1580. *Grants & Certificates (Harl. MS 1,441; Stowe MS 703)*
A dexter gauntlet fesseways Proper holding a sword erect Argent hilt Or on the blade a man's head couped Proper issuing drops of blood at the neck, with a scroll behind the sword with this motto 'Ex merito'.
  CHESTON, of Mildenhall. *Visitation 1612. Reyce, 155. Davy, A. Washbourne*, 'Suff.' Proc.S.I.A. II. 47. Fairbairn*, 'Suff.'* Saracen's head, no scroll 'A Capt. in Mildenhall Suff. His Crest on a wreath g.O.& Erm. a right hand armd, holding upright a Sword, thereon a mans head full faced, all proper, wth this word, Ex merito. The right hand gauntlet is blew, or harnefs colour, nayled O. ye pomell & hilt of ye sword A. ye Sword po. above ye crown of the head, the face of dead color ye head & beard browne. Y^e neck coupde bleeding & dropping. Commanded in this sort to be borne by his Soveraigne, for y^t his great valor & desert, in bringing in ye head of y^t Archtraytor E Desmond'
  CHESTON, of Mildenhall. *MS Fairfax (Tyl.)*
A gauntlet Proper holding a broken sword Argent hilt and pommel Or.
  CHEWT, of Ellough, Wrentham. *MS Ordinary of Arms, fo. 229*. Davy, A., Ellough church*
A gauntlet Proper studded Or grasping a sword in bend sinister Argent hilt and pommel Or.
  GEE, of London. *Gee, 14. Undated Docket of Grant p' Cooke, Clar.; Another Docket, 1592. Coll. of Arms, Misc.Grants. I. 127b. and IV, 118*
A gauntlet erect Or lined Gules grasping a sword Proper hilt and pommel Or.
  GEE, Samuel, of London. Patent 1592. *Grants & Certificates (Harl. MS 1,359)*
A dexter gauntlet erect Proper grasping a sword Argent.
  GEE, of Mildenhall. *Visitation 1664–8.*
A gauntlet Argent garnished at the wrist Or holding a sword Argent hilt and pommel Or.
  GEE, of Mildenhall. *Davy, A.*
A gauntlet erect grasping a sword all Proper garnished Or.
  VANE, Sir Thomas, of Badsell, co. Kent. Patent 15 May 1574. *Grants & Certificates (Stowe MS 703)*
A gauntlet Or holding a broken sword hilt and pommel Or.
  FANE [VANE]. *Davy, A. (Edms.)*
A dexter gauntlet brandishing a sword Proper.
  VANE, William John Frederick, 3rd Duke of Cleveland, died 1864. *Her.Suff.Ch., Hatchment, Santon Downham*

GED see FISH, PIKE

GLOBE see SPHERE

GLOVE

On a dexter glove Argent bound and tasselled Or a falcon wings expanded Or between two branches leaved Vert fructed Sable.
JENNEY, JENNY, of Knodishall. *Visitation 1561 (MS G.7*)*
On a glove in fesse Argent a falcon belled Ppr.
JENNEY, of Knodishall. *Visitation 1561 (ed. Metcalfe)*
On a glove Argent a hawk Or belled Or.
JENNEY, of Theberton, Knodishall, Hasketon, Herringfleet, Bredfield. *Page. Davy, A. Washbourne*, 'Middx, Linc. and Suff.' Burke, L.G. 1853 ed. Fairbairn*, 'of Bredfield House, Suff.' Glove in fesse*
On a glove Argent a falcon close belled Or.
JENNY, Arthur, died 1667. *Her.Suff.Ch., Slab, Knodishall*
On a glove lying fesseways a hawk all Proper.
JENNEY, Arthur, died 1729. *Her.Suff.Ch., Hatchment, Bredfield.* Arthur Jenney, of Rendlesham, died 1742. *Hatchment, Bredfield.* [No glove shown, the talons rest on the wreath]
On a glove in fesse a falcon close armed Or.
JENNEY, Edmund, of Hasketon and Bredfield, died 1852; sister Anne, died 1857. *Her.Suff.Ch., Glass, Hasketon*

GRENADE see FIRE-BALL

HALBERD, HALBERT see AXE

HAMMER

A hammer Argent handle Or.
PETTUS, Bart., of Cheshton. *Davy, A.*

HAND

A hand couped fesseways Proper.
BLACKE, of Suffolk. *Davy, A. Washbourne*, 'Suff.' Fairbairn*, 'Suff. and Essex'*
A hand issuing from a cloud fessewise reaching to a garland of laurel Proper.
BUCTON, of Brome, Oakley. *Davy, A. Washbourne**
Out of a cloud a dexter hand erect pointing to a star all Proper.
BUMSTED, of Sotterley. *Davy, A., church. Washbourne*, 'Bumstead or Bumsted, Suff.'*
A dexter hand couped at the wrist and erect Proper over it a crescent reversed Argent.
HARVEY, of Leiston. *Davy, A. Washbourne*, 'Harvey, G.C.B., Ess.' The hand 'apaumee' [in illustration open, palm forward]*
A dexter hand erect Proper.
MOULD, Henry, late of Appleby, co. Leic. (married Sarah, sister of John Moore, of Kentwell Hall), died 1715. *Her.Suff.Ch., Ledger stone in Clopton chapel, Long Melford*

HAND, holding: [Objects in alphabetical order]

A dexter hand Proper holding an annulet Or.
NOTTINGHAM, of Bury, Ipswich. *Davy, A.*
A hand holding a sheaf of arrows points downward Proper.
BOONE, of Barking. *Davy, A., church*
A hand in armour Proper holding an arrow Or headed and feathered Argent.
CLARKE. *Davy, A.*
A dexter hand in mail holding a battle-axe handle Gules blade Argent.
LEVESON, LEWSON, of Blundeston. *Davy, A., church*

A hand holding a billet Azure.
PATTISHALL, PATESHULL, of Euston. *Davy, A.*
A falconer's gloved hand in fesse couped Proper thereon a falcon perched Or.
JENNEY, . . . , of Knodishall, co. Suffolk; Confirmation by Sir W. Segar, Garter. *Grants & Certificates (Add. MSS 4,966 and 12,225)*
A falconer's hand in a glove in fesse Proper bearing a falcon perched thereon Or.
JENNEY. *Davy, A. Washbourne*, 'Jenny. Suff.' Fairbairn*, 'Jenny. Suff.'*
A dexter hand couped at the wrist holding a book.
APPLEWHAITE, Henry, died 1740; Henry Applewhaite, died 1765. *Her.Suff.Ch., Ledger stones, Huntingfield*
A hand couped at the wrist erected holding a book its leaves open Proper.
MACRO, of Bury. *Bokenham*
A hand holding two branches of laurel meeting at the top Proper.
COOPER, Bart., of Worlington. *Davy, A. (Burke)*
A hand couped at the wrist lying fesseways holding a branch of laurel fructed Proper.
GRANT. Vicar of Wickhambrook. *Davy, A.*
A dexter hand holding a branch of oak Proper.
GRANT, of Darlway, Scotland. *Her.Suff.Ch., Ledger stone, Wickhambrook. No inscription given*
A hand vested [*sic* hand and arm] barry Argent and Sable holding a holly branch Proper
HILTON, of Waldringfield. *Davy, A.*
A hand holding two branches of palm in orle Proper.
JACOMB, of Ipswich. *Davy, A.*
A dexter hand holding a rose branch all Proper.
LE HEUP, of Hessett, Bury. *Davy, A.*
A dexter hand erect couped at the wrist Or supporting a crescent the horns downward Argent.
HARVEY, Sir Daniel, of Comb Nevile, co. Surrey; Grant by Sir W. Segar, Garter. *Grants & Certificates (Add. MS 12,225)*
A dexter hand Proper holding a cross paty fitchy Azure.
CORBEN, CORBIN, CORBYN, of Suffolk. *Davy, A.*
Out of a cloud in the sinister a dexter hand fesseways Proper holding a cross paty fitchy Azure.
CORNELIUS, of Ipswich, Nacton. *Davy, A.*
A hand erect holding a cross crosslet fitchy in pale.
ILLEY, ILLEGH, ILNEY, of Brent Eleigh. *Davy, A. (Burke)*
A dexter hand Proper holding up a cross crosslet fitchy Sable.
SHEPHEARD. *Davy, A.*
A hand Proper holding a cross of five mascles Gules.
TINDALL, of Rattlesden. *Davy, A.*
A hand couped at the wrist in fesse holding a curling stone.
BIDWELL. *Davy, A. Washbourne, 'of Dev.'*
A dexter hand holding a fish all Proper.
HADDOCK. Perpetual Curate of Thorpe by Ixworth. *Davy, A. (Burke). Heraldry of Fish, 165*, a haddock*
A hand erect holding a fish.
SOLEY. Mary, wife of John Soley, clerk, died 1737. *Partridge, 33 (Darby, 1830), Chediston churchyard*
An arm couped at the wrist [*sic*] and erect holding in the hand a fish as in the arms [a sole, Or or Gules].
SOLLEY, Rev. Benjamin, A.M., Rector of Barsham, died 1714. *Her.Suff.Ch., Ledger stone, Barsham*

A hand Proper holding a fleur-de-lis per pale Argent and Sable.
> NELSON, of Bungay, Bramfield. *Davy, A., Bramfield church*

A dexter hand Proper holding a fleur-de-lis Sable.
> NELSON, Richard, Gent., died 1718; son Richard Nelson, Gent., died 1768. *Her.Suff.Ch., Tablet, Holy Trinity, Bungay*

A hand issuing [*sic*] pulling a thistle.
> BOXTED. *Davy, A. Washbourne, issuant from the wreath*

A hand issuant [*sic*] plucking a rose.
> FREISELL, FREYZELL. *Davy, A. Washbourne*, *'Fresell, Fresill', issuant from the wreath*

A dexter hand holding a thistle all Proper.
> GIFFARD. *Davy, A.*

A hand holding a cinquefoil stalked.
> HOWCHIN, of Eye. *E.A.N. & Q. I. 312, Stone in church*

A dexter hand Argent holding a bunch of wheat ears Or.
> DENNY. 'John denny of Howe' *MS Knight's Visitations, Norf.* *

A dexter hand cuffed Argent holding four ears of wheat, or barley, Or.
> DENNY. '? Dennye' *MS Philpot's Visitations, Norf.* *

A dexter hand Proper holding a bunch of wheat ears Or.
> DENNY, of Occold. *Davy, A., church*

'on a healme forth of a wreath of their coullers [Sable and Or] a hand proper houlding a fuzill of the second' [Or].
> ESSINGTON. William and Thomas Essington of Cowley, co. Glos.; Grant of Arms and Crest by Segar, Garter, 28th July 1610. *Misc.Gen. et Her. 4th S. I. 3* *

A hand Proper holding a fusil Or.
> ESSINGTON, of Brightwell. *Davy, A., church*

A dexter hand holding a gamb erased.
> BROWN, John, died 1693. *Her.Suff.Ch., Slab, Framlingham*

A hand issuing from a cloud fesseways lifting a garb Proper.
> LARK. *Davy, A.*

A hand holding a glove Proper.
> INGE, of Alpheton. *Davy, A.*

A hand Gules holding a grenade fired Proper.
> HALLUM, of Ipswich. *Davy, A.*

A dexter hand couped at the wrist Proper holding a serpent's head erased Argent.
> SAYER, of Eye. *Sharpe*

A hand Proper holding a dragon's head erased Argent.
> SAYER, John, died 1761; widow Grace, died 1775. *Her.Suff.Ch., Hatchment, Eye*

A hand holding a hunting horn Proper.
> HACKLUYT, of Wetheringsett. *Davy, A.*

A hand in armour [*sic* gauntlet] Proper lying fesseways grasping a lance Or headed Argent.
> LAUNCE, of Halesworth. *Davy, A., 'Granted 8 Nov. 1580. Grant pen. Mr. B.' Washbourne, 'Suff.' Fairbairn, 'of Halesworth, Suff.'*

A dexter hand holding a lancet Proper.
> CRAWFORD, of Haughley. *Davy, A.*

A hand erect holding an eagle's leg erased à la quise [erased at the thigh].
> BROWNE. Elizabeth, wife of John Browne of Woodbridge, died 1732 aged 28; widower died 1735 aged 42; three infant sons. *Green, 151, Marble slab, Framlingham church*

A hand Proper holding an eagle's leg erased at the thigh Gules.
> GERVIS, JERVYS, of Bradfield St. Clare, Whepstead. *Davy, A.* Jervys of Whepstead. *Her.Suff.Ch., Glass, Whepstead*

A dexter hand holding a hawk's lure Proper.
> ALDRINGTON. *Davy, A., St. Cross church*

A dexter hand Proper sleeved Argent [*sic* hand and arm] holding a millrind Sable.
> KINGSMILL, of Cretingham. *Davy, A.*

A hand Proper clothed Azure [*sic* hand and arm] grasping a buck's scalp Gules.
> PARKER. *MS Martin's Crests*

A dexter hand Proper holding a spear in bend.
> CAMPBELL, of Achanduin & Barbreck, co. Argyll. Colin and Duncan Campbell, both killed in action, 1917. *Her.Suff.Ch., Wall tablet, Holy Trinity, Ipswich. Called 'the Badge'*

A dexter hand armed [*sic* gauntlet] throwing a dart [spear].
> GODBOLD. *Davy, A.*

On a Bible open a hand couped close holding a sword erect.
> ALLIN, Bart., of Lowestoft, Somerleyton. *Davy, A.*

A dexter hand couped at the wrist holding a sword erect.
> CAMPE, of Kessingland, Ellough. *Davy, A., both churches*

A dexter hand couped at the wrist barwise holding a sword erect.
> CAMPE, John, died 1699. *Her.Suff.Ch., Ledger stone, Kessingland*

A dexter hand holding a sword.
> CHAPMAN. *Davy, A., St. Mary Tower church, Ipswich*

Out of a cloud a dexter hand brandishing a scimitar Proper.
> CHARTRES. Elizabeth, widow of the Rev. James Chartres, M.A., Vicar of Godmanchester and West Haddon, died 1840. *Her.Suff.Ch., Monument, Mettingham*

A dexter hand brandishing a scimitar Proper.
> DAMANT, of Eye, ?Cransford. *Davy, A.*

A dexter hand holding a scimitar indented on the back cutting at a pen all Proper.
> DURWARD. *Davy, A. Washbourne. Fairbairn*, 'a seax'*

A dexter hand holding a sword in pale all Proper.
> KIRKETOT, CRIKETOT. *Davy, A.*

A hand holding a scimitar in pale Proper.
> MONTCHENSY, of Edwardstone. Sir William de Montchensy, temp. Edw. I. *Davy, A.*

A dexter hand grasping a dagger.
> SKIPPON, of Wrentham, Marlesford, Stratford St. Mary. *Davy, A.*

A sinister hand holding an inflamed torch.
> MCDOUALL, Rev. William, M.A., Rector 1854–death 1902. *Her.Suff.Ch., Wall tablet, Ousden*

TWO HANDS [Alphabetically by name]

Two dexter hands conjoined supporting a human heart Proper.
> DE LA LAND, DE LAND. About Debenham c.1407. *Davy, A. Fairbairn*, 'Deland, Suff.'*

Two hands couped at the wrists and clasped the dexter Or the sinister Argent.
> LE STRANGE, STRANGE. *MS Ordinary of Arms, fo. 51* *

A dexter and sinister hand issuing in bend couped

Proper holding a sword in pale Argent pommelled
Or on its middle a boar's head Sable tusked Argent
erased Gules.
    MITFORD. *Davy, A.*
Two hands couped at the wrist conjoined and erect.
    NELSON. *Davy, A.*
Two hands couped at the wrist erect.
    NELSON, Edward, died 1744. *Her.Suff.Ch., Wall*
    slab, Bramfield
A dexter hand in bend couped at the wrist in the act
of conveying to another dexter hand issuant from
the wreath Argent a torch erect Gules fired Or.
    WHEWELL, of Lowestoft. Master of Trinity
    College, Cambridge. *Davy, A.*

HAND, where armoured, see GAUNTLET

HAT see CAP, CHAPEAU

HEAD
A horned head couped Or. [*sic* ?].
    ROWNING. *Sharpe*

BEAST

ANTELOPE [Alphabetically by name]
An antelope's, or goat's, head.
    COLMAN, of Hacheston, Laxfield, Brent Eleigh.
    Davy, A.
An antelope's, or goat's, head erased Argent.
    FAULKES, of Exning, Mildenhall. *Davy, A.*
An antelope's head erased Argent attired Or about
its neck a wreath Argent and Sable.
    GLASCOCK, of Barton Mills. *Bokenham*
An antelope's head erased Argent collared with a
belt Sable buckled and rimmed Argent attired Or.
    GLASCOCK, of Lt. Barton, Aldham, Stoke,
    Ipswich. *Davy, A., Lt. Barton church*
An antelope's head erased gorged with a ducal
coronet.
    GORTON. Rector of Badingham. *Davy, A.*
An antelope's head erased Argent armed Or.
    OGLE. *MS Ordinary of Arms, fo. 269**
An antelope's head erased.
    OGLE, Henry Meade Ogle, of Ireland, died 1823.
    Green, 145, Marble slab, Framlingham church
An antelope's head Sable.
    RANDALL. *MS Martin's Crests*
An antelope's head couped, or erased, Or.
    RANDALL, RANDOLPH, of Beccles. *Davy, A.*
An antelope's head couped Or.
    RANDALL. Maria, wife of William Randall, died
    1706. *Her.Suff.Ch., Monument, Beccles*
An antelope's head erased per fesse wavy Argent
and Azure.
    RAPER, Richard, of Langthorn, co. York., citizen
    and merchant of London; Grant by Sir T. St.
    George, Garter and Sir H. St. George, Clarenceux,
    6 February 1701. *Grants & Certificates (Add. MS*
    14,831)
In front of a springbok's head Proper three mullets
Argent.
    VESTEY. Ronald, Arthur and William, sons of Sir
    Edmund Hoyle Vestey, 1st Bart.; the former, of
    Thurlow Hall, died 1987; the latter died 1971.
    Her.Suff.Ch., Wall tablets, Gt. Thurlow

APE
An ape's head erased Proper ducally gorged Or.
    CHAMBERLAIN, of Gedding. *Davy, A., Capel*
    church. Washbourne, 'of Camb.'

ASS [Alphabetically by name]
An ass's, or hind's, head Argent.

ASCOUGH. 'Ascu' *Wall's Book*
An ass's head erased Argent.
    ASCOUGH. 'ffraunc Ayscoughe of Holsey' *MS*
    Knight's Visitations, Linc.*
An ass's head per pale Argent and Sable.
    ASTON. *Wall's Book*
'to his crest an asses hed ptyd in pale ar/sa/'
    ASTON. *MS Alphabet of Crests, fo. 3*
An ass's head couped Argent.
    BARNARDISTON, of Kedington, Clare. 'Sr
    Nathaniell Barnardeston Knight' *MS Lilly's*
    Visitation of Suffolk*, second of two crests given.
    Gipps, 'anciently'
An ass's head Argent.
    BARNARDISTON, of Kedington, Clare. *Davy, A.*
    Washbourne*, 'Suff.' Fairbairn*, 'of Kiddington
    [sic], Suff.'*
An ass's head couped.
    BARNARDISTON, Sir Thomas, died 1619; wife
    Elizabeth (Hanchet), died 1584. *Her.Suff.Ch.,*
    Effigy monument, Kedington
An ass's head erased Argent ducally gorged Or.
    CHAMBERLAIN, of Suffolk. *Davy, A.*
An ass's head couped Argent polled Azure collared
between two barrulets Or the collar charged with
three roses Gules all between two branches.
    LATTON. *MS Heraldic Collections, fo. 41**
An ass's head couped Ermine ducally gorged Or.
    MALLET. *MS Ordinary of Arms, fo. 207**
An ass's head couped Azure the mane – charged on
the neck with a fesse between three bezants above
the first a martlet Or.
    ST. AMAND. 'Sainctamond' *Wall's Book.*
    'Anthony St Amand' *MS Ordinary of Arms,*
    fo. 70*, bezants one above and two below fesse,
    mane Or.
'to his crest an asses hed b/ the mane a fesse on the
necke betwene iij besants above ye fyrst a marlet or/'
    ST. AMAND. 'Saintamond' *MS Alphabet of*
    Crests, fo. 118
An ass's head couped collared charged on the neck
with three roundels one above and two below the
collar.
    ST. AMAND. *MS Heraldic Collections, fo. 82b**

BEAR
A bear's head Sable bezanty muzzled Gules.
    BRERETON. *Wall's Book*
'to his crest a beres hed sa/ moseled g/bezanty'
    BRERETON. *MS Alphabet of Crests, fo. 7*
A bear's head Proper muzzled Gules.
    CRADOCK, Walter, born 1656, died aged c.75;
    Rev. Samuel Cradock, B.D., Rector of North
    Cadbury, co. Somerset, died 1706. *Her.Suff.Ch.,*
    Ledger stones, Wickhambrook
A bear's head Sable muzzled Gules between two
wings erect.
    HEARD, of Seckford Hall in Gt. Bealings, Lt.
    Bealings. *Davy, A.*
A bear's head.
    MORLEY, of Framsden. *Davy, A.*
A bear's head muzzled.
    MORLEY, Thomas, Lord Morley, Marshal of
    Ireland. *Davy, A. (Blomefield, II. 441. Seal of*
    1420)

BEAR'S HEAD, Couped
A bear's head couped Azure collared Sable
garnished and studded Or.
    CAVENDISH, of Trimley. *Bokenham*
A bear's head couped Sable maned and muzzled Or
the leash hanging down before with a ring at the end.

COLLINGS. 'Henry Collynge of Bury' *MS Knight's Visitations, Suff.* *
A bear's head couped Sable muzzled Or.
CRADOCK, of Wickhambrook. *Davy, A.*
A bear's head couped Argent muzzled Gules.
CRADOCK. *Davy, A. (Barrett MS)*
A bear's head couped Or muzzled Gules.
DEANE, of Alton Hall, Stutton, Hintlesham. *MS Heraldic Alphabet. Davy, A.*
A bear's head couped Sable muzzled Or, a crescent for difference.
DEANE, of Gt. Maplestead in Essex. *Muskett. I. 154 (Harl. MSS 6071 and 1542)*
A bear's head couped in fesse.
DOWNING, of Spexhall. *Davy, A., church. Washbourne, 'of Norf.'*
A bear's head couped per pale Argent and Gules muzzled Sable.
ONEBY, ONEBYE, of Lowdham [*sic*]. *Davy, A., Monument, Ufford church.* Robert Oneby, late of Loudham Park, High Sheriff of Suffolk 1750, died 1753. *Her.Suff.Ch., Monument and Hatchment, Ufford.* 'a head bridled'
A bear's head couped Sable semy of estoiles Or.
TRYON or TRYUNE, Peter, of London, a Dutchman; Grant by W. Camden, Clarenceux, 1 June (?July) 1610. *Grants & Certificates (Harl. MSS 1,441 and 6,059; Stowe MSS 706 and 707)*
A bear's head couped Argent muzzled Gules collared dancetty Ermines.
WHITE, John, of London; Confirmation by W. Dethick, Garter, 2 February 1588. *Grants & Certificates (Stowe MS 676)*

BEAR'S HEAD, Erased
A bear's head erased Gules muzzled Or.
BARKER, of Clare. *Davy, A., St. Peter's church, Sudbury*
A bear's head erased Sable muzzled Or.
BARKER, of Clare, Thorndon. *Davy, A.* Lt. Col. J. Barker, of Clare Priory, died 1804; John, son of John C. Barker, of Clare Priory, died 1837. *Her.Suff.Ch., Hatchment and Wall tablet, Clare*
A bear's head erased Sable muzzled Or charged with two swords in saltire Argent hilts and pommels Or.
BARKER. Gen. Sir George Barker, of Clare Priory, died 1914. *Her.Suff.Ch., Wall tablet, Clare*
A bear's, or wolf's, head erased and collared.
BARRY. Lambe Barry, Esq., died 1768; daughters Anne and Isabella, died 1808 and 1825; Others. *Her.Suff.Ch., Altar tomb in churchyard and Wall tablet in church, Syleham*
A bear's head erased Proper.
BEAUMONT. *Washbourn, 'Suff.' Fairbairn*, 'Suff.'*
A bear's head erased Sable muzzled and billety Or.
BETTENHAM, of Barningham. *Davy, A.*
A bear's head erased Sable muzzled Gules.
BRERETON. 'Sir Randolf Brereton of Ipston' *Banners & Standards*, with a crescent for difference.* 'Gilbert Brerton of Norwiche' *MS Knight's Visitations, Norf.* * 'Cutbert Brereton' *MS Philpot's Visitations, Norf.* *
A bear's head erased and muzzled.
BRERETON. *MS Heraldic Collections, fo. 83b* *
A bear's head erased Sable muzzled Or.
BRERETON. 'Brewerton' *MS ex-Taylor Coll.* *
A bear's head erased Azure.
BREWSTER, *Washbourne, 'Suff.'* 'Humphyre Brewster, Lord of the Manor, died 1593'

Her.Suff.,Ch., Wall brass, Wrentham. Humphrey Brewster, died 1735; Philip Brewster, died 1765, both of Wrentham Hall. *Hatchments, Wrentham*
A bear's head erased Argent charged on the neck with three hurts.
FARR, of Beccles, North Cove. *Davy, A., North Cove church*
'to his crest on a beres hed rased Vert moseled or/ iij Dropes ar/ John fford of hadley in Suff/ to Robt fford by C hawley 31 h 8' [1539/40].
FORD. 'fford of hadley in Suff' *MS Alphabet of Crests, fo. 40*
'uppon his healme on a torse silver & sable on a bears head rased vert moseled gold three dropps silver'
FORD. Robert Forde of Hadley in Suffolk; Grant of Arms and Crest by Thomas Hawley, Clarenceux, 10th. December 1539. *Muskett. I. 108. Rylands MS 154–5* *
'vpon his healme on a torse siluer and sable on a bere hed Rasy vert moseled gold thre dropps siluer manteled gewles dobled siluer'
FORD. Robert Forde of Hadley, co. Suffolk, Gentleman; Grant of Arms and Crest by Thomas Hawley, Clarenceux, 10th Dec. 1539. *Miscellaneous Grants (H.S.) I. 81–2 (MS Queen's Coll. 139, No. 39)*
A bear's head erased Sable muzzled Argent.
FORD, FORTH. 'Sr William Foorde of Butley in Com Suffolke Knight' *MS Lilly's Visitation of Suffolk* *
A bear's head erased Sable muzzled Or.
FORD, FORTH, of Butley, Hadleigh. *MS Fairfax (Tyl.) Bokenham. Davy, A. Washbourne, 'Forth, Suff. Muzzled Or or Gules'. Muskett. I. 9. E.A. Misc. 1910. 7, head untinctured. Fairbairn*, 'Forth, Suff. Muzzled Or or Gules'*
A bear's head erased Sable ducally gorged Or.
LITTLE, of Shrubland Hall. *Davy, A., Barham church*
A bear's head erased Sable muzzled Or.
MILBURN, of Long Melford. *Davy, A. (Berry)*
A bear's head erased Sable muzzled Or.
MILES, of Woodbridge. *Davy, A.*
A bear's head erased muzzled and collared.
SWATMAN, of Beccles, Dunwich. *Davy, A.*
A bear's head erased Sable semy of mullets Or.
TRYON. *MS Martin's Crests, 'Essex and Lond.'*

BEAVER
'upon a wreathe argent and sable a Bevers head razed azure purfelled golde mantelled gules dobled argent'
BREWSTER, of Rushmere. Humphrey Brewster of Rushmere; Exemplification of Arms and Grant of Crest by William Hervey, Clarenceux, 3 July 1561. *Misc.Gen. et Her. N.S. II. 326*. E.A. Misc. 1908, 104–5*
A beaver's head Sable garnished and studded Or [*sic* ? a collar].
CAVENDISH, of Trimley St. Martin. *Davy, A. (Harl. MS 4686)*

BOAR [Alphabetically by name]
A griffin's head erased grasped at the neck by the head and mouth of a boar.
BACON, of Suffolk. *Farrer (Seals), 'on Lord Keeper Bacon's copy of the letters patent relating to Redgrave estate'*
A boar's head erect between two ostrich feathers.
BRADBURY. *Washbourne, 'Ess. and Suff.'*
A boar's head Proper.

BORTON. *Washbourne*, 'Suff.' Fairbairn*, 'Suff.'*

A boar's head and neck Azure armed and bristled Or.

CALTHORPE, of Ampton, Erwarton, etc. 'John Calthorp' *MS Philpot's Visitations, Norf.* Davy, A. Washbourne*, 'Calthorp and Calthrop, Suff. and Norf.' Fairbairn, 'Calthorp, Calthrop, Norf. and Suff.'*

A boar's head erect Sable.

CAMPBELL, of Kinlick. *Her.Suff.Ch., Glass, Old Felixstowe*

A tower Argent issuing from the port a boar's head Sable.

CANTRELL, of Bury, Hemingstone. *Berkshire Visitation 1623 (H.S.) I. 77*. Visitation 1664–8*. MS Fairfax*

A castle triple-towered Argent issuing out of the port a boar's head Sable and the words 'Pectus fidele et opertium'.

CANTRELL, of Hemingstone. *E.A. Misc. 1916, 21 (Conder MS 43–4)*
'beryth to his crest a boores hed in pal sylver swallowyng a pecockes tayle in hys kynde'

TYRELL, TYRRELL. 'Terell of Heron in Essex' *Wall's Book*
'to his Crest a bores hed in pale ar/ swalowing a pecocks tayle in his pryde   S thom tyrell'

TYRELL, TYRRELL. 'Terell of Heron in Essex'. *MS Alphabet of Crests, fo. 127b*

A boar's head in pale, or erect, Argent swallowing a peacock's tail Proper.

TYRELL, TYRRELL, of Gipping, Essex, etc. *MS ex-Taylor Coll.* Fairbairn, 'Tirrell, Gepynge [sic], Suff., Essex, etc.' Bookplate**

A boar's head erect Argent out of the mouth a peacock's tail Proper.

TYRELL, TYRRELL, of Gipping, Wetherden, Haughley, Polstead. *MS Fairfax. Bokenham. Page. Davy, A. Bright, 229. Proc.S.I.A. IX. 221. E.A. Misc. 1929, 83*

A boar's head erect Argent out of a plume of five feathers.

TYRELL, of Lavenham. *Davy, A., church*

A boar's head erect issuant from a plume of feathers.

TYRELL, Charles, Surgeon, of Castle Hedingham, co. Essex, died 1750; Others. *Her.Suff.Ch., Floor slab partly hidden by choir stalls, Lavenham*

A boar's head Gules langued Azure.

URQUHART, of Hobland Hall. *Davy, A., Belton church.* David Urquhart, of Hobland Hall, Esq., died 1774. *E.A.N. & Q. II. 326*

Issuant from a demi mural tower Gules charged with three crosses paty Argent a boar's head Argent tusked and maned Or charged on the neck with a cross paty Gules.

WHITE, Eaton, J.P., of Boulge Hall, Woodbridge, Suffolk. *Fairbairn*, [blazoned from the illustration, better than text]*

A boar's head Sable.

WORLD, of Yoxford. *Sharpe*

BOAR'S HEAD, Couped [Alphabetically by name]

A boar's head couped Or tusked Gules in the mouth a griffin's head erased Azure.

BACON, Nicholas; Grant by Barker. *Grants & Certificates (Stowe MS 692)*

A boar's head couped and twisted [sic tusked] Or having in his mouth a griffin's head erased Argent.

BACON. *Bacon, 16, 'Grant p' Barker, before 1549'*

A boar's head couped holding in his mouth a griffin's head erased.

BACON, of Drinkstone, Redgrave. *Visitation 1561 (MSS G.7* and Iveagh Copy*)*
'his Crest a bores hed coupey tusked g/ having in his mouth a gryffyns hed rased b/   S nycolas bacon'

BACON. *MS Alphabet of Crests, fo. 14b*

A boar's head couped Or langued Azure.

BADLEY, BADELY, of Stutton. *Sharpe*

A boar's head couped at the neck Argent.

BADLEY, BADELEY, of Chediston, Halesworth, Yoxford. *Davy, A. Washbourne*, 'of Ess. and Suff.' Fairbairn*, 'Baddeley, Essex and Suff.'*

A boar's head couped and erect Proper.

BARLEY. *MS Heraldic Collections, fo. 59**

A boar's head couped close sandy colour bristled Or holding a broken spear which is thrust through the neck Or.

BORRETT. *Davy, A.*

A boar's head couped.

BORRETT, Giles, late of Bungay, died 1749. *Her.Suff.Ch., Ledger stone, Stradbroke*

A boar's head couped Or in his mouth a branch of laurel erect Vert.

BORTON, of Bury, Uggeshall. *Davy, A.*

A boar's head couped.

BORTON. Capt. John Henry Borton, died 1852. *Her.Suff.Ch., Wall tablet, St. Mary's, Bury*

A boar's head couped Gules bristled Or.

BROKESBY, of Suffolk. *Davy, A.*

A bear's [sic should be boar's] head couped supported by two wild men the sinister one turned backwards.

CALTHORPE. Probably for Sir Philip Calthorpe, died 1551, buried at Erwarton. *Her.Suff.Ch., Wall monument, Erwarton*

A bear's [sic boar's] head couped.

CALTHORPE, Henry, son of Jacob Calthorpe, of Cockthorpe in Norfolk died 1637; James Calthorpe, Esq., died 1784. *Her.Suff.Ch., Monumental and Wall tablets, Ampton*

A boar's head couped at the neck Azure bristled and tusked Or between two woodmen with clubs over their shoulders wreathed about the temples and loins with leaves all Proper.

CALTHORPE, Henry, 1st Baron Calthorpe, died 1798. *Her.Suff.Ch., Hatchment, Ampton*

A boar's head couped.

CAMELL, of Gislingham. *Davy, A.*

A boar's head couped close.

CAMPBELL. *Bookplate**

A boar's head couped in fesse Argent langued Gules.

CARTER, of Ipswich. *Davy, A., St. Nicholas church vestry*

A boar's head couped Ermine holding in the mouth a griffin's head erased Azure.

COOKE. *Davy, A.*

A boar's head couped fesseways.

DERSHAM. *Davy, A.*

A boar's head couped Sable pierced with an arrow.

ELLIOT. *Bokenham. MS Martin's Crests.*

A boar's head couped close Sable lying fesseways pierced with an arrow point downwards.

ELLIOT. 'James Elyott, Es. Groom of his Majestyes most Hon[ble] Privy Chamber . . . in y[e] Year of our Lord 77' [?1677]. *Martin's Church Notes, Frag. Gen. IX. 91*, Wall monument in All Saints church, Newmarket.* [Drawn in margin, not blazoned] 'the Creast upon a healme, a Boares head Gules, about his Necke a Coller, about his necke a Cheyne gould enarmed of the same, and a Boare Speare broken in his mouth the head silver, and the shaft sable'

GOUGH, William, of co. Chester, gent.; Grant of Arms and Crest by Thomas Holme, Clarenceux, 12 December 1481. *Miscellaneous Grants (H.S.) I. 92–3 (Harl. MS 1571, fo. 449)*
A boar's head and neck couped Gules collared and chained Or holding a boar spear in his mouth shaft Sable head Argent.

GOUGH. *Wall's Book*
'to his crest a bores hed w^t necke coupey g/ a coller and a chayne hangyng at yt or havinge a bore spere in his mouth/ the shaft sa/ the hed ar/'

GOUGH. *MS Alphabet Of Crests, fo. 47b*
A boar's head couped close devouring a broken lance.

GOUGH. *MS Ordinary of Arms, fo. 104**
A boar's head couped pierced through the neck with a boar spear broken at the head.

GOUGH. *MS Martin's Crests*
A boar's head couped Argent devouring a broken spear Gules.

GOUGH, of Ampton. *Davy, A.*
A boar's head couped at the neck Azure bristled and tusked Or between two woodmen with clubs over their shoulders all Proper.

GOUGH, of Ampton. *Davy, A.*
A boar's head couped close pierced through the head by a tilting spear.

GOUGH. *Fairbairn, 'of Clensmore House, Woodbridge, Suff.'*
A boar's head couped Argent armed Or transfixed with a sword.

HALLIDAY, of Halesworth. *Davy, A.*
A sword erect Argent hilt Or on the blade a boar's head couped Sable.

HALSEY, of Woodbridge. *Davy, A. Fairbairn**
A boar's head couped close Sable armed Or holding in the mouth a branch of oak Vert fructed Or.

HILL, William, of Bury. *MS Knight's Visitations, Suff., fo. 108**. 'Will Hill' *MS Philpot's Visitations, Suff.**
A boar's head couped Sable in the mouth an oak bough Vert fructed Or.

HILL, of Suffolk. *Visitation 1612. Not given as couped. Bokenham. Washbourne, 'Suff. an acorn Or, leaved Vert.'*
A boar's head couped Sable in his mouth a thistle branch Proper.

HILL, of Bury, Needham. *Davy, A., 'Granted by Cooke, Clar., 17 Sept. 1576'*
A boar's head and neck couped Sable with a demi-spear in his mouth in pale Or.

HILL, of Bury, Needham. *Davy, A.*
A boar's head couped, or erased, Sable in his mouth an acorn Or leaved Vert.

HILL, of Bury, Needham. *Davy, A. Fairbairn*, 'of Bury St. Edmunds, Suff. Boar's head couped'*
A boar's head couped close.

HOVEL, HOVELL, of Ashfield. *Davy, A., church.* William Hovell, Esq., died 1769. *Her.Suff.Ch., Slab, Badwell Ash, 'recorded by Davy, not found 1987'. Given as ? Hovenell*
A boar's head couped at the neck per pale Or and Gules.

JUDD, of Brandon. *Bokenham*
A boar's head couped and erect Argent in the mouth a cross crosslet fitchy Gules between two branches

of oak fructed Proper.

LOFFT, of Troston Hall near Bury. *Burke, L.G. 1900 ed.* 'Henry Capell Moseley-Lofft, of Glemham House, Suff.' *Fairbairn. Second of two crests.*
A boar's head Or couped Gules.

LOWNSFORD, of Suffolk. *Davy, A.*
A boar's head couped oblique Or tusked Argent breathing fire Proper.

MALTBY, of Stonham Aspal. *Davy, A., 'Granted by Camden, 29 May 1612'*
A boar's head couped and erect breathing fire.

MAUTEBY, MAUTEBEY. *MS Heraldic Collections, fo. 90**
A boar's head couped at the neck Gules langued Azure crined and tusked Or collared Erminois.

NOTTIDGE. Rector of St. Helen's, Ipswich. *Davy, A.*
A boar's head couped erect collared Gules rimmed Or.

PEMBERTON, of Ipswich. *Davy, A., St. Lawrence church*
A boar's head couped Or pierced through the neck with a spear Argent embrued with blood Proper.

SPOONER, Edward, M.A., Rector of Hadleigh and Co-Dean of Bocking, died 1899. *Her.Suff.Ch., Brass, St. Bartholomew's, Ipswich.*
A boar's head couped and erect Argent.

SWINBORNE, SWINFORD. *Davy, A., Stanningfield church.*
A boar's head couped and erect Argent armed Or out of the mouth a peacock's tail Proper.

TYRREL, TYRRELL, of Gipping. 'Thomas Tyrell de gyppyng' *Banners & Standards* Visitation 1561 (MS G.7*) Harl. 772*, untinctured. Visitation 1664–8.** Edmund Tyrell, of Gipping Hall, died 1799. *Her.Suff.Ch., Hatchment, Gipping chapel.* Rev. Charles Tyrell, of Gipping Hall, Rector of Thurston, died 1811. *Hatchment, Stowmarket.* Charles Tyrell, of Gipping Hall, died 1872; wife Elizabeth (Ray), died 1826. *Ledger stone and Hatchment, Haughley. Livery button*, untinctured.*
A boar's head couped in pale, or erect, Argent swallowing a peacock's tail Proper.

TYRREL, TYRRELL. 'John Tyrell' *MS Philpot's Visitations, Suff.* Washbourne* 'Tirrell, Suff., Essex, etc.'*
A boar's head partly erect and couped Sable armed langued and gorged with a ducal coronet Or.

? TYRELL. *Her.Suff.Ch., Glass in east window, Gipping chapel*
A boar's head couped Gules.

URQUHART, David, of Hobland Hall, died 1774. *Her.Suff.Ch., Wall tablet, Belton*

BOAR'S HEAD, Erased [Alphabetically by name]

A boar's head erased Or charged on the neck with a cross paty and holding in the mouth a trefoil slipped.

BARLEE, Rev. Charles, LL.B., Rector for 35 years, died 1831. *Her.Suff.Ch., Ledger stone, Worlingworth*
A boar's head erased holding in the mouth a quatrefoil Azure [and charged on the neck with a cross paty, added when a canton was also added to the coat, in ink].

BARLEE. 'Charles Barlee LL.B.' *Bookplate**
A boar's head erased Or holding in the mouth a sword Argent pomelled Or.

BARRETT, Thomas, son of Thomas Barrett, of

Cransford Hall, died 1913. *Her.Suff.Ch., Wall tablet, Cransford*

A boar's head couped close, or erased, sandy colour bristled Or holding a broken spear which is thrust through the neck Or.

BORRETT. *Davy, A.*

A boar's head erased and erect between two ostrich feathers.

BRADBURY. *Fairbairn*, 'Essex and Suff. Feathers Proper'*

In front of a sword erect the blade entwined by two serpents respecting each other Proper a boar's head erased Sable.

BROOKE, of Sibton Park. *Crisp's Visitation, I. 73*, serpents shown addorsed. Burke, L.G. 1900 ed. Fairbairn*, 'of Sibton Park, near Yoxford, Suff.'*

A boar's head erased Ermine tusked and crined Or.

FISH. 'Walter fyshe of Stowe Market' *MS Knight's Visitations, Suff.**

In front of three roses Argent stalked and leaved Proper a boar's head erased Argent.

'GUTCH, John, M.D., 28 Fonnereau Road, Ipswich' *Fairbairn**

A boar's head couped, or erased, Sable in his mouth an acorn Or leaved Vert.

HILL, of Bury, Needham. *Davy, A.*

A boar's [wolf's in illustration] head erased quarterly Ermine and Azure gorged with a collar Or charged with three lozenges Azure and holding in the mouth a cross crosslet fitchy Gules.

IMAGE, of Herringswell House, Mildenhall, Whepstead. *Burke, L.G. 1900 ed.**

A boar's head erased quarterly Ermine and Azure holding in the mouth a cross crosslet fitchy Gules.

IMAGE. *Fairbairn, 'of Herringswell House, Mildenhall, Suff.'*

A boar's head erased and erect Gules.

KEBLE, of Tuddenham. *Davy, A. church.*

A lion's, tiger's, or boar's head erased Gules charged on the neck with a crescent.

KEBLE, of Stowmarket, Newton, Halesworth, Tuddenham. *Davy, A., Halesworth and Tuddenham churches*

A boar's head erased Azure ducally gorged Or.

KELL, of Woodbridge, Shottisham. *Davy, A. (Berry)*

A boar's head erased Gules armed and gorged with a collar of the last [*sic*] charged with three escallops Sable.

SAMPSON, of Kersey, Oulton. *Davy, A., Oulton church. Fairbairn, 'Sampson of Kersey, Suff. armed and gorged Or.'*

A boar's head erased and erect Argent armed Or out of the mouth a peacock's tail Proper and charged on the neck with a mullet – [for difference].

TYRRELL, of Gipping. *Visitation 1561 (Iveagh Copy*)*

A boar's head erased in pale, or erect, Argent swallowing a peacock's tail Proper.

TYRRELL. 'Thomas Tirrell of Gippinge esquier' *MS Lilly's Visitation of Suffolk**

A boar's head erased Sable snout tusks and ears Or earhole Gules.

VERNON. 'Syr Henry Vernon' *Banners & Standards**

A boar's head erased Sable eared Gules.

VERNON. 'S. Harry Vernon' *Harl. MS 6163* 'beryth to his crest a long bores hede sable rased tusked geules'

VERNON. *Wall's book*

'to his Crest a Long Bores hede sa/ rased tusked g/' VERNON. *MS Alphabet of Crests, fo. 132*

A boar's head erased Gules ducally gorged Or.

VERNON. *MS Martin's Crests*

A boar's head erased Sable ducally gorged Or.

VERNON, of Aldeburgh. *Davy, A., church.* Leveson Vernon, died 1831. *Her.Suff.Ch., Hatchment, Aldeburgh*

A boar's head erased Sable ducally gorged and bristled Or.

VERNON-WENTWORTH, of Aldeburgh Lodge, Saxmundham. *Burke, L.G. 1900 ed. The crest of Vernon*

A boar's head erased.

WALL, of Holton, Stratford St. Mary. *Davy, A., both churches. E.A.N. & Q. XII. 147.* Daniel Wall, died 1667; Rev. Daniel Wall, died 1670. *Her.Suff.Ch., Ledger stone and in churchyard, Stratford St. Mary.* Bartholomew Wall, died 1745; daughter Mary Wall, died 1763. *Slab in the tower, Holton St. Mary*

A ?boar's head erased and erect.

WEBSTER, of North Cove. *Davy, A., church*

BUFFALO

A buffalo's head erased Gules.

HENCHMAN, of Earl Soham, Brandeston. *Davy, A.*

A bull's, or buffalo's, head erased Argent.

HOUGHTON. 'Jo. Houghton, M.D., of Ipswich' *MS Fairfax*

A buffalo's head Sable gorged with a wreath of roses Proper.

ORGILL, of Beccles, Worlingham, Brampton. *Davy, A. Fairbairn, 'of Beccles, Suff.'*

CAMEL [Alphabetically by name]

A camel's head couped Sable.

ABBERBURY, of Suffolk. *Washbourne*, 'Suff.'*

A camel's head Proper bezanty erased Gules.

BURGESS, BURGESS-LAMB, Bart., of Ixworth Thorpe. *Davy, A. Washbourne*

A camel's head per pale Argent and Or eared Gules charged on the neck with a fesse between three annulets Sable.

CHAMBER. 'Chambur of – in Essex'. *Wall's Book*

'to his crest a camelles hed ar/ and or/ p pale the eyres g/ on the necke a fece bet iij anneletts sa/'

CHAMBER. 'Chambur of Essex' *MS Alphabet of Crests, fo. 21b*

A camel's head erased Or.

COLLINGS, COLLINS. *Davy, A. (Barrett)*

A camel's head Or vulned in the neck Gules.

COURTHOPE. *Davy, A.*

A camel's head Or wounded in the neck Gules.

CROWE. *Davy, A.*

'his crest a Camelles hed copey [ermine spot drawn. ?flecked] sa/ brydeled and the mayne hangyng Downe or/ to thom Draper of grete marloo in bokynghm by C Cooke'

DRAPER. *MS Alphabet of Crests, fo. 30*

A camel's head Ermine bridled Or maned Sable.

DRAPER. *Davy, A.*

A camel's head erased Azure bezanty.

FRAMLINGHAM. *Davy, A. Washbourne, 'Framyngham, Suff.' Fairbairn, 'Framyngham, Suff.' Her.Suff.Ch., Effigy tomb, Debenham*

A camel's head erased Or bridled lined ringed and gorged with a ducal coronet Sable.

PEPYS, of Stoke by Clare. 'Thomas pepys of Southe Creke' *MS Knight's Visitations, Norf.**

MS Martin's Crests. Davy, A. Pepys, 9. Hon. &
Rev. Henry Leslie Pepys, Bart., son of Sir Lucas
Pepys, Bart., Rector for 35 years, died 1849.
*Her.Suff.Ch., Wall tablet, Wetherden. Second of
two crests*

A camel's head couped Or holding in the mouth an
oak branch Proper.
  PHILIPSON. *Sharpe*

A camel's head Or holding in the mouth an oak
branch Proper.
  PHILLIPSON, of Ipswich. *Davy, A., St. Helen's
  church*

A camel's head Proper.
  WOODTHORPE. *Davy, A.*

CAT
A cat's head guardant erased holding in the mouth a
rat.
  DAWSON. *MS Heraldic Collections, fo. 87b* *

A cat's head full-faced Argent with a rat in the
mouth Sable.
  DAWSON, Suff. *MS Martin's Crests*

A cat's head guardant erased tabby in the mouth a
rat Proper or Sable.
  DAWSON, of Edwardstone, Groton. *Davy, A.,
  both churches. Burke, L.G. 1853 ed. Fairbairn,
  'of Edwardstone Hall, Suff. Rat Sable'* Thomas
  Dawson, late merchant of London, of
  Edwardstone Hall, died 1807; George Augustus
  Dawson, Vicar of Edwardstone, died 1848.
  Her.Suff.Ch., Wall tablets, Edwardstone

A cat's head full-faced and erased near the shoulders
Argent spotted Sable holding in the mouth a rat
Sable.
  DAWSON, of Edwardstone. *Her.Suff.Ch.,
  Mentioned under Gt. Waldingfield*

The head of a cat-a-mountain erased half guardant
Argent spotted Gules.
  HOBSON, of Suffolk. *Davy, A.*

DEER

HIND or DOE, FAWN [Without antlers]
A hind's head Proper.
  ALFORD, of Ipswich, Suffolk. *Davy, A. (Edms.)
  Washbourne*, 'Suff.' Fairbairn*, 'Suff.'*

'A hind's head Azure on the neck three bezants
between two bars gemells Gold standing betwixt
two branches of hazel Vert nuts Or'
  ALVARD, of Ipswich, Suffolk. Grant by Barker.
  Grants & Certificates (Stowe MS 692)

A hind's head Azure on the neck three bezants
between two bars gemel Or standing between two
branches of hazel Proper.
  ALVARD. 'Alvard of Gyppyswyche in Suffolke'
  Wall's Book

'To his crest a hyndes hede b/ on the necke bezanty
betwene ii gemelles or/ standing betw ii branches of
hasell in there color'
  ALVARD. 'Alvard of Ipswyche in Suff.' *MS
  Alphabet of Crests, fo. 2*

An ass's, or hind's, head Argent.
  ASCOUGH. 'Ascu' *Wall's Book*

A hind's head Argent.
  BARROW, of Westhorpe, Barningham. *Visitation
  1664–8*

A hind's head Argent collared Or.
  COLLETT. Henry Pymont Collett, c.1911.
  Her.Suff.Ch., Glass, Brightwell

A hind's head Gules.
  CRISP, of Bury. *Bokenham*

A doe's head.

CRISP, of Bury. Clopton Crisp, died 1711.
  *Martin's Church Notes, Frag.Gen. IX. 63, St.
  James's in Bury. Davy, A.*

Issuing out of eight park pales Or and Gules a hind's
head Argent.
  HALL. *MS Martin's Crests, 'looking over pales'.
  Davy, A. (Barrett MS)*

A hind's head Or.
  HARPEDON, of Aspal. *Davy, A.*

A hind's head Or pellety.
  KENE, of Ipswich, North Cove. *Davy, A.*

'A hyndes head silver and sable p'ty p' pale on the
Neck three dropps enterchanged of the same
between two Hawthornes branches leaved vert
flowered (silver in *Add. MS 7098*) holding the third
in his mouth'
  MILDMAY. 'Thomas Myldmay, of Moulsham, co.
  Essex, gent.; Grant of Arms and Crest by Thomas
  Hawley, Clarenceux, 15 March 1542 (15 May
  1542 in *Add. MS 7098, fo. 76*). *Miscellaneous
  Grants (H.S.) II. 152–3 (Harl. MS 1507, fo. 433)*

'a hyndes hed ar/ sa/ Pty P pale on the necke iij
Dropes entd of the same betw ij hethorne braunches
Leved Vert/ flowed ar/ holding the 3 in her mouth/
Thom myldmay of Mulessheyam in Essex/ dat p C
hawley 34 of h 8' [1542/3].
  MILDMAY. *MS Alphabet of Crests, fo. 81b*

A hind's, or horse's head.
  PAVELEY, of Stutton. *Davy, A.*

A hind's head.
  THWAITES, THWAYTE. *Davy, A.*

A hind's head Or.
  UNDERWOOD, of Ipswich. *Visitation 1664–8*

A hind's head Argent pierced through the neck by
an arrow Proper head and feathers Argent.
  VERE. 'John Verre, of Blakenham, co. Suffolk'.
  Patent by R. Cooke, Clarenceux, 1584. *Grants
  & Certificates (Harl. MS 1,359)*

A hind's head pierced through the neck with an
arrow.
  VERE, of Stradbroke. *Davy, A.*

HIND'S HEAD, Couped
'to his crest a hynds hede ar/ coupey'
  BARROW. 'Barroo of Suff.' *MS Alphabet of
  Crests, fo. 12*

A hind's head couped Argent.
  BARROW, of Westhorpe, Barningham.
  *Bokenham. Davy, A. Muskett. II. 238 (Harl. MS
  1552) Washbourne*, 'Suff.' Fairbairn*, 'Suff.'*
  William Barrow, Esq., died 1613. *Her.Suff.Ch.,
  Effigy monument, Westhorpe.*

A hind's, or roe's, head couped Argent.
  BARROW, of Westhorpe. *Davy, A.*

'on a Helmet and Wreath of their Colours, a Hind's
Head coupé Argent, with a Coller ingrailed Sable,
mantled Gules, doubled Argent'.
  COLLETT. Anthony and Samuel Collett, of
  Westerfield; Grant of Arms and Crest by Edward
  Bysshe, Clarenceux, 14th August 1664. *Muskett.
  II. 352*

A hind's head couped Argent gorged with a collar
engrailed Sable.
  COLLETT, of Westerfield, Walton, Kelsale,
  Grundisburgh, Thorndon, Dennington. *Visitation
  1664–8. Davy, A. Fairbairn, 'Suff.'*

A hind's head couped and gorged with a fesse
engrailed.
  COLLETT, Samuel, of Westerfield, died 1681; son
  Samuel, died 1710. *Her.Suff.Ch., Ledger stones,
  Westerfield.* Anthony Collett, late of Eyke, died

1785; widow Mary, died 1799. *Ledger stone, Eyke*

A hind's head couped Gules ducally gorged and lined Or.

    FORSTER *MS Martin's Crests*

A hind's head couped Argent.

    HALL, of Clopton, Wherstead, Ipswich, Hadleigh, Melton. *Davy, A.*

A hind's head (couped) Or pellety.

    KENE. *Washbourne*, 'Suff.'* [Head couped in illustration]

A fawn's head couped.

    MOUNTJOYE, DE 'Mr Isaac De Remy De Mountjoye', died 1747. *E.A.N. & Q. IX. 214, Slab outside St. Margaret's church, Ipswich*

A doe's, or hind's, head couped Argent charged on the neck with two chevronels Azure.

    PIERSON, . . . , of London, draper; Grant by Sir W. Segar, Garter. *Grants & Certificates (Add. MS 12,225)*

A hind's head couped Argent charged with two chevrons Azure.

    PIERSON, of Framlingham. *Davy, A., church*

A hind's head couped Proper between a pair of wings Gules.

    TICHBORNE. Impaled by Tasburgh. *Her.Suff.Ch., Ledger stone, Flixton*

A hind's head couped Or gorged with a chaplet of oak leaves Vert.

    UNDERWOOD. 'Robart Onderwood' *MS Philpot's Visitations, Norf.**

A hind's head couped, or erased, Or.

    UNDERWOOD, of Lowestoft, Bury, Ipswich. *Davy, A.*

A hind's head couped pierced through the neck with an arrow.

    VERE, VERRE, of Stradbroke. 'Jo: Verre of Blakenham in Suff.' *MS Heraldic Collections, fo. 84b.* Fairbairn, 'Vere, Stanbroke [sic], Suff. All Proper'*

A hind's head couped Gules.

    WHITBREAD. 'John Whitebread of writtle in Essex' *MS Philpot's Visitations, Essex*.* [In a different hand]

HIND'S HEAD, Erased

A hind's head erased at the neck Argent gorged with a mural crown Sable.

    COLLETT. *Washbourne, 'Suff.' Fairbairn, 'Collet, Suff.'*

A hind's head erased in the mouth a cross crosslet and gorged with two chevrons.

    COLVIN, of Gt. Bealings. *Davy, A.*

A hind's head erased.

    CONRAN, of Bury. *Davy, A.*

A hind's head erased Or in the mouth a branch of holly Vert fructed Gules.

    FINCHAM, of Brantham. *Davy, A.*

A hind's head erased Proper gorged with a wreath of laurel Vert.

    GARNHAM, of Buxhall, South Town. *Davy, A.*

A hind's head erased Or pellety.

    KENE, of Thrandeston, North Cove. *Visitation 1561 (MSS G. 7* and Iveagh Copy*) and (ed. Metcalfe). Harl. 772*. MS Knight's Visitations, Suff.* Visitation 1664–8*. MS Fairfax*

A hind's head erased Or pellety charged on the neck with a trefoil.

    KENE. 'Myles Kene of Yarmouthe' *MS Knight's Visitations, Norf.* 'Myles Kene' MS Philpot's Visitations, Norf.**

A hind's head erased Gules bezanty plain collared Or studded Sable.

    KENE. 'Thomas Kene' *MS Philpot's Visitations, Norf.**

A hind's head erased Argent pellety charged with a trefoil Or.

    KENE, KEENE, of Suffolk. *Davy, A. Washbourne, 'Norf. and Suff.' Fairbairn, 'Kene, Suff.'*

A hind's head erased Sable bezanty.

    KENE, KEEN, KEENE. *Washbourne, 'Suff.' Fairbairn, 'Keen, Keene, Suff.' Her.Suff.Ch., on bench end in chancel, Bentley*

A hind's head couped, or erased, Or.

    UNDERWOOD, of Lowestoft, Bury, Ipswich. *Davy, A.*

A hind's head erased pierced through the neck with an arrow.

    VERE. *Washbourne, 'Suff.'*

A hind's head erased Gules.

    WHITBREAD, of Loudham Park. *Davy, A., Pettistree church. Burke, L.G. 1900 ed. Fairbairn*, 'of Landham [sic] Park, Suff.'* Anne Elizabeth, wife of Jacob Whitbread, of Loudham Hall, died 1792. *Her.Suff.Ch., Hatchment recorded by Farrer, Pettistree. Not found 1981.*

STAG'S, BUCK'S, HART'S HEAD
[Alphabetically by name]

A buck's head trunked [*sic*] and attired Or.

    ALABASTER. 'Arbalaster' *MS Heraldic Alphabet*

A stag's head Argent.

    ANDREWS, of Bury. *Davy, A.*

A buck's head Proper

    BUXTON. *Bokenham*

A stag's head Argent attired Or gorged with two bars gemel Gules.

    CARR, of Ipswich. *Gloucestershire Visitation 1582–3 (H.S.), 224*

A stag's head Gules gorged with a fesse between two gemelles Argent charged with three fleurs-de-lis Sable.

    DRAPER, of Bury. *Davy, A., St. Mary's church*

A stag's head holding in the mouth a snake encircling the neck.

    GORDON-FINLAYSON, Gen. Sir Robert, of Wickerstreet House, Kersey, died 1956. *Her.Suff.Ch., Wall tablet, Kersey. Crest of Finlayson*

A stag's head Argent gorged with a bar gemel Gules.

    GRANDGEORGE. Rector of Bradfield St. Clare. *Davy, A. Washbourne, 'Linc.'*

A stag's head Azure attired Or.

    GREEN, of Wilby, Ipswich. *Bokenham, Davy, A.*

A buck's head Or issuing out of pales Proper.

    GREEN. Rector of Burgh Castle, 1840. *Davy, A.* 'beryth to his crest a buckes hede ermyn horned goold'

    GREEN. 'Greene' *Wall's Book*
'to his crest a Bucks hed [ermine spot drawn] horned or/ h 7'

    GREEN. 'Grene' *MS Alphabet of Crests, fo. 46*

A stag's head.

    GREEN, Capt. Samuel, Mariner of this parish, died at Smyrna 1685. *Her.Suff.Ch., Wooden tablet, St. Clement's, Ipswich*

A stag's head Proper attired Or.

    GRIMSTON, of Rishangles, Ipswich. *Davy, A.*

A stag's head Sable gutty Or attired Or.

    HARNEYS, of Coddenham. *Davy, A.*

A stag's head Gules attired Or gorged with a wreath Argent.

HOWORTH. Capt. Thomas Orton Howorth, 44th Reg., died 1865. *Her.Suff.Ch., Brass tablet, Whitton*

A stag's head, or 'animal with antlers'.

KERRINGTON. 'Alexander Kerrington of Thorpe Moreux'. *E.A. Misc. 1931, 67, Seal of 1646*

A stag's head with two wings behind it.

LIFE, of Brandon. *Davy, A., churchyard*

A stag's head attired charged with two chevrons Gules.

PEIRSON, of Framlingham. *Green, 145, church tablet*

A stag's head charged with two chevronels.

PEIRSON, Jasper, died 1888. *Her.Suff.Ch., Slab, Framlingham*

'The Crest upon the helme an herts hed sable set wth in a wrethe of Silver & goules the hornes of golde, the Mantle goules lyned wth Ermine'

POWER. Confirmation of Arms and Crest to John Power of co. Bucks., by Thomas Holme, Clarenceux, 1478. *Misc.Gen. et Her. 4th S. III. 273**

A hart's head Sable armed Or.

POWER. 'Power of Bukkynghamshire' *Wall's Book*

'to his Crest a harts hed sa/ armed or/'

POWER. 'Power of Bokynghm' *MS Alphabet of Crests, fo. 99*

A stag's head Proper.

PYTCHES. 'John Thomas Pytches, of The Little Grange, Woodbridge, Suff.' *Fairbairn*

A buck's head Azure attired Or.

RAINSFORD. 'Raynford of Essex' *MS Heraldic Alphabet*

A stag's head Argent and collared Or between tufts of grass Or.

REDE, Robert, died 1822. *Her.Suff.Ch., Hatchment, Barsham*

A stag's head Sable attired and charged on the neck with a bar gemel Or between branches Vert.

REDE, Robert (formerly Cooper), died before 1855. *Her.Suff.Ch., Hatchment, Barsham*

A stag's head Proper.

ROANE, of Layham. *Davy, A.*

An embattled wall on it a stag's head Or.

SAY, Lord *Davy, A.*

A stag's head Proper.

SPRINGE. *Fairbairn*, 'Suff.'*

'beryth to his crest a hertes hede silver tynyd gold'

STANLEY. 'Stanley of Hutton' *Wall's Book*

'to his crest a harts hed ar/ tyned or.'

STANLEY. 'Stanley of Hutton' *MS Alphabet of Crests, fo. 116b*

A stag's head Proper between the attires a pheon Argent.

STUBBE, of Laxfield. *Davy, A. Fairbairn, 'of Laxfield, Suff.'*

A stag's head Proper.

WHATELEY. Rector of Halesworth, Archbishop of Dublin. *Davy, A.*

STAG'S HEAD, Cabossed

A stag's head cabossed between the attires a bugle horn stringed Argent.

BEAUCLER, ? of Lidgate. *Davy, A.*

A buck's head cabossed Argent attired Or.

DOYLEY, of Hadleigh. *Bokenham*

A stag's head cabossed between the attires a cross.

FITZEUSTACE, of Hawstead. *Davy, A.*

A stag's head cabossed Proper between two roses Argent barbed and seeded Proper.

NORTON, of Kentwell Hall in Long Melford, died 1906. *Church monument, Long Melford*

A stag's head cabossed between two roses.

NORTON. Henry Turton Norton, of London; of Kentwell Hall, 1895–death 1906. *Her.Suff.Ch., Tablet, Long Melford*

A stag's head cabossed Or within the attires an escallop Or charged with a plain cross Gules.

POWER, of Gifford's Hall. *Davy, A.*

A stag's head cabossed Proper between the attires a pheon Argent.

STUBBE. *Washbourne*, 'Suff.'*

A stag's head cabossed Proper.

SULYARD. *Fairbairn*, 'Sulyard, Bart., Suff.'*

STAG'S HEAD, Couped [Alphabetically by name]

A stag's head couped.

[ASTON]. Hon. & Rev. John Hervey, D.D., married Catherine Aston in 1730, after which he assumed the name of Aston. Dated 1745. *Her.Suff.Ch., Over south door, Shotley. Unidentified in source.* [But see S.H.A. Hervey's *'Shotley Parish Records,' Suff. Green Bks, 353 and 329–332,* in which he states that the Hon. Henry Hervey was the man concerned and gives his biography]

A buck's head couped.

BETTS, George, died 1713; widow Susan, died 1719; Edmund Betts, gent., died 1733; Rev. George Betts, LL.B., died 1766. *Her.Suff.Ch., Ledger stones, Wortham*

A hart's head couped Argent attired Or gorged with two bars Azure.

BROOKSBANKE. *MS Heraldic Alphabet*

A hart's head couped Proper attired Or gorged with two bars wavy Azure.

BROOKSBANK, of Gt. Bradley. *Davy, A.*

A buck's head couped Gules attired Or.

BUXTON, of St. Margaret South Elmham, Syleham, Sudbury. *MS Ordinary of Arms, fo. 30*. London Visitation 1633 (H.S.) I. 130*. Davy, A., Tomb, Syleham churchyard. E.A. Misc. 1931, 19.* Thomas Buxton, A.M., son of John Buxton of South Elmham, Incumbent of Syleham for 21 years, died 1738. *Her.Suff.Ch., Altar tomb in churchyard, Syleham*

A buck's head couped Argent the neck barry Argent and Gules attires Argent with the three upper tynes Or coupled by an annulet Argent.

CARR. 'Care' *Banners & Standards **

A stag's head couped Argent attired Or gorged with two bars gemel Gules.

CARR, of Ipswich. *MS Martin's Crests*

A stag's head couped Proper.

CRAWFORD, William, of Haughley Park, died 1835. *Her.Suff.Ch., Hatchment, Haughley*

A stag's head couped.

DRAGE. Rector of Westerfield. *Davy, A.*

A stag's head couped collared and chained.

DRAPER, Edmund, died 1732. *Her.Suff.Ch., Ledger stone, St. Mary's, Bury*

A stag's head couped gorged with a bar gemel.

GRANDGEORGE, GRANDORGE. *MS Heraldic Collections, fo. 83b**

A stag's head couped per pale and charged with gutties holding in the mouth an ear of wheat.

GRANDGEORGE, GRANDORGE. *MS Heraldic Collections, fo. 83b**

A buck's head in profile couped Or.

GREEN. 'S. Thomas Green' *Harl. MS 6163*

A buck's head couped Or.
  GREEN, of St. Clement's, Ipswich. *MS Heraldic Collections, fo. 16*. Davy, A.*
A roebuck's head couped Ermine attired Or.
  GREENE. *MS Heraldic Alphabet*
A stag's head couped Proper
  GRIMSTON, of Rishangles. *Visitation 1561 (MS G. 7*). Sharpe*
A buck's head and neck couped Proper horned Azure.
  GRIMSTON, of Rishangles, Thorndon. *MS Fairfax*
A roebuck's head couped Proper attired Azure.
  GRIMSTON, of Rishangles. *Bokenham*
A stag's head couped Or.
  GRIMSTON. *MS Martin's Crests*
A buck's head couped Gules attired Argent the tops Or from the dexter antler a branch of a tree suspended Vert.
  HARLESTON. *Banners & Standards**
A buck's head couped Gules armed Argent.
  HARLESTON, of Bardwell, Denham. *Davy, A.*
A stag's head couped.
  HAWORTH. Bernard John Haworth, 1897–1969. *Her.Suff.Ch., Headstone in churchyard, Hitcham*
A stag's head couped Gules attired Or gorged with a wreath Argent.
  HOWORTH. Master of the Grammar School, Ipswich. *Davy, A.*
A stag's head couped Argent attired Or.
  KNIGHTLEY. 'George Knyghtley' *MS Knight's Visitations, Essex**. 'George Knightley' *MS Philpot's Visitations, Essex**
A stag's head couped and winged.
  LIFE. Caesar Life, gent., died 1739; wife Martha (Bedingfield), died 1736. *Partridge, 117 (Darby, 1829), Brandon churchyard*
A buck's head couped behind it a pair of wings addorsed.
  LIFE, Caesar, Gent., died 1739. *Her.Suff.Ch., Altar tomb in churchyard, Brandon*
A stag's head couped Proper.
  MAXWELL. Brigadier Richard H. Maxwell. No date given. *Her.Suff.Ch., Glass, St. Mary's, Bury*
A stag's head couped.
  ORDE. Charles Somerville Orde, died 1937. *Her.Suff.Ch., Tombstone in churchyard, Hopton*
A stag's head couped Proper.
  PALEY. Rector of Freckenham, 1840. *Davy, A.*
In front of a stag's head couped Proper a cross crosslet Or.
  PALEY, of Freckenham, Ampton. *Burke, L.G. 1952 ed.**
A stag's head couped Proper.
  PARKER, of Sproughton. *Davy, A.*
A buck's head couped Argent attired Or with an arrow through the attires Argent.
  PARKER. Rector of Ringshall. *Davy, A.*
A buck's head couped.
  PARKHURST, of Ipswich. *MS Fairfax*
A buck's head couped Argent attired Or.
  PARKHURST. Vicar of Yoxford, died 1707. *Davy, A., church*
A buck's head couped Proper.
  ROWE. 'Row' *MS Martin's Crests*
A buck's head couped Proper attired Or with an acorn in its mouth Or slipped Vert.
  ROWE. *Davy, A.*
A stag's head couped per pale Gules and Sable.
  SEAGO. 'William Rix Seago, Oulton Hall, Oulton, Suff.' *Fairbairn.*

A buck's head couped Or.
  SKINNER, of Monks Eleigh. *Davy, A.*
A stag's head couped.
  SORRELL. Catherine, daughter of Sir William Gage, Bart., wife of Henry Sorrell, M.D. No date given. *Her.Suff.Ch., Ledger stone, St. Mary's, Bury*
A stag's head couped.
  SPRING. Sir William Spring, 4th Bart., died 1736. *Her.Suff.Ch., Ledger stone, Pakenham*
A stag's head couped Argent.
  SULYARD, of Eye, Wetherden. *Visitation 1561 (MS G. 7*)*
A stag's head couped Proper.
  SULYARD, of Eye, Wetherden. *Visitation 1561 (MS Iveagh Copy*)*
A stag's head couped Proper attired Or.
  SULYARD, SULIARD, of Haughley, Wetherden. *Harl. 772*. Visitation 1664–8*. Bokenham. Davy, A., Wetherden church. Washbourne*, 'Sulliard, Ess. and Suff.' Fairbairn*, 'Sulliard, Haughley, Suff.'* Sir John Sulyard, Kt., died 1574; Edward Sulyard, of Haughley Park, died 1799. *Her.Suff.Ch., Effigy monument and Hatchment, Wetherden*
A stag's head couped Proper between the attires a pheon Argent.
  STUBBE, of Laxfield. *Visitation 1664–8*
A buck's head couped at the neck.
  THEXTON, Sir William, died 1649; wife Dame Dorothy (Tasburgh), died 1641. *Her.Suff.Ch., Ledger stone, Flixton*
'beryth to his crest a hertes hede silver coppe.'
  WINDSOR. 'Wyndesore of Stanwel' *Wall's Book*
'to his crest a harts hed ar/ coupey armed or/'
  WINDSOR. 'Wyndesore of Stawell knight by h 8' *MS Alphabet of Crests, fo. 137*
A buck's head affronty couped at the neck Argent attired Or.
  WINDSOR, Earl of Plymouth. Of Parham Lodge, Tendring Hall in Stoke by Nayland. *Davy, A., Stoke church. Torlesse, 54* [garbled blazon]

STAG'S HEAD, Erased [Alphabetically by name]

A stag's head erased Or gorged with a wreath Argent and Sable tied at the end.
  AMYAS, of Beccles, Henstead. 'Thomas Amyas' *MS Knight's Visitations, Norf.*, attired Sable.* 'Thomas Amyas' *MS Philpot's Visitations, Norf.* Davy, A., (Edms.), Beccles church*
A stag's head erased Argent.
  ANDREWS. *MS Knight's Visitations, Norf.**
A stag's head erased Argent charged with a crescent.
  ANDREWS, ANDREWES, of Baylham, Bury. 'Edmond Andrewe' *MS Philpot's Visitations, Norf.*, crescent Sable. Davy, A. Washbourne, 'Andrewes of Suff.' Fairbairn*, 'Suff. Crescent for diff.'*
A stag's head erased Or.
  ANDREWS. *Fairbairn*, 'Suff.'*
A stag's head erased pierced through the neck with an arrow holding a sprig of three leaves in the mouth.
  BATE. *MS Ordinary of Arms, fo. 12**
A stag's head erased pierced through the neck with an arrow.
  BATE. *MS Heraldic Collections, fo. 87b**
A stag's head erased transfixed by an arrow Proper.
  BATES, George, died 1857. *Her.Suff.Ch., Wall tablet, Blaxhall*

A stag's head erased Argent antlered Or pierced through the throat by an arrow Or.

BATES, Ernest. *Her.Suff.Ch., Wooden shield in vestry, Dennington*

A stag's head erased Or attired and ducally gorged Gules.

BEDELL, of Herringfleet. *Davy, A. (Edms.), church*

A stag's head erased Argent attired Or gorged with two bars wavy Azure.

BROOKSBANK. *MS Ordinary of Arms, fo. 272**

A stag's head erased Proper.

BUCK, BUCKE, of Worlington. *Davy, A.*

A stag's head erased Argent armed and ducally gorged Or.

COPLEDIKE, of Horham. *Davy, A.*

A stag's head erased Proper.

COTMAN. 'John Sell Cotman' *Bookplate**

A stag's head erased per pale dancetty Or and Sable.

DIXON. 'Raulf dixon' *MS Knight's Visitations, Norf.**

A stag's head erased per pale dancetty Or and Sable attires counterchanged.

DIXON. 'Raffe Dixon' *MS Philpot's Visitations, Norf.**

A stag's head erased per pale dancetty Sable and Or attires counterchanged.

DIXON, of Suffolk. *Davy, A.*

A stag's head erased Proper attired Or.

ELWIN, of Gt. Glemham. *Davy, A.*

A buck's head erased Or billety Sable attired Sable.

EVERTON, of Newton, Battisford. *Visitation 1561 (MS G. 7*) and (ed. Metcalfe)*

A buck's head erased Sable bezanty.

EVERTON, of Battisford. *Bokenham*

A buck's head erased Or pellety and attired Sable.

EVERTON. *Washbourne, 'Suff.' Fairbairn, 'Suff.'*

Between two saltires Azure a stag's head erased Argent gorged with a collar Azure thereon three crescents Argent and between the attires a fleur-de-lis Azure.

FLORY, of Bramford, Gt. Bealings. *Crisp's Visitation I. 253**

A stag's head erased.

FORSTER. *Washbourne*, 'Suff. and Warw.'*

A stag's head erased.

GREEN, GREENE. *MS Heraldic Collections, fo. 88b*. Green of Wilby, 1730–1862. Her.Suff.Ch., Tomb, Tablet, Brass and Hatchment, Wilby*

A stag's head erased Proper.

GREEN, of Wilby, Ipswich. *Green Memoir, 'buck's head'. Davy, A., Wilby church*

A buck's head erased Azure attired Or.

GREENE, Robert, Gent., died 1640. *Her.Suff.Ch., Ledger stone, Braisworth*

A stag's head erased Proper attired Or.

GRIMSTON, of Suffolk. *Davy, A.*

A buck's head erased Vert attired Or gorged with a collar Argent charged with a fret Gules and in the mouth a sprig of oak Proper.

HARGREAVES, of Drinkstone Park. *Burke, L.G. 1900 ed.* and 1952 ed.*

A buck's head erased gorged with a collar and holding in the mouth a sprig of oak.

HARGREAVES, John Reginald, of Drinkstone Park, died 1934; widow died 1951. *Her.Suff.Ch., Tomb in the churchyard, Drinkstone*

A stag's head erased.

HEMENHALE. *Davy, A.*

A stag's head erased Proper.

HUNTER. *Bookplate**

A stag's head erased transfixed through the neck by an arrow in bend point to the dexter all Proper between the attires a horseshoe Or.

KITCHENER, of Lakenheath, Bury, Newmarket, Mildenhall, Aspal Hall. Lord Kitchener of Khartoum. *Crisp's Visitation VII. 1*, Pedigree*

A roebuck's head erased Sable bezanty attired Or gorged with a coronet Argent.

LAWRENCE. William Lawrence, of St. Ives, co. Hunts., Esq.; Confirmation of Arms and Grant of Crest by W. Hervey, Clarenceux, 30 October 1562. Copied 18 August 1688 by H. St. George, Clar. *Grants & Certificates (Add. MS 14,295)*

A buck's head erased and attached to its neck on the sinister side a pair of wings addorsed (Edmund Farrer).

LIFE, Caesar, Gent., died 1739. *Her.Suff.Ch., Altar tomb in churchyard, Brandon*

A stag's head erased Proper.

LODER, of Woodbridge. *Davy, A.*

A stag's head erased Proper ducally gorged Or.

MACHELL, of Newmarket, Kentford. *Burke, L.G. 1900 ed.*

A stag's head erased.

OAKES. Rev. Abraham Oakes, LL.D., Rector of Withersfield and of Melford, died 1756. *Her.Suff.Ch., Ledger stone, Withersfield. A small Hatchment formerly in the church and stated to have been 'very badly and incorrectly restored' could not be found in 1988*

A stag's head erased.

PALEY. *Her.Suff.Ch., on water trough outside church, Ampton. Not found 1988*

A roebuck's head erased Proper attired Or.

PARKHURST, Sir William. Patent by Sir W. Segar, Garter. *Grants & Certificates (Add. MSS 4,966 and 12,225)*

A buck's head erased Argent charged on the neck with a collar dancetty Gules.

PENNING, of Ipswich. *Bokenham*

A stag's head erased per fesse indented (no colours, but ? Argent and Gules).

PENNING (or PENNYNGE), Anthony, of Ipswich, in Suffolk, gent. A gift by W. Dethick, Garter (no date given). *Grants & Certificates (Harl. MSS 1,359 and 6,169; Add. MS 14,295)*

A buck's head erased per fesse indented Argent and Gules attired Gules.

PENNING, of Ipswich. *Davy, A., St. Matthew's church monument. Washbourne, 'Penyng, Suff.' Haslewood, 4. Proc.S.I.A. VII. 206. Fairbairn, 'of Ipswich, Suff.' also 'Penyng, Kettleburgh and Ipswich, S.'*

A buck's head erased Argent.

PENNING, of Ipswich, Kenton's in Kettleburgh. *Davy, A,. 'Granted by Dethick, Garter, 1 June 1594.'*

A buck's head erased.

PENNING, of Ipswich. *E.A.N. & Q. IX. 362. Copinger, IV. Anthonie Penning, died 1630. Her.Suff.Ch., Effigy monument, St. Matthew's, Ipswich. 'stag's head'*

A buck's head erased Sable attired and ducally gorged Gules.

RANDALL, RANDELL. *MS ex-Taylor Coll.**

A buck's head erased Azure armed ducally gorged and lined Or.

RANDALL, of Orford. *Davy, A.*

A stag's head erased.

RANDALL. Maria (Castell) married, secondly, William Randall, she died 1693. *Her.Suff.Ch., Ledger stone, Beccles.*

A buck's head erased Or holding in the mouth a pear Or stalked and leaved Vert.

RAPER, ROPER. 'Robart Roper' *MS Philpot's Visitations, Norf.**

A buck's head erased Sable attired Or charged on the neck with three bezants in pale and three bars gemel Or all within two branches Or.

READE, REDE, of Beccles, Weston. *Visitation 1561 (MS G. 7*)*

A buck's head erased Argent attired Or charged on the neck with three bezants in pale and three bars gemel Or all within two branches Or.

REDE, of Beccles. *Visitation 1561 (Iveagh Copy*)*

A buck's head erased Argent attired Or between two palm branches Vert charged on the neck with three bars gemelle Or.

REDE, of Beccles. *Visitation 1561 (ed. Metcalfe). Washbourne, 'Suff. and Norf.'*

A buck's head erased Sable attired Or collared and charged on the neck with three bezants in pale and between two branches.

REDE, of Weston, St. Margaret's South Elmham. *Visitation 1664–8*. E.A. Misc. 1927, 30*

A buck's head erased Sable attired Or charged with three bars gemelles Or.

READE, of Rendham, St. Margts., Ilketshall. *Bokenham*

A buck's head erased brown colour (Proper) collared with two bars gemelle Ermine.

READ, of Bardwell. *Bokenham*

A buck's head erased triple-collared between two branches.

REDE, of Beccles. *Davy, A., church*

A buck's head erased Sable attired Or the nose Or collared with three bars gemelles Or three bezants in pale upon the neck and between two branches.

REDE, of Beccles, Rendham, Weston. *Davy, A.*

A buck's head erased Argent attired Or between two palm branches Or and charged on the neck with two bars gemelles Or.

REDE, of Beccles, Rendham, Weston. *Davy, A. (Edms.) Burke, L.G. 1853 ed., 'three bars g.'*

A stag's head erased.

REDE. *Washbourne*, 'Suff.' Fairbairn*, 'Suff.'*

A buck's head erased Azure attired Or between two reeds Or and charged on the neck with three bars gemelles Or and three bezants in pale.

REDE. *Fairbairn, 'of Norwich and Beccles, Suff.'*

'A Roo Bucks hed rasy in his prop coler horned or/ P g dethyke to Antony Rone of houndesloo in mydelsex'

ROAN. *MS Alphabet of Crests, fo. 110*

A stag's head erased Proper armed Or holding in his mouth a branch of oak leaved Vert fructed Or.

ROAN, ROANE. 'Rone' *MS Knight's Visitation, Suff.**

A stag's head erased Or.

ROBINSON, of Southwold. *Davy, A., church. Washbourne*, 'Suff.' Fairbairn*, 'of Southwold, Suff.'* John Robinson, died 1802. *Her.Suff.Ch., Hatchment, Southwold*

A stag's head erased.

SORRELL, of Ipswich, Bury. *Davy, A., St. Peter's in Ipswich, St. Mary's in Bury. Tymms, 201*

A stag's head erased Argent armed Or, on the neck a crescent – ? for difference.

STANLEY, of Beccles. 'Wyll Stanley' *MS Philpot's Visitations, Norf.*, without the crescent. Davy, A.*

A roebuck's head erased Or.

STAVELEY. *MS Martin's Crests*

A stag's head erased Sable pierced through the neck with an arrow feathered and armed Or.

STAVERTON. *Davy, A., Chillesford and St. Lawrence in Ipswich churches*

A stag's head erased Or gorged with a garland of roses Gules leaved Vert.

TIPTOFT, of Nettlestead. *Davy, A.*

A buck's head erased Sable attired Or billety Or.

VILLERS, VILLIERS. 'John Villers . . . com.Leyc.' *Banners & Standards**

'beryth to his crest a robuckes hede sable rased byllsted all over and armed gold'

'VILLERS of –' *Wall's Book*

'to his crest a roo bucks hed sa/ rased bylleted all over and armed or /'

VILLERS. 'Vyllers' *MS Alphabet of Crests, fo. 132b**

A stag's head erased Gules gutty Or attired Or.

WRIGHT, of Ipswich, Bury. *Visitation 1561 (MSS G. 7* and Iveagh Copy*) and (ed. Metcalfe). Harl. 772*. Davy, A. Washbourne, 'Kent and Suff.' Fairbairn, 'St. Edmundsbury, Suff.'*

A stag's head erased charged on the neck with four gouttes.

WRIGHT. *MS Heraldic Collections, fo. 46**

A stag's head erased Or charged with four gutties in cross Gules.

WRIGHT, of Ipswich, Bury. *Davy, A.*

A stag's head erased Or charged with three guttes in cross [*sic*] Gules.

WRIGHT. *Washbourne, 'of Kent and Suff.'*

A stag's head erased.

WRIGHT, of Freston. *E.A.N. & Q. VIII. 69. Proc.S.I.A. XIII. 385.* John Wright, 'pastor of this church', died 1723. *Her.Suff.Ch., Ledger stone, Freston*

DEER'S HEAD [Continued]

CHAMOIS

A chamois's head Sable.

COPINGER, COPPINGER, of Suffolk. *Davy, A. (? Edms.) Washbourne, 'Copinger, Suff. chamois deer's head', untinctured*

A chamois deer's head Sable.

COPINGER, Rev. Henry, Rector of Lavenham, died 1622. *Her.Suff.Ch., Effigy monument, Lavenham* 'There is a plain torse but no crest (A chamois deer's head Sable)'

COPINGER, Raphe, citizen & mercer of London, died 1658. *Her.Suff.Ch., Slab, Bramford*

REINDEER

A reindeer's head erased Argent attired Or.

DRAKE. 'Wyll Drake' *MS Philpot's Visitations, Norf.**

A reindeer's head couped Proper collared and chained Or.

EDGE. Richard Edge, of Strelley, co. Notts.; Grant by Sir H. St. George, Garter and P.le Neve, Norroy, 9 May 1709. *Grants & Certificates (Add. MS 14,830)*

A reindeer's head Proper, collared and ringed Or.

EDGE, of Ipswich, Rushmere, Nedging, Waldringfield, Drinkstone, etc. *Sharpe. Davy, A.*

A reindeer's head couped Proper collared and chained Or.

EDGE. Peter Edge, A.M., Rector of Drimoleague in Ireland, died 1782. *Her.Suff.Ch., Wall tablet, Rushmere.* 'Rev[d] W[m]. Edge' *Bookplate**

A reindeer's head Proper collared and chained Or.
> EDGE, of Lavenham, Nedging Hall, Naughton. *Bildeston, 96. E.A. Misc. 1918, 14*

A reindeer's head Argent attired Or.
> GARDINER. *Davy, A.*

DOG

A dog's head Argent langued Gules gorged with a collar indented Azure.
> HICKMAN. Henry Hickman, D.C.L., Chancellor of the Bishop of Peterborough; By W. Dethick, Garter, 1 December 1590. *Grants & Certificates (Stowe MS 676)*

A dog's head Argent collared Azure to the collar a line nowed Azure.
> LEE, of Livermere, Lawshall. *Davy, A.*

HOUND

'his crest is a hounds hed ar/ his heyres/ g/'
> DEVEREUX. 'Sr Water Devereux' *MS Alphabet of Crests, fo. 29d*

A hound's head erased Argent langued Gules collar and line Azure.
> LEE. Robert Lee, of Lee, Alderman of London. *Grants & Certificates (Harl. MS 1,359; Add. MS 14,295; Stowe MS 676)*

'uppon the heaulme on a wreathe Silver and Sables, a hownde's heade razed Golde bettwen two ostriche fethers Silver, mantled Gules dubled Silver'
> SUDBURY, Borough of Grant by Cooke, Clarenceux, 20 September 1576. *Proc.S.I.A. I. 200*

A hound's head erased Or between two ostrich feathers Argent.
> SUDBURY. 'The Towne of Sudbery' *MS Knight's Visitations, Suff.* *

A hound's head couped Or the ear and collar Argent.
> WHETTELL, of Ampton manor. *Copinger, Manors, VI., 'Grant by Cooke, Clar., 1657' [sic ?1567]*

BLOODHOUND

A 'bludhoundes' head Sable erased and eared Argent holding in the mouth a hog's foot Or.
> BACON. *Wall's Book*

'to his crest a blodhounds hed rased sa/ eared ar/ having a hoggs foote in his mouth/ in bend or/ the foote downward'
> BACON. *MS Alphabet of Crests, fo. 12b*

A bloodhound's head per pale Gules and Sable eared Ermine langued Gules teeth Argent.
> MOLL. 'Mol of . . . Staffordshire' *Wall's Book*

'to his Crest a Blud hounds hed Pty P Pale/ g/ sa/ eared [ermine spot drawn] Langed b/ Dented ar/'
> MOLL. 'Moll of Codsall in Staff/' *MS Alphabet of Crests, fo. 80b*

GREYHOUND

A marigold in pale one leaf Argent one other Purpure stalked and leaved Vert issuing therefrom a greyhound's head per pale Argent and Sable on the neck three gutties counterchanged.
> CAVE. *Wall's Book*

'to his crest a mary gold in pale the on leve ar/ the other purpur stalked and Leved vert/ owt of the mary gold doth issu a grehounds hede p pale ar/sa/ on the neck iij Dropes count i ij'
> CAVE. *MS Alphabet of Crests, fo. 21b*

A greyhound's head collared.
> COLEMAN, of Axfield [sic Laxfield]. *Bokenham*

A greyhound's head Sable charged with three bezants Or.
> COMBER. *Washbourne, 'Suff.' Fairbairn, 'Suff. bezants two and one'*

A greyhound's head between two wings displayed holding in his mouth a horse-shoe.
> EDGAR. *E.A. Misc. 1910, 106, 'formerly in Sternfield ch.'*

A greyhound's head Argent collared and chained Or.
> FORSTER, FOSTER, of Copdock. *Davy, A.*

A greyhound's head Proper collared Gules studded bordered and ringed Or.
> GORGE. 'S.Edmond Gorge' *Harl. MS 6163* *

A dun greyhound's head langued Gules collared Gules a buckle 'and a payre of tyrrettes hangyng by hit' Or.
> GORGE. 'Gorges' *Wall's Book*

'to his crest a Dun grehounds hed wᵗ a coller a bowt his necke g/ a buckle and a payre of Tyrretts hangyng by yt or/ knight by h 8'
> GORGE. *MS Alphabet of Crests, fo. 46b*

A greyhound's head Argent charged on the neck with a bugle horn Sable garnished Or stringed Gules and holding in the mouth a divining rod Proper.
> HUNTER, Sir Cecil Hunter Rodwell, G.C.M.G., of Woodlands, Holbrook, Governor of Fiji, etc., died 1953. *Her.Suff.Ch., Wall tablet, Holbrook*

A greyhound's head.
> JERMYN. Edmund Jermyn, Esq., died 1573, Portrait at Rushbrook. *Suff. Green Bks, Rushbrook*

A greyhound's head Proper, collared Or.
> JERMYN, of Rushbrook. *Muskett. II. 243 (Burke)*

A greyhound's head Sable gorged with a bar gemelle Or.
> JERMYN, of Rushbrook. *Davy, A. Washbourne, 'Suff.' Fairbairn, 'Suff.' Muskett. II. 243 (Burke). Her.Suff.Ch., Sibton.* Rev. Edward Jermyn, M.A., Rector for 41 years, died 1848. *Wall tablet, Carlton Colville*

A greyhound's head Argent.
> PENNING, of Ipswich. *Proc.S.I.A. VII. 206, Monument in St. Matthew's church*

A greyhound's head erect.
> RODWELL, ROTHWELL, of Livermere, Ipswich. *Davy, A.*

A greyhound's head quarterly Argent and Sable collar counterchanged.
> TAYLER. Rector of Otley, 1850. *Davy, A.*

GREYHOUND'S HEAD, Couped

A greyhound's head couped Argent gorged with a wreath of laurel Proper.
> BROWNE. *MS Heraldic Alphabet*

A greyhound's head couped plain collared and ringed.
> COLMAN. *Bookplate* *

A greyhound's head couped Argent collared Gules.
> GORGE. 'Gorges' *MS Martin's Crests*

A greyhound's head Pean couped at the neck collared Or.
> HALFORD. Charles Douglas Halford, of West Lodge, East Bergholt, c. 1861. *Her.Suff.Ch., Brass, East Bergholt. Not found 1978*

A greyhound's head couped Sable collared studded and ringed Argent.
> JERMYN. 'Sr Thomas Jermin' *MS Lilly's Visitation of Suffolk* *

A greyhound's head couped and collared.
> JERMYN, Henry, son of Peter Jermyn and his wife Sarah (Bitton), died 1819. *Partridge, 44 (Darby, 1825)*

A greyhound's head couped Sable gorged with a bar gemel Or.

JERMYN. *Bookplate**
A greyhound's head couped per pale Azure and Argent holding in his mouth a stag's leg erased Or.
LENHAM. 'Leynham' *Banners & Standards**
A greyhound's head couped.
LLOYD, of Stanstead. *Davy, A.*
A greyhound's head couped per pale Argent and Sable thereon three gutties counterchanged in the mouth a rose Gules slipped and leaved Vert all between two branches of oak Proper.
MILDMAY. Thomas Mildmay, of Moulsham, co. Essex. Patent from T. Hawley, Clar., 15 May 1542. *Grants & Certificates (Harl. MSS 1,359 and 1,484)*
A greyhound's head couped Or collared Sable.
NORTON, of Hundon. *Davy, A.*
A greyhound's head couped Vert in the mouth a laurel branch Vert.
PHILLIPSON. *Davy, A.*
A greyhound's head couped Or in the mouth a holly branch Proper.
WARREN, of Long Melford, Gt. Thurlow. *Davy, A.,* 'Granted by Hawley, 1538'
A greyhound's head couped (or erased) Sable holding in the mouth a rose Gules slipped Vert.
WELLER. Capt. Francis Weller, R.A. *Her.Suff.Ch., Tomb in churchyard, Waldringfield. Covered in brambles*

GREYHOUND'S HEAD, Erased
A greyhound's head erased quarterly Argent and Gules charged with four gutties counter-changed 'remainder imperfect'.
BABINGTON. 'Babyngton' *Banners & Standards**
A greyhound's head erased Sable collared Argent holding in the mouth a stag's foot Or.
BACON, of Hessett. *Visitation 1612*
A greyhound's head erased in the mouth a horseshoe.
BAKER, of Wattisfield. *E.A.N. & Q. I. 135, church monuments*
A greyhound's head erased Proper on the neck two chevrons Gules and in the mouth a cross crosslet fitchy Or.
COLVIN, James, died 1847; two sons, in the Indian Civil Service, both died 1857. *Her.Suff.Ch., Wall tablet, Lt. Bealings*
A greyhound's head erased Argent collared Gules ringed Or.
CUTTS. 'Sr. John Cuttes Knyght' *MS Knight's Visitations, Essex**. 'Sr. John Cutt' *MS Philpot's Visitations, Essex**. *Davy, A., Clare church*
A greyhound's head erased Argent collared studded ringed and lined turned behind the neck nowed Gules.
DAY. Vincent Day, of London; Grant of Crest by William Dethick, Garter, 20th March 1582. *MS Heraldic Alphabet*
A greyhound's head erased Argent.
FORD, of Suffolk. *Davy, A.*
A greyhound's head erased.
FULLER, Will., gent., died 1758; Osborn Fuller, esq., died 1794; Mary Fuller, spinster, died 1802; Others. *Partridge, 102 (Darby, 1826), Palisaded tomb in churchyard, Carlton*
A greyhound's head erased Gules.
FULLER, of Carlton near Saxmundham. *Sharpe. Davy, A., churchyard.* William Fuller, died 1758; Osborne Fuller, died 1794. *Her.Suff.Ch., Altar tomb in churchyard and Hatchment, Carlton*

A greyhound's head erased Argent collared and lined Or.
GOTTES, of Hawkedon. *Davy, A.*
A greyhound's head erased Sable round the neck a double chain Or pendent therefrom an escutcheon Or charged with a bugle-horn stringed Sable.
GRISSELL, of Redisham Hall. *Burke, L.G. 1952 ed.**
A greyhound's head erased Azure ducally gorged Or.
TANY, of Bures. *MS Ordinary of Arms, fo. 138**, 'de Essex'. *Davy, A.*
A greyhound's head erased Sable holding in the mouth a rose Gules slipped and leaved Vert.
WELLER, WELLER-POLEY, of Boxted Hall. *Davy, A. Burke, L.G. 1900 ed. Fairbairn. Second crest, for Weller.* Rev. William Weller-Poley, died 1887. *Her.Suff.Ch., Wall tablet, Hartest.* Captain Francis Weller, R.A. *Tomb in the churchyard, Waldringfield. Covered in brambles, no date given*
A greyhound's head erased.
WRIGHT, John, of Ipswich or Freston; Portman, Bailiff and Burgess, died 1683. *Her.Suff.Ch., Wall tablet, St. Clement's, Ipswich*

TWO GREYHOUND'S HEADS
'A brace of Greyhounds heads couped & endorsed ye 1st Arg. ye 2d Sab each wth a Collar counterch.'
ATKINS. *MS Martin's Crests*
Two greyhound's heads endorsed Argent and Sable collared and ringed counterchanged.
ATKINS. 'Attkyns' *MS ex-Taylor Coll.* Davy, A.*

TALBOT
A talbot's head Ermine.
ALLINGTON. *Davy, A.*
A talbot's head per fesse Sable and Argent holding in the mouth a deer's leg Or.
BACON, of Hessett, Loudham, Erwarton. *Davy, A. Proc.S.I.A. V. 51*
A talbot's head.
CLARKE, of Mellis, Bury. *Bokenham. MS Martin's Crests.* 'Johannes Clarke, Armiger, died 81' [*sic* ?1681]; Others. *Martin's Church Notes, Frag.Gen. IX. 100, 'in the Church yard upon neat Altar Tombs', St. Mary's, Bury*
A talbot's head collared.
CLARKE, of Bury. *Davy, A., St. Mary's church*
A talbot's head Or langued Gules.
COPLAND, of Sibton, Yoxford. *Davy, A.*
A talbot's head Erminois gorged with a mural coronet of the first [*sic* Or].
LINGWOOD, of Honington, Bury. *Davy, A.*
A talbot's head Argent collared Gules ringed Or.
MAXEY, Anthony, of Bradwell, co. Essex. *Grants & Certificates (Add. MS 4,966; Harl. MS 1,359)*
From a tower Proper a talbot's head Argent collared Vert ringed Or.
RICKARDS. Rector of Stowlangtoft. *Davy, A.*
Issuing from a tower Or a talbot's head Sable.
SHEPPARD. John Sheppard, of Ash, died 1669; Lt. Frederick Sheppard, died 1812. *Her.Suff.Ch., Wall tablet and Altar tomb in churchyard, Campsea Ash. Fairbairn, 'of Campsey Ashe, Suff.'*
A talbot's head Or issuing from a triple-turreted tower Sable.
SHEPPARD. Bridget, wife of Thomas Sheppard, gent., died 1748; daughter Dorothy, died 1752. *Her.Suff.Ch., Ledger stone, Wetheringsett cum Brockford*

A talbot's head.
TIDDIMAN, of Lowestoft. *Gillingwater, 379. Davy, A. Lees, 280*

TALBOT'S HEAD, Couped

A talbot's head couped Sable eared and charged with gutties Or.
ASLACK. 'Wm aslake' *MS Knight's Visitations, Norf.*

A talbot's head couped Sable eared and charged with gutties Argent.
ASLACK. 'Thomas Aslake' *MS Philpot's Visitations, Norf.*

A talbot's head couped Argent eared Gules.
BARRELL, of Suffolk *Davy, A. Washbourne*

A talbot's head couped Or.
COPLAND, of Yoxford. *Sharpe.* Daniel Copland, A.M., Vicar of Yoxford, died 1793. *Her.Suff.Ch., Wall tablet, Yoxford. Photograph*

A talbot's head couped.
JEAFFRESON, John, died 1759. *Her.Suff.Ch., Altar tomb in churchyard, Bawdsey*

A talbot's head couped Sable collared Or.
KINGE, of Long Melford. *Burke, L.G. 1900 ed.*

A talbot's head couped plain collared and ringed.
LEE. 'Bap^st Lee Esq.' *Bookplate*

A talbot's head couped per pale Gules and Sable eared Ermine.
MELL, of Bramfield. *Davy, A. (Barrett)*

A talbot's head couped Gules eared and gorged with a collar gemel Or pierced in the breast with a pheon Or.
PARKE, Lord Wensleydale. Daughter Charlotte married William Lowther. *Her.Suff.Ch., Glass, Campsea Ash*

In front of a talbot's head couped Gules a cinquefoil Ermine all between two trefoils slipped Vert.
SMITH-REWSE, Rev. Gilbert, M.A., Rector of St. Margaret's & St. Peter's, South Elmham, Suffolk. *Fairbairn. Second crest, for Smith*

A talbot's head couped Or collared and eared Argent.
WHETTEL, WHETTELL. 'William Whittell, of London 1587' (F.13, fol. 19, Coll. of Arms). *Grants & Certificates (Stowe MS 670; Harl. MS 1,359)*

A talbot's head couped Or collared.
WHETTELL, William, Esq., died 1628. *Her.Suff.Ch., Wall tablet with effigy bust, Ampton*

A talbot's head couped charged on the ear with one and on the neck with four torteaux.
WHISTLER. Edward John Whistler, Esq., died 1868. *Her.Suff.Ch., Wall brass, Ilketshall St. John*

TALBOT'S HEAD, Erased [Alphabetically by name]

'one a wreath Argent and Sables a Talbots head rased Gold, with Collor Sables, ye line Gules: mantled gules doubled Argent'
ALDHAM, John, of Shimpling and co. Norfolk; Confirmation of Arms and Grant of Crest by Wm. Hervey, Clar., 20 April 1563. *Misc.Gen. et Her. 5th S. VIII. 192*

A talbot's head erased Or gorged with a collar Sable lined Gules.
ALDHAM. 'John Aldham' *MS Philpot's Visitations, Norf.*, lined and ringed Gules. *Visitation 1664–8, end of line tied in a knot. Davy, A. (Blois MS)*

A talbot's head erased gorged with a collar and lined.

ALDHAM, John, A.M., 'Rector of this parish', died 1727. *Her.Suff.Ch., Ledger stone, Market Weston*

A talbot's head erased Argent collared Sable.
ALEXANDER, of Framlingham, Badingham. *Visitation 1664–8. Davy, A. Misc.Gen. et Her. 5th S. IX. 134–8, Pedigrees*

A talbot's head erased Argent collared Gules.
ALEXANDER, Of Framlingham, Badingham. *Bokenham. Geen, 138.* Joseph Alexander, died 1644; John Alexander, died 1661. *Her.Suff.Ch., Hatchment, Framlingham*

A talbot's head erased.
ALEXANDER. Jane, wife of Waldegrave Alexander, died 1720. *Her.Suff.Ch., Ledger stone, Ubbeston*

A talbot's head erased Sable gutty d'eau.
ASLACK, of Willingham. *Davy, A. Washbourne, 'Aslake, Suff.' Fairbairn, 'Aselock, Aslake, Suff.'*

A talbot's head erased per fesse Sable and Argent holding in the mouth the leg of a deer Or.
BACON, of Hessett. *Visitation of Northants., 1618–9 (ed. Metcalfe), 66, 'To Thomas Baken of Hessett in Suffolk p. Thomas Wriothesley, Garter, and Thomas Benolt, Clarenceux, 9 of May A° 1514, 6 H.8.'*

A talbot's head Sable eared and erased Argent holding in the mouth a deer's leg couped hoof downward Or.
BACON. 'Edmond Bacon' *MS Philpot's Visitations, Suff.*

A talbot's head erased per fesse Sable and Argent holding in the mouth a nag's foot Or.
BACON, of Hessett. *Bokenham*

A talbot's head erased Sable holding in the mouth a horse's leg couped in pale Or.
BACON, of Hessett, Loudham, Erwarton. *Davy, A. (Barrett)*

A talbot's head erased Argent eared ducally crowned and charged on the neck with two gemel bars Or.
BOZUN, BOZOUN. 'Adam Bozun' *MS Knight's Visitations, Norf.*

A talbot's head erased Argent eared Or ducally crowned Or.
BOZUN, BOZOUN, of Chelmondiston. *Davy, A.*

A talbot's head erased.
CHITTING, of Wortham, Bury. Henry Chitting, Chester Herald 1618–death 1638. *Davy, A., Engraved portrait. Proc.S.I.A. XXXIV. 103–128, Article 'Henry Chitting's Suffolk Collections', by D.N.J. MacCulloch; Portrait c.1620 in Coll. of Arms*

A talbot's head erased Argent.
CHITTING, of Wortham, Bury. *Davy, A.*

A talbot's head erased Or.
CHITTING, of Wortham, Bury. *Davy, A.*

A talbot's head erased Ermine.
CHITTY, Michael, died 1816; widow Elizabeth, died 1856. *Her.Suff.Ch., Ledger stone, Gorleston*

A talbot's head erased Or.
CLARKE, Bart., of Freckenham. *MS Heraldic Alphabet. Davy, A.*

A talbot's head erased Argent eared Gules.
DEVEREUX, Viscount Hereford Of Earl Soham, Ipswich. *Bokenham*

A talbot's head erased Sable.
HALL. *MS Ordinary of Arms, fo. 111*

A talbot's head erased.

HALL, Joseph, Bishop of Norwich 1641–56.
Rector of Hawstead. *MS Martin's Crests.*
Bedford, 2nd ed., 94
A talbot's head erased Ermine.
HUNT, of Harwich in co. Essex *Sharpe*
A talbot's head erased Argent eared Gules.
JEAFFRESON, of Tunstall, Clopton, Brandeston,
Ufford, Bawdsey. *Davy, A., Tunstall, Clopton
and Bawdsey churches. Bildeston, 85. Crisp's
Visitation. II. 52–3. Frag.Gen. IV. 33*.
Fairbairn*, under 'Robinson, of Denston Hall,
Suff. 2nd Crest'. E.A. Misc. 1910, 66.* John
Jeaffreson, gent., died 1746; widow Ann, died
1751. *Her.Suff.Ch., Wall tablet, Clopton.* Chris.
Jeaffreson, Rector of Tunstall, died 1789. *Wall
tablet, Tunstall*
A talbot's head erased Argent langued and eared Or.
JEAFFRESON. *Her.Suff.Ch., Glass, Denston*
A talbot's head erased Argent pellety.
KEENE, of Ipswich. *Bokenham, 'p. Harvey,
Clar., 1561'*
A talbot's head erased Sable collared and eared Or.
KING, Alexander, of London; Grant by R. Cooke,
Clar., in 1592. *Grants & Certificates (Harl. MS
1,359)*
A talbot's head erased Sable collared Or.
KING. *Davy, A.*
A talbot's head erased Argent collared and ringed
Gules.
MAXEY, MAXIE, of Holton in Samford Hundred,
Shotley. *Visitation 1664–8. Bokenham. Davy, A.
Washbourne, 'Ess. and Suff.' Fairbairn*, 'Maxey,
Maxie. Shotley, Suff.' Suff. Green Bks, Shotley*
A talbot's head erased Sable.
RYLEY, John, died 1672/3. *Her.Suff.Ch., Wall
tablet, Whepstead*
A talbot's head erased ducally gorged.
SMYTH, John, died 1650. *Tymms, 200, Slab in
St. Mary's church, Bury*
A talbot's head erased Or collared Sable between
two ostrich feathers erect Argent.
SUDBURY, Town of *Her.Suff.Ch., Brass shield on
chest, St. Gregory's (probably removed from St.
Peter's); Glass, St. Peter's, Sudbury*
A talbot's head erased Or eared collared and ringed
Argent the collar studded.
WHETTEL, of Ampton. *Davy, A. Washbourne*,
'Suff.' In Addenda II.*

ELEPHANT

An elephant's head quarterly Gules and Or.
CLARKE, of Hadleigh, Kettlebaston. *Davy, A.
Washbourne, 'Suff.' Fairbairn, 'Suff.'*
An elephant's head Or eared and armed Gules.
ELLIOT, of Boxted. *Davy, A. Washbourne,
'Elliot, Elliott, Suff.'*
An elephant's head Argent gorged with a coronet
Or.
HAMMOND, of North Cove. *E.A.N. & Q. II. 346,
'Hamonde 1576' in window of old farmhouse at
N. Cove*
An elephant's head.
SAUNDERS. 'Sanders' *MS Martin's Crests*
An elephant's head.
THROCKMORTON, THROGMORTON, of South
Elmham All Saints. *MS Martin's Crests. Davy, A.*
An elephant's head Proper.
THROCKMORTON. 'S. Throgmorton' *Harl. MS
6163*
An elephant's head 'in his coulours graye'
THROGMORTON. *Wall's Book*

ELEPHANT'S HEAD, Couped

An elephant's head couped Sable eared and tusked,
or toothed, Or in the mouth a snake Vert wreathed
about the trunk.
APPLETON, APULTON, of Waldingfield. *Visitation
1577. MS Knight's Visitations, Suff.* * 'Thomas
Apulton' MS Philpot's Visitations, Suff.* * MS
Fairfax (Tyl.) MS Martin's Crests, 'serpent
Proper' Davy, A. Washbourne*, 'Suff.' Muskett. I.
322. Fairbairn, 'Appleton, Apleton, Suff.'*
An elephant's head couped Sable ears and tusks Or.
APPLETON, of Preston. *Visitation 1664–8*
An elephant's head couped Or holding in the trunk a
snake Proper.
APPLETON, of Waldingfield. *Bokenham*
An elephant's head couped quarterly Gules and Or
tusks of the last [*sic* Or].
CLARKE, Edward, of Kettlesdon [*sic* Kettlebaston],
co. Suffolk, gent.; Confirmation 20 June I Elizabeth
[1558/9]. *Grants & Certificates (Stowe MS 703)*
An elephant's head couped Argent.
ELLIOT. *MS Ordinary of Arms, fo. 272**
An elephant's head couped Or ear Gules.
ELIOTT, . . . , of Suffolk. Patent November 1614.
Grants & Certificates (Stowe MS 706)
An elephant's head couped Argent (should be
collared Gules).
ELLIOTT, Charles, F.R.S., died 1856; son William
H. Elliott, died 1870. *Her.Suff.Ch., Wall tablet,
Tattingstone*
An elephant's head couped Ermine eared Sable
armed Or.
GARDINER, of Walberswick, Wrentham.
Visitation 1561 (MS G. 7) and (ed. Metcalfe).
Washbourne, 'Linc. and Suff.'*
An elephant's head couped Ermine.
GARDINER, of Stoke Ash. *Bokenham*
An elephant's head couped Ermine.
GARDINER, of Walberswick. *Davy, A.*
An elephant's head couped Ermines.
GARDINER, of Wrentham, Walberswick, Stoke
Ash, Exning. *Davy, A.*
An elephant's head couped Argent ducally gorged
eared and tusked Or.
HAMMOND, of Ufford. 'Hamonde' *MS Knight's
Visitations, Norf.* * 'John Hamonde' MS
Philpot's Visitations, Norf.* * Davy, A.*
An elephant's head couped Sable eared and tusked Or.
THROCKMORTON. 'Mayster Frogmorton'
*Banners & Standards**
An elephant's head couped.
THROCKMORTON. 'Thomas Throgmorton' *MS
Heraldic Collections, fo. 15**

ELEPHANT'S HEAD, Erased

An ?elephant's head erased Erminois charged on the
neck with a plate thereon a mullet.
KIRBY. Rector of Gt. Waldingfield. *Davy, A.*
An elephant's head erased Gules plain collared Or
studded Sable.
PIGEON. 'John pigoot' *MS Philpot's Visitations,
Norf.**
An elephant's head erased Gules eared tusked
collared lined and ringed Or.
PIGEON. *Davy, A.*
An elephant's head erased Sable eared Argent armed
Or.
SAUNDERS, of Blaxhall. *Visitation 1561 (MS
G. 7*)*
An elephant's head erased Sable eared and armed
Argent.

SAUNDERS. 'Sanders' *MS Heraldic Alphabet*
An elephant's head erased per chevron
counterchanged [*sic*] Argent and Sable.
    SAUNDERS. *Druery, 142, Gorleston church slab*
An elephant's head erased Sable.
    SAUNDERS, of Blaxhall. *Davy, A., Blaxhall and
Gorleston churches.* Francis Saunders, of
Blaxhall, died . . . *Her.Suff.Ch., Wall tablet,
Blaxhall. Elephant's trunk broken off.* Capt.
Francis Saunders, died 1679; widow Catherine,
died 1696. *Ledger stone, Gorleston*
An elephant's head erased Argent eared and gorged
with a coronet Or.
    SQUIRE, William, of London, 1584. *Grants &
Certificates (Harl. MS 1,359)*
An elephant's head erased Argent ducally gorged
Or.
    SQUIRE, of Lavenham. *Davy, A., church*
An elephant's head erased Argent ducally gorged
Gules.
    SQUIRE. *MS Ordinary of Arms, fo. 151**
An elephant's head erased ducally gorged.
    SQUIRE, Rev. John, M.A., Rector for 33 years,
died 1763. *Her.Suff.Ch., Floor slab partly
hidden by choir stalls, Lavenham*
An elephant's head erased Gules ducally gorged Or
charged on the neck with a martlet Sable.
    VERNON. 'William Vernon' *MS Knight's
Visitations, Essex*.* [Drawn as the usual boar's
head, but with a trunk]
An elephant's head erased Gules ducally gorged Or.
    VERNON. 'William Vernon' *MS Philpot's
Visitations, Essex*.* [Drawn with ears like a
talbot]

ELK

An elk's head [unfinished, bottom of neck not
drawn].
    ORD. *MS Ordinary of Arms, fo. 253**
An elk's head erased Argent attired Or.
    ORD. *MS Martin's Crests*
An elk's head couped Proper.
    ORD, of Fornham, Hopton House. *Davy, A.
Washbourne*
An elk's head Proper.
    ORD. Capt. William St. George Ord, of Fornham
House, Suff. *Fairbairn. Burke, L.G. 1853* and
1900 eds.**

FOX

A fox's head Azure.
    WALLER, of Ramsholt. *Davy, A., Ramsholt and
St. Stephen's Ipswich churches. Washbourne*,
'Suff.' Fairbairn*, 'of Boklesham [sic
Bucklesham], Suff.'*
A fox's head.
    ZOUCHE. *MS Martin's Crests*

FOX'S HEAD, Couped

A fox's head couped Argent.
    BRAHAM, of Ash, Wickham Skeith. *Bokenham*
A fox's head couped per pale Or and Azure.
    CLOPTON, of Long Melford. *MS Knight's
Visitations, Suff.**
A fox's head couped at the neck Azure.
    WALLER, of Bucklesham. *Visitation 1664–8*

FOX'S HEAD, Erased

A fox's head erased Vert bezanty.
    BAMBOROUGH. 'Bamburgh' *MS Martin's Crests*
A fox's head erased Argent.
    BARRY, of Syleham. *Bokenham*
A fox's head erased Argent collared Gules.

BARRY, of Syleham. *Davy, A.*
A fox's head erased Sable.
    BELET, of Elmswell, Buxhall. *Davy, A. (Edms.)*
A ? fox's head erased.
    CUMBERLAND, of Bury. *Davy, A.*
A fox's head erased Or.
    EDWIN. *Davy, A., St. Mary Tower, Ipswich
church*
A fox's head erased Or.
    GOWER. *MS Martin's Crests*
A fox's head erased Gules.
    HIGHGATE. 'Heygate or Hyegate, Raynold, of
Ferring [*sic* Feering], co. Essex'; Confirmation by
Sir C. Barker, Garter, 9 Nov. 1549; 'Copied from
the original 19 March 1687/8, per H. St. George,
Clar.' *Grants & Certificates (Add. MS 14,295)*
'his crest a fox hed rased g/ to Riagnold heigat of
fferryng in Essex'
    HIGHGATE. 'Heigat' *MS Alphabet of Crests,
fo. 59*
A fox's head erased Gules.
    HIGHGATE. 'Heygatt' *MS Knight's Visitations,
Suff.** 'Reynolde Hygate' *MS Knight's Visitations,
Essex*. Bokenham*
A fox's head erased – collared Or.
    MOORE, of Stanstead. *Davy, A.*
A fox's head erased Proper.
    REASON, of Hadleigh. *Davy, A.*
A fox's head erased gorged with a collar charged
with three roundels and charged on the neck with a
martlet (for difference).
    REYNOLDS, RAYNOLDE, of East Bergholt, Shotley.
Visitation 1561 (MS G. 7*)
A fox's head erased Sable gorged with a collar
rimmed Or and charged with three roundels – on the
neck a martlet (for difference).
    REYNOLDS, REIGNOLDE, of Shotley. *Visitation
1561 (MS Iveagh Copy*)*
A fox's head erased Sable collared Or charged with
three torteaux.
    REYNOLDS, REIGNOLDE, of Shotley, East
Bergholt. *Visitation 1561 (ed. Metcalfe), a
martlet for difference. Harl. 772*. Davy, A.
Washbourne, 'Reynolds, of Shotley, Suff. On the
neck a martlet'.*
A fox's head erased Sable collared Or.
    REYNOLDS. *Fairbairn, 'of Belstead, Suff.'*
A fox's head erased Argent gutty Vert.
    RUSH, RUCHE, of Ipswich, Orford, Chapmans [in
Orford]. *Harl. 772*. Davy, A. Washbourne*,
'Rushe, Suff.' Fairbairn, 'Rushe, Suff. . . . gutty
d'olive'*
A wolf's, or fox's, head erased ducally gorged.
    SMYTH, John, Gent., died 1650. *Martin's Church
Notes (Frag.Gen. IX. 78), St. Mary's, Bury*
A wolf's, or fox's, head erased Argent ducally
gorged Or.
    SMITH, of Bury, Tuddenham. *Davy, A., St.
Mary's church, Bury*
A fox's head erased Sable fretty Or collared Or.
    STYLE. *Bokenham*
A fox's head erased Azure.
    WALLER, of Bucklesham, Parham, Wortham,
Ramsholt. *Davy, A.*
A fox's head erased Gules and Blue [*sic*] per pale
gutty d'Or.
    WIGSTON, WIGSON, of Horsecroft in Horringer.
Proc.S.I.A. IV. 39
A fox's head erased in its mouth a wing.
    WILKINSON, Dr. H.W., Principal of Magdalen
Hall, Oxford, died 1690. *Her.Suff.Ch., Floor*

slab, Milden. (Wilkinson of co. Derby, A fox's head couped per pale Vert and Or holding in the mouth a dragon's wing Argent)

A wolf's, or fox's, head erased gorged with a ducal coronet.

YOUNG, of Bradfield Combust. *Davy, A.*

A fox's head erased ducally gorged.

YOUNG. 'Arthur Young' *Bookplate*

GOAT

A goat's head Argent.

ANTHONY. *Davy, A.*

A goat's head Or.

ANTHONY. *Davy, A.*

A goat's head Gules.

ANTHONY. *Davy, A. Fairbairn*, 'Antony, Antonie, Suff.' E.A. Misc. 1918, 15*

A goat's head Argent attired Or.

CHESTER. Heneage Charles Bagot Chester, of Henstead Hall and Southwold, died 1912. *Her.Suff.Ch., Wall tablet, Henstead. The crest of Bagot*

A goat's, or antelope's, head.

COLMAN, of Hacheston, Laxfield, Brent Eleigh. *Davy, A.*

A goat's head Argent.

COLMAN, of Ipswich. *E.A.N. & Q. IX. 168, Monument, St. Lawrence church.*

A goat's head Sable bezanty armed and maned Gules.

COOKE. *Davy, A.*

A goat's head Sable.

COPINGER, of Lavenham, Buxhall. *MS Fairfax*

A goat's head Argent attires and beard Or.

LAMPLOW, LAMPLUGH. *Davy, A.*

'to his Crest a gotts hed or/ is of Yorkshᵣ'

WARD. *MS Alphabet of Crests, fo. 139.* [The arms given are those of Ward or Warde, of Ipswich and Lidgate]

GOAT'S HEAD, Couped

A goat's head couped Argent armed Or.

BARDWELL, BERDEWELL, BURDWELL, of Bardwell, Tostock. *Davy, A., Bardwell church. Her.Suff.Ch., Glass, Bardwell*

A goat's head couped Sable armed Sable.

COPINGER. 'Thomas Copinger of buxall' *Harl. 772**

A goat's head couped Sable without a beard.

COPINGER. 'Coppinger, of Buxhall' *Bokenham*

A goat's head couped Azure attired Or.

JACKSON, of Suffolk. *Davy, A.*

A goat's head couped Argent.

METHOLD, of Stonham. *Sharpe*

A goat's head couped Argent attired Or.

SIDLEY. *MS Martin's Crests*

GOAT'S HEAD, Erased [Alphabetically by name]

A goat's head erased Sable armed Argent ducally gorged Argent.

BACON. 'Nicholas Bacon of Shrobland in Suffolk Esquier' *MS Lilly's Visitation of Suffolk**

A goat's head erased Argent armed Or.

BARDWELL, of Bardwell, Tostock. *Davy, A. (Gage)*

A goat's head erased Gules attired Or.

BARDWELL, of Bardwell. *Copinger. I*

A goat's head erased Argent gorged with a mural crown Gules.

BEWICKE. Master of Bungay School. *Davy, A.*

A goat's head erased Argent gorged with a mural coronet Gules.

BEWICKE, Rev. Thomas, died 1842; widow Sarah, died 1849. *Her.Suff.Ch., Wall tablet, St. Mary's, Bungay*

A goat's head erased Sable.

COPINGER, COPPINGER, of Buxhall. *Davy, A. Copinger Family, 399*

A goat's head erased Or.

COPPINGER. *Fairbairn*, 'Suff.'*

A goat's, or antelope's, head erased Argent.

FAULKES, of Exning, Mildenhall. *Davy, A.*

A goat's head erased.

FAULKES, FOLKES, FFOLKES, of Cheveley co. Cambs., Mildenhall. *Muskett. II. 106 (Cole's MSS XXI., fo. 37)*

An Indian goat's head erased.

FOWKE. 'Eliz. w. of Will Fowke esq. 22 March 1820 ag. 66' *Partridge, 79 (Darby, 1826), Palisaded tomb, Chelsworth churchyard*

An Indian goat's head erased Argent.

FOWKE, of Chelsworth, Weston Market. *Davy, A. (Edms.), Chelsworth churchyard. Her.Suff.Ch., Altar tomb, Chelsworth churchyard. Hatched [sic]*

'upon his healme on a wreath silver and azure a goates head Razy purple plated Silver, horned and bearded gold holding in his mouth an aglington branche verte, the flowers silver'

FULMERSTON, Richard, of Thetford, co. Norfolk, Esq.; Grant of Arms and Crest by Gilbert Dethick, Garter, 15 June 1556. *Miscellaneous Grants (H.S.) I. 86–7 (MS Queen's Coll. 140, No. 69)*

A goat's head erased Purpure semy of plates armed Or in the mouth a rose slip Proper with two roses Argent.

FULMERSTON. 'Tulmerstone [sic] Richard, of Thetford, co. Norf., Esq.; Grant by Sir G. Dethick, Garter, 15 June 2 & 3 Phil. and Mary [1555/6]. *Grants & Certificates (Harl. MS 1,359)*

A goat's head erased Purpure charged with roundels Argent armed and bearded Or holding in his mouth a spray of ?eglantine Vert flowered Argent.

FULMERSTON. *Visitation 1561 (MS G. 7*)*

'his crest a gots hed rased purpure/ plated horned and berded or/ holding in his mouth by the branche Vert ij ar/ [sic] Sʳ Rychᵈ ffulmerston'

FULMERSTON. *MS Alphabet of Crests, fo. 40b*

A goat's head erased Azure plated Argent horned and bearded Or holding in his mouth an eglantine branch Vert flowered Argent.

FULMERSTON, of Thetford manor. *Martin's Thetford, 286. Monument, St. Mary the Less church*

A goat's head erased Azure platy horned and hoofed Or holding in his mouth a rose branch Vert flowered Argent.

FULMERSTON, FULMESTON, of Thetford. *Davy, A.*

A goat's head erased Or attired Sable holding in his mouth a holly branch Vert fructed Gules.

FUTTER, of Stanton. 'Robert Futter' *MS Knight's Visitations, Norf.*, 'a branch Vert'. 'Robart Futter' MS Philpot's Visitations, Norf.*, attired Or. Davy, A. Washbourne, 'Norf. and Suff.' Fairbairn, 'Norf. and Suff.'*

A goat's head erased Gules.

GOATE, Edward, died 1803. *Her.Suff.Ch., Wall monument, Brent Eleigh.*

A goat's head erased Ermine gorged by a chaplet Vert roses Gules.

HALEY. John Haley, of co. Middlesex; Grant by Sir W. Dugdale, Garter and Sir H. St. George, Norroy, 27 January 1679. *Grants & Certificates (Add. MS 14,831)*

A goat's head erased Argent gorged with a chaplet Gules.

HALEY, of Ipswich. *Davy, A.*

A goat's head erased Argent attired Or.

HAY. Lord Thomas Hay. Rector of Rendlesham. *Davy, A.*

A goat's head erased Argent attired Or.

LAMPLOW, LAMPLUGH. *Davy, A.*

A goat's head erased.

MACHIN, Thomas, Surgeon, died 1784; son William Machin, died 1797. *Her.Suff.Ch., Tombstones on south side of church, Pakefield*

A goat's head erased Or.

METHWOLD. 'Methwold, . . ., who died 2 March 1653–4. No authority given' *Grants & Certificates (Harl. MS 5,869)*

A goat's head erased Argent.

METHWOLD, METHOLD. Rector of Stonham Aspal. *Davy, A., church*

A goat's head erased Proper.

METHOLD. Rector of Stonham Aspal and Wetheringsett, died 1836. Of Hepworth. *Crisp's Visitation. I. 145–7, Pedigree*

A goat's head erased Argent attire and beard Sable.

METHWOLD, of Norfolk. *Muskett. I. 292 (Harl. MS 1552)*

A goat's head erased Argent armed and crined Sable and charged with an escallop.

METHOLD. Frederick J. Methold, Thorn Court, Bury St. Edmunds. *Fairbairn*

A goat's head erased per fesse Or and Azure.

RAPER, of Clopton. *Davy, A.*

A goat's head erased Argent horns and beard Azure gorged with a crest coronet Gules.

THURSTON, THRUSTON. John Thruston, of Hoxne, co. Suffolk, gent.; Grant by W. Dethick, Garter, 5 May 1573. *Grants & Certificates (Stowe MS 676, fo. 42). Apparently after this grant was made it was discovered that the family was entitled to an older coat – Confirmed by Dethick, 10 February 1586/7* [See Bird, Crane or Stork]

A goat's head erased.

WRIGHT, of Ipswich, Bury. *Bokenham. Davy, A.*

A goat's head erased.

WRIGHT, Abraham, Gent., died 1702; widow Elizabeth, died 1705. *Martin's Church Notes, Frag.Gen. IX. 103*

HARE

A hare's head erased Or.

HAREWELL, of Lt. Blakenham, Felsham. *Davy, A. Washbourne, 'Suff. and Worcs.' In Addenda II. Fairbairn, 'Suff. and Worcs.'*

HORSE

A horse's head per pale bay and Argent on its head two feathers tips Azure bottoms Or counterchanged.

BUTTS, of Redgrave, Levington. *Davy, A.*

A horse's head caparisoned all Proper from the top of the head issuant two feathers the dexter Or the sinister Sable.

BUTTS. *Washbourne, 'Suff.' Fairbairn, 'Suff.'*

A horse's head Argent armed and bridled Or on the head a plume of three feathers Argent and Or.

BUTTS. Fairbairn, 'Suff. and Norf.'

A nag's head Sable bridled Or.

COLLINS, COLLYNGS. *Washbourne, 'Suff.' Fairbairn, 'Collyngs, Suff.'*

A nag's head Ermine.

COLT. *Washbourne, 'Suff.'*

A horse's head Or.

DENARDESTON. *Davy, A., Clare church*

A horse's head between two wings displayed.

FLACK, William, died 1766. *Her.Suff.Ch., Memorial tablet, Chattisham. Recorded by Farrer in 1899, but not found 1978*

A nag's head.

HEIGHAM. 'Sir John Heigham, benefactor of this church' *Her.Suff.Ch., Glass, Clare*

A nag's head Argent with his mane flowing Or holding in his mouth a broken spear Or.

JEX, JAQUES, of Lowestoft. *Gillingwater, 336. Fairbairn, 'Jex, Lowestoft, Suff.'*

Out of a wreath of laurel Or a horse's head paly of six Sable and Argent.

LLOYD, LLOYD-ANSTRUTHER, of Hintlesham Hall. *Burke, L.G. 1900 ed.*

A horse's head Argent.

PAVELEY. Sir Walter Paveley, Founder K.G., died 1375. *Stall Plates, plate VI.* [Appears more like an ass's head and is cabossed]

A hind's, or horse's, head.

PAVELEY, of Stutton. *Davy, A.*

A horse's head per chevron Or and Sable.

SMITH. *Fairbairn, 'of Walsham, Suff.'*

A horse's head Argent bridled Gules.

TWENTYMAN. Rector of Elmsett. *Davy, A.*

A horse's head Or gorged with a chaplet Vert.

UNDERWOOD. *MS Martin's Crests, 'Norf.'*

HORSE'S HEAD, Couped

A horse's head couped of a bay colour armed on the face and neck with a spike in the forehead Argent and Or on the head two feathers Azure and Or.

BUTTS. 'Sr. Will. Buttes of Tornage' *MS Knight's Visitations, Norf.* 'Sr Wyll Buthe' *MS Philpot's Visitations, Norf.* Spike Or, feathers dexter Or sinister Azure. MS Heraldic Collections, fo. 46*. Head couped 'sorell'*

A bay horse's head couped Proper armoured on the back of the neck Argent with two ostrich feathers one Or one Azure.

BUTTS, of Levington, Brockford. 'Butes' *MS Philpot's Visitations, Norf.* [second given]. *Visitation 1664–8, of Brockford. Davy, A., (Barrett MS 137), Feathers tinctures of sides counterchanged. Of Levington*

A horse's head couped 'baye Cullor' armed on neck and face Argent and Or the chamfron spike Or with two ostrich feathers Or and Azure their tops counterchanged.

BUTTS [under Bacon]. 'Sʳ Buttes Bacon Knight Barronett' *MS Lilly's Visitation of Suffolk*

A bay horse's head couped bridled and comparisoned [*sic* caparisoned] Or and Azure on his head a plume of feathers Or and Azure his mane adorned with ribbons Or and Azure.

BUTTS, of Mendlesham. *Bokenham*

A horse's head couped Argent.

CHAMBERLAYN. *Banners & Standards* [Drawn more like an ass's head]

A horse's head couped Sable bridled Or.

COLLINGE, of Bury St. Edmunds. *Visitation 1577*

A horse's head couped Sable bridled Or the rein hanging down before with a ring at the end of it.

COLLINGE, COLLINGS, COLLINS, of Bury, Ipswich, Gt. Thornham, Lowestoft. 'Henry Collinge' *MS Philpot's Visitations, Suff.* Maned Or.

[Drawn more like a camel's head.] *MS Fairfax, untinctured. Davy, A.*
A horse's head couped Sable tied with a halter Argent.
    COLLINGE, COLLING, of Bury. *Bokenham*
A colt's head couped Ermine.
    COLT, of Colt's Hall in Cavendish. *Davy, A.*
A horse's head couped Argent.
    DETHICK. 'Delhike' *Wall's Book.* 'Edmond dethyke of Wormgay' *MS Knight's Visitations, Norf.* * 'Sr Geffry Dethike' *MS Philpot's Visitations, Norf.* *
'for his crest a horsse hed copey ar/'
    DETHICK. 'Dethyke of Darbyshyre' *MS Alphabet of Crests, fo. 30*
A horse's head couped Argent.
    FLETCHER, of Hutton in the Forest, co. Camb. *MS Heraldic Alphabet*
A horse's head couped Argent bridled and tasselled – chamfron Or spiked Or.
    HORSEY. *MS Heraldic Collections, fo. 31* *
A horse's head couped Argent maned Or holding in the mouth the butt end of a broken tilting spear Or.
    JAKES, JAQUES. John Jakes or Jaques, of London. *Grants & Certificates (Harl. MS 1,359; Stowe MS 670)*
A horse's head couped Argent bridled and maned Or charged on the neck with a bezant [all] between two wings Or.
    MILNER. *Fairbairn, 'of Sefton Lodge, Newmarket'*
A horse's head couped at the shoulders.
    MOUNTJOYS, DE   Isaac De Remy De Mountjoys. *Her.Suff.Ch., Ledger stone outside north transept door, St. Margaret's, Ipswich*
A horse's head couped Argent.
    REDMAN. *MS Martin's Crests*
A horse's head couped Argent.
    ROXBURGH. 'Sir Francis Roxburgh, Q.C., J.P., The Beach House, Aldeburgh, Suff.' *Fairbairn*

HORSE'S HEAD, Erased [Alphabetically by name]

A horse's head erased Ermines.
    CLARKE, of Ipswich, Claydon, Norton, Friston. *Visitation 1664–8. Davy, A.*
A horse's head erased Sable.
    CLARKE, of Ipswich, Claydon, Norton, Friston. *Davy, A. Washbourne, 'Suff.' Fairbairn* *, 'Suff.'*
A horse's head erased and bridled Proper.
    COOKSON, of Ipswich. *Crisp's Visitation. III. 129*
A horse's head erased per fesse couped Or and Sable.
    CRABTREE, of Halesworth. *Davy, A.*
A horse's head erased Argent.
    DETHICK, of Framsden. *Davy, A.*
A horse's head erased Argent.
    FLETCHER, of Ipswich. *Sharpe*
A horse's head erased Argent.
    HEIGHAM, HIGHAM, of Barrow, Cavenham, Rougham, Gislingham, Hunston, Gazeley, Higham Green, Wickhambrook. *Visitation 1561 (MSS G. 7* and Iveagh Copy*) and (ed. Howard) II. 210*, 219*, 234, 310*, Bookplate.* Sir Clement Heigham, Brass of 1570. *Cotman's Suffolk Brasses plate 28*, in Barrow church. MS Heigham Pedigree Roll, 1579*; Corder MS 87.* 'John Higham of Barrowhall in Com Suffolke Esquier' *MS Lilly's Visitation of Suffolk*.* *Bokenham.* Gage (Thingoe). *Davy, A.* Burke, L.G. 1853 and 1900 eds. *Proc.S.I.A. VIII. 223. Fairbairn*, 'of Hunston Hall, Suff.' *Copinger. VII.*

Thomas Heigham, died 1630. *Her.Suff.Ch., Effigy monument, Wickhambrook.* Arthur Heigham, Esq., died 1787; Rev. Henry Heigham, of Hunston Hall, Patron and Incumbent of Hunston, died 1834. *Wall tablets and Hatchment, Hunston*
A horse's head erased Or.
    HEIGHAM, George, R.N., died in action 1794. *Her.Suff.Ch., Wall tablet in the tower, St. Mary's, Bury*
A horse's head erased Or plumed Azure.
    HORSEY, of Bury. *Davy, A.*
A horse's head Argent erased Gules maned Or holding in the mouth a broken spear Argent headed Or.
    JAQUES, JEX, of Lowestoft. *Davy, A.*
A horse's head Argent maned Or erased Gules holding in the mouth a broken tilting spear Or.
    JAQUES, JEX, of Lowestoft. *Crisp's Visitation. XIX. 37*
A nag's head erased Sable.
    KITSON, of Hengrave. *Bokenham*
A horse's head erased Argent.
    LLOYD, of Hintlesham. *Davy, A., Church hatchment. E.A.N. & Q. XIII. 86.* Capt. Heneage Lloyd, died 1776. *Her.Suff.Ch., Hatchment, Hintlesham*
A horse's head erased Argent.
    MEYNELL, of Thurlow, Lt. Blakenham. *Davy, A.*
A horse's head erased Azure.
    MILLER. Major-General Charles H. Miller, C.B., D.S.O., died 1974. *Her.Suff.Ch., Glass, Badingham*
A horse's head erased per pale indented Argent and Azure.
    PAGE. *MS Heraldic Collections, fo. 78a* *
A horse's head Sable erased Gules crined Or.
    PARTRIDGE. *MS Knight's Visitations, Suff.* *
Robart Partrige' *MS Philpot's Visitations, Suff.* *
A horse's head erased per fesse Sable and Gules crined Or.
    PARTRIDGE, of Finborough. *Visitation 1577. Bokenham. Davy, A. Washbourne, 'Glouc. and Suff.' Fairbairn, 'of co. Glouc. and Finbarrow [sic], Suff.' Muskett. II. 161*
A horse's head erased.
    RUSH, of Ipswich, Orford. *Davy, A., St. Stephen's in Ipswich and Orford churches*
A horse's head erased Vert gutty Argent.
    RUSH. *Fairbairn, 'Rushe, Suff.'*
A horse's head erased Sable.
    SLADE, of Ipswich. *Davy, A., St. Clement's church*
A horse's head erased.
    SMEAR, of Gislingham. Incumbent of Wyverstone, 1704. *E.A. Misc. 1920, 108*
'And to his Creaste vppon the heaulme, on a wreath or and sable a horffe hedd razed, par cheveron unde golde and sables, mantelled gules doubled argent'
    SMITH, SMYTH. 'Thomas Smyth of owld buckenham in the countie of Norff. gentilman'; Grant of Arms and Crest by 'Will hervy als Clarenceulx King of Armes, the vvᵗʰ of Auguste, 1562' *Original Grant, in my possession; Corder MS 80*
A horse's head erased per chevron nebuly Or and Sable.
    SMITH, SMYTH, of Helmingham. *MS Philpot's Visitations, Norf.* * Davy, A., 'Granted 1563 [sic] to Thos. Smith, of old Buckenham, Norf.' Fairbairn, 'Smyth, of Walsham & Old Buckenham, Norf.'*
A horse's head erased Gules between two wings

expanded Or pellety.

TALMACHE, TOLLEMACHE, of Helmingham,
Bentley, Gt. Fakenham. *Visitation 1561 (MSS
G. 7*, Maned Or; Iveagh Copy*) and (ed.
Metcalfe). Harl. 772**. 'Lyonell Talmage of
Bentley' *MS Knight's Visitations, Suff.** 'Sr
Lyonell Tallemache Knight Barronett' *MS Lilly's
Visitation of Suffolk*. Visitation 1664–8**

A horse's head erased Argent between two wings
Sable.

TOLLEMACHE. 'Tolmach' *MS Martin's Crests*

A horse's head erased Argent between two wings Or
pellety.

TOLLEMACHE, Earl of Dysart. Of Bentley,
Helmingham. *Davy, A. Washbourne, 'Talmach,
Suff.'* 'Tollemache, Baron, Helmingham Hall,
Suff.' *Fairbairn**. Tollemache of Helmingham.
*Her.Suff.Ch., Monuments and Tablets,
Helmingham*

A horse's head erased Sable semy of mullets Or.

TRYON. *Bokenham*

LEOPARD

On a leopard's head a falcon rising belled all Or.

AUSTEN, AUSTYN. *MS Ordinary of Arms,
fo. 166**

On a leopard's head Azure a falcon Or.

AUSTEN, of Chelsworth. *Davy, A.*

A leopard's head Gules.

CHARLTON. *MS Heraldic Alphabet*

A leopard's head Argent.

COOKE. 'Sr. James, South Elmham' *Bokenham*

A leopard's head Or pierced through the cheeks with
a sword chevronwise (broken) Proper.

FITCH, FYTCH. 'Fytch' *MS Martin's Crests*

A leopard's head.

HARRINGTON, Joseph, died 1758; Others.
Her.Suff.Ch., Floor slab, Lavenham

A leopard's head Gules between two wings Or.

HARVEY, HERVEY. *MS Ordinary of Arms, fo. 85**

A leopard's head Or gorged with a collar Azure
rimmed Or and charged with three bezants.

PAYNE. *Davy A.*

A leopard's head and neck affronty Or.

SLAPP, of Botesdale. *Davy, A.*

A leopard's head Or charged on the neck with a
fleur-de-lis Gules.

SMYETH, of Suffolk. *Davy, A.*

LEOPARD'S HEAD, Cabossed

A leopard's face Or transfixed by two crossed
swords in saltire points upward blades Argent hilts
and pomels Or.

BUNBURY. Sir Thomas Charles Bunbury, Bart.,
died 1821. *Her.Suff.Ch., Wall tablet, Mildenhall.*
Lt. Gen. Sir Henry Bunbury, Bart., died 1860; Sir
Charles Bunbury, Bart., died 1886. *Monumental
and Brass tablets, Gt. Barton.* Sir Henry
Bunbury. *Glass, St. Mary's, Bury.* 'Henry Edward
Bunbury' [Bart., died 1860]. *Bookplates*,
untinctured*

A leopard's face Gules jessant a fleur-de-lis Or.

CANTELUPE, CANTELOW, of Finborough.
Davy, A.

A leopard's face Or.

CHARLTON. *Sharpe*

A leopard's face cabossed Argent.

COOKE, of Bury, St. James South Elmham.
MS Fairfax

A leopard's face Argent.

EADE, EADES, of Saxmundham, Cotton,
Badingham, Metfield. 'Rev. John Eade, c.1734–

death 1811, son of Thomas Eade, farmer, of
Saxmundham; graduated from Emmanuel Coll.,
Cambridge, 1756 (B.A.), Vicar of Tannington
1772 and Rector of Cotton 1793, both until
death.' *Bookplate*, (Lee's British Bookplates,
92) Davy, A. Washbourne*, 'Eades, Middx. &
Suff.'*

A leopard's head cabossed Or in the mouth a sword
Proper hilt Gules.

FITCH, of Ipswich, 1840 *Davy, A.*

A leopard's face per pale Argent and Sable between
two wings counterchanged.

GURDON, of Assington. *Davy, A., 'three wings'
[sic error]. Muskett. I. 273 (Harl. MS 1560)*

A leopard's face between two wings Sable.

GURDON, Robert, died 1577; son John Gurdon,
died 1623. *Her.Suff.Ch., Effigy monument,
Assington*

A leopard's face Argent.

HARRINGTON, of Clare, Lavenham. *Davy, A.,
both churches*

A leopard's face affronty Argent.

HARRINGTON, James, died 1788. *Her.Suff.Ch.,
Wall tablet, Clare*

A leopard's face Or.

HASELEY, HASLEY, of Suffolk. *Davy, A.*

A leopard's face between two wings erect.

IMPEY. Physician at Gt. Yarmouth, died 1852.
E.A.N. & Q. IV. 269

A leopard's face Sable between two wings Or.

IMPEY, Alfred, Esq., M.D., Physician in Gt.
Yarmouth for 11 years, died 1852. *Her.Suff.Ch.,
Altar tomb in churchyard, North Cove*

A leopard's face Sable crowned Or.

LEE, of Suffolk, Coddenham. *MS Fairfax*

A leopard's face Gules surmounted by an eagle's
claw erased Or.

PARSONS, of Hadleigh. *Visitation 1664–8. MS
Heraldic Collections, fo. 20*, claw untinctured*

A leopard's face Sable in front of three crosses as in
the arms (crosses calvary botonny) Argent one in
pale and two in saltire.

PECKHAM, Piers, of London; Confirmation by
Roger Machado, Richmond alias Clarenceux.
Clarenceux 30 June 1494. *Grants & Certificates
(Harl. MS 1,359)*

LEOPARD'S HEAD, Couped

A leopard's head couped.

BRAHAM, Anthony, son of John Braham, gent.,
died 1713, aged 41. *Partridge, 97 (Darby,
1828), palisaded altar tomb in churchyard,
Wickham Skeith*

A leopard's head couped Azure purfled Or.

BREWSTER, of Wrentham. *Visitation 1664–8*

A leopard's head couped at the neck and reguardant
Argent ducally collared and lined Or.

CATELYN, of Wolverstone. *Davy, A.*

A leopard's head couped collared and ringed.

MEENE, of Weybread. *Davy, A., churchyard*

A leopard's head couped at the neck and affronty.

MEEN, James, gent., died 1751; widow Elizabeth,
died 1765. *Partridge, 113 (Darby, 1825),
Weybread churchyard*

A leopard's head couped at the shoulders Argent
collared Sable.

MYNNE, of Ilketshall St. Margaret's. *Bokenham*

A leopard's head couped at the neck Proper.

TRIVETT. *Washbourne, 'Suss. and Suff.'
Fairbairn*, 'Sussex and Suff.'*

LEOPARD'S HEAD, Erased

A leopard's head erased.
BREWSTER, of Wrentham, Brantham House, Ipswich. 'Humphrey Brewster, Esq.' *Brass of 1593 in Wrentham church. Cotman's Suffolk Brasses, plate 35*, p.23. Crisp's Visitation XIII. 17*

A leopard's head erased Azure purfled Or.
BREWSTER, of Wrentham. *Davy, A., church. Burke, L.G. 1853 ed.*

A leopard's head erased affronty Argent.
COOKE, of Langham, South Elmham St. James. *Visitation 1577. MS Knight's Visitation, Suff, fo. 106b*, 'of Bury'. 'Wyll Cooke' MS Philpot's Visitations, Suff*. Visitation 1664–8*

A leopard's head guardant erased at the neck.
DAWSON. *Davy, A.*

A leopard's head guardant erased Or semy on the neck with hurts pomeis and torteaux.
FRAMLINGHAM. 'James Fframlyngham de debenhm armyger Suff' *Banners & Standards**

A leopard's head guardant erased Or semy of roundels Azure and Gules.
FRAMLINGHAM. 'Framingham of Norfolk' *MS Ordinary of Arms, fo. 170**

A leopard's, or lion's, head guardant erased Or semy on the neck with roundels Azure Vert and Gules.
FRAMLINGHAM. *Davy, A.*

A leopard's head affronty erased Azure ducally gorged chained and ringed Or.
HARVEY, HERVEY. 'Sr George Harve' *MS Knight's Visitations, Suff.**

A leopard's head erased Proper collared Or.
JOHNSON, of Bury, Saxmundham, Bildeston, Kelsale. *Davy, A. Bildeston, 13. Fairbairn, 'of Bury, Saxmundham and Bildeston, Suff.'*

A leopard's head erased Azure.
KETT, of Henstead. *Davy, A.*

A leopard's head guardant and erased Sable charged with torteaux [sic].
ROBERTS. *Davy, A. Washbourne, 'of Ess., etc. Head Argent'*

LION

A lion's head affronty.
CAMPBELL, of Ipswich. *Davy, A. Washbourne*, 'Suff.'*

A lion's head affronty Proper.
CAMPBELL. *Fairbairn, 'Suff.'*

A lion's head per pale Vert and Sable charged with an escallop Argent.
CLAY, of Bury. *Davy, A. (Edms.)*

A lion's face [sic] between two wings Proper.
COKEREL, of Ashfield. *Davy, A.*

A lion's head Erminois murally crowned Gules.
HART, Sir Percival. *Davy, A.*

A lion's head guardant Argent collared Sable.
MYNN, of Cratfield. *Davy, A.*

A lion's head Or pierced through the side of the head with an arrow in fesse the point coming out at the mouth Or feathered and headed Argent.
PEAKE, of Gt. Thornham. *Davy, A.*

Issuing from a tower Or a lion's head Sable.
SHEPPARD, of Mendlesham, Campsey Ash. *Visitation 1664–8. Bokenham.* John Sheppard of Ash, died 1669; son John Sheppard, died 1671. *Partridge, 129 (Darby, 1825), Campsey Ash churchyard. Untinctured. Davy, A. Burke, L.G. 1853 ed. Fairbairn, 'Shepard, Mendlesham, Suff.'*

Issuing from a triple-turreted tower a lion's head.
SHEPPARD. Ann (Coell), wife of Edmund Sheppard, junr., died 1679; Edmund Sheppard, senr., gent., died 1676; Edmund Sheppard, Esq., died 1708; John Sheppard, Esq., died 1747. *Her.Suff.Ch., Ledger stones, Mendlesham*

LION'S HEAD, Couped

A lion's head couped Argent semy of hurts and crowned Or.
HENLEY, Robert, of Hendlegh, co. Somerset, High Sheriff 1613. Patent 26 February 1612. *Grants & Certificates (Stowe MSS 706 and 707; Harl. MSS 1,359 and 1,441)*

A lion's head couped Or thereon a cap of estate Azure turned up Ermine the points forward.
HOLMES. 'Holme' *MS Heraldic Alphabet*

A lion's head couped Or thereon a cap of maintenance Azure turned up –.
HOLMES. 'Hulme' *MS ex-Taylor Coll.* Washbourne*, 'turned up Ermine'*

A lion's head couped Gules charged with a cross crosslet fitchy Or.
MAUDE. Rector of Hasketon. *Davy, A.*

A lion's head couped Gules (may be gutty Or).
MAY. Sir Francis H. May, of Clare Priory, died 1922. *Her.Suff.Ch., Wall tablet, Clare*

A lion's head couped Gules charged with a bend Ermine.
MILBANKE. Rt. Hon. Ralph G.N. Milbanke, D.L., Baron Wentworth, of Nettlestead, Suffolk. *Fairbairn*

A lion's head couped at the neck affronty Argent collared Sable rimmed and studded –.
MYNN, of Cratfield. *Visitation 1664–8**

A lion's head couped Ermine ducally crowned Or.
PECHE. 'Syr John Peche, knyght' *Banners & Standards**

A lion's head couped Or vomiting flames of 'fier' Proper.
WAKEMAN, of Kelsale. *Gloucestershire Visitation, 1623 (H.S.) 174*

LION'S HEAD, Erased [Alphabetically by name]

A lion's head erased Gules in the mouth a quatrefoil Vert.
ANGERSTEIN, of Brandon. *Davy, A.*

A lion's head erased Gules collared and lined Argent charged on the neck with a cinquefoil Argent.
BALAM. *Davy, A.*

A lion's head erased Gules collared and lined Or charged on the neck with a cinquefoil Argent.
BALAM. *Fairbairn, 'Norf. and Suff.'*

A lion's head erased Or discharging from his mouth a trefoil slipped Argent and charged on the neck with a cross paty Sable.
BARLEE, of Worlingworth, Wrentham, Framlingham. *Davy, A.*

A lion's head erased Argent.
BENJAFIELD, BENEVILE, of Bury. *Davy, A.*

A lion's head erased Gules charged with a bezant.
BENNET, 'of Camb.' *MS Martin's Crests*

A lion's head erased Or gutty Azure crowned per pale Argent and Gules.
BRANDON. 'Syr Charles Brandon, Vycount Lysle' *Banners & Standards** [as badges]. 'Brandon Duke of Suffolke' *Wall's Book* 'his crest a lyons hede rased or/ crowned p pale ar/ g/ the hede dropey b.'

A lion's head erased Or gutty Sable crowned per pale Argent and Gules.
BRANDON. 'Charles Brandon Duke of Suff' *MS Alphabet of Crests, fo. 7*

A lion's head erased Or gutty Sable crowned per pale Argent and Gules.

BRANDON, Charles. Duke of Suffolk. *MS Ordinary of Arms, fo. 25**
A lion's head erased Or gutty de larmes crowned per pale Argent and Gules.
BRANDON, Duke of Suffolk. Of Westhorpe. *Bokenham. MS Martin's Crests*
A lion's head erased Or ducally crowned per fesse Argent and Gules.
BRANDON, Duke of Suffolk. Of Westhorpe, Henham, West Stowe. *Davy, A.*
A lion's head erased Or gutty Sable crowned with a ducal coronet party per fesse Argent and Gules.
BRANDON. *Washbourne, 'Suff.' Fairbairn, 'Suff.'*
A lion's head erased Or.
BRANSBY, of Ipswich. *Davy, A.*
A lion's head erased.
BROWNE. Rev. Lancelot R. Browne, Rector of Kelsale and Carlton for 58 years, died 1868. *Her.Suff.Ch., Wall tablet, Kelsale*
A lion's head erased Argent.
BURGHILL, of Bungay. *Visitation 1664–8. Bokenham. Davy, A. Washbourne*, 'Suff.' Fairbairn*, 'Suff. and Wales'*
A lion's head erased.
CADOGAN. Lt. Col. Hon. Henry Cadogan, killed at Battle of Vittoria, 1813. *Her.Suff.Ch., Wall tablet, Santon Downham*
A lion's head erased Or.
CARTER, of Woodbridge, Melton, Kelsale, Sudbury, Tunstall. *Sharpe. Davy, A., Tunstall church. E.A.N. & Q. IV. 225. E.A. Misc. 1910, 68. Untinctured.* Rev. Samuel Carter, A.M., Incumbent of three Norfolk parishes, died 1832. *Her.Suff.Ch., Monument, Worlingham*
A lion's head erased reguardant.
CARTER. Bessy, Countess of Rochford, married, secondly, Rev. Philip Carter. She died 1746. *Her.Suff.Ch., Ledger stone in chancel, Tunstall*
A lion's head erased Argent langued Gules.
CHEVALLIER, of Aspal, Badingham, Ellough, Cransford. *Davy, A. Fiske, 180* Crisp's Visitation. XX. 8, Pedigree.* Clement Chevallier, Gent., died 1762; Rev. Temple Chevallier, died 1804. *Her.Suff.Ch., Ledger stone and Hatchment, Aspal.* 'Rev.d Temple Chevallier' *Bookplate**
A lion's head erased Or langued Azure charged on the neck with three trefoils slipped Vert.
CODENHAM. *E.A.N. & Q. (N.S.) II. 207*
A lion's head guardant erased Argent.
COOKE, of South Elmham St. James, Langham. *Davy, A. Washbourne, 'erased and affronty. Of Suff.' Fairbairn, 'Suff.'*
A lion's head erased Azure on the head a chapeau.
COWLING, of South Cove. *Davy, A. (Burke)*
A lioness's head erased Gules collared and chained Or on the neck a cinquefoil Argent (? for difference).
CRESSENOR, of Hawkedon. *Davy, A.*
A lion's head erased.
CROSS, of Bradwell. John Cross gent., of this parish, died 1813. *Partridge, 144 (Darby, 1832), Bradwell churchyard. Davy, A. E.A.N. & Q. II. 326.* Judith, wife of John Cross, died 1789; John Cross, died 1813. *Her.Suff.Ch., Slabs in churchyard, Bradwell. Not found 1979*
A lion's head erased Argent.
CROSS, of Gorleston. *Kett*, pedigree V.*
A lion's head erased Or langued Gules.
CROSS, of Bradwell, Gorleston, Somerleyton. *Misc.Gen. et Her. 5th S. IX. 6–9, Pedigree*

A lion's head erased.
EATON, of Worlington, Newmarket. *Davy, A.*
A lion's head erased Gules.
ELLIS. 'Elley, Elly' *MS Ordinary of Arms, fo. 269**
A lion's head erased Sable.
FAIRFAX, of Bury, Halesworth, Barking, Woodbridge. *MS Fairfax*
A lion's head erased Gules semy of billets Or.
FAIRWEATHER, Josias, of Brisitt [*sic* Bricett], co. Suffolk, late of Henley-on-Thames. Patent 1604. *Grants & Certificates (Add. MS 12,225)*
A lion's head erased Gules billety Or.
FAIRWEATHER, FAYREWEATHER, of Bricett. *Davy, A. Fairbairn, 'of Brissett [sic], Suff.'*
A lion's head erased in the bow of a fetterlock.
FELBRIGGE, of Playford. *Davy, A.*
A lion's head as in the arms [erased Or murally crowned Argent] charged with a collar dancetty Ermine.
FELLOWS, William, of Lincoln's Inn, co. Middlesex, Esq., one of the Masters of the Court of Chancery; Confirmation by Sir H. St. George, Garter and J. Vanbrugh, Clarenceux, 28 July 1713. *Grants & Certificates (Add. MS 14,830; Stowe MS 716)*
A lion's head erased Or crowned Argent gorged with a fesse dancetty Ermine.
FELLOWES. 'Fellows' *MS Martin's Crests*
A lion's head erased Or murally crowned Argent charged with a fesse dancetty Ermine.
FELLOWES, of Nacton. *Crisp's Visitation XV. 113*. Burke, L.G. 1853 ed.*
A lion's head erased Or.
GIBBONS. *Sharpe*
A lion's head erased.
GOATE, John, late of Thrandeston, died 1736; widow Ann (Cullum), died 1739. *Her.Suff.Ch., Ledger stone in churchyard, Redgrave*
A lion's head erased Gules between two palm sprigs erect Vert.
GOODWIN alias GOODEN. *MS Heraldic Alphabet*
A lion's head erased imperially crowned Proper.
GOODYER, of Suffolk. *Davy, A.*
A lion's head erased.
GREENE, of Ipswich. *Northumberland Visitation, 1615 or 1666 (ed. Foster), 60*
A lion's head erased Or collared Gules.
HARRINGTON. *MS Martin's Crests. Two given, one as above, the second 'collar studded gold'. MS ex-Taylor Coll.*, collar buckled and ringed Or*
A lion's head erased gorged and chained Or.
HARRINGTON, of Clare, Lavenham. *Her.Suff.Ch., Funeral board, Layham*
A lion's head erased charged with hurts and ducally crowned Or.
HENLEY. Rector of Rendlesham. *Davy, A.*
A lion's head erased Or.
HENSLOW. Rector of Hitcham. *Davy, A.*
A lion's head erased.
HENSLOW. 'J.S. Henslow' *Bookplate**
A lion's head erased Argent.
HINDE. *Davy, A.*
A lion's head erased Gules.
HOCKMORE or HUCKMORE, of co. Devon. On Keble monument. *Her.Suff.Ch., Wall tablet, Tuddenham. Second of two crests, both called Huckmore – but neither given in Washbourne or Fairbairn*
A lion's head erased Sable charged with a chevron

Or 'as in the arms' ['surmounted by a cross formy fitchy at the foot'].

HOLBROOK, HOLBROOKE, of Suffolk. *Davy, A. Fairbairn*

A lion's head erased Sable charged with a chevron Gules [*sic*].

HOLBROOKE. *Washbourne*, 'Suff.'*

A lion's head erased Or.

HOLMES, of Bury. *Davy, A.*

A lion's head erased Or.

HOUBLON, of Thorndon, Alpheton. *Davy, A.*

On a quatrefoil quarterly Gules and Vert a lion's head erased Argent.

HUNINGES. 'Hunynge' *MS Ordinary of Arms, fo. 19**

'to his crest a lyons hed rased ar/ a bowt his necke ij gemelles and gowted sa/ Langed g/ Willm Hunyngs Clerk of the Counsell in the time of Edward the 6/'

HUNYNGS, HUNYNGS. *MS Alphabet of Crests, fo. 58*

A lion's head erased Argent collared with two bars gemel Sable.

HUNINGES, HONINGS, HONNYNGS, of Norfolk, Suffolk. 'Edwarde Honnynge' *MS Knight's Visitations, Suff.** 'Wylliam Honnyngs' *MS Knight's Visitations, Norf.** 'Edward Honnynges' *MS Philpot's Visitations, Suff.* MS ex-Taylor Coll.**

A lion's head erased Argent collared Sable.

HUNINGES, HONINGS, of Darsham, Eye. *Bokenham. Davy, A. Washbourne, 'Huninges. Ches. & Suff.' Fairbairn*, 'Huninges, Chesh. and Carsam [sic Darsham], Suff.'*

A lion's head erased per pale Argent and Sable collared Gules lined and ringed Or.

HUNT. Vicar of Mildenhall, died 1736. *Davy, A., church*

A lion's head erased.

JEAFFRESON, JEFFRAYSON, JEFFERSON. *MS Heraldic Collections, fo. 53**

A lion's head erased.

JOHNSON. Vicar of Stradbroke, Rector of Horham, died 1782. *Davy, A.*

A lion's, tiger's, or boar's head erased Gules charged on the neck with a crescent.

KEBLE, of Stowmarket, Newton, Halesworth, Tuddenham. *Davy, A., Halesworth and Tuddenham churches*

A lion's head erased Or pierced through with arrows Sable.

KEMOR. *Davy, A.*

A lion's head erased Erminois collared and line Azure.

KENT, John, son of Roger Kent, of Coppenhall, co. Chester; Patent by R. St. George, Norroy, 1615. *Grants & Certificates (Stowe MS 706)*

A lion's head erased Erminois collared lined and ringed Azure.

KENT, Bart., of Fornham. *Davy, A.*

A lion's head erased.

KENT, Bart., of Fornham St. Genevieve, Lackford. *Gage (Thingoe)*

A lion's head erased and collared.

KENT, Bart., of Fornham. *Davy, A. Washbourne*, 'Kent-Egleton, Bart., Suff.' Fairbairn*, 'Kent-Egleton, Bart., Suff.'* William Kent, of Limpsfield in Surrey, died 1708. *Her.Suff.Ch., Ledger stone, Wangford*

A lion's head erased gutty.

KYNASTON. 'Kinaston' *MS Martin's Crests*

A lion's head erased Sable gutty Or.

KYNASTON, Bart., of Risby. *Davy, A.*

A lion's head erased Or charged with a crescent for difference.

LANCASTER. *MS Heraldic Alphabet*

A lion's head erased Argent.

LANCASTER, of Bury. *Davy, A.*

A lion's head erased Argent charged with a crescent.

LANCASTER, of Lidgate, Cattawade. *Davy, A.*

A lion's head erased Gules.

MAY, . . . , draper, of London; Patent by Sir W. Segar, Garter. *Grants & Certificates (Add. MS 12,225)*

A lion's head erased affronty.

MEEN. 'Eliz., relict of James Meen, died 176?3.' *Her.Suff.Ch., Ledger stone in churchyard, Weybread.*

A lion's head erased Or collared and lined Azure ringed Or below the collar three ogresses.

MILDMAY, Sir Walter, descended from Thomas Mildmay, of Chelmsford in Essex; Confirmation of Arms and Grant of Crest by Sir G. Dethick, Garter, 10 November 1558. *Grants & Certificates (Harl. MS 1,359)*

A lion's head erased Sable.

MORTLOCK, of Woodbridge. Rector of Moulton. *Davy, A.*

'to his crest a lyons hed rased sa/ Langed g/ theron iij trefoyles ar Willm Naunton of Suff'

NAUNTON. *MS Alphabet of Crests, fo. 90*

A lion's head erased Gules.

NEWDIGATE. *Sharpe*

A lion's head erased.

PACKARD, Edward, K.B., High Steward of Ipswich and Freeman, died 1932. *Her.Suff.Ch., Wall monument, Bramford*

A lion's head erased Or collared Sable on the collar three cinquefoils Argent with an ermine spot on each petal.

PACKE, of Melton Lodge. *Crisp's Visitation VII. 165**

A lion's head erased Argent.

PALGRAVE, of Ipswich. *Davy, A.*

'Upon ye Heaulme on a wreath Or and vert, A Lyons head rased gold thereon three Gowtes Gules persed through the head with a broad Arrow Golde, feathered silver Mantled vert, doubled or.'

PEAKE, Robert, of Warton, co. Lincoln; Confirmation of Arms and Grant of Crest by William Hervey, Clarenceux, 16th March 1562. *Misc.Gen. et Her. 5th S. IX. 42 (Soc. of Ant. MS 378, fo. 551)*

A lion's head erased Or langued Gules pierced through the neck by an arrow in bend sinister point downwards feathered Argent.

PEAKE. *MS Ordinary of Arms, fo. 77**

A lion's head Or erased Gules pierced through the cheek with the point coming out of the mouth by an arrow Or feathered and headed Argent.

PEAKE. *MS ex-Taylor Coll.**

A lion's head erased issuing flames of fire Proper.

PLAIZ, PLAYZE, of Chelsworth. *Davy, A.*

A lion's head erased.

PREEDY. Lt. Col. Benjamin Preedy, died 1828; widow Isabella (Crick), died 1861. *Her.Suff.Ch., Wall tablet, Lt. Thurlow*

A lion's head erased Argent.

RACKHAM, of Bungay. *Davy, A.*

A lion's head erased Argent.

STEBBING, of Wisset, Brandeston, Kettleburgh, Earl Soham, Woodbridge. *Davy, A.(Edms.) Washbourne*, 'London and Suff.' Proc.S.I.A. II.*

146. *E.A.N. & Q. I. 312. Bildeston, 83.*
Untinctured. Fairbairn*, 'London and Wisset,
Suff.' E.A. Misc. 1924, 79–80. Untinctured.
Henry Stebbing, of Brandeston, died 1721.
Her.Suff.Ch., Slab, Brandeston. Robert Stebbing,
of Eye, died 1758; wife Mary, died 1754. *Ledger*
stone, Eye
A lion's head erased Or.
STEBBING, Samuel, Rose Rouge Pursuivant 1698,
Somerset Herald 1700, died unmarried 1719,
buried at Eltham. Of Woodbridge. *H.S. London*
A lion's head erased Argent ducally gorged Or.
SUMNER. Rector of Copdock. *Davy, A.*
A lion's head erased Purpure gorged with a coronet
Or.
THORNTON, Robert, of East Newton, co. Yorks.;
Grant dated 4 October 1563. *Grants &*
Certificates (Harl. MS 1,359)
A lion's head erased – collared Vert rimmed Or on
the collar five ermine spots Argent.
TILYARD, of Thorington. *Davy, A. Washbourne,*
'Tilyard of Norf.'
A lion's head erased.
WALTER. *MS Ordinary of Arms, fo. 135**
A lion's head erased Argent.
WALTER. *MS Martin's Crests*
A ? lion's head erased.
WARNER. Elinor, wife of J. Warner, died 1719.
Her.Suff.Ch., Slab, St. Gregory's, Sudbury
'his crest a lyons hed rased b/ the rasures g/ John
Wendy of Clare in Suff'
WENDEY. 'Wendy' *MS Alphabet of Crests,*
fo. 138b
A lion's head erased Azure gorged with a collar
dancetty Or.
WENDEY, of Clare. *Davy, A.*
A lion's head erased Argent charged with three
gutties de sang.
WILSON, William, of Welbourn, co. Lincs.; Grant
by W. Flower, Norroy, 24 March 1586. *Grants*
& Certificates (Add. MS 14,295; Harl. MSS 1,359
and 6,169)
A lion's head erased Argent langued Gules.
WILSON. Vicar of Holy Trinity, Bungay, died
1774. *Davy, A.*
A lion's head erased.
WILSON, Rev. Thomas, A.M., Vicar for 40 years,
died 1774. *Her.Suff.Ch., Monument, Holy*
Trinity, Bungay
A lion's head erased Sable.
WOGAN. *Davy, A., Fressingfield church*
A lion's head erased Azure through the neck a spear
Or headed Gules.
WRENN, Matthew. Bishop of Norwich, 1635–8;
Bishop of Ely, 1638–67. *Bedford, 2nd ed., 47*
A lion's head guardant and erased Argent crowned
Or.
WROTH, of Hempnall's Hall in Cotton. *MS*
Ordinary of Arms, fo. 81*, 'Wroth de Com
Midlesx.' Davy, A. Washbourne, 'Kent, Ess.,
Herts. and Suff.' Fairbairn,' of Hempneyshall
[sic], Suff., Kent, Essex, Herts.'
A lion's head erased Argent crowned Or.
WROTH, of Essex. *MS Martin's Crests*
A lion's head erased Or within a fetterlock Or the
bow countercompony Or and Azure.
WYNDHAM, WINDHAM, of Aldeburgh, Felbrigge
Hall in Norfolk. 'Sr. Edmonde Wyndham of
Folbridge' *MS Knight's Visitations, Norf.**
Edmond Wyndam' *MS Philpot's Visitations,*
Norf.* Davy, A. Washbourne*, 'London, Suff.,

Norf., etc.' Fairbairn, 'Suff., Norf., London, etc.'
A lion's head erased Or within an arch chequy Or
and Azure.
WYNDHAM. 'Windham' *MS Martin's Crests*
A lion's head erased Or within a fetterlock Or.
WYNDHAM. 'Windham' *MS ex-Taylor Coll.**

TWO LION'S HEADS

Two lion's heads erased and addorsed Azure and
Argent collared Or.
GREGORY. Sir Wm. Gregory, Lord Mayor of
London, 1451. Of Mildenhall. *Davy, A.*
Two lion's heads erased and endorsed the first Or
the second Azure each gorged with a plain collar
counterchanged.
PETRE. Lord Petre. Of Kentford. *Davy, A.*

LYNX

A lynx's head erased Vert gutty Argent.
RUSH. 'Ruche' *Wall's Book*
'to his crest a Lynx hed rased Vert dropey ar/'
RUSH. 'Ruche' *MS Alphabet of Crests, fo. 109*
A lynx's head erased per pale Gules and Azure gutty
Or.
WIGSTON. 'Wygsten' *Wall's Book*
'to his Crest a lyncks hed rased g/ and b/ P Pale
Dropey or/'
WIGSTON. 'Wygston' *MS Alphabet of Crests,*
fo. 136b

MULE

A mule's head couped Argent.
CHAMBERLAIN. Sir William Chamberlain, K.G,
died 1463. *Stall Plates, plate LXV*, 'Recorded*
in the Visitation of Suffolk'
A mule's head couped Gules gorged with a coronet
and chained Or.
FORSTER. *MS Martin's Crests*
A mule's head erased Argent.
THWAYTES. *Bokenham*
A mule's head erased.
UNDERWOOD, of Bury. *Bokenham*

OTTER

An otter's head and neck erased Sable.
MERKS, of Reydon. *Davy, A.*

OUNCE

An ounce's head erased Azure 'shaddowed' Or
langued Gules.
BREWSTER, of Wrentham Hall. *MS Fairfax*
An ounce's head erased Gules gorged with a collar
dovetail Argent thereon three mullets Sable (or
Gules).
GRIGBY, of Drinkstone. *Davy, A., Drinkstone*
and St. Mary's Bury churches
An ounce's head erased Proper collared Argent the
edges dovetailed and charged with two mullets Gules.
GRIGBY, George, son of Joshua Grigby, of
Drinkstone, Capt. 11th Foot, died 1811.
Her.Suff.Ch., Wall tablet, Drinkstone

OX

A bull's head Argent.
BARBER *MS Fairfax (Tyl.), St. James's church,*
Bury
A bull's head.
GOSNOLD, GOSNELL, of Otley. *Visitation 1561*
(ed. Metcalfe)
A bull's head affronty per pale Or and Vert.
GOSNOLD, of Suffolk. *Buckinghamshire*
Visitation 1634 (H.S.), 65*
A bull's head per pale Or and Vert horns
counterchanged.

GOSNOLD. Anna, daughter of Robert Gosnold, of Otley, married Edmund Warner; she died 1652. *Her.Suff.Ch., Ledger stone, Parham*

A bull's head Gules.

HOUGHTON. 'Hoghton' *Wall's Book*

'to his crest a Bulles hed g'

HOUGHTON. 'Houghton' *MS Alphabet of Crests, fo. 54*

A bull's head.

MACLEOD. Malcolm Bonar Macleod, Surgeon Captain, R.N., died 1951. *Her.Suff.Ch., Arm rest on pew, Hollesley.*

A bull's head Sable ducally gorged and horned Or.

RADCLYFFE. '1683' *Her.Suff.Ch., Glass formerly in chancel window, Hacheston. Not found 1982*

OX'S HEAD, Cabossed

A bull's head cabossed between two wings Or.

BULL. *MS Heraldic Collections, fo. 20*, wings untinctured. Davy, A. Washbourne, 'Oxon.'*

A bull's head cabossed Argent armed Or.

CROFTS. *Washbourne*, 'Norf. and Suff.'*

A bull's head cabossed Sable armed Or.

CROFTS. *Fairbairn*, 'Suff.'*

A bull's head cabossed per pale Or and Azure.

GOSNOLD, of Otley. *Bokenham*

OX'S HEAD, Coupled

A bull's head couped.

ALPE, of Framlingham, Lt. Bealings. *Davy, A., Slab in Lt. Bealings church. E.A.N. & Q. XIII. 279.* Edward Alpe, 'medical doctor', died 1700. *Her.Suff.Ch., Ledger stone, Lt. Bealings*

A bull's head couped Or armed Argent tips of the horns Sable.

ASTON *MS Martin's Crests*

A bull's head couped Sable horned Or.

BOLEYN. 'Bulleyn' *MS Martin's Crests*

A bull's head couped Argent langued Gules charged on the neck with a crescent Or.

BOLEYN, BOLEINE. *Davy, A.*

A bull's head couped Sable armed Or.

CROFTS. *Washbourne*, 'Norf. and Suff.'* Charles Crofts, Esq., son and heir of Thomas Crofts, of Bardwell, died 1616. *Her.Suff.Ch., Wall tablet, Ixworth Thorpe. Not 'armed'.* Sir Charles Crofts, Kt., died 1660; first wife Cecilia (Poley), died 1626. *Part of Altar tomb and Wall tablet, Bardwell.* Frances Crofts married Edmund Poley, of Badley; she died 1661. *Slab in sanctuary, Badley.* Crofts of Lt. Saxham; Several, 1677, 1694. *Effigy monument and Tablets, Lt. Saxham*

A bull's head couped.

CROFTS, Ernest, R.A., Keeper of the Royal Academy, died 1911. *Her.Suff.Ch., Wall tablet, Blythburgh*

A bull's head guardant couped at the neck per pale Or and Azure.

GOSNOLD, of Otley, Ipswich. *Davy, A. Washbourne, 'Gosnall, Gosnold, Suff.'*

A bull's head couped per pale Or and Azure.

GOSNOLD, John, died 1628. *Her.Suff.Ch., Monumental tablet, Otley.*

A bull's head couped.

HASTINGS. Sir Hugh Hastings, Elsing, co. Norfolk. Brass of c. 1347. *Cotman's Norfolk Brasses, plate 1, page 3 *.* [Head shown without horns]

A bull's head couped Or armed Gules.

HASTINGS, Earl of Pembroke   Of Lidgate. *Davy, A. (Burke)*

A bull's head couped.

HORN. Frederick Edward Horn, Rector of Drinkstone for 48 years, died 1914. *Her.Suff.Ch., Wall tablet, Drinkstone*

A bull's head couped between two wings.

MATTHEWS, Richard, late of March in the Isle of Ely, died 1840. *Her.Suff.Ch., Wall tablet, Hadleigh*

A bull's head couped.

WAINWRIGHT, John, late of Woodbridge, butcher, died 1724. *Her.Suff.Ch., Ledger stone, Woodbridge. 'Possibly suggesting the arms (and crest) of the Worshipful Company of Butchers'*

A bull's head couped Sable armed Argent the points Gules.

WHITNEY, of Bardwell. *Davy, A.*

A bull's head couped Sable armed Or.

YAXLEY, of Yaxley. *Davy, A.*

OX'S HEAD, Erased [Alphabetically by name]

A bull's head erased.

ALPE, of Framlingham. *Bokenham. Bookplate**

A bull's head erased quarterly Argent and Gules.

BEAUMONT. *MS Ordinary of Arms, fo. 28*. Washbourne, 'Lond.'*

A bull's head and neck erased Sable.

BULL, of Sproughton, Hacheston. *Davy, A.*

A bull's head erased Or attired Sable.

BURMAN, of Smallbridge. *Davy, A. (Edms.), Wiston churchyard.* 'Thomas Burman of Smallbridge gent. 1750' *Partridge, 20 (Darby, 1828), Wiston churchyard. Untinctured.*

A bull's head erased Sable bezanty.

COELL, COLE, of Depden, Bildeston. *Visitation 1664–8*. Davy, A., Depden and Wattisham churches*

A bull's head erased Sable.

CROFTS, Lord   Of Saxham. *Bokenham*

A bull's, or buffalo's, head erased Argent.

HOUGHTON. 'Jo. Houghton, M.D., of Ipswich.' *MS Fairfax*

A bull's head erased Argent crined Sable the horns twisted Or and Sable.

JENKINSON, JENKENSON, Of Oulton, Saxmundham. *Visitation 1664–8*. Bokenham. Davy, A. Washbourne, 'Jenkinson, Norf. and Suff.' Fairbairn, 'Jenkinson, Norf. and Oulton, Suff.'*

A bull's head erased.

JENKINSON, Henry, son of Richard Jenkinson, died 1709. *Partridge, 35 (Darby, 1830), Halesworth churchyard*

A bull's head erased Gules ducally gorged chain and ring Or.

MANNERS. George Manners, Lord Roos. *Banners & Standards **

A bull's head erased Argent collared Or.

MUNDEFORD, of Barrow. *Gage (Thingoe)*

A bull's head Argent horned crined and erased Gules.

NOON, NUN, NUNNE. 'George Noune, of Tostock, co. Suffolk'; Patent by R. Cooke, Clarenceux. *Grants & Certificates (Harl. MS 1,359)*

A bull's head Argent armed crined and erased Gules.

NOON, NUNN, of Tostock. 'Noone of Tostock' *MS Heraldic Alphabet. Davy, A., 'armed Or'*

A bull's head erased Or armed Argent.

NOON. 'Nun of Tostock' *Bokenham*

A bull's head erased per fesse Argent and Gules armed Gules.

NOON, NUNN, of Tostock, Martlesham. *Davy, A. Washbourne, 'Noone, Suff. and Norf.' Fairbairn, 'Noone, Noune, Nunne, of Norf. and Suff. and of Tostock, Norf.' [sic]*

A bull's head erased Or horns Gules.
> OGLE, Richard, of Pinchbeck in Holland, co. Linc., Esq.; Grant by Sir C. Barker, Garter. *Grants & Certificates (Stowe MS 692)*

A bull's head erased Or armed Gules gorged with a chaplet Vert.
> OGLE, of Wicken in Bardwell. 'Thomas Ogylle of pynchbeke' *MS Knight's Visitations, Linc.* Davy, A.*

A bull's head erased Sable armed Or.
> OGLE. *MS Heraldic Alphabet*

A bull's head erased Sable armed Or gorged with a garland Proper.
> ORGILL. Rev. Naunton Thomas Orgill, later Leman, died 1837. *Her.Suff.Ch., Hatchment, Charsfield.* Rev. N.T.O. Leman, Rector for 43 years, died 1837. *Wall monument, Brampton, Orgill quartered by Leman. Horns not tinctured.*

A bull's head erased Sable armed Or ducally gorged Or lined and ringed Argent, charged on the neck with an annulet upon a crescent – (for difference).
> RADCLIFFE, RATELIFFE, of Hundon. *Visitation 1561 (MSS G. 7* and Iveagh Copy*)*

A bull's head erased Sable armed Or ducally gorged lined and ringed Argent, charged on the neck with a torteau on a crescent – (for difference).
> RADCLIFFE, RATCLIFE, RATTLYFFE, RATLYFE, of Hundon. *Visitation 1561 (ed. Metcalfe). Harl. 772**

A bull's head erased Sable horned and collared Or a chain cast over the neck Argent.
> RADCLIFFE, Earl of Sussex. *MS Fairfax (Tyl.)*

A bull's head erased Sable armed and maned [*sic*] Or ducally gorged lined and ringed Argent.
> RADCLIFFE. 'Radclife' *MS Heraldic Collections, fo. 53**

A bull's head erased Sable armed ducally gorged lined and ringed Or.
> RADCLIFFE. *MS ex-Taylor Coll.**

A bull's head erased Sable horned Azure from the mouth fire Proper.
> TRUMBULL, William, of East Hampsted, co. Berks. Patent by Sir E. Walker, Garter. *Grants & Certificates (Harl. MS 15,832)*

A bull's head erased Sable breathing fire Proper.
> TRUMBULL. *Proc.S.I.A. IX. 207, Hadleigh church paten*

A bull's head erased Sable ducally gorged and armed Or.
> WALCOT. *MS Ordinary of Arms, fo. 110**

A ?bull's head erased.
> WALL. *E.A.N. & Q. XII. 197, Slab, Holton St. Mary church*

A bull's head erased Sable armed Or.
> YAXLEY. 'Yaxlee' *E.A.N. & Q. I. 313, Tomb in Yaxley church*

RHINOCEROS

In front of a rhinoceros's head couped Proper a crescent Or.
> HOVELL, of Wyverstone. *Muskett. II. 102. Correction, without the crescent for difference, II. 404*

A rhinoceros's head couped Proper.
> LAMB, of Ixworth. *Davy, A.*

SHEEP

A ram's head Argent.

BELGRAVE. Rev. George Belgrave, D.D., Rector of Cockfield, died 1831; widow died 1844. *Her.Suff.Ch., Monument in chancel, Cockfield*

A ram's head Or charged on the neck with a rose Proper.
> CAPPER, of Earl Soham, Wherstead, Martlesham. *Davy, A.*

'beryth to his crest a rammes hede silver armed vert'
> COPE. 'Cope of –' *Wall's Book*

'to his crest a rammes hed ar/ armed Vert'
> COPE. *MS Alphabet of Crests, fo. 22*

A ram's head Sable attired Or.
> COPE, of Glemsford. *Misc.Gen. et Her. 3rd S. IV, 211, Pedigree*

A ram's head the horns forming a hoop from which hangs a bell.
> MUSARD, of Denham, Hoxne. *Davy, A.*

A ram's head and neck guardant.
> RAMSEY, of Kettleburgh. 'S Radulfi Rammeseye' *E.A.N. & Q. (N.S.) III. 175, Seal of II Ric. 2. [1387/8]*

SHEEP'S HEAD, Couped

A ram's head couped Sable armed Sable.
> COPINGER, of Buxhall. *Visitation 1561 (MSS G. 7* and Iveagh Copy*)*

A ram's head couped Sable.
> COPINGER, COPPINGER, of Buxhall, Lavenham, London. *London Visitation 1633 (H.S.) I. 187*. Visitation 1664–8. Davy, A.*

A ram's head couped Gules.
> CURTIS. 'Thomas Curtes of Ely' *MS Knight's Visitations, Linc.**

A ram's head affronty couped per pale Or and Azure.
> GOSNOLD, of Otley, Ipswich. *Visitation 1664–8*. Davy, A.*

A ram's head couped Argent.
> GRAY, GREY. *MS Ordinary of Arms, fo. 35*. Washbourne, 'Ess.'*

SHEEP'S HEAD, Erased

A ram's head erased Gules armed Or charged on the neck with a rose Argent.
> CAPPER, of Earl Soham. *Sharpe*

A ram's head erased Sable horned Argent.
> COPPINGER, of Buxhall, Bramford. *Visitation 1561 (ed. Metcalfe), horns untinctured. Visitation 1664–8*

A ram's head erased Azure bezanty horned Or.
> JOURS. 'Luke Jowers (Jours), of Ipswich, 1664, 'out of France to London' *Grants & Certificates (Harl. MSS 1,085 and 1,105)*

A ram's head erased Argent charged with a chevron Azure.
> RAM. 'Francis Rame, of Hornchurch, co. Essex, 1590.' *Grants & Certificates (Harl. MS 1,359)*

A ram's head erased Argent charged with a chevron Azure.
> RAM. *Bokenham*

A ram's head erased – armed Or charged on the neck with a cinquefoil Argent.
> SACKVILLE, SACKVILE. *MS Heraldic Collections, fo. 33**

A ram's head erased Sable attired Or.
> SACKVILLE. *Davy, A. Washbourne**

TIGER

A lion's, tiger's, or boar's, head erased Gules charged on the neck with a crescent.
> KEBLE, of Stowmarket, Newton, Halesworth, Tuddenham. *Davy, A., Halesworth and Tuddenham churches*

A tigress's head erased quarterly Argent and Sable.
MANNOCK. Sir Francis Mannock, Bart., died
1634. *Her.Suff.Ch., Effigy monument,
Stoke-by-Nayland*

WOLF

A wolf's head Argent.
BARHAM, BRAHAM. *Washbourne, 'Suff. and
Surr.' Fairbairn, 'Barham, Braham, Suff. and
Surrey'*

A wolf's head Argent charged with a crescent Sable.
BRAHAM, of Wickham Skeith, Surrey. *Surrey
Visitation 1530 (H.S.) 29*

A wolf's head per pale Or and Azure.
CLOPTON, of Kentwell. *Visitation 1561 (ed.
Metcalfe).* Rev. Walter Clopton, died 1711.
*Her.Suff.Ch., Slab in the vestry, Rattlesden.
Partially covered 1980*

A wolf's head.
CLOPTON, of Suffolk. *MS Fairfax*

A wolf's head Argent charged on the neck with a
mullet Or.
DOWNES, of Debenham. *Davy, A. Washbourne,
'Suff. & Norf.' Mullet untinctured. Fairbairn,
'Suff. and Norf.' Mullet untinctured*

A wolf's head Or collared Gules.
GARNON, CANDISH alias GARNON, of Cavendish.
Davy, A.

A wolf's head Sable collared Or.
GARNON, of Cavendish. *Davy, A.*

A wolf's head Azure.
IRELAND. *MS Fairfax (Chesh.)*
'beryth to his crest a woulves hede silver and sable
par pall langued and ered geules on his necke a fece
contercoloured standyng betwene two branches of
ooke in the colours the fece plated and pelleted'
PRATT. 'Pratte of Royston' *Wall's Book*
'to his crest a wolves hed ar/ sa/ p pale Langed and
eared g/ on his necke a fece count standing bet ij
braunches of oke in the collers the fece plated and
peleted'
PRATT. 'Pratte of Royston' *MS Alphabet of
Crests, fo. 99*

A wolf's head per pale Argent and Sable collared
counterchanged.
PRATT, of Yoxford. *Bokenham*

A wolf's head.
REYNOLDS. *Davy, A. (Barrett MS)*

A wolf's head.
RUSH. *Davy, A. (Barrett)*

WOLF'S HEAD, Couped

A wolf's head couped Argent.
BRAHAM, of Brantham, Ash, Wickham Skeith.
Davy, A. (Barrett MS)

A wolf's head couped Azure collared Or.
CANDISH, CAVENDISH, of Suffolk. 'Candyshe'
*Visitation 1561 (ed. Metcalfe), collared and
ringed. Davy, A.*

A wolf's head couped Azure collared Sable ringed
[*sic* rimmed] Or.
CANDISH alias GARNON, CAVENDISH. *Harl.
772*, rimmed and studded Or. Davy, A.*

A wolf's head couped per pale Or and Azure
charged on the neck with a crescent on a mullet –
(for difference).
CLOPTON, of Liston Hall in Essex, Kedington.
Visitation 1561 (MSS G. 7 and Iveagh Copy*)
and (ed. Metcalfe)*

A wolf's head couped per pale Or and Azure
charged on the neck with a mullet – (for difference).
CLOPTON, of Sudbury. *Visitation 1561 (MS*

G. 7*). Of Melford *(ed. Metcalfe). Harl. 772*,
mullet Or*

A wolf's head couped per pale Or and Azure.
CLOPTON, of Kentwell, Kedington, Melford,
Ipswich, Clopton. *Visitation 1561 (MS G. 7*, of
Kentwell Hall) and (ed. Howard*)* 'Sr William
Clopton of Kentwell in Com Suffolke Knight' *MS
Lilly's Visitation of Suffolk*. Visitation 1664–8.
MS Heraldic Collections, fo. 54*. Gage
(Thingoe), Seal. Davy, A. Washbourne, 'Suff.'
Muskett. I. 136. Fairbairn, 'Suff.'*

A wolf's head couped Sable collared and ringed Or.
GARNON. 'Sir Rychard Garnon of Candyshe'
Banners & Standards*

A wolf's head couped Azure gorged with a collar
ringed Or and charged with three roundels Sable.
GARNON, GERNON alias CAVENDISH, of Trimley
St. Martin. *Visitation 1561 (MSS G.7* and
Iveagh Copy*)*

A wolf's head couped Azure collared and ringed Or.
GARNON, of Suffolk. *MS ex-Taylor Coll.**

A wolf's head couped Proper.
LAWRENCE. *Davy, A. Washbourne*, 'Suff.,
Lanc., Glouc. and Devon'*

A wolf's head couped at the neck barry of four Or
and Gules holding in the mouth an ostrich feather
erect Proper.
ORMEROD. Archdeacon of Suffolk. *Davy, A.
Washbourne*

A wolf's head couped per pale Argent and Sable
gorged with a collar charged with three roundels and
ringed counterchanged.
PRATT, of Yoxford. 'George Pratt of Ryston'
MS Knight's Visitations, Norf. Visitation
1664–8**

A wolf's head couped per pale Argent and Sable
collared plain charged with three roundels all
counterchanged.
PRATT, PRATTE. 'Edward Pratt' *MS Philpot's
Visitations, Norf.* 'Thomas Pratt' MS Philpot's
Visitations, Norf.* London Visitation 1633 (H.S.)
II. 176*. Davy, A.*

A wolf's head couped Sable gorged with a collar Or
the neck below the collar fretty Or.
STYLE, of Ipswich, Hemingstone. *Visitation
1664–8. Davy, A. Washbourne, 'Ess., Kent and
Suff.' Fairbairn, 'of Ipswich, Suff. and Essex'*

A wolf's head couped Argent charged with a
lozenge shaped buckle tongue to the dexter Azure.
THORROWGOOD. 'Nicholas Throgood, of
Thornhaugh, co. Northants.'; Grant by R. Lee,
Clarenceux, 1594. *Grants & Certificates (Add.
MS 14,195; Harl. MS 1,359)*

A wolf's head couped, or erased, Argent charged on
the neck with a lozenge buckle tongue fesseways
Azure.
THORROWGOOD, of Kersey. *Davy, A., church.
Proc.S.I.A. IX. 209, church cup and silver spoon.
Untinctured*

A wolf's head couped Argent charged on the neck
with a lozenge Azure.
THORROWGOOD. 'Thoroughgood' *MS ex-Taylor
Coll.**

A wolf's head couped Argent the neck charged with
a mascle shaped buckle tongue fessewise Azure.
THORROWGOOD, John, of Sampson's Hall, died
1734; Sir Thomas Thorrowgood, died 1794.
Her.Suff.Ch., Hatchments, Kersey

A wolf's head couped Proper.
WEBBER, of Hopton. *Crisp's Visitation. IV. 158,
Pedigree*

WOLF'S HEAD, Erased [Alphabetically by name]

A wolf's head erased Vert bezanty.
> BAMBOROUGH, BAMBROUGH, of Rendlesham, Suffolk. *Visitation 1561 (MS G. 7*) Yorkshire Visitation 1584 (ed. Foster), 85 note, 'This coate, with a wolfes head erased vert bezantee, for the crest, was granted by William Harvey unto William Bamburgh, of Suffolk'. Davy, A., 'Granted 1602'*

A wolf's head erased Proper collared embattled counter-embattled Gules ring Or thereon three bezants.
> BARNWELL. 'Edward Barnewell, of Cranesley'; Grant by W. Camden, 1566. *Grants & Certificates (Stowe MS 707)*

A wolf's head erased Argent collared Gules studded and chained Or.
> BARNWELL, TURNOR-BARNWELL. *Her.Suff.Ch., Glass, St. Mary's, Bury. 'Granted in 1826 to the late Frederick Henry Barnwell, Esq., of Bury St. Edmunds, on his taking the additional name and arms of Turnor'. First crest, for Barnwell*

A wolf's head erased Argent gorged with a collar embattled counter-embattled Gules chained Or the collar charged with three bezants.
> BARNWELL, TURNOR-BARNWELL, of Bury, Cockfield. *Gage (Thingoe). Davy, A., Monument in Fornham All Saints church. Fairbairn, 'Turnor-Barnwell, of Bury'. Bookplate*. 'Frederick Henrici Turner Barnwell, died 1843' Her.Suff.Ch., Wall tablet, St. James's, Bury*

A wolf's head erased and collared.
> BARNWELL. 'Barnewell of Mileham, co. Norfolk' *Her.Suff.Ch., Glass, Herringfleet*

A wolf's head erased Proper collared Gules.
> BARNWELL, Rev. H.S. Turnor-Barnwell. *Her.Suff.Ch., Glass, St. Mary's, Bury*

A wolf's head erased Argent.
> BARRY, of Syleham. *Visitation 1664–8, 'from Devon'*

A wolf's head erased Argent collared Gules.
> BARRY, of Syleham. *Davy, A.*

A wolf's head erased.
> BARRY, Lambe, of Syleham, died 1768. *Partridge, III (Darby, 1828), Syleham churchyard*

A wolf's, or bear's, head erased and collared.
> BARRY, Lambe, Esq., died 1768; daughters Anne and Isabella, died 1808 and 1825; Others. *Her.Suff.Ch., Wall tablet and Altar tomb in churchyard, Syleham*

A wolf's head erased Ermine.
> BARTON, of Woodbridge. *Davy, A.*

A wolf's head erased Argent ducally gorged Or.
> BRETT, of Hepworth. *Davy, A., 'Born also by Smith, of Bury' [q.v.]*

A wolf's head erased Or pierced through the neck with a broken lance Proper.
> CARTWRIGHT, of Ipswich. *Sharpe*

A wolf's head erased Argent pierced through the neck with a broken spear Sable headed Argent the wound issuing blood Proper.
> CARTWRIGHT, of Ipswich, Ixworth. *Davy, A., St. Mary Stoke church, Ipswich*

A wolf's head erased Or pierced through the neck with a spear Argent.
> CARTWRIGHT, Thomas, Esq., died 1754; widow died 1756. *Her.Suff.Ch., Ledger stone, St. Mary Stoke, Ipswich*

A wolf's head erased Or pierced through the neck with a sword blade broken off at the hilt Argent.
> CARTWRIGHT, of Ixworth Abbey. *Burke, L.G. 1853 ed.*

A wolf's head erased Sable langued Gules armed Argent ducally gorged –.
> CARVER, of Halesworth. *Davy, A., church*

A wolf's head erased Argent ducally gorged Or.
> COCKE, of Withersfield. *Misc.Gen. et Her. 5th S. III. 253*

A wolf's head erased Argent ducally gorged Or.
> COOKE, of Yoxford. *Davy, A. (Barrett MS)*

A wolf's head erased Argent ducally gorged Gules.
> COOKE, of Yoxford. *Davy, A. Washbourne, 'Suff.' Fairbairn, 'Suff.'*

A wolf's head erased Or collared Gules the collar charged with three bezants.
> D'EWES, of Stowlangtoft. *Visitation 1561 (ed. Howard) I. 130*. Her.Suff.Ch., Stowlangtoft, quoting first source*

A wolf's head erased collared.
> D'EWES. 'Dews of Stowlangtoft' *Bokenham*

A wolf's head erased.
> D'EWES, Paul, died 1616; Sir Willoughby D'Ewes, died 1685; Delariviere, wife of Sir Symond D'Ewes, died 1708. *Her.Suff.Ch., Effigy monument, Wall tablet and Ledger stone, Stowlangtoft*

A wolf's head erased.
> DONNE. *MS Martin's Crests*

A wolf's head erased Or.
> DONNE, of Wilby. *Davy, A.*

A wolf's head erased Proper.
> DONNE. 'W.B. Donne' *Bookplate**

A wolf's head erased Proper charged on the neck with a mullet Argent.
> DOWNES. *Washbourne, 'Suff.' In Addenda II.*

A wolf's head erased with a sprig in his mouth.
> FINCHAM, John, of Haverhill, 1794. *Golding, 83, Tradesman's token*

In front of a wolf's head erased Argent a staff raguly fessewise Or.
> GATHORNE. GATHORNE-HARDY, Viscount Cranbrook. *Burke, Peerage, 1891 ed.* Her.Suff.Ch., Wall brass of 1915, Gt. Glemham*

A wolf's head erased Argent.
> GOLTIE, GOLTY. *Bokenham*

A wolf's head erased.
> GOLTIE, GOLTY, of Belstead. *Davy, A., church*

A wolf's head erased Or.
> GOWER, of Ipswich. *Davy, A.*

A wolf's head erased quarterly Or and Azure.
> HAMMOND, of Hawkedon, Boxted. *Muskett. I. 260, on Hatchments, Monuments, etc. in both churches.* Philip Hamond, died 1679; son Philip Hamond, died 1735. *Her.Suff.Ch., Wall monument, Boxted*

A wolf's head erased quarterly Gules and Or.
> HAMMOND, of Hawkedon, Ufford, Boxted. *Davy, A.*

A wolf's head erased quarterly and per fesse indented Or and Azure.
> HAMMOND. *Davy, A.*

A wolf's head erased per pale indented Or and Azure.
> HAMMOND. Henry Lewis Hammond, Esq., of the Vinery, Bury St. Edmunds, Suff.' *Fairbairn*

A wolf's head erased quarterly per fesse indented.
> HAMMOND, John, died 1721; widow Catherine, died 1740. *Her.Suff.Ch., Ledger stone, Pettistree*

A wolf's head erased Ermine.
> HANKEY, of East Bergholt. *Sharpe. Davy, A., church.* Sir Joseph Hankey, Kt., died 1769; Rev.

Harry Hankey, Rector for 28 years, died 1782.
*Her.Suff.Ch., Tablet in north chapel, East
Bergholt. Inscription not found 1978*
A wolf's head erased Erminois.
HANKEY. *Davy, A.*
A wolf's head erased Gules.
HIGHGATE, HIGATE, HEYGATE, of Rendlesham.
Davy, A. E.A.N. & Q. I. 35. Washbourne,
'Highgate, Midd. and Suff.' Burke, Peerage, 1891
ed.* Fairbairn*, 'Highgate, Middx. and Suff.'*
A wolf's head erased Azure gorged with a collar
Argent charged with three roundels and holding in
the mouth a cross crosslet fitchy.
IMAGE, of Whepstead, Bury. *Davy, A. Fairbairn,
'Whepstead & Bury. Cross flory fitchy'*
A boar's head [wolf's in illustration] erased
quarterly Ermine and Azure gorged with a collar Or
charged with three lozenges Azure and holding in
the mouth a cross crosslet fitchy Gules.
IMAGE, of Herringswell House, Mildenhall,
Whepstead. *Burke, L.G. 1900 ed.*
A wolf's head erased quarterly Ermine and Sable
gorged with a collar Argent charged with three fusils
and holding in the mouth a cross crosslet fitchy
Gules.
IMAGE, Capt. John, died in India, 1870.
Her.Suff.Ch., Brass tablet, St. Mary's Bury
A wolf's head erased per pale embattled Argent and
Gules.
JOHNSON, William of Ingham, co. Norfolk; Grant
by R. St. George, Clarenceux, 20 July 1633.
Grants & Certificates (Harl. MS 1,105)
Two lion's gambs erased the dexter Sable gutty
Argent the sinister Argent gutty Sable holding a
wolf's head erased –.
KINWELLMARSH. 'Kymelmarche' *MS Ordinary
of Arms, fo. 26*
Two lion's gambs united at the bottom gutty Argent
and Sable counterchanged holding a wolf's head
erased.
KINWELLMARSH. 'Kynnelmarch' *Washbourne*
A wolf's head erased Sable ducally gorged Or.
LITTLE. Helen, daughter of Thomas Little, of
co. Berks., married Edward Bacon, died 1646.
Her.Suff.Ch., Altar tomb in vestry, Barham
A wolf's head erased Argent.
LLOYD. Rector of Thrandeston, died 1750.
Davy, A.
A wolf's head erased Or.
LOUTH, LOWTH, LOWTHE. *MS Ordinary of
Arms, fo. 8*
A wolf's head erased Gules.
MANNERS, of Sutton. *Davy, A.*
A wolf's head erased collared.
MILLER. *MS Martin's Crests*
A wolf's head erased Argent.
MILLER, of Walsham-le-Willows. *Davy, A.*
A wolf's head erased Gules gorged with a collar
ringed Or spiked Sable.
MOORE, of Stanstead. *Visitation 1561 (MSS
G. 7* and Iveagh Copy*)*
A wolf's head erased Gules gorged with a collar
Sable spiked and ringed Or.
MOORE, of Stanstead. *Visitation 1561 (ed.
Metcalfe)*
A wolf's head erased Sable gorged with a collar
dancetty Or.
MOORE. 'More of Stanstead' *Harl. 772*.
Washbourne, 'Suff.' Fairbairn, 'Suff.'*
A wolf's head erased Gules langued Azure collared
and ringed Or.

MOORE, of Bury, c.1619. *Dugdale's Yorkshire
Visitations 1665–6. III. 444*
A wolf's head erased.
MOORE, MORE. *MS Fairfax (Tyl.)*
A wolf's head erased Or collared Sable.
MOORE. 'Moor' *MS Martin's Crests*
A wolf's head erased Sable collared Or.
MOORE. 'More' *MS Heraldic Alphabet*
A wolf's head erased Gules gorged with a collar
dancetty Or.
MOORE, MOOR. *Davy, A.*
A wolf's head erased Sable ducally gorged Or.
NORTH, of Benacre, Lt. Glemham. *Davy, A.*
A wolf's head erased Azure bezanty.
PAYNE, of Hengrave, Nowton, Worlington.
Visitation 1561 (MSS G. 7 and Iveagh Copy*)
and (ed. Metcalfe) and (ed. Howard. II. 64*)
Harl. 772*. Bokenham. Gage (Thingoe)*
A wolf's head erased Azure charged with five
bezants saltirewise.
PAYNE, of Hengrave, Nowton, Worlington.
*Davy, A. Washbourne, 'Leic. and Suff.' Fairbairn,
'of Leics. and of Paine [sic], Suff.'*
A wolf's head erased Azure.
PAYNE, of Lt. Waldingfield. *Davy, A., church
monument*
A wolf's head erased.
PAYNE, of Lt. Waldingfield. *Proc.S.I.A. IX. 128.*
William Payne, Merchant of London, born Lt. W.,
1643, died in London 1723. *Her.Suff.Ch., Slab in
chancel, Lt. Waldingfield*
A wolf's head erased.
PIGOTT. 'Pigot, Lord' *MS Ordinary of Arms,
fo. 262* MS Martin's Crests*
A wolf's head erased Proper collared Or.
PIGOTT, of Denston Hall. *Davy, A. Her.Suff.Ch.,
Glass, Denston*
Between an oak branch and a pine branch each
fructed Or a wolf's head per pale Argent and Sable
gorged with a collar charged with three roundels all
counterchanged langued and erased Gules.
PRATT, of Ash. *Davy, A.* Rev. Jermy Pratt,
Rector of Campsea Ash, died 1867.
*Her.Suff.Ch., Glass, Campsea Ash. 'Roger Pratt'
Bookplate*. As above, but both branches of oak*
A wolf's head erased Proper.
REEVE, Bart., of Thwaite. *Davy, A., church*
A wolf's head erased Sable eared and langued Gules
charged on the neck with three gutties cotised Or in
fesse.
REYNOLDS. 'Reignolt' *Wall's Book*
'to his crest a Wolves hed rased sa/ eyred and
Langed g/ on the necke iij Dropes betwene ij coteses
or/ in fece'
REYNOLDS. 'Raynolt' *MS Alphabet of Crests,
fo. 109*
A wolf's head erased Sable charged with three
gutties d'or between two barrulets Or.
REYNOLDS, Henry, of Belstead, in Suffolk, son of
Robert of the same place; Confirmation of Arms
with an alteration and Grant of Crest by R.
Cooke, Clar., 1584. *Grants & Certificates (Add.
MS 14,295; Stowe MS 670; Harl. MS 1,359)*
A wolf's head erased Sable collared Gules studded
Or.
REYNOLDS. 'Reignolds of Belstead' *Bokenham*
A wolf's head erased Sable collared per pale Sable
and Argent rimmed Or.
REYNOLDS. *Davy, A.*
A wolf's head erased Sable collared Or charged with
three gutties Sable.

REYNOLDS, of Belstead. *Davy, A. Washbourne, 'Reygnales, Reynolds, Suff.' Fairbairn, 'Reygnales, Reynolds, Suff.'*
A wolf's head erased Sable collared Or.
REYNOLDS. *Washbourne, 'Suff.'*
A wolf's head erased Vert gutty Argent.
RUSH, RUSHE. *Visitation 1561 (Iveagh Copy*) Davy, A.*
A wolf's head erased Argent charged with three gutties Vert.
RUSH, of Thornham. *Bokenham*
'On a Wreath Argent and Gules a Wolf's Head erased Vert, guttè d'or, gorged with a Collar Gold thereon three Torteaux'
RUSH, Sir William Beaumarice Rush, of Wimbledon, co. Surrey, Knt.; Grant of new Crest by Sir George Nayler, Garter and Ralph Bigland, Clarenceux, dated 28th December 1826; Extension of limitations of Crest, dated 11th April 1827. *Miscellaneous Grants (H.S.) II. 183–4, Grants Book. XXXVI. pp. 180 and 203*
A wolf's head erased Vert langued Gules gutty Or gorged with a collar Or charged with three torteaux.
RUSH, of Benhall. *Davy, A.*
A wolf's head erased holding in the mouth a trefoil slipped.
SCRATTON, of Belstead. *E.A.N. & Q. II. 320*
A wolf's head erased per pale Sable and Or ducally gorged counterchanged.
SHARP. 'Syr John Sharp de Coggeshall essex' *Banners & Standards*.* 'Sharp' *Wall's Book, 'langued Gules'*
'to his Crest a Wolfes hed rased Pty P Pale sa/ or/ a bowt his neck a crowne counter color Langed g/ Knight by h 8'
SHARP. *MS Alphabet of Crests, fo. 117b*
A wolf's head erased per pale Azure and Or charged on the neck with a horse-shoe counterchanged.
SHARPE, of Melton, Woodbridge. *Davy, A.*
A wolf's head erased per pale Or and Azure on the neck a horse-shoe Argent.
SHARPE, of Melton, Woodbridge. *Davy, A., 'Grant by Bigland, Clar.' Burke, L.G. 1853 ed. Fairbairn, 'of Melton, Suff.'*
A wolf's head erased per pale Or and Azure.
SHARPE. Charles Thomas Rissowe, later Sharpe, died 1821. *Her.Suff.Ch., Hatchment, Melton*
A wolf's head erased.
SHARPE. Anne, wife of Rev. Charles Sharpe, clerk, of Melton, died 1843. *Her.Suff.Ch., Ledger stone, Martlesham*
A wolf's head erased per fesse embattled Argent and Sable.
SMALPEECE, of Metfield, Gt. Worlingham. *Visitation 1664–8. Davy, A. Fairbairn, 'Smalpeece, Smallpiece, of Worlingham, Suff.'*
A wolf's, or fox's, head erased ducally gorged.
SMYTH, John, Gent., died 1650. *Martin's Church Notes (Frag.Gen. IX. 78), St. Mary's, Bury*
A wolf's, or fox's, head erased Argent ducally gorged Or.
SMITH, of Bury, Tuddenham. *Davy, A., St. Mary's church, Bury*
A wolf's head erased Argent ducally gorged Or.
SMITH, of Bury, Tuddenham. *MS Fairfax (Tyl.). Bokenham. Washbourne*, 'Suff.' Fairbairn*, 'of Tuddenham and Edmondsbury'*
A wolf's head erased – collared Or the neck below the collar fretty Or.
STYLE, STILE. *MS Heraldic Collections, fo. 55**
A wolf's head couped, or erased, Argent charged on

the neck with a lozenge buckle tongue fesseways Azure.
THORROWGOOD, of Kersey. *Davy, A., church. Proc.S.I.A. IX. 209, church cup and silver spoon. Untinctured*
On a wolf's head erased a buckle.
THORROWGOOD. *E.A. Misc. 1934, 70, on dessert spoon, 1753*
A wolf's head erased per fesse Or and Azure.
WARD, John, M.P. for Ipswich; father of Knox Ward, Clarenceux; Grant by John Anstis, Garter and John Vanbrugh, Clarenceux, 8 September 1722. *Misc.Gen. et Her. 5th S. X. 54, note*
A wolf's head erased per pale (or per fesse) Or and Azure.
WARD, of Ipswich. *Davy, A., St. Stephen's church*
A wolf's head erased Proper holding in the mouth a key.
WARD, of Chediston. *Davy, A. Washbourne, 'Bucks. and Suff.'*
A wolf's head erased Sable.
WHITE, WHITE-CORRANCE, of Bury, Parham, Ipswich. *Bokenham. MS Heraldic Alphabet. Davy, A., 'now Corrance'. Washbourne*, 'White-Corrance, Parham & Loudham Hall, Suff.' Fairbairn*, 'Corrance-White, of Parham and Loudham Hall, Suff.' First crest, for White*
A wolf's head erased holding in the mouth an oak branch fructed Or.
WILKINSON, of Holton, Halesworth, Holbrook. *Davy, A.*
A wolf's, or fox's, head erased gorged with a ducal coronet.
YOUNG, of Bradfield Combust. *Davy, A.*

HEAD. BIRD
A bird's head erased Gules.
STEELE. James Rivers Steele, eldest son of Rev. Thomas Steele, Rector of Whepstead, died 1858 in his 11th year. *Her.Suff.Ch., Wall tablet, Whepstead*

CORNISH CHOUGH
A Cornish chough's head and neck wings displayed.
AYLMER. *Davy, A. (G.B.J.)*

COCK
A cock's head.
MARTYN, of Long Melford. *Bokenham*
A cock's head Gules holding in the beak a branch of holly and charged on the neck with three bezants between two cotises in fesse Or standing between two wings chevronny of four pieces Or and Sable.
NORTH. 'North of Felcham.' *Wall's Book*
'to his crest a Cocks hed g/ holding in his beke a braunche of holly vᵉᵗ/ beryes g/ on his necke iij besants bet ij coteses in fece or/ standing bet ij wyngs chevronney of iiij pecs or/ sa/ Dat P garter wyrotheslay & Clarencioulx benolt six [?] of h 8/ to Edward north of felsham in ?'
NORTH. 'North of Ffelcham' *MS Alphabet of Crests, fo. 90*

COCK'S HEAD, Couped
A cock's head and neck couped between its two wings displayed Or comb and wattle Gules issuing from a chaplet of roses Gules.
JODRELL, Paul, of Duffield, co. Derby, Esq., Clerk of the House of Commons; Grant by Sir H. St. George, Garter and P. le Neve, Norroy, 10 July 1707. *Grants & Certificates (Add. MS 14,831)*
A cock's head and neck couped the wings erect Or

combed and wattled Gules issuant out of a chaplet of roses Gules barbed and seeded Proper.
JODRELL, Rev. Henry, M.A., Rector of Gisleham. *Crisp's Visitation. I. 33–4*, Pedigree*
A cock's head couped wings Or charged on each wing with two chevrons Sable collared and holding in the beak a branch of holly Proper.
NORTH, of Felsham. *Davy, A.*
A cock's head couped between two wings elevated Sable.
PARKER. *MS Heraldic Alphabet*
A cock's head couped Gules combed and wattled Or charged on the neck with four billets Or.
SALTER, of Battisford. *Visitation 1664–8*, but corrected and in the Appendix.* [It is a pheasant's head.] *Davy, A. Washbourne, 'Bucks., Northamp. & Suff.'* Edmund Salter, died 1724. *Her.Suff.Ch., Wall tablet, Battisford*
A cock's head couped Or comb and wattle Gules.
TAYLOR, John, of London, Captain of Bartholomew Ward in the White Regiment; Certificate by W. Riley, Lancaster Herald. *Grants & Certificates (Harl. MS 5,810)*

COCK'S HEAD, Erased
A cock's head erased Sable crested and jelloped Or.
ALCOCK. *Bokenham. MS Martin's Crests, 'crested etc. Or'*
A cock's head erased Gules combed and wattled Or holding in the beak a branch of columbines Argent leaved Vert.
FIRMIN. 'Farmour de London' in MS [but arms given are those of Firmin, of Hawkedon]. *MS Ordinary of Arms, fo. 77**
A cock's head erased Ermine combed and wattled Gules holding in the beak a trefoil slipped Vert.
MAIDSTONE. 'Maydstone' *MS Heraldic Collections, fo. 55**
A cock's head erased per pale Or and Vert combed and wattled Gules.
SECKFORD, SEKFORD, of Gt. Bealings. *Visitation 1561 (MS G. 7*) and (ed. Metcalfe) Visitation 1561 (MS Iveagh Copy*, untinctured).* 'Thomas Sackforde' *MS Philpot's Visitations, Suff.*, 'and beaked Gules'*
A cock's head erased per pale Or and Vert charged on the neck with a mullet – for difference.
SECKFORD, SEKFORD, of Lt. Bealings. *Visitation 1561 (MS G. 7*) and (ed. Metcalfe). Visitation 1561 (MS Iveagh Copy*, untinctured)*
A cock's head erased per pale Gules and Vert? beaked Gules charged with a label and crescent for difference.
SECKFORD. Deed Poll of Grant of Arms and Crest by Charles Seckford of Seckford Hall, co. Suffolk, Esq., to his kinsman Gibbon Seckford and his heirs, dated 3 January 1575. *Miscellaneous Grants (H.S.) II. 225–6. Note on this attempted Grant*
A cock's head erased.
SECKFORD. *Bokenham*
A cock's head erased Vert combed and wattled Gules.
SECKFORD. 'Sr Thomas Sackford of Seckford Knight' *MS Lilly's Visitation of Suffolk*. Second of two crests drawn. Davy, A. (Edms.) Washbourne*, 'Seckford, Seckforde, Suff.' Fairbairn*, 'Seckford, Seckforde, Suff.'*
A cock's head erased Azure combed and wattled Or.
WAYNMAN, Richard, of Witney, co. Oxford; Grant by T. Wriothesley, Garter and R. Machado alias Richmond, Clar., in 1509. *Grants & Certificates (Harl. MS 1,359)*

A cock's head erased.
WAYNMAN. *MS Heraldic Collections, fo. 15**
A cock's head erased Azure combed and wattled Or.
WAYNMAN, WAYNEMAN, WAYMAN, of Bury. *Davy, A.*

CRANE see also HERON, STORK
A crane's head erased Azure pierced through the back of the neck with an arrow Proper barbed and plumed Argent the neck vulned Gules.
CRANMER, of Loudham. *Davy, A.*
A crane's, heron's, or stork's, head and neck erased between two wings Argent.
GODFREY. *MS Ordinary of Arms, fo. 174**
A crane's head.
RYLEY. *Davy, A.*
A crane's head erased Argent.
WAREYN, of Wilby, Kenton. *Davy, A., both churches*
A crane's head erased between two wings erect Argent.
WARING, of Edwardstone, Groton. *Davy, A. E.A. Misc. 1932, 72, Alms dish of 1729 in Groton church*
A crane's head and neck couped Argent holding in the beak a branch of holly Vert.
WARREN. 'Jaspar Warren' *MS Philpot's Visitations, Suff.**

CROW
A crow's head erased Proper.
VAUX, Lord Of Eye. *Bokenham*

DUCK
A drake's head erased Proper.
CRICKITT, of Ipswich. *Davy, A. Washbourne, 'of Essex'*

EAGLE
An eagle's head vairy Argent and Gules.
DALLENDER. *Washbourne, 'Suff. and Surr.'*
From rays of the sun Or an eagle's head Proper.
GILBERT, Thomas, of Mayfield, co. Sussex; Grant by Sir W. Segar, Garter, 8 November 1616. *Grants & Certificates (Harl. MS 6,140; Add. MS 12,225)*
An eagle's head Proper issuing out of rays Or.
GILBERT. *Davy, A. Washbourne, 'Suss. and Suff.' Fairbairn, 'Sussex and Suff.'*
An eagle's head between two wings.
JERNINGHAM, JERNEGAN. *Davy, A. (Barrett MS)*
An eagle's head between two wings Argent biting an arrow standing upright Gules feathered Argent.
LACEY. 'Lacye ? of Spelman's Hall' *MS Fairfax (Tyl.)*
An eagle's head Sable.
RUSSELL, of Kelsale. *Davy, A.*
An eagle's head.
SLATER, of Nayland, Bury. *Davy, A.*
An eagle's head between two wings expanded.
WILLIAMS. Rev. Edward Williams, 35 years Rector, died 1775; Rev. Henry Williams, 47 years Rector, died 1823; widow died 1841 aged 94; Others. *Her.Suff.Ch., Wall tablets, Marlesford*
An eagle's head Or between two wings displayed Vair.
WILMER. Bradford Wilmer, Esq., of Reydon Hall, died 1886. *Her Suff.Ch., Glass, Reydon*

EAGLE'S HEAD, Couped
An eagle's, or griffin's, head couped Argent beaked Or charged on the neck with two chevronels Azure.
BURROUGH, BURROUGHE, of Wickhambrook.

Visitation 1561 (ed. Howard) II. 233, on brass of 1597
An eagle's head couped Sable.
    CUDMORE. *MS Martin's Crests*
An eagle's head couped Proper.
    ELINGHAM, of Bealings. *Davy, A.*
An eagle's head couped Or holding in the beak the leg of a fowl erased à–la–quise [erased at the thigh] Gules.
    ESSEX. *MS Martin's Crests*
An eagle's head couped between two wings Or.
    KNOX, of Nacton. *E.A. Misc. 1913. 79*
An eagle's head couped between two wings elevated Or.
    MARTYN, of Thornham. *Bokenham*
An eagle's head couped Or crowned Gules holding in the beak a cinquefoil slipped Or.
    PIKE. *MS Heraldic Alphabet*
An eagle's head couped enfiled by a coronet.
    WATSON, Herbert, M.A., Rector for 27 years, died 1915. *Her.Suff.Ch., Wall tablet, Cransford*
An eagle's head couped Or beaked Gules wings elevated Argent between them a mullet Argent.
    WINGFIELD. 'Syr Rychard Wyngfeld' *Banners & Standards** [the 'mullet' is shown as a star of sixteen points]

EAGLE'S HEAD, Erased [Alphabetically by name]

An eagle's head erased ducally gorged holding in the beak an acorn slipped and leaved.
    ARNOLD.. *MS Heraldic Collections, fo. 81b**
An eagle's head erased.
    AUBERY. 'Awbrey' *MS Martin's Crests*
An eagle's head erased Or beaked Gules.
    BISHOP. 'Byshop' *MS Heraldic Alphabet*
An eagle's head erased Or collared Gules.
    BISHOP. *Bokenham*
An eagle's head erased Sable holding a snake Argent on the eagle's breast two chevrons Argent.
    BROUGHTON, of Stonham Aspal. *Davy, A. (Burke)*
An eagle's head erased Ermine ducally crowned Or between two wings Sable.
    CLAGGET, of Bury. *Davy, A., St. Mary's church*
An eagle's head Argent erased Gules gorged with a mural coronet Gules.
    ELLISTON. *MS Heraldic Alphabet*
An eagle's head erased Proper gorged with a ducal coronet Argent.
    ELLISTON, of Gedgrave, Orford. *Davy, A.*
An eagle's head erased Sable charged with a crescent Ermine.
    GOSLING, of Ellough. *Davy, A. (Edms.), church*
In front of an eagle's head erased Or holding in the beak a sprig of three trefoils slipped Vert two annulets Azure between two bezants.
    GREENE, of Nether Hall, Bury. *Burke, L.G. 1900 ed.*
An eagle's head erased.
    HARDING, of Eye. Mary, daughter of Richard and Ann Harding, died 1695 aged 14; Richard Harding, died 1719; widow Ann, died 1733. *Partridge, 86 (Darby, 1825), Eye churchyard*
An eagle's, or griffin's, head erased.
    HARDING, Mary, died 1695; Richard Harding, died . . . *Her.Suff.Ch., Ledger stone in churchyard, Eye*
'And to the Creast upon the healme on a wreath golde and asur an Egles head rased argent pellatie a crowne about the neck asur manteled gules dobled silver'

HEYNES, Simon, of Mildenhall, son and heir of John Heynes, gent.; Grant of Arms and Crest by Robert Cooke, Clarenceux, 20 September 1575. *Misc.Gen. et Her. I. 250–1. E.A. Misc. 1914. 40–1*
An eagle's head erased Argent gorged with a coronet Azure and semy of ogresses.
    HEYNES, Simon, of Mildenhall, co. Suffolk, gent., son of John Heynes; Grant by Rob. Cooke, Clar., 20 Sept. 1575. *Grants & Certificates (Stowe MS 677)*
An eagle's head erased Ermine ducally gorged Or.
    HEYNES, of Mildenhall. *Davy, A.*
An eagle's head erased Sable gorged with a bar gemelle Or.
    HOARE, of Bury. *Davy, A.*
An eagle's head erased Or.
    MADAN. Rector of Gt. Bradley, 1783–6. *Crisp's Visitation. XIX. 30*
An eagle's head erased Argent armed Gules.
    MICKLETHWAITE. 'Micklethwayte' *MS Martin's Crests*
An eagle's head erased Or.
    MIGHELLS, of Lowestoft. *Gillingwater, 304. Lees, 108. Davy, A., church.* James Mighells, Vice Admiral, died 1733. *Her.Suff.Ch., Monument, Lowestoft.* [Crest gone, but given as above by Gillingwater]
An eagle's head erased holding in the beak an escallop.
    MUDD, of Lavenham. *Davy, A., church.* Hannah, wife of John Mudd, died 1807. *Her.Suff.Ch., Floor slab, Lavenham*
An eagle's head erased per fesse Sable and Azure gutty Or holding in the beak two annulets interlaced Or.
    RAWSON, TRAFFORD-RAWSON. Major Henry Trafford-Rawson, Coldham Hall, Bury St. Edmunds. *Fairbairn, first crest- for Rawson.* Lt. Col. Henry Trafford-Rawson, of Coldham Hall, died 1912; only son Capt. J.H.E. Trafford-Rawson, killed in action 1916. *Her.Suff.Ch., Wall tablet, Lawshall*
An eagle's head erased Or collared Sable.
    REEVE, of Bury. *Davy, A. Washbourne. Muskett. III. 1 (Harl. MS 1177, fo. 24), 'crow's, eagle's or griffin's head.'*
An eagle's head erased Proper.
    ROLLESTON, of Kettleburgh. *Davy, A.*
An eagle's head erased Argent gorged with a ducal coronet Or in the mouth a pheon Argent.
    SHARPE, ? of Yorkshire. *Her.Suff.Ch., Shield on tile in chancel, Sotherton*
An eagle's head erased Or collared Ermine cotised Gules.
    SNELLING, of Whatfield. *Bokenham, 'per Dethick, Gr. 1594'*
An eagle's head erased Azure purfled Or holding in the beak Or a slip of strawberry plant Vert fructed Gules.
    TASSELL, of Bury St. Edmunds. *Visitation 1561 (MSS G. 7* and Iveagh Copy*)*
An eagle's head erased purfled Or holding in the beak a pine branch Vert fructed Gules.
    TASSELL, of Bury. *Visitation 1561 (ed. Metcalfe). MS Heraldic Alphabet, 'of Norf.' Not purfled*
An eagle's head erased Sable ducally gorged Or.
    VAUX. *Davy, A. (Burke)*
An eagle's head erased Ermine beaked Or.
    WESTHORP, of Rattlesden, Ipswich, Yoxford, Sibton, Stansfield. 'Westhrop' *Berkshire*

Visitation 1665–6 (H.S.) 305*, unfinished and beak untinctured. Davy, A.

An eagle's head erased Or beak Gules, on the neck a crescent Gules for difference.

WESTON, Sir John *Grants & Certificates (Add. MS 12,225)*

An eagle's head erased Or beaked Gules.

WESTON, Earl of Portland, Baron of Sudbury. *Davy, A.*

An eagle's head erased per fesse Argent and Gules.

WESTON, of Thorington. *Davy, A.*

An eagle's head erased – beaked Gules charged on the breast with a crescent.

WESTON. *Washbourne, 'Suff.'*

An eagle's head erased Argent.

WESTON. Col. Thomas Weston, of Shadowbush, died 1843. *Her.Suff.Ch., Hatchment, Poslingford*

An eagle's head erased Sable holding in the beak an annulet Or.

YOUNG. Vicar of Stowmarket, Master of Jesus Coll., Camb. *MS Fairfax (Lev.)*

TWO EAGLE'S HEADS

Broken – probably two eagle's heads erased Argent.

BARLOW, Elisha, died 1755. *Her.Suff.Ch., West end of churchyard, St. Margaret's, Lowestoft. Not found 1979*

Two eagle's heads erased and addorsed beaked Or each holding an annulet Gules, arising from a crescent Argent.

CROOKE. Lt. Col. Charles D. Parry Crooke. No date. *Her.Suff.Ch., Glass, St. Mary's, Bury*

FALCON or HAWK [Alphabetically by name]

A hawk's head erased Sable charged with three bezants.

BRIDON, BRYDON, of Bury, Suffolk. *Davy, A. Golding, 87, untinctured, 'bezants one and two'.* [Not a tradesman's token, but fully described.] *Washbourne, 'Bridon, Suff.' Fairbairn, 'Bridon, Suff. bezants one and two'*

A falcon's head couped Sable.

HACKET, of Mickfield. *Bokenham.* 'Hackett' *MS Martin's Crests*

A hawk's head erased collared Gules rays issuing Or.

HAMMOND. *Her.Suff.Ch., Enamelled shield on post in cemetery, Ufford*

'The Creaste ys a fawcons hed coupe or betwene two winges gobone wavey of eight pecs.'

HARBOTTLE, of Crowfield. *Visitation 1561 (MS Iveagh Copy)*

A falcon's head Or between two wings undy of eight pieces Argent and Azure.

HARBOTTLE. 'Harbottell of Crowfield' *MS Fairfax, 'p. Hervey, Clar. 1559. I saw yᵉ Grant of these Arms & Crest'*

A falcon's head erased.

GLEMHAM. 'Sr Thomas Glemham of Glemham Knight' *MS Lilly's Visitation of Suffolk*, second of two crests drawn. Davy, A.*

A hawk's head erased Or pellety.

PUPPLET, of Ipswich. *Bokenham*

A hawk's head erased Or pellety and beaked Sable collared Argent and Sable.

PURPETT, of Newbourne. *MS Fairfax (Tyl.)*

A hawk's head couped Or pellety beaked Sable.

PURPETT, of Newbourne. *Davy, A.*

A hawk's head erased Sable in the beak an annulet Or.

RANSON, of Suffolk. *Davy, A.*

A hawk's head erased Azure in the beak an annulet Or.

RANSON. *Washbourne*, 'Suff.' Fairbairn, 'Suff.'*

A merlin's head erased Proper.

RICE, Richard, of Preston, co. Suffolk; Exemplification by . . . , Rouge Crois, 1586. [Rouge Croix Pursuivant in 1586 was Ralph Brooke] First of two crests. *Grants & Certificates (Stowe MS 670)*

A 'Merleon's' head erased Or.

REYCE, of Preston. *Bokenham*

A falcon's head erased Proper beaked Or.

ROLLESTON. 'Rollston' *MS Heraldic Alphabet*

A hawk's head erased holding in its mouth a branch of a tree.

TASSELL. *Bokenham*

A hawk's head erased Azure holding in the beak a pine branch Vert fructed Gules.

TASSELL, of Bury. *Davy, A. Washbourne, 'Tasell, Suff.' Fairbairn*, 'Tasell, Suff.'*

A hawk's head erased Azure holding in the beak a branch of strawberries.

TASSELL. *Davy, A.*

HERON

A crane's, heron's, or stork's, head and neck erased between two wings Argent.

GODFREY. *MS Ordinary of Arms, fo. 174**

OSTRICH [Alphabetically by name]

An ostrich's head and neck couped between two ostrich feathers.

ALFRAY. *MS Heraldic Collections, fo. 86b.**

An ostrich's head and neck gorged with a ducal coronet Or between two ostrich feathers.

ALFRAY, of Henley. *Davy, A.*

A (? ostrich) camel's head erased Or holding a horse shoe.

BAKER. . . . Baker, Gent., no date; Saml. Baker, Esq., no date; baby son, died 1712/3. *Her.Suff.Ch., Ledger stone partly covered by seats, Wattisfield. Washbourne, 'ostrich head'*

An ostrich's head Azure gorged with a collar Sable rimmed Or and charged with three bezants.

CAVENDISH, CANDISH, of Suffolk. *Davy, A. Washbourne, 'Candish, Suff.' Fairbairn, 'Candish, Suff.'*

An ostrich's head holding in the beak a horse-shoe all between two feathers Proper.

DE LA MOTE, of Willisham. *Davy, A.*

An ostrich's head and wings expanded bendy of four Or and Azure beaked Gules holding in the beak a horse-shoe Argent.

EDGAR, of Ipswich. *Sharpe*

An ostrich's head between two wings expanded Or each charged with two bends Azure in the beak a horse-shoe Argent.

EDGAR, of The Red House in Ipswich. *Davy, A. Washbourne, 'Suff.' Burke, L.G. 1853 ed. Fairbairn, 'of the Red House, near Ipswich, Suff.' Her.Suff.Ch., Gt. Glemham*

An ostrich's head and neck couped wings displayed holding in the beak a horseshoe.

EDGAR. *Livery buttons**

An ostrich's neck erased Argent gorged with a coronet Azure beak Sable.

KING, Richard, of Stansfield, in Suffolk. Patent 1589. *Grants & Certificates (Harl. MS 1,359)*

An ostrich's head couped Argent ducally gorged Azure.

KING, of Shelley, Witnesham, Ipswich. *MS Knight's Visitations, Suff.* Davy, A., Shelley church*

An ostrich head Argent gorged with a mural coronet Azure.

KING, of Stansfield. *Bokenham, 'Confirmed to R. King p' Cooke, Clar. 1589'*
From five ostrich feathers Azure the head and neck of an ostrich Or.

> PAYNE. 'Thomas Paine, of Dunham, in Norfolk'; Patent by R. Cooke, Clarenceux. *Grants & Certificates (Stowe MS 670; Harl. MS 1,359; Add. MS 4,966)*

An ostrich's head erased Or between two wings expanded Sable holding in the beak a horse-shoe Sable garnished Or.

> PAYNE, John *MS Philpot's Visitations, Norf.**

An ostrich's head erased Or between two wings expanded Sable in the beak a horse-shoe Sable.

> PAYNE. Rector of Hepworth, 1840. *Davy, A.*

An ostrich's head between two palm branches.

> SMART. *Davy, A.*

An ostrich's neck quarterly Sable and Argent eared Or holding in the beak a horse-shoe Or and between two wings displayed Gules.

> SMITH. *MS Heraldic Alphabet*

An ostrich's head erased.

> WRIGHT, of Ipswich, Bury. *Davy, A., St. Clement's Ipswich and St. Mary's Bury churches*

PEACOCK

A peacock's head erased Or holding in the beak a serpent entwined about the neck Proper between two wings Azure each charged with three bezants in pale.

> BECK. Edward Bigsby Beck, of Creeting St. Mary, Needham Market; Grant of Arms and Crest by Ralph Bigland, Garter and William Woods, Clarenceux, 17 September 1835. [Seen by me in 1958, since sent to family representatives in Canada.] *Fairbairn, 'of Creeting St. Mary and Needham Market, Suff.'*

Between two wings Gules a peacock's neck Or holding in the beak Gules a snake Azure its head Or.

> PEACOCK. 'Pecocke of Ireland' *Wall's Book*

'to his crest a pecocks necke or/ standing bet ij wyngs & membred g/ holding a snake in his mouth b/'

> PEACOCK. 'Pecocke of Waterford in Irland' *MS Alphabet of Crests, fo. 99b*

A peacock's head and neck Or between two wings displayed Azure holding in the beak a snake entwined about the neck Azure.

> PEACOCK, PECOCKE. *MS Ordinary of Arms, fo. 152**

Between two wings expanded a peacock's head erased holding in the beak a snake twisted about the neck.

> PEACOCK, of Ipswich. *Davy, A., Monument, St. Matthew's. Proc.S.I.A. VII. 204. E.A.N. & Q. IX. 380.* Capt. Eustace Peacock, died 1727. *Her.Suff.Ch., Carved slab, St. Matthew's, Ipswich. Not found 1979*

A peacock's head erased holding in the beak a snake entwined round the neck all Proper between two wings erect Or.

> RANBY, of Bury. *Davy, A., Brent Eleigh church*

Between two wings erect a peacock's head erased entwined round with a serpent all Proper.

> RANBY. John, of Bury (married Mary Goate), died 1820. *Her.Suff.Ch., Wall monument, Brent Eleigh*

A peacock's head and neck couped Azure between two wings erect Or.

> SEYMOUR. 'Syr John Semer' *Banners & Standards**

PELICAN

A pelican's head erased Argent vulning itself an arrow pierced through the neck Or barbed and feathered Argent.

> CHEKE, CHEEKE, of Debenham, Framlingham. *Bokenham. Davy, A., Debenham church*

A pelican's head erased Or.

> GODFREY, of East Bergholt. *MS Martin's Crests. Davy, A.*

A pelican's head erased Azure.

> PERNE. Rector of Norton, died 1772. *Davy, A.*

PHEASANT

A ?pheasant's head erased Sable in the beak and entwined about the neck a snake Proper.

> ELYS. *Harl. 772**

A pheasant's head and neck couped Gules beaked and wattled Or [now appearing Argent] charged all over with ten billets Or.

> SALTER. 'Thomas Salter of Oswaldstre in the County of Salop in the fift yeare of king Hen. 8 [1513/4] from whom Edwarde Salter of Monks Illeigh in the county of Suff clerke doth derive himself and so is regestred in the visitatio of Suff remayninge in the Office of Armes. Dated the 22th daye of Maye 1623. Confirmation of Coat and Creast'. Signed William Penson Lancaster. Hen. St. George Richmond. Hen Chittinge Chester. [Original vellum in my possession; *Corder MS 82*]

'to his crest a ffeasants hed g/ powdered wt byllets or/ his beke of the same. gylbert Salter & robt salter'

> SALTER. 'Salter of Oswestre' *MS Alphabet of Crests, fo. 118b*

A pheasant's head and neck couped Gules beaked Or charged on the neck with ten billets Or.

> SALTER, of Battisford. *Visitation 1664–8**. *Fairbairn, 'Suff. billets 1. 2. 3. & 4.'*

A pheasant's head erased Gules billeted Or.

> SALTER, of Battisford. *Bokenham*

A pheasant's head couped Gules charged with four billets, 1. 2. 1.

> SALTER, Edmund, died 1724. *Wall tablet, Battisford. Coloured photograph**

RAVEN

A raven's head erased Or.

> REYCE, RICE, of Preston. *Davy, A. Washbourne, 'Rice, Baron Dynevor. Suff.' Fairbairn, 'Rice, of Preston, Suff.'*

SEAGULL

'to his crest a sey goynes [*sic* ? seagull] hed coupey in her proper kynd beked g/ holding in her beke a braunche of holly on threy Leves vert. Dat p C hawley 30 of h 8 [1538/9] to Robt Waren of long melford in Suff & now in London'

> WARREN. 'Waren' *MS Alphabet of Crests, fo. 141*

STORK

A stork's head.

> ALFORD. Rector of Ampton. *Davy, A.*

A stork's head chevrony Sable and Argent beaked and erased Or in the beak an eel Azure.

> BROUGHTON. Grant of Crest by Barker. *Grants & Certificates (Stowe MS 692)*

A crane's, heron's, or stork's head and neck erased between two wings Argent.

> GODFREY. *MS Ordinary of Arms, fo. 174**

A stork's head erased holding a snake in the beak all Proper.

> MERCER. *Sharpe*

A stork's head erased enclosed by a pair of wings.
> WARING. *Proc.S.I.A. IX. 206, Alms dish, Groton church*

SWAN

A swan's head erased Or beaked Azure holding in the beak a fish Argent.
> COBB. 'ffrancys Cobbe of Burnham' *MS Knight's Visitations, Norf.* * 'Will Cobbe' *MS Philpot's Visitations, Norf.* *

A swan's head holding in the beak a fish Argent.
> COBB, of Suffolk. *Davy, A.*

A swan's neck couped gorged with a ducal collar.
> KING, of Stansfield. *E.A. Misc. 1908, 85 and 1911, 25, 'Granted 1589'*

A swan's head and neck erased Ermine ducally gorged and beaked Or.
> MELLISH, MILLS. *MS Ordinary of Arms, fo. 153* *

A swan's neck Argent beaked Or between two wings Ermine.
> MOORE, Thomas, of Wiggenhall St. German, co. Norfolk. *Grants & Certificates (Stowe MS 703)*

A swan's head and neck between two wings Argent ducally gorged Gules.
> TALBOT. Rector of Icklingham. *Davy, A.*

A ?swan's head and neck couped Or beaked Gules between two wings displayed Argent.
> WINGFIELD. 'Sr. Tho: Wingfeild de Suff.' *MS Ordinary of Arms, fo. 200* *

HEAD. FISH

DOLPHIN

A ?dolphin's head.
> SPOURNE, of Lavenham. *Davy, A., church*

EEL

A conger eel's head erased and erect Gules collared with a bar gemelle Or.
> CLARKE, of Ipswich. *Davy, A. Washbourne, 'Suff.' Fairbairn, 'Suff.'*

LUCY [PIKE]

A lucy's head couped erect Or.
> GASCOYNE. 'S. Welye Gasgon' *Harl. MS 6163*

A lucy's head in pale Argent.
> GASCOYNE. 'Gascoign' *Wall's Book*
'to his crest a Lucy hed ar in pale'
> GASCOYNE. 'Gascon' *MS Alphabet of Crests, fo. 46*

A lucy's head erect.
> GASCOYNE. 'Gascoign' *MS Martin's Crests*

A lucy's head erased and erect Gules collared with a bar gemelle Or.
> GILLET, GILLET alias CANDLER, of Ipswich, Coddenham, Woodbridge, Yoxford, etc. 'William gyllot of Bradfyld' *MS Knight's Visitations, Norf.* * 'William Gyllott' *MS Philpot's Visitations, Norf.* * Visitation 1664-8. MS Fairfax. Page. Davy, A. Washbourne, 'Gillet, Suff.' Fairbairn*, 'Gillet alias Chandler, of Ipswich, Suff. & Broadfield [sic], Norf.'*

A lucy's head erased and erect Gules collared with a bar gemel Gules [sic].
> GILLET alias CANDLER, Philip, died 1689; Rev. Philip, A.M., died 1739. *Her.Suff.Ch., Ledger stones, Woodbridge*

WHALE

A ?whale's head couped devouring a ton [sic tun or barrel].
> EATON. 'Robert Eton' *MS Knight's Visitations, Essex*, against the neck 'Whal'*

HEAD. HUMAN

MAN, Unspecified or Couped [Alphabetically by name]

A man's head affronty couped at the neck Proper.
> ADAIR, Bart., of Flixton Hall. *MS Ordinary of Arms, fo. 13*. Davy, A. Burke, Peerage, 1891 ed.* Fairbairn, 'Adair, Bart., of Flixton Hall, Suff.'* Alexander Adair, Esq., of Flixton Hall, lord of the manor of South Elmham, died 1834; Robert Shafto Adair, 5th Bart., of Flixton Hall, died 1949. Her.Suff.Ch., Monument and Wall brass, Flixton. Carved on end of choir stall, Mendham*

A man's head bearded Proper on his head a cap Gules.
> ASPALL, of Gt. Thurlow. *Davy, A., church*

The bust of a man Proper crined Sable band Argent vested paly Or and Azure.
> BARRINGTON. *MS Martin's Crests. MS Heraldic Alphabet*

A man's head couped sideways Proper between two branches Vert.
> BLACKERBY, of Stow [sic Stowmarket]. *Bokenham*

A man's bust in profile couped at the shoulders Proper hair Sable habited Gules collared Or on his head a cap Or turned up Ermine.
> BLAGE. *Davy, A.*

A man's head couped at the shoulders half sideways – hair and beard grey.
> BOCKING, BOCKYNGE, of Ashbocking. *Visitation 1561 (Iveagh Copy*)*

A man's head affronty couped at the shoulders Argent hair Vert.
> BOCKING. 'Edmunde Bekyng of ashe bekyng in com Suff.' *Harl. 772* *

A man's head affronty couped at the shoulders Proper hair grey.
> BOCKING, BOKINGE, of Ashbocking. *Visitation 1577. Davy, A.*

A man's head full-faced couped at the breast Proper beard and hair 'duskish'.
> BOCKING, of Ashbocking. *Bokenham*

A man's head couped at the shoulders Argent hair Vert.
> BOCKING, BOKING. *Washbourne, 'Suff.' Fairbairn, 'Bokinge, Boking, of Boking [sic], Suff.'*

An old man's head full-faced Proper habited Vert collared Or couped at the shoulders on his head a ducal coronet Or out of which a long cap hanging forwards tasselled Or.
> BOURCHIER, Earl of Bath. Of Hengrave. *Davy, A. Bookplate* [as above but head in profile]*

A man's head Proper one lock of hair braided band round head Argent.
> BREWSE, of Little Wenham. *Sharpe*

A man's head in profile Proper filletted Argent.
> BREWSE, of Little Wenham. *Davy, A.*

An old man's head couped Proper hair in a pigtail tied Or a turban round the head Argent.
> BREWSE, Sir, John, died 1585. *Her.Suff.Ch., Effigy monument, Lt. Wenham*

A man's head and shoulders in profile vested paly wreathed about the temples.
> BRIDGES. 'Sr Gyles de Brugis' added 'Brydges'. *MS Ordinary of Arms, fo. 92* *

The bust of a bearded man in profile wreathed about the temples the ends flotant Or and Gules vested paly Or and Azure semy of roundels.

BRIDGES. 'Anthony Briges' *MS Philpot's Visitations, Essex**
A man's head couped in profile Proper hair and beard Sable wreathed about the temples Argent and Azure.

BRIDGES. *MS ex-Taylor Coll.**
The bust of an old man in profile wreathed about the temples Argent and Azure vested paly Argent and Gules and semy of roundels counterchanged.

BRIDGES, Duke of Chandos. Of Ashfield, Debenham, Thornham, etc. *Davy, A.*
A man's head full-faced wearing a helmet the vizor open all Proper.

BUCKWORTH. *MS Heraldic Alphabet*
A man's head couped at the shoulders.

BURROUGHS, of Ipswich, near Bures. *MS Fairfax, '1662'*
The bust of a man Proper.

BURROUGHS. 'Burrowe of Ipswich' *Davy, A.*
A man's head side-faced in a helmet.

CANHAM, of Bradfield Combust. 'Barth. Canham gent., 16..' *Partridge, 212 (Darby, 1829), churchyard. Davy, A., churchyard*
A man's head couped below the shoulders and side-faced 'swartish' habited Vert collared Or on his head a cap bendy wavy Or and Azure turned up Argent and Sable.

COCKET, COCKETT, of Ampton. *Addit. Suff. Peds.*
A man's head in profile couped at the shoulders Proper habited Vert collar Or wreathed round the temples Argent and Sable on his head a cap bendy wavy of six Or and Azure.

COCKETT, of Ampton. *Worcestershire Visitation 1569 (H.S.), 38*
A man's head couped below the shoulders in profile Proper habited Vert collared Or on his head a cap bendy wavy Or and Azure turned up indented Sable.

COCKET, of Suffolk. *Davy, A. Washbourne, 'Herts., Norf. & Suff.'*
A man's head couped at the shoulders in profile.

COTTINGHAM, John; children 'who dyed in there childhood of ye Small Pox 1723' *Partridge, 108 (Darby, 1826), Laxfield churchyard, 'worn out'*
A man's head in profile couped at the shoulders on his head a cap.

COTTINGHAM, of Laxfield. *Davy, A.*
A man's head affronty.

COTTINGHAM. *Her.Suff.Ch., Ledger stone in churchyard, Laxfield. Not found 1981*
A man's head in profile Proper.

DUNSTON, of Hopton. *Davy, A., Worlingworth church. Washbourne*
A man's head in profile about his temples a fillet.

ELDRED, of Gt. Saxham. *Davy, A.*
A man's head 'charnu' [flesh colour] a close coif about his ears Gules an 'albanois' hat Or fretty Sable.

EVERARD, of Suffolk. *Wall's Book*
'to his crest a mans hed Charnu/ a closse coyff a bowt his eyres g/ an albonays hat or ffreted sa/'
'EVERARD, of Suff/' *MS Alphabet of Crests, fo. 34*
A man's head affronty couped at the shoulders – wearing over a coif Gules a tall cap Or fretty Sable.

EVERARD, EVERAD, of Gt. Linstead. *Visitation 1561 (MS G. 7, fo. 68*).* Head and shoulders Argent (*MS Iveagh Copy**)
A man's head affronty couped at the shoulders and wearing a conical spiralled cap all Argent, charged on the neck with a crescent Sable for difference.

EVERARD. *Visitation 1561 (MS G. 7, fo. 82b.)*
A man's head affronty couped at the shoulders Argent having on a cap Or fretty Sable.

EVERARD, of Linstead. *Visitation 1561 (ed. Metcalfe). Harl. 772*, bottom of cap edged Gules.* [? part of coif.] *Visitation 1577. Visitation 1664–8*
A man's head couped at the shoulders affronty Proper on the head a cap Sable fretty Or.

EVERARD, of Linstead, Denston. 'Henry Everad' *MS Philpot's Visitations, Suff.*.* Henry Everard, Esq., brass of 1524. *Cotman's Suffolk Brasses, plate 25*, Denston church. Davy, A. E.A. Misc. 1916, 3*
A man's head Proper on the head a cap barry Argent and Sable.

EVERARD, of Linstead. 'Rychard Everard' *MS Philpot's Visitations, Norf.* Davy, A.*
A man's head couped at the shoulders affronty Proper on the head a pointed cap barry Argent and Sable.

EVERARD, of Linstead. *Visitation 1664–8*
A man's head couped at the shoulders Proper on his head a cap wavy barry of eight Or and Sable turned up of the second [*sic*].

EVERARD. *Washbourne, 'Ess., Suff., Norf., etc.'*
A man's head couped at the shoulders and on the head a long cap.

EVERARD, James, died 1846. *Her.Suff.Ch., West end of churchyard, Lowestoft St. Margaret. Not found 1979*
A man's head full-faced with beard and moustache wreathed about the temples and knotted.

GLEANE. 'Glean' *MS Ordinary of Arms, fo. 56**
A man's bust full-faced Proper wreathed about the temples Argent and Sable.

GLEANE. *Davy, A.*
An old man's head in profile Proper habited round the shoulders Gules on his head a cap Or turned up Ermine and charged with three gutties Gules.

HEVENINGHAM, of Heveningham. *Davy, A. Washbourne, 'Suff. and Staff. cap . . . gutty Gules'. Fairbairn, 'Heningham, Staffs. & Suff.'*
An old man's head in profile Proper vested Gules on his head a cap Azure gutty Or.

HEVENINGHAM. *Washbourne, 'Suff. and Staff.' Fairbairn, 'Suff. and Staffs.'*
The bust of a man full-faced bearded Proper bound about the temples and knotted.

LAMBE. *MS Ordinary of Arms, fo. 18** [the coat given is that of Lambe of Troston]
A man's head full-faced couped at the shoulders Proper banded about the temples with a ribbon Or and Azure the ends extended each side.

NORTON, of Ixworth. *Bokenham*
A man's head couped at the shoulders Proper.

NORTON, Richard, Esq., died 1708. *Her.Suff.Ch., Ledger stone, Ixworth*
A man's head side-faced Gules hair and beard Or round his head a fillet Or jewelled Azure and Argent.

POLE, DE LA POLE. Sir William de la Pole, Duke of Suffolk, K.G., died 1450. Buried at Wingfield. *Stall Plates, plate L**
A man's head side-faced Gules hair and beard Or round his head a fillet Or jewelled Sable and Argent.

POLE, DE LA POLE. Sir John de la Pole, Duke of Suffolk, K.G., died 1491. Buried at Wingfield. *Stall Plates, plate LXXIX**
A man's head in profile Gules collared Azure bordured Or and wreathed about the temples Or.

POLE, DE LA POLE. 'Pole, Lord of Suffolke, Great Chamberlain' *Harl. MS 6163*
The head of a bearded man wearing a round cap or hat with side pieces covering the ears.

POLE, DE LA POLE. Below head of the effigy of Michael de la Pole, Earl of Suffolk, died at Harfleur, 1415. *Effigy Monument, Wingfield. Photograph**
A man's bust in profile couped Proper with a long cap Gules on it a Catherine wheel Or.

ROBSART, of Henham, Bulcamp. *Davy, A.*
A helmet Or feather Or the vizor open showing a man's face Proper.

ROGERS, Christopher, of Sutton, in Kent; Patent 1593. *Grants & Certificates (Harl. MS 1,359)*
A man's head Argent beard hair and whiskers Sable on the head a cap Sable tied with ribbons Argent.

ROUS, ROUSE, of Hasketon, Woodbridge. *Davy, A. Washbourne, 'Norf. and Worc.'*
The bust of a man couped at the shoulders Proper hair beard and whiskers Sable the head surrounded and crossed by a ribbon knotted at the top the ends flowing from either temple Argent.

ROUS, ROUSE. 'Rev. Rolla Rouse, M.A., The Rectory, Rayleigh [sic], Suff.' *Fairbairn*
A man's head affronty Proper hair and beard Sable.

ROUS, Sir Thomas, died 1603. *Effigy wall monument, Dennington. Photograph**
A man's head side-faced couped at the shoulders Proper hair and beard Sable.

SHELTON. 'Shellton' *MS ex-Taylor Coll.**
A man's head affronty couped at the shoulders Proper.

SHELTON, of Brent Eleigh, Mettingham Castle. *Davy, A.*
A bearded man's head and shoulders couped affronty cloaked- collared Ermine and regally crowned.

SOUTHWOLD. 'Borough of Southwold' *Visitation 1561 (MSS G. 7.* and Iveagh Copy*)*
On a wreath the bust of a man affronty couped at the breast vested and regally crowned.

SOUTHWOLD. 'Town of Southwold' *Visitation 1561 (ed. Metcalfe).* 'Sotheldtonne or sothel towne' *Harl. 772*. E.A.N. & Q. IV. 166*
A helmet Or feathers Azure the vizor open showing a man's face Proper.

SYMS, Edward, of Daventry, co. Northants., 1592. *Grants & Certificates (Harl. MS 1,359)*
A head in a helmet beaver up Proper plumed Azure.

SYMMES, of Whepstead. *Davy, A.*
A man's head couped at the neck crined and bearded Argent on his head a chapeau Gules turned up Ermine.

THORPE. 'Thorpp' *MS Heraldic Alphabet*
A man's head Proper wreathed about the temples.

UFFORD, assumed by WILLOUGHBY. *Davy, A., Ufford church*
A man's head affronty Proper crowned Or.

UFFORD. *Davy, A.*
The bust of a man in profile couped Proper ducally crowned Or on his head a long cap Gules thereon a Catherine wheel Or.

WALPOLE, Earl of Orford. *Davy, A. Burke, Peerage, 1891 ed*. Wagner, 83**
A man's head and shoulders couped affronty long hair and beard Sable wreathed about the temples Or and Gules issuing therefrom a plume of three ostrich feathers Or, round the neck a label of three points –.

WARBURTON, John, of Melford. *MS Knight's Visitations, Suff.*, wreath Gules only. MS Heraldic Collections, fo. 54**

A man's head full-faced Proper wreathed about the temples Argent and Gules adorned with a plume of feathers Or.

WARBURTON. *MS Martin's Crests*
A man's head with long black hair and black beard wreathed about the temples Argent and Gules on his head a plume of three feathers Or.

WARBURTON, of Long Melford. *Davy, A.*
A man's head and shoulders full-faced Proper beard and hair – wreathed about the temples and tied Argent and Gules.

WARNER. *MS Ordinary of Arms, fo. 222**
A man's head Proper couped at the shoulders habited chequy Or and Gules wreathed about the temples Or and Gules and on his head a cap Argent turned up Or.

WARNER, of Parham, Wickhambrook, Framlingham, Cratfield. *Davy, A., Wickhambrook church. 'Grant by Camden'*
A man's head couped below the shoulders habited chequy Or and Azure wreathed about the temples Or and Gules on the head a cap Argent.

WARNER. Dorothy Warner, wife of Edmund Poley, of Badley; she died 1625. *Her.Suff.Ch., Floor slab in sactuary, Badley.* Elizabeth (Rous), wife of Francis Warner, died 1649; Edmund Warner, died 1617. *Ledger stones, Parham., no mention of cap.* Andrews Warner, died 1717; Poulett Warner, died 1721; Nathaniel Warner, died 1753. *Ledger stones, Wickhambrook*
The bust of a man couped at the shoulders and affronty Proper ducally crowned Or.

WILLOUGHBY. *Her.Suff.Ch., On monument of Hon. Lindsey Burrell, died 1848 (Mother a Willoughby), St. Mary Stoke, Ipswich*

MAN'S HEAD, Erased

A man's head in profile erased bearded and crowned.

UFFORD. *Davy, A.*
A man's head erased Proper bearded and crowned Or.

UFFORD, Earl of Suffolk (extinct). *Fairbairn*

MOOR'S HEAD, Unspecified or Couped [Alphabetically by name]

A Moor's head.

ALFORD. *Davy, A.*
A black Moor's head couped Proper.

ANDREWS. *MS Heraldic Alphabet*
A Blackamoor's head in profile couped at the shoulders Proper in the ear a pendant.

ANDREWS, of St. Pernells in Bury. Rector of Herringswell, 1578. *Muskett. III. 22 (Harl. MS 1553, fo. 212–217b.)*
A Blackamoor's head and shoulders couped Sable on his head a chapeau Gules turned up Argent surmounted by a fleur-de-lis Or.

BANKS. 'Bankes of Lincolns Inn' *MS Ordinary of Arms, fo. 224**
A 'moreans' [sic called variously Moor or Satyr] head between two wings 'in maner of devylles wyngs' Sable.

BAWDE. 'Baud of Essex' *Wall's Book*
'to his crest a moryans hed betw ii wyngs in manner of dyvelles wyngs sa/'

BAWDE. 'Bawde of Essex' *MS Alphabet of Crests, fo. 8*
A Blackamoor's head couped at the shoulders with a pair of dragon's wings conjoined to his neck.

BAWDE. 'Baud' *MS Martin's Crests*
'for their Crest on a helme and wreath of their

Cullers a Blackamore head between two Lawrell
branches proper Mantled gules doubled Argent'
> BLACKERBY, James, of London and Thomas
> Blackerby of Shakerland Hall, co. Suffolk,
> gentlemen, and to the descendants of John
> Blackerby of Worlington, co. Suffolk, their
> grandfather'; Grant by Sir Edward Bysshe,
> Clarenceux, 10 June 1664. *Miscellaneous
> Grants (H.S.) I. 30–31 (Harl. MS 1470, fo. 103)*

A Blackamoor's head between two laurel branches
Proper.
> BLACKERBY, of Stowmarket, Shakerley Hall in
> Badwell Ashe. *MS Fairfax, 'from the Grant
> itself, 1664'*

A Moor's head in profile couped at the shoulders
filleted and jewelled between two palm branches.
> BLACKERBY, of Stowmarket. *Davy, A., church*

A Moor's head in profile couped at the neck Proper
wreathed about the temples Or and Azure jewelled
Or.
> CANNING, of Ipswich, St. Helen's. ? Minister of
> St. Lawrence, Ipswich, 1778. *Davy, A.*

A Moor's head couped in profile Proper wreathed
round the temples Argent and Azure.
> CANNING. 'Richard Canning, M.A., 'many years
> minister of the parish of St. Lawrence in this
> town', died 1775. *Her.Suff.Ch., Monument in St.
> Helen's Ipswich*

'beryth to his crest a 'morions' [*sic* ? Moor] hede
with a towell about hit'
> CONWAY. 'Conwey' *Wall's Book*

'to his crest a 'moryans' hed wᵗ a towell a Bowt yt'
> CONWAY. 'Conway' *MS Alphabet of Crests,
> fo. 19*

The bust of a Moor in profile couped at the
shoulders Proper wreathed at the temples Argent
and Sable, or Azure.
> CONWAY, SEYMOUR-CONWAY. Francis, 2nd
> Marquess of Hertford, K.G., died 1822; Francis
> Charles, 3rd Marquess of Hertford, K.G., died
> 1842. *Her.Suff.Ch., Hatchments, Sudbourne*

A Moor's head couped Sable wreathed about the
temples Ermine, and charged on the neck with a
crescent – (for difference).
> CONYERS, CONYERS alias NORTON, of
> Halesworth. *Visitation 1561 (MS G. 7*)*

A Blackamoor's head wreathed round the temples
Argent and Azure, on the breast a crescent.
> CONYERS, CONYERS alias NORTON, of
> Halesworth. *Davy, A.*

A Moor's head couped at the shoulders Proper
wreathed about the temples Ermine and Gules.
> CONYERS, CONYERS alias NORTON. *Davy, A.
> (Barrett)*

A Moor's head couped at the shoulders Proper
crowned with coronet 'such as is painted on ye
heads of our Saxon kings' Or set on a turban Argent
and Azure.
> COWPER, John; Confirmation by W. Dethick,
> Garter, 23 April 1593. *Grants & Certificates
> (Stowe MS 676), 'descent given for John Cowper,
> of Okey, co. Somerset'*

A Blackamoor's head in profile Sable couped at the
shoulders vested – wreathed about the temples and
knotted Or and Gules.
> HERBERT. 'Sʳ Geofry Harburt' *MS Ordinary of
> Arms, fo. 55**

On a pedestal a Blackamoor's head.
> HUNLOCK, ? of Wissett. *Davy, A.*

A Blackamoor's head.
> JENNINGS. *Davy, A. (Barrett)*

A Moor's head in profile Proper wreathed about the
temples.
> MOOR, MOORE, of Gt. Bealings, Woodbridge,
> Bury. *Davy, A.*

A Moor's head in profile couped at the shoulders.
> MOOR. 'George Moor, Esq., of Java Lodge, near
> Wickham Market, Suff.' *Fairbairn*

A Moor's head in profile couped at the shoulders
wreathed and knotted.
> MOOR. Canon Edward Moor, Rector of Gt.
> Bealings, 1844–1886. *Carved on choir stall,
> Gt. Bealings. Booklet, 'Hassocks for your
> Church'**

A Moor's head affronty Proper bound about the
forehead with a fillet wreathed and tied in a knot
Argent Azure and Gules.
> NORTON, of Ixworth. *Davy, A. (Edms.)*

A Moor's head in profile Proper bound about the
temples with a fillet wreathed and tied in a knot
Argent Azure and Gules, on the top of the head two
eagle's heads erased.
> NORTON. Rector of Alderton, Vicar of Eyke.
> *Davy, A.*

A Moor's head couped at the shoulders Proper.
> NORTON. *Washbourne*, 'Suff., York. and Hants.'*

The bust of a Moor in profile couped at the
shoulders Proper wreathed about the temples Argent
and Azure.
> SEYMOUR-CONWAY, Marquis of Hertford. Of
> Sudbourne. *Davy, A.*

A Moor's head couped Sable wreathed about the
temples Gules.
> TANNER. Vicar of Lowestoft, Rector of Hadleigh.
> *Davy, A.*

A Blackamoor's head couped Proper wreathed at the
temples Argent and Gules drops in the ears Argent.
> TANNER. Thomas Tanner, D.D., Rector of
> Hadleigh, died 1786. *Her.Suff.Ch., Hatchment,
> Hadleigh*

A Negro's head Proper.
> WESTON, of Landguard Fort. *Sharpe*

MOOR'S HEAD, Erased

A Moor's head in profile erased at the neck Sable.
> IVESON, of Brantham, Rattlesden, Grundisburgh,
> Hitcham. *Davy, A.*

A blackamoor's head in profile erased.
> WARNER, of Sudbury. *Davy, A., St. Gregory's
> church*

SARACEN'S HEAD, Unspecified or Couped
[Alphabetically by name]

A Saracen's head bearded his cap Gules.
> ASPALE. *Gage (Thingoe), 'formerly in Lt.
> Thurlow, Flempton and Lt. Bradley churches'*

A Saracen's head in profile Argent wreathed Or.
> AUDLEY. 'S. Jamys Audeley' *Harl. MS 6163*

A Saracen's head Proper ducally crowned Or.
> BERTIE. Lord Willoughby of Eresby. Crest for
> Willoughby. *Davy, A.*

A Saracen's head Proper couped at the shoulders
bearded and crined Sable wreathed tasselled and
necklaced Argent.
> BOCKING. Edmund Bocking, lord of the manor of
> Ashbocking, died 1585. *Her.Suff.Ch., Effigy
> brass, Ashbocking*

A Saracen's head.
> BOURCHIER, Earl of Bath. *Her.Suff.Ch., on
> Kitson effigy monument, Hengrave*

A Saracen's head half-faced Proper hair and beard
Sable wreathed about Or and Azure.
> BREWSE, of Wenham. *Bokenham*

A Saracen's head Proper.

BURROWE, BURROWS. *Davy, A. (Barrett MS)*

Out of a castle Argent charged with three cross
crosslets Sable a Saracen's head affronty Proper
wreathed Argent and Gules.

CATON. Rev. Redmond Caton and Rev. Thomas
Caton, Rectors of Gt. Fakenham and Denham.
Burke, L.G. 1900 and 1952 eds.

Issuant from a castle with two towers Argent
charged with three crosses crosslet fitchy in fesse
Sable a Saracen's head affronty Proper wreathed
round the temples Or and Gules.

CATON. 'Rev. R.B. Caton, Gt. Fakenham Rectory,
Suff.' *Fairbairn*

A Saracen's head Argent with a 'towail' [*sic* turban]
about it.

COTTINGHAM. 'Cotyngham' *Wall's Book*

'to his crest/ a Saracyns hed ar/ w^t a towell a bowt
yt'

COTTINGHAM. 'Cottyngham' *MS Alphabet of
Crests, fo. 19*

A Saracen's head Proper.

CRESWELL. *Davy, A. (Edms.) Washbourne,
'Northamp.'*

A Saracen's head Proper.

GLEANE. *Davy, A.*

A Saracen's head affronty Proper wreathed about
the temples Argent and Sable.

GLEANE, John, Gent., died 1664. *Her.Suff.Ch.,
Ledger stone, South Elmham St. Cross or St.
George*

A Saracen's head in profile couped at the shoulders
habited Azure charged on the neck with two barrulets
Or and on his head a pointed cap Azure turned up
Ermine tasselled and charged with five gutties Or.

HEVENINGHAM. 'Sr Arthur Henyngham' *MS
Knight's Visitations, Suff.*

A Saracen's head and shoulders couped Gules on his
head a cap Or turned up Ermine and charged with
three gutties Gules.

HEVENINGHAM, of Heveningham Manor.
*Copinger. II. 93, 'Their crest is a Saracen's head
and shoulders couped [etc., as above]; the origin
of which bearing is ascribed to Sir William
Heveningham, Knt., who 'going with King
Richard I. overcame Safer, the daring Saracen,
captain of the Castle in Palestine. Since that they
gave his head for a crest' (Suckling. II. 387)*

A Saracen's head in profile Proper wreathed Argent
and Sable.

IRBY, Lord Boston. Of Gisleham, Hinkley [*sic*].
Davy, A.

A Saracen's head Proper.

MURE, of Saxham, Herringswell. *Gage
(Thingoe). Davy, A. Burke, L.G. 1853 ed.
Fairbairn, 'of Herringswell House, Suff.'*

A Saracen's head Gules covered with a cap and fillet
Or.

POLE, DE LA POLE. Dukes and Earls of Suffolk.
Of Wingfield. *Davy, A.*

A Saracen's head.

POLE, DE LA POLE. John de la Pole, 2nd Duke of
Suffolk, died 1491. *Her.Suff.Ch., Effigy
monument, Wingfield.* [Photograph*, shows the
head of a bearded man couped with wavy hair
bound with a jewelled fillet and ear ring in right
ear]

A Saracen's head in profile couped at the shoulders
on the head a chapeau Azure turned up Argent.

PRIDEAUX. Dean of Norwich 1685; Archdeacon
of Suffolk. *Davy, A.*

A Saracen's head in profile Proper bound round the
temples with a fillet Or.

ST. CLERE. *Sperling, 147, All Saints church
Sudbury, Eden wall pedigree. Her.Suff.Ch., Eden
wall pedigree, All Saints Sudbury. Photograph*

A Saracen's head Argent habited Or.

SHELTON. 'S. Rafe Shelton, Norff.' *Harl. MS
6163*

A Saracen's head couped at the breast Proper.

SHELTON, of Barningham, Brent Eleigh.
Bokenham. Copinger. I

A Saracen couped below the shoulders.

SHELTON. Margaret (Randall) married Maurice
Shelton, of Barningham Hall, she died 1727.
Her.Suff.Ch., Ledger stone, Barningham

A Saracen's head in profile couped at the neck and
wreathed round the temples Or and Azure.

SHIRLEY, of Barnham. *Davy, A.*

A Saracen's head in profile Sable ducally crowned Or.

UFFORD. 'Lord Broke' *Harl. MS 6163*

A Saracen's head affronty couped at the neck Sable
wreathed about the head Argent and Gules issuing
therefrom a plume of three ostrich feathers Or.

WARBURTON. 'Mayster Warburton . . . Chesshyre'
Banners & Standards [shown as a badge]

A Saracen's head affronty couped at the shoulders
Sable wreathed about the temples Argent and Gules
issuing therefrom three ostrich feathers Or, on the
neck a label of three points the centre point charged
with a crescent – for difference.

WARBURTON, of Long Melford. *Visitation 1561
(MSS G. 7* and Iveagh Copy*) and (ed. Howard)
I. 308*, without the difference*

A Saracen's head affronty couped at the shoulders
Proper wreathed about the temples Argent and
Gules issuing therefrom three ostrich feathers Or, a
label of three points Azure.

WARBURTON, of Melford. *Visitation 1561 (ed.
Metcalfe)*

A Saracen's head Proper couped at the shoulders
wreathed round the head Argent and Gules on the
head a plume of feathers Argent.

WARBURTON. *Washbourne*, 'Chesh., Cumb.,
Suff. & Notts.' Fairbairn*, 'Chesh., Cumb., Suff.
& Notts. Feathers Or.'*

A Saracen's head couped below the shoulders
habited chequy Or and Gules wreathed about the
temples Or and Gules on the head a cap Argent.

WARNER. 'Warner of Essex now of Parham in
Suffolk'; Confirmation by Camden, Clarenceux,
1609. *Sir Thomas Warner, 88**

A Saracen's head affronty Proper (wreathed about
the temples Or and Gules).

WARNER, Robert, died 1641 aged 29; father
Robert Warner, died 1654 aged 80. *Her.Suff.Ch.,
Ledger stones, Cratfield*

A Saracen's head affronty couped at the shoulders
Proper vested Gules on the head a cap chequy
Argent and Gules in front thereof three roses.

WARNER, of Brettenham Hall. *Burke, L.G. 1900
ed.* Lieut. Cornwallis Warner, killed in action
1915. Her.Suff.Ch., Bronze tablet, Brettenham*

A Saracen's head affronty couped at the breast
bearded grey vested Gules on his head a conical cap
chequy Argent and Gules on the breast three roses
fessewise Argent.

WARNER, Lieut. Cornwallis J., killed in action
1915; father Col. Sir Thomas Warner, Bart., died
1934; mother died 1947. *Her.Suff.Ch., Bronze
tablet and Hatchment, Thorpe Morieux; Glass,
Brettenham*

A Saracen's head affronty Proper hair and beard Sable a band round his neck Or and wreathed about the temples Argent and Azure.

> WESTON. 'Syr Rychard Weston' *Banners & Standards**

A Saracen's head couped Proper wreathed about the temples and tied in a bow Argent and Azure.

> WESTON, of Shotley. *London Visitation 1633 (H.S.) II. 339**

A Saracen's head full-faced Proper crined Sable.

> WESTON. *MS Martin's Crests*

A Saracen's head cabossed Sable langued Gules crowned Or.

> WILLOUGHBY. 'Baron' *Wall's Book*
>
> 'to his crest a Sarazyns hed cabossed sa/ crowned or/ Langed g/'
>
> WILLOUGHBY. 'Baron Wylloughby/ knight by h 8' *MS Alphabet of Crests, fo. 137*

A Saracen's head affronty the tongue hanging out Proper ducally crowned Or.

> WILLOUGHY, Lord Of Parham. *Davy, A.*

MAN'S HEAD. VARIOUS [Alphabetically by name]

A Capuchin friar couped below the shoulders affronty Proper habited paly of six Argent and Gules.

> BARRINGTON. 'Mayster Nycollas Baryngton . . . com. Essex' *Banners & Standards**

A Capuchin friar affronty Proper couped below the shoulders habited paly of six Argent and Gules on his head a cap Proper.

> BARRINGTON, of Exning. *Davy, A., Yoxford church*

A Capuchin friar affronty Proper couped below the shoulders habited paly of six Argent and Gules on his head a cap hanging down behind and striped as the habit.

> BARRINGTON. *Davy, A.*

A hermit's bust in profile vested and having on the head a cowl paly of six Argent and Gules.

> BARRINGTON. Vicar of St. Mary Tower church, Ipswich, 1890–1904. *Crisp's Visitation XXI. 121*, Pedigree*

A man's head and shoulders Argent long hair and beard Sable a 'sowdain's' hat Or lined Ermine the 'becke' backwards habited Gules collared Or.

> BLAGE. 'Blagge of . . . Kent' *Wall's Book*
>
> 'to his Crest a hed fro the shoulders face and necke ar/ Long hare and Berd sa/ A Sodans hat or/ Lyned [ermine tail drawn] the Beke backward his apell g/ bound a bowte the coller or/'
>
> BLAGE. 'Blagge of Dartford in Kent' *MS Alphabet of Crests, fo. 8*
>
> 'to his crest a ded mans hed in the fasshon of Deth/ holding in his mouth a candell or/ at ether end the fflaminge fyer issuing'
>
> BOLNEY. 'of Sussex' *MS Alphabet of Crests, fo. 11*

A skeleton's head couped at the shoulders Proper holding in the mouth a firebrand Or flamant at both ends Proper.

> BOLNEY, of Suffolk. *Davy, A.*

A death's head with a firebrand in the mouth Proper.

> BOLNEY, of Wetheringsett. *Davy, A. (Barrett)*

A 'soldan's' head side-faced Argent hair and beard Azure on the head a ducal coronet out of which a pointed cap hanging forward Gules.

> BOURCHIER. Sir John Bourchier, K.G., died 1400. *Stall Plates, plate XIV**

A 'soldan's' head side-faced Proper hair and beard Sable on his head a ducal coronet Or encircling a cap hanging forward Gules with a roundel Or on its point and turned up Argent charged with three water bougets Sable.

> BOURCHIER. Sir Henry Bourchier, K.G., died 1483. Earl of Essex. *Stall Plates plate LXI**

The head of a savage couped at the shoulders and affronty Proper.

> BURROUGH, of Ipswich. *Visitation 1664–8*
>
> 'ffor his crest or cognizaunce Upon a wreathe of his saide cullores [Or and Sable] Arabians head proper beaded & coyffed sables tyed about with a band and the pendant argent'
>
> ELDRED. 'John Eldred of London gentleman ye fourth sonne of John Eldred of Buckenham sonn of John Eldred of Knet-sell sonne of William who was the sonne of Nicholas Eldred of Knetsell in ye countie of Norff. Gentleman'; Confirmation of Arms and Grant of Crest by William 'Dethecke als Garter', 10 June 1592. *Misc.Gen. et Her. 5th S. VII. 308 (Harl. MS 1754, 113a.)*

An Arabian's head couped at the shoulders in profile Proper hair and beard Sable banded about the head Argent the ends hanging down at the back charged near the edges with a bar gemell Gules.

> ELDRED, John, of London, gent. [continued as above, but 'John Eldred of Buckingham']. Patent from Sir W. Dethick, Garter, 10 June 1592. *Grants & Certificates (Harl. MS 6,140)*

An Arabian's head couped Proper bearded and crined Sable tied about with a band and pendant Argent the end fringed Gules.

> ELDRED. John Eldred, of Great Saxham, lord of the manor, died 1632. *Her.Suff.Ch., Effigy brass, Gt. Saxham. Untinctured*

A warrior's head in profile couped at the shoulders helmeted Proper garnished Or between two wings Argent, in front thereof a short bow stringed of the first [*sic*].

> HARTCUP, of Upland Grove House, Bungay. *Burke, L.G. 1853, 1900 and 1952 eds.** William Thomas Hartcup, Esq., of Upland Hall, Bungay, Suff. and Old Catton, Norf. *Fairbairn*

A savage's head in profile Proper habited round the shoulders Gules on his head a cap Or turned up Ermine and charged with three gutties Gules.

> HEVENINGHAM. 'Heningham, Staff. and Suff.' *Washbourne*

A monk's head Proper hood Or.

> HOPTON. 'S. George Hopton, Norff.' *Harl. MS 6163*

A Savage's head couped and distilling blood Proper.

> MUSARD. *Davy, A.*

A chieftain's head half-faced Or his headpiece Gules.

> PRIDEAUX. *MS Martin's Crests*

A 'soldan's' head Argent hair Azure plaited and tasselled with beard Azure on his head a ducal coronet above which a pointed cap Gules surmounted by a Catherine wheel Azure spoked and rimmed Or.

> ROBSART. 'Sir Lewis Robessart, K.G., died 1431.' *Stall Plates, plate XXIX**

A chieftain's head armed with a headpiece.

> ROUSE. *MS Martin's Crests, 'Worc.'*

A hermit Proper couped below the shoulders vested russet his hood pendent at his back.

> SHEDDEN, of Aldham. *Davy, A.*
>
> 'beryth to his crest an hermetes hedde with a hoode over hit and a nother of hit in his necke silver' [*sic ?*]

SHELTON. *Wall's Book*
'to his Crest an ermyns hed w^t a hode over y$^{t/}$ and an other of yt in his necke ar/'
SHELTON. 'of Norff.' *MS Alphabet of Crests, fo. 116b*
A King's head crowned with an Imperial crown.
SOUTHWOLD, Town of *E.A.N. & Q. IV. 166*
A 'soldan's' head side-faced Sable hair and beard Sable bound about the head with a ribbon Azure knotted and the ends flotant.
STAPLETON. Sir Miles Stapleton, founder K.G., died 1364. *Stall Plates, plate XXXIX**
A friar's head side-faced Proper couped at the shoulders habited grey.
SWILLINGTON, of Yoxford, Blythburgh. *Davy, A. (Berry)*
A Capuchin friar's head Proper couped at the shoulders vested Argent.
THURLAND. *Davy, A.*
A 'soldan's' head side-faced Sable hair and beard Or ducally crowned Or.
WILLOUGHBY. 'Sir William; Lord Willoughby d'Eresby, K.G., died 1409' *Stall Plates, plate XX**

WOMAN'S HEAD

A maid's head couped at the shoulders Proper crined Or clothed Azure.
BOROUGH of Ipswich. *Bokenham*
A maiden's head Proper hair Or garlanded with violets and leaves.
BRAYBROOK, James, of Suffolk, Esq., of the Privy Chamber to Henry VII; Grant of Arms [and Crest] 7 March 1504. *Misc.Gen. et Her. 3rd S. III. 242, Pedigree. Davy, A., 'Grant 20 March 1504' [sic]. Washbourne, 'Braybroke, Braybrook, Suff. violets and leaves Proper' Fairbairn, 'Braybroke. violets and leaves Proper'*
'to his crest upon the helme a maydens hed w^t a garland of vyolet flowers and leves vert'
BRAYBROOK. 'Braybroke' *MS Alphabet of Crests, fo. 11b*
A maiden's head couped at the shoulders affronty Argent crined Or on her head a garland of flowers Azure leaved Vert.
BRAYBROOK. 'Braibrooke, of Suffolk' *Berkshire Visitation 1532 (H.S.) I. 3*, 'these Armes (and Crest) were gyven by Roger Machado als Richemond King of Armes Clarencieulx [sic] bearing date at London the vijth daye of the monethe of Marche . . . a thousand fyue hundrethe and foure . . .'*
A woman's head couped at the breast Proper hair flotant Or.
GRIFFIN, of Suffolk. *Davy, A. Washbourne*, 'Staff.'*
A woman's bust three quarter faced Sable crined wreathed and tasselled Or.
HERBERT. 'S. Water Harberd' *Harl. MS 6163*
A maid's head Proper within a gold ring.
HOO. *MS Martin's Crests*
A female head couped below the shoulders habited Azure on the head a wreath of roses alternately Argent and Gules.
PARR, Marquis of Northampton. Of Bildeston. *Davy, A.*
Three fleurs-de-lis Or in front of the bust of a woman Proper vested Gules crined and on the head a crown vallary Or issuing from the crown five thorn leaves Vert.
THORNHILL. Sir Thomas Thornhill, Bart., J.P.,

D.L., M.P., of Pakenham Lodge. *Burke, Peerage, 1891 ed.** Compton-Thornhill, Bart., J.P., D.L., of Pakenham Lodge, Suffolk and Riddlesworth Hall, Norfolk. *Fairbairn*, first crest – for Thornhill*

CHILD'S HEAD [CHERUB see MONSTER]

A child's head couped at the shoulders full-faced Proper on the head a basket Or fretty Sable.
EVERARD. 'Everad, of Linstead' *Bokenham*

HEAD. MONSTER

HERALDIC ANTELOPE

'Vpon the Helme one a Wreath Argent and Sables, an Antilops head erased Or, Pellety, Horned Mained tongued Gules, ye Torsh Argent and Sables, Mantled Gules Doubled Silver'
COOKE, Nicholas, of Linstead, co. Suffolk; Confirmation of Arms and Crest by Robert Cooke, Clarenceux, 15th July 1560. *E. Counties Collectanea, 43. (17th Century MS penes A.W. Morant, Esq.)*
An antelope's head erased Or armed maned and langued Gules tusked Argent charged with roundels Sable.
COOKE, of Gt. Linstead. *Visitation 1561 (MSS G. 7* and Iveagh Copy*)*
An antelope's head erased Or charged with torteaux tusked horned and tufted Gules.
COOKE, of Linstead. *Visitation 1561 (ed. Metcalfe). Fairbairn, 'Cooke, Suff. heraldic antelope'*
An antelope's head erased Or charged with torteaux, or pellety, tusked Or horned and tufted Gules.
COOKE, of Linstead. *Davy, A.*
An antelope's head erased Or tusked horned and tufted Gules.
COOKE. *Washbourne, 'Suff.'*
An antelope's head erased Argent attired and maned Or gorged with a belt Gules studded Or.
GLASCOCK, of Suffolk. *MS ex-Taylor Coll.*, 'p. Rich. St. George'*

CAMELEOPARD [Giraffe]

'on a Wreath A. and S., a Cameleopardes head erased A. spotted S. horned and a Crowne about the neck or.'
SOTHERTON, Thomas, of Norwich, gent.; Confirmation of Arms and Grant of Crest by W. Harvy als Clarencieux, 29 April 1562. *Misc.Gen. et Her. 5th S. IX. 128 (Soc. of Ant. MS 378, fo. 499), Pedigree. [Much information regarding earlier generations of the Sothertons of Sotherton in Suffolk given in Grant]*

CHERUB

A cherub's head between two wings Proper.
BUSSELL, of Finborough Hall. *Davy, A.*
A cherub's head winged.
BUSSELL, D^r., owner of Shelland, died c.1932. Of Finborough Hall. *Her.Suff.Ch., On processional staff in vestry, Shelland*
A cherub's head Proper.
CARRUTHERS. Rev. William Mitchell-Carruthers, M.A., The Rectory, Holbrook, Ipswich. *Fairbairn*, 'on the dexter side, crest of Carruthers'*
A cherub's head between two wings Proper.
WHINCOPP, of Woodbridge, Bredfield. *Davy, A.*

COCKATRICE

A cockatrice's head couped beaked and crowned with wings displayed Or.

BIGG. Rev. John Bigg, A.M., Rector of Hardwicke, co. Cambs., died 1765. *Her.Suff.Ch., Wall tablet, Glemsford*
On a wreath Argent and Azure the head of a cockatrice erased Proper (Vert toned to pink) combed and wattled Gules, on the neck a trefoil Argent.
HENSLOW. Thomas Henslowe, of West Borehunt, co. Hants.; Confirmation by W. Dethick, Garter. *Grants & Certificates (Stowe MS 676), notes on family of Henslow*
A cockatrice's head erased Proper beaked combed and wattled Gules, on the neck a trefoil Argent.
HENSLOW. *Davy, A.*
A cockatrice's head between its two wings displayed Vert combed and wattled Gules.
JESSUP. 'Thomas Jessope, of Gillingham, co. Dorset.' Patent by R. Cooke, Clar. *Grants & Certificates (Harl. MSS 1,359 and 1,422; Add. MS 4,966)*
A cockatrice's head couped Or beak and wattles Gules between its wings Vert.
MARTIN, or MARTYN, Sir Roger, Lord Mayor of London 1568. *Grants & Certificates (Harl. MS 1,463)*
A cockatrice's head Or beak and wattles Gules between two wings expanded Vert.
MARTIN, 'Martyn, Long Milford [*sic*], Suff.' *Fairbairn**
A cockatrice's head between two wings.
MARTIN, Bart. *Washbourne*, 'Suff.' Fairbairn*, 'Martin, Bart., Suff. One of two Martin crests'*
'to his crest a koketryce hed rased Vert beked g/ croned wateled & crest or/ 1559 to thom Sacford of Sackford hall in Suff.'
SECKFORD. 'Sacford' *MS Alphabet of Crests, fo. 122*

DRAGON [Alphabetically by name]

A dragon's head Or between two aspin [*sic*] branches Proper.
ASPIN. *Her.Suff.Ch., Hatchment recorded by Farrer in 1912, not now in church, Cockfield*
A dragon's head between two dragon's wings Gules.
BABINGTON, of Halesworth. *Crisp's Visitation. VIII. 89**. Francis Evans Babington, Esq., of South Lodge, Halesworth, Suff. *Fairbairn*
A dragon's head Argent gutty de sang.
BONHAM, of Suffolk. *Davy, A. (Berry)*
A dragon's head Gules vomiting flames of fire Proper collared and lined Or.
BRIGHT. Thomas Bright, of Nether Hall, Pakenham, died 1736; Others. *Her.Suff.Ch., Ledger stones, Thurston*
A dragon's head between two wings expanded Gules.
CASTLETON. Rev. Sir John Castleton, Bart., Vicar of Gorleston, died 1777. *Druery, 143, 'dragon's wings'. Washbourne, 'Surr., Suff. & Linc.' Fairbairn, 'Surrey, Suff. & Lincs.'*
A dragon's head Gules transfixed through the breast with a lance Or headed Argent.
COLDHAM, of Bury. *Davy, A.*
A dragon's head Argent charged with three bars Gules on each as many mascles Or and in the mouth a teazle Or.
CONSTABLE, of Bures, East Bergholt. *Davy, A.*
A dragon's head Or collared and with a crown Gules.
CUTLER. 'Cutteler of Suffolk' *MS Fairfax (Tyl.)*
A dragon's head Vert langued Gules.
DALTON. *Wall's Book*

'to his Crest a Dragons hed Vert'
DALTON. *MS Alphabet of Crests, fo. 29*
'for his crest a dragons hed vert bet ij wyngs or/ on the neck wreth ar/ b/ confyrmed by norry hawley the 6 yere of k h 8/ to george Dalton Cytizen & goldsmyth of London'
DALTON. *MS Alphabet of Crests, fo. 30.* [The date is wrong, Hawley was Norroy 1534–6, therefore should be 26 Hen. 8]
A dragon's head Vert wings Or gorged with a collar nebuly.
DALTON, of Bury. *Davy, A.*
A dragon's head Vert holding in the mouth a sinister hand Gules.
FITZHUMFREY, of Clare. *Davy, A.*
A dragon's head.
GREY, of Cavendish. *Davy, A.*
A dragon's head Sable collared Or.
HODELOW, HODILOW, of Lt. Cornard, Sudbury. *Davy, A.*
A dragon's head between two wings Azure.
KNEVETT. 'Knyvet' *Wall's Book*
A dragon's head between two wings expanded Sable.
KNEVETT, KNEVET, of Suffolk. *Davy, A. Washbourne, 'Knevett, Knevit, Corn., Norf. and Suff.' Fairbairn, 'Knevett, Knevit, Corn., Norf. and Suff.'* ? John Knevet, 1417. *Her.Suff.Ch., Effigy brass, Mendlesham, Biographical notes on John Knevit by Edmund Farrer*
A dragon's head between two wings expanded Sable gutty Argent.
MANN, of Syleham, Weybread, Ipswich. *Davy, A., Weybread churchyard*
A dragon's head issuing from the wreath in bend Or from its mouth flames of fire Proper.
MAUTEBY. 'Mautby' Patent May 1612. *Grants & Certificates (Harl. MS 1,441; Stowe MS 706)*
A dragon's head Or vulned in the neck Gules.
NEALE. *Davy, A.*
A dragon's head between two wings Ermine.
POYNINGS, of Wrentham. *Davy, A.*
A dragon's head Vert armed Gules.
SYER, of Kedington. *Davy, A., Lavenham and Lt. Waldingfield churches*
A dragon's head Proper.
SYER, John, died 1774; Others. *Her.Suff.Ch., Wall tablet, Lavenham*
A dragon's head between two wings Ermine.
VALOINES. *Davy, A., 'also Poynings'*
In front of two spears in saltire Proper a dragon's head Gules gorged with a collar gemel Argent.
WARE, CUMBERLEGE-WARE, of Poslingford Hall, Clare. *Burke, L.G. 1900 and 1952 eds.** 'Charles Edward Cumberlege-Ware, of Poslingford, Suff. and Middx.' *Fairbairn*
A dragon's head Gules.
WARREN. Rector of Cavendish, died 1748. *Davy, A.*
A dragon's head Gules.
WESTROPP, of Melford. *Davy, A.*
Out of a cinquefoil Gules a dragon's head Sable bezanty langued Gules holding in the mouth a 'dartes ende' erased Or head upwards Argent embrued Gules.
WHITTINGTON. 'Whitingdon' *Wall's Book*
'to his crest a Dragons hed sa/ bezanted comyng owt of a cynckfoil g/ holding in his mouth a Darts end rased or/ the hed upward ar/ the poynt & the Dragons tong g/'
WHITTINGTON. 'Whytingdon' *MS Alphabet of Crests, fo. 137b*

DRAGON'S HEAD, Couped

A dragon's head couped Or.
ASPALL, of Talmach Hall in Lt. Bricett. *Davy, A. E.A. Misc. 1919, 5.*

A dragon's head couped at the neck Vert gorged with a crown Argent.
BLAKEY, of Huntingfield. *Davy, A. Fairbairn*, 'Suff. Coronet Argent'*

A dragon's head couped Gules vomiting flames of fire Proper collared and lined Or.
BRIGHT, of Bricett, Pakenham, Bury. *Visitation 1664– 8*. Davy, A. Bright, 15, 75. Fiske*. Fairbairn, 'Suff.' Muskett. II. 136*

A dragon's head couped.
BRIGHT. Thomas Bright, of Lt. Bricett, married Mary Revett, who died 1666. *Her.Suff.Ch., Slab in chancel, Brandeston*

A dragon's head couped at the neck Gules.
CASTELL. *Davy, A.*

A dragon's head couped Vert.
DRAYCOT, of Suffolk. *Davy, A.*

A dragon's head couped Or the mouth embrued Gules.
NEALE. Richard Neale, D.D., Dean of Westminster. Patent November 1612, another dated January 1613 where called 'Bishop of . . .' [Bishop of Lichfield and Coventry 1610–14]. *Grants & Certificates (Harl. MS 6,059; Stowe MS 706)*

A dragon's head couped Or bristled Gules in his mouth an anchor roped all Proper.
PLEIJS. Rector of Gislingham, died 1781. *E.A. Misc. 1916, 92*

A dragon's head couped Or in the mouth an anchor Or roped Proper.
PLEIJS, Charles, Rector, died 1743; Rev. Charles Bedingfeld Pleijs, Patron of the living, died 1781. *Her.Suff.Ch., Wall tablet and Ledger stone, Gislingham*

A dragon's head couped Gules fretty Argent ducally gorged and chained Or.
ROLFE, of Hadleigh, Kersey Priory. *Davy, A. Fairbairn, 'of Hadleigh, Suff.'*

A dragon's head couped.
RUSSELL. Thomas Russell, died 1730; widow died 1754. *Her.Suff.Ch., Wall tablet, Kelsale. Crest gone 1980*

A dragon's head couped Proper gorged by a coronet per pale Or and Azure from the mouth fire Proper.
SOUTH, Thomas, of Swallowcliff, Wilts., Esq.; Confirmation by Sir G. Dethick, Garter. *Grants & Certificates (Harl. MS 1,441; Stowe MS 703)*

A dragon's head couped, or erased, Proper ducally gorged per pale Or and Azure out of the mouth flames of fire issuing of the last [sic].
SOUTH, of North Cove. *Davy, A. (Burke), tomb in churchyard, 1732*

A dragon's head couped Gules.
WARREN, M.D., 'Phisician to K. Geo. II. & III.' *MS Ordinary of Arms, fo. 26*. [In a later hand]*

A dragon's head and neck couped Argent ? pellety.
WRIGHT, of Downham. *Visitation 1664–8*

A dragon's head couped.
WYARD, James, died 1715; James Wyard, died 1741. *Her.Suff.Ch., Ledger stones, Brundish*

DRAGON'S HEAD, Erased [Alphabetically by name]

A dragon's head erased Or between two aspen branches Proper.
ASPIN, of Cockfield. *Davy, A.*

A dragon's head erased Azure pierced through the neck with a broken spear Or holding a piece of the same in his mouth headed Argent.
BERESFORD, Lord George. *Davy, A.*

A dragon's head erased Or pellety eared and langued Gules.
BLACKE, BLAKE. 'Rychard Blake' *MS Knight's Visitations, Essex**

A dragon's head erased Or pellety.
BLACKE, BLAKE. 'Richard Blake' *MS Philpot's Visitations, Essex**

A dragon's head erased Vert ducally gorged Or.
BLACKLEY, of Bury. *Davy, A.*

'upon his healme on a torse silver & sable a dragons head rasie vert langued gueles dented silver mantled gueles dobled silver'
BOYLAND, Richard, of Margaretting, co. Essex; Grant of Arms and Crest by Gilbert Dethick, Garter, 2 July I Elizabeth [1558/9]. *Misc.Gen. et Her. 3rd S. III. 128**

A dragon's head erased Gules collared Or line of the last vomiting fire Proper.
BRIGHT, Thomas, of S. Edmund's Bury, son of Robert Bright, of Nether Hall, Suff. Patent 10 May 1615. *Grants & Certificates (Stowe MS 767)*

A dragon's head erased Gules breathing flames of fire collared and lined Or.
BRIGHT, of Pakenham, Bricett. *Bokenham*

A dragon's head erased bendy of four Vert and Or between two bird's wings 'standing in pal pal' [sic] the first Argent the second Sable.
CARILL. *Wall's Book*

'to his Crest a Dragons hed bendey of iiij pecs rased vert or/ bet ii byrds wyngs standing in pale the fyrst ar/ the second sa/'
CARILL. 'Caryll' *MS Alphabet of Crests, fo. 21b*

A dragon's head erased Azure between two dragon's wings Argent.
CURSON. *Grants & Certificates (Stowe MS 700)*

A dragon's head erased Or langued Azure gorged with a coronet Gules.
CUTLER, Nicholas, of Eye, co. Suffolk; Grant by Barker. *Grants & Certificates (Stowe MS 692)*

A dragon's head erased Or ducally gorged Gules.
CUTLER, of Eye. *Visitation 1561 (MSS G. 7* 'langued azure' and Iveagh Copy*) and (ed. Metcalfe). Harl. 772*. Davy, A., Eye church monument. Washbourne*, 'Suff.' Proc.S.I.A. II. 142. Fairbairn*, 'Suff.'*

A dragon's head erased Gules collared.
CUTLER, of Eye. *Bokenham*

A dragon's head erased Gules.
DRAYCOT. *Davy, A.*

A dragon's head erased collared on the collar three escallops.
FENN. 'Fenn of Lincolnshire' *MS Ordinary of Arms, fo. 206**

A dragon's head erased Azure collared Argent on the collar three escallops Azure.
FENN, of Worlingworth. *Davy, A., All Saints Sudbury and Finningham churches. Washbourne, 'Suff.' Fairbairn, 'Suff.'*

A dragon's head erased gorged Ermine.
FENN, Sir John, Kt., F.A.S., of East Dereham in Norfolk. On tablet he erected in memory of Tom Martin, F.A.S., died 1771. *Her.Suff.Ch., Wall tablet in the porch, Palgrave*

A dragon's head erased collared (A dragon's head erased Azure collared Argent on the collar three escallops Azure).

FENN, Thomas, died 1818; daughter Anna, died 1833; Others. *Her.Suff.Ch., Wall tablet in chancel, All Saints Sudbury*
A dragon's head erased.
GOATE, of Thrandeston, Redgrave. *Davy, A., Redgrave churchyard.* John Goate, late of Thrandeston, gent., died 1736; widow Ann (Cullum), died 1739. *Partridge, 91 (Darby, 1826), Redgrave churchyard*
A dragon's head erased Vert gutty Argent collared Or with a large ring on either side of the collar.
GOLDING. 'Gorge Goldinge' *MS Philpot's Visitations, Suff.* *
A dragon's head erased Vert.
GOLDING, of Poslingford, Thorington. *Davy, A.*
A dragon's head erased Vert gutty de l'armes [*sic* should be d'eau] collared Argent.
GOLDING. *Davy, A. (Barrett MS)*
A dragon's head erased Vert collared and lined Or.
GOLDING, of Poslingford, Cavendish. *Davy, A. Fairbairn*, 'of Essex and Postingford [sic] and Cavendish, Suff.'* Frances, wife of Thomas Golding, died 1641; he died 1652. *Her.Suff.Ch., Monumental tablet, Poslingford. Shown as a dog's head*
A dragon's head erased Sable gutty collared and ringed Or.
GOLDING, George, of Poslingford and Thorington Hall, died 1803. *Her.Suff.Ch., Hatchment, Thorington*
A dragon's head erased quarterly per fesse dancetty Or and Azure.
HAMMOND, of Whitton. *Bokenham*
A dragon's head erased ducally gorged.
NORTH. *Visitation 1561 (ed. Howard) I. 195**
'to his crest a Dragons hed rasy sa/ open mouthed/ Langed g/ dented ar/ purfled or/a bowt his necke a cronall of the same   p C hawley'
NORTH. 'Sr Edward North knight lord of kyrtlynge in Cambrydgsh^{r}' *MS Alphabet of Crests, fo. 90b*
A dragon's head erased Sable ducally gorged Or.
NORTH, of Benacre, Lt. Glemham. *Sharpe. Davy, A.*
As above, with slight variations.
NORTH. *Berry, Sussex Genealogies, 221*, 'scaled'. Tymms, 200. Fairbairn, 'of Rougham Hall, Norf.' [sic]. E.A. Misc. 1910, 102.* Mary North, daughter of Dudley, 4th Baron North, married Sir William Spring, Bart., she died 1662. *Her.Suff.Ch., Ledger stone, Pakenham.* Henry North, of Laxfield, died 1674; widow Elizabeth (Wingfield), died 1706. *Ledger stone, Letheringham.* Hon. Sir Dudley North, died 1691; widow died 1715; Dudley North, died 1764. *Wall tablets, Lt. Glemham*
A dragon's head erased.
NORTH, Isabella, died 1701; Thomas North, died 1715. *Her.Suff.Ch., Ledger stone, St. Mary's Bury. Bookplates* *
A dragon's head erased gorged with a ducal coronet.
PIERSON. *Davy, A., Seal*
'upon a healme on a torse gold and azure a Dragons head rased gold, about his neck a Coronall langued gu manteled gules doubled argent'
RAYMOND. John Raymond of Dunmowe, co. Essex, gentleman; Grant of Arms and Crest by Gilbert Dethick, Garter, 15 November, 2 & 3 Philip & Mary (1555). *Miscellaneous Grants (H.S.) II. 178 (MS Queen's Coll. 140, No. 60)*
A dragon's head erased Or gorged with a coronet Gules.

RAYMOND, John, of Little Dunmow, co. Essex; Grant by Sir G. Dethick, Garter, 15 Nov., 2 & 3 Philip and Mary [1555/6]. *Grants & Certificates (Harl. MS 1,359)*
'a Dragons hed rased or/ a bowt his neck a coronall Langed g/ P garter Dethyke to John Remond of lytel Donmoo'
RAYMOND. 'Reymond of Lytell Donmowe' *MS Alphabet of Crests, fo. 109b*
A dragon's head erased Or ducally gorged Gules.
RAYMOND, of Belchamp Hall near Melford, Middleton. 'George Raymond' *MS Knight's Visitations, Essex*.* 'George Raymond' *MS Philpot's Visitations, Essex*. E.A. Misc. 1918, 33. Her.Suff.Ch., Hopton*
A dragon's head erased Argent.
REEVE, REVE, of Thwaite. *Visitation 1664–8**
A dragon's head erased Argent collared Or.
REEVE, REVE, of Monewden. *Davy, A., church brass. Washbourne*, 'Reve, Suff.' Fairbairn*, 'Reve, of Malden [sic], Suff.'* William Reve, died 1587; third son Thomas Reve, died 1595. *Her.Suff.Ch., Brass plates, Monewden*
A dragon's head erased Vert gutty –.
RUSH, of Benhall Lodge. *Sharpe*
A dragon's head erased Gules bezanty.
RYLEY. 'Riley, . . . , of London' *Grants & Certificates (Add. MS 12,225)*
A dragon's head erased.
RYLEY. *MS Heraldic Collections, fo. 29**
A dragon's head erased Ermine ducally gorged Gules breathing fire Proper.
SMITH, of Nettlestead, Elmsett, Chelsworth. *Davy, A.*
A dragon's head couped, or erased, Proper ducally gorged per pale Or and Azure out of the mouth flames of fire issuing of the last [*sic*].
SOUTH, of North Cove. *Davy, A. (Burke), Tomb in churchyard, 1732*
A dragon's head erased gorged with a ducal coronet.
SOUTH, Thomas, of this parish, Gent., died 1732; widow Judith (Aldred), died 1749; Others. *E.A.N. & Q. IV. 267, Churchyard tomb, North Cove. Her.Suff.Ch., Churchyard, North Cove*
A dragon's head erased.
SYER, of Lt. Waldingfield. *Proc.S.I.A. IX. 129, Slab in church.* Dey Syer, of Lt. Waldingfield, died 1740. *Her.Suff.Ch., 'as given by Davy – slab in north aisle, within the rails'. Not seen by Farrer, or in 1979*
A dragon's head erased quarterly Argent and Vert.
WEBSTER. *Davy, A.*
A dragon's head erased quarterly Or and Vert.
WEBSTER. Jane (Sparrow), wife of Richard Webster, died 1700 (Suckling). *Her.Suff.Ch., Ledger stone in churchyard, North Cove. Not found 1985*
A dragon's head erased Argent pelletty langued Gules.
WRIGHT, WRIGHT alias REVE, of Thwaite. *Visitation 1561 (MS G. 7*)*
A dragon's head erased Argent pelletty.
WRIGHT, of Santon Downham, Burnt Bradfield. 'Edmonde Wryght' *MS Knight's Visitations, Norf.* * 'Edmond Wright' *MS Philpot's Visitations, Norf.* Davy, A.*
A dragon's head erased Sable bezanty.
WRIGHT, Thomas, of Santon Downham, died 1757; Others. *Her.Suff.Ch., Wall tablet, Santon Downham*
A dragon's head erased Argent ducally gorged Or.

YOUNG. *Davy, A., Bradfield Combust church*
A dragon's head erased Or ducally gorged Argent.
YOUNG, of Bradfield Combust. *Davy, A.*
A dragon's head erased ducally gorged.
YOUNG, Arthur *Bookplate**

TWO DRAGON'S HEADS

Two dragon's heads erased and addorsed one Or the
other Azure enfiled by a coronet per pale
counterchanged.
POPE, Thomas, of Dodington, Esq., Grant by Sir
C. Barker, Garter. *Grants & Certificates (Stowe
MS 692)*

GRIFFIN

A griffin's head Proper.
ALDRED, ALRED, of Tannington. *Davy, A.*
A griffin's head Or.
BEDWELL, of Ipswich, Holton. *Davy, A.*
A griffin's head.
BRYAN. Sir Guy Bryan, of Acton, died 1390.
Davy, A.
A griffin's head.
ELMRUGGE, of Fakenham. *Davy, A.*
A griffin's head per pale Argent and Sable.
GODSALVE. *Davy, A., Blundeston church*
A griffin's head Or holding in the beak a sprig of
three trefoils Vert.
GREENE. John Wollaston Greene, of Bury, died
1925. *Her.Suff.Ch., Wall tablet, St. James's Bury*
A griffin's head.
HARSANT, of Wickham, Earl Soham, Dennington,
Brandeston. *Davy, A., Seal, Brandeston
churchyard*
A griffin's head holding in the beak a key Proper.
HILLARY, of Hadleigh. *Davy, A.*
A griffin's head between two wings Or holding in its
beak a 'sowned or a plomet' Sable.
JENNENS. 'Jenyns Maior of London at the
Coronacion H. viijth.' *Wall's Book*
'to his crest a gryffyns hede betwene ij wyngs or/
holding in his mouth a sowned or a plomet sa/'
JENNENS. 'Jennyns Maior of London/ knight by h
8/' *MS Alphabet of Crests, fo. 64*
A griffin's head per pale Or and Gules between two
wings Azure.
MASHAM, of Badwell Ash, Southolt. *Davy, A.
Washbourne, 'Suff.' Fairbairn, 'Suff.'*
A griffin's head Gules between two wings Or.
MONTACUTE, Earl of Salisbury. Of Kelsale,
Staverton, Bungay, Kessingland. *Davy, A.*
A griffin's head between two wings Proper.
MONTHERMER, of Clare. *Davy, A.*
A griffin's head with wings displayed Ermine.
POYNINGS, of Wrentham. *Davy, A.*
A griffin's head and neck wings elevated Sable
collared Ermine.
SHORT, of Boulge. *Davy, A.*
A griffin's head Or collared Gules studded Or.
SNELLING, of Whatfield, Ipswich, Elmsett. *Davy,
A. Washbourne, 'Surr., Suss. & Suff.' Fairbairn,
'Surrey, Sussex and Wheatfield [sic], S.'*
A griffin's head chevronny of four Argent and Sable
beaked Or langued Gules holding a branch of roses
Gules stalk and leaves Vert.
WATSON, Edward, of Liddington, co. Rutland,
gent. *Grants & Certificates (Stowe MS 693;
Add. MS 14,830)*
A griffin's head wings indorsed Azure issuing from
a plume of ostrich feathers two Argent and three Or.
WYE. *Washbourne*, 'Glouc. and Suff.' Fairbairn,
'of Ipswich, Suff. and co. Glouc. wings addorsed.'*

GRIFFIN'S HEAD, Couped

An eagle's, or griffin's head, couped Argent beaked
Or charged on the neck with two chevronels Azure.
BURROUGH, BURROUGHE, of Wickhambrook.
*Visitation 1561 (ed. Howard) II. 233, on a brass
of 1597*
A griffin's head couped Argent charged on the neck
with two chevrons Vert.
BURROUGHS, of Ipswich, Wickhambrook.
*Davy, A., St. Margaret's church Ipswich. E.A.N. &
Q. IX. 213, 293*
'apon his healme on a torse argent and vert a
griffons heade cowpey of the fielde [Argent] beaked
d'or, charged with too Cheuernels of the coulor as in
the armes [Vert], manteled gules, dowbled argent.'
BURROUGH, Thomas, of Wickhambrook; Grant of
Arms and Crest by Cooke, Clarenceux, 20 June
1586. *Muskett. I. 294, 308, 'on brass at
Wickhambrook, painted'*
A griffin's head and neck couped Gules pierced
through with an arrow Proper.
COLDHAM. *Sharpe*
A griffin's head erased [shown couped in plate].
DAGWORTH. Sir Nicholas Dagworth, Blickling,
co. Norfolk. Brass of 1401. *Cotman's Norfolk
Brasses, plate 13*, p. 11*
A griffin's head couped gorged with a ducal coronet.
FOXWELL, Rev. John, A.M., died 1731.
Her.Suff.Ch., Slab in the vestry, Rattlesden
A griffin's head couped Or.
GREY, of Cavendish. *Davy, A.*
A griffin's head couped winged Or holding in its
mouth a plummet Sable.
JENNENS. 'Jennings' *MS Martin's Crests*
A griffin's head couped between two wings
endorsed Proper in the beak a plummet pendent
Sable.
JENNENS, of Acton. *Davy, A. Bookplate**
A griffin's head couped between two wings
endorsed Argent in the beak a plummet pendent
Sable.
JENNENS. 'Wm. Jennens, Esq., of Acton Place,
Sheriff of Suffolk 1753, died unmarried 1798
aged 98' *E.A.N. & Q. IV. 252*
A griffin's head couped between two wings inverted
Proper holding in the beak a plummet pendent
Sable.
JENNENS. *Fairbairn, 'of Acton, Suff.'*
A griffin's head couped Gules beaked Or between
two wings Azure each charged with a billet Or.
MASHAM, 'William, of Shackerland Hall in
Badwell Ash, co. Suffolk, and now citizen
alderman and haberdasher, of London';
Confirmation by Sir G. Dethick, Garter, 12 June
1583. *Grants & Certificates (Harl. MS 1,441;
Add. MS 26,753; Stowe MS 703)*
A griffin's head couped wings expanded Or.
MONTAGUE, of Marlesford, Gunton, Beccles.
Davy, A.
A griffin's head couped Vert gutty Argent.
RUSH, of Benhall, Sudbourne. *Davy, A.*
A griffin's head couped Gules winged Argent.
WALL, of Aldeburgh. *Sharpe*

GRIFFIN'S HEAD, Erased [Alphabetically by name]

A griffin's head erased Proper.
ACKWORTH, of Suffolk. *Davy, A. (Edms.)*
A griffin's head erased Gules.
ALVERD, of Woodbridge, Ipswich. *Davy, A., St.
Stephen's church Ipswich*

A griffin's head erased Argent beaked Azure.

ALVERD, ALUARD, of Ipswich. *Proc.S.I.A. XXVII. 150 (Dandy Pedigree)*

A griffin's head erased grasped at the neck by the head and mouth of a boar.

BACON, of Suffolk. *Farrer (Seals), 'on Lord Keeper Bacon's copy of the letters patent relating to the Redgrave estate'*

A griffin's head erased Or.

BATELL, BATTELY, BATTELEY, of South Elmham St. James, Bury, Gt. Whelnetham. *Davy, A., Gt. Whelnetham church monument.* Charles Battely, Esq., died 1722; widow Elizabeth, died 1752. *Suff. Green Bks, Gt. Whelnetham, 164. Her.Suff.Ch., Wall tablet, Gt. Whelnetham*

A griffin's head erased Sable ducally collared lined and ringed Or.

BOOTH, BOWTH. *MS Heraldic Collections, fo. 36**

A griffin's head erased Sable collared and studded Argent.

BROWN. 'Browne' *MS Heraldic Alphabet*

A griffin's head erased Proper.

BROWN. Rector of Kelsale. *Davy, A.*

A griffin's head erased.

BROWN. *Livery button**

A griffin's head erased Argent charged on the neck with a chevron Vert surmounted of a chevron Argent.

BURROUGHES, of Melton, Kessingland, etc. *Davy, A.*

A griffin's head erased charged with two chevrons on the neck.

BURROUGHS, Thomas, died 1597; two wives. *Her.Suff.Ch., Effigy brass, Wickhambrook*

A griffin's head erased charged with two chevrons.

BURROUGHS, Charles, gent., died 1690; widow Amy, died 1701. *Her.Suff.Ch., Ledger stone, St. Margaret's Ipswich*

A griffin's head erased Argent.

BURWELL. 'Francis Burwell of Sutton, Suffolk, died about 1627' *Durham Visitations, 1666 (ed. Foster), 56**

A griffin's head erased.

BURWELL, of Shottisham. *Davy, A., Shottisham and Sutton churches. E.A. Misc. 1921, 40.* Francis Burwell, son of Francis Burwell of Sutton, died 1678; Charles Burwell, died 1741. *Her.Suff.Ch., Ledger stones, Sutton.* Francis Burwell, died 1702. *Ledger stone, Shottisham*

A griffin's head erased Argent beaked Azure collared with three lozenges Azure.

BURWELL. *Davy, A.*

A griffin's head erased thrust through the neck with a dart.

CARTWRIGHT, Thomas, died 1754. *Her.Suff.Ch., Ledger stone in nave, St. Mary Stoke Ipswich. Not found 1983*

A griffin's head erased Argent ducally gorged Or.

CHAPLIN, of East Bergholt, Sudbury, Bury, Levington [*sic* ?Chevington]. *Davy, A., East Bergholt church and Chevington churchyard.* 'Will. Chaplin of Bury S. Ed. gent. ?1718' *Partridge, 220 (Darby, 1831), untinctured*

A griffin's head erased.

CHAPLIN. 'Chaplyn of Sudbury' *Golding, Tradesman's token, 1667.* William Chaplin, of Bury St. Eds., died 1713. *Muskett. III. 112 (Davy, Add. MSS 19, 017), churchyard monument, Chevington*

'on a wreath of the colours a griphons head erased Or, gorged with a mural crown Vert'

CHAPLIN. 'Francis Chaplyn, of London, Clothworker'; Grant of Arms and Crest to Sir Francis Chaplyn by Edward Bysshe, Clarenceux, 6 August 1668. *Muskett. III. 118 (Herald's College, Miscellaneous Grants V. 241 and 280)*

A griffin's head erased ensigned with a ducal coronet.

CHAPLIN. 'Joseph Chaplin Esqʳ Late of This Parish, Lord of the Mannors of old Hall And the Comandre, Patron of Brantham Cum Bergholt, and Here to Fore High Sherif of the County of Suffolk . . . died 1728' *E.A.N. & Q. XII. 334, Altar tomb in north chapel, East Bergholt. Muskett. III. 101*

A griffin's head erased Argent ducally collared Or.

CHAPLIN, Joseph, Lord of the manor, died 1728. *Her.Suff.Ch., Altar tomb, East Bergholt*

A griffin's head erased Argent.

COTTON, of Gt. Barton, Exning, Finningham, Ashfield. 'Sr. John Cotton' *MS Knight's Visitations, Cambs.* MS Ordinary of Arms, fo. 124* MS Heraldic Alphabet. Davy, A. Washbourne*, 'Suff.' Fairbairn*, 'Suff.'*

A griffin's head erased holding in the mouth a sinister hand couped.

CROUGHTON, of Clare. *Davy, A.*

A griffin's head erased Sable.

CUDMORE, CUDNOR. *Davy, A. Washbourne*, 'Ess. and Suff.'*

A griffin's head erased [shown couped in plate].

DAGWORTH. Sir Nicholas Dagworth, Blickling, co. Norfolk. Brass of 1401. *Cotman's Norfolk Brasses, plate 13*, p. 11*

A griffin's head erased per fesse.

DASHWOOD. *Visitation 1561 (ed. Howard), II. 130*, Bookplate*

'and for his Creast on a Helmet and Wreath of his Colours A Griffons Head Erminoys beakt and erazed Gules Mantled Gules doubled Argent'

DASHWOOD, Francis, of London; Grant of Arms and Crest by Bysshe, Clarenceux, 24th October 1662. *Misc.Gen. et Her. 3rd S. V. 137*

A griffin's head erased Erminois erasures Gules.

DASHWOOD. *MS Heraldic Alphabet*

A griffin's head erased per fesse Erminois and Gules.

DASHWOOD, of Bury. *Davy, A., St. James's church*

A griffin's head erased per fesse Or and Gules.

DASHWOOD, of Bury, Honington, Peyton Hall, Beccles, *Davy, A.*

A griffin's head erased Ermine.

DASHWOOD. *Bookplate**

A griffin's head erased Argent ducally gorged Or.

DYCER, of Wrentham. *Middlesex Visitation 1663 (ed. Foster), 58*

A griffin's head Argent beaked and erased Gules gorged with a mural coronet Azure.

ELLISTON, Joseph, of Tillingham, second son of Matthew Elliston of Heveningham Castle, co. Essex [*sic* ?Hedingham Castle]; Confirmation by Sir R. St. George, Clarenceux. *Grants & Certificates (Add. MS 14,293)*

A griffin's head erased Argent charged on the neck with three hurts.

FARR, of North Cove. *E.A.N. & Q. IV. 265, church monument*

A griffin's head erased Argent on the neck three pellets in pale.

FARR, John, Esq., Magistrate and J.P., died 1824; widow Hannah, died 1839. *Her.Suff.Ch., Monument, North Cove*

A griffin's head erased Argent.
> FARR, of North Cove. *E.A.N. & Q. IV. 265, Hatchment, North Cove.* Thomas Farr, of Beccles, died 1850 aged 87. *Her.Suff.Ch., Hatchment, North Cove, 'langued Gules'*

A griffin's head erased Vert beaked Gules.
> FETTIPLACE. *Davy, A. (Edms.) Misc.Gen. et Her. 5th S. II. 290**

A griffin's head erased.
> FOWLE. *Proc.S.I.A. XXVII. 123, Stone shield, Shrubland Park*

A griffin's head erased Argent pierced through the neck with an arrow Gules barbed Argent the neck vulned Gules.
> FOWLE. Mary, wife of John Fowle, of Brome Hall, co. Norfolk, died 1722. *Her.Suff.Ch., Slab in chancel, Blythburgh*

A griffin's head erased Argent pierced through the neck with an arrow Or.
> FOWLE, FOWLE-MIDDLETON, Baronets, of Shrubland Park, 1829–1887. *Her.Suff.Ch., Hatchments and Glass, Barham.* Sir William Fowle Fowle-Middleton, 2nd Bart., died 1860; widow died 1867. *Hatchment, Crowfield*

A griffin's head erased Argent pierced through the neck with a spear Or embrued Gules.
> FOWLE-MIDDLETON, Sir William, died 1860. *Her.Suff.Ch., Brass in south aisle, Coddenham*

A griffin's head Or erased Gules gorged with a crest coronet Argent.
> FOXWELL, FOXALL. 'John Foxall, of London, gent.' Patent 29 November 1579. *Grants & Certificates (Harl. MS 1,359; Add. MSS 4,966 and 12,225)*

A griffin's head erased with wings endorsed.
> FULLER, John, of Yarmouth, died 1743. *Her.Suff.Ch., Ledger stone, Gorleston*

A griffin's head erased Azure charged with three chevrons Argent.
> GAINSBOROUGH, of Sudbury. *Davy, A.*

A griffin's head erased Sable.
> GARDINER. *Davy, A. (Barrett)*

A griffin's head erased Argent surmounted by two branches of laurel in saltire Proper.
> GARDNER, DUNN-GARDNER. Algernon C.W. Dunn-Gardner, of Denston Hall and Chatteris, died 1929. *Her.Suff.Ch., Glass, Denston. First crest – for Gardner*

A griffin's head erased Or.
> GARTON. *MS Ordinary of Arms, fo. 123**

A griffin's head erased.
> GEDDING. *Davy, A.*

A griffin's head erased paly wavy of four Argent and Sable erasures and beaked Or holding a branch of 'jelofres' [gillyflowers. July flowers or pinks] Gules stalked Vert.
> GODSALVE. *Wall's Book*
> 'to his crest a gryffyns hed pale of iiij pecs wavey ar/sa/ the rasures and membred or holding a braunche of Juleflowers g/ stalked Vert'
> GODSALVE. 'Godsalff of Norwyche' *MS Alphabet of Crests, fo. 47*

A griffin's head erased paly wavy Argent and 'g als s' holding in the beak a bunch of three gillyflowers Gules slipped Or.
> GODSALVE. *MS Heraldic Collections, fo. 87b**

A griffin's head erased paly wavy Argent and Sable eared Sable beaked Or holding therein a branch of gillyflowers Gules leaved Proper.
> GODSALVE, of Suffolk. *Davy, A.*

A griffin's head erased Vert in the beak a fleur-de-lis Gules.
> GODSALVE, Thomas, of Norwich, gent.; Grant by Barker. *Grants & Certificates (Stowe MS 692)*

A griffin's head erased langued Gules.
> GOLTY, Richard, A.M., died 1733. *Her.Suff.Ch., Slab, Belstead*

A griffin's head erased quarterly Or and Vert holding in the beak a trefoil Sable.
> GREEN. 'Grene' *Wall's Book*

A griffin's head erased quarterly Or and Sable holding in the beak a trefoil slipped Sable.
> GREEN, GREENE, of Bury. *MS Heraldic Collections, fo. 31*. Davy, A.*

In front of a gryphon's head erased Or holding in the beak three trefoils Vert two annulets interlaced fesseways Azure between two bezants [sic].
> GREENE. *Fairbairn, 'of Nether Hall, Bury St. Edmunds'*

A griffin's head erased Or.
> GREY, of Cavendish. *Davy, A.*

A griffin's head erased per pale Argent and Gules charged with a rose counterchanged.
> GRUBBE, of Southwold. *Crisp's Visitation. I. 27–32*, Pedigree. Fairbairn, 'of Southwold, Suff.'*

A palm branch in bend sinister Vert in front of a griffin's head erased Or charged with a gemel Gules and holding in the beak a hawk's lure Argent lined and ringed Or.
> HALL. Rector of Glemsford, c.1875. *Crisp's Visitation. IV. 29*. 'Rev. H. Hall, The Rectory, Glemsford, Suff.' Fairbairn*

A griffin's head erased.
> HALLWARD, of Milden. *Davy, A.*

A griffin's head erased Gules.
> HALLWARD, of Assington, Milden. *Davy, A.*

A griffin's head erased per pale.
> HAMMOND, of Pettistree, Ipswich. *Davy, A., Pettistree church and St. Clement's Ipswich churchyard*

A griffin's head erased Or.
> HANHAM. *MS Heraldic Collections, fo. 8**

A griffin's head erased Or beaked and eared Sable.
> HANHAM, of Hitcham, Bildeston. *Davy, A.*

A griffin's head erased Ermine.
> HANKEY, of East Bergholt. *E.A.N. & Q. XII. 335, Church monuments*

A griffin's head erased.
> HARDING, of Eye. *Davy, A.*

An eagle's, or griffin's, head erased.
> HARDING. Mary, daughter of Richard Harding, died 1695; Richard Harding, died . . . *Her.Suff.Ch., Ledger stone in churchyard, Eye*

A griffin's head erased.
> HARSANT. 'John Harsant gent. of this par. 10 Nov. 1778 ag. 65.' *Partridge, 128 (Darby, 1825), Headstone, Brandeston churchyard*

A griffin's head erased Ermine collar line and ring Or.
> HAWES. 'Henry Hawe, of Dudlington, co. Norfolk'; Grant by Sir G. Dethick, Garter, 15 November 2 Eliz. [1559/60]. *Grants & Certificates (Harl. MS 1,359; Add. MS 26,753; Stowe MS 703, which gives date of Grant as 10 November.)*

A griffin's head erased Ermine collared ringed and lined.
> HAWES. 'Hawe of Norfolk' *MS Heraldic Alphabet*

A griffin's head erased Or beaked Gules.
> HAWES. 'Haw' *MS Heraldic Alphabet*

A griffin's head erased collared and chained.

HAWES, of Brandeston, Framlingham. *Davy, A., Brandeston church*
A griffin's head erased Ermine collared and lined Or.

HAWES, Henry, died 1717; Thomas Hawes, died 1746. *Her.Suff.Ch., Slabs, Brandeston*
A griffin's head erased Argent murally gorged Gules thereon three escallops Argent.

HUDSON. *MS Heraldic Collections, fo. 43**
A griffin's head erased Argent beak and ears Sable on the neck three pellets in pale.

HUMBERSTON, of Dunwich, Bawdsey. *Davy, A.*
A griffin's head erased Argent gutty de poix.

JACKMAN, of Ipswich. Rector of Falkenham. *Davy, A.*
A griffin's head erased Sable gutty Or.

JACKMAN, of Ipswich. Rector of Falkenham. *Davy, A.*
A griffin's head erased (now defaced).

JOHNSON, William, Rector of Horham for 36 years, Vicar of Stradbroke for 29 years, died 1782; sister Hannah Johnson, died 1795. *Her.Suff.Ch., Ledger stones, Stradbroke*
A griffin's head erased Or.

KEBLE. Probably for John Keble, of Halesworth, died 1652/3. *Her.Suff.Ch., Hatchment, Halesworth*
A griffin's head erased.

LANE. Elizabeth, daughter of Samuel Lillingstone of Beccles, wife of Samuel Lane, died 1831. *Her.Suff.Ch., Monument, Barsham*
A griffin's head erased Proper charged with a fleur-de-lis Or.

MCCALMONT, of Chevely Park in Newmarket. *Burke, L.G. 1900 ed.**
A griffin's head Argent erased Gules gorged with a collar compony Gules and Argent.

MICKLETHWAITE. *Davy, A.*
A griffin's head erased Gules charged with three crescents in pale Argent.

PERIENT, PERYN. *Davy, A.*
A ?griffin's head erased in front of a pair of wings addorsed.

POSTLE. Elizabeth (Betts), wife of Jehosophat Postle, gent., of Norwich; she died 1777. *Her.Suff.Ch., Ledger stone, Wortham*
A griffin's head erased Pean.

RAIKES, of Battisford, Yoxford. *Davy, A.*
A griffin's head erased Azure beak and ears Or.

READ, William and Thomas, of Wickford, co. Essex; Confirmation by Sir E. Bysshe, Garter, 20 January 1653. *Grants & Certificates (Add. MS 26,758)*
A griffin's head erased Azure purfled [garnished] Or.

READ, of Halesworth. *Davy, A.*
A griffin's head erased.

READ. *Livery button**
A griffin's head erased Gules.

REEVE. *Washbourne*, 'Suff.' Fairbairn*, 'Suff.'*
A griffin's head erased Gules beaked Or.

ROSSINGTON, of Framlingham, Yoxford. *Davy, A.*
A griffin's head erased Sable collared Or langued Gules.

RYLEY, of Whepstead. *Davy, A., church*
A griffin's head erased Argent collared Azure thereon a fret Argent.

SANDBY. Rector of Flixton. *Davy, A.*
A griffin's head erased Argent ducally gorged and beaked Or.

SHELLEY. *MS Ordinary of Arms, fo. 208**
A griffin's head erased Argent ducally gorged Or.

SHELLEY, of Bury. *Visitation 1664–8. Bokenham. MS Martin's Crests. Davy, A. Fairbairn, 'Shelly, Suff.'*
A griffin's head erased Argent in the beak a dexter gauntlet Azure garnished Or.

SKINNER, . . . , of . . . ; Grant by R. Lee, Clarenceux, August 1594. *Grants & Certificates (Harl. MS 6,169)*
A griffin's head erased Argent holding in the beak a hand couped Gules.

SKINNER. Rector of Sweffling, 1869. *Davy, A., Church paten.* [Arms only]
A griffin's head erased Argent.

SKINNER. Unidentified. *Her.Suff.Ch., Hatchment, Elmsett*
A griffin's head erased Or langued Azure gorged with a fesse Ermine cotised Gules.

SNELLING, Richard, of . . ., near Ipswich, co. Suffolk; Grant by W. Dethick, Garter, 23 April 1594. *Grants & Certificates (Stowe MS 676)*
A griffin's head erased Or collared Gules.

SNELLING, Charles, of East Horsley, Surrey; Grant 1631. *Grants & Certificates (Add. MS 12,225)*
A griffin's head erased Or collared Gules.

SNELLING, of Whatfield, Ipswich, Elmsett, Blakenham. *Visitation 1664–8*, 'To Rob' Snelling of Whatfeld by Ipswich p' Wm Dethick G 23 Aprill 1594 (Harl. MS 1085, p. 19b)', collar studded. MS Fairfax (Lev.)*
A griffin's head erased Gules beaked Argent charged on the neck with a bezant and debruised by a staff reguly Or.

STEWARD, of Norfolk. *MS Ordinary of Arms, fo. 37**
A griffin's head erased.

SUTTON, of Bury. *Davy, A., St. Mary's church. Bookplate**
A griffin's head erased and collared.

SYER. Rev. William Henry Syer, died 1868; Rev. Barrington Bloomfield Syer, B.A., Rector of Kedington 1869–death 1909. *Her.Suff.Ch., Wall tablets, Kedington*
A griffin's head erased party per pale Argent and Sable.

TEMPEST. 'Henry T.D. Tempest, F.S.A., Bridge House, Brockford, Nr. Stowmarket, Suff.' *Fairbairn*
A griffin's head erased Gules eared Or holding in the beak a gem-ring Or.

TILNEY. *MS Ordinary of Arms, fo. 124**
A griffin's head erased.

VAUX. Lord Vaux of Harroden. *Davy, A., Eye church*
A griffin's head erased ?Sable.

VAUX, of Ipswich, Melton. *Davy, A., St. Nicholas church vestry, Ipswich*
A griffin's head erased Ermine gorged with a wreath or chaplet.

VOYCE, of Sudbury. John Voyce, died 1690; Will. Voyce, late of London, linen-draper, died 1728; Roger Voyce, clothier, of this town, died 1734; Others. *Partridge, 19 (Darby, 1827), Tomb, Sudbury All Saints churchyard. Davy, A., All Saints church*
A griffin's head erased collared.

VOYCE, Roger, clothier of Sudbury, died 1731; Others. *Her.Suff.Ch., Altar tomb in churchyard, All Saints Sudbury*
A griffin's head erased chevronny of four Argent and Sable holding in the beak a branch of roses Gules stalked and leaved Vert.

WATSON. *MS Ordinary of Arms, fo. 192**
A griffin's head erased Argent.
WATSON. *MS Ordinary of Arms, fo. 192*. MS Fairfax*
A griffin's head erased Or ducally gorged of the same [*sic*].
WATSON, of Glemsford. *Davy, A. (Edms.) Bookplate*, untinctured*

TWO GRIFFIN'S HEADS

Two griffin's heads erased and addorsed Or and Azure ducally gorged counterchanged.
POPE. *MS Martin's Crests*
Two griffin's heads erased and addorsed Or and Azure with plain collars counterchanged.
POPE, Earl of Down. *Davy, A.*

IBEX

An 'ilex's' or ibex's, head Or issuing out of the centre of a rose Gules barbed Vert.
BEWLEY, of Suffolk. *Davy, A. Washbourne*, 'Suff. ibex's head'. Fairbairn, 'Suff. ibex's head.'*

PANTHER

'Upon hys healme on a Torse silver and geules A Panthers hedd Rasyd Acordynge to ye first [Proper] manteled sable dobled silver'
CLERKE, Edward, of Kettlebaston; Grant of Arms and Crest by Thomas Hawley, Clarenceux, 2nd May, 2 & 3 Philip and Mary [1555/6]. *MS Suffolk Armorial Families**
'to his crest on a wreth ar/g/ a panthers hed rasy pp color p C hawley the 2 & 3 of Phelyp and Mary'
CLERKE. 'Edward Clarke of the manner of kettell Baston' *MS Alphabet of Crests, fo. 23b*
A panther's head Proper gorged with a collar counter-embattled Argent charged with two mullets Gules.
GRIGBY, of Ipswich. *Sharpe*
A panther's head erased the mouth closed Or spotted Azure and Gules.
FRAMLINGHAM. 'Framelyngham' *Wall's Book*
'to his Crest a panthers hede closse mouthed or/ Spotted g/ rased knight of h 8 Sr James fframlynghm'
FRAMLINGHAM. 'Fframlynghm' *MS Alphabet of Crests, fo. 39*
A panther's head erased Argent semy of torteaux.
HOBSON. 'Hobsun' *Wall's Book*
'to his crest a panthers hed rased ar/ full of torteaulx'
HOBSON. *MS Alphabet of Crests, fo. 55*

PEGASUS

A Pegasus head Gules winged Argent pellety.
TOLLEMACHE. 'Tolmach, Earl of Dysart. Of Helmingham. *Bokenham*

PHOENIX

A 'phenix' head and neck Or crested Azure wings displayed Azure the inner parts Or.
SEYMOUR. *MS Ordinary of Arms, fo. 200**
A phoenix's head issuing from flames.
SHAFTO. Theodosia (Meade), wife of Sir Robert Alexander Shafto Adair, 2nd Bart., later Baron Waveney. She died 1871. *Her.Suff.Ch., Statue in chapel at end of north aisle, Flixton. Second crest – for Shafto*

SATYR

A Satyr's head side-faced [with ears drawn as dragon's wings] Sable.
BAWDE. 'S. Thomas Bawde of Essex' *Harl. MS 6163**

A Satyr's head in profile Sable wings to it and the tongue hanging out of the mouth.
BAWDE, of Bures. *Davy, A.*

HERALDIC TIGER

A tiger's head erased Sable armed Or gorged with a fesse wavy Argent.
BALES, of Wilby. *Davy, A.*
A tiger's head erased Sable armed Or gorged with a fesse wavy Azure [*sic*].
BALES. *Fairbairn, 'Wilby, Suff.'*
A tiger's head Ermines.
BARTON. 'Barton of Grimston in –' *Wall's Book* 'to his crest a tygers hed ermyns'
BARTON. 'Barton of Grymston' *MS Alphabet of Crests, fo. 11*
A tiger's head couped Azure collared Sable [*sic*] ringed Or.
CAVENDISH, CANDISH alias GARNON. *Davy, A.*
Issuing out of a quatrefoil Or a tiger's head erased per pale indented Argent and Sable tusked Or langued Gules.
EYRE. 'Robert Eyer, of Eye, co. Suffolk. Descended paternally of the house of Hope, co. Derby, and of Eyers, by his mother'; Confirmation by Barker. *Grants & Certificates (Stowe MS 692)*
An heraldic tiger's head erased Erminois.
FISH. 'Walter Fysh, of Stow Market, Suff.'; Grant by R. Cooke, Clarenceux, 1586. *Grants & Certificates (Stowe MS 670; Harl. MS 1,359; Add. MS 14,297, which last says 'Per Chester')*
A tiger's head erased Ermine maned and tufted Or.
FISH, of Stowmarket. *Davy, A.*
A tiger's head erased Argent.
GOLTIE, GOLTY, of Dennington, Framlingham, Ashbocking, Sweffling. 'Goltie. rector of fframlingham and of Ash bocking (in his house). The Crest, a Tygers head erased Argent'. *MS Golty's Ordinary, fo. 129. Davy, A.*
'A Tygers head'.
GOLTIE, GOLTY. 'Rich. Goltye: Recto^r of Framlinghā. his grandfather was of Ipsw^{ch} his wife dā of Sam. Ward B.D. ye famous preacher in Ipsw^{ch}.' *MS Fairfax*
An heraldic tiger's head erased Azure tufted collared and lined Or.
LENTON, John, of Aldwinckle, co. Northants.; Confirmation by R. Cooke, Clarenceux, 21 May 1584. *Grants & Certificates (Stowe MSS 670 and 700; Add. MS 14,295)*
A tiger's head erased Azure collared lined and ringed Or.
LENTON, LINTON, of Hasketon. *Davy, A., church, 1737*
A tiger's head erased quarterly Argent and Sable armed maned and tufted Or.
MANNOCK. 'Sr Francis Mannock of Giffords hall in Sokenayland Knight Barronett' *MS Lilly's Visitation of Suffolk**
A tiger's head erased quarterly Argent and Gules.
MANNOCK, of Giffard's Hall in Stoke. *Davy, A. Washbourne, 'Suff.' Fairbairn, 'of Gifford's Hall, Suff. heraldic tiger's head.'*
A tiger's head couped maned and tufted Or.
MANNOCK. *Davy, A. (Barrett MS)*
A tiger's head Argent erased Gules tusked and crined Sable.
MARSHALL. 'Rychard Marshall of Barking' *MS Knight's Visitations, Essex*. 'Richard Marshall' MS Philpot's Visitations, Essex**

From rays of the sun Or a tiger's head Sable collar chain and tufts Or.

MILESON. 'Edmund Militon, of St. Edmund's Bury, Suffolk'; Grant by R. St. George, 1611. *Grants & Certificates (Harl. MS 6,140)*

Issuing out of a fire Or a tiger's head Sable collared and lined Or.

MILESON, MELLISENT, of Bury, Ipswich, Norton. *Visitation 1664–8*, 'p' Ric. St. George, Norroy, 1612 (Harl. MS 1085, p. 25). Davy, A., St Mary Tower church, Ipswich*

A tiger's head Sable collared and lined Or, behind the rays of the sun issuing from a cloud Proper.

MILESON. 'Milleson, of Norton' *Bokenham, 'p. R. St. George Norroy'*

Issuing out of rays a tiger's head collared and studded lined and ringed.

MILESON. 'Edmon milison of St. edmunds Bury' *MS Heraldic Collections, fo. 88b**

A tiger's head erased Argent crined and armed Or shot through the neck with a barbed arrow Or feathered and headed Argent.

MORE. *MS Heraldic Alphabet*

A tiger's head erased Argent tusked tufted and gorged by two bars all Or.

REEVE, Francis, of Maldon, in Essex. Patent 1590. *Grants & Certificates (Harl. MS 1,359; Stowe MS 670)*

A tiger's head erased Argent collared Or.

REEVE, REVE, of Monewden. *Bokenham. Davy, A. Washbourne, 'Reeve, Suff. Armed, maned and collared Or'. Fairbairn, 'Reeve, Suff. Armed, maned, collared Or'*

A tyger's head couped Argent collared and crowned Or.

ROLFE, of Hadleigh. *MS Fairfax (Tyl.)*

A tiger's head Or.

SCRIVENER, of Sibton. *Dade MS. (Davy, Suff. Coll.: Add. MS 19,126, fo. 9)*

An heraldic tiger's head erased Or gorged with a coronet Argent.

YOUNG. 'Lancelot Young, the Queen's Glazier'; Exemplification by R. Cooke, Chester. *Grants & Certificates (Stowe MS 670)*

UNICORN

A unicorn's head Or between two ostrich feathers Argent.

ABBOT, of Sudbury. *Misc.Gen. et Her. 5th S. IX. 12, Pedigree*

A unicorn's head between two branches of laurel in orle.

BRADSTREET, of Bentley, Raydon, etc. *Davy, A.*

A unicorn's head Argent armed and crested [*sic* ?crined] Or.

CARRINGTON, KERRINGTON, of Glemsford, Thorpe Morieux, St. Nicholas Ipswich. *Davy, A.*

A unicorn's head issuing Proper.

COLLYER. Rector of Gisleham, Vicar of Bungay, Trimley and Raydon. *Davy, A.*

A unicorn's head Or winged Azure.

COOKE. 'John Cooke de gedehall essex' *Banners & Standards**

A unicorn's head Argent horned Or.

CUNNINGHAM. Charles Cunningham, Gent., 1788; Rear Admiral Sir Charles Cunningham, K.G.H., died 1834. *E.A.N. & Q. I. 311–12, Monuments, Eye church*

A unicorn's head Or.

CUNNINGHAM. Vicar of Lowestoft, 1830–60. *Davy, A.*

A unicorn's head Argent horned bearded and maned Or.

CURWEN. 'Curuen' *Wall's Book*

'to his Crest an Unycorine hed ar the horne berd and mayne or/'

CURWEN. *MS Alphabet of Crests, fo. 20*

A unicorn's head Argent maned and horned Or.

DANIEL. *Davy, A.*

A unicorn's head Ermine armed and attired Or.

DOGGET, DOGET, of Groton, London. *London Visitation Peds. 1664 (H.S.), 56. Misc.Gen. et Her. 5th S. VIII. 226 (Harl. MS 1086)*

A unicorn's head Ermine maned Or horned Argent.

DOGGETT, 'of London from Groton', Boxford. *Muskett. I. 337 (Harl. MS 1086)*

A unicorn's head.

HOWE, of Stowmarket. *MS Fairfax (Tyl.)*

'vpon a heaulme on a Torce of his coulers an vnicornes hedde sable issuant out of a Son golde'

KITSON, Thomas, of Hengrave; Grant of Alteration of Arms and Crest by Sir Gilbert Dethick, Garter, Robert Cooke Clarenceux and William Flower, Norroy, 13 February 1568. *Visitation 1561 (ed. Howard), II. 98–9**

From rays of the sun Or a unicorn's head Sable.

KITSON, Thomas, of Hengrave, Suffolk. New Arms and Crest granted in place of the older ones, by Sir G. Dethick, R. Cook and W. Flower, 13 Feb. 1568. *Grants & Certificates (Harl. MSS 1,359 and 1,441; Add. MS 26,753; Stowe MS 703)*

Out of park pales Or a unicorn's head Sable maned and armed Or.

KITSON, KYTSON. *Visitation 1561 (ed. Howard), II. 83**

Issuant out of a demi-sun Or a unicorn's head Sable.

KITSON, KYTSON, of Hengrave. 'Kittson' *MS ex-Taylor Coll.*, 'unicorn armed Or'. Gage (Hengrave)*

From a demi-estoile of six points Or a unicorn's head Sable maned and armed Or.

KITSON. *Davy, A.*

A unicorn's head Argent attired and maned Or environed with palisades Or.

KITSON, of Hengrave. *Davy, A. Washbourne, 'Suff.' Fairbairn, 'Kitson, Kittson, Suff.'*

A unicorn's head Sable armed and maned Or.

KITSON. *Fairbairn, 'Hengrave, Suff.' Her.Suff.Ch., Effigy monument, Hengrave, mane and horn untinctured*

A unicorn's head Argent armed and crined Or.

KNOTT, of Suffolk. *Davy, A. (Berry)*

A unicorn's head ducally gorged in a tuft of five ostrich feathers.

UPCHER, of Sudbury, Willisham, Gt. Yarmouth. *Davy, A. Misc.Gen. et Her. 3rd S. III. 80, bookplate*, 'Peter Upcher Esq.'*

A unicorn's head Argent armed Or.

WHITE, William, A.M., Rector, died 1841. *Her.Suff.Ch., Wall tablet and Glass, Stradbroke*

A unicorn's head.

WILDE, of Lowestoft. *Davy, A., church. Lees, 27*

UNICORN'S HEAD, Couped

A unicorn's head couped Or between two ostrich feathers Argent.

ABBOT, ABBOTT, of Hawkedon, Somerton, Mildenhall, Sudbury. *Visitation 1664–8. Bokenham. Davy, A. Abbot, of Swan Hall, Hawkedon, 1568–1764. E.A. Misc. 1926, 12*

A unicorn's head couped Sable horned and maned Or.

CARLETON, CHARLTON. *MS ex-Taylor Coll.* *
A unicorn's head couped Or between two wings
Azure.

COOKE. *MS Martin's Crests*
A unicorn's head couped Argent armed and maned
Or.

CUNNINGHAM, of Eye. *Davy, A., Church
monuments. Proc.S.I.A. II. 145.* Rear Admiral Sir
Charles Cunningham, died 1834. *Her.Suff.Ch.,
Tablet and Hatchment, Eye, Tablet not found
1987.* Francis Cunningham, M.A., Hon. Canon of
Norwich and Rural Dean, 42 years Rector of
Pakefield, Vicar of Lowestoft from 1830, died
1863. *Altar tomb at east end of churchyard,
Lowestoft St. Margaret*
A unicorn's head couped Or.

DANIEL, of Acton. *Sharpe*
A unicorn's head couped.

DANIEL. 'Danniell' *MS ex-Taylor Coll.* *
A unicorn's head couped Sable.

FILIOL, of Ashfield. *Davy, A.*
A unicorn's head couped Azure.

LEWKENOR. 'S Roger Lewkenore' *Harl. MS
6163*
A unicorn's head couped Argent roundelly Azure
and Sable horned Or.

LEWKENOR, of Denham. 'Lewknor' *MS Fairfax
(Tyl.) Bokenham*
A unicorn's head couped Sable [*sic* should be
Argent] semy of hurts and pellets maned and armed
Or.

LEWKENOR. *Davy, A.*
A unicorn's head couped Argent armed and maned
Or.

RAMSEY, of Kettleburgh, Easton. *Davy, A.*
A plume of five ostrich feathers alternately Argent
and Or before them a unicorn's head couped Azure
gorged with a ducal coronet Or.

UPCHER. Rector of Halesworth. *Crisp's
Visitation. III. 25*, Pedigree*
A unicorn's head couped Argent.

WOMBWELL. Rt. Hon. Lady Anne Wombwell,
died 1808. *Her.Suff.Ch., Monumental tablet,
Stowlangtoft*

UNICORN'S HEAD, Erased [Alphabetically by name]

A unicorn's head erased Argent thrust through the
neck with an arrow and charged on the breast with
three annulets.

ADDISON, of Sudbury, Chilton. *Davy, A. Burke,
L.G. 1853 ed. Fairbairn, 'Addison, Sudbury'*
A unicorn's head Sable erased Gules armed and
crined Or.

BEALE, of Woodbridge. *Surrey Visitation 1530
(H.S.) 78*
A unicorn's head erased Or semy of estoiles Gules.

BEALE, of Bildeston. *Davy, A.*
A unicorn's head Or erased Gules mane horn and
heart [*sic*] Sable.

BEALE, of Woodbridge. *Davy, A. (Barrett MS)*
A unicorn's head erased Argent.

BURLEIGH, of Haverhill. *Davy, A.*
A unicorn's head erased Argent horned Gules
maned Or.

BURWOOD, of Woodbridge. *Sharpe*
A unicorn's head erased Or.

DANIEL, of Acton. 'Daniel of Yorkshire' *MS
Ordinary of Arms, fo. 262*. Bokenham. MS
Martin's Crests. Washbourne*, 'of Herts., York.
and Wilts.'*

A unicorn's head erased quarterly Argent and Gules.

ERRINGTON. 'Erington' *MS ex-Taylor Coll.* *
Washbourne
A unicorn's head erased Sable.

FILIOL. 'Fyloll' *Wall's Book*
From rays of the sun a unicorn's head erased Argent
collared Gules holding in the mouth a cross paty
fitchy Or.

GWILT, of Icklingham. *Davy, A.*
From rays of the sun a unicorn's head erased Argent
collared Gules ringed Or.

GWILT. 'Gwylt. Rector of Icklingham' *Burke,
L.G. 1853 ed.*
A unicorn's head erased per fesse Argent and Gules
charged with three escallops counterchanged 2.1.

IBBOTSON, of Bosmere House. *Davy A.*
A unicorn's head erased charged with three
escallops.

IBBOTSON. *Livery button* *
'A son ty'bre la teste dune licorne rasee de sable les
oreilles et la barbe dor sur son col trois besantz les
rasures de gueules estât sur vng demy soleil dor'

KITSON. 'Thomas Kytson of Hengrave'; Grant of
Arms and Crest by Sir Thomas Wroithesley,
Garter and Thomas Benolt, Clarenceux, 14 April
1527. *Visitation 1561 (ed. Howard), II. 96–7* *
On a demi sun a unicorn's head erased Sable ears
and beard Or on the neck three bezants the erasures
Gules.

KITSON, KYTSON, of Hengrave. 'Kytson' *Wall's
Book. Gage (Hengrave), 'the original crest'*
'to his crest a half a sonne or/ in fece over yt an
unecornes hed sa/ rased g/ on the necke iij besants
eared armed and berded g/ of Essex'

KITSON. 'Kytson' *MS Alphabet of Crests, fo. 68b*
A unicorn's head erased holding in his mouth an
olive branch Or.

LOMAX. *Davy, A.*
A unicorn's head erased having a leaf in his mouth.

LOMAX *Proc.S.I.A. II. 144*
A unicorn's head erased holding in the mouth a
sprig.

LOMAX. Isabella (Haydon), wife of Lawrence
Lomax, died 1702. *E.A.N. & Q. I. 312.*
Her.Suff.Ch., Ledger stone, Eye. No date given
A unicorn's head erased quarterly Argent and Sable
horned Or.

MANNOCK, of Gifford's Hall. *Bokenham*
A unicorn's head erased Or armed and maned Gules
on the neck a chevron vairy Argent and Gules.

MATHEW, of Bury. *Davy, A. (Mr. B.)*
'on a wreath argent and sable an unicorns head rased
Argent thereon a cheveron varry argent & Gules
mayned bearded Gules ye horne wreathed gules &
argent mantled Gules doubled Argent'

MAYHEW. Robert Mayhew, of Clippesby, co.
Norfolk; Confirmation of Arms and Grant of
Crest by William Hervey, Clarenceux, 6th
November 1558. *Misc.Gen. et Her. 5th S. IX. 16
(Soc. of Ant. MS 378, fo. 529)*
A unicorn's head erased Gules horned Gules and
charged on the neck with a chevron Vair.

MAYHEW. 'Robert Mahewe of Clypesby' *MS
Knight's Visitations, Norfolk* 'Thomas Mayhew'
MS Philpot's Visitations, Norfolk*, the horn
untinctured*
A unicorn's head erased Gules maned bearded and
armed Or on the neck a chevron Vair.

MAYHEW, of Brundish, Hemingstone, Clopton.
MS Fairfax. Visitation 1664–8, the horn
untinctured. Davy, A., Brundish church, 1605.*

Fairbairn, 'of Hemington [sic], Suff.' Thomas
Mayhew, died 1861. *Her.Suff.Ch., Wall tablet,
Saxmundham*
A unicorn's head erased.
   NORMAN, of South Elmham St. Margaret,
Rumburgh. *Davy, A., Rumburgh church.* John
Norman of Rumburgh. *Proc.S.I.A. XXII. 164*.*
'John Norman, Gent.', of St. Margaret's South
Elmham, died 1837' *Her.Suff.Ch., Ledger stone,
Rumburgh*
A unicorn's head erased Argent armed and maned
Or.
   PARIS, PARISH, of Ipswich. *Sharpe. Davy, A., St.
Helen's and St. Lawrence churches*
A unicorn's head erased.
   PARIS, PARISH. 'Edward Clark Parish, Esq.,
Merchant, of London, died 1764; widow
Elizabeth, died 1776' *E.A.N. & Q. IX. 169,
Tablet, St. Lawrence Ipswich. Her.Suff.Ch.*
A unicorn's head erased Argent horned and maned
Or.
   SAVAGE. *MS ex-Taylor Coll.**
A unicorn's head erased Ermines.
   SPARROW. *Bokenham*
A unicorn's head erased Or ducally gorged and
armed Azure.
   TAYLOR, of Lidgate. *Davy, A.*
A unicorn's head erased Azure horn mane and
crowned with a crest coronet Or between two wings
Or.
   WELLS or WELLES, . . . , of Caius College,
Cambridge. Patent November 1614. *Grants &
Certificates (Stowe MSS 706 and 707)*
A unicorn's head erased Azure crined armed and
ducally crowned Or between two wings Or.
   WELLES. Rector of Huntingfield, died 1758.
Davy, A. 'John Welles, Clerk, late Rector, died
1758.' *Her.Suff.Ch., Ledger stone, Huntingfield*
A unicorn's head erased.
   WILDE. Helen, wife of James Wilde, died 1704.
*Her.Suff.Ch., Ledger stone, St. Margaret's
Lowestoft*
A unicorn's head erased per chevron Or and Gules
armed Or.
   WILKINSON. 'Hugh Wilkinson of Old bukenham'
MS Philpot's Visitations, Norf.*
A unicorn's head erased.
   WILKINSON, of Sibton, Bramfield, Mildenhall,
Redgrave. *Davy, A.*
'Vpon his helme one atorse argent and gules a
Unycornes hede argent Rased maned horned and
berded golde and gules manteled gules dubled
argent'
   WOMBWELL, LAWEVELL alias WOMBWELL. Grant
of Crest p' Wm. Flower, Norroy, 9th July 1565.
Misc.Gen. et Her. 5th S. VII. 357
A unicorn's head erased Argent.
   WOMBWELL, Bart., of Stowlangtoft. *Davy, A.* Sir
George Wombwell, 1st Bart., died 1780.
Her.Suff.Ch., Hatchment, Haughley
A unicorn's head erased.
   WOMBWELL. *Her.Suff.Ch., Slab in the chancel,
Drinkstone*

WYVERN

A wyvern's head couped.
   BARRY. '. . . Barry . . . ham, Gent . . . life Oct. 30
1701' *Her.Suff.Ch., Ledger stone inside altar
rail, Syleham. Partly covered*
A wyvern's head couped Gules run through the neck
with the lower part of a lance Argent.

   COLDHAM. *MS Heraldic Alphabet*
'to his crest a Wyvers hed rased or/ a crowne a bowt
the necke g/ Nycolas Cutler of Eye in Suff'
   CUTLER. *MS Alphabet of Crests, fo. 23b*
A wyvern's head Proper.
   DE GREY, Baron Walsingham. Of Copdock.
Davy, A. 'Hon. John Augustus de Grey, of
Leiston Old Abbey, Suff.' *Fairbairn.* Thomas de
Grey, Baron Walsingham, died 1839.
Her.Suff.Ch., Glass in the tower, Washbrook
A wyvern's head couped Or.
   DE GREY, WALSINGHAM. Of Copdock. *Crisp's
Visitation. XVI. 17**, as Walsingham, Pedigree
'to his crest a Wyvers hed betwene ij Wyngs b/ '
   KNEVET. *MS Alphabet of Crests, fo. 69*
'for his crest a Wevers hed rased Sa/ a bowt the neck
a crowne or/ Langed g/ to sʳ Edward north of
kyrtelyng in Cambrydgeshʳ '
   NORTH. *MS Alphabet of Crests, fo. 91*
A wyvern's head erased chained.
   NORTH, of Laxfield. *Davy, A.*
A ?wyvern's head erased holding in the beak an
arrow.
   WHITTINGTON. *Davy, A.*
A wyvern's head couped.
   WYARD, of Brundish. *Davy, A., church*

HEART

A human heart Gules between two wings Argent
charged with estoiles Gules.
   BARRETT. *MS Ordinary of Arms, fo. 272**
A human heart Gules ducally crowned Or.
   CORDEROY, of Earl Soham. *Davy, A. (Edms.)*
A human heart between two wings.
   DOUGLAS. *MS Ordinary of Arms, fo. 6*
A heart Gules winged Or.
   DRIVER, of Earl Stonham. *Davy, A.*
A winged heart Proper.
   FITZWALTER. *Davy, A.*
A heart Gules winged Or.
   FITZWALTER. *Davy, A.*
Upon a heart Or a raven Sable gorged with a collar
gemel Argent.
   JONES, of Pakenham, Barton Mere. *Crisp's
Visitation. I. 286–7*, Pedigree*
Standing on a heart Or a raven Proper collared
gemelle Argent.
   JONES. Rev. Preb. H. Jones, M.A.,
Chaplain-in-Ordinary to the Queen, of Barton
Mere, Pakenham, Suff. and Rev. C.W. Jones,
M.A., of Pakenham. *Fairbairn**
A human heart Gules pierced with a pile, or nail,
Azure.
   LOGAN, of Kentwell Hall in Long Melford.
Davy, A., church
A human heart ducally crowned Or.
   TRUEMAN. *Davy, A.*
Over a human heart two batons in saltire.
   TYE, William, Gent., died 1759. *Her.Suff.Ch.,
Headstone outside the church, Grundisburgh*

HELMET

A military helmet Proper.
   BAMBOROUGH. 'Bamburgh' *MS Martin's Crests*
A skull-cap Argent.
   BAMBOROUGH, of Rendlesham. *Davy, A.
Washbourne, 'Bambury, of York. and Suff.'
Fairbairn, 'Bambrough, Rendlesham, Suff.'*
An esquire's helmet Proper garnished Or with a
plume of feathers hanging down behind it Or and
Azure.
   BARRETT, of Westhall, Blythburgh. *Davy, A.*

A helmet Argent garnished and plumed with feathers Or.

> BARRETT. *Davy, A., St. Mary's church, Bury. Washbourne, 'Suff.' Fairbairn, 'Suff.'*

On a helmet two ostrich feathers one Or the other Argent.

> BARRETT, Thomas, of Norwich. *Muskett. II. 160 (Visitation of Norfolk 1664, Harl. MS 1085).* [But in the *Visitation (H.S.), I. 15,* the helmet is Argent and the feathers Or and Gules.]

A man's head full-faced wearing a helmet the vizor open all Proper.

> BUCKWORTH. *MS Heraldic Alphabet*

A man's head side-faced in a helmet.

> CANHAM, of Bradfield Combust. *Davy, A., churchyard.* 'Barth. Canham gent . . . 16 . .' *Partridge, 212 (Darby, 1829), Bradfield Combust churchyard*

A close helmet surmounted by a mural crown Gules thereout a star of seven points.

> FOX, of Stradbroke, Fressingfield, Yoxford. *Davy, A., Stradbroke churchyard*

A helmet surmounted by a mural coronet.

> FOX. Several members of the Fox family. *Partridge, 110 (Darby, 1825), Large altar tomb in churchyard, Stradbroke. E.A.Misc. 1929, 40,63. Full description of tomb in Stradbroke churchyard*

An esquire's helmet Proper.

> HALSHAM, of Woodbridge. *Davy, A. (Burke)*

A helmet the vizor up.

> PENDRED, of Cransford. *Davy, A.*

A helmet Or feather Or the vizor open showing a man's face Proper.

> ROGERS, Christopher, of Sutton, in Kent. Patent 1593. *Grants & Certificates (Harl. MS 1,359)*

Upon an esquire's helm a bull's scalp Or armed Argent.

> SHERLAND. *MS Ordinary of Arms, fo. 34**

A helmet Or feathers Azure the vizor open showing a man's face Proper.

> SYMS, Edward, of Daventry, co. Northampton, 1592. *Grants & Certificates (Harl. MS 1,359)*

A head in a helmet beaver up Proper plumed Azure.

> SYMMES, of Whepstead. *Davy, A.*

HEMP – BRAKE

A hemp-brake Or.

> BRAY, BREE, of Stowmarket. *MS Heraldic Collections, fo. 20*. Davy, A.*

A hemp-brake Argent.

> BRAY, BREE. *MS Martin's Crests.* 'Bree' *Bookplate**

HOOKS

Two tenter hooks in saltire Azure.

> TAY. 'Sr. Henry Tay' *MS Ordinary of Arms, fo. 189**

Two rack hooks in saltire.

> TAY. *MS Heraldic Alphabet*

HORN

A cock Gules standing on a trumpet Proper.

> ACHESON, Earl of Gosford, Viscount Acheson of Worlingham. *Davy, A.*

A cock Gules standing on a trumpet Or.

> ACHESON, Earl of Gosford, Baron Worlingham, of Beccles, co. Suffolk. *Burke, Peerage, 1891 ed.**

A bugle horn.

> LOWDE, of Fressingfield. 'Rob. Lowde gent. 1729 ag. 63' *Partridge, 104 (Darby, 1825), the horn stringed. Davy, A., churchyard*

A hunting horn.

> LOWDE, Robert, Gent., died 1729; widow Elizabeth (Betts), died 1739. *Her.Suff.Ch., Tomb in churchyard, Fressingfield*

On a trumpet Or a swan wings expanded Argent.

> LYTE, of Gt. Yarmouth, Bradwell. *Crisp's Visitation. V. 153, Pedigree*

A hunting horn of Durham Annuld [*sic*] tasselled Or. (Given to the Scarletts by the Prince Bishop of Durham, 1402)

> SCARLETT. *Sharpe*

A bugle horn Gules stringed Or between two wings expanded per fesse Or and Agent.

> VANNECK, Lord Huntingfield. Of Heveningham Hall. 'Van-Neck Bart.' *MS Ordinary of Arms, fo. 247*; un-named on fo. 259*, horn stringed Gules. Page. Davy, A.*

A bugle horn Gules stringed Or between two wings expanded Argent tipped Or.

> VANNECK, HUNTINGFIELD, Baron. Of Heveningham Hall. *Burke, Peerage, 1891 ed.* Fairbairn*, 'Huntingfield, Baron (Vanneck), of Heveningham Hall, Yoxford, Suff.'*

A hunting horn Gules between two wings per fesse Or and Argent.

> VANNECK, Sir Joshua, 1st Bart., died 1777; Sir Gerard, 2nd Bart., died 1791; Joshua, 1st Baron Huntingfield, died 1816; Joshua, 2nd Baron Huntingfield, died 1844. *Her.Suff.Ch., Hatchments, Huntingfield*

A bugle horn stringed Gules.

> VANNECK, Lord Huntingfield. *Her.Suff.Ch., Tiles on chancel floor, Huntingfield*

A bugle horn stringed.

> WHIMPER, of Glevering Hall, Wickham Market, Woodbridge. *Davy, A.*

TWO [COW'S] HORNS

Out of a coronet two horns one Or the other Sable.

> CLOPTON. *MS Knight's Visitations, Suff.**

Two horns one Or the other Sable.

> CLOPTON. *MS Knight's Visitations, Suff.**

Two horns one Or the other Gules.

> CLOPTON, of Kentwell. *MS Lilly's Visitation of Suffolk*, the third of four crests drawn*

Two horns one Or the other Gules out of a coronet Or.

> CLOPTON, of Clopton. 'Clopton of Kentwell' *MS Lilly's Visitation of Suffolk*, the fourth of four crests drawn. Davy, A.*

HORSE – SHOE

A horse-shoe Sable between two wings Argent.

> FARRER, of Cratfield. *Davy, A.*

A horse-shoe Argent between two wings Or.

> FARRER. *Davy, A.*

A horseshoe between two wings.

> FARROW. 'Mr. Will. Farrow, late of city of London, goldsmith, died 1748 ag. 48; Anne, w. of above Will., died 1763 ag.75'; Others. *Partridge, 14 (Darby, 1826), Monk's Eleigh churchyard. Davy, A., Monk's Eleigh churchyard*

A horse shoe Sable between two wings erect Argent.

> FARROW, William, late of London, goldsmith, died 1748; Others. *Her.Suff.Ch., Altar tomb at east end of churchyard, Monks Eleigh*

HUMAN FIGURE

DEMI-MAN [Alphabetically by name]

A demi- Moor Proper in his dexter hand an arrow Or feathered and headed Argent on his sinister arm a shield Or and over his Shoulder a sash Gules.

BARKER. *Fairbairn, 'of Ipswich, Suff.'*
A demi-wild man with a ragged staff.
BATTIE. Rector of Alderton, 1660. *E.A.Misc.
1933. 18, (Candler MS)*
A demi- savage Proper in his hands a branch of
gleton [*sic*] Vert flowered Or on his breast three
ogresses.
BORREL, BORRELL. 'John Borell, of Wormeley,
co. Herts., gent.'; Grant by Barker. *Grants &
Certificates (Stowe MS 692)*
A demi-friar holding in his hand a crucifix.
BOVILE, of Letheringham, Badingham. *Davy, A.
Washbourne. Fairbairn, 'Bovil, Bolvile, Suff.'*
A demi-man couped wearing a laurel wreath Proper.
BOYS. Rev. William Boys, Rector of
Grundisburgh, Rector of Kelsale, died 1700.
E.A.N. & Q. (N.S.) IV. 248, Kelsale
A demi-wild man Proper bound round the head with
a wreath Argent and Azure in his dexter hand an oak
branch fructed Or.
COLLIN, of Groton. *Davy, A.*
A demi-Moor Proper vested Gules semy of billets
Argent girdle Or turban Gules turned up Argent
surmounted by a crescent Or holding in the dexter
hand a mace with a crescent at the top Or.
COLMER. 'James Cullymoore, of London'. Patent
January 1611. *Grants & Certificates (Stowe
MS 707)*
A demi-man vested Sable under-vest Gules on his
head a Scotch bonnet Azure over his shoulder a staff
Proper.
DRUMMOND. Rector of Hadleigh, died 1829.
Davy, A.
A demi-naked man on his head a round cap left
hand on his hip and holding over his right shoulder
an ox-yoke.
DRUMMOND. 'Edw.ᵈ Auriol Hay Drummond,
D.D.' *Bookplate**
A demi-man vested grey capped Azure waistcoat
Gules bearing on his shoulder an ox-yoke Proper.
DRUMMOND. Very Rev. Edward Auriol
Hay-Drummond, died 1829. *Her.Suff.Ch.,
Hatchment, Hadleigh*
A demi-knight in armour holding in the right hand a
scimitar/machete and in the left hand a sword Or.
DUNKIRK VETERAN'S ASSOCIATION, Bury St.
Edmunds Branch. *Her.Suff.Ch., Small oak
shield, St. Mary's Bury*
A demi-savage holding a scimitar Proper.
GEDDING, of Suffolk. *Davy, A.*
A demi-naked man holding in his dexter hand a
cross crosslet fitchy.
GODFREY. *MS Heraldic Collections, fo. 48**
A demi-Saracen Proper holding in his dexter hand a
cross crosslet fitchy Argent.
GODFREY, of Risby, Old Hall in East Bergholt.
Davy, A., Risby church. Burke, L.G. 1853 ed.
A demi-old man Proper beard and hair Argent
wreathed about the head with leaves Vert in his
dexter hand the stump of a tree erased Vert purfled
[garnished] Or chained round his body with the end
of the chain in his sinister hand Or.
HARMAN, of Rendlesham, Mutford, Ipswich.
Visitation 1664–8. Davy, A. Fairbairn, 'of
Rendlesham and Mulford [sic], Suff. tree fructed
Or'. Bookplate*, untinctured*
A demi-naked man issuing out of water holding in
his dexter hand a sword with wavy blade and on his
sinister arm a shield of the arms of Hotham [Barry
of ten Argent and Azure on a canton Or a Cornish
chough Proper].

HOTHAM. 'Henry Hotham', with mullet for
difference. 'Sir Henry Hotham', with K.C.B.,
died 1833. *Bookplates**
A demi-seaman issuing out of water Proper holding
in his dexter hand a flaming sword and in his other
hand a shield of the Hotham arms [as above].
HOTHAM. Rector of Dennington. *Davy, A.*
A demi-savage Sable collared Or wreathed about the
temples and knotted Or and Vert holding in his
dexter hand a halbert staff Gules headed Argent.
JENNINGS, JENNYNGS, of Dennington. *Visitation
1561 (MS G. 7*)*
A demi-naked man collared wreathed about the
temples and knotted holding in his dexter hand a
halbert.
JENNINGS, JENNYNGE. *Visitation 1561 (Iveagh
Copy*)*
A demi-savage Sable collared Or wreathed round
the temples Or and Vert holding in his dexter hand a
halbert Azure staff Gules.
JENNINGS, JENNYNGS, of Dennington. *Visitation
1561 (ed. Metcalfe). Washbourne, 'Jenynges,
Suff. wreath Or'. Fairbairn, 'Jenynges, Suff.'*
A demi-savage Sable wreathed round the head
Argent holding in his dexter hand a halbert Azure
staff Gules.
JENNINGS, of Suffolk. *Davy, A.*
A demi-savage holding a sheaf of arrows in his
dexter hand and pointing with the sinister to a ducal
coronet all Proper.
LARGE, of Saxham. *Davy, A.*
Out of a tower a demi-man in armour in profile
holding in the dexter hand a sword by the blade
erect.
LONDON. *Washbourne**. 'William London, of
Quay House, Woodbridge' *Fairbairn*
A demi-man.
LOUTH, Lionel, died 1532; monument erected by
daughter Margaret in 1596. *Her.Suff.Ch., Effigy
monument, Cretingham*
A demi-man kneeling affronty habited Sable with a
chain about his neck Or.
LOUTH, Lionel, died 1532. *Photograph**
A demi-savage grasping in the dexter hand a sheaf
of arrows and pointing with the sinister hand to an
Imperial crown Proper.
MACFARLANE. 'Willelmus Comyn Macfarlane,
M.A., Rector and Lord of the Manor, died 1884'
Her.Suff.Ch., Brass wall shield, Elmswell
A demi-man shooting an arrow from a bow Proper.
MOLLINGTON. *Davy, A.*
A demi-man in armour holding a halbert or
battle-axe.
MORSE, of Belton, North Cove, Lound,
Blundeston. *Davy, A., Belton and North Cove
churches.* Francis Morse, wife Margaret. No date.
E.A.N. & Q. II. 326, Slab, Belton. Sarah, wife of
John Morse, died 1762. *E.A.N. & Q. IV. 268,
Tomb in churchyard, North Cove*
A demi-man in complete armour Proper garnished
Or his helmet open and surmounted by a plume of
three ostrich feathers Azure on his breast a
cross-belt Sable and holding in his dexter hand a
halbert Proper.
MORSE. 'Alfred Herbert Morse, Esq., of Copdock,
Ipswich' *Fairbairn**
A demi-man in armour Proper on the helmet a
plume of ostrich feathers Azure grasping in the
dexter hand a battle-axe Proper.
MORSE, Francis and wife Margaret, c.1750.
Her.Suff.Ch., Ledger stone, Belton. John Morse,

died 1779; Others, 176.–1835. *Altar tomb in churchyard, North Cove. Untinctured*
A demi-savage Proper wreathed about the head and waist Vert holding in his dexter hand a dagger Proper pomelled and hilted Or and in his sinister hand a key Or.
MURRAY, of Eriswell. *Davy, A. Burke, L.G. 1853 ed. Fairbairn*, 'of Eriswell Lodge, Suff.'*
A demi-savage wreathed about the middle holding over his shoulder a club and round his sinister arm a serpent entwined.
PLOWMAN, of Bungay, Oulton. *Davy, A.*
A demi-figure of St. Nicholas vested in pontificals Proper mitred and holding in his dexter hand a pastoral staff and in his sinister hand three purses Or.
ROYAL SCHOOL OF CHURCH MUSIC. Granted 1950. *Her.Suff.Ch., Certificate in frame, Gt. Waldingfield. Notice on the organ, Reydon*
The demi-figure of St. Edmund, King and Martyr.
SOUTHWOLD, Borough Council. *Scott-Giles, 346**
On the top of a castle Argent a demi-man bareheaded and in mail Proper holding in his right hand an arrow point downwards Sable headed Or and on his left arm a round shield Or.
WISEMAN. 'Thomas Wiseman son of John Wiseman of Canfield in Suff.' *MS Philpot's Visitations, Suff.** [In a different hand]
A demi-woodman Proper holding in both hands a club Sable.
WODEHOUSE. 'Woodhouse' *MS Martin's Crests*
A savage man couped at the knees Proper crined Or wreathed about the middle Argent and Sable holding a club erect Sable.
WODEHOUSE, of Ashbocking. *Davy, A.*
A demi-man Proper vested Or on his head a cap Sable in his dexter hand a cutlass Proper.
WOODVILLE. *Davy, A.*

MAN [Alphabetically by name]
A man in armour holding in his hand a pole-axe Argent handle Gules.
ALENÇON, also DALLISON, of Badingham. *Davy, A.*
A mower per pale Sable and Argent with a scythe Argent the helve Or in his hand 'his stroke striken'.
ASHTON. 'Asheton of Asheton' *Wall's Book*
'to his crest/ a Man Mower pty par pale sa/ ar/ w^t a Sythe in his hand ar/ the helve or/ his stroke stryking'
ASHTON. 'Ashton of Ashton' *MS Alphabet of Crests, fo. 3*
A mower habited per pale Sable and Argent scythe Proper.
ASHTON. 'S. Thomas Asheton, Lanc.' *Harl. MS 6163*
A mower counter-habited per pale Argent and Sable his cap and stockings Sable and Argent palewise the scythe Or.
ASHTON. *MS Ordinary of Arms, fo. 118**
A mower counter-habited Argent and Sable and Argent palewise the scythe Proper.
ASHTON. *MS Martin's Crests, 'ye original Crest'*
A mower with his scythe habited quarterly Argent and Sable on his head a cap Vert scythe Or blade Argent.
ASHTON, of Halesworth, Bury. *Davy, A. Suckling. II. 343*
A mower with his scythe face and hands Proper habit and cap counterchanged Argent and Sable the handle of the scythe Or blade Argent as in action.

ASHTON, Richard, son of Raphe Aston, of Kirkley, co. Yorks., died 1641. *Her.Suff.Ch., Funeral board, Halesworth*
A naked man holding in his hand a willow wand Proper.
BATES, of Marlesford, Blaxhall, Eyke. *Davy, A.*
A wild man bearing a club raguly Vert.
BATTIE, of Woodbridge, Hitcham, Alderton. *MS Fairfax (Candler). Davy, A.*
On a tiger Argent a naked man astride Proper wreathed about the temples Argent and Gules.
BRAMPTON, of Brampton in co. Norfolk. *Davy, A.*
An archer Proper habited Vert shooting an arrow from a bow Proper.
CLIFFE, of Dunwich, Westleton. *Davy, A.*
A knight in full armour with baton in hand Proper.
CLOUN, CLUN. *Davy, A.*
An Indian king armed in mail crowned Or kneeling on his left knee and rendering up his sword.
CRADOCK, of Wickhambrook. *Bokenham*
An armed man holding out a battle-axe all Proper.
DALLISON. *MS Martin's Crests*
A man in a military habit Proper holding a flag displayed Argent, or Azure.
DANFORD, DANFORTH, of Framlingham. *Davy, A.*
A Moor full-faced wreathed round the temples holding in his dexter hand a rose slipped and leaved all Proper.
HEYMAN, Bart. Vicar of Fressingfield, 1797–1808. *Davy, A.*
A man on horseback at a charge holding a broken tilting spear Proper.
JESSUP, of Theberton, Leiston, Woodbridge. *Davy, A.*
A Turk kneeling on one knee habited Gules legs and arms in mail Proper at his side a scimitar Sable hilted Or on his head a turban with a crescent and feathers Argent holding in his sinister hand a crescent Argent.
MINSHULL, MYNSHULL. Granted to Sir Robert Minshull by Le Neve in 1642 instead of the 'original' crest [q.v.] *Davy, A., St. Stephen's church Ipswich. Fairbairn, 'Minshall, Mynshall, Minshull, Bucks., Chesh., Suff. etc.'*
An armed man.
NEVILL, of Long Melford. *E.A.N. & Q. X. 128, Slabs, Lavenham church.*
A man issuing from a tower holding an arrow in his right hand and a shield in the left.
NEVILL, Isaac, died 1768; Others. *Her.Suff.Ch., Slab in chancel, Lavenham.*
A mower per pale Argent and Sable fetching his stroke with a scythe Argent 'maunched' [*sic*] Gules.
PILKINGTON. 'Pylkyngton' *Wall's Book*
'to his crest a man mowyer ar/ sa/ party par pale feching his stroke w^t his sythe ar/ manched g/'
PILKINGTON. 'Pylkyngton' *MS Alphabet of Crests, fo. 98*
A mower Argent with his scythe Sable blade Azure.
PILKINGTON, of Swilland. *Lincolnshire Visitation 1634, Notes (Gibbons), 275*
A mower with his scythe clothed paly Argent and Sable.
PILKINGTON. *MS Martin's Crests*
A mower with his scythe Proper habited quarterly Argent and Gules.
PILKINGTON, of Stanstead, Ipswich. *Davy, A.*
A man clothed in doublet and hose quartered Argent and Gules with hat quartered Gules and Argent with

the dexter arm extended and the sinister arm resting on the waist.

PILKINGTON. Catherine, daughter of Sir Thomas Pilkington, married James Blake, of Thurston House, who died 1874. *Her.Suff.Ch., Glass, Thurston. Second crest, for Pilkington*
A savage man Proper wreathed about the loins and temples Vert holding in his dexter hand a tall club Vert.

SPELMAN, of Bury, Framsden. 'John Spelman, Esq., at Narburgh co. Norfolk' Brass of 1581. *Cotman's Norfolk Brasses, plate 81*, untinctured. Top of club sprouting leaves.* 'Erasmus Spylman of Byston' *MS Knight's Visitations, Norf.* Davy, A.*
A wild man holding in his dexter hand a staff.

SYDNOR, William, died 1613. *Druery, 221, Slab with brass, Blundeston church. Davy, A., Blundeston church*
'beryth to his crest a man threschar party par pale silver and geules with a flayll in his honde gold'

TRAFFORD. *Wall's Book*
'to his crest a man thresher Ppy P pale ar/g/w^t a flele in his hand or'

TRAFFORD. 'Trayford' *MS Alphabet of Crests, fo. 126*
A thrasher Proper his coat breeches and stockings party per pale Argent and Gules holding in his hands a flail Proper the head Or over a garb fesseways Or.

TRAFFORD- RAWSON, Major Henry, Coldham Hall, Bury St. Edmunds. *Fairbairn, second crest, for Trafford.* Lt. Col. Henry Trafford Rawson, of Coldham Hall, died 1912; only son, Capt. J.H.E. Trafford Rawson, killed in action 1916. *Her.Suff.Ch., Wall tablet, Lawshall*
On the front of a castle Argent the portcullis shut down Gules a Moor Proper wreathed about the temples Argent and Gules clothed in mail in his right hand a broad arrow Argent in his left a shield Or.

WISEMAN, of Thornham. *Bokenham*
A woodsman Proper a club in his dexter hand resting on the ground on his sinister arm a shield Argent charged with a cross Gules.

WOOD, of Woodbridge, Melton. *Davy, A.*
A wood-man Proper wreathed about the middle Vert a club in his dexter hand and on his sinister arm a shield Argent charged with a cross Gules.

WOOD, of Loudham. *Davy, A., Ufford church*
A wild man Proper.

WOODEHOUSE. 'Woudhouse of Norffolk' *Wall's Book*
A naked savage wreathed about the temples and loins holding in front of him in bend the trunk of a tree eradicated all Proper.

WOODFORD. *MS Ordinary of Arms, fo. 82**

DEMI-WOMAN [Alphabetically by name]
A demi-maiden from the navel upwards habited per pale indented Sable and Or the 'sleves strayte and endented' her girdle counterchanged standing in a daisy Proper her hands on its stalk with two leaves Vert her hair Or a garland about her head Gules budded Or.

BALDRY, 'Baldry Maior of London' *Wall's Book*
'to his Crest a demy mayden fro the navell upward her apell sa/ and or p pale endented/ the sleves strete and endented and her gyrdell count. standing in a daysy in his coullor/ and her hands upon yt stalked w^t ij leves vert her here or/ a garland a bowt her hede g/ boded or/ knight by h 8/'

BALDRY. 'Baldry maior of London' *MS Alphabet of Crests, fo. 9b*
A demi-maiden habited Gules crined crowned and holding in her dexter hand a Catherine wheel Or in her sinister hand a dagger point downwards Argent.

BOOTH, BOWTH. *MS Heraldic Collections, fo. 36**
'to his crest a demy moryan b/ ij annoletts in the Left eyre holding in the Left hand a branche of Acornes or/ to Robt Collyar of Darleston in Staff'

COLLYER. 'Collyar' *MS Alphabet of Crests, fo. 25*
A demi-negress rings in her ears holding in her right hand a sprig of oak with acorns.

COLLYER. Rev. Thomas Collyer, A.M., Cantab., died 1890. *Her.Suff.Ch., Wall brass in chancel, Gislingham*
A demi-woman hair dishevelled Proper habited Or square neck Argent cuffed Purpure round her neck a ribbon Purpure suspended therefrom a quatrefoil Azure holding in her dexter hand two roses Gules slipped and leaved.

DARCY. 'Darsy of Essex' *Banners & Standards**
A maiden couped at the knees Proper crined Or clothed Gules a caul on her head knotted Or holding in her right hand three cinquefoils two Gules the midmost Azure stalked and leaved Vert.

DARCY. *MS Martin's Crests*
A demi-virgin holding in her right hand a bunch of cinquefoils all Proper.

DARCY, Lord Of Norton, Elmswell, Woolpit. *Davy, A., Eden wall pedigree, All Saints church, Sudbury*
A demi-virgin vested Gules holding in her dexter hand three cinquefoils Gules.

DARCY. Elizabeth, daughter of Thomas Lord Darcy, married Thomas, 1st Viscount Savage, who died 1635. *Proc.S.I.A. XXVI. 216, Savage Hatchment, Long Melford*, 'crined Or'. Her.Suff.Ch., Savage Hatchment, Long Melford*
A demi-virgin habited Or holding in her right hand a branch of cinquefoils all Proper and charged on the breast with a crescent Sable for difference.

DARCY. *Sperling, 147, Eden wall pedigree, All Saints church Sudbury, 'with golden tresses'. Her.Suff.Ch., Eden wall pedigree*
A demi-woman couped at the waist Proper hair flotant Or holding in each hand a sprig of laurel Vert.

GREY, of Thrandeston. *MS Heraldic Collections, fo. 78b.*, untinctured. Davy, A.*
A demi-lady richly attired Azure in her dexter hand a garland of laurels Vert.

LODINGTON, of Beccles. *Davy, A.*
A demi-lady holding a pair of scales.

LOVETOFT, LOVETOT, of Bramford. *Davy, A. (Berry)*
The figure of St. Margaret half-length holding in her hands a pearl all Proper.

LOWESTOFT, Borough Council *Scott-Giles, 346*, 'Granted 1913'*
'beryth to his crest a demy mayden fro the navel upward in a surcote geules voyded ermyns her here gold a chappelet about her hede and an other in her right hond holdyng it up geules standyng in a garlond geules'

SEXTON. 'Saxton of –' *Wall's Book*
'to his crest a demy maydon fro the Navell upward in a Surcot g/ Voyded [ermine spot drawn] Her hare or/ a chapelet a bowt her hed and an other in her ryght hand holding yt up g/ standing in a garland g/'

SEXTON. 'Saxton' *MS Alphabet of Crests, fo. 118*

A woman couped at the waist Proper habited Gules holding in her dexter hand a chaplet Vert.

SEXTON, of Lavenham. *Davy, A. (Barrett)*

A female figure (the emblem of Ceres) couped below the waist Proper vested Azure wreathed about the temples with wheat Or holding on her dexter arm a garb Or in her sinister hand a sickle erect Proper.

VERNON, Earl of Shipbrooke Of Orwell Park. *Davy, A. Fairbairn, 'Vernon of Herringswell, Suff. A cross crosslet Or on her breast for difference.'*

A demi-woman Proper vested Azure wreathed about the temples with wheat Or in her dexter hand a sickle in the sinister a garb Or.

VERNON, of Hundon. *Misc.Gen. et Her. 2nd S. IV. 204, church monument. Her.Suff.Ch., Gt. Thurlow*

A demi-Ceres Proper habited Or and Purpure hair Purpure [*sic*] and wreathed about the temples with wheat holding in her arms a garb Or.

VERNON, James, lord of the Manor, repaired church in 1741; Henry Vernon, died 1776. *Her.Suff.Ch., Wall tablet and Glass, Gt. Thurlow*

A demi-woman holding under her left arm a garb and in the right hand a sickle.

VERNON, Rev. Charles, D.D., of Worstead [*sic*] Park, died 1863. *Her.Suff.Ch., Wall tablet, Wherstead*

WOMAN

A woman with golden tresses.

DARCY, Thomas, died 1614. *Her.Suff.Ch., Effigy monument in north chapel, Hengrave*

DEMI-CHILD

The bust of a child a fillet round the head.

BOYS, William, Rector of Kelsale, died 1700. *Davy, A.*

A boy couped at the navel Sable on his head a wreath with tassels pendent Or leaning his left hand on his hip and holding in his right hand a halbert Gules headed Proper.

JENNINGS. *Bokenham*

CHILD

On a child in swaddling clothes lying fesseways an eagle seizing it wings elevated Or.

LATHAM, of cos. Cambridge and Essex. *MS Heraldic Alphabet*

In a cradle Or a child in swaddling clothes at the head of the cradle an oak sprig erect Vert with an acorn Or an eagle perched on the child seizing it wings elevated Or.

LATHAM, of co. Essex. *MS Heraldic Alphabet*

TWO CHILDREN

Two naked boys with rods in their hands between them a boar's head.

CALTHORPE. 'Calthorp' *Wall's Book*

'to his crest ii naked Boyes w^t rodds in their hands betwene them both a bores hed'

CALTHORPE. 'Calthorp' *MS Alphabet of Crests, fo. 19b*

HURT see ROUNDEL, Azure

INSECT

A grasshopper Proper.

GRESHAM. *MS ex-Taylor Coll.*

A grasshopper Or.

GRESHAM, of Battisford, Ringshall. *Davy, A.*

A glow-worm Proper.

NERFORD, NEREFORD, of Stansfield, Wissett. *Davy, A. Washbourne*

A scorpion in pale tail in chief Or between two elephant's tusks the upper part chequy Argent and Azure the bottom part Gules each charged with a cross formy Sable.

SHERRINGTON. *Davy, A.*

LANCE see SPEAR

LEAVES [Alphabetically by name]

A bunch of leaves.

ELLIS, ELSE. *Davy, A.*

A plume of five ostrich feathers, or oak leaves.

FARR, John, Gent., Attorney-at-Law, died 1727; widow Martha, died 1733. *Her.Suff.Ch., Altar tomb in churchyard, Beccles*

A pyramid of ten bay leaves Proper.

PHELIP, Lord Bardolf, of Dennington. *Davy, A., 'Later assumed by Rous'*

A cone of bay leaves Vert, charged with a crescent – for difference.

ROUS, of Cransford. *Visitation 1561 (MS G. 7*)*

A bunch of bay leaves piled in the form of a cone Vert.

ROUS, Earl of Stradbroke. Of Dennington, Darsham, Henham, Cransford. *Visitation 1561 (MS G. 7*) and (ed. Metcalfe). MS Ordinary of Arms, fo. 269*. Visitation 1664–8*. Page. Davy, A., 'the crest of Phelip, Lord Bardolph, assumed by Rous from an intermarriage'. Burke, Peerage, 1891 ed.* Fairbairn*, 'Stradbroke, Earl of (Rous), Henham Hall, Wangford, Suff.'*

Nine bay leaves Vert, or Proper.

ROUS, ROUSE, of Henham, Dennington, Badingham. *MS Fairfax (Tyl.) Bokenham*

Six laurel leaves Vert.

ROUSE, Bart., of Henham. *Sharpe*

A pyramid of bay leaves per pale Argent and Vert.

ROUS, of Cratfield. *Davy, A., church*

A bunch of bay leaves piled in the form of a cone Vert.

ROUS, Lucie, wife of William Cotton, died 1621; Laurence Rous and wife Elizabeth. *Her.Suff.Ch., Effigy monument and two Ledger stones, Badingham. Judeth, wife of Edward Rous, Gent., died 1697. Ledger stone in churchyard, Horham. Sir John Rous, Bart., died 1730. Wall tablet, Wangford. Silver harness crest*, untinctured*

From leaves Vert a cubit arm in armour Proper the gauntlet grasping a battleaxe staff Gules headed Argent the arm tied round with a scarf of the second [*sic*].

WORLICHE, Charles, of Cowling, co. Suffolk; Confirmation by R. Cooke, Clarenceux. *Grants & Certificates (Harl. MS 1,359)*

LEG

BIRD [Alphabetically by name]

'to his Crest an egles Legge the foote Donward b/'

DRAYTON. 'Drayton of London' *MS Alphabet of Crests, fo. 29b*

An eagle's leg couped at the thigh Azure the leg Or.

DRAYTON, of Pakefield. 'Rob Drayton de Com̄ Norff' *MS Ordinary of Arms, fo. 19*. Davy, A. (Berry)*

A falcon's leg Or erased at the thigh Gules belled Argent.

JOSSELYN. 'Thomas Josselyn' *MS Knight's Visitations, Essex*. 'Thomas Josselyn' MS Philpot's Visitations, Essex**

A falcon's leg erased at the thigh Gules belled Or.
JOSSELYN, JOSCELIN, JOCELYNE, of Ipswich, Belstead, Sproughton, Bury, Copdock, Leiston. 'Jocelyn' *MS Martin's Crests. Davy, A. Josselyn*, untinctured; bookplate*. Fairbairn*, 'Josselyn, Fornham, near Bury St. Edmunds, Suff. also Ipswich, Suff.'*

A falcon's leg erased at the thigh Proper belled Or.
JOSSELYN, of Ipswich, Belstead, Copdock, Sproughton, etc. *Crisp's Visitation. II. 42, Pedigree*

An eagle's leg Gules armed Or carrying a bell Or thonged Proper.
JOSSELYN, Ernest William, restored the tower c.1956. *Her.Suff.Ch., Tablet on wall of tower, Trimley St. Mary*

An eagle's leg couped at the thigh on the top two wings erect endorsed.
VICTORYN, of Stowmarket. *Davy, A., church*

An eagle's leg couped at the thigh on the top two pairs of wings [sic] erect addorsed.
VICTORYN, John, son of Peter Victoryn, a Dutch merchant in London, died 1720. *Her.Suff.Ch., Ledger stone, Stowmarket*

HUMAN

A leg in armour couped at the thigh flexed at the knee the foot in chief toe pointing to the dexter Proper the spur Or.
COPINGER, of Cockerell's Hall in Buxhall. *Burke, L.G. 1900 ed.** 'Walter Arthur Copinger' *Bookplates**

'to his crest a mans Legge quarterly or/ g/ w^t a Spurre or/ 1558 to Robt Eyre of Eye'
EYRE. *MS Alphabet of Crests, fo. 35*

A man's leg in armour couped at the thigh Proper.
EYRE. *MS Ordinary of Arms, fo. 220*, spur Or. MS Martin's Crests*

A leg in armour couped at the thigh.
EYRE, of Stuston, East Bergholt, Gt. Whelnetham. 'John Eyer, of Narburgh, co. Norfolk' Brass of 1561. *Cotman's Norfolk Brasses, plate 72*. E.A.N. & Q. XII. 337, Wall tablet, East Bergholt. Whelnetham Registers (Suff. Green Bks) 180, churchyard. Bookplate*.* Joseph Eyre, died 1789. *Her.Suff.Ch., Tablet, East Bergholt.* Rev. C.J.P. Eyre, Incumbent, 1844. *Glass, St. Mary's Bury,* 'leg palewise'

A man's leg couped at the thigh Proper.
GODMANSTON. *Davy, A.*

A leg erased at the middle of the thigh Proper.
RAINE, of Yoxford. *Davy, A.*

LOCK

A square padlock Azure.
FAKENHAM, of Fakenham. *Davy, A. Washbourne,* 'Fakenham, Feckenham' *Fairbairn*,* 'Fakenham, Feckenham'

A square padlock Azure.
FITZRALPH. *Davy, A., Rendlesham church. Washbourne. Fairbairn*,* 'Fitz-Ralph'

The Fitzwalter fetterlock supporting an estoile Or between a pair of wings Gules.
FITZWALTER. 'My Lorde Fu-ater' *Harl. MS 6163**

A fetterlock Or the chain archwise links alternately Or and Azure in its centre an escutcheon per fesse Argent and Azure charged with a lion's head erased Or.
WYNDHAM. 'Tho: Wyndham' *MS Ordinary of Arms, fo. 78**

LOZENGE

A lozenge Gules between two wings erect Argent.
BLOMFIELD, of Stonham Aspal, Badingham, Bury, Ipswich, Wattisham, Sternfield. *Davy, A. Blomfield Family, Title page and Bookplate*, untinctured*

Five lozenges conjoined fessewise Or thereon a Cornish chough Proper.
TAUNTON, of Coldham Hall near Bury. *Crisp's Visitation. IV. 167**

LURE

A 'leure' [sic ?lure] Azure fretty Argent with a heart in the midst thereof.
ECHINGHAM. *Davy, A.*

A hawk's lure Proper.
HAROLD, of Suffolk. *Davy, A.*

On a lure feathers Argent cap and line Gules ring Or a falcon belled Or.
SOAME, Sir Stephen, of London. *Grants & Certificates (Harl. MS 5,869)* Thomas Soame, of Brent Eleigh, co. Suffolk. The same crest *(Harl. MS 1,359)*

On a lure Argent garnished and lined Gules a hawk close Or.
SOAME, Bart., of Lt. Bradley, Kedington, Haughley, Thurlow, Hundon, etc. *London Visitation 1633 (H.S.) II. 250*. Bokenham. Davy, A. Washbourne*,* 'Lond. and Suff.' *Fairbairn,* 'London and Suff.' *Misc.Gen. et Her. 5th S. VIII. 343*

A hawk's lure Argent.
WINGFIELD. 'Sr. Tho: Wingfeild de Suff.' *MS Ordinary of Arms, fo. 200*, one of three crests drawn. Washbourne**

MAST see SHIP

MAUNCH

A maunch per pale Argent and Vert between two wings Or.
WING, of Bury. *Davy, A.*

Two maunches Sable and Argent between a pair of wings Gules.
WING, Frederick, of Bury, died 1864. *Her.Suff.Ch., Wall tablet, Mildenhall*

MILL – RIND

A mill-rind Or.
ALVERD. *Davy, A. Fairbairn*,* 'Alvarde, Alverd, Alured, of Ipswich'

MITRE

A mitre.
BARCLAY, of Henstead. *Davy, A., Seal*

A mitre Or.
BARCLAY, of Higham, Bury St. Edmunds. *Burke, L.G. 1900 ed.*

A mitre Proper.
BARCLAY. Robert Barclay, of Higham, Bury St. Edmunds. *Fairbairn*

A mitre Gules charged with the arms of Berkeley [Gules a chevron between twelve crosses paty Argent] and seamed and crossed Argent.
BERKELEY, of Wixoe. 'S. Edward Berkeley' *Harl. MS 6163* Davy, A., church*

A mitre carved with a chevronel and on each point a cross paty.
BERKELEY, Samuel, Barrister-at-Law, died 1764. *Her.Suff.Ch., Wall tablet, Wixoe*

A bishop's mitre Gules charged with a chevron as in the arms [Gules on a chevron Argent fimbriated Or three escallops Sable].

HARDING. 'Nicholas Hardinge' Patent 22
November 1711. *Grants & Certificates (Stowe
MS 716). See also Miscellaneous Grants (H.S.) I.
99–101*
A mitre Gules charged with a chevron Argent
fimbriated Or thereon three escallops Sable.
HARDING. *MS Martin's Crests.* Hardinge, Rector
of Theberton. *Davy, A., (Burke)*
A bishop's mitre Or banded Gules charged with a
chevron Argent thereon three bezants [*sic*].
SPALDING, of Framlingham. *Davy, A.
Washbourne* *

MONSTER

DEMI-HERALDIC ANTELOPE
A demi-antelope salient Gules billety Argent attired
tufted and unguled Or.
REPINGTON, of Waldingfield. *Warwickshire
Visitation 1619 (H.S.) 188**
A demi-antelope Gules billety Argent maned
bearded tusked and hoofed Or.
REPINGTON, of Waldingfield. *Davy, A.*
A demi-heraldic antelope rampant Azure armed Or
collared Or studded Gules.
ROCHESTER. 'John Rochester' *MS Knight's
Visitations, Essex**

HERALDIC ANTELOPE
An antelope seiant Argent attired tufted and maned
Sable gorged with a label of three points Gules.
BURGOINE. *Davy, A.*
An heraldic antelope statant Ermine horned tusked
maned and hoofed Or.
BYNG, of Thorington, Yoxford. *Davy, A.
Washbourne, 'of Middx.'*
An antelope passant Argent mane and flecks Or.
FORTESCUE, of Chilton. *Davy, A.*
An antelope sejant – armed tufted and maned Or.
PARKYNS. 'Parkins, Perkins' *MS ex-Taylor
Coll.* *
An heraldic antelope passant Proper collar line
hooves and horns Or.
WARDE, Edward, late of Postwick, now of Binley
(? Bilney), co. Norf.; gent; Confirmation by Sir G.
Dethick, Garter, 22 February 1575. *Grants &
Certificates (Harl. MS 1,441; Stowe MS 703)*

BASILISK
A basilisk Proper.
NAUNTON, of Alderton and Letheringham Abbey,
Suffolk. *Fairbairn*
A wyvern Azure membered and scaled Or with a
second head at the end of the tail [*sic* therefore a
basilisk].
WORSLEY, Sir Robert, of Worsley, co. Lanc.;
Confirmation of Arms and Grant of Crest by L.
Dalton, Norroy, 25 November 1561. *Grants &
Certificates (Harl. MS 1,359)*
A wyvern wings elevated on the end of the tail the
head of a wyvern [*sic* as above].
WORSLEY. 'Worseley' *MS Heraldic Alphabet*

CAMELEOPARD [Giraffe] see BEAST,
CAMELEOPARD

CENTAUR
A Sagittarius Gules human part Or bow Or.
BASSETT, of Bradwell. *Davy, A., 'a centaur'*
A centaur shooting an arrow from a bow Proper.
CRULL. *Davy, A.*
A centaur.
METCALFE. Rector of Stonham Aspal. *MS
Fairfax*

DEMI-COCKATRICE
A demi-cockatrice Vert combed wattled and ducally
gorged Or between two wings displayed Argent.
BOTELER. *MS Knight's Visitations, Cambs.* *
A demi-cockatrice wings addorsed Proper.
COOKE. *Washbourne, 'Suff.' Fairbairn, 'Suff.'*
A demi-cockatrice wings addorsed Proper.
FAULKNER. *Washbourne, 'Suff.' Fairbairn,
'Suff.'*
A demi-cockatrice Or on the breast an escallop and
on each wing a cross paty.
KILDERBEE. *Washbourne, 'Suff.' Fairbairn,
'Suff. Escallop and crosses Gules'*

COCKATRICE
A cockatrice sejant Or winged Vert.
ARNOLD. *MS ex-Taylor Coll.* *
A cockatrice Sable.
BURES, of Bures, Acton. *Davy, A., Acton church*
'Upon his Healm on a Tors Argent and Gules a
Cockatrice standing Vert posled gold, comed beaked
and bearded Geuls, his Tayl tortoled'
CORDELL, John, of Long Melford; Grant of Arms
and Crest by an un-named Clarenceux, no date.
Visitation 1561 (ed. Howard) I. 246
A cockatrice wings close Vert beaked combed and
wattled Gules gorged with a ducal coronet Or.
CORDELL, Bart., of Long Melford. *Visitation
1561 (MSS G. 7* and Iveagh Copy*) and (ed.
Metcalfe). Davy, A.*
'to his crest on a wreth ar/g/ a Coketryce in his pp
collers/ beked Combed and Berded g.'
CORDELL. 'Cordall the queenes Solysyter' *MS
Alphabet of Crests, fo. 22*
A cockatrice close.
CORDELL. 'Cordall' *MS Heraldic Collections,
fo. 88a**
A cockatrice Vert.
CORDELL. 'Cordall of Long Melford' *Bokenham*
A cockatrice wings close Vert combed and wattled
Gules.
CORDELL, CORDALL, of Long Melford. *MS
Heraldic Collections, fo. 54*. Davy, A. Fairbairn,
'Cordall, Norf. and Suff.'* Sir William Cordell,
Master of the Rolls, Speaker of the House of
Commons, died 1581. *Her.Suff.Ch., Effigy
monument, Long Melford*
A cockatrice Argent.
GOLDING, of Poslingford. *Bokenham*
A cockatrice Vert comb wattles and sting at tail
Gules.
KILDERBEE. *Sharpe*
A cockatrice Or charged on the breast with an
escallop Argent.
KILDERBEE. 'Saml. Kilderbee, Esq. died 1813'
*E.A. Misc. 1911. 45, 50; Wall tablet and
Hatchment, Gt. Glemham*
A cockatrice wings elevated Or beaked Gules.
LEEDES. 'Leeds' *MS Heraldic Alphabet*
On a staff raguly Vert a cockatrice with wings
endorsed Or combed and wattled Gules.
LEEDES, of Oulton, Eyke, Staverton. *Davy, A.*
A cockatrice Sable comb and wattle Gules.
MELTON, William, son of William Melton, late of
Chester; Grant by L. Dalton, Norroy, 2 January
1560. *Grants & Certificates (Harl. MS 1,359)*
'for his crest a Coketryce closse bryght in prop coler
his hed Upright his combe Spotted or/g/ his tayle Up
behynd flamyng burnyng/ his feete lyke to cokes
fete   To William Naunton in the tyme of Edward
the thryde'

NAUNTON. *MS Alphabet of Crests, fo. 90b*
A cockatrice with unbarbed tail wing 'sad greene' front part 'yellowish' beak 'russett' long crest and legs Sable.

NAUNTON. *MS Lilly's Visitation of Suffolk, fo. 17b*; Second, smaller, crest drawn, beneath it 'This ye Righ Crest'*
A cockatrice close Proper tail nowed.

NAUNTON. 'Sr Robart Naunton Knighte Secretary of State to King James and one of the Privie Cownsell to the saide Kinge' *MS Lilly's Visitation of Suffolk, fo. 17b.* Larger of two crests drawn*
A cockatrice Proper.

NAUNTON. 'William Nawnton'; Confirmation by Sir C. Barker, Garter. *Grants & Certificates (Stowe MS 692)*
A cockatrice per pale Gules and Sable out of its mouth a scroll with these words 'ut vidi ut vici'
NAUNTON, of Letheringham. *Bokenham*
A cockatrice close Proper wings Sable.

NAUNTON, of Letheringham, Alderton, Rendlesham, Rougham. *Davy, A. Washbourne*, 'Nanton, Suff.'*
A cockatrice.

SECKFORD. *Davy, A. (Barrett)*

CUPID
A cupid Or quiver and bow Gules tipped Argent.

SEWSTER. 'Sr Robert Sewster, Knight and Dame Ann (Fletcher) his wife, he died the 25th and she died 29th February 1675' *Tymms, 204, Gravestone, St. Marys church Bury. Arms only.* Sewster, of cos. Hunts. and Cambs. *Misc.Gen. et Her. 5th S. VII. 333*

DEMI- DRAGON [Alphabetically by name]
A demi-dragon wings expanded Gules.

BABINGTON. 'Syr Antony Babyngton' *Banners & Standards**
A demi-griffin, or demi-dragon, segreant Ermine.

BLOSS, BLOSSE, of Belstead, Ipswich. *Visitation 1664–8*. MS Fairfax. Davy, A. E.A.N. & Q. VII. 244*
A demi-dragon salient Ermine.

BLOSS, of Belstead. *Bokenham*
A demi-dragon.

BLOSS. Thomas Blosse, died 1662. *Her.Suff.Ch., Slab, Belstead*
'for his Crest or Cognizance vpon the Helme a demy Dragon volant gold rising from the top of a Castle gules, scituated vpon a wreath of his Colours arg: & gu: with mantelles appendant gu: doubled or lyned argent'

BOWYER. 'William Bowyer, of Knypersley, co. Staff.'; Grant of Crest by William Flower, Norroy, 12 June 1574. *Miscellaneous Grants (H.S.) I. 37–8 (MS Ashmole 858). See Notes*
A tower Gules out of the top a demi-dragon Or.

BOWYER. 'R.. Bowyer, Esq., son of William Bowyer, of co. Stafford'. Grant 18 Elizabeth [1575/6]. *Grants & Certificates*
A dolphin embowed Proper in front of a demi-dragon Azure armed and langued Gules.

BUNN. Albert Edward Bunn, 1887–1959. *Her.Suff.Ch., Wooden shield on chair, Beccles*
A demi-dragon segreant Gules.

CASTLETON, of Stuston. *MS Knight's Visitations, Suff.* 'William Castelton' MS Philpot's Visitations, Suff.* Bokenham. Davy, A.*
A demi-dragon Gules wings expanded and armed Or.

CASTLETON, Sir John, Bart., died 1705. *Her.Suff.Ch., Effigy monument, Stuston. Erected 1727*
A demi-dragon Gules.

CASTLETON, Sir Robert, descended from Sir William Castleton, Bart., of Stuston Hall, died 1715. *Her.Suff.Ch., Monument, Beccles*
A demi-dragon wings endorsed.

CASTLETON. Mary, wife of John Castleton, died 1737; Rev. Sir John Castleton, A.M., Rector of Gorleston, died 1777, aged 80. *Her.Suff.Ch., Ledger stone in chancel, Gorleston*
A demi-dragon rampant Gules.

COMPTON. *MS ex-Taylor Coll.**
A demi-dragon Azure wings displayed Or.

DALTON. *MS ex-Taylor Coll.**
A demi-dragon volant Gules wings and claws Or.

DOYLEY. *MS Fairfax (Staveley)*
A demi-dragon with wings expanded Vert.

ECHINGHAM, of Barsham. 'Mayster Ichyngham' *Banners & Standards*. Davy, A.*
A demi-dragon Vert.

FITZOSBORNE, FITZOSBERT, of Somerleyton, North Cove. *Davy, A.*
A demi-dragon couped wings endorsed Azure.

KNEVETT. *Visitation 1561 (ed. Howard) I. 130*.* 'Knyvett' *MS Martin's Crests*
A demi-dragon winged.

LUCAS. *MS Martin's Crests, 'of Horringer Suff.'*
A demi-dragon Gules gutty Or.

MANN. 'John Man, of Bolingbroke, co. Linc., J.P. and feodary of the Duchy of Lancaster in the co. of Lincoln'; Grant by L. Dalton, Norroy, 5 April 1561. *Grants & Certificates (Harl. MS 1,359)*
'for his crest a Demy Dragon the wyngs Dyspled g/ gowty or/ langed and membred b/ to John Manne of Bolyngbroke in Lyncolnsh^{re}.'

MANN. 'Manne' *MS Alphabet of Crests, fo. 83b*
A demi-dragon Gules gutty Or armed Azure.

MANN. 'Man of Bramford' *MS Fairfax*
'a Demy dragon rampant Sable gutty Argent'

MANN. Edward Mann, of Ipswich; Grant of Arms and Crest by Bysshe, Clarenceux, 2 March 1662/3. *Muskett. III. 76 (Harl. MS 1470)*
A demi-dragon.

MANN, Edward, died 1680. *Muskett. III. 80e, Floor slab, St. Nicholas church, Ipswich. Davy, A.*
A demi-dragon wings endorsed Sable gutty Argent.

MANN, of Syleham, Weybread, Ipswich. *Visitation 1664–8*. Bokenham. Davy, A., 'inside of the wings and talons Proper'*
A demi-dragon Gules gutty Or, on his shoulder a mullet Or [for difference].

MANN, of Framsden. *Bokenham*
A demi-dragon wings indorsed Argent gutty Sable.

MAN, MANN. *Washbourne, 'Suff.' Fairbairn, 'Man, Mann, Ipswich, Suff. Wings addorsed'*
A demi-dragon Gules gutty Or.

MANN, Thomas, of the Inner Temple and Yoxford, died 1669. *Her.Suff.Ch., Hatchment, Yoxford*
A demi-dragon Sable gutty Or.

MANN, John, died 1715. *Her.Suff.Ch., Ledger stone in churchyard, Weybread*
A demi-dragon wings endorsed Sable langued Gules.

PONYNGES. *Harl. MS 6163*
A demi-dragon rampant sans wings.

SALKELD, of Woodbridge. *Davy, A.*

DEMI- DRAGON, holding: [Objects in alphabetical order]
A demi-dragon Vert holding in the dexter paw [*sic*]

an arrow Or headed and flighted Argent.
> COLE, of Sudbury. *Surrey Visitations 1530, etc. (H.S.) 134*

A demi-griffin, or demi-dragon, segreant holding in the dexter claw an arrow.
> COLE, COELL, of Depden, Bildeston. *Bokenham. Davy, A.*

A demi-dragon Vert holding an arrow point downwards Or barbed and feathered Argent.
> COLE. *MS Heraldic Collections, fo. 42*. Washbourne*, 'of Cornw.' Dragon untinctured*

A demi-dragon holding between its paws [*sic*] an arrow point downwards head and feathers Argent.
> COLE, COELL. Thomas Coell, of Depden Hall, son of Sir John Coell, Kt., died 1698. *Her.Suff.Ch., Altar tomb in churchyard, Depden. Not found 1988*

A demi-dragon wings expanded Sable holding in its dexter claw a battle-axe erect Proper.
> LILLINGSTON, of Sproughton, Ipswich, Southwold. *Davy, A.*

A demi-dragon Or holding in its claws a cross paty Gules.
> EVETT. 'Edmund Evett of Woodhall in Hallow, descended from an ancient family in Suffolk, temp. H. 7' *Worcestershire Visitation 1634 (H.S.) 33*

A demi-dragon without feet its tail nowed Vert holding in its mouth a cross paty Gules.
> SANDCROFT, of Fressingfield. *Bokenham*

A demi-dragon without wings Vert holding a rose branch flowered Argent stalked and leaved Vert.
> EDEN, of Sudbury. *Visitation 1561 (ed. Howard) I. 1*. Davy, A. Washbourne, 'Ess. and Suff.' Fairbairn, 'Essex and Suff.'*

A demi-dragon without wings Vert holding a bunch of strawberries Proper.
> EDEN. *Davy, A. (Barrett)*

A demi-dragon Vert holding a slip of a rose bush in flower Proper.
> EDEN. *Her.Suff.Ch., Eden wall pedigree, All Saints church, Sudbury*

A demi-dragon wings indorsed Vert holding between its feet a garb Or.
> FIRMIN, of Hawkedon. *Davy, A. Washbourne, 'of London'*

TWO DEMI-DRAGONS

Two demi-dragons without wings rampant addorsed their necks interlaced the first Or the second Gules.
> MOYLE. *Wall's Book*
> 'to his Crest ij Demy Dragons endossed rampant their necks enterlased the fyrst or the 2 g/ the wyngs not seen'
> MOYLE. *MS Alphabet of Crests, fo. 81*

Two demi-dragons without wings endorsed and the necks interwoven sinister Argent dexter Gules.
> MOYLE, of Bury. *Davy, A., Rushbrook church.* Captain Robert Moyle, died 1742. *Suff. Green Bks., Rushbrook, in the church, untinctured*

Two demi-dragons addorsed with necks entwined the dexter Gules the sinister Or.
> MOYLE. Hon. Major-General John Moyle, died 1738; Isabella Moyle, died 1746. *Her.Suff.Ch., Ledger stone in chancel, Rushbrooke*

DRAGON [Alphabetically by name]

A dragon and on its back a pelican vulning herself all Proper.
> ATKINS. *MS Heraldic Alphabet*

A dragon passant with wings endorsed Vert.
> CASTLETON. *Davy, A. Fairbairn*, 'Suff. Wings addorsed'*

A dragon passant the tail extended wavy Ermine.
> CHESTER. *MS Martin's Crests*

A dragon passant Argent.
> CHESTER, of Melford. *Davy, A.*

A dragon passant Ermine.
> CHESTER, of Sudbury, Paddock Hall in Melford. *Burke, L.G. 1900 ed.**

A dragon Sable 'the myddes of her body' Gules.
> CROFTS. 'Crofte' *Wall's Book*
> 'to his Crest a Dragon sa/ the mydes of her body g/'
> CROFTS. 'Crofte' *MS Alphabet of Crests, fo. 19b*

A dragon with wings displayed Sable.
> CROFTS. *MS Martin's Crests*

A dragon seiant Proper
> CROFTS. 'Croft' *MS Heraldic Alphabet*

A halbert in pale Or sticking on the point a dragon volant without feet Sable bezanty 'casting fyre at her tayle'
> DAWES. 'Daweus (Sheriff) of London, temp. H.7.' *Wall's Book*

A dragon sans wings the head looking upwards Argent gorged with a coronet Gules chain Or the tail long and nowed.
> FARRINGTON, William, of Worden, co. Lanc.; Confirmation of Arms and Alteration of Crest by L. Dalton, Norroy, 17 December 1561. *Grants & Certificates (Harl. MS 1,359)* 'Sʳ Nic. Farington of Suff.' *MS Fairfax (Lev.), arms only given*

A dragon passant Argent.
> LOWTHER. *Davy, A.* 'Hon. William Lowther, High House, Campsea Ashe, Wickham Market' *Fairbairn*.* James Lowther, 1st Viscount Ullswater, died 1949; Others. *Her.Suff.Ch., Wall monument, Glass and Tombstone in churchyard, Campsea Ash*

A dragon passant Sable.
> PRATT. *Davy, A.*

A dragon with wings tail nowed.
> QUINCY, Earl of Winchester. *Davy, A.*

A lizard, or dragon, passant Vert collared and crowned Or.
> WARNER. 'Will Warner' *MS Philpot's Visitations, Suff.* Davy, A.*

A dragon Gules collared and chained Or.
> WELD. *MS Martin's Crests*

DEMI-GRIFFIN [Alphabetically by name]

A demi-griffin Gules wings endorsed Argent.
> CASTLETON, CASTILTON, of Rattlesden. *Visitation 1577*

A demi-griffin Argent.
> CASTLETON. *MS Heraldic Alphabet*

A demi-griffin Argent beaked and legged Gules.
> CATER, of Ixworth. *Davy, A.*

A demi-griffin Or beaked Gules collared Ermine.
> COLLINGE, of Bury. *Davy, A. (Mr. Barnwell), Wenhaston church*

A demi-griffin Gules.
> DENT. *Sharpe*

A demi-griffin Vert.
> FAULKNER, of Long Melford. *Davy, A.*

A demi-griffin erased wings erect.
> FULLER, of Gorleston. *Davy, A., church*

Out of a tower a demi-griffin Proper.
> KERDISTON, of Henham. *Davy, A.*

A demi-griffin Proper.
> LESLIE. Hon. & Rev. Sir Henry Leslie, Bart., Rector of Wetherden for 35 years, died 1849. *Davy, A. Her.Suff.Ch., Wall tablet, Wetherden*

A demi-griffin wings expanded Gules.
> LUCAS. *Davy, A.*

'to his crest a Demy gryffen p pale or/g/ a coller a bowt necke count/ Edward page of Suff gentelman Usher to quene Elizabeth'

PAGE. *MS Alphabet of Crests, fo. 102*

A demi-griffin.

POSTLE, of Wortham. *Davy, A., church*

A demi-griffin Or.

WYTHE. Vicar of Eye, died 1835. *Proc.S.I.A. II. 144, church monument*

DEMI- GRIFFIN, holding: [Objects in alphabetical order]

'And for his Creast on a healme & wreath of his Colours a demy Griffin Or holding a Danish Hatchet handled Gules, head Proper Mantled Gules doubled silver'

BROND. 'Benjamin Brond of Edwardstone in the county of Suffolke son of John Brond of Boxford in the said County, and Jacob, Samuell and James his brethren'; Confirmation of Arms and Crest by William Camden, Clarenceux, dated 10th March 1612–13. *Miscellaneous Grants (H.S.) I. 40–1 (Harl. MS 1441, fo. 52b)*

'on an healme and wreath of his Colours a Demy Griphin Or, holding a Danish Hatchet handled Gueles, mantled Gueles doubled silver'

BROND, Benjamin, of Edwardstone; Grant of Arms and Crest by William Camden, Clarenceux, 10th March 1612. *MS Suffolk Armorial Families**

A demi-griffin holding a halberd Or.

BROND, BRAND, of Polstead, Tattingstone. *Sharpe.* Samuel Brand, A.M., Rector of Tattingstone, son of William Brand of Polstead, died 1725. *E.A.N. & Q. VIII. 158, Arms on wooden tablet, crest on floor slab, untinctured. Her.Suff.Ch., Tattingstone*

A demi-griffin Or holding a battle-axe handle embowed Gules head Argent.

BROND, BRAND, of Boxford, Edwardstone. *Davy, A. Washbourne, 'Lond. and Suff.' Fairbairn*, 'Brond, Brounde, London and Suff.' Axe handle not embowed. Her.Suff.Ch., Brass and Slab, Edwardstone*

A demi-griffin Argent holding between its paws [*sic* claws] a buckle Sable.

BILNEY. *Davy, A.*

A demi-griffin Argent collared Azure holding between its claws an escallop Or.

CUTTING, of Mettingham. *Davy, A. (Edms.)*

A demi-griffin Or wings Gules between the claws an escallop shell Argent.

HOLBECH, Roger, of Witchingham, co. Norfolk, son of Thomas Holbech, of Suffolk. Patent June 1613. *Grants & Certificates (Harl. MS 1,441; Stowe MSS 706 and 707)*

A demi-griffin Or winged Gules holding an escallop Argent.

HOLBECK, of Coddenham, Dennington, Bedfield. *Davy, A.*

A demi-griffin reguardant holding a flag charged with a saltire.

BRÉAUTÉ, Fulk de temp.Hen.3. Honour of Eye. *Davy, A.*

A demi-griffin holding in his claws a fleur-de-lis.

GIRLING. Thomas Girling of Horham gent., died 1694. *Patridge, 105 (Darby, 1826), Stone in Horham churchyard*

A demi-griffin Azure holding between its feet [*sic*] a fleur-de-lis Gules.

GIRLING, of Stradbroke. *Davy, A. E.A.Misc. 1927, 69*

A demi-griffin Azure holding between its paws [*sic* claws] a fleur-de-lis Gules and Azure.

GIRLING, Thomas, of Horham, died 1694. *Her.Suff.Ch., Ledger stone in churchyard, Horham. Fleur-de-lis now indecipherable*

A demi-griffin Argent holding in its beak a Guernsey lily Proper.

DE BEAUVOIR, BENYON – DE BEAUVOIR, of Culford Hall. *Davy, A., 'dragon or griffin'. Burke, L.G. 1853 ed.*

A demi-griffin holding between his talons a wheat sheaf [or garb].

FIRMAN, of Ipswich. *Sharpe*

A demi-griffin wings elevated Argent ducally gorged chain and ring Or holding in its beak a horse-shoe Or.

WELLYS, Lord *Harl. MS 6163*

A demi-griffin wings close Or holding in its beak a griffin's leg erased foot downwards Gules.

ESSEX. *Wall's Book*

'to his Crest a demy gryffyn/ the wyngs closse or/holdyng in his beke a gryffens Legge rased g/ the ffoote donward knight by h 8/'

ESSEX. *MS Alphabet of Crests, fo. 34*

A demi-griffin Argent holding between its claws a saltire Sable.

MALTIWARD. *Fairbairn, 'of Rougham, Suff.'*

A demi-griffin holding in the dexter claw a sword erect Proper.

ELWES, Bart. *Davy, A.*

Rampant or Segreant
[Alphabetically by name]

A plume of ostrich feathers Argent issuing therefrom a demi-griffin segreant Gules.

ALDERSON, of Lowestoft, Badingham. *Davy, A.*

A demi-griffin rampant.

ATHILL, of Halesworth, Rumburgh. *Davy, A.*

A demi-griffin, or demi-dragon, segreant Ermine.

BLOSS, BLOSSE, of Belstead, Ipswich. *Visitation 1664–8*. MS Fairfax. Davy, A. E.A.N. & Q. VII. 244*

A demi-griffin rampant Ermine.

BLOSS. *E.A. Misc. 1921. 65, Glass, Framsden Hall*

A demi-griffin segreant.

BLOSS, BLOSSE. Elizabeth (Darcy), wife of Thomas Blosse, died 1653. *Her.Suff.Ch., Wall tablet, Belstead.* Thomas Blosse, of Belstead, died 1722. *Wall tablet, Belstead.* 'demi griffin sejant' [*sic*]

A demi-griffin segreant Gules winged Or.

CASTLETON, Bart. *E.A.N. & Q. I. 257, Stuston church monument*

A demi-griffin segreant Or collared and chained Argent.

COLLINS. *MS Martin's Crests*

A demi-griffin segreant.

DOYLEY. *MS Martin's Crests*

A demi-griffin segreant Gules winged Or.

FELGATE, of Stonham Aspal, Yaxley. Andrew Felgate, died 1598. *E.A. Misc. 1918. 94, Glass dated 1591 in Yaxley church*

A demi-griffin segreant.

KIRKMAN. Keeper of Melton Lunatic Asylum. *Davy, A.*

A demi-griffin rampant wings displayed Sable.

LEATHES, of Herringfleet. *Page. Davy, A.*

A demi-griffin rampant Or.

LEATHES, of Herringfleet. *Davy, A., church.* George Leathes of Herringfleet Hall, died 1817.

Her.Suff.Ch., Hatchment, Herringfleet, 'armed and langued Gules'

A demi-griffin segreant Or on the head two fleurs-de-lis in pale Gules.

> LEATHES. 2nd Lieut. Robert H. de M. Leathes, killed at Arras 1917 aged 18; sister Dulcibel Leathes, died 1920 aged 18. *Her.Suff.Ch., Wall monument, Herringfleet*

A demi-griffin segreant Gules.

> LESTER, of Wenhaston. *Davy, A., church*

A demi-griffin segreant.

> MAN, MANN, of Ipswich, Weybread. John Man, gent., died 1715. *Partridge, 113 (Darby, 1825), Weybread churchyard. E.A.N. & Q. X. 55, Monument, St. Nicholas church, Ipswich, churchyard.* Edward Mann, Esq., died 1680. *Her.Suff.Ch., Ledger stone, St. Nicholas, Ipswich. Missing 1983*

A demi-griffin rampant couped per pale Gules and Azure collar counterchanged on the shoulder three gutties Argent.

> PAGE, William, of Hegesett (? Hessett), co. Suffolk; Grant by G. Dethick, Garter, 16 September 1552. *Grants & Certificates (Stowe MS 676)*

A demi-griffin segreant couped wings addorsed plain collared.

> PAGE. *Bookplate**

A demi-griffin segreant Argent beaked and armed Gules.

> PARSON, of Botesdale. *Davy, A. (Burke), Redgrave church*

A demi-griffin segreant Proper.

> RIX, of Beccles, Ipswich. *Davy, A.*

A demi-griffin segreant Sable beaked and legged Or.

> SCOTT, of Glemsford. *MS Heraldic Collections, fo. 48*. Davy, A., Carlton church*

A demi-griffin segreant Azure in front of a plume of five feathers alternately Or and Argent.

> WYE, of Ipswich. *Visitation 1664–8*

A demi-griffin segreant Azure in front of a plume of five feathers alternately Or and Azure.

> WYE, of Ipswich. *Bokenham. Davy, A.*

A demi-griffin segreant.

> WYTHE, of Eye, Framsden. *Davy, A. Bookplate**. Rev. Thomas Wythe, M.A., Vicar of Eye over 50 years, died 1835. *Her.Suff.Ch., Wall tablet, Eye*

DEMI- GRIFFIN, Rampant or Segreant, holding: [Objects in alphabetical order]

A demi-griffin segreant holding an arrow.

> COELL, COLE. 'Tho. Coel esq. of Depden Hall, s. and heir to Sir John C. knight [marriages given], 5 Oct. 1698 ag. 57' *Partridge, 183 (Darby, 1831), Depden churchyard*

A demi-griffin [segreant] Or holding a battleaxe Gules head Argent.

> BRAND, BROND. 'Benjamin Brounde, of Edwardeston co. Suffolk'. Patent by W. Camden, March 1610. *Grants & Certificates (Stowe MS 707)*

A demi-griffin segreant Or holding a battle-axe, or halbert, embowed handle Gules headed Argent.

> BRAND, BROND, of Edwardstone, Polstead, Boxford, London. *London Visitation 1633 (H.S.) I. 108*. Visitation 1664–8*. Bokenham, 'p.Camden'. Davy, A.*

A demi-griffin segreant holding a battleaxe all Or.

> BRAND, of Polstead. *Her.Suff.Ch., Hatchments, Polstead.*

A demi-griffin segreant Gules holding between his paws [*sic* claws] a crown imperial Or.

> LANE, of Campsey Ash. *Bokenham*

A demi-griffin segreant Azure winged Or beaked Gules holding in its claws a fleur-de-lis Gules.

> GIRLING. 'Wyll Girlynge' *MS Philpot's Visitations, Norf.**

A demi-griffin segreant holding in its claws a fleur-de-lis Gules.

> GIRLING, of Horham. *Davy, A.*

A demi-griffin segreant Argent holding in its claws a garb Or.

> FIRMIN, of Ipswich. *Davy, A., St. Lawrence church*

A demi-griffin couped Argent segreant wings erected bezanty in his dexter paw [*sic* claw] a mullet Or.

> CHOPPYNE, of Coddenham. *MS Fairfax (Tyl.)*

A demi-griffin rampant Gules supporting a mullet Or.

> CHOPPYNE, of Coddenham. *MS Fairfax (Candler)*

A demi-griffin rampant Sable holding in its claws a mullet Gules.

> CREED, of Bury, Mellis. *Davy, A.*

A demi-griffin rampant holding in its dexter claw a mullet.

> GUMBLETON, Maxwell H. M. Gumbleton, D.D., sometime Bishop of Dunwich and Archdeacon of Sudbury, Rector of Hitcham 1935–49, died 1952. *Her.Suff.Ch., Wall tablet in chancel, Hitcham*

A demi-griffin rampant Gules bezanty between the paws [*sic* claws] a bezant.

> LANE. *Washbourne, 'Suff.' Fairbairn, 'Suff. griffin segreant'*

A demi-griffin rampant wings erect holding in his paws [*sic* claws] a saltire Or, on a scroll over the griffin 'Ab aquila'.

> GILLY, of Hawkedon. *Davy, A., church*

A demi-griffin segreant wings erect Argent holding in the dexter paw [*sic* claw] a saltire Or. Same motto as above, but no scroll.

> GILLY. *Fairbairn, 'Hawkdon [sic], Suff.'*

A demi-griffin segreant Argent holding between its claws a saltire Sable.

> MALTIWARD, MALTYWARD, MALTWOOD, of Hawkedon, Rougham. *Bokenham. Sharpe. Davy, A., Hawkedon and Buxhall churches. Washbourne, 'Maltiward, Suff.'*

A castle Sable issuing therefrom a demi-griffin segreant Argent holding in its dexter claw a sword Argent hilted Or.

> HIGGINS, of Bury. *Davy, A.*

GRIFFIN

A griffin Or.

> BEVAN, of Rougham. *Davy, A.*

A griffin reguardant with wings elevated Gules.

> CHETHAM. *MS Martin's Crests*

A griffin with wings expanded Gules.

> JERMY, of Brightwell, Stutton, Metfield. *Davy, A. Washbourne, 'Suff. and Norf.'* Thomas Jermy, Esq., son and heir of Sir Thomas Jermy, died 1652. *Her.Suff.Ch., Ledger stone, Metfield.* Sir Isaac Jermy, date of death unrecorded; son John Jermy, died 1662. *Effigy monuments, Stutton*

Out of a castle a griffin.

> REDE. *Her.Suff.Ch., Bench end, Hollesley*

Rampant or Segreant [Alphabetically by name]

A griffin segreant.

ALDRICH, of Suffolk. *Davy, A. (Burke)*
A griffin rampant segreant [*sic*] Or.
COOKE, of Semer. *Sharpe.*
A griffin segreant Or winged Argent.
COOKE, of Lavenham, Semer. *Davy, A.*
A griffin rampant Sable.
COOKE. *Washbourne*, 'Suff.' Fairbairn*, 'Suff. segreant'*
A griffin segreant reguardant with wings expanded Argent.
COPLEY, of Suffolk. *Davy, A. Fairbairn, 'Suff.'*
A griffin segreant.
CROSS, CROSSE, William, died at Onehouse Hall, 1861. *Her.Suff.Ch., Wall tablet, Lt. Finborough*
A griffin segreant Proper wings endorsed
DOLBEN, Bart., of Bury, Denham in Risbridge Hundred. *Davy, A.*
A griffin segreant quarterly Argent and Gules winged and armed Or.
DUFFIN, of Yoxford. *Davy, A.*
A griffin segreant the dexter claw raised Gules pierced through the breast with a broken arrow headed Or feathered Argent the top part held in the beak.
FELGATE. *MS Knight's Visitations, Suff., fo. 107b**
A griffin segreant with wings expanded ducally gorged.
HEARING. *Fairbairn, 'of Eye, Suff.'*
A griffin segreant Or winged Ermine.
LOUND, of Lound. *Davy, A.*
A griffin segreant Or.
PEYTON, of Peyton Hall in Ramsholt, Boxford. *Page. Davy, A.*
A griffin segreant wings expanded Ermine legged and beaked Or.
PLEASANCE, PLEASAUNCE, of Tuddenham, Brandon Ferry. *Visitation 1664–8*. Davy, A.*
A griffin segreant per fesse Or and Sable.
SANDYS. *MS Martin's Crests.*
A griffin segreant per fesse Or and Gules.
SANDYS, Lord Of Somerton. *Davy, A.*
A griffin segreant Or pierced in the breast with a broken sword blade Argent vulned Gules.
SHUTE. Vicar of Stowmarket, died 1687. *Davy, A.* 'The creast on a wreath or.b. a Gryffin Segreant [with] a coller & armed and beaked or'
WENTWORTH, of Nettlestead. *Visitation 1561 (Iveagh Copy)*
A griffin segreant Or.
WOODHOUSE, WOODHOUSE alias PORE. 'Sr. William Woodhouse of Hyklynge' *MS Knight's Visitations, Norf.** 'Sr. thomas wodhose' *MS Philpot's Visitations, Norf.**

Rampant or Segreant, holding: [Objects in alphabetical order]

A griffin segreant Argent supporting a book Sable garnished –.
GARDINER. *MS Heraldic Collections, fo 56**
A griffin segreant with wings endorsed Or holding in its beak a chaplet Gules.
PASTON, of Huntingfield. *Davy, A., church*
A griffin segreant holding an escarbuncle all Proper.
PAGENHAM, PAKENHAM, of Suffolk. *Davy, A. Washbourne, 'Iri. and Suff.'*
A griffin segreant Argent holding a fleur-de-lis Or.
SHERLAND, of Woodbridge, Lavenham. *Davy, A., Woodbridge and Elmsett churches.* Edward Sherland, of Gray's Inn, Esq., died unmarried 1609. *E.A.N. & Q. VII. 169, Effigy monument,*

Elmsett. The fleur-de-lis called 'a small object, or'.

Passant [Alphabetically by name]

A griffin passant Argent.
ASHFIELD. *Fairbairn*, 'Norf. and Suff.'*
A griffin passant Argent.
BATLEY, of Ipswich. *Davy, A., St. Nicholas church vestry*
A griffin passant Ermine.
BAYLIE. Rector of Kelsale and Wrentham, died 1770. *Davy, A.*
A griffin passant per pale Or and Azure.
BLEADON, of Ipswich. *Davy, A., St. Mary Stoke church*
A griffin passant reguardant Gules winged and beaked Or, charged on the breast with a crescent on a crescent – [for difference].
CHETHAM, of Gt. Livermere. *Visitation 1561 (MSS G. 7* and Iveagh Copy*).* 'John Chethum' *Harl. 772*, one crescent only*
A griffin passant reguardant Gules wings endorsed and membered Or.
CHETHAM, CHITTAM, of Livermere, Bury. *Visitation 1561 (ed. Metcalfe and ed. Howard, II. 59*, tuft of tail Or). MS Fairfax*
A griffin passant reguardant with wings endorsed Argent winged Or, charged on the shoulder with a crescent Gules.
CHETHAM, CHETTHAM, of Livermere. *Davy, A. Fairbairn, 'Suff.'*
A griffin passant disclosed Azure.
COOKE, of Lavenham, Semer. *Davy, A. (Barrett)*
A griffin passant Or.
CUDMORE, CUDNOR, of Suffolk. *Davy, A. Washbourne, 'Ess. and Suff.'*
A griffin passant Argent.
ELRINGTON, of Suffolk. *Davy, A.*
A griffin passant Sable.
FINCH, Earl of Aylesford. Of Withersfield, Gazeley. *MS Ordinary of Arms, fo. 115*. MS ex-Taylor Coll.*, 'of Kent'. Davy, A.*
A griffin passant.
FINCH. 'Simon H.M. Ffinch, 1937–41' *Her.Suff.Ch., Bench end, Hollesley*
A griffin passant Argent.
HOPTON. *Bokenham*
A griffin passant Proper.
JERMY, of Brightwell, Foxhall, Coddenham, Creeting, Stonham. *Page*
A griffin passant Or winged Argent.
PEERES, Robert, of West Downe, co. Kent; Confirmation of Arms and Grant of Crest by R. Cooke, Clar., in 1588. *Grants & Certificates (Harl. MSS 1,144 and 1,359)*
A griffin passant.
PRESS, of Hoxne, Syleham. *Davy, A., Capel church.* William Press, ? of Hoxne, died 1807. *Her.Suff.Ch., Tablet, Capel*
A griffin passant with wings addorsed Argent.
SHULDHAM, of Marlesford, Beccles. *Davy, A.*
A griffin passant Argent.
SHULDHAM. *Burke, L.G. 1853 ed. Fairbairn*, 'of Shuldham and Kettlestone, Norf. and Marlesford, Suff.'*
A griffin passant Argent armed Gules.
SHULDHAM, Lemuel, Cornet in the Scots Greys, killed at Waterloo, 1815; William Shuldham, of Marlesford Hall, died 1845 aged 102. *Her.Suff.Ch., Wall tablet and Hatchment, Marlesford*

A griffin passant Argent winged Azure collared Or.
>   WENTWORTH. *Bokenham*

A griffin statant, or passant, Argent collared per pale
Or and Argent.
>   WENTWORTH, Lord Of Nettlestead. *Davy, A.*

A griffin statant, or passant, Argent ducally gorged
Gules.
>   WENTWORTH, Lord Of Nettlestead. *Davy, A.*
>   *(Barrett)*

Passant, holding: [Objects in alphabetical order]

A griffin passant holding in the beak an arrow.
>   WHITTINGTON, of Theberton, Yoxford, Orford.
>   *Davy, A.*

A griffin passant per pale Ermine and Or beaked and
membered Or holding in the beak a key Or.
>   HOBSON. *Davy, A.*

A griffin passant Or the dexter claw resting on a
bezant (or globe) Or.
>   BISHOP. Elizabeth, daughter of Rev. Thomas
>   Bishop, married – King; she died 1813.
>   *Her.Suff.Ch.*, Wall tablet, Witnesham

A griffin passant Argent holding in the dexter claw a
pellet.
>   HOPTON, of Blythburgh. *Visitation 1561 (MSS*
>   *G. 7* and Iveagh Copy*) and (ed. Metcalfe).*
>   *Somersetshire Visitation 1623 (H.S.) 56, 'a ball'.*
>   *Davy, A. Misc.Gen. et Her. 3rd S. III. 9, 'armed*
>   *Or'. Fairbairn, 'of Somers. and Blithbon [sic],*
>   *Suff. A stone Sable'*

A griffin passant per pale wavy Gules and Argent
collared Or wings elevated Erminois the dexter claw
resting on a woolpack Argent.
>   BACK, of Oulton Broad. *Crisp's Visitation. VI.*
>   *124*, of Curat's House, Norwich and Oulton,*
>   *Suffolk, Pedigree.* 'Philip Edward Back, Esq., of
>   Curat's House and Mancroft Towers, Oulton,
>   Suff.' *Fairbairn, 'supporting a woolpack'*

Statant

A griffin statant.
>   ASTY, of Market Weston, Bury. *Davy, A.*

A griffin statant Gules armed and legged Azure.
>   JERMY. 'Sr. Thomas Jermy' *MS Knight's*
>   *Visitations, Norf.**

A griffin statant Gules.
>   JERMY. 'Sr Thomas Jermy of Brightwell K^t of the
>   Bathe' *MS Lilly's Visitation of Suffolk**

A griffin statant wings inverted Argent plain
collared per pale Or and Argent.
>   WENTWORTH. 'Syr Rychard Wentworthe of
>   netylstede in Suffe' *Banners & Standards**

A griffin statant wings expanded Argent forelegs
beak and ears Or ducally gorged Gules.
>   WENTWORTH, of Mendham. *Visitation 1561*
>   *(MSS G. 7* and Iveagh Copy*)*

A griffin statant Argent beak and forelegs Or gorged
with a collar per pale Or and Gules.
>   WENTWORTH, of Nettlestead. *MS Humfry*
>   *Pedigree Roll*; Corder MS 91.* 'Lord Wentworth'
>   *Proc.S.I.A. XXVII. 151 (Dandy Pedigree)*

A griffin statant, or passant, Argent collared per pale
Or and Argent.
>   WENTWORTH, Lord Of Nettlestead. *Davy, A.*

A griffin statant, or passant, Argent ducally gorged
Gules.
>   WENTWORTH, Lord Of Nettlestead. *Davy, A.*
>   *(Barrett MS)*

Sejant [Alphabetically by name]

A griffin sejant.

>   BAILEY, John, of The Priory, died 1813; Sir
>   Joseph Bailey, died 1850. *Her.Suff.Ch., Carved*
>   *shield on bench end, Gt. Wenham*

A griffin sejant Gules winged legged beaked and tail
tufted Argent.
>   BREWSE. 'Thomas Brewse of Wenham in Com
>   Suffolke esquier' *MS Lilly's Visitation of*
>   *Suffolk*, first of two crests drawn*

A griffin sejant reguardant wings displayed and
depressed Argent.
>   COPLEY, Thomas, of Gatton, co. Surrey, Esq.;
>   Confirmation by Dethick, Camden and Flower,
>   16 February 1568. *Grants & Certificates (Stowe*
>   *MS 703)*

A griffin sejant reguardant wings expanded Argent.
>   COPLEY. *Washbourne, 'Suff.'*

A griffin sejant Gules wings erect Or pierced
through the breast with a broken spear Or holding
the pointed end in its beak.
>   FELGATE. 'Andrew felgate' *MS Philpot's*
>   *Visitations, Suff.*, griffin beaked and legged Or*
>   *spear Or headed Argent.* 'Fieldegate of Yaxley'
>   *Visitation 1664–8*

A griffin seiant Gules wings elevated Or its forefeet
rampant in its body a spear broken the two ends
appearing.
>   FELGATE, of Stonham, Yaxley. *Bokenham*

A griffin seiant salient Or pierced through the breast
with a broken spear and holding the top point in his
mouth.
>   FELGATE, of Stonham Aspal, Yaxley. *Davy, A.*

A griffin sejant salient Argent pierced through the
breast with a broken spear Or the point in the
mouth.
>   FELGATE. 'Fellgate' *Washbourne*.* 'Fellgate'
>   *Fairbairn*, 'Suff.'*

A griffin sejant Gules winged Or pierced through
the breast with a broken spear Or holding the point
Argent in its mouth.
>   FELGATE, Andrew, son of John Felgate, of
>   Stonham Aspal, died 1598. *Her.Suff.Ch., Brass*
>   *and Glass, Yaxley*

A griffin seiant wings expanded Or gutty de poix
armed Sable.
>   GOODING, GOODWIN, GOODWYNE, of Wherstead,
>   Hasketon, Charsfield, Debach, Hollesley,
>   Marlesford, Freston. *Visitation 1577.* 'Goding of
>   Ipswiche' *MS Knight's Visitations, Suff.** 'Edward
>   Goddinge' *MS Philpot's Visitations, Suff.* London*
>   *Visitation 1633 (H.S.) I. 324*. Visitation 1664–8.*
>   *Bokenham. Davy, A., Wherstead church.*
>   *Washbourne, 'Gooden, Gooding, Suff.' Muskett. I.*
>   *200 and 232. Fairbairn, 'Gooden, Gooding, Suff.'*

A griffin sejant wings extended Sable gutty Or.
>   GOODWIN. 'William Goodwyn, late of Hasketon,
>   died 1663/4'; two sons, both died in Smyrna,
>   1664 and 1665. *Her.Suff.Ch., Wall tablet,*
>   *Hasketon.* 'William Goodwin, died 1663/4'; John
>   Goodwin, of Martlesham and Grundisburgh, died
>   1742; son John Goodwin, died 1758. *Hatchments,*
>   *Martlesham*

A griffin sejant wings expanded Or gutty de poix
claws and beak Sable.
>   GOODWIN, John, died 1742; son John, died 1758.
>   *Her.Suff.Ch., Ledger stone, Martlesham*

A griffin seiant wings elevated Sable.
>   HALSEY. 'Halse' *MS Martin's Crests*

A griffin seiant wings addorsed Or.
>   HALSEY, of Bury. *Davy, A., St. Mary's church*

A griffin seiant rising Ermine ducally gorged ringed
and lined Gules.

HAVERS, of Norfolk. 'Thomas Havers of Winfarthing' *MS Knight's Visitations, Norf.* * *MS Heraldic Alphabet*
A griffin seiant Argent beak and fore-legs Or ducally collared and lined Or.
HAVERS, of East Bergholt. *Davy, A.*
A griffin seiant with wings expanded Argent ducally gorged.
HEARING, of Eye. *Davy, A., Cretingham church*
A griffin seiant Gules armed Argent.
HOLBROKE. *Bokenham*
A griffin seiant Argent beaked legged and winged Azure pierced through the breast with a broken tilting spear Proper and holding the bottom part of the broken spear in the sinister claw.
HOWELL, HOVELL. *Fairbairn, 'of Northamp., Warw., and Suff.'*
A griffin seiant Proper.
LAWRENCE, of South Elmham St. James. *Davy, A.*
A griffin seiant with wings endorsed Proper.
LOVENEY, of Stratton. *Davy, A.*
A griffin seiant wings endorsed Gules armed Or.
MULSO, of Cretingham. *Davy, A.*
A spear in pale Or beside it a griffin sejant Vert.
PASHLEY. *MS Ordinary of Arms, fo. 32* *
A griffin seiant Argent the dexter claw raised beaked and membered Or.
PESCOD. *Davy, A.*
A griffin sejant Or.
PEYTON, of Bury, Worlingworth. 'Payton of Suffolk' *Wall's Book. Visitation 1561 (ed. Howard) II. 109* *. Warwickshire Visitation 1619 (H.S.) 378* *. Visitation 1664–8* *. Sharpe.* Peyton, Bart., of Bury. *Davy, A.*
'to his Crest a gryffyn seant or /'
PEYTON. 'Payton of Suff.' *MS Alphabet of Crests, fo. 98b*
A griffin sejant wings addorsed.
PEYTON, PAYTON, of Bury St. Edmunds. *Visitation 1561 (MS G.7*). Washbourne* , 'Payton, Suff. wings indorsed'. Fairbairn* , 'Payton, Suff. wings addorsed'*
A griffin seiant Or the tail between the hind legs and reflexed over the back.
PEYTON. 'Sr Henry Payton of Bery St Edmond' *MS Lilly's Visitation of Suffolk* *
'a griffin Seiant or, ye tail betwn ye hinder legs over ye back Vert'
PEYTON. *MS Martin's Crests*
A griffin sejant wings expanded Ermine.
PLEASANCE, of Tuddenham. *Visitation 1577. MS Knight's Visitations, Suff.* * 'Thomas Pleasannes' *MS Philpot's Visitations, Suff.* *, 'armed and beaked Or'. MS Fairfax (Tyl.) Washbourne* , 'Suff. wings addorsed'. Fairbairn* , 'of Tudenham [sic], Suff. wings addorsed'*
A griffin sejant Ermine.
PLEASANCE. 'Pleasants of Brandon' *Bokenham, 'p. Cooke, Clar., 1576'*
A griffin sejant Argent beak claws and wings Or pierced by a spear Sable head Argent.
SHUTE, Christopher, of Giggleswick in Craven, co. Yorks.; Confirmation of Arms and Grant of Crest by Sir W. Segar, Garter, April 1616. *Grants & Certificates (Harl. MS 6,059; Stowe MS 706)*
A griffin sejant Argent winged Or pierced through the breast and protruding from the back with a spear Sable.
SHUTE, of Cambridge. 'Shute of ?' *MS Knight's Visitations, Cambs.* * MS Ordinary of Arms, fo. 133* *

A griffin seiant Azure beaked and membered Or.
SYDNOR, of Norfolk. *MS Heraldic Alphabet*
A griffin seiant wings expanded Azure legged armed and tailed Or.
SYDNOR, of Blundeston. *Davy, A.*

Sejant, holding: [Objects in alphabetical order]
A griffin sejant Or collared Sable in the claw an arrow Argent.
HICKS. 'Mr. Hicks, of London' *Grants & Certificates (Stowe MS 706)*
A griffin seiant Argent gorged with a collar embattled counter-embattled Or beaked and legged Or holding in its dexter claw an arrow Or.
HICKS, of Beccles. *Davy, A.*
A griffin sejant Azure gorged with a collar embattled counter-embattled Or beaked and legged Or holding in its dexter claw an arrow Or.
HICKS. *Fairbairn, 'of London and Beccles, Norf.' [sic]*
A griffin sejant holding a battleaxe all Or.
BRAND. William Beale Brand, died 1799. *Her.Suff.Ch., Hatchment, Polstead.*
'A gryphon sejant wings expanded, tail cowed or, holding in the beak a chain gold'
PASTON. 'S. John Paston, Norff.' *Harl MS 6163*
'A gryphon sejant, wings elevated, tail cowed or, in his beak a circular chain of the last'
PASTON. 'Syr Wyllm Paston de Paston Norff.' *Banners & Standards* *
A griffin sejant holding in its beak a chain.
PASTON. *Wall's Book*
'to his Crest a gryffyn Seant holding in his mouth a chayne wound or/'
PASTON. *MS Alphabet of Crests, fo. 98b*
A griffin seiant holding in its dexter claw an escutcheon Argent.
BISHOP. *MS Martin's Crests*
A griffin seiant resting its dexter claw on an escutcheon Azure.
BISHOP. *MS Heraldic Alphabet*
A griffin seiant Argent resting the dexter claw on an escutcheon.
BISHOP. Elizabeth, daughter of Rev. Thomas Bishop, married – King; she died 1813. *Her.Suff.Ch., Wall tablet, Witnesham*
A griffin sejant Gules wings elevated and addorsed barry of six Or and Azure in its beak a rose Argent slipped and leaved Proper and resting the dexter claw on a portcullis with chains Sable.
BARRY. Rectors of Gosbeck and Badingham. Of Ipswich. *Crisp's Visitation. XIV. 1* *
A griffin sejant Or collared with an Eastern crown Gules holding in its beak a Guernsey lily Proper.
BENYON. Quartered by De Beauvoir. *Burke, L.G. 1853 ed.*
A griffin sejant Or holding a bezant in his dexter claw.
BISHOP, of Ipswich. *Sharpe*
A griffin seiant Sable holding in the dexter claw a sword erect Proper pommel and hilt Or.
HOY, of Higham. *Davy, A. Fairbairn, 'of Higham Lodge, Suff.'*

Volant
A griffin volant Argent winged and membered Or holding up in one claw a pellet.
HOPTON. *Wall's Book*
'to his crest an gryffyn ar/ Volant/ holding in on foote Up a pellet/ the wyngs and membred or/ made knight by h 8'

HOPTON. *MS Alphabet of Crests, fo. 55*

HARPY
A harpy with wings expanded Argent crined and belled Or on the breast a mullet.
ALLINGTON. *Davy, A.*
A harpy with wings expanded Proper.
HURRY, of Rumburgh, Yarmouth. *Davy, A.*
A harpy with wings Proper full-faced and tail twisted round the leg.
POCHIN. Rector of Lt. Cornard. *Davy, A. 'Pochin of Barkby'* [See Dennys, *The Heraldic Imagination, p. 128*,* drawn as a lizard's tail]

IBEX
A demi-ibex erect quarterly Azure and Gules maned and tufted Or holding in his mouth an apple Purpure stalked and leaved Vert.
APPLEYARD. 'Mayster appellyerd' *Banners & Standards**
An ibex passant Sable bezanty maned armed and attired with two straight horns Or.
EDWARDS, of Bradfield Combust. *Davy, A.*
An ibex seiant Argent tufted armed and maned Or.
NIGHTINGALE. 'Nyghtingall' *MS Knight's Visitations, Essex*.* 'Nyghtingall' *MS Philpot's Visitations, Essex*, not tufted or maned. Davy, A. (Edms.)* Nightingale, Bart., of Cambridge. *Washbourne**
An ibex sejant Argent maned and horned Or.
WROTT. 'Wrotte of Gunton' *Addit.Suff.Peds.*
An ibex sejant Argent maned tufted and with two straight horns.
WROTT, WROTE. 'Wrote, John, of Bungay in co. Suffolke gent., Robert Wrote of Gunton in Com.Suff.esq^r., ffran Wrote of Gunton in Co. Suffolke now living 1634' *London Visitation 1633 (H.S.) II. 373*, 'A Patent vunder the hand and seale of Robert Cooke Clar. A° 1581'*
An ebeck (a beast like a tiger) seiant Argent with two horns mane and hooves Or.
WROTT. WROTE, of Gunton, Bungay. *Davy, A.*

LION DRAGON
The fore part of a lion Gules maned Argent breathing fire Gules and Or joined to the hind part of a dragon Vert salient.
BRENDE, of Beccles. *Visitation 1561 (MS G. 7*)*
The fore part of a lion Gules conjoined with the hind part of a dragon seiant Vert the centre part Argent.
BRENDE. *Harl. 772**
The forepart of a lion Gules conjoined with the hind part of a dragon seiant Vert.
BRENDE, of Beccles. *Davy, A. Washbourne*, 'Suff.' Fairbairn, 'Suff.'*
A lion dragon sejant Ermine.
HOVELL. *MS Knight's Visitations, Suff., fo. 110b.* 'Rychard Hovell' MS Philpot's Visitations, Suff.**

LION, WINGED
A winged lion rampant with rays round his head Or 'a Glory' holding in both paws a lyre Azure.
MARKHAM. *MS Ordinary of Arms, fo. 50**
A winged lion seiant Or circled round the head Argent supporting a lyre Or.
MARKHAM, MARKANT, of Ipswich. *Davy, A., St. Peter's church*

DEMI- MERMAID
A demi-mermaid.
AYLMER. *Davy, A.*

MERMAID
A mermaid with her glass and comb Proper.
AYLMER, of Claydon. *Bokenham*
A mermaid with glass, or mirror, and comb Proper.
ELMY. *Davy, A.* Henry Elmy, died 1730; brother John Elmy, died 1734. *Her.Suff.Ch., Altar tomb in churchyard, Rickinghall Superior, untinctured.* 'James Elmy, of Beccles, 1757' *Bookplate**
A mermaid with glass, or mirror, and comb Proper.
GARNEYS, GARNISH, of Redisham, Ringsfield. *Visitation 1664–8*. Suckling. I. 63 and 68*. Davy, A. Washbourne*, 'Garnish, Suff.' Fairbairn *, 'Garneshe, Garnishe, Suff.' Muskett. II. 259 (Harl. MS 1085).* John Garneys, Lord of the Manor, died 1524, son of Thomas Garneys of Kenton. *Her.Suff.Ch., Effigy brass in vestry, Kenton. Mutilated.* Nicholas Garneys, Lord of the Manor of Lt. Redisham in Ringsfield, died 1623. *Brass on outside wall of church, Ringsfield.* 'Thomas Garneis, Esq., died 1701' *Ledger stone, Weston.*
A mermaid Argent crined and finned Or holding in her dexter hand a comb Or.
GARNEYS. *Muskett. I. 189 (Harl. MS 1820, fo. 43)*
A mermaid Proper crined Or comb and mirror Or.
HASTINGS. 'S. John Hastyngs' *Harl. MS 6163. MS Heraldic Collections, fo. 14**
A mermaid Proper.
HASTINGS. *MS Martin's Crests*
'And to the Crest vppon the healme a marmaide fynned flasshed & hearid golde a wreathe abowte her hed argent and vert holdinge in her hand a bell golde atache with a lace of the wreathe of her hed on a wreathe argent and sables mantellid gules dobled argent'
LANY. 'John Lanye of Cratfield'; Confirmation of Arms and Crest by William Hervy, Clarenceux, 12 July 1561. *Frag.Gen. XIII. 13–14*
A mermaid Argent tail and hair Or tied round the temples with two ribbons Argent and Vert holding in her dexter hand a hawk's bell Or hung to two strings Argent and Vert.
LANY, LANYE, of Cratfield. *Visitation 1561 (MSS G. 7* and Iveagh Copy*) and (ed. Metcalfe). Harl. 772**
A mermaid Proper on her head a wreath Argent and Azure holding in her right hand a branch of two acorns.
LANY. 'Laney' *Bokenham*
A mermaid Proper crined Or tailed Vert holding a mirror in her right hand.
LANY, of Ipswich. *E.A.N. & Q. IX. 203, Monument in St. Margaret's church.* John Lany, son of John Lany of Cratfield, Recorder of Ipswich, died 1633. *Her.Suff.Ch., Wall monument, St. Margaret's, Ipswich*
A mermaid Proper her waist encircled by a mural crown Or.
MYLES, of Willisham. *Davy, A.*
A mermaid Proper crined Or comb and mirror frame Or.
NEWMAN. 'George Newman, of . . .'; Grant June 1611. *Grants & Certificates (Stowe MSS 706 and 707)*
Out of a ducal coronet Or a mermaid Proper crined Or conjoined to a dolphin hauriant Or devouring her sinister hand.
THORNE. *Washbourne, 'Suff.' Fairbairn, 'Suff. and Shropsh.'*

MERMAN

A merman, or triton, Proper holding in his hand an escallop Or.

ELDRED, of Ipswich, Saxham. *Gage (Thingoe). Davy, A.*

A merman.

ELMES, ELMY, of Rickinghall Superior. Henry Elmy, died 1730; brother John Elmy, died 1734. *Partridge, 93 (Darby, 1828), churchyard*

A merman Proper tail Argent fins and hair Or tied round the temples with two ribbons Argent and Azure holding in his hand a hawk's bell hung to two strings Argent and Or.

LANY, of Ipswich, Cratfield. *Davy, A. Washbourne*, 'Lond., Leic. and Suff.'*

A merman Proper tail Argent fins and hair Or wreathed round the temples Argent and Azure holding in his hand a hawk's bell Proper suspended from a string Vert tasselled Argent.

LANY. *Fairbairn, 'London, Leics. and Suff.'*

OX, WINGED

A bull courant Sable winged collared and armed Or.

COLE. *MS Heraldic Collections, fo. 42**

A bull courant winged.

COLE. *Washbourne. Elvin**

PANTHEON or THEOW

'A best lyke a woulf' Sable semy of stars Or eared and legged Gules 'his fete cloven lyke a hogge'

BAYNHAM. *Wall's Book*

'to his crest a beast lyke a wolff sa/ full of starres or/ his eyres and legs g/ his fete cloven lyke a hogge/. Sr Crystofer Baynam.'

BAYNHAM. 'Baynam' *MS Alphabet of Crests, fo. 9*

[See Dennys, *The Heraldic Imagination, 159* and 161*, where the late Hugh Stanford London, Norfolk Herald Extraordinary, is credited with having identified these rare crests, the Pantheon being shown as semy of estoiles but the Theow as being a species of wolf, both with ears and lower legs Gules and with cloven hooves. In *Banners & Standards, 154**, Sir Christopher Baynham's crest is drawn and described as having a lamb's head and tail]

DEMI-PANTHER

A demi-panther Argent spotted Azure Or and Gules holding in his paws a branch Vert flowered Gules.

HACKET, HAGGITT, of Ipswich, Bury. *Davy, A. Washbourne, 'Hacket, of London and Bucks.'*

A demi-panther rampant guardant Argent flames issuing from his mouth Gules semy of roundels Azure Sable and Gules holding in his dexter paw a ?vine branch Vert with fruit Gules.

PALMER. 'Thomas Palmar' *Banners & Standards**

A demi-panther Argent 'wounde pellete' breath Azure holding between his feet in pale a branch of vine Vert the grapes Purpure.

PALMER. 'Pawlmer' *Wall's Book*

'to his crest a Demy panther ar/ spotted p/ & sa/ the breth b/ holding bet his fete in pale a braunche of Vyne vert the grapes purpure'

PALMER. *MS Alphabet of Crests, fo. 99b*

A demi-panther rampant flames issuing from his mouth and ears holding in his paws a holly branch Proper.

PALMER, of Gt. Yarmouth. Several members of the Palmer family, 1672–1834. *E.A.N. & Q. II. 325, Altar tombs in churchyard, Gt. Yarmouth*

A demi-panther rampant guardant issuing flames

from ears and mouth Proper holding a branch Vert fructed Gules.

PALMER. Walpole D. Palmer, of Shrubland House, Southtown, died 1901. *Her.Suff.Ch., Brass wall tablet in chancel, Gorleston*

A demi-panther rampant guardant spotted Sable fire issuing from his ears and mouth.

SPARKES. *Bookplate**

PANTHER

A panther sejant Or spotted Sable collar and line Or.

POTT. John Pott, of Lincoln's Inn, son of Roger Pott; Grant by R. Cooke, Clar., 1583. *Grants & Certificates (Stowe MSS 670 and 700; Add. MS 14,295)*

A panther Argent spotted of various tinctures fire issuing from his mouth and ears Proper.

SOMERSET, of Wickhambrook. *Davy, A. Washbourne, 'Suff.' Fairbairn, 'of Suff. panther incensed Proper'*

DEMI-PEGASUS

A demi-pegasus semy of estoiles.

BOND. *MS Martin's Crests*

A demi-pegasus rampant wings addorsed Argent.

BOND, of Freston. *Davy, A., church*

A demi-pegasus Azure winged and semy of estoiles Or.

BOND. Rev. William Bond, Rector of Wheatacre, Mutford, Barnby, died 1832 aged 86. *Crisp's Visitation. III. 72. Her.Suff.Ch., Freston*

A demi-pegasus winged.

BOND. Henrietta Maria (Jermyn), wife of Thomas Bond, died 1698. *Suff. Green Bks, Rushbrook. Her.Suff.Ch., Ledger stone, Rushbrook*

A demi-pegasus.

BOND. Rev. John Bond, Rector of Freston for 36 years, died 1831; daughter Laura Bond, died 1860. *E.A.N. & Q. VIII. 69, church monument. Her.Suff.Ch., Wall tablet, Freston. Crest missing 1982*

A demi-pegasus Or.

COURTHOPE – MUNROE, Dame Ellen, of Manor House, Kelsale, died 1930. *Her.Suff.Ch., Wall tablet, Kelsale*

A demi-pegasus Or.

MYNN. *Washbourne*. Fairbairn*, 'of Cratfield, Suff.'*

PEGASUS

A pegasus volant Gules winged Azure ducally gorged and chained Argent.

BROOKE, of Southolt, Worlingworth. 'John Brooke' *MS Knight's Visitations, Essex*. MS Philpot's Visitations, Essex*. Davy, A., 'p' Cooke'*

A pegasus courant with wings endorsed Argent charged on the shoulder with a cross avellane Vert.

PEPPIN, of Ringshall. *Davy, A. (Burke)*

PHOENIX

A phoenix close Proper.

EYRE, of Burnham, Suffolk. *Davy, A.*

A phoenix in flames Proper.

NEEDHAM, of Barking. *Davy, A.*

SALAMANDER

A salamander Vert in flames Proper.

SHAFTO, of Framlingham. *Davy, A. (Edms.)*

SEA CONEY

A sea coney sejant Gules maned Or among reeds Vert.

CONYERS alias NORTON, NORTON, of Halesworth. *Visitation 1561 (Iveagh Copy*)*

A sea coney seiant Gules maned Or finned Argent
out of a tuft of grass and rushes Proper.
NORTON, of Halesworth. *Davy, A.*

DEMI- SEA DOG

A demi-sea dog guardant Sable finned and collared
Or.
DODGE. 'John dodge of Mannyngton' *MS Knight's
Visitations, Norf.*
A demi-sea dog Azure collared finned and purfled Or.
DODGE, of Suffolk. *Davy, A.*

DEMI- SEA HORSE

A demi-sea horse rampant per pale indented Or and
Azure.
PAGE, of Clopton, Woodbridge. *MS Ordinary of
Arms, fo. 163*. Davy, A., Hemingstone church*
A demi-sea horse assurgent.
PAGE, of Woodbridge. *Burke, L.G. 1853 ed.*
A demi-sea horse Argent hooves and mane Or
holding an anchor.
SAMSON. Col. Arthur Oliver Samson, C.B.E.
Her.Suff.Ch., Glass, St. John's church, Felixstowe
A demi-sea horse rampant quarterly Gules and Or
ducally gorged per pale Or and Gules.
TOOKIE, TOOKY. *Davy, A. (Burke)*

SEA HORSE

A sea horse Sable scaled finned and crined Or.
WISEMAN, Thomas, of Felstead, co. Essex, gent.,
son and heir of John Wiseman, of the same place,
Esq.; Confirmation by R. Cooke, Clarenceux,
22 February 1574. *Grants & Certificates*
([Harl.] *MS 1,359*)

SEA LION

A sea lion holding a cross patonce.
BENSTED, of Icklingham, Tuddenham. *Davy, A.*
On a wave of the sea a sea lion erect Azure with a
ducal coronet Or holding an anchor Sable.
HARLAND. *Sharpe*
Issuing from the sea Proper a sea lion supporting an
anchor Sable beam Or.
HARLAND, Bart., of Sproughton, Nacton,
Wherstead. *Davy, A.*
A sea lion Sable supporting an anchor Proper.
HARLAND, Bart. *Washbourne*, 'Suff.'
Fairbairn, 'Suff.'*
A sealion ducally crowned supporting an anchor.
HARLAND. Ann, wife of Captain Robert Harland,
Junr., died 1747. *Her.Suff.Ch., Slab in chancel,
Sproughton*
A sealion erect on its tail Azure ducally crowned Or
holding between the paws [*sic*] an anchor Or fluked
Sable.
HARLAND. Sir Robert Harland, Bart., died 1848;
widow died 1860. *Her.Suff.Ch., Tablet, Glass
and Altar tomb in churchyard, Wherstead*
A sea lion seiant Ermine.
HOVEL, HOVELL, HOWELL, of Stratford Hall,
Ashfield. *Addit.Suff.Peds. London Visitation
1633 (H.S.) I. 396*. Davy, A., Mildenhall church.
Muskett. II. 10 (Harl. MS 1103) and 44 (London
Visit. 1633)*
A sea lion.
HOVELL, Hugh, 'of Keningall Parke in Norfolk',
died 1690. *Her.Suff.Ch., Ledger stone,
Mildenhall*
A sea lion Proper finned Or holding a cross paty
from each arm a fleur-de-lis issuing [a cross fleury]
Sable.
NORRIS. Patent 1622. *Grants & Certificates
(Stowe MS 706)*

A sea lion sejant supporting with the dexter paw
[*sic*] a cross fleury.
NORRIS. *MS Heraldic Collections, fo. 86a**
A sea lion seiant per pale Or and Argent gutty de
poix finned Or.
SHERMAN, of Ipswich. *Davy, A. Washbourne,
'Suff.' Fairbairn, 'of Ipswich, Suff.'*
A sea lion seiant Or semy of plates [*sic*].
SHERMAN. *Davy, A. (Barrett MS)*
A sea lion seiant Sable charged on the shoulder with
three bezants 2.1.
SHERMAN, of Ipswich, Yaxley. *Davy, A. St.
Stephen's church Ipswich. Washbourne, 'Suff.'
Fairbairn, 'Suff.'*

SEA UNICORN

A sea unicorn.
PAGE, of Ipswich, 1824. *Davy, A.*

SERPENT WOMAN

A serpent nowed Proper with a woman's head
full-faced hair Or.
BONHAM. *Davy, A. [See Dennys, The Heraldic
Imagination, 129*]*

SPHINX

A sphinx couchant guardant.
ARGALL, of London. *MS Ordinary of Arms,
fo. 80** [beside it, in a later hand 'Harpy' but
clearly drawn as a sphinx]
A sphinx with wings expanded Proper.
ARGALL, of Halesworth. *Davy, A.*

DEMI-HERALDIC TIGER [Alphabetically by
name]

'A demi-tiger quarterly Azure and Gules the mane
and the end of the tail and 'a busche of here in the
myddes of hit' Or holding the stalk of an – Vert in
his mouth the apple Purpure the tail countercoloured'
APPLEYARD. 'Applyard' *Wall's Book*
'to his crest a demy tigre qtrly b/g/ the mayne and
end of the tayle and a bush of hare in the mydes of
yt or/ holdyng the stalke of – in his mouth the aple
p. the tayle count/ K by H 8'
APPLEYARD. 'Aplyard' *MS Alphabet of Crests,
fo. 3b*
A demi-tiger quarterly Gules and Azure the tail
Azure tufted Or in his mouth a rose Gules stalked
and leaved Vert.
APPLEYARD, of Framlingham. *Davy, A.*
A demi-heraldic tiger Azure armed and tufted Or
collared of the first [*sic*] holding a broken sword
Proper.
BLOMEFIELD, Bart. *Washbourne, 'Norf.'*
A demi-heraldic tiger rampant Argent holding
between its paws a broken sword.
BLOMFIELD. *Fairbairn, 'Suff.'*
A demi-heraldic tiger Sable. 'He had afore from
Clarencieux a coat that had no lions and the crest
per pale Or and Sable, in the paws an appletree
branch'
PAGET. 'Sir William Pagett, of Bromley, co.
Stafford'; Grant by Sir C. Barker, Garter. *Grants
& Certificates (Stowe MS 692)*
'his Crest a demy tigre sa/ armed & langed g/ tusked
ffafed [?] and Crowned a bowt the neck ar/ to S[r]
Willm Paget of Bromley in Staff'
PAGET. *MS Alphabet of Crests, fo. 101b*
A demi-heraldic tiger salient Sable ducally gorged
armed and tufted Argent.
PAGET, of Levington. 'William Dominus Pagett
de Beaudesert in Com Staff' *MS Ordinary of
Arms, fo. 42* Davy, A.*

A demi-tiger guardant issuing flames from his mouth Proper holding a branch Vert.

PALMER, of Burgh Castle, Yarmouth. *Davy, A.*

A demi-tiger Azure collared Or.

ROCHESTER. 'John Rochester' *MS Philpot's Visitations, Essex**

A demi-tiger Azure horned maned hooved and collared Or studded Gules.

ROCHESTER. 'Sir Rob. Roucester, K.G.' Of Gt. Ashfield. *Davy, A.*

HERALDIC TIGER

On an heraldic tiger Or collared a naked man astride Vert wreathed about the temples Sable and Argent the ends of the wreath flotant.

BRAMPTON. 'Thomas Brampton of Blownorton' *MS Knight's Visitations, Norf.**

An heraldic tiger.

FORTESCUE. *Davy, A.*

A tiger Or crined Sable charged on the shoulder with a crescent Sable.

OSBORNE. 'Osborn' *MS Heraldic Alphabet*

Rampant or Salient

An heraldic tiger rampant.

FRENCH. John French, of London, a Governor of Bart's Hospital, died 1734; son John French, of Groton. *Her.Suff.Ch., Altar tomb in churchyard, Groton*

A monster [unknown to the College of Arms] resembling an heraldic tiger salient Or langued Gules without forelegs but with three straight tapering spikes protruding from the breast each banded alternately Sable and Or.

WEST, of Sudbury. Visitation 1561 (MS G. 7*, crest not blazoned but drawn). Ralph West of Sudbury in Suffolk, descended from West of Brustwyk, co. Yorks.; Confirmation of Arms by Roger Durroit, Lancaster King of Arms, in 1386; again Confirmed by Roger Legh, Clarenceux, 23 July 1446; again Confirmed by John Wrexworth, or Wrixwourthe, Guyenne King of Arms, 12 March 1446/7. [See Dennys *The Heraldic Imagination, 167** and my edition of *The Visitation of Suffolk 1561. I. 14–17,* where the full Patent, in French, and translation are given]

Passant

A tiger passant holding in his jaws the leg of a man couped at the thigh.

CHICHELY, CHICHELEY. 'Chichly' *MS Knight's Visitations, Cambs.**

A tiger passant reguardant tail extended Sable langued Gules, charged on the shoulder with a crescent – for difference.

DANIEL. 'Danyell of Acton' *Visitation 1561 (MSS G. 7* and Iveagh Copy*)*

A tiger passant reguardant Sable, a crescent for difference.

DANIEL. 'Danyell of Acton' *Visitation 1561 (ed. Metcalfe)*

A tiger passant reguardant tail extended Sable, charged on the shoulder with a martlet – for difference.

DANIEL. 'Danyell of Stoke juxta Clare' *Visitation 1561 (MSS G. 7* and Iveagh Copy*)*

A tiger passant reguardant Sable, a martlet for difference.

DANIEL. 'Danyell of Stoke juxta Clare' *Visitation 1561 (ed. Metcalfe)*

A tiger passant reguardant Sable.

DANIEL, of Acton, Stoke by Clare. *Harl. 772** 'Danyell' *MS Knight's Visitations, Suff.** *MS Martin's Crests. Davy, A. (Barrett)*

A tiger passant Or tufted and maned Sable.

DEREHAUGH, DERHAUGH, of Colston Hall in Badingham. *Addit.Suff.Peds. Davy, A. Washbourne, 'Derhaugh, Suff.' Fairbairn**, *'Suff. An heraldic tiger'*

An heraldic tiger passant Or tufted and maned Sable.

OSBORNE, of Somerleyton. *Davy, A.*

Statant

A tiger statant Sable.

DANIEL, DANIELL. 'John Daniell, late of Messing in Essex, Esq., died 1584.' *Her.Suff.Ch., Brass, Wetherden*

A tiger statant reguardant Sable.

DANIEL, DANIELL. Col. William Daniell and Grace his wife. No dates given. *Her.Suff.Ch., Glass, Yoxford*

Sejant

A tiger seiant Argent tufted and maned Sable.

BURGOINE. 'Burgoyn' *MS Knight's Visitations, Camb.**

An heraldic tiger sejant the dexter paw raised Or gorged with a coronet tufted maned and tusked Sable.

RANT, Roger, of the Pipe Office and of North Walsham, co. Norfolk, gent. son of Robert Rant, of the same place; Confirmation of Arms and Grant of Crest by R. Cooke, 26 January 1580. *Grants & Certificates (Add. MS 14,295; Harl. MS 1,359; Stowe MS 700)*

A tiger sejant reguardant Argent tufted Sable in the mouth an arrow pierced through the shoulder Or headed and feathered Argent.

SIDAY. 'William Sidey, of Bures S. Mary, co. Suffolk'. Patent 1536. *Grants & Certificates (Harl. MS 1,105)*

A tiger seiant Argent maned Sable.

THETFORD. 'Andrewe Thetford' *MS Knight's Visitations, Norf.** *MS Heraldic Alphabet*

A tiger seiant Or maned and tufted Sable.

THETFORD, of Thetford. 'Christofer Thetford' *MS Philpot's Visitations, Norf.** *Davy, A. (Edms.)*

An heraldic tiger seiant Gules ducally gorged chained and ringed Or.

TOTHILL. 'Tothill' *MS Knight's Visitations, Norf.**

TRITON

A merman, or triton, Proper holding in his hand an escallop Or.

ELDRED, of Ipswich, Saxham. *Gage (Thingoe). Davy, A.*

DEMI-UNICORN

A demi-unicorn Argent.

CRIKETOT, KIRKETOT, of Suffolk. *Davy, A.*

A demi-unicorn Argent horn mane and hooves Or in the mouth a branch of oak Vert with three acorns Or and gorged with a collar of roses Gules.

HARWOOD, Henry, of Kensington, co. Middx. and of Crawford [*sic* Crowfield] Hall, co. Suff.; Grant and Confirmation by J. Anstis, Garter and Sir J. Vanbrugh, Clarenceux, 13 August 1722. *Grants & Certificates (Add. MS 14,831)*

A demi-unicorn Gules armed and crined Or supporting a lozenge Or.

SMYTH. *Washbourne, 'Suff.'*

A demi-unicorn Argent collared gobony Or and Azure armed and crined Or.

YAXLEY, YAXLEE, of Yaxley. *Visitation 1664–8*.
Davy, A.*
A demi-unicorn Argent collared gobony Sable and
Or.
  YAXLEY. *Fairbairn, 'of Boston, Lincs., and Suff.'*

Rampant or Salient
A demi-unicorn rampant Or armed Proper crined
Or.
  BAYNARD, Lord   *Davy, A.*
A demi-unicorn rampant holding in its mouth a
branch.
  HARWOOD, of Crowfield. *Davy, A., church*
A demi-unicorn rampant.
  HARWOOD, of Crowfield Hall. *E.A.N. & Q. XII.
  227, Slab, Crowfield church.* Henry Harwood,
  late of Crowfield Hall, died 1738. *Her.Suff.Ch.,
  Ledger stone, Crowfield*
A demi-unicorn salient Ermine.
  JOBSON. *Bokenham*
Between two wings a demi-unicorn salient with an
olive branch in his mouth.
  LOMAX. *Bokenham*

UNICORN
A unicorn.
  CUNNINGHAM. Vicar of Lowestoft, 1830–60.
  Lees, 191
A unicorn Argent.
  DAWTREY, of Bricett. *Davy, A.*
A unicorn Ermine horned and crined Or.
  GREY, 'Lord Marq. Dorset' *Harl. 6163*
A unicorn Ermine in a sun Or.
  GREY. 'Grey Marquys Dorset' *Wall's Book*
'to his Crest an Unycorne [ermine spot drawn] / in a
son gold/'
  GREY. 'Gray marquis Dorset' *MS Alphabet of
  Crests, fo. 47b*
A unicorn Ermine armed unguled and surrounded
by rays of the sun Or.
  GREY, Marquis of Dorset, Duke of Suffolk. Of
  Hengrave, Haverhill. *Davy, A.*
A unicorn.
  HOWE, of Stowmarket. *MS Fairfax (Tyl.)*

Rampant or Salient
In front of a sun Or a unicorn salient Ermine.
  GREY, Lord   *MS ex-Taylor Coll.**

Passant
A unicorn passant Azure gutty Or ducally gorged
Argent foreleg resting on a shield Or charged with a
pale Vair.
  BLAKELEY. John Rix Blakeley, Esq., died 1810.
  E.A.N. & Q. I. 257, Hatchment, Thrandeston
A unicorn passant Azure gutty Or ducally gorged
Argent resting on the dexter leg on an inescutcheon Or
charged with a pale Vair.
  BLAKELEY, John Rix, of Goswold Hall, died 1810;
  probably for his son, William Rix Blakeley, died
  1842. *Her.Suff.Ch., Hatchments, Thrandeston*
A unicorn passant Or.
  GOUSHILL, GOSELL, of Suffolk. *Davy, A.*
A unicorn passant Gules gorged with a coronet Or
horned and hooved Or.
  GREY. 'Henry Gray, of Eye, co. Suffolk'; Grant
  by R. Cooke, Clarenceux, 1576. *Grants &
  Certificates (Stowe MS 670)*
A unicorn passant Gules bezanty crined armed
hooved and ducally gorged Or.
  GREY, of Eye, Thrandeston, Hitcham, Kersey,
  Cavendish. *MS Fairfax. Davy, A., Cavendish
  church. Washbourne, 'Suff.' Fairbairn, 'Suff.'*

A unicorn passant Gules bezanty gorged with a
mural coronet and armed Or.
  GREY, of Eye, Thorndeston [*sic* Thrandeston].
  Bokenham
A unicorn passant ducally gorged.
  GREY, Rev. Thomas, Rector for 50 years, died
  1704/5. *Her.Suff.Ch., Ledger stone, Cavendish*
A unicorn passant Or horn twisted Or and Sable
gorged with a coronet and line Sable.
  OSBORNE. 'John Osbourne, of Suffolk'; Grant
  1578. *Grants & Certificates (Harl. MS 1,359;
  Add MS 4,966)*
A unicorn passant Or ducally gorged ringed lined
armed and crined Sable.
  OSBORNE, OSBOURN, of Debenham, Rickinghall,
  Wattisfield. *MS Knight's Visitations, Suff.*
  MS Ordinary of Arms, fo. 126* Visitation
  1664–8* Bokenham. Davy, A. Washbourne,
  'Osborne, Suff.' Fairbairn, 'Osborne, Debenham,
  Suff.'* John Osborne, late of Wattisfield, died
  1691. *Her.Suff.Ch., Wall tablet, Wattisfield*

Statant
A unicorn statant Gules ducally gorged spotted and
attired [*sic*] Or.
  GREY, of Eye. *Visitation 1577.* 'Henry Graye'
  MS Philpot's Visitations, Suff.*
A unicorn statant – armed and ducally gorged Or.
  GREY. *MS Knight's Visitations, Suff.**

Sejant
A unicorn seiant reguardant Or ducally gorged
armed maned and tufted Argent.
  LIMESI, 'Edward Lymsey' *MS Knight's
  Visitations, Norf.** 'Edward Lymsey' *MS Philpot's
  Visitations, Norf.**

Couchant
A unicorn at layer Argent armed and membered Or.
  CLAYTON, of Dennington, Bedfield. *MS Fairfax*
A unicorn couchant.
  CLAYTON, James, late of the city of Norwich,
  gent., died 1699; Robert Clayton, late of this
  parish, gent., the grandfather, and Robert Clayton
  late of Bedfield, gent., the father of the above
  James Clayton. *Partridge, 110 (Darby, 1826),
  Southolt churchyard*
A unicorn couchant Argent armed and maned Or.
  CLAYTON, of Yoxford, Sibton, Southolt, Bedfield.
  Davy, A., Southolt churchyard. Elizabeth (Eyre),
  married John Clayton, of Sibton Park, died 1802.
  Her.Suff.Ch., Hatchment, Yoxford
A unicorn couchant Argent armed hooved and
maned Or under the dexter hoof a bezant.
  CLAYTON, of Southwold, Finningham. *Burke,
  L.G. 1853 ed.* James Clayton, Gent., no date
  given. *Her.Suff.Ch., Altar tomb in churchyard,
  Southolt*

DEMI-WYVERN
A demi-wyvern
  DALTON, of Bury. *Davy, A.*
A demi-wyvern wings expanded charged on the
breast with an escallop and on each wing with a
cross paty.
  KILDERBEE, of Framlingham, Ipswich, Gt.
  Glemham. *Davy, A. Bookplate*, escallop and
  crosses Gules*
A demi-wyvern issuant tail nowed Sable wings
expanded and elevated Or charged with an ermine
spot Sable and on the breast two annulets conjoined
in pale Or.
  LILLINGSTON, of The Chantry in Ipswich, The

Lodge in Southwold. *Burke, L.G. 1900 ed.**
Crisp's Visitation. IX. 33*, Pedigree
A demi-wyvern wings displayed Vert armed and
wattled [*sic*] Gules.
   MARTYN, Bart., of Long Melford. *Davy, A.*

WYVERN [Alphabetically by name]
A wyvern Argent langued Gules.
   ARCHER. Charles Archer, M.A., Rector of
   Alderton for 54 years, died 1910. *Her.Suff.Ch.,*
   Wall tablet in chancel, Alderton
A wyvern Gules.
   ASTY, of Market Weston, Bury. *Davy, A.*
A wyvern Vert.
   BUERS. *Bokenham*
A wyvern with wings expanded Sable.
   CROFTS. *Davy, A.*
A wyvern Or.
   CROMWELL. Thomas Lord Cromwell, of
   Elmham, co. Norfolk; his daughter married
   Lionel Tollemache. *Her.Suff.Ch., Wall tablet,*
   Helmingham
A wyvern with tail nowed Proper pierced through
the neck with a spear Or headed Argent.
   GARRARD, of Peasenhall. *Davy, A.*
A wyvern.
   RICH. *Bookplate**
A wyvern with wings expanded Argent.
   RICH. Sir Robert Rich, Kt. and Bart., died 1699.
   Her.Suff.Ch., Altar tomb in churchyard, Beccles
A wyvern wings displayed Vert.
   STOPFORD, Earl of Courtown, Viscount Stopford.
   Burke, Peerage, 1891 ed.
A wyvern Gules legged Sable beaked Or.
   THEOBALD, of Barking, Henley. *Davy, A.*
A wyvern Sable gutty Or collar line ring and
charged with a martlet all Or.
   WELD. Sir Humphrey Weld, Lord Mayor of
   London; Confirmation by W. Camden, Clar.,
   1606. *Grants & Certificates (Harl. MSS 1,441*
   and 6,059; Stowe MSS 706 and 707)
A wyvern with wings expanded Sable gutty Or
collared and ringed Or.
   WELD, of Bury. *Davy, A., St. Mary's church*
A wyvern Sable gutty Or ducally gorged and
chained Or.
   WELD. Wixstead Weld, Esq., died 1699.
   Her.Suff.Ch., Ledger stone, Moulton, 'indistinct'
A wyvern Azure membered and scaled Or with a
second head at the end of the tail [*sic* a basilisk].
   WORSLEY, Sir Robert, of Worsley, co. Lanc.;
   Confirmation of Arms and Grant of Crest by L.
   Dalton, Norroy, 25 November 1561. *Grants &*
   Certificates (Harl. MS 1,359)
A wyvern with wings indorsed Azure armed and
legged Gules.
   WORSLEY. *Davy, A.*

WYVERN, holding:
A wyvern Vert ducally gorged and lined Or in his
mouth a sinister hand couped at the wrist Gules.
   HERBERT, of Glemham. *Davy, A., church*
A wyvern Vert holding in his mouth a sinister hand
couped at the wrist Gules.
   HERBERT. Percy Mark Herbert, Bishop of
   Norwich 1942. *Burke, Peerage, 1953 ed., under*
   'Powis'. Bookplate*
A wyvern with wings elevated Vert holding in the
mouth a sinister hand couped at the wrist Gules.
   HERBERT. Hon. Nicholas Herbert, married Ann
   North, of Glemham Hall, died 1775.
   Her.Suff.Ch., Wall tablet, Lt. Glemham

Rampant or Segreant
A wyvern segreant.
   WYARD. *MS Heraldic Alphabet*

Passant
A wyvern passant wings addorsed Proper.
   CROFT. *MS Ordinary of Arms, fo. 44**
A ?wyvern passant.
   YAXLEY. *Davy, A.*

Statant
A wyvern statant Argent.
   ASHFIELD. *Fairbairn, 'Suff.'*
A wyvern statant with wings addorsed Sable.
   CROFT. 'William Croft de Com Hereforde'
   MS Ordinary of Arms, fo. 47*

Sejant
A wyvern displayed sejant affronty Or.
   BATEMAN, of Flixton. *Davy, A. (Barrett MS), St.*
   Cross church

Volant
A halberd erect Or on the point a flying dragon, or
wyvern, without legs tail nowed Sable bezanty
vulned Gules.
   DAWES, of Stowmarket. *Davy, A. Washbourne*,*
   'Lond., Suff., etc. A wyvern'

TWO WYVERNS
Two wyverns entwined Azure langued Gules tails
knit in saltire.
   CHAPMAN, Alexander, of Bordon, co. Kent.; Grant
   by Barker. *Grants & Certificates (Stowe MS 692)*

ON A MOUNT

BEAST. BOAR
On a mount Vert a boar passant Azure.
   BORRETT, of Stradbroke. *Bokenham*
On a mount Vert a boar passant –.
   BORRETT, of Stradbroke. *Davy, A., church*
On a mount a boar passant.
   BORRETT, John, of Stradbroke, died 16 . . ;
   Thomas Borrett, died 1694. *Her.Suff.Ch., Ledger*
   stones, Stradbroke
On a mount Vert a boar passant Proper.
   QUAPLOD. *Davy, A. Washbourne*

CAMEL
On a mount Vert a camel statant Proper charged on
the shoulder with a horse-shoe Argent and holding
in its mouth a rose Gules slipped and leaved Proper.
   CRIPPS, CRIPPS-DAY, of Newmarket. *Crisp's*
   Visitation. VIII. 50*
On a mount Vert a camel couchant Argent mane feet
and humps Or.
   MAWE. *MS Knight's Visitations, Suff.** 'Symon
   Mawe' *MS Philpot's Visitations, Suff*, 'feet*
   humps and tail Or'
On a mount Vert a camel seiant Argent the bunch
[*sic* ?hump] and tail Or.
   MAWE. *Bokenham*
On a mount Vert a camel couchant Gules maned and
tailed Or.
   MAW, MAWE, of Rendlesham. *Davy, A.*
On a mount Vert a camel couchant Argent the lump
on the back and end of the tail Or.
   MAW. *Washbourne*, 'Lanc. and Suff.'*
   Fairbairn*, 'Lancs. and Suff.'

DEER
On a mount Vert a stag reguardant Argent attired
Sable.
   COCKS, of Norton. *Davy, A.*

Springing. Rampant or Salient

On a mount Vert a stag salient Argent attired Or with a branch of laurel growing from the dexter side of the mount Vert.

HITCHAM. 'Sir Robert Hicham, Attorney to Q. Anne, Consort of K. James'; Confirmation1604. *Grants & Certificates (Harl. MSS 1,441 and 6,059; Stowe MSS 706 and 707)*

On a mount a stag springing on the dexter side of the mount a sprig of laurel.

HITCHAM. 'Sr. Robert Hitcham, Sergeant att Law' *MS Heraldic Collections, fo. 89a**

On a mount a buck springing Proper.

HITCHAM, of Framlingham. *Bokenham*

On a mount Vert a stag springing Gules attired and unguled Or on the dexter part of the mount a branch of laurel Proper.

HITCHAM, of Levington, Framlingham. *Green, 131, Framlingham church*

Courant

On a mount a stag courant.

COCKS, of Norton. *Davy, A., church*

On a mount Vert a roebuck courant Or.

DREW, of Long Melford. *Davy, A.*

Trippant. Passant

On a mount a stag trippant all Proper.

GLANVILLE, of Elmsett. *Sharpe*

On a mount Vert a stag trippant Proper.

PARKER. *Fairbairn*, 'of Arwerton [sic Erwarton], Suff.'*

On a mount Vert a buck trippant per pale Argent and Proper attired Or the dexter fore-leg bearing a flag staff in bend sinister Proper thereon hoisted a banner Or fringed and charged with an escallop Gules.

WHITE. 'Capt. Joseph H.L. White, J.P., D.L., Bredfield House, Woodbridge, Suff.' *Fairbairn**

At Gaze. Statant

On a mount Vert a stag at gaze Proper under a vine Vert fructed Gules.

BRADSHAIGH, Rev. Thomas, A.M., Rector of Stratford St. Mary for 42 years, died 1752. *Davy, A. E.A.N. & Q. XII. 148. Her.Suff.Ch., Stratford St. Mary, 'vine Vert fructed Or'*

On a mount Vert a buck at gaze Azure with an olive branch rising from his hinder part and encircling him Vert.

BRADSHAW. *MS Heraldic Alphabet*

On a mount Vert a hind statant Proper.

FITZRALPH. *Davy, A.*

On a mount Vert a roe buck statant guardant Gules attired and hoofed Or between the attires a quatrefoil Or.

ROE, Bart., of Brundish. *Davy, A. Washbourne, 'Suff. roe buck untinctured.' Fairbairn, 'of Brundish, Suff. roe buck at gaze'*

On a mount Vert a stag at gaze Argent attired Or.

STAPLEY. *Washbourne, 'Suff.'*

On a mount Vert a stag statant Proper collared Azure studded Argent.

WINGFIELD. 'Harbotell Wyngfild of Wantisden in Com Suffolke Esquier' *MS Lilly's Visitation of Suffolk** [one of three crests drawn, the usual 'Bull' and 'Cap' Wingfield ones also given]

Lodged. Couchant

On a mount Vert a stag lodged reguardant Argent.

CARRILL, of Ixworth. *Davy, A.*

On a mount Vert a stag lodged Argent attired Sable.

COCKS, of Harkstead, Norton. *Davy, A., Norton church. Washbourne, 'Glouc. and Suff.'*

Fairbairn*, 'Glouc. and Suff.'

On a mount Vert a buck couchant reguardant Argent attired Sable.

COCKS, of Norton. *Bokenham, 'mount Proper' Bookplate*, untinctured*

On a mount Vert a stag lodged reguardant Argent attired Sable.

COCKS, Charles, died 1667 (or 1669); Leicester Cocks, died 1681. *Her.Suff.Ch., Ledger stone, Norton*

On a mount Vert a stag lodged reguardant Argent attired Or gorged with a chaplet of laurel Vert and vulned on the shoulder Gules.

CORNWALLIS, CORNWALLYS, of Brome. *Visitation 1561 (ed. Metcalfe).* John Cornwallis, Esq., J.P., D.L. and High Sheriff of Suffolk, died 1698. *Her.Suff.Ch., Ledger stone, Wingfield*

On a mount Vert a stag lodged reguardant Argent gorged with a chaplet Vert and vulned in the shoulder Gules.

CORNWALLIS, Marquis. Of Brome, Cretingham, Oakley. *Visitation 1664–8. Bokenham. Page. Davy, A.*

On a mount Vert a hind couchant reguardant Or.

HAWKINS. *MS Ordinary of Arms, fo. 225**

On a mount Vert a buck lodged Proper.

KINSMAN. 'Kingsman' *MS Ordinary of Arms, fo. 271**

On a mount Vert a stag lodged Sable attired Or.

NEEDHAM. *Davy, A.*

On a mount Vert a hart lodged at the foot of a tree all Proper.

USBORNE, Henry, of Branches Park, died 1840. *Her.Suff.Ch., Hatchment, Cowlinge*

'upon a helme on a wreath Silver and azure on a Mount vert a hinde lying silver; Mantled Gules, doubled Silver'

WARD. Richard Ward, of Gorleston; Confirmation of Arms and Crest by Robert Cooke, Clarenceux, 7th July 1593. *Misc.Gen. et Her. 5th S. IX. 171 (Soc. of Ant. MS 378, fo. 560)*

On a mount Vert a hind couchant Argent.

WARD, Richard, of Gorleston, Suffolk; Grant 1593. *Grants & Certificates (Add. MS 4,966; Harl. MS 1,359)*

On a mount Vert a hind couchant Argent.

WARD, of Homersfield, Gorleston. *London Visitation 1633 (H.S.) II. 321* Davy, A. Washbourne, 'Ward, Warde, Suff.' Fairbairn*, 'Ward, Warde, Gorleston, Suff. hind lodged.'*

DOG

GREYHOUND

On a mount Proper a greyhound sejant Argent collared and lined Or the line reflexed over the back and in front of a tree Proper.

KYNARDESLEY. 'Kinardby' *MS Ordinary of Arms, fo. 30**

On a mount Vert a greyhound seiant Argent collared Or under a bush Vert fructed Gules.

KYNARDESLEY. *Davy, A.*

On a hill Vert a greyhound passant Sable collared and chained Argent.

LONG, of Parham. *Davy, A.*

On a mount Vert a greyhound seiant Argent spotted of a brown colour collared Argent.

PROCTOR, BEAUCHAMP-PROCTOR, of West Creeting. *Davy, A. Washbourne, 'Proctor, Bart., Norf.'*

On a mount Vert a greyhound sejant Argent collared Sable rim and studs Or ears Sable from the dexter side of the mount a branch of laurel growing Proper.

WILKINSON. 'Richard Wilkinson, of Wateringbury in Kent, one of the six clerks in Chancery'; Grant by W. Camden, Clarenceux, 14 September 1605. *Grants & Certificates (Stowe MSS 700 and 706–7; Harl. MS 1,441)*

On a mount a greyhound sejant collared and ringed on the dexter side a branch of laurel.

WILKINSON. *MS Heraldic Collections, fo. 89b**

TALBOT

On a mount Vert against a halbert erect in pale Gules headed Argent a talbot seiant Or collared and tied to the halbert Gules.

HUNT, of Walsham-le-Willows, Wherstead. *Davy, A., both churches.* John Hunt Esq., died 1726. *Her.Suff.Ch., Walsham-le-Willows.* John Hunt, died 1764. *Wherstead*

On a mount Vert a talbot couchant Ermine.

MOTHAM, of Drinkstone. *Davy, A. Washbourne, 'Suff.' Fairbairn, 'of Drinkston [sic], Suff.'*

On a mount Vert a talbot seiant Ermine collared –.

SMITH, of Leiston, Bury. *Davy, A., Leiston church, 'the Actor'*

On a mount Vert a talbot seiant Sable.

TEMPLE, of Mutford. *Davy, A.*

On a mount a talbot couchant guardant against a tree all Proper.

TOPSFIELD, of Fressingfield, Gislingham. *Davy, A., Fressingfield church. Washbourne, 'Suff. and Norf.'*

ERMINE

On a hill Vert an ermine trippant Proper.

ARMYNE. 'Ayrmin' *MS Martin's Crests*

On a mount Vert an ermine Proper.

ARMYNE. *Davy, A.*

On a mount Vert an ermine Proper holding in his mouth a trefoil slipped Or.

SYMONS, of Bury. *Davy, A.*

On a mount Vert an ermine Proper holding in his mouth a cinquefoil Or.

SYMONS, of Bury. *Davy, A., St. Mary's church*

FOX

On a mount Vert a fox statant Argent brush Ermine holding in his mouth a rose Gules stalked –.

SYMONS, SYMONDS. *MS Heraldic Collections, fo. 21**

HARE

'a Hare pper running on a mount vert sett upon a helmet in a wreathe of his coullors'

WINTHROP. 'John Wynethrop of Groton'; Confirmation of Arms and Crest by William Dethick, Garter, 24th June 1592. *Facsimile of Grant*. 'John Wynthrope' Grants & Certificates (Stowe MS 676). Muskett. I. 2–3. Fairbairn*, 'of Groton, Suff.' Her.Suff.Ch., Tomb outside south wall of church, Glass, Groton*

HORSE

On a mount a horse passant Argent against a tree Proper.

ARUNDEL. *Davy, A.*

On a mount Proper a brown horse.

BATHURST. *MS Heraldic Alphabet*

On a mount Vert a horse passant Argent in his mouth an oak branch Proper.

FITZALAN, Earl of Arundel. *Davy, A.*

On a mount Vert a horse passant Argent holding in the mouth a slip of oak fructed Proper.

HOWARD, Bernard, 12th Duke of Norfolk, died

1842. *Her.Suff.Ch., Hatchment, Fornham St. Martin. Third crest shown, for Fitzalan*

LEOPARD

A demi-leopard Argent an increscent Ermine on mount held by sinister paw dexter paw on mount.

HARVEY. *Visitations of Cambridgeshire 1575 and 1619 (H.S.) 60, 'true'.* [Two MS Visitations of 1619 in my possession *(Corder MSS 13 and 14)* do not show any mount]

On a mount Vert a leopard passant Gules spotted Sable [*sic*] ducally crowned gorged lined and ringed Or.

TUTHILL, of Halesworth. *Davy, A.*

LION [Alphabetically by name]

On a mount Vert a lion seiant Ermine.

BALES, of Wilby. *Bokenham, 'p' Cooke, Clar. 1576'. Davy, A. Fairbairn, 'of Wilby, Suff.'*

On a mount Vert a lion passant guardant Argent holding in his dexter paw a fer-de-moline, or millrind, Sable and charged on the side with a fret Sable.

BARNWELL, TURNOR-BARNWELL, of Horsecroft in Horringer, Bury St. Edmunds. *Gage (Thingoe) 514, note. Licence to add name of Turnor to that of Barnwell granted 17 May 1826. Davy, A. Fairbairn, 'fret Gules'*

On a mount Vert a lion seiant Argent.

BOND, of Bury. *Bokenham*

On a mount Vert a lion seiant guardant in his dexter paw a caltrap Proper.

DE LIGNE, of Weybread, Nowton. *Davy, A.*

On a mount Vert a lion rampant guardant Argent holding in his paw a slip of laurel Vert.

GREENE, of Ixworth Thorpe. *Davy, A.*

On a mount Vert within a crown vallary Or a lion rampant Gules.

STEWARD, STEWART, of Ipswich, Blundeston. *Davy, A. Fairbairn, 'Steward, of Stoke Park, Suff.' and 'Stewart, Blundeston, Suff.'* Thomas Fowler Steward, of Gt. Yarmouth, died 1880. *Her.Suff.Ch., Wall brass, Gunton*

On a mount Vert a lion passant per pale Gules and Argent crowned Or holding in his dexter paw an arrow Vert.

TRUSSON, of Kelsale. *Sharpe*

On a mount a lion passant crowned collared and lined.

TUTHILL. 'Tuttell' *Bookplate**

On a mount Vert a lion passant Erminois the dexter paw resting on an escutcheon Azure charged with a fleur-de-lis Or.

VENN, of Ipswich, Freston, Cotton. *Davy, A. Burke, L.G. 1853 ed. Fairbairn, 'of Freston Lodge & Ipswich, Suff.'*

On a mount Vert a lion rampant Or supporting a lance erect Proper tassels Gules headed Argent.

WARREN, Thomas, of Newbourne, co. Suffolk. 'Crest given at the request of Drury in 1589, but the Arms by patent from W. Harvey, Clar., at the Visitation of Suffolk, entered and a crest'. *Grants & Certificates (Stowe MS 670).* [The Crest of Warren of Newton and Newbourne, given by Hervey in his Visitation and drawn in MS G. 7 is a demi-greyhound salient Ermine collared counter-compony Or and Azure. See my edition of the Visitation. II. 236–7]

On a mount Vert a lion rampant Or holding a spear Gules headed Argent.

WARREN, of Newton, Newbourne. *Davy, A., 'Granted 1589' Washbourne, 'Suff.' An obituary* of Canon Frederick Warren, D.D., F.S.A., in 1930, gives both crests, but the head of the spear is Or. Proc.S.I.A. XX. 317–8

MARTEN
On a mount Vert a martin [sic] passant Argent in the mouth a cinquefoil Or slipped Vert on the tail an ermine spot Sable.

SYMONS. 'William Symonds, of Lyme Regis, co. Dorset, 1587' Grants & Certificates (Harl. MS 1,359)

OTTER
On a mount an ?otter passant Vert collared Or.

LANGDON. 'Cristofer Langdon' MS Philpot's Visitations, Norf.*

OUNCE
On a mount Vert an ounce seiant Proper collared and chained Or.

POTT, of Bury. Davy, A.

On a mount Vert an ounce passant Proper.

RAYNE, of Stradishall Place. Davy, A. Fairbairn, 'Rainer, of Stradeshall [sic] Place, Suff.'

OX
On a mount Vert a bull passant Gules supporting with his dexter foreleg a spear erect Proper.

RIDLEY, of Clare, Bury. Crisp's Visitation. XIII. 89*

SHEEP
'and to the Crest or Cognizant on a Helme a wreth of his Cullors, Or and Azure a mount vert, thereon a lambe standing argent, holding a banner Azure with a woolsacke argent, the staffe Or mantelled argent doubled gules, tasselled Or'

HADLEIGH, Town of Grant of Arms and Crest by William Camden, Clarenceux, 18 February 1618. Proc.S.I.A. III. 311–13*. Scott-Giles, 348*

SQUIRREL
On a mount Vert a squirrel seiant cracking a nut of the last [sic]

CORBET, of Assington. Davy, A.

On a mount Vert a squirrel sejant cracking a nut Or leaved Proper.

CORBET. Washbourne*, 'Lond.'

TIGER
On the ground Vert a tiger passant Proper collared and lined Or supporting with his dexter paw a caltrap Or.

KERRISON, of Bungay. Davy, A.

On a mount Vert a tiger passant Proper collared and lined Or the dexter forepaw resting on a caltrap Or.

KERRISON. Washbourne*, 'Bart., Suff.' Fairbairn, 'of Hoxne and Brome, Suff.' Matthias Kerrison, Esq., Magistrate for the County, died 1827. Her.Suff.Ch., Monument, Holy Trinity Bungay. Gen. Sir Edward Kerrison, Bart., of Oakley Park, Hoxne, died 1853; Others. Wall tablet, Hoxne. Sir Edward Clarence Kerrison, Bart., died 1886. Glass, Oakley

WOLF
On a mound Vert a wolf passant Argent.

BRACEBRIDGE, of Suffolk. Davy, A. Washbourne, 'Suff.' Fairbairn, 'Suff.'

On a mount a wolf sejant collared and chained supporting with his dexter paw a circular escutcheon and behind him a sword point downwards in the mount.

TODD. Livery button (Pitt Collection, 79/2)

BIRD. BITTERN
On a mount Vert a bittern between four reeds on the one side and four on the other.

BARNARDISTON. Gipps, 'Modern crest'

CORNISH CHOUGH
On a mount Vert a Cornish chough wings elevated between two reeds all Proper.

READ, READE, of Holbrook, Crowe Hall in Stutton. Davy, A. Fairbairn*, 'Reade of Holbrooke House, Suff.' Burke, L.G. 1952 ed.*

On a mount Vert a Cornish chough wings extended between two stalks of wheat all Proper.

READE, of Crowe Hall in Stutton. Burke, L.G. 1900 ed.* Col. James Reade, of Crowe Hall, Stutton, Suff. Fairbairn*

On a mount Vert a chough standing among reeds Proper.

READE, John, of Holbrook House, died 1843; two sons and one daughter. Her.Suff.Ch., Wall tablet and Hatchment, Holbrook. Reade, of Stutton and Crowe Hall. Glass, Pew end and 'The vault of Crow Hall Sept. 1825' on altar tomb in the churchyard, Stutton

COCK
On a mount Vert a cock Gules legged wattled and combed Or charged on the breast with a saltire Or.

LELAM, of Bury. Davy, A. Washbourne, 'of Northamp. & York.'

On a mount Vert a cock Argent combed legged and wattled Gules.

NORWICH of Mettingham. MS Heraldic Alphabet. Davy, A. Washbourne*, 'Ess., Norf., Suff.'

CRANE
On a mount Vert a crane, heron, or stork Ermine legged Or.

RICHMAN, of Ellough. 'Robert Rychman' MS Knight's Visitations, Norf.* 'Robart Richmanne' MS Philpot's Visitations, Norf.* Visitation 1664–8* Davy, A.

CROW
On a mount Vert a crow Proper supporting with its dexter claw a staff Or erect and environed by a serpent Proper.

CROWFOOT, of Beccles. Davy, A. Crisp's Visitation. I. 26*, Pedigree

CURLEW
On a hill Vert a curlew Proper.

EWEN. 'Ewens.' MS Heraldic Alphabet

EAGLE
On a mount Vert an eagle volant Argent ducally gorged and membered Or.

BARNE, of Sotterley Park, Grey Friars in Dunwich. Crisp's Visitation VII. 158*, Pedigree. Burke, L.G. 1900 ed.

On a mount Vert a demi-eagle displayed Argent.

GILBERT, William, Dr. of Physick; Confirmation by Robert Cooke, Clarenceux, 27 November 1577. Grants & Certificates (Stowe MS 676). 'William Gilberte of Clare' MS Knight's Visitations, Norf.* Washbourne, 'Ess. and Suff. charged on the breast with a mullet Or'

On a mount Vert a demi-eagle displayed Azure charged on the breast with a mullet Or.

GILBERT. Fairbairn, 'Essex and Suff.'

On a mount Vert an eagle displayed Argent.

GILBERT, of Clare, Brent Eleigh, Badley Hall, Long Melford, Lavenham. *Visitation 1664–8*. Bokenham, 'p. Cooke, Clar. 1577'. Davy, A. (Barrett MS) Gilbert, 204*

Rising from a mount Vert an eagle Sable.
  NORREYS, Lord Of Wrentham, Thorington. *Davy, A.*

On a mount Vert an eagle displayed Ermine beaked and legged Or.
  WARD. 'Thomas Ward of broke' *MS Philpot's Visitations, Norf.**

FALCON
On a mount Proper a falcon rising Or.
  BARKER. *MS Martin's Crests*
On a mount Vert a falcon volant Argent ducally gorged and membered Or.
  BARNE. *Fairbairn, 'of Sotterley, Suff.'*
On a mount Vert a falcon Ermine beaked and belled Or in its mouth [*sic*] a trefoil slipped Vert.
  BOLTON, of Nedging, Ipswich. *Davy, A., 'Granted 1803'. Muskett. II. 214. To Thomas Bolton, of Woodbridge, Confirmation of earlier Grant of 1610 [q.v.]; Crest as above, with a mount and trefoil for difference, allowed 1803*
On a mount Vert a falcon Proper belled Or collared and charged on the breast with a cross flory Gules.
  LACON, Bart., of Gt. Yarmouth. *Druery, 116*
A mount Vert thereon a falcon Proper beaked and belled Or charged on the breast with a cross flory and gorged with a collar Gules.
  LACON. 'Sir Edmund Lacon, Bart., of Gt. Yarmouth, Norf. [*sic*]; Henry Edmund Lacon, Esq., of Ackworth House, East Bergholt, Suff.' *Fairbairn*
On a mount Vert a falcon rising Or gorged with a ducal coronet Gules.
  PAULET, PAWLETT. William Pawlett, late of Kings Lynn, Norfolk, died 1746; Others. *Her.Suff.Ch., Altar tomb in churchyard, Rickinghall Inferior*
On a mount Vert a falcon volant Or gorged and belled Gules.
  ST. JOHN. *MS Martin's Crests*
On a mount Vert a falcon rising belled Or ducally gorged Gules.
  ST. JOHN, of Ramsholt, Cavendish. *MS ex-Taylor Coll.*, bells untinctured. Davy, A.*
On a mount a falcon close holding in the beak an oak branch fructed.
  SPRIGGS. Rector of Brockley, 1829. *Davy, A., Gt. Bealings church*
On a mount Vert a falcon close Or collared Gules the dexter claw on an escutcheon Azure charged with a bezant.
  WALKER, of Lowestoft. *Gillingwater, 423. Davy, A.*

HERON
On a mount Vert a crane, heron, or stork Ermine legged Or.
  RICHMAN, of Ellough. 'Robert Rychman' *MS Knight's Visitations, Norf.** 'Robart Richmanne' *MS Philpot's Visitations, Norf.* Visitation 1664–8*. Davy, A.*

MOORCOCK
On a mount Vert a moorcock rising Sable winged Or.
  HOLDEN. Rev. John S. Holden, M.A., Lackford Manor, Bury St. Edmunds. *Fairbairn**
On a mount Vert a moorcock Proper.

MATTHEW. Dorothy, wife of William Matthew, of Onehouse Lodge, died 1868. *Her.Suff.Ch., Headstone in churchyard, Woolpit. Not found 1980*

OSTRICH
On a mount Vert an ostrich Argent legs Or beak Sable holding a key Or.
  BAYNING, of Spexhall, Chediston, Cookley. *Misc.Gen. et Her. 5th S. II. 277*, 'Grant p' Cooke, Clar., 1588'*

PEACOCK
On a mount Vert a peacock Proper.
  KETT, William, of Kelsale; Grant by Garter, 1756. *Davy, A. Washbourne, 'Suff.' Fairbairn, 'Kelsall [sic], Suff.' Kett, 73*, Pedigree*
On a mount a peacock Proper.
  SOMER, SOMNER, of Suffolk. *Davy, A. Fairbairn, 'of Kent and Suff.'*

QUAIL
Upon a mount Vert a quail between two bulrushes Proper.
  QUAYLE. Rector of Trimley St. Martin, resigned 1896. *Crisp's Visitation. II. 40**

RAVEN
'and for Crest on a Wreath of the Colours, Upon a Mount Vert a Raven Sable supporting with the dexter claw a Staff erect and entwined with a Snake as in the Arms' [Proper]
  CROWFOOT. Dr. William John Crowfoot, of Beccles; Grant of Arms and Crest by George Nayler, Garter, 14 February 1831. *Misc.Gen. et Her. N.S. IV. 40.* 'Crowfoot, of Beccles' and 'William Miller Crowfoot, Esq., of Beccles, Suff.' *Fairbairn, 'staff erect Or . . . snake Proper'*

STORK
On a mount Vert a stork statant Proper.
  EWEN, of Raydon. *Davy, A., church, 1724*
On a mount Vert a crane, heron, or stork Ermine legged Or.
  RICHMAN, of Ellough. 'Robert Rychman' *MS Knight's Visitations, Norf.** 'Robart Richmanne' *MS Philpot' Visitations, Norf.* Visitation 1664–8*. Davy, A.*

HEAD [Alphabetically by name]
'Crest 2 greyhounds heads nekes indorsant sylver & sables collered & terets Counterchanged the wreth gold & gowles sett uppon a mountayne vert mantles syluer lyned sables bottoned gold'
  ATKINS. 'Thomas Atkins, of Hempstead in the Countye & sytee of Glocester, gent'; Grant of Arms and Crest by Sir Christopher Barker, Knt., Garter, 26 November 1548. *Miscellaneous Grants (H.S.) I. 11–12 (Stowe MS 606, fo. 60)*
On a mount Vert two greyhound's heads couped and addorsed one Argent the other Sable collared counterchanged ringed Or wreath Or and Gules mantled Argent lined Sable.
  ATKINS. 'Thomas Atkyns, of Hemsted, in the city and co. of Gloucester, gent.' Patent by Sir Christopher Barker, Garter, 26 Nov. 1648 [*sic* 1548]. *Grants & Certificates (Stowe MSS 677 and 692)*
On a mount Vert a greyhound's head erased Argent collared and lined Gules, in front a fountain.
  DAY, CRIPPS-DAY, of Newmarket. *Crisp's Visitation. VIII. 50**

Upon a mount Vert a boar's head couped Or in front of a flagstaff erect Proper therefrom flowing to the dexter a flag Gules charged with a naval coronet Or.

PLUMRIDGE. *Fairbairn, 'of Hopton Hall, Suff.'*

MONSTER. HERALDIC ANTELOPE

On a mount Vert a tiger, or antelope, seiant Ermine ducally gorged crined and tufted Or armed or attired Argent.

JOHNSON, of Lavenham. *Davy, A.*

COCKATRICE

On a mount Vert a cockatrice Argent ducally gorged and lined Or.

BALDENSON, BALDWIN, of Assington. *Davy, A.*

On a mount Vert a cockatrice Argent wattled ducally gorged and lined Or.

BALDWIN, John, Gent., died 1712. *Her.Suff.Ch., Ledger stone, Worlington*

On a mount Vert a cockatrice displayed Argent.

RICH, Edward, of Horndon on the Hill, co. Essex; Confirmation of Arms and Grant of Crest by R. Cooke, Clar., 30 May 1579. *Grants & Certificates (Harl. MS 1,359)*

DRAGON

On a mount a dragon Argent gorged with a ducal coronet and chained Or.

BALDWIN, of Worlington. *Bokenham*

On a mount Vert a demi-dragon rampant.

WATSON, of Woolpit. *Davy, A. Washbourne, 'Kent and Suff.' Fairbairn, 'of Walpett [sic], Suff. and Kent'*

GRIFFIN

On a mount Vert a griffin seiant Argent.

BENYON, of Denston Hall. *Davy, A. Washbourne. Fairbairn, 'of Sussex and Suff.'*

On a burning mount Proper a griffin sejant Or armed Gules.

CLEMENTS, of Harwich. *Sharpe*

On a mount Vert a griffin passant Or armed Or wings endorsed Ermine.

LOUNDE. *'Richard Lownde' MS Knight's Visitations, Cambs.**

On a hill Vert a griffin couchant Argent wings elevated Ermine.

LOUNDE. *MS Heraldic Alphabet*

IBEX

On a mount Vert an ibex sejant Ermine ducally gorged Gules armed langued crined and tufted Or.

JOHNSON. *MS Knight's Visitations, Suff.** 'Wyll Johnson' *MS Philpot's Visitations, Suff.**

On a mount Vert an ibex seiant Ermine ducally gorged crined and tufted Or attired Argent.

JOHNSON, of Lavenham. *Davy, A. Washbourne*, 'of Staff. and Suff.' Fairbairn, 'Staffs. and Suff.'*

PEGASUS

'And for his Creast, on a Wreath Argent and Gules, a Pegasus volant Sable, on a mount proper'

HOWMAN. 'Dr. Roger Howman of Norwich Dr. of Physick'; Grant of Arms and Crest by William Dugdale, Garter, and Henry St. George, Clar., 5th May 1684. *Misc.Gen. et Her. N.S. I. 397**

On a mount Proper a pegasus volant Sable.

HOWMAN, of Shipmeadow. *Davy, A.*

SEA LION

On a mount Vert a sea lion sejant Ermine.

BALES, of Wilby. *Visitation 1664–8**

HERALDIC TIGER

On a mount Vert a tiger, or antelope, seiant Ermine ducally gorged crined and tufted Or armed or attired Argent.

JOHNSON, of Lavenham. *Davy, A.*

UNICORN

On a mount Vert a demi-unicorn erased chequy Argent and Azure winged Gules.

COOKE, of Semer. *Davy, A.*

On a mount Vert a unicorn sejant Ermine ducally gorged Gules horned and maned Or.

JOHNSON, of Lavenham. *Visitation 1577*

WYVERN

On a mount Vert a wyvern wings endorsed Argent beaked combed ducally gorged and lined Or.

BALDWIN, of Worlington. *Visitation 1664–8*

On a mount Vert a wyvern with wings expanded Argent.

RICH, Bart., of Rose Hall, Beccles. *Davy, A.*

On a mount Vert a wyvern with wings addorsed Sable gutty Argent collared ringed and lined reflexed over the back Or.

WELD. 'Welde vel Wylde' *MS ex-Taylor Coll.**

VARIOUS [Objects in alphabetical order]

On a mount Vert an arm couped at the elbow erect vested Erminois holding in the hand Proper a battle-axe Or handled Sable.

CUDWORTH, of Southolt. *Davy, A.*

On a mount Vert a beacon Sable issuing flames Proper propped against the dexter side a ladder Sable.

COMPTON. *MS Ordinary of Arms, fos. 65* and 235**

A mount Vert thereon a beehive Or charged with a chaplet of roses in chief alighting on the hive a bee Proper and in base around the hive three bees Proper.

BULLOUGH, Sir George, Bart. *Her.Suff.Ch., Wall brass, Moulton. No date given*

On a mount a caltrap.

KERRICH. *MS Ordinary of Arms, fo. 204**

On a mount, or hill, Proper a caltrap Sable.

KERRICH, KERRIDGE, of Bury, Shelley Hall, Geldeston Hall near Beccles. *Bokenham, 'p. R. St. Geo., Clar., to Capt. Tho. Kerridge for service in the Gt. Mogul's Country, 1620'. Sharpe. Davy, A., Monuments and Hatchment, Shelley church. Burke, L.G. 1853 ed. E.A.N. & Q. VI. 91. Fairbairn, 'Kerrich, of Geldeston Hall, Suff. The mount Vert.'*

On a mount Proper a caltrap Or.

KERRICH, of Geldeston Hall near Beccles. *Burke, L.G. 1900 ed.*

On a mount Vert a caltrap Sable.

KERRIDGE, of Shelley Hall. Lords of the manor of Shelley, 1657–1743. *Her.Suff.Ch., Ledger stones, Hatchment, Shelley*

On a mount Vert a caltrap Or.

RAVEN. 'John Raven, M.D., Fellow of the College of Physicians of London, sworn physician to the late Queen Anne and King Charles, eldest son of John Raven, late Richmond Herald'. Grant to the father by W. Camden, Clar., of Crest A raven close Sable perched on a torteau [q.v.]; this altered for the son to On a mount Vert a caltrap Or. *Grants & Certificates (Add. MS 12,225; Stowe MS 677)*

On a mount Vert a caltrap Or.

RAVEN. John Raven, Richmond Herald. of Creeting St. Mary. *London Visitation 1633 (H.S.) II. 187*, 'Vnder the hand of Will Camden Clarenceux King of Armes the Creast'*. [But see H.S. London's *'College of Arms', 145–6*, where he states that the Raven and Torteau crest was granted to John Raven senior, Richmond Herald, and gives a short biography]. Of Hadleigh. *Davy, A.*

On a hill a steel gad [caltrap] erect Or.
RAVEN, of Creeting in Suffolk. *MS Heraldic Alphabet, 'P. Wm Camden, Clar.'*

Issuing from a mount Vert a column Sable entwined Or issuing therefrom on the dexter side an arm embowed in armour holding in the hand the hilt of a sword Or.
SMYTH. Joseph Burch Smyth, of Stoke Hall and Sproughton, died 1852. *Farrer MS II. 161, Monument Sproughton church. Her.Suff.Ch., 'Crest on south wall of chancel, much faded. Missing 1980', Sproughton*

On a mount Proper within a coronet Argent an eagle Proper holding in the dexter claw a fleur-de-lis Or.
BOWEN. *Sharpe*

On a mount Proper issuing out of a coronet a stag at gaze Argent.
ROBINSON. *MS Martin's Crests*

On a mount issuing out of a ducal coronet Vert a stag at gaze Or.
ROBINSON, Bart. Of Kentwell Hall. *Sharpe*

On a mount Vert three cross crosslets fitchy one in pale and two in saltire enfiled with an annulet Or.
RUSTAT. Rector of Stutton, died 1793. *Davy, A., church. Crisp's Visitation. Notes. I. 87, 'Grant by William Dugdale, Norroy, 30 December 1676'*

On a mount Vert a thistle Proper.
DOBREE. Rector of Bucklesham. *Davy, A.*

Out of a mount Vert in front of two battle-axes in saltire a pine-apple Proper.
TANQUERAY, of Halesworth, Gorleston. *Davy, A.*

On a mount Vert a garb Or.
NEWCE, of Gazeley. *MS Heraldic Collections, fo. 54*. Davy, A., 'arms granted 1575'*

On a mount Vert a hand Proper couped at the wrist holding a sword Argent hilted Or.
BOOTY, of Lackford, Suffolk. *Davy, A., 'Granted 3 January 1300' [sic]. Washbourne, 'Suff.' E.A.N. & Q. VIII. 16 (Fairbairn) Fairbairn, 'Suff.'*

On a mount Or in flames Proper a unicorn's head Sable.
KITSON. *Davy, A. Washbourne, 'Suff.'*

A naked savage affronty standing on a mount wreathed about the head and waist with leaves and holding in the right hand a studded club.
SYDNOR, William, Esq., died 1613. *Her.Suff.Ch., Brass on chancel floor, Blundeston*

On a mount Vert a grasshopper Or.
GRESHAM. *MS Ordinary of Arms, fo. 95*, 'Gresham of Surrey granted by Christopher Baker [sic] Garter King at Arms 30 Novʳ 1537'. Misc.Gen. et Her. N.S. IV. 253*

On a mount a grasshopper all Vert.
GRESHAM. *MS Heraldic Collections, fo. 56**

Upon a mount Vert five palisades conjoined Sable in front of a leopard's head couped Proper.
WARREN. *Fairbairn, 'of Hopton, Suff.'*

On a mount Vert a panther couchant guardant Argent spotted various fire issuing from the mouth and ears Proper gorged with a collar and line Gules ringed Or.

REYNOLDS, Anthony, of London, Esq., fined for Sheriff 1706, and to his nephews Anthony and John Reynolds; Grant by Sir H. St. George, Garter and Sir J. Vanbrugh, Clarenceux, 22 May 1714. *Grants & Certificates (Add. MS 14,830)*

On a mount Vert a panther couchant guardant Argent spotted various fire issuing from the mouth and ears Proper gorged with a collar and line Gules ringed Or.
REYNOLDS, of Lavenham. *Davy, A., churchyard.* '... Reynolds, died 1720; widow Ann, died 1727' *Partridge, 12 (Darby, 18..), Palisaded tomb outside south chancel wall, Lavenham, untinctured. E.A. Misc. 1934. 79–80*

On a mount Vert a snake coiled up and environed with rushes Proper.
ANGUISH, ALLIN, of Somerleyton. *Page. Davy, A.*

On a mount Vert a sun Or charged with a rose Gules.
CROWLEY, of Barking. *Davy, A., church.* Sir Ambrose Crowley, of London, granted Arms 14 June 1707; son John Crowley, Alderman of London, of Barking Hall through marriage, died 1727. *Her.Suff.Ch., Wall monument (nothing of Crest remaining) and on a Helmet, Barking*

From a mount Vert the sun rising in splendour Proper therefrom issuant a unicorn's head couped Sable armed and crined Or holding in the mouth a cross paty fitchy Or.
GWILT. *Fairbairn*, 'of Icklingham, Suff.'*

On a mount Vert an ash tree Proper hanging from the branches by a riband Azure an escutcheon Sable charged with a leopard's face Or.
GIPPING, Rural District Council. *Scott-Giles, 349*, 'Granted 1951'*

On a mount Vert a dead tree.
PAYNE. *Davy, A.*

On a mount an oak tree fructed Proper surmounted by a beehive also Proper.
NUNN, of Bury. *Davy, A.*

Upon a mount Vert in front of an oak tree Proper a beehive Or.
NUNN, Elias, of Bury St. Edmunds, Suff. *Fairbairn*

On a mount Vert an oak tree Proper fructed Or encircled by iron palisades Proper.
OAKES, of Nowton Court. *Burke, L.G. 1952 ed.* Her.Suff.Ch., Brass shield in tower, Glass, Nowton*

On a mount in front of an oak tree fructed the trunk of a tree fessewise eradicated and sprouting all Proper.
WOOD, of Hengrave Hall. *Burke, L.G. 1900 ed.* 'John Wood, Esq., J.P., D.L., of Hengrave Hall, Bury St. Edmunds. *Fairbairn*, untinctured*

On a mount a walnut tree all Proper.
WALLER, of Hollesley. *Davy, A.*

MOUNTAIN

A mountain in flames Proper.
CREVEQUER. *Davy, A.*

A goat Argent attired Or salient against a mountain Proper.
GURDON, of Assington. 'Gourdon' *MS Knight's Visitations, Suff.*, 'mountain Vert'. Davy, A. Washbourne*, 'of Hants., Suff., Wilts. mountain Vert'. Fairbairn, 'Hants., Suff. & Wilts. mountain Vert'*

MULLET [Alphabetically by name]

A mullet of six points Or between two wings Azure.

AUDLEY, Earl of Gloucester. Of Gazeley, Haverhill. *Davy, A.*
A mullet Sable.
DOUGHTY, of Theberton, Martlesham, Woodbridge. *Davy, A. Burke, L.G. 1853 ed. Fairbairn*, 'of Theberton Hall, Suff.' Her.Suff.Ch., Over doorway, Theberton*
A mullet Argent.
DOUGHTY, George, Rector of Martlesham, died 1832. *Bildeston, 73*
A mullet Sable pierced Argent.
DOUGHTY, Samuel, died 1749; George Doughty, of Theberton Hall, died 1798; Rev. George Doughty, M.A., Rector of Martlesham and Vicar of Hoxne, died 1832. *Her.Suff.Ch., Wall tablets in chancel, Martlesham*
A pierced mullet Or.
DRURY. *Her.Suff.Ch., Glass, Bardwell. Photograph**
A mullet of six points Gules.
LAYER, of Bury. *Davy, A.*
A mullet pierced Or.
ROWLEY, of Tendring Hall in Stoke-by-Nayland, Holbecks in Hadleigh. *MS Ordinary of Arms, fo. 163*, [in a later hand 'Rowley Knt of the Bath & Admiral ob 1768'] Washbourne*, 'Suff.' Burke, Peerage, 1891 ed.* 'Sir Joshua Thellusson Rowley, Bart., J.P., D.L., of Tendring Hall, Suff.' Fairbairn. Rowley, Barts., of Tendring Hall, 1786–1918. Her.Suff.Ch., Wall tablets and Glass, Stoke-by-Nayland*
A mullet Or pierced Sable.
ROWLEY, Bart. *Davy, A.*
A mullet Or charged with a crescent between two wings expanded Gules.
SMITH, of Elmsett, Suff. *Fairbairn*, 'without crescent'*
A mullet of six points Or between two wings conjoined and displayed Argent.
SPURLING, of Gt. Cornard, Burgh, Stratford. *Davy, A.*
A mullet Or.
VAREY, of Ixworth. *Davy, A.*

MULLETS
Three mullets two at bottom one at top.
BOKENHAM, of Thornham. *Davy, A.*

PALES, PALETS, PALY [Alphabetically by name]
A buck's head Or issuing out of park pales Proper.
GREEN. Rector of Burgh Castle, 1840. *Davy, A.*
From eight park pales alternately Or and Gules a hind's head Argent.
HALL. Bartholomew Hall, of Ipswich, Suffolk, son of Thomas Hall, Clerk of the Hanaper and Chancellor, son of Thomas Hall, of Sherbourne, co. York.; Grant to the said Bartholomew and the descendants of the said Thomas Hall by W. Flower, Norroy, 8 February 1587. *Grants & Certificates (Stowe MS 677). Miscellaneous Grants (H.S.) I. 97–8, 'Latin text, arms & crest tricked in MS'*
Issuing out of eight park pales Or and Gules a hind's head Argent.
HALL. *MS Martin's Crests, 'looking over pales'. Davy, A. (Barrett MS)*
Out of park pales Or a unicorn's head Sable maned and armed Or.
KITSON, KYTSON. *Visitation 1561 (ed. Howard) II. 83**
Out of park pales Or a cubit arm erect habited Gules

lined Ermine holding in the hand Argent a roll of paper Argent, charged on the wrist with a crescent – [for difference].
SCOTT, of Leiston, Essex. *Visitation 1561 (MSS G. 7* and Iveagh Copy*)*
Six palets arranged fanwise alternately Ermines and Ermine.
STUTEVILLE, STOTEVYLL, of Dalham. *Visitation 1561 (MSS G. 7* and Iveagh Copy*)* 'Thomas Stoteville' *MS Philpot's Visitations, Suff.**
Paly of six Ermine and Ermines shaped like a plume of feathers.
STUTEVILLE, STOTEVILL, of Dalham. *Visitation 1561 (ed Metcalfe). Visitation 1577.* Sir Martin Stuteville, died 1631. *Effigy wall monument, Dalham. Photographs**
Paly of five shaped like feathers Ermines.
STUTEVILLE. 'Stotavyll' *Harl. 772**

PAW see also GAMB
A bear's paw erased and erect charged with a bird.
BANYARD, BAYNARD. 'John Banyard' *MS Philpot's Visitations, Norf.**
A bear's paw erect holding a plume of three ostrich feathers Proper.
SQUIRE, of Barton Place near Mildenhall. *Burke, L.G. 1853 ed. Fairbairn*, 'of Barton Place, Suff. paw erased and erect'*

TWO PAWS
Two bear's paws erased and erect supporting a crescent.
MINSHULL. *Washbourne, Addenda. 'Granted to Michael de Minshull, at Acre, in 1191'*

PEDESTAL
On a pedestal a Blackamoor's head.
HUNLOCK, ? of Wissett. *Davy, A.*

PELLET see ROUNDEL, Sable

PHEON see also ARROW
A pheon Sable.
BELWARD, of Mettingham. *Davy, A., church*
A pheon point down Azure the staff broken off Or and entwined by a snake Vert.
EWRE. '. . Ewer, of Langley'; Grant by R. Cooke, Clarenceux. *Grants & Certificates (Stowe MS 706)*
A pheon's head with a piece of the shaft thereon Or enwrapped with a snake Vert.
EWRE. *MS Heraldic Collections, fo. 82*, untinctured. MS Martin's Crests*
A pheon Or headed Argent environed with a snake Proper.
EWRE, EWAR, of Bury. *Davy, A., St. James's church*
A pheon Or between two sprigs, or branches, of laurel Vert.
LANGLEY, of Somersham, Bury. *Shropshire Visitation 1623 (H.S.) II. 310, 'Langley of Bury St. Eds.' Crisp's Visitation II. 101*, 'laurel vert fruited proper'*
A pheon Sable.
OLDERSHAW. *Washbourne*, 'Suff.'*
A pheon Sable a snake turned about it Proper.
OLDERSHAW. *Washbourne, 'Suff.'*
A pheon Sable entwined by a snake Proper.
OLDERSHAW. *Fairbairn*, 'Suff.'*
A pheon shafted and feathered in pale Argent entwined by a snake Proper.
WHITBY. *MS Ordinary of Arms, fo. 243**
A pheon Or between two wings Argent.

YALLOP. *Dade MS, Dade monument, Tannington church*

PIKE see SPEAR

PILLAR see COLUMN

PINE APPLE or FIR CONE see FRUIT

PLATE see ROUNDEL, Argent

POMEY see ROUNDEL, Vert

POPINJAY see BIRD, PARROT

PORTCULLIS
A portcullis Azure chained Or.
BUCK. *MS Heraldic Alphabet*
A portcullis Argent chains and studded Or the chains in fret.
PORTER. 'Richard Porter, of S. Margaret in South Elmham, co. Suffolk, son of Nicholas, son of John Porter, gent., being descended of an ancient family'; Confirmation by Sir W. Segar, Garter, in 1606. *Grants & Certificates (Add. MS 12,225)*
A portcullis chained.
PORTER, of Metfield, Framlingham. *MS Ordinary of Arms, fo. 247*. Richard Porter, of Framlingham, died 1702. E.A.N. & Q. X. 56, Ledger stone, St. Nicholas church Ipswich. Crisp's Visitation XVI. 164. Bookplate*. Richard Porter, of Framlingham, died 1702. Her.Suff.Ch., Ledger stone, St. Nicholas Ipswich*
A portcullis Argent nailed and chained Or the chains cast over it in fret.
PORTER, of St. Margaret South Elmham, Halesworth, Framlingham. *Visitation 1664–8*. Davy, A. Washbourne, 'Linc. and Suff.' Fairbairn, 'Lincs. & St. Margarets in Southernam [sic], Suff.'*
A portcullis Argent chained and toothed Or.
PORTER, of Halesworth. *Bokenham, 'p. Segar, Garter. 1606'*
A portcullis Or nailed Azure with chains pendent thereto Or.
SOMERSET, Duke of Beaufort. Of Gt. Waldingfield. Somerset, Earl of Worcester. Of Wickhambrook. *Davy, A., 'as for the Duke of Beaufort'*

POT

VARIOUS [Alphabetically by name]
A vase.
BELL, Samuel, late of Hopton, died 1844. *Her.Suff.Ch., Wall tablet, Lound. 'This may not be a crest but there is a torse beneath it'*
A vase containing four flowers.
GOLDWELL, Henry, Burgess of Bury St. Edmunds, died 1693; widow Frances (Shelley), died 1712. *Her.Suff.Ch., Ledger stones, Tuddenham. 'Out of a well Or a vine and two columbine branches Proper Goldwell'*
Out of a pot Or five roses parted per . . . Argent and Gules stalked Vert.
MACKWILLIAMS. 'Mac-William' *MS Fairfax*
Out of a flower pot Or a branch of five roses per bend Argent and Gules.
MACKWILLIAMS. *MS Martin's Crests*
A wine pot with a towel tied to the handle Argent.
WENTWORTH. 'Wentwourth of Suffolk' *Wall's Book*
'to his Crest a Wyne pot with a towell knyt to the hand ar/'
WENTWORTH. 'Wentworth of Suff   knight by h 8'

MS Alphabet of Crests, fo. 137
A covered pot or ewer Argent garnished Or tied about the handle with a flowing riband Or.
WENTWORTH, of Nettlestead. *Visitation 1561 (MS G. 7*)*

REEDS, BULRUSHES, FLAGS [Alphabetically by name]
A stork among bulrushes all Proper.
BARHAM. *Davy, A.*
A bittern Or standing among bulrushes Proper.
BARNARDISTON, of Kedington, Brightwell. 'Sr Nathaniell Barnardeston Knight' *MS Lilly's Visitation of Suffolk*, first of two crests shown. MS Heraldic Alphabet. Crisp's Visitation VIII. 41, of the Ryes in Sudbury, Pedigree. Fairbairn, 'of The Ryes, Sudbury, Suffolk'. Her.Suff.Ch., Monuments, Tablets and Hatchments, Kedington; Funeral helm, Hatchments and Vault, Brightwell*
A bittern Or in bulrushes legged and beaked Gules.
BARNARDISTON. *Proc.S.I.A. VIII. 224, Clare church glass*
A stork Or amid rushes Proper.
BARNARDISTON, of Kedington, Clare, Brightwell. *Davy, A., Brightwell church, Wyverstone church flagon. Proc.S.I.A. VIII. 323. E.A.N. & Q. XIII. 327, 'a crane'. 'Sir . . . Barnardiston Kt. Benefactor of this . . .' Her.Suff.Ch., Glass, Clare*
A swan among bulrushes.
HEARD, Thomas, Churchwarden c.1834. *Carved on bench end, Gt. Bealings church. Photograph. Heard, of Seckford Hall for 60 years. Church booklet*
A bittern within a heap of reeds.
LITTON. *MS Martin's Crests*
A bittern among flags seeded all Proper.
LYTTON, of Shrubland Hall. *Davy, A.*
A sea coney sejant Gules maned Or among reeds Vert.
NORTON, CONYERS alias NORTON, of Halesworth. *Visitation 1561 (MS Iveagh Copy*)*
A demi-horse salient Gules maned Or issuing out of a heap of rushes Vert.
NORTON, of Chediston. *Bokenham*
A sea coney seiant Gules maned Or finned Argent out of a tuft of grass and rushes Proper.
NORTON, of Halesworth. *Davy, A.*

REPTILE

CROCODILE
A demi-crocodile, or lizard, Sable.
BRISE, of Cavendish. *Davy, A., church*

LIZARD
A demi-crocodile, or lizard, Sable.
BRISE, of Cavendish. *Davy, A., church*
A demi lizard Proper holding in his paws [sic] a bush of hawthorn Vert flowers Argent.
EDEN. 'Eden of Bury in Suffolk' *Wall's Book*
'to his Crest a Demy Lyzard in his coullers holding in his pawes [sic] a bush of hathorne Vert fflowers ar'
EDEN. 'Edon of Bury in Suff/' *MS Alphabet of Crests, fo. 34*
A 'lisorde' passant Vert collared Or.
LONGDEN. 'Langdon' *MS Knight's Visitations, Norf.*
A lizard.
LONGDEN. Rector of Brent Eleigh for 35 years, died 1895. *Crisp's Visitations. IX. 41*
A lizard Vert ducally gorged and lined Or.
PRATT, of Ipswich, Yoxford, Ash. *Visitation*

1577. 'Thomas Pratte of Ipswiche' *MS Knight's Visitations, Suff.** 'Thomas Pratt' *MS Philpot's Visitations, Suff.**, *'line reflexed over the back and ringed'. Bokenham. Davy, A. Washbourne, 'Suff.' Fairbairn, 'Suff.'*

A lizard Vert collared Or.

WARNER, of Framlingham, Cratfield. *MS Knight's Visitations, Suff.** *Bokenham, 'collared and chained Or'*

A lizard, or dragon, passant Vert collared and crowned Or.

WARNER. 'Will Warner' *MS Philpot's Visitations, Suff.** *Davy, A.*

A lizard Vert.

WARNER, of Cratfield. *Davy, A. Washbourne, 'Suff.' Fairbairn**, *'Suff.'*

SNAKE [Alphabetically by name]

On a mount Vert a snake coiled up and environed with rushes Proper.

ANGUISH, ALLIN, of Somerleyton. *Page. Davy, A.*

An anguis (or snake) coiled in grass.

ANGUISH, of Somerleyton. *Suckling. II. 45. Burke, L.G. 1853 ed.*

A snake coiled up and environed with flags or rushes Proper.

ALLIN *Fairbairn, 'Suff.'*

A pheon point down Azure the staff broken off Or and entwined by a snake Vert.

EWRE. '. . . Ewer of Langley' By R. Cooke, Clarenceux. *Grants & Certificates (Stowe MS 706)*

A pheon's head with a piece of the shaft thereon Or enwrapped with a snake Vert.

EWRE. *MS Heraldic Collections, fo. 82**, *untinctured. MS Martin's Crests*

A pheon Or headed Argent environed with a snake Proper.

EWRE, EWAR, of Bury. *Davy, A., St. James's church*

A serpent Proper entwined round five arrows shafts Or feathered and barbed Argent one in pale and four saltirewise.

HALE. 'Hales' *MS Ordinary of Arms, fo. 272**

Seven arrows six in saltire and one in pale Or heads and feathers Argent entwined by a snake Vert.

HALES, HALLES, of London. Patent February 1605. *Grants & Certificates (Stowe MSS 706 and 707; Harl. MSS 1,115, 1,442, 5,829, 6,095)*

A serpent Proper entwined round five arrows shafts Or headed Sable feathered Argent one in pale and four saltirewise.

HALE, of Bury. *Davy, A.*

A snake Proper entwined round a broken column Argent.

HARRISON, of Martlesham. *Davy, A.*

A Corinthian column broken Argent entwined with a snake Proper.

HARRISON, of Palgrave. *Davy, A.*

A pheon Sable a snake turned about it Proper.

OLDERSHAW. *Washbourne, 'Suff.'*

A pheon Sable entwined by a snake Proper.

OLDERSHAW. *Fairbairn**, *'Suff.'*

A serpent Vert holding in its mouth a Jerusalem cross (paty) Gules.

SANCROFT *Davy, A.*

A pheon shafted and feathered in pale Argent entwined by a snake Proper.

WHITBY. *MS Ordinary of Arms, fo. 243**

SNAKES

Two snakes coiled Vert from the centre of them an arm in armour embowed Proper holding in the hand a brand fired at both ends Proper.

BRAND, of Wherstead, Hemingstone, Woodbridge. *Davy, A.*

Three snakes interlaced two heads in chief and one in base.

CLOUN, CLUNE, of Tunstall. *Davy, A., 'Hune more properly Clun'*

Two demi-snakes couped holding a pomegranate Proper.

CORNELIUS, of Ipswich. *MS Fairfax*

Two demi-snakes couped Proper holding in their mouths a pomegranate.

CORNELIUS, of Ipswich. *Bokenham*

Five snakes erect on their tails tied together by one snake in fesse all Azure.

DUNNE. *MS Heraldic Collections, fo. 34b**

ROCK [Alphabetically by name]

On a rock Proper an eagle preparing to fly.

BINGHAM. *MS Martin's Crests. Washbourne**, *'eagle rising Or. Of Dorset'*

On a rock Proper an eagle rising Argent winged Azure.

BLATHWAYT. P.C. [Perpetual Curate] of Leiston. *Davy, A.*

On a rock Proper an eagle rising Argent.

BRANTHWAITE, of Lavenham. *Gage (Thingoe). Davy, A. 'Miles Branthwayt, Esq.' Bookplate**, *untinctured*

Upon a rock an auk Proper holding in the beak a bezant.

CARTHEW. 'Radulphus John Carthew, J.P., of Woodbridge Abbey Suffolk and London' *Fairbairn**

On a rock a wyvern wings endorsed Proper.

CHETTLE, of Suffolk. *Davy, A.*

In front of two wings Argent each charged with an estoile Azure a rock Proper thereon a caltrap Or.

COLMAN, of Corton. *Crisp's Visitation VIII. 142** *and 148**. *Bookplate**, *the caltrap untinctured*

On a rock a beacon fired in front thereof a helmet all Proper.

COMPTON, 'COMPTON-THORNHILL, Bart., of Pakenham Lodge, Suff. and Riddlesworth Hall, Norfolk' *Fairbairn**

'And for the Crest On a Wreath of the Colours Upon a Rock proper a Cameleopard statant Sable semé of Annulets gorged with a Collar with Chain reflexed over the back and holding in the mouth a Horse-shoe all Or.'

CRISP. 'Frederick Arthur Crisp of the Hall in the Parish of Playford in the County of Suffolk . . . Gentleman, eldest son of Frederick Augustus Crisp late of the Hall aforesaid . . . deceased'; Grant by Albert W. Woods, Garter and Walter Aston Blount, 4 November 1884. *Family of Crisp. N.S. I. 89–90**

Upon a rock Proper a cameleopard statant Sable semy of annulets gorged with a collar with chain reflexed over the back and holding in his mouth a horseshoe all Or.

CRISP, of Rendlesham, Melton, Sternfield, Chillesford, Butley Abbey, Lt. Wenham Hall, Gt. Bealings, Playford Hall. *Crisp's Visitation. XIII. 115**, *Pedigree. Fairbairn**, *'of Playford Hall and The Cedars, Great Bealings, Suff.' Livery button**, *untinctured*

Upon a rock Proper a lion sejant Sable gutty Or
gorged with a collar Or supporting with his dexter
paw an escutcheon Argent charged with a cross flory
Sable surmounted of another –.

DICKEN. Rector of Norton, 1831–79. *Crisp's
Visitation VII. 138**

A rock Proper thereon a falcon belled Or wings
displayed Azure on the insides supporting with the
dexter claw a banner Azure charged with a garb Or.

EAST SUFFOLK, County Council. *Scott-Giles,
343**

Upon a rock a cubit arm erect in armour Proper
grasping an escutcheon Gules charged with a caltrap
Argent.

GILSTRAP, Bart., of Fornham St. Genevieve.
*Burke, Peerage, 1891 ed.** Sir William Gilstrap,
Bart., of Fornham Park, died 1896. *Her.Suff.Ch.,
Hatchment, Fornham St. Martin*

A goat climbing up a rock all Proper.

GURDON, of Norfolk, Suffolk. *Washbourne**.
Fairbairn, 'of Norf. and Suff.' and 'Assington
Hall, Suff.'*

A goat Argent horned Or climbing a rock Proper
with a sprig issuing from the top Vert.

GURDON, of Assington Hall. *Burke, L.G. 1853,
1900 and 1952 eds.** Muskett. I. 272 (Harl. MS
1560). Crisp's Visitation XVII. 121, 'all Proper'*

A goat Argent climbing a rock therefrom sprouting
sprigs of laurel Proper.

GURDON, Baron Cranworth. Patron of Culpho.
*Crisp's Visitation. X. 90**

A goat climbing a rock with a sprig issuant from the
top all Proper.

GURDON, of Assington. *Her.Suff.Ch.,
Monuments and Tablets, Assington*

A goat climbing a rock with a tree issuant
therefrom.

GURDON. Robert Brampton Gurdon, Coldstream
Guards, killed in action 1942; son Charles, died
1945, aged 9. *Her.Suff.Ch., Wooden wall tablet,
Grundisburgh*

In front of a rock Proper a fasces fesseways also
Proper thereon a goat salient Sable.

KEMBALL. 'Charles Gurdon Kemball, of
Mettingham Castle, Bungay, Suff.' *Fairbairn**

On a rock Proper an eagle with wings elevated
Erminois preying on a child Proper swaddled Azure
banded Argent.

LATHAM, of Ipswich. Vicar of Bedingfield, Rector
of Westley. *Davy, A.*

On a rock Proper a martlet rising or.

TONG, of Haverhill, Tuddenham. *Davy, A.*

A bird on a rock.

WENYEVE, of Brettenham. *Davy, A.*

ROUNDEL [Alphabetically by name]

In front of a pelican in her piety Proper five bezants
fesseways.

GATAKER, of Mildenhall. *Burke, L.G. 1952 ed.**

On a roundel Azure a stag's head erased Or.

GREEN. Georgina Lindsay, daughter of the last
Thomas Green of Wilby, died 1923.
Her.Suff.Ch., Brass in south aisle, Wilby

A bezant charged with a lion's head erased and
collared.

JAQUES, of Framsden, Wetheringsett. *Davy, A.*

A bezant between two wings Azure each wing semy
de lis Or.

MONEY. Rector of Sternfield. *Davy, A.*

A torteau between two wings Or.

MORTIMER, of Cavendish. *Davy, A.*

A bezant.

RAYDON. *Davy, A.*

A bezant.

ROWDON. *Washbourne*, 'Suff.' Fairbairn,
'Suff.'*

ROUND TOP see SHIP

RUDDER see SHIP

RUSHES see REEDS

RYE see FRUIT

SAIL see SHIP

SALTIRE

A saltire Or.

LE HUNTE, of Bradley. *Davy, A.*

SCALING LADDER

A double scaling-ladder Or.

BENNET, Earl of Arlington. Of Euston, Bury,
Rougham, Boxford. *Davy, A.*

A scaling ladder Argent.

GREY, Lord Powis. Of Kersey, Layham. 'Sʳ Ed
Gray de Werke de Chillingham' *MS Ordinary of
Arms, fo. 35*, a double ladder shown. Davy, A.*

A scaling ladder.

GREY, GRAY. *MS Heraldic Collections, fo. 61**

A tower with a ladder leaning against the sinister
side.

LUGG. 'Thomas Lugg of this parish, died 1748';
Others. *Partridge, 177 (Darby, 1825), Tomb in
churchyard, Sternfield. E.A. Misc. 1926. 17*

A tower embattled against it a scaling ladder.

LUGG, of Sternfield. *Davy, A., Tomb in
churchyard. E.A. Misc. 1910. 104*

A triple-turreted tower and leaning thereto a scaling
ladder.

LUGG, Thomas, died 1748; son Thomas Lugg,
died 1791. *Her.Suff.Ch., Altar tomb in
churchyard, Sternfield. Not found 1980*

SCALP

The scalp and attires of a stag Or between them an
eagle displayed Argent.

BARENTINE. 'Sʳ Wᵐ Barrantyne' *MS Ordinary
of Arms, fo. 131* Washbourne**

A bear's scalp Sable.

HEMENHALE, of Wickham Skeith. *Davy, A.*

SCEPTRE

A sword Argent hilt and pommel Or and a sceptre
Or in saltire enfiled with a civil crown Vert.

CARLOS, of Sotterley, Frostenden. *Davy, A.
Washbourne*

SCIMITAR see SWORD

SEA

On a wave of the sea a sea lion erect Azure with a
ducal coronet Or holding an anchor Sable.

HARLAND. *Sharpe*

Issuing from the sea Proper a sea lion supporting an
anchor Sable beam Or.

HARLAND, Bart., of Sproughton, Nacton,
Wherstead. *Davy, A.*

A demi-seaman issuing out of water Proper holding
in his dexter hand a flaming sword and in his other
hand a shield of the Hotham arms [Barry of ten
Argent and Azure on a canton Or a Cornish chough
Proper]

HOTHAM. Rector of Dennington. *Davy, A.*

Upon waves of the sea the wreck of the 'Dutton'
East Indiaman upon a rocky shore off Plymouth

garrison all Proper.

PELLEW. Minister of St. James's, Bury. *Davy, A.*

SEAX see SWORD

SHIELD see ESCUTCHEON

SHIP, parts of SHIP [Alphabetically by name]
A round top Or thereout a demi-lion rampant issuant Sable.

CAREW. 'S. Welye Carow' *Harl. MS 6163. Banners & Standards*, with and without a mullet for difference*

'to his crest/ a Demy lyon sa/ comyng owt of the top of a ship or/'

CAREW. *MS Alphabet of Crests, fo. 19*

The round top of a ship Or issuing therefrom a demi-lion rampant Sable between six spears three in bend and three in bend sinister Or.

CAREW. *MS Ordinary of Arms, fo. 53**

Issuing from the top mast head of a ship Or a demi-lion rampant between six half-pikes bendways dexter and sinister.

CAREW. *MS Martin's Crests*

A main mast the round top set off with palisadoes Or issuant therefrom a lion rampant Sable.

CAREW. *MS Heraldic Alphabet*

A mainmast the round top surrounded with spears and a demi-lion issuant from the centre Sable.

CAREW, of Bury. *Davy, A., St. Mary's church*

The sail of a ship Proper

EXTON. Vicar of Cretingham, Rector of Athelington. *Davy, A.*

A rudder.

HELMES, of Bury. *Davy, A., St. Mary's church, 1725*

A rudder.

HOLMES. Merelina (D'Ewes), wife of Richard Holmes, Junior, died 1725. *Tymms, 204, Slab in St. Mary's church*

'Vppon the healme a demy lyon golde supportinge a shyppe sables on a wreathe argent and sables ma'teled gulz dobled argent'

IPSWICH. 'John Gardener and Jeffery Gylbert at this present baylyffs of the towne of Ypswyche'; Confirmation of Arms and Grant of Crest and Supporters by W. Hervy, Clarenceux, 20 August 1561. *Proc.S.I.A. VI. 456*. Misc.Gen. et Her. 2nd S. II. 343–4**

A demi-lion rampant Or holding a three masted ship with sails furled Proper.

IPSWICH, Borough of *Scott-Giles, 29.* Ipswich, Town of *Her.Suff.Ch., Glass, St. James's, Bury; Tooley brass, formerly in St. Mary Quay church, now in Ipswich Museum.* [Differing in details of ship]

The mast of a ship broken with a top Sable darts in it Or the heads Argent the sail in cross bound up fastenings Gules.

MERRY. 'Meery' *Wall's Book*

'to his crest the mast of a shyp broken/ with a toppe sa/ vj Darts in yt or/ they heded ar/ the seale in crosse bound up and the ffastening g/'

MERRY. 'Mery of North hall in Essex' *MS Alphabet of Crests, fo. 81b*

The mast of a ship rompu and erect thereto a yard with sail furled in bend sinister above it a round top with three arrows issuing therefrom on each side saltirewise points upward all Proper.

MERRY, of Herringfleet. *Davy, A. Washbourne, 'Norf.' Fairbairn, 'of Herringfleet Hall, Norf.' [sic]*

The stern of a Spanish line-of-battle ship flotant upon waves all Proper inscribed under the gallery 'San Josef'

NELSON. Horatio, Lord Nelson. Of Round Wood in Ipswich, 1798. *Davy, A. Wagner's Historic Heraldry of Britain, 91, plate XXV*, Biography, Grant, etc.*

Upon waves of the sea the wreck of the 'Dutton' East Indiaman upon a rocky shore off Plymouth garrison all Proper.

PELLEW. Minister of St. James's, Bury. *Davy, A.*

A ship in full sail.

SHARDELOW. *Davy, A.*

A ship under sail Proper.

TENDRING, of Boxford. *Davy, A.*

SLIP, SPRIG see BRANCH

SPEAR [Alphabetically by name]
A spear head Argent consanguined and within a chaplet of oak fructed all Proper.

BROADRICK. 'George Broadrick, Esq., of Broughton House, Broughton Road, Ipswich' *Fairbairn*

A spear's head erect.

KNIGHTS, Thomas, of Woodbridge, died 1707. *Her.Suff.Ch., Ledger stone in chancel Woodbridge*

A lance Or headed Argent environed with a laurel branch Vert.

MINGAY, of Ashfield. *Davy, A., St. Mary's church, Thetford*

A spear in pale Or beside it a griffin sejant Vert.

PASHLEY. 'Sʳ Ric: Pashley' *MS Ordinary of Arms, fo. 32**

SPEARS
Two spears in saltire Or headed Argent tasselled Gules.

BULBROKE, BULBROOKE, of Tostock, Drinkstone, Whepstead. *Davy, A. (Barrett), Tostock church*

Two lances in saltire each having a pennoncelle thereon.

BULBROKE. 'John Bulbrooke, Gent., of Tostock, died 1641' *E.A. Misc. 1907, 86. and 1918, 83. Her.Suff.Ch., Slab in churchyard, Tostock*

The butt ends of three tilting spears broken off one in pale and two in saltire Or interlaced with a wreath Argent and Sable.

GIBBS. '. . . Gibbs, of co. Warwick'. Per Portcullis. *Grants & Certificates (Add. MS 14,297)*

Two tilting spears in saltire Or each with a pennant Gules.

LOMBE. Rev. Henry Evans Lombe, J.P. for Norfolk and Suffolk, died 1897. *Crisp's Visitation XIX. 85*, Pedigree. Livery button*, untinctured*

Two lances in saltire Or headed Argent on each a pennoncelle Gules charged with a cross paty Or the lances entwined with a wreath of laurel Vert.

PECK. 'William Peck, of Wood Dalling, co. Norfolk, gent'; Confirmation by Sir W. Segar, Garter. *Grants & Certificates (Stowe MS 677; Add. MS 12,225)*

Two lances in saltire Or headed Argent pennons hanging to them Or each charged with a cross formy Gules the lances enfiled with a chaplet Vert.

PECK, of North Cove, Chediston, Halesworth. *Davy, A.*

In front of two spears in saltire Proper a dragon's head Gules gorged with a collar gemel Argent.

WARE, CUMBERLEGE-WARE, of Poslingford Hall, Clare. *Burke, L.G. 1900 and 1952 eds.* * 'Charles Edward Cumberlege Ware, of Poslingford, Suff. and Middx.' *Fairbairn*

SPHERE
A sphere Or in a frame Sable.
CARPENTER, of Rumburgh. *Davy, A. (Edms.)*
A globe under a rainbow with clouds at each end.
HOPE. Stephen Charles Hope, J.P., of co. Essex and Walton, died 1871. *Her.Suff.Ch., Brass, Walton.* Adrian C.F. Hope, died 1904; widow Laura, died 1929. *Tombstone on north side of church, Hopton*
A sphere Or at the North and South Poles an estoile Or.
PEERES, of Gazeley. *Davy, A., church*

SPIRE
A spire of a church within the tower of it a bell all Proper.
PORTER, of Framlingham. *Bokenham*

SPUR
A spur Or strap Gules between two wings Or.
JOHNSON, of Long Melford. *Davy, A. Fairbairn* *, 'Johnson, Long Melford, Suff. and Lancs.'*
A winged spur Or leathered Gules.
JOHNSTONE. *Bookplates* *, untinctured. Fairbairn* *, 'Johnstone of Beaulieu, co. Louth.'*
Standing on a spur leathered 'lyng' [?lying in fesse] Or a hawk volant per fesse Azure and Argent wings Or membered Gules.
KNIGHT. 'Knyght' *Wall's Book*
'to his crest a hawke Volant b/ar/ p fece membred g/standing on a Spurre Lethered lying and her wyngs or/'
KNIGHT. 'Knyght' *MS Alphabet of Crests, fo. 68b*
A spur-rowel Azure between two wings Or.
ROSSELINE, ROSCELIN, of Kelsale, Yoxford, Cookley. *Davy, A. Washbourne, 'Rosseline, Rosselyne'*

STAFF
A staff raguly Or.
EWERS, of Chediston. *Davy, A.*
On a staff raguly Vert a cockatrice with wings endorsed Or combed and wattled Gules.
LEEDES, of Oulton, Eyke, Staverton. *Davy, A.*
On a staff raguly fesseways Vert a falcon rising Proper beak and bells Or.
READE, Thomas, of Barton, co. Berks. *Grants & Certificates (Harl. MS 1,359)*
A staff with scrip hanging on it Sable garnished Or.
TASBURGH, of Flixton. *Davy, A. (Barrett MS)*

TWO STAVES
Two staves raguly in saltire enfiled by a crest coronet all Or (? the staves Sable).
REYCE. 'Richard Rice, of Preston, co. Suffolk'; Exemplification by . . . Rouge Crois, 1586. *Grants & Certificates (Stowe MS 670). The second of two Crests given.* [Rouge Croix in 1586 was Ralph Brooke]

STAR see ESTOILE

SUN [Alphabetically by name]
The sun rising in glory therein an eye gutty Argent.
BLOUNT. 'Blunt' *MS Heraldic Alphabet*
An armed foot in the sun.
BLOUNT. *MS Heraldic Alphabet*

The sun rising Proper.
BLUNDESTON. *Davy, A. Washbourne* *, 'Blundestone, Blunstone, Suff.' Fairbairn, 'Blundestone, Blunstone, Suff.'*
The sun Or between two wings Azure on each a crescent Argent.
CLERE, of Norfolk. 'Sr de Cleere de Norffe' *MS Ordinary of Arms, fo. 136* *
The sun Or between two wings Azure on each a crescent Or.
CLERE. *Davy, A.*
On a mount Vert a sun Or charged with a rose Gules.
CROWLEY, of Barking. *Davy, A., church.* Sir Ambrose Crowley, of London, granted Arms 14 June 1707; son John Crowley, Alderman of London, of Barking Hall by marriage, died 1727. *E.A.N. & Q. III. 95–6.* John Crowley, died 1727. *Her.Suff.Ch., Wall monument (nothing of Crest remaining) and on a Helmet, Barking*
The sun shining on the stump of a tree Proper.
D'URBAN, of Halesworth. *Davy, A. Washbourne* *, 'Durban'*
The sun Proper.
FONNEREAU, of Christ Church Park and The Moat, Ipswich. *Grants & Certificates (Add. MS 14,831). Sharpe. Davy, A., St. Margaret's church Ipswich. Burke, L.G. 1853 and 1900 eds. E.A.N. & Q. IX. 233. Fairbairn, 'of the Moat, near Ipswich'. Crisp's Visitation XVII. 161*
The sun in splendour Or.
FONNEREAU, of Christ Church, Ipswich. Several, 1785–1855. *Her.Suff.Ch., Hatchments, St. Margaret's Ipswich*
From rays of the sun Or an eagle's head Proper.
GILBERT, Thomas, of Mayfield, co. Sussex; Grant by Sir W. Segar, Garter, 8 November 1616. *Grants & Certificates (Harl. MS 6,140; Add. MS 12,225)*
An eagle's head Proper issuing out of rays Or.
GILBERT. *Davy, A. Washbourne, 'Suss. and Suff.' Fairbairn, 'Sussex and Suff.'*
From rays of the sun a unicorn's head erased Argent collared Gules holding in the mouth a cross paty fitchy Or.
GWILT, of Icklingham. *Davy, A.*
From rays of the sun a unicorn's head erased Argent collared Gules ringed Or.
GWILT, GWYLT. Rector of Icklingham. *Burke, L.G. 1853 ed.*
The sun in glory.
KEMPE. *Bokenham*
'A son ty'bre la teste dune licorne rasee de sable les oreilles et la barbe dor sur son col trois besantz les rasures de gueules estãt sur vng demy soleil dor'
KITSON. 'Thomas Kytson of Hengrave'; Grant of Arms and Crest by Sir Thomas Wroithesley, Garter and Thomas Benolt, Clarenceux, 14 April 1527. *Visitation 1561 (ed. Howard) II. 96–7* *
On a demy-sun a unicorn's head erased Sable ears and beard Or on the neck three bezants the erasures Gules.
KITSON, KYTSON, of Hengrave. 'Kytson' *Wall's Book. Gage (Hengrave), 'the original crest'*
'to his crest a half a sonne or/ in fece over yt an unecornes hed sa/ rased g/ on the necke iij besants eared armed and berded g/ Of Essex'
KITSON. 'Kytson' *MS Alphabet of Crests, fo. 68b*
The sun in splendour surmounted of a dexter arm in armour embowed holding in the hand a sword all Proper.

KYNASTON, Bart., of Risby. *Davy, A. (Burke). Washbourne*, 'of Salop.' Fairbairn*, 'of Salop.'*
From rays of the sun Or a tiger's head Sable collared chained and tufted Or.

MILESON. 'Edmund Militon, of St. Edmunds Bury, Suffolk'; Grant by R. St. George, 1611. *Grants & Certificates (Harl. MS 6,140)*
Issuing out of rays a tiger's head collared and studded lined and ringed.

MILESON. 'Edmon milison of St. edmunds Bury' *MS Heraldic Collections, fo. 88b**
The sun in splendour Or.

PITCAIRNE. Rector of Burgh Castle and Belton, died 1753. *Davy, A., Slab, Burgh Castle. E.A.N. & Q. II. 327*
The sun in splendour rising from clouds all Proper, above 'Clarior e Tenebris'

PURVIS, of Darsham. *Sharpe. Davy, A. Burke, L.G. 1853 ed.*
The sun breaking from behind a cloud Proper, with motto as above.

PURVIS, Charles, of Darsham House, died 1808. *Washbourne. Her.Suff.Ch., Wall tablet and Hatchment, Darsham*

SWORD [Alphabetically by name]

A sword in pale point upwards.

ALLEN, of Lowestoft. *Gillingwater, 312. Druery, 271–2*
A dagger erect point upwards.

ALLEN. Anne, daughter of Captain Thomas Allen, died 1664 aged 17. *Her.Suff.Ch., Monument, Lowestoft*
A sword erect Argent hilt and pommel Or.

ALLIN, Bart., of Lowestoft, Somerleyton. *Bokenham. Davy, A.*
A seax Azure hilted Or.

BELSTEDE. *Davy, A.*
On the point of a sword in pale a mullet.

BLANCHARD, of Heveningham. *Davy, A.*
In front of a sword erect the blade entwined by two serpents respecting each other Proper a boar's head erased Sable.

BROOKE, of Sibton Park. *Crisp's Visitation. I. 73*, serpents shown addorsed. Burke, L.G. 1900 ed. Fairbairn*, 'of Sibton Park, near Yoxford, Suff.'*
A sword erect in pale environed with a snake all Proper.

BROWNRIG, of Ipswich, Willisham, Beccles, Rishangles. *Davy, A.*
A sword Argent hilt and pommel Or and a sceptre Or in saltire enfiled with a civil crown Vert.

CARLOS, of Sotterley, Frostenden. *Davy, A. Washbourne*
A sword paleways ensigned with a cross paty.

CHEEKE, of Suffolk. *Davy, A. Washbourne, 'Somers. and Suff.' Fairbairn, 'Somers. and Suff.'*
A cutlass Argent hilt and pommel Or environed with two branches of laurel Vert.

CHESTER, of Loudham. *Davy, A. Washbourne, 'Ess.'*
A sword Argent hilted Or stuck pommel upwards in a panache of nine ostrich plumes in two heights of four and five blue and white alternately the midmost feather being blue.

DUKE, of Brampton, Worlingham, Shadingfield. *Surrey Visitation 1530 (H.S.) 70. Surrey Visitation 1662 (H.S.) 37**
A sword Argent hilted Or thrust into a plume of five ostrich feathers alternately Azure and Argent.

DUKE, of Brampton, Shadingfield. *Visitation 1561 (MSS G. 7* and Iveagh Copy*)*
A sword thrust into a plume of five ostrich feathers.

DUKE, of Worlingham. *Visitation 1561 (MS Iveagh Copy*)*
A sword Argent hilt Or stuck in a plume of five feathers three Azure two Argent.

DUKE, of Brampton, Worlingham. *Visitation 1561 (ed. Metcalfe). Harl. 772*. 'Duke of Suffolk' MS Philpot's Visitations, Suff.*, [in a different hand.] Washbourne, 'Suff.' Fairbairn, 'Suff. On a plume..' Her.Suff.Ch., Benhall, Worlingham*
A sword point downwards Proper behind a plume of feathers Argent.

DUKE, of Benhall, Bentley. *Bokenham*
A dagger issuing haft uppermost from a plume of five ostrich feathers.

DUKE, of Bentley. *E.A.N. & Q. VII. 221, Slab in church*
A sword Argent hilted Or stuck into a plume of five feathers Sable.

DUKE. 'Mrs. Parnell Rous alias Duke, wife of John Duke, of Wallingham. Epitaph made 1658' *Her.Suff.Ch., Memorial board, Worlingham. Photograph**
A sword Argent hilt Or stuck into a plume of five feathers three Gules and two Argent.

DUKE, Tollemache, died 1713 aged 23. *Her.Suff.Ch., Slab in chancel, Bentley*
An anchor and cable Sable and a sword Azure hilted Or in saltire.

FITZURSE, FITZOURSE. *Davy, A.*
A sword Proper hilted and pommelled Or and an olive branch also Proper in saltire.

FRASER. 'Fraser of Farraline, co. Inverness' *Her.Suff.Ch., Enamelled shield on post in cemetery, Ufford*
A sword erect Argent hilt Or on the blade a boar's head couped Sable.

HALSEY, of Woodbridge. *Davy, A. Fairbairn**
A sword and an ear of wheat in saltire Proper.

SOMERI, SOMERY, of Gt. Bradley. *Davy, A.*
A scimitar erect Argent hilt and pommel Or grip Sable.

TATNALL. 'Tattnall' *MS ex-Taylor Coll.**
A scimitar erect Argent hilt and pommel Or round the grip a ribbon Gules.

TATNALL, of Leiston. *Davy, A., churchyard.* 'Will Tatnall, esq., died 1826 aged 86' *Partridge, 40 (Darby, 1826), untinctured*
A cutlass erect Argent hilt and pommel Or a ribbon tied round the grip Gules.

TATNALL, William, died 1826; widow died 1837. *Her.Suff.Ch., Altar tomb in churchyard, Leiston*
A sword erected in pale Proper between two wings elevated and erected Argent.

VENTRIS, of Sproughton. *Bokenham*
A sword erect Argent hilt and pommel Or between two wings expanded Azure.

VENTRIS, of Sproughton, Ipswich. *Davy, A. Her.Suff.Ch., St. Nicholas Ipswich*

SWORDS

Two swords in saltire Argent hilted Or pierced through a leopard's head Or.

BUNBURY, Bart., of Gt. Barton, Mildenhall. *MS Heraldic Alphabet. Sharpe. Davy, A. Burke, Peerage, 1891 ed.**
Two swords in saltire the points upward Proper pommels and hilts Or tied with a riband Vert

pendant therefrom a key Sable.

DUNN, DUNN-GARDNER. *Washbourne, 'Dunn, Dunne, ribbon Azure.'* Algernon C.W. Dunn-Gardner, of Denston Hall and Chatteris, died 1929. *Her.Suff.Ch., Glass, Denston*

A dagger and sword in saltire Proper.

FINCHINGFIELD, of Suffolk. *Davy, A.*

A dagger and sword in saltire Proper.

HUNTINGFIELD, of Huntingfield. *Davy, A., Mettingham and Sternfield churches*

Two swords erect in saltire.

KEDINGTON. *Davy, A.*

Two scimitars in saltire points upward.

KEDINGTON, of Rougham. *Davy, A., church*

A pair of falchions saltirewise.

KEDINGTON, KERINGTON. Roger Kerington, died 1705; Anne, died 1717. *Her.Suff.Ch., Ledger stone in nave and Altar tomb in churchyard, Rougham*

Two swords in saltire.

KEDINGTON, KERINGTON. 'Roger Kerington, armiger, died 1705'; Others. *Partridge, 216 (Darby, 1827), Altar tomb in churchyard, Rougham*

Two swords crossed in saltire Argent hilted Or knotted with a ribbon Sable.

TONYN. Forth Tonyn, died 1748. *Her.Suff.Ch., Wall monument, St. Mary Tower Ipswich*

TAIL

A peacock's tail displayed Proper supported by two eagles Or.

LEAKE, LEEKE, of Yaxley Hall, Hadleigh, Willisham. *MS ex-Taylor Coll.*, 'of Lincolnsh^r.' Davy, A., Yaxley church. E.A.N. & Q. I. 313. Proc.S.I.A. XVI. 151** Rev. Seymour Leeke, of Yaxley Hall, died 1786; Francis Gilbert Yaxley Leeke, died 1836. *Her.Suff.Ch., Hatchments, Yaxley*

A peacock's tail erect Proper.

LOVELL. 'Thomas Lovell' *MS Knight's Visitations, Norf.**

A peacock's tail erect and bound with a wreath Proper.

LOVELL. 'Sr gregory Lovell' *MS Philpot's Visitations, Norf.**

A boar's head couped and erect Argent armed Or out of the mouth a peacock's tail Proper.

TYRREL, TYRRELL, of Gipping. 'Thomas Tyrell de gyppyng' *Banners & Standards* Visitation 1561 (MS G. 7*) Harl. 772*, untinctured. Visitation 1664–8**. Edmund Tyrell, of Gipping Hall, died 1799. *Her.Suff.Ch., Hatchment, Gipping chapel.* Rev. Charles Tyrell, of Gipping Hall, Rector of Thurston, died 1811. *Hatchment, Stowmarket.* Charles Tyrell, of Gipping Hall, died 1872; wife Elizabeth (Ray), died 1826. *Ledger stone and Hatchment, Haughley. Livery button*, untinctured*

A boar's head couped in pale, or erect, Argent swallowing a peacock's tail Proper.

TYRREL, TYRRELL. 'John Tyrell' *MS Philpot's Visitations, Suff.* Washbourne*, 'Tirrell, Suff., Essex, etc.'*

A boar's head erased and erect Argent armed Or out of the neck with a mullet – [for difference].

TYRRELL, of Gipping. *Visitation 1561 (MS Iveagh Copy*)*

A boar's head erased in pale, or erect, Argent swallowing a peacock's tail Proper.

TYRRELL 'Thomas Tirrell of Gippinge esquier' *MS Lilly's Visitation of Suffolk**

TORCH

A flaming torch Proper.

PRESCOTT. *Bokenham*

TORTEAU see ROUNDEL, Gules

TOWER see also CASTLE [Alphabetically by name]

On a wreath Argent a tower Or.

ALMACK. *Her.Suff.Ch., Glass, Long Melford*

A tower Or charged with a fret Gules.

BENCE, of Aldeburgh, Benhall, Ringsfield, Thorington, Kentwell Hall. *Visitation 1664–8*. Davy, A. Thorington, Pedigree*. Burke, L.G. 1900 ed.* 'Edward Starkie Bence, of Kentwell Hall, Suff.' *Fairbairn. Crisp's Visitation. XXI. 97* Her.Suff.Ch., Benhall, Carlton, Heveningham, Ringsfield.* Alexander Bence, son of Alexander Bence, of Thorington Hall, died 1742. *Wall tablet, Thorington.* Lawrence Bence, died 1746. *Hatchment, Henstead.* Harriot (Elmy), wife of Rev. B. Bence, Rector of Beccles, died 1815. *Monument, Beccles*

A tower Argent charged with a fret Gules.

BENCE. *Washbourne*, 'Suff.'* Alexander Bence, son of Alexander Bence, of Thorington Hall, died 1742. *Her.Suff.Ch., Hatchment, Thorington. Without the fret*

A tower.

BENCE, Thomas, Rector for over 50 years, died 1757. *Partridge, 102 (Darby, 1826) Palisaded tomb in churchyard, Carlton.* Edmund Bence, died 1672. *Her.Suff.Ch., Slab, Benhall.* John Bence, died 1718. *Ledger stone, Heveningham.* Thomas Bence, 50 years Rector of Carlton, died 1757. *Slab at east end of church, Carlton.* Edward Starkie Bence, of Kentwell Hall, Long Melford, died 1889. *Wall brass, Thorington*

A triple tower.

BESTNEY. Johanna, daughter of Edward Bestney, Esq., married Simon Steward. She died 1583. *Her.Suff.Ch., Wall tablet, Lakenheath*

A tower triple-towered Sable purfled Or.

CASTLE, of Parham. 'Castell' *MS Knight's Visitations, Cambs.** 'Castell of Cambs' *MS Heraldic Alphabet. Davy, A. (Edms.)*

A tower triple-towered.

LONGCHAMP. *Davy, A.*

A tower with a ladder leaning against the sinister side.

LUGG. 'Thomas Lugg of this parish, died 1748'; Others. *Partridge, 177 (Darby, 1825) Tomb in churchyard, Sternfield. E.A. Misc. 1926, 17*

A tower embattled against it a scaling ladder.

LUGG, of Sternfield. *Davy, A., Churchyard tomb. E.A. Misc. 1910, 104*

A triple-turreted tower and leaning thereto a scaling ladder.

LUGG, Thomas, died 1748; son Thomas Lugg, died 1791. *Her.Suff.Ch., Altar tomb in churchyard, Sternfield. Not found 1980*

A tower, or castle, of three towers chequy Or and Azure.

MARTIN. 'Sir Christopher Martin, of Bourton (? Burton), co. Cambridge.' Knighted at the Tower by K. James, 15 March 1604. Patent of Arms June 1604. *Grants & Certificates (Stowe MSS 707 and 714)*

A tower triple-towered chequy Or and Azure.

MARTIN, of Sudbourne. *MS Heraldic Collections, fo. 77b* Davy, A., church. E.A. Misc. 1911, 65*
A tower chequy Or and Azure.
MARTIN, Leicester, died 1732; wife Anne (Devereux). *Her.Suff.Ch., Hatchments, Sudbourne*
A tower.
MORRIS. Elizabeth, daughter of John Dade, M.D., married Bacon Morris, Esq., she died 1722. *Haslewood, II. E.A.N. & Q. IX. 380. Her.Suff.Ch., Slab, St. Matthew's, Ipswich. Not found 1979*
A tower Or from the top fire Proper.
PADDON. 'Robert Paddon, of Hinton Dawbeney, co. Hants.'; Grant by R. Cooke, Clar., in 1590. *Grants & Certificates (Harl. MS 1,359)*
A tower Or flammant Proper.
PADDON, of Bungay, Southwold. *Davy, A.*
A tower Or transfixed with six darts in saltire and inflamed Proper.
RUGGLES, of Clare. *Davy, A. Burke, L.G. 1853 ed.*

ON A TOWER

BEAST
A tower Argent on the battlements a lion couchant Ermine crowned Or.
SKRINE. 'John Skryne, of Warleigh in the parish of Bathford in Somerset'; Grant by Sir William Dugdale, Garter and Sir Henry St. George, Clarenceux, 8 November 1682. *Grants & Certificates (Stowe MS 677). Washbourne, 'Skrine, Somers. and Suss.'*
A tower Argent on the battlements thereof a lion combatant [*sic* ? rampant] Ermine ducally crowned Or.
SKRINE, of Gt. Finborough. *Davy, A.*

BIRD
On a tower Argent a dove rising Proper.
DOVE, of East Bergholt, Ipswich, Gosbeck, Scole, Stradbroke, Dallinghoo. *Visitation 1664–8. Davy, A.*
A tower Or over it a dove volant.
DOVE, of Barham. *Sharpe*
On a tower Argent a dove with wings expanded Proper.
DOVE, of Gosbeck. *Washbourne*, 'Suff.' E.A.N. & Q. V. 313.* John Dove, died 1753; Others. *Her.Suff.Ch., Ledger stone, Gosbeck*
On a broken tower Proper an eagle reguardant wings expanded Sable holding a millrind Sable.
TURNER, of Ipswich. *Sharpe*
On a tower Argent broken in the battlements an eagle reguardant with wings expanded Sable grasping in the dexter claw a millrind Sable.
TURNER, of Stoke by Ipswich, Ipswich. *Sharpe, Stonham Aspal church*

FLAG
On a tower Sable a flag Azure with the word 'Pax' Argent.
ALMACK, of Long Melford. *Davy, A.*
A tower Argent thereon a flag having inscribed on it 'Pax'.
ALMACK. *Washbourne, 'Suff.' Fairbairn, 'Suff.'*
A tower Proper with flag Gules.
CASTELIN, of Groton. *Davy, A.*
A tower Sable cupola and flag Gules.
ENGAINE, *Davy, A.*
A tower Proper ensigned with a flag Azure flotant to the sinister staff Sable.

HOXTON, of Hoxne. *Davy, A. Fairbairn, 'of Sutterton Hoxton [sic], Suff.'*
A tower with a flag flying from the summit.
POWELL. Thomas Harcourt Powell, of Drinkstone Park, died 1892. *Her.Suff.Ch., Tomb on south side of church, Drinkstone*

ISSUANT FROM TOWER

ARM
Out of a tower Or an arm in armour Argent garnished Or wielding in the gauntlet a dagger Argent hilt and pommel Or.
BEESTON. *MS Heraldic Alphabet*
Out of a tower a dexter arm embowed habited Azure holding in the hand Proper a sword Azure hilted Or.
BEESTON, of Sproughton, Ipswich. *Davy, A., Sproughton church*
Issuant from a tower an arm in armour wielding a scimitar all Proper.
FITZURSE, FITZOURSE. *Davy, A.*
Issuant from the battlements of a tower Proper a cubit arm erect vested and cuffed Or the hand Proper holding an antique lamp Sable fired Proper.
LUCAS. John Seymour Lucas, F.S.A., of London and Blythburgh, Suffolk. *Fairbairn*.* John Seymour-Lucas, died 1923. *Her.Suff.Ch., Wall tablet, Blythburgh*

BEAST
A tower Argent issuing therefrom a lion rampant Gules.
BEVERSHAM, of Holbrook Hall. *Davy, A.*
A tower Argent issuing therefrom a demi-lion rampant Gules.
BEVERSHAM. *Washbourne*, 'Suff.' Fairbairn*, 'of Holbrook Hall, Suff.'*
A tower triple-towered Argent port Sable a boar issuing therefrom Sable.
CANTRELL, of Bury. *Davy, A., Hemingstone church*
Out of a tower Gules a lion rampant issuant Argent.
HIGGENS, of Bury. *Davy, A.*
A tower Argent with a demi-lion rampant issuing from the battlements Or ducally gorged Gules holding between his paws a grenade fired Proper.
RATCLIFFE. *Davy, A.*
'his crest a demy lyon regardant or/ sa/ P pale holding in his pawes a sword ar/ garneshed or/ issant owt of a tower ar/'
SIMPSON. 'Sympson Under mareshall of Calles' *MS Alphabet of Crests, fo. 122*
A demi-lion rampant per pale Or and Sable holding in the dexter fore-paw a sword erect Sable arising from a tower Azure.
SIMPSON. Rear-Admiral C.H. Simpson and his wife. *Her.Suff.Ch., Wall tablet, Stoke-by-Nayland. Erected 1956*
Out of the top of a tower Gules a demi-lion rampant Or armed and langued of the second [*sic*].
SKINNER. 'John Skinner, of London, Sheriff of that City'; Confirmation by Sir W. Dethick, Garter, 29 September 1587. *Grants & Certificates (Stowe MS 676)*
Out of a tower Gules a lion rampant Or.
SKINNER. *MS Heraldic Alphabet*
A tower Azure portal Or issuing from the battlements thereof a demi-lion rampant Or ducally crowned Gules holding between his paws a ? Azure [unidentifiable object].

STANHOPE. 'Sr Mychaell Stanhope of Orfforde Knight of the Bathe' *MS Lilly's Visitation of Suffolk* *
A tower Argent issuing from the battlements thereof a demi-lion rampant Or ducally crowned Gules holding between his paws a grenade fired Proper.
STANHOPE, of Sudbourne. *Davy, A., church*
On a tower Azure a demi-lion issuant from the battlements Or ducally crowned Gules holding between the paws a grenade fired Proper.
STANHOPE, Sir Michael, Privy Councillor to Queen Elizabeth and King James. *Her.Suff.Ch., Effigy monument in chancel, Sudbourne*
A demi-lion issuing from a tower Sable, or Gules.
VERDON, of Martlesham, Brundish. *Davy, A.*
A demi-lion Gules issuing from a tower Sable.
VERDON. *Washbourne*
The upper part of a tower Azure therefrom a demi-lion issuing Or supporting a banner Argent charged with a cross Gules staff Proper.
WEDDALL. 'John Weddall, of Stepney, co. Midd., Captain of the 'Rainbow', a principal ship in the King's Navy, who did good service in the East during a voyage and employment before 1627'; Grant 3 May 1627 *Grants & Certificates (Add. MS 12,225)*

HEAD
A tower Argent issuing from the port a boar's head Sable.
CANTRELL, of Bury, Hemingstone. *Berkshire Visitation 1623 (H.S.) 77* Visitation 1664–8* MS Fairfax*
From a tower Proper a talbot's head Argent collared Vert ringed Or.
RICKARDS. Rector of Stowlangtoft. *Davy, A.*
Issuing from a tower Or a talbot's head Sable.
SHEPPARD. *Washbourne, 'Shepard, Sheppard, Suss. and Suff.' Fairbairn, 'Sheppard, of Campsey Ashe, Suff.'* John Sheppard, of Ash, died 1669; Lieut. Frederick Sheppard, died 1812. *Her.Suff.Ch., Wall monument and Altar tomb in churchyard, Campsea Ash*
A talbot's head Or issuing from a triple-turreted tower Sable.
SHEPPARD. Bridget, wife of Thomas Sheppard, gent., died 1748; daughter Dorothy, died 1752. *Her.Suff.Ch., Ledger stone, Wetheringsett cum Brockford*
In front of a demi-tower Gules issuant therefrom a boar's head Argent tusked and maned Or charged on the neck with a cross paty Gules and on the tower three crosses paty Argent.
WHITE. 'Eaton White, J.P., of Boulge Hall, Woodbridge, Suff.' *Fairbairn* * [garbled blazon, see illustration for clarity]

HUMAN FIGURE
Out of a tower a demi-man in armour in profile holding in the dexter hand a sword by the blade erect.
LONDON. *Washbourne*. William London, of Quay House, Woodbridge. *Fairbairn*
A man issuing from a tower holding an arrow in his right hand and a shield in the left.
NEVILL, Isaac, died 1768; Others. *Her.Suff.Ch., Slab in chancel, Lavenham*
A tower Argent from the top thereof issuing a demi-Moor Sable wreathed about the head Argent and Azure in mail Proper on the left arm an oval shield Or in the dexter hand an arrow Sable headed and feathered Argent.

WISEMAN. 'Thomas Wiseman, third son of John Wiseman of Canfield, co Essex; Exemplification by Rouge Crois 1586.' [Ralph Brooke, Rouge Croix]. *Grants & Certificates (Harl. MS 1,359; Stowe MS 670)*

VARIOUS
A tower Gules out of the top a demi-dragon Or.
BOWYER. 'R. . . Bowyer, Esq., son of William Bowyer, of co. Stafford'; Grant 18 Elizabeth [1575/6]. *Grants & Certificates*
A tower per bend indented Argent and Gules from the battlements flames issuant Proper.
HOPKINS, of Alderton, Hinton. *Davy, A.*
Out of a tower a demi-griffin Proper.
KERDISTON, of Henham. *Davy, A.*
A tower Or flames issuing from the top Proper behind the tower four arrows in saltire Argent.
RUGGLES. *Washbourne* *, 'Ess. and Suff.' Fairbairn, 'of Spain's Hall, Essex and Clare, Suff.'*

TREE [Alphabetically by name]
On the trunk of a tree lying fesseways Or a fleur-de-lis Azure between two sprigs Vert.
ATWOOD, of Suffolk. *Davy, A.*
On the stump of a tree couped a stork close all Proper.
BANKS, of Metfield. *MS Ordinary of Arms, fo. 226*, the stump issuing leaves from both sides. Davy, A.*
On the stump of a tree a pelican Or vulning herself Gules, or Proper.
BRIGGES, BRYGGES, of Euston. *MS Heraldic Alphabet. Davy, A.*
A stump of a tree erased raguly and couped [*sic*].
BURLZ. *Davy, A.*
On the trunk of a tree raguly Or a falcon close Gules.
FRANK. 'Thomas Francke of hatfeild Bodoke' *MS Philpot's Visitations, Essex* *
A goat rampant Argent attired Or supporting the stump of a tree Proper with a branch sprouting from it Vert.
GURDON. *Davy, A.*
A falcon close Argent beaked legged and belled Or standing on the branch of a tree couped and raguly Or.
HEWETT, Bart., of Brightwell Hall. *Davy, A.*
A buck salient Proper attired Or among leaves and the trunk of a tree also Proper.
HITCHAM, of Framlingham. *Loder, 304, Tomb in church. Copinger IV. 282*
On a mount Proper a greyhound sejant Argent collared and lined Or the line reflexed over the back and in front of a tree Proper.
KYNARDESLEY. 'Kinardby' *MS Ordinary of Arms, fo. 30* *
A tree Vert in the midst of its branches a pelican Or.
LEMAN, of Charsfield, Wenhaston. *Bokenham*
A pelican in her piety Or under a tree Vert fructed Or.
LEMAN, of Ipswich. *E.A.N. & Q. XII. 130, Monument, St. Stephen's church, Ipswich*
On the stump of a tree erased Proper a martlet Sable.
LOCKWOOD. Vicar of Lowestoft. *Druery, 269, Glass in church*
A martlet sitting on the stump of a tree between two branches all Proper.
LOCKWOOD. Vicar of Yoxford and Lowestoft. *Davy, A.*
Upon the stump of a tree eradicated Proper

surmounted by an anchor in bend sinister Or a martin-cat sejant supporting between the paws a mirror Proper and gorged with a naval crown therefrom a chain reflexed over the back Or.

MARTIN. 'Major-General William G. Martin, of Hemingstone, Ipswich, Suffolk; Col. Sir Richard Martin, of Aldeburgh, Suff.' *Fairbairn**

Upon the stump of a tree eradicated Proper surmounted by a martin cat sejant supporting between the paws a mirror also Proper and gorged with a naval crown thereon a chain reflexed over the back Or.

MARTIN, of Hemingstone Hall. *Burke, L.G. 1900 and 1952 eds.*

A tree.

PINE, Horace, died 1770. *Her.Suff.Ch., Ledger stone, Nacton*

A dead tree erased at the roots and erect Proper.

PLAYNE, PLAINE, of Sudbury, Preston. *Visitation 1612. MS Fairfax (Tyl.) Davy, A. Washbourne, 'Playne, Suff.' Fairbairn, 'Playne, Sudbury, Suff. a withered tree'*

A bull with tail erect standing before a leafless tree whose trunk is divided into two branches.

RIDLEY. Sir Jasper Ridley, son of 1st Viscount Ridley, died 1951; son Patrick Conrad Ridley, died 1952; widow Nathalie, died 1968. *Her.Suff.Ch., Tombstone in the churchyard, Claydon*

On the stump of a tree raguly and branched Proper a falcon volant Or.

THURSTON, of Wenham. *Bokenham*

A talbot couchant guardant against a tree all Proper.

TOPSFIELD, of Fressingfield, Gislingham. *Davy, A., Fressingfield church. Washbourne, 'Suff. and Norf.'*

A tree.

UHTHOFF. Rector of Huntingfield and Cookley. *Davy, A.*

A doe couchant at the foot of a tree all Proper.

USBORNE, of Branches Hall in Cowlinge. *Davy, A., church*

On the stump of a tree erased a stag statant collared and lined.

WIGHTMAN. *MS Ordinary of Arms, fo. 250**

On the stump of a tree Proper a buck trippant Argent collared chained and attired Or.

WIGHTMAN, of Framlingham, Cransford, Saxted, Clare. *Wightman, 16*, 19, 106*, etc.**

Against a tree leaved Vert fructed Or, or Proper, a wolf passant Or.

WOLVERSTON, WOLFERSTON, WOLVESTON, of Wolverston, Culpho. *Harl. 772* Davy, A. Washbourne, 'Wolverstone, Suff. and Staff. tree Proper'*

A wolf passant tied to a tree [*sic*].

WOLVERSTON. 'Wolferston' *MS Martin's Crests*

Leaning against a tree Vert a wolf Or.

WOLVERSTON. 'Wolverton' *MS Heraldic Alphabet*

ASH

'An ashe plant' erased at the roots erect and leaved Proper.

PLAYNE. 'Apollo Playne of Sudbury' *MS Knight's Visitations, Suff.**

BAY

A hound reguardant lying down against a bay tree Proper.

TOPPESFIELD, of Fressingfield. *Bokenham*

BEECH

A beech tree Proper within a row of pales Or.

BEACHCROFT. 'Beechcroft' *MS Martin's Crests*

A beech tree Proper behind six park pales Or.

BEACHCROFT, of Preston, Kettlebaston. *Davy, A.*

HAZEL

A branch of a tree barways Vert thereon a squirrel Gules cracking a nut Or between two sprigs of hazel nuts Vert fructed Or.

CRESWELL. *Davy, A. Washbourne, 'of Northamp.'*

A nut tree Proper the trunk raguly, on either side a squirrel salient Gules.

LITTLER. *Davy, A. Washbourne*, 'Litler, Littler.'*

HOLLY

A holly tree Vert fructed Gules.

HOLMES, of Stowmarket, South Elmham All Saints and St. Nicholas, Fressingfield Hall, etc. *Davy, A. Crisp's Visitation XIX. 204–5*

'to his crest a ffagot of holly Vert w^t the Beryes g/ alibi blased a bush of holly'

STRICKLAND. 'Stryckland' *MS Alphabet of Crests, fo. 116*

A holly bush fructed Proper.

STRICKLAND, of Reydon near Southwold. *Davy, A.*

LAUREL

A talbot statant reguardant Argent in front of a laurel tree Vert.

TOPESFIELD. 'Symond Toppesfeld' *MS Knight's Visitations, Norf.**

A talbot couchant reguardant Argent against a laurel tree Vert.

TOPESFIELD, of Essex. 'Symond Toppsfild' *MS Philpot's Visitations, Suff.* MS Heraldic Alphabet*

LEMON

A lemon tree Vert fructed Or therein a pelican Argent on its nest of the last [Argent].

LEMAN, John, of London, Alderman; Patent 25 January 1615. *Grants & Certificates (Harl. MS 6,059; Stowe MS 706)*

In a lemon tree Proper a pelican in her nest Or feeding her young Proper.

LEMAN, of Wenhaston, Brampton, Bury. *Visitation 1664–8. Davy, A., St. Stephen's church, Ipswich. Fairbairn, 'Brampton Hall, Suff.' Robert Leman, died 1637. Her.Suff.Ch., Effigy Monument, St. Stephen's, Ipswich*

In a lemon tree a pelican in her piety.

LEMAN, of Wenhaston, 1672–1735. *Her.Suff.Ch., Ledger stones, Wenhaston. 'N.T.O. Leman, Clerk' Glass, Wrentham. Recorded by Farrer, all Proper*

In a lemon tree a pelican in her nest feeding her young all Proper.

LEMAN, of Brampton, 1640–1837. *Her.Suff.Ch., Wall monument and Ledger stones, Brampton.* Matthew Leman, died 1678; Charles Leman, died 1687; Matthew Leman, died 1692. *Ledger stones, Beccles.* William Leman, died 1730. *Wall tablet, Charsfield*

In a lemon tree leaved and fructed Proper a pelican Argent feeding her young in a nest Proper.

LEMAN, Rev. Naunton T. Orgill (later Leman), died 1837. *Her.Suff.Ch., Hatchment, Charsfield*

OAK

A stump of an oak tree couped and erased from the top issuing flames of fire from the sinister side a

sprig with one acorn and leaves all Proper.
> BRANDLING, of Ipswich. *Davy, A., St. Clement's church.* 'Brandling 1683' *Her.Suff.Ch., Glass shield formerly in window of chancel, Hacheston. Not found 1982*

A wild boar sticking between the cleft of an oak tree fructed all Proper with a lock and chain holding the cleft together Azure.
> DOUGLAS, of Halesworth. Vicar of Kenton. *Davy, A.*

In front of an oak tree Proper a beehive Or.
> NUNN, of Bury. *Davy, A.*

An oak tree fenced round.
> OAKES. James Oakes, Esq., of Bury, died 1829. *Tymms, 195, Biography, Wall tablet, St. Mary's church*

An oak tree Proper the trunk enclosed in a circular iron palisade.
> OAKES, of Bury, Nowton. *Davy, A. Bookplate**

An oak tree Proper fructed Or encircled with palisades.
> OAKES, of Nowton Court near Bury. *Burke, L.G. 1853 and 1900 eds. Fairbairn, 'of Newton [sic] Court, Suff.'*

An oak tree Proper fructed Argent surrounded by a palisade Or.
> OAKES. 'J.H. Porteous Oakes' *Her.Suff.Ch., Glass, St. Mary's, Bury*

An oak within pales all Proper.
> OAKES, James, died 1829. *Her.Suff.Ch., tablet, St. Mary's, Bury.* Charles Tyrell Oakes, of East Bergholt, died 1846. *Wall tablet, East Bergholt*

A stump of an oak tree couped and sprouting leaves all Proper.
> RODDAM. George Roddam, M.D., Naval Physician and to the Royal Family, died at Aldeburgh, 1838; widow died 1884. *Her.Suff.Ch., Hatchment recorded by Farrer, Falkenham. Not found 1982*

An oak Proper.
> STISTED. 'Stysted, of Ipswich, Kesgrave' *Bokenham*

An oak tree erased Vert acorned Or.
> WOOD. *MS Heraldic Alphabet*

PALM

A palm tree Proper.
> STISTED, of Kesgrave, Ipswich. *Visitation 1664–8. MS Fairfax (Mr. Candler) Davy, A. Washbourne*, 'Stysted, Suff.', untinctured. Fairbairn*, 'Stysted of Kisgrave [sic], & Ipswich, Suff.', untinctured*

PINE

A pine tree Proper.
> BERTIE, Lord Willoughby of Eresby. *Davy, A.*

A pine tree Vert fructed Or.
> PINE. 'Pyne' *MS Heraldic Alphabet*

A pine tree with fruit all Proper.
> PINE, of Nacton. *Sharpe*

PLANE

A plane tree dead without leaves.
> PLAYNE. 'Apollo playne of Sudbery' *MS Philpot's Visitations, Suff.*, the tree couped. Bokenham*

ROSE

A rose tree bearing roses Proper.
> LIMESI, LINDESEI, LYNDSEY, of Cavendish. *Davy, A.*

VINE

A buck and vine both Proper.
> BRADSHAIGH. *MS Heraldic Alphabet*

TWO TREES

Two ? stumps of trees in saltire enfiled with a ducal coronet.
> REYCE, RYECE, of Preston. *Davy, A., church*

Two stems of trees raguly in saltire enfiled with a ducal coronet.
> REYCE. Robert Ryece, died 1638. *Her.Suff.Ch., Brass in sacrarium, Preston*

TRIANGLE

'On a Helmet a Torse argent and gules, a Triangle, argent, above the upper angle an Estoile or, mantelled gules, doubled, argent'
> FISKE. 'Nicholas ffiske, of Studhaw in the Parish of Laxfield in the countie of Suffolk Professor in Phisick, son of Mathew Fiske of the same, son of William, son of Thomas, son of William Ffyske of Studhaw aforesaid that lived in the raignes of King Henry the sixt, Edward the iiij Richard the third and King Henry the 7th'; Confirmation of Arms and Grant of Crest by Sir W. Segar, Garter, 16 November 1633. *Grants & Certificates (Add. MS 12,225; Stowe MS 703). MS Suffolk Armorial Families*. Fiske, 67–8**

A triangle Argent on the apex an estoile Or.
> FISKE, of Studhaw in Laxfield. *Addit.Suff.Peds. Washbourne*, 'Fyshe, Suff. and Herts.' Fairbairn*, 'Fyshe, Suff. and Herts.'*

A triangle Argent voided and surmounted with an estoile Or.
> FISKE. Of Clopton Hall in Rattlesden, 1684–1799. *Her.Suff.Ch., Floor slabs, Rattlesden*

A triangle voided surmounted by an estoile of six points Or.
> FISKE, of Rattlesden, Shimpling, Laxfield. *Davy, A., Rattlesden church*

A triangle erected Sable on the vertex an estoile Proper.
> FISKE. *Washbourne*, 'Suff.' Fairbairn*, 'Suff.'*

A triangle erected Or on the vertex an estoile Proper.
> FISKE. Rev. John Fiske, A.M., Rector of Thorpe Morieux, died 1778. *Her.Suff.Ch., Wall tablet in chancel, Thorpe Morieux*

A triangle erected on the vertex a mullet (estoile) Sable.
> FISKE. Susan, wife of Rev. John Fiske, Rector of Shimpling, died 1797. *Her.Suff.Ch., Wall tablet, Shimpling*

TRUMPET see HORN

TUN [Barrel]

On a tun Or a crow Proper holding in its beak a rose branch Proper.
> BRAMPTON, BRAMSTON. *Davy, A.*

On a tun Or a dove Proper holding in its beak a branch Vert fructed Gules.
> BRAMPTON, BRAMSTON. *Davy, A.* 'Thomas Brampton, gent., died 1712.' *Her.Suff.Ch., Ledger stone, Eye.* This crest [not the lion sejant as on the stone, q.v.], *stated to be for Brampton of London*

WALL

An embattled wall on it a stag's head Or.
> SAY, Lord *Davy, A.*

WELL

Out of a well Or a branch of columbine stalked and leaved Vert flowered Proper.

GOLDWELL, GOULDWELL, of Bury. *MS Ordinary of Arms, fo. 21*, two branches, the flowers Gules. Davy, A. Fairbairn, 'Gouldwell, Bury St. Edmunds, Suff. and Wisbeach [sic], Cambs.'*
A golden well.

GOLDWELL. *Bokenham*
A golden well with a bunch of leaves and flowers placed in it.

GOLDWELL, James, Bishop of Norwich 1472– 98. *Blomefield's Norfolk. III. 540*

WHEEL

A Catherine wheel Gules between two wings erect per fesse Argent and Gules.

DREYER, of Coney Weston. *Davy, A., church*
A wheel Proper.

HASTED, HAWSTEAD, of Bury, Hawstead. *Davy, A. (Burke)*
A mill wheel Or.

MOLINS. *MS Martin's Crests*

WING [Alphabetically by name]

A wing pierced with an arrow Or.

BARTHROPP, of Hacheston, Cretingham. *Davy, A.*
A single wing extended Gules thereon a chevron Argent charged with a lion rampant Sable crowned Or.

BROOK, of Allington. *Bokenham*
A wing erect.

COLLINS. *Davy, A.*
'upon his healme on a Torce gould & azure an Angells winge gules'

CONYERS. 'Sr George Conyers Knight'; Grant of Arms and Crest by Gilbert Dethick, Norroy, 18 May 1548. *Miscellaneous Grants (H.S.) I. 54–5 (Harl. MS 1507, fo. 450)*
A wing Gules.

CONYERS. *MS Ordinary of Arms, fo. 251**
A sinister wing erect per pale Argent and Or.

EDMONDS, of Suffolk. *Davy, A.*
A wing erect per pale Or and Argent.

EDMONDS. *Washbourne, 'Lond. and Suff.'*
A wing erect.

HENGRAVE, HEMGRAVE, of Hengrave. *Davy, A.*
A sinister wing erect – charged with a chevron Gules.

HETHERSET, of about Buxhall. *Davy, A.*
'And to his Creast upon a healme or, a Wreath silver & sable a Wing Argent with a pale as in his Armes thereon [on a pale Sable three crescents Argent], mantled gules dubled Argent.'

HEYWARD. 'Edward Heyward, of the Inner Temple London Gent . . . . the Sonne of Richard Heyward of Kerdeston in the County of Norff. Gent.'; Confirmation of Arms and Crest by William Camden, Clarenceux, 21 June 1611. *Misc.Gen. et Her. 5th S. X. 12 (Soc. of Ant. MS 378, fo. 471). Grants & Certificates (Stowe MSS 706 and 707; Harl. MS 6,059)*
On a wing a pale charged with three crescents.

HEYWARD, of Norfolk. *MS Heraldic Collections, fo. 86**
On a wing Argent a pale Sable charged with three crescents Argent.

HEYWARD, of Bury. *Davy, A.*
On a wing Argent a pale Sable charged with three crescents Argent.

HOWARD, of Brundish. *Davy, A.*
A wing per pale indented Sable and Ermine.

MACKWORTH, Bart. *MS Martin's Crests. Davy, A.*
A dexter wing per pale dancetty Sable and Ermine.

MACKWORTH-PRAED, of Ousden Hall. *Burke, L.G. 1952 ed.**
An eagle's wing Sable semy de lis Or vulned Proper pierced by an arrow embrued in bend point upwards.

PEARSON. Vicars of Henley, 1850–94; 1894–. 'Rev. William Pearson, Henley Vicarage; Rev. Arthur Pearson, Ringsfield, Beccles, Suff.' *Fairbairn. Crisp's Visitation. XV. 164**

WINGS [Alphabetically by name]

A 'moreans' [*sic* called variously Moor or Satyr] head between two wings 'in maner of devylles wyngs' Sable.

BAWDE. 'Baud of Essex' *Wall's Book*
'to his crest a moryans hede betw ii wyngs in manner of dyvelles wyngs sa/'

BAWDE. 'Bawde of Essex' *MS Alphabet of Crests, fo. 8*
A Blackamoor's head couped at the shoulders with a pair of dragon's wings conjoined to his neck.

BAWDE. 'Baud' *MS Martin's Crests*
A Satyr's head in profile Sable wings to it and the tongue hanging out of the mouth.

BAWDE, of Bures. *Davy, A.*
Two wings erect Argent.

BELLMAN, of Helmingham, Earl Soham. *Davy, A.*
Two wings endorsed Argent on each a chevron engrailed Sable charged with a chaplet Or.

BRIDGE. *Davy, A.*
Two wings one Or the other Gules.

CLOPTON, of Clopton. 'Clopton of Kentwell' *MS Lilly's Visitation of Suffolk*, second of four crests drawn. Davy, A.*
In front of two wings Argent each charged with an estoile Azure a rock Proper thereon a caltrap Or.

COLMAN, of Corton. *Crisp's Visitation. VIII. 142*, 148*. Bookplate*, caltrap untinctured*
Two wings conjoined Proper.

DESPENSER, Earl of Gloucester. Of Clare. *Davy, A.*
Two wings displayed and elevated Or.

D'EYE, of Eye. *Bokenham. E.A.N. & Q. I. 312, Ledger stones and Monument, Eye*
Two wings joined in lure Or and Azure.

D'EYE. *Proc.S.I.A. II. 146, 'wings joined in lever' [sic]*
Two wings expanded Or.

D'EYE. Mary (Cowper), married Nathaniel D'Eye, died 1749. *Her.Suff.Ch., Hatchment, Eye*
A Catherine wheel Gules between two wings erect per fesse Argent and Gules.

DREYER, of Coney Weston. *Davy, A.*
A horse-shoe Sable between two wings Argent.

FARRER, of Cratfield. *Davy, A.*
A horse-shoe Argent between two wings Or.

FARRER. *Davy, A.*
Two wings conjoined Proper.

FITZRAYNOLD, of Suffolk. *Davy, A.*
Two wings displayed Azure semy of stars Or.

GIPPS, of Horringer, Gt. Whelnetham. *Bokenham*
Two wings addorsed Or.

GRAHAM, of Holbrook Hall, Waldingfield. *MS Ordinary of Arms, fo. 207*. Davy, A., Waldingfield church*
Two wings extended sideways.

GRAHAM. *MS Martin's Crests*
Two wings addorsed Or.

HOSTE. *Washbourne*, 'Suff.' Fairbairn*, 'Suff.'*
A stag's head with two wings behind it.

LIFE, of Brandon. *Davy, A., churchyard*
A stag's head couped and winged.
  LIFE, Caesar, gent., died 1739; wife Martha
  (Bedingfield), died 1736. *Partridge, 117 (Darby, 1829), Brandon churchyard*
Three [*sic*] wings erect Argent one behind another the outer one charged with two mullets Gules.
  PENRICE, of Yarmouth, Hopland Hall. *Davy, A.*
A wing elevated surmounting another Argent the former charged with two mullets of six points in pale Gules.
  PENRICE. Washbourne, 'of Yarmouth, Norf. and Hopland Hall, Suff.' *Fairbairn, 'of Great Yarmouth, Norf.'*
Two wings sideways.
  PEYTO. *MS Martin's Crests*
Two wings addorsed and erect.
  PEYTO. 'S. Morton Peto' [Bart. added].
  Bookplates*
A ? griffin's head erased in front of a pair of wings addorsed.
  POSTLE. Elizabeth (Betts), wife of Jehosophat Postle, gent., of Norwich. She died 1777.
  Her.Suff.Ch., Ledger stone, Wortham
Two wings conjoined Azure.
  REEVE, of Oulton. *Davy, A.*

Two wings conjoined in lure Or ensigned by a ducal coronet Or.
  SEYMOUR. *MS Ordinary of Arms, fo. 200*. MS Heraldic Collections, fo. 15* Washbourne*
Two wings displayed and elevated Argent.
  WINGFIELD. *Bokenham*

WOOLPACK
A woolpack, or a cushion tasselled.
  STEBBING, George, died 1733; Others.
  Her.Suff.Ch., Ledger stone, Framsden

WREATH see also CHAPLET, GARLAND
Out of a wreath of laurel Or a horse's head paly of six Sable and Argent.
  LLOYD, LLOYD-ANSTRUTHER, of Hintlesham Hall. *Burke, L.G. 1900 ed.*
A dexter arm in armour erect Argent garnished Or out of a wreath Vert bound with a ribbon in the centre of the arm Sable holding in the gauntlet a battle-axe Argent handle Gules garnished Or.
  WORLICHE, of Cowlinge. *Davy, A.*

YOKE
An ox yoke Or.
  FYNDERNE, of Wiston. *Davy, A., Haverhill church*

Egleston to his Crest a hummers hed rased fayrd a
coller or fire of forbeare in a voreth or g m ag d

Egerlon to his crest a park hed arsed or voreth ar/a
m g d or

Egertoun to his crest a Bores hede raboffed ar on a
voreth or 6 m g d or

Edon of Bury in Suff to his crest a demy Lyzard in
his coullors foting in his parret a Buff of haforme brst
fflowers in on a voreth or g m g d ar

Edard g yotefger knyght or g d to his crest a catte pafant
or o yurferly in a voreth or fa m g d ar

Effer knyght or g d to his crest a demy greffon the voynge
rloff or foldyng in his oft a greffens legge rafed g
fe fote donward in a voreth or fa m 6 d ar

Efyngote to his crest a armis & foldyng up heir fude
or on a voreth or g m 6 d ar

Edward y Suff to his crest a maub hed yferour a
roff cryff a back his gris g an albonays fat or
frotid fa

Eldorton to his crest y Salamonders in doffd 6 or
out of a Crovone Jnterganged f or c ye flyms g the
faylds enterganged affo g rafe

SOURCES

Addit.Suff.Peds.
Additional Suffolk Pedigrees, contained in
Harl. MSS 1560 and 1449. Appendix to the
Visitations of Suffolk, 1561, 1577 and 1612.
Edited by Walter Metcalfe, F.S.A. 1882
MS Alphabet of Crests [Corder MS 05]
Copy, the last entry dated 1580, of *Wall's
Book of Crests of 1530* [q.v.] Greatly
enlarged and possibly in the hand of
William Flower, Norroy King of Arms from
1562 until appointed a Poor Knight of
Windsor in 1580 when he might well have
gone into semi-retirement; he died in 1588
aged about 90, being succeeded as Norroy
in 1590 by Edmund Knight [*Knight's
Visitations,* q.v.] Another likely compiler of
this MS is Hugh Cotgrave, Richmond
Herald from 1566 to death in 1584
Bacon.
*The False Pedigree & Arms of the Family
of Bacon of Suffolk.* Walter Rye. 1919
Badham.
*The History and Antiquities of All Saints
Church, Sudbury.* Rev. Charles Badham,
M.A. 1852
Banners & Standards.
*Banners Standards and Badges from a
Tudor manuscript in the College of Arms.*
Edited by Lord Howard de Walden;
published as a volume of The De Walden
Library. 1904
Barlow.
Barlow Family Records. Rt. Hon. Sir
Montague Barlow, Bart., K.B.E., LL.D.
1932
Mr. Barnwell.
Rev. Frederick Henry Turnor Barnwell, of
Bury, F.R.S., F.S.A. 1770–1843. Received
Grant of Arms and Crest in 1826. See *The
Topographers of Suffolk.*
Barrett.
Jos. Barrett, compiler of MS of Suffolk
Pedigrees and Arms; internal note dated
1773. See *E.A.N. & Q. IX. 57*
Bedford, 1st and 2nd eds.
The Blazon of Episcopacy. Rev. W.K. Riland
Bedford, M.A. First ed., 1858; 2nd ed., 1897
Berkshire Visits., 1532, 1566, 1623, 1665–6.
The Four Visitations of Berkshire. Edited by
W. Harry Rylands, F.S.A. Harleian Society.
Two volumes, 1907 and 1908
Berkshire Visit., 1664–6.
The Visitation of Berkshire 1664–6. Edited by
Walter C. Metcalfe, F.S.A. 1882
Berry.
Encyclopaedia Heraldica. William Berry.
Three volumes. 1828

Betts.
*The Betts of Wortham in Suffolk,
1480–1905.* Katherine Frances Doughty.
1912
Bildeston.
*Materials for a History of the Parish of
Bildeston.* Frederic Salmon Growse, M.A.
1892
**Blois MS [Corder MS 24. A photographic
copy of SRO Ipswich GC17:755]**
*The Arms of All the Antient Families in
Suffolk.* William Blois of Grundisburgh,
1600–1673. See *Proc.S.I.A. XIV. 147– 226;
Topographers of Suffolk.*
Blomef.
*Topographical History of the County of
Norfolk.* Rev. Francis Blomefield,
1705–1752. Eleven volumes, three
completed by Rev. Charles Parkin after
Blomefield's death. 1805–10. See *Norfolk
Archaeology. II. 201; Topographers of
Suffolk.*
Blomfield Family.
*A Suffolk Family, Being an Account of the
Family of Blomfield in Suffolk.* Reginald
Blomfield, R.A. 1916
Bohun.
*The Diary and Autobiography of Edmund
Bohun Esq.* S. Wilton Rix. 1853
**Bokenham [Corder MSS 33 and 43. From
transcripts made by Hugh Stanford
London]**
*An Alphabetical List of ye Arms & Crests of
ye Gentry in ye County of Norfolk as well
Ancient as Modern. Part ye 1st. As also of
ye Arms of ye Gentry of Suffolk. Part ye
2nd. Collected from ye Best Authors & most
Authentick Manuscripts.* Rev. Joseph
Bokenham, Rector of Stoke Ash, Lt.
Thornham and Market Weston. Died 1728.
See *E.A.N. & Q. IX. 11–12*
Bokenham Family.
*Notes and Extracts from numerous
authorities respecting the Family of
Bukenham or Bokenham, of Norfolk and
Suffolk.* Henry Maudslay and W.P. Ivatts.
1884
Booty.
The Booty Family. Harold Booty. 1951
Bright.
The Brights of Suffolk, England. J.B.
Bright. Boston, 1858
Bucks. Visitation, 1634.
*The Visitation of the County of Buckingham
made in 1634 by John Philipot, Esq.,
Somerset Herald and William Ryley,
Bluemantle Pursuivant . . . Together with*

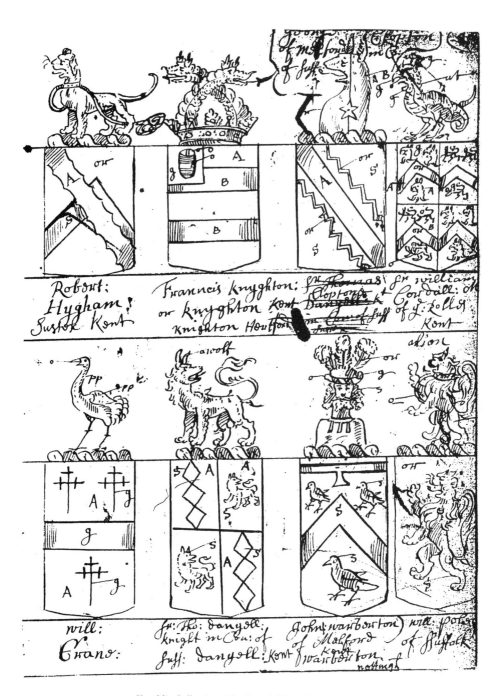

Robert:
Hygham:
Suffok Kent

Franncis knyghton: Sr Thomas   S^r william
or knyghton Kent Cloptone + Cordall: oF
knighton Houfton   Kon^t of suff of y^e Rolla
                                        Kent

will:
Crane

S^r: Tho: danyell: John: warburton will: pole
knight m Con: of   of Malford   of Suffolk
suff: danyell: Kent warburton
                    nottingh

Heraldic Collections [Corder MS 11] p. 54 (upper part)

Pedigrees from the Visitation made in 1566 by William Harvey, Esq., Clarenceux. Edited by W. Harry Rylands, F.S.A. Harleian Society. 1909

Burke Ill. Her. Illust.
Illuminated Heraldic Illustrations, with Annotations. Sir Bernard Burke, Ulster King of Arms. 1856

Burke, L.G., 1853 ed.
Genealogical and Heraldic Dictionary of the Landed Gentry of Great Britain and Ireland. J. Bernard Burke. 1853

Burke, L.G., 1900 ed.
A Genealogical and Heraldic History of the Landed Gentry of Great Britain. Edited by Sir Bernard Burke, C.B., LL.D., Ulster King of Arms. 1900

Burke, L.G., 1952 ed.
Burke's Genealogical and Heraldic History of the Landed Gentry. Edited by L.G. Pine, F.S.A. Scot., F.R.S.A. 1952

Burke, Peerage, 1891 ed.
A Genealogical and Heraldic Dictionary of the Peerage and Baronetage. Edited by Sir Bernard Burke, C.B., LL.D., Ulster King of Arms. 1891

Burrell Coll.Cat.
Stained and Painted Heraldic Glass in the Burrell Collection. The Corporation of the City of Glasgow; Art Gallery and Museum Catalogue. 1962

Caerlaverock Poem.
The Siege of Carlaverock, in the XXVIII Edward I. A.D.MCCC; with the Arms of the Earls, Barons, and Knights, who were present on the occasion; with a translation, a history of the castle, and memoirs of the personages commemorated by the poet. Nicholas Harris Nicholas. 1828

Cambs. Visits., 1575 & 1619.
The Visitation of Cambridge Made in A.^{0} 1575 . . . Wth the Vissitation of the same County made by Henery St George . . . in A.^{0} 1619. Edited by John W. Clay, F.S.A. Harleian Society. 1897

Candler.
Matthias Candler, 1604–1663; son Philip Candler, died 1689. Father was Vicar of Coddenham from 1629; son was Headmaster of Woodbridge School from 1670. Both compilers of extensive MS collections of Church and Parish notes, Norfolk and Suffolk pedigrees, etc. See *Topographers of Suffolk.*

Chesh.
The Vale Royall of England, or the County Palatine of Chester Illustrated. Daniel King, engraver. 1656

Coe.
Robert Coe, Puritan. His Ancestors and Descendants, 1340–1910. J. Gardner Bartlett. 1911

Colvile.
History of the Colvile Family. Sir Charles, Charles Robert and Zélie Colvile. 1896

Copinger.
The Manors of Suffolk. W.A. Copinger, M.A., LL.D., F.S.A., F.R.S.A. Seven volumes. 1905–1911

Copinger Family.
History of the Copingers or Coppingers of the County of Cork, Ireland, and the Counties of Suffolk and Kent, England. Walter Arthur Copinger. 1883–4

Corbould.
The Corbould Genealogy. George C.B. Poulter. 1935

Cotman.
Engravings of Sepulchral Brasses in Norfolk and Suffolk. John Sell Cotman. Two volumes. 1839

Crisp's Visitation.
Visitation of England and Wales. Edited by Joseph Jackson Howard, LL.D., Maltravers Herald Extraordinary and Frederick Arthur Crisp. Twenty one volumes. 1893–1921

Dade MS [Corder MS 63]
Collection of rough notes, brass rubbings, extracts from Davy's church notes, letters to Dr. J.J. Howard relating to the family of Dade, etc. See below

Dade.
Genealogical Memoranda relating to the Family of Dade of Suffolk. Anonymous [Dr J.J. Howard] 1888

Darby.
Rev. John Wareyn Darby, 1791–1846. Vicar of Wicklewood, Norfolk 1823; Rector of Shottisham, Suffolk 1832. Transcribed monumental inscriptions in Suffolk churches in the 1820s., the churchyard inscriptions later published by Charles Partridge [q.v.] See *Topographers of Suffolk.*

Davy, A. [Corder MSS Extra 1 & 2]
David Elisha Davy, 1769–1851. Of Yoxford and Ufford. Receiver General for Suffolk from 1795. Compiler of vast MS collections relating to Suffolk, now in the B.L. His *Armoury of Suffolk*, Add. MS 19,158 [Corder MS Extra I., microfilm and photographic copies] is dated 1848. See *Topographers of Suffolk* and *A Journal of Excursions through the County of Suffolk 1823–1844*, edited by John Blatchly; Suffolk Records Society volume 24. 1982

Debenham.
A Record of the Family of Debenham of Suffolk. Walter Debenham Sweeting, M.A. 1909

Druery.
Historical and Topographical notices of Great Yarmouth in Norfolk; and the half Hundred of Lothingland in Suffolk. John Henry Druery. 1826

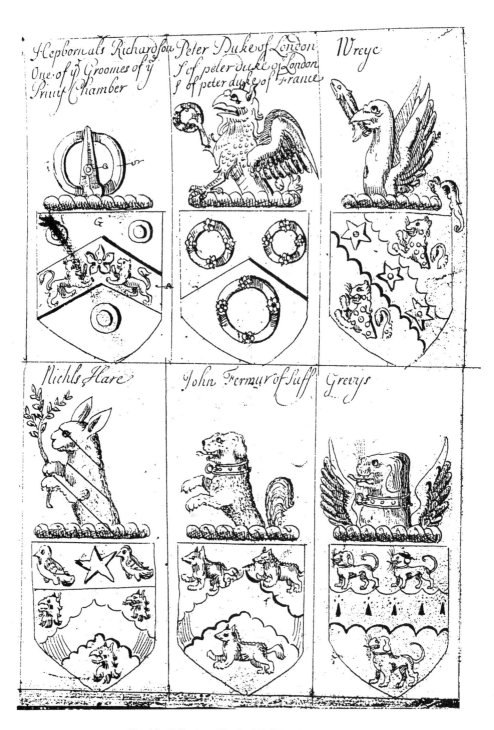

Heraldic Collections [Corder MS 11] fo. 87 (lower part)

Dugdale's Visit. of Yorkshire.
Dugdale's Visitation of Yorkshire. Edited by
J.W. Clay, F.S.A. Three volumes.
1899–1917

Durham Visits. (Foster).
*Durham Visitation Pedigrees; 1575, 1615 &
1666.* Edited by Joseph Foster. 1887

E.A. Misc.
*East Anglian Miscellany upon matters of
History, Genealogy etc. relating to East
Anglia.* Reprinted from the *East Anglian
Daily Times.* 1907–1935. [Work actually
commenced 1901, complete sets in SRO]

E.A.N. & Q.
*The East Anglian; or Notes and Queries on
subjects connected with the Counties of
Suffolk, Cambridge, Essex & Norfolk.*
Original series, vols. 1–4; edited by Samuel
Tymms, F.S.A., F.G.H.S. 1864–9. New
series, vols. 1–13; edited by C.H. Evelyn
White, F.S.A., F.R.Hist.S. 1885–1910

E. Counties Collectanea.
*The Eastern Counties Collectanea: being
Notes and Queries on subjects relating to
the counties of Norfolk, Suffolk, Essex and
Cambridge.* Edited by John L'Estrange.
1872–3

Edms.
The Complete Body of Heraldry. Joseph
Edmondson. Two volumes. 1780

Elvin.
A Dictionary of Heraldry. Charles Norton
Elvin, M.A. 1889

Emerson.
*Penultimate Notes on the Emersons alias
Embersons of Ipswich, Massachusetts Bay
Colony, 1638, and of Bishops Stortford,
Co.Herts., England, 1578.* P.H. Emerson,
B.A., M.B. 1925

Essex Visit. 1634.
*The Visitations of Essex 1552, 1558, 1570,
1612 and 1634, etc.* Edited by Walter C.
Metcalfe, F.S.A. Harleian Society. Two
volumes. 1878 and 1879

Ewen.
*The Families of Ewen of East Anglia and
the Fenland.* C. L'Estrange Ewen. 1928

Fairbairn.
*Fairbairn's Book of Crests of the Families
of Great Britain and Ireland.* Fourth
edition, two volumes. 1905

MS Fairfax [Corder MS 28]
Catalogue of Arms of Many Authors.
Compiled by Dr. Nathaniel Fairfax,
1637–1690; Perpetual curate of Willisham
until ejected in 1662, after which he
practised as a physician in Woodbridge,
where he is buried. A full description of
this MS and a critical analysis of its
contents by Leslie Dow, F.S.A. under the
title *A Suffolk Heraldic Manuscript* is in
Proc.S.I.A. XXV. 288–96. See
Topographers of Suffolk.

Farrer (Seals).
Rev. Edmund Farrer, F.S.A., 1848–1935.
Held livings in Norfolk and Suffolk,
1878–1914. Compiled extensive collections
relating to Seals, Parish histories, Heraldry,
etc., now in Record Offices of Bury and
Ipswich. Author of *Church Heraldry in
Norfolk* 1885–93; *Norfolk Brasses* 1890;
Suffolk Brasses 1903. See *Proc.S.I.A. XXI.
I.* and *XXII. 228*; *Topographers of Suffolk.*

Fauconberge.
The Fauconberge Memorial. S. Wilton Rix.
1849

Fiske.
The Fiske Family Papers. Henry Ffiske.
1902

Foster.
*Some Feudal Coats of Arms, from Heraldic
Rolls 1298–1418.* Edited by Joseph Foster,
Hon. M.A. 1902

Frag. Gen.
Fragmenta Genealogica. Edited by
Frederick Arthur Crisp. Thirteen volumes.
1889–1909

Gage (Hengrave).
*The History and Antiquities of Hengrave, in
Suffolk.* John Gage, F.S.A. 1822

Gage (Thingoe).
*The History and Antiquities of Suffolk,
Thingoe Hundred.* John Gage, F.R.S.,
Dir.S.A. 1838

Gawdy.
The Gawdys of Norfolk and Suffolk. Percy
Millican, F.S.A. 1939

Gee.
Gee of Freshford and London. Henry Gee,
D.D., F.S.A. 1916

Gent's Mag.
*The Gentleman's Magazine Library, English
Topography, Part XI. (Staffordshire,
Suffolk).* Edited by F.A. Milne, M.A. 1899

Gilbert.
*The Family and Arms of Gilbert of
Colchester.* Silvanus P. Thompson, F.R.S.
*Transactions of Essex Arch.Soc. IX.
197–211*; Paper read at Meeting 1903

Gillingwater.
*An Historical Account of the ancient town
of Lowestoft, in the County of Suffolk.. and
a general account of the Island of
Lothingland.* Edmund Gillingwater,
c.1735–1813. Stationer and bookseller of
Harleston; published *Lowestoft* in 1790 and
History of Bury St. Edmunds in 1804.
Biography in *E.A.N. & Q. IV. 253–5.* See
Topographers of Suffolk.

Gipps.
Sir Richard Gipps of Gt. Whelnetham,
1659–1708. Compiler of MS collections for
Suffolk, his *Antiquitates Suffolciences*
published as *The Ancient Families of
Suffolk* in *Proc.S.I.A. VIII. 121–214.* See
Topographers of Suffolk.

Gloucs. Visit.
The Visitation of the County of Gloucester 1623, with Pedigrees from the Herald's Visitations of 1569 and 1582–3. Edited by Sir John Maclean, F.S.A. and W.C. Heane, M.R.C.S. Eng. Harleian Society. 1885

Golding.
The Coinage of Suffolk; Regal Coins, Leaden Pieces, and Tokens. Charles Golding. 1868

MS Golty's Ordinary [Corder MS 23]
Richard Golty, c.1594–1678, of Framlingham, Rector of Dennington 1630–45 and 1660–death, was almost certainly the compiler of this fine Ordinary of Arms, containing 2,376 emblazoned coats, with a strong East Suffolk bias; of c.1655 with additions in other hands up to 1660. I named the MS when it came into my possession as the first recorded owner named on the fly-leaf is given as 'Mr. Gouter of Donnington' and also because the only crest noted is that of 'Goltie'

Grants & Certificates.
Grants and Certificates of Arms. Edited by Arthur J. Jewers. Reprinted from The Genealogist. 1913

Green.
The History, Topography and Antiquities of Framlingham and Saxsted. R. Green. 1834

Green Memoir.
A Memoir of Thomas Green, esquire, of Ipswich; with a critique on his writings, and an account of his Family and Connections. I.F. [James Ford] 1825. Rev. James Ford, 1779–1850, Perpetual curate of St. Lawrence, Ipswich for 22 years; compiler of extensive MS collections of Suffolk Topography, Genealogy, etc. See *Topographers of Suffolk.*

Harl. 772 [Corder MS 03; a photographic copy]
Harleian MS 772; B.L. naming *Arms of Suffolk Families.* A manuscript of 26 pages and index, the first 14 pages relating to Suffolk. The arms, many with quarterings, are in trick, with names, marriages and in many cases crests above. Date c.1565, with additions and corrections by Cooke, Clarenceux, dated 1578

Harl. 6163.
A Tudor Book of Arms. Being Harleian Manuscript No. 6163. Edited by Joseph Foster, Hon. M.A. Oxon. Published as a volume of The De Walden Library. 1904 Stated by Sir Anthony Wagner in *Catalogue of English Mediaeval Rolls of Arms* to be a copy of Peter Le Neve's Book and compiled c.1480–1500. Peter Le Neve, 1661–1729, Pres.S.A., F.R.S., Richmond Herald and Norroy King of Arms, see *Topographers of Suffolk.*

Haslewood.
The Monumental Inscriptions in the Parish of Saint Matthew, Ipswich, Suffolk. Rev. Francis Haslewood, A.K.C. 1884

Hatchments [Corder MS EXTRA 9]
Hatchments in Britain 2, Norfolk and Suffolk. General Editor of series and of Norfolk section, Peter Summers, F.S.A.; of Suffolk section, Joan Corder, F.S.A. 1976

Herald & Genealogist.
The Herald and Genealogist. Edited by John Gough Nichols, F.S.A. Eight volumes. 1863–1874

MS Heraldic Alphabet [Corder MS 36]
Unpaginated semi-alphabetical collection of Arms and Crests in various hands, many thumb-nail sketches and dates in 17th and 18th centuries. Spine label *Herald: Alpha: bet* and date 1750 at bottom

MS Heraldic Collections [Corder MS II]
Collection of Arms in trick, Crests and Pedigrees from different manuscripts; almost certainly partly the work of several Heralds. Some Arms crudely drawn and others very finely so, the latter on fos. 81–90. Approximate date c.1700

Her.Suff.Ch.
The Heraldry of Suffolk Churches. A series of forty nine typescript booklets, with index of Armigers and of Parishes, issued to members of The Suffolk Heraldry Society. A modern perambulation of the County and with reference to the work of the Rev. Edmund Farrer, F.S.A. [q.v.] Edited by Dr. David Reynolds, Ph.D. and Peter MacLachlan. 1978–88

Herts. Visit., 1634.
The Visitations of Hertfordshire, 1572 and 1634. Edited by Walter C. Metcalfe, F.S.A. Harleian Society. 1886

Heylyn.
A Help to English History. Peter Heylyn, D.D.; a later edition by Paul Wright, B.D. 1786

MS Humfry Pedigree Roll [Corder MS 91]
Untitled copy, on paper, of an earlier Roll by Charles Humfry of Rishangles, July 1644; additional material added by William Radcliffe, Rouge Croix, 28 December 1815. One hundred and six emblazoned Coats and nine Crests. Includes Pedigrees of Muskett, Frere, Baxter, Daundy, Fastolf, Poley and Wentworth

Ickworth Reg. (S.G.B.)
Ickworth Parish Registers, 1566–1890. Edited by S.H.A.H. (Rev. Sydenham Hervey). *Suffolk Green Books.* 1894

G.B.J.
Rev. Dr. George Bitton Jermyn, LL.D., 1789–1857. Curate of Hawkedon, Littleport and Swaffham Prior. Compiler of much manuscript material relating to Suffolk including the twenty six volumes of

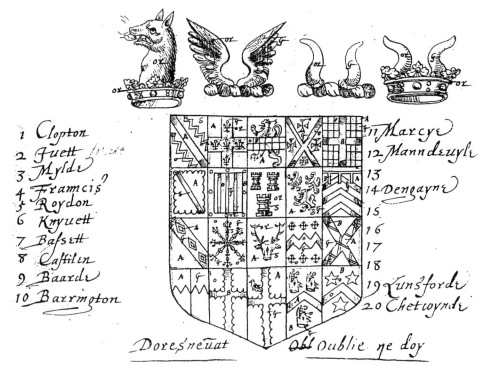

All these 20 Cottes are quartered by Clopton of Kentwell

1 Clopton
2 Juett
3 Mylde
4 Framcis
5 Roydon
6 Knyuett
7 Bassett
8 Castilen
9 Baardi
10 Barrington

11 Marcye
12 Manndeuyle
13
14 Dengayne
15
16
17
18
19 Lunsfordi
20 Chetwyndi

Doresneuat   Oublie ne doy

Lilly's Visitation [Corder MS 21] fo. 16v (top)

Heraldic Insignia of Suffolk Families,
jointly with his first wife Catherine; now in
Bury Record Office. See *Topographers of
Suffolk.*

Josselyn.
*Genealogical Memoranda relating to the
Family of Josselyn.* John H. Josselyn. 1903

Kent Visit., 1619.
The Visitation of Kent 1619–1621. Edited by
Robert Hovenden, F.S.A. Harleian Society.
1898

Kett.
The Ketts of Norfolk. L.M. Kett. 1921

Kirby's Map.
A New Map of the County of Suffolk.
Engraved by Joshua and William Kirby.
1766

MS Knight's Visitations [Corder MS 06]
Faintly, on spine and front cover *I.K.
Visitations of Cornwall Hamshire Norfolk
Lincolnsh Essex Cambridge Suffolk.*
Repeated on seventh fly-leaf, with signature
above 'E. Knyght Norroy'. Limp vellum,
drawn and tricked Arms and Crests with
names, on one hundred and twenty seven
folios, Suffolk mainly from the Visitation of
1577. Main index in Knight's hand,
additions at end stated to be 'in the hand
writing of Gregory King Esq.[r] Lancaster
Herrauld who dyed 1712'. Edmund Knight,
created Norroy King of Arms pat. 29 April
1590, creation 26 March 1592; died 1593,
buried at Twickenham 30 October. I.K.
possibly John Knight, a relative of Edmund
Knight and who knew Gregory King. Date
of MS c. 1580–90

Lees.
*The Chronicles of a Suffolk Parish Church,
Lowestoft St. Margaret.* Hugh D.W. Lees.
1948

Lev.
Zaccheus Leverland or Letherland,
schoolmaster of Framlingham. Compiler of
MSS referred to by Blois, Golty and Fairfax
[all q.v.] Biography see *Proc.S.I.A. XXV.
294*

MS Lilly's Visitation [Corder MS 21]
Visitation of Suffolk. Manuscript in Lilly's
hand, Arms and Crests with quarterings,
names and marriages. The coats two or three
to the page, superbly drawn and tricked;
many pages blank or with partition lines only
drawn. Henry Lilly, c. 1589–1638, appointed
Rose Rouge Pursuivant 1634 and Rouge
Dragon Pursuivant in January 1638; died the
following August. From internal evidence it
appears that the MS was compiled
c. 1627–post 1630

Linc. Visit. Notes (Gibbons).
*Notes on the Visitation of Lincolnshire
1634.* A. Gibbons, F.S.A. 1898

Loder.
The History of Framlingham, in the County

*of Suffolk; including brief notices of the
Masters and Fellows of Pembroke Hall, in
Cambridge.* Begun by the late Robert
Hawes, Gent. Edited and published by
Robert Loder. 1798

H.S. London.
Hugh Stanford London, M.A., F.S.A.,
1884–1959. Diplomat, Norfolk Herald
Extra-ordinary, served on the Croft Lyons
Committee of the Society of Antiquaries
from 1941 to his death; an authority on
medieval heraldry in particular, he
transcribed over a hundred rolls of arms
and wrote more than 10,000 cards for the
great *Dictionary of British Arms,* at
present being published by the Society of
Antiquaries

London Visitation 1568.
The Visitation of London in the year 1568.
Edited by J.J. Howard, LL.D., F.S.A. and
G.J. Armytage, F.S.A. Harleian Society.
1869. *Visitation of London 1568.* Edited by
H. Stanford London, F.S.A. and Sophia
Rawlins, F.S.A. Harleian Society. 1963

London Visitation 1663–4.
The Visitation of London, 1633–4. Edited
by J.J. Howard, LL.D., F.S.A. and Joseph
Lemuel Chester, LL.D. Harleian Society.
Two volumes. 1880 and 1883

London Visit. Peds., 1664.
London Visitation Pedigrees 1664. Edited
by J.B. Whitmore, F.S.A. and A.W. Hughes
Clarke, F.S.A. Harleian Society. 1940

MS Martin's Crests [Corder MS 35]
Crests in an- (A) alphabetical order.
Modern title *Crests & Quarterings. Tom
Martin.* Thomas Martin of Thetford, 1697–
1771. Attorney's clerk, but from 1723
antiquary, of Palgrave where he is buried.
F.S.A. 1720. Compiler of valuable Church
Notes, which are mainly in the Record
Offices at Bury and Norwich. See
Topographers of Suffolk.

Martin's Ch. Notes. Frag. Gen.
Fragmenta Genealogica. Vol. IX. Edited
by Frederick Arthur Crisp. 1903. On p.
116, at the end of the church notes, is
printed: From a MS [now SRO Bury
1183], entitled *Epitaphs chiefly in the
County of Suffolk, Collected by Thomas
Martin of Palgrave, Vol. II.* On the cover
is written: *Funeral Monuments. . .* On the
fly-leaf are the autographs of Thomas
Martin and John Fenn. See above

Martin's Thetford.
*The History of the Town of Thetford, in the
Counties of Norfolk and Suffolk. By the late
Mr. Thomas Martin, of Palgrave, Suffolk,
F.A.S.* Edited by R.G. [Richard Gough].
1779. See above

Middlesex Visit., 1663.
The Visitation of Middlesex . . . 1663.
Edited by Joseph Foster. 1887

Darnel	(2 a Lyon head erased Az. betw. 2 wings displ. Or
Dacres	(1 a Bull Gu gorged w a coronet & chained Or
	(2 a Dove betw. 2 Branches
Doleman	(1 a garb Or
Dixy	a leopard seiant pp gorged w a Coronet Or Motto Quod dixi dixi
Donne	a Wolfs head erased, motto Fiat voluntas Dei
Dalziel	a demy man armed compleat in all points brandishing his Sword above
	his head, over w on a Scroll I dare
Doyley	(1 a demy griffin Segt.
Dockwray	a demy Lion Ramp. Sab. w 2 taily erect de Or holding betw. his paws
	a plate charged w a pallet Sab
Dyer	out of a Coronet Or a goats head erased Gu
Dolies	out of a ducal Coron. pp a demy Eagle displ Arg, (in some a Boar Arg
	(motto Ie ne puy, in some Ie dofie Fortune)
Dryden	a demy Lion holding a Sphere Or
Dallison	an armed Man holding out a battle Axe all pp
Dent	a demy Lion Ramp.
Downing	an arm armed holding a broken spear Or pp
Dugdale	a demy Griffin 2 wings displ
Dabridgcourt	out of a Coronet a plume of feathers
Damant	a demy Lion Ramp guard Sab holding ye truncheon of a broken Spear or
Denham	a Lyon head erased Ermine
Deane	(4 a tortoise or
Dushe	or 3 Lyon heads erased Gu (R on a mount V a falcon volant Az armed or
Dawson	(first Az a hew w betw 3 annows or on a chief Arg 2 cornish choughs pp on a canton
	Gu a mullet or, (R a Cats head full faced Arg w a Rat in ye mouth Sab
Davy	2 Lyons paws erased holding a round buckler or
Dunston	a Lion past Or armed Gu
Denton	a Lion couchant Or Gu
Egerton	(1 3 ostrich feathers Arg & Sab. Motto Supra Spem Spero
	another) an Harts head erased Or
Estmond	out of a Coronet mural, a mans head armed w an helmet plumed pp
Elton	(1 a dexter arm armed ye hand holding a Sword pp
Estcourt	out of a Coronet mural Az a demy falcon displ Arg
Eyre	(1 a mans leg couped at ye thigh armed pp
Edwards	(1 out of a Coronet a Tyger past Or erined Sab
Evelyn	a demy mule Saliant erm
Eastoft	an Ostrich w a Key in its mouth
Evans	an arm clowthed ye hand holding a July flower — (3 Lys)
Elroys	3 arrows enwrapped about w a snake Vert
Elkinston	a hand holding a Sword pp

Martin's Crests [Corder MS 35] fo. 4v

Misc.Gen. et Her.
Miscellanea Genealogica et Heraldica, and The British Archivist. Edited by J.J. Howard, LL.D., F.S.A.; W. Bruce Bannerman, F.S.A. and A.W. Hughes Clarke, F.S.A. Thirty one volumes. 1868–1938

Miscellaneous Grants of Arms.
A Collection of Miscellaneous Grants, Crests, Confirmations, Augmentations and Exemplifications of Arms . . . Edited by Willoughby A. Littledale, M.A., F.S.A. Harleian Society. Two volumes. 1925 and 1926

Moule.
Heraldry of Fish. Thomas Moule. 1842

Muskett.
Suffolk Manorial Families. Edited by Joseph James Muskett and, after Muskett's death in 1910, by Frederic Johnson. Two volumes (Muskett), 1900 and 1908; three parts (Johnson), 1910–1914

Norfolk Visitation 1563 (Dashwood).
The Visitation of Norfolk in the year 1563. Edited by Rev. G.H. Dashwood, F.S.A. (1801–1869); W.E.G.L. Bulwer; G.A. Carthew, F.S.A.; Rev. W. Grigson, M.A.; Rev. Augustus Jessopp, D.D. *Norfolk Archaeology.* Two volumes. 1878 and 1895

Northants. Visitation, 1618–19.
The Visitations of Northamptonshire made in 1564 and 1618–19. Edited by Walter C. Metcalfe, F.S.A. 1887

Northumberland Visitations.
Pedigrees recorded at the Herald's Visitations of the County of Northumberland, 1615 and 1666. Edited by Joseph Foster. 1891

MS Ordinary of Arms [Corder MS 08]
Acquired as a collection of loose sheets, offset, damp-stained and charred at the edges; bound up and titled *Ordinary of Arms.* Compiled c. 1595–1600, this MS is particularly useful for the number of crests given; the whole emblazoned

Page.
A Supplement to the Suffolk Traveller; or Topographical and Genealogical Collections concerning that County. Augustine Page. 1844. See *Topographers of Suffolk.*

Partridge.
Suffolk Churchyard Inscriptions copied from the Darby transcription (made about 1825–34). Edited by Charles Partridge, M.A., F.S.A., F.R.G.S. Reprinted from *Proc.S.I.A., 1913, 1920 and 1923*

Pepys.
Genealogy of the Pepys Family, 1273–1887. Walter Courtenay Pepys. Second edition. 1951

Perlustration.
The Perlustration of Great Yarmouth, with Gorleston and Southtown. Charles John Palmer, F.S.A. Three volumes. 1872, 1874 and 1875

MS Philpot's Visitations [Corder MS 19]
Visitations of eight counties including Norfolk, Suffolk and Essex, in all probability the work of John Philpot, Rouge Dragon Pursuivant 1618–23, who signs on fo. 4 of the Berkshire Visitation. A total of some nine hundred coats and crests in trick, with additions in several hands. Modern blind-stamped morocco binding and title *Heraldic Collec-tions*

Portrait (of Henry Chitting).
Henry Chitting of Bury St. Edmunds and Islington, 1580–1638; son of Thomas Chitting, of Wortham. Chester Herald 1618–38. Compiler of MS Collections for Norfolk and Suffolk; his *Suffolk Pedigrees and Notes* collected in twenty two Churches and eight houses edited by Dr. Diarmaid MacCulloch, M.A., F.S.A. in *Proc.S.I.A. XXXIV. 103–128 (1978).* See *Topographers of Suffolk.*

Proc.S.I.A.
Proceedings of the Bury and West Suffolk Archaeological Institute, later the Suffolk Institute of Archaeology and History. 1848–ongoing

Ray.
Pedigree of Ray of Denston, Wickhambrook, and other places in Suffolk; together with Oakes, Rawlinson, Heigham, Hasted, etc., all of the said County. Gery Milner-Gibson-Cullum, F.S.A. 1903

Reyce.
Robert Ryece or Reyce of Preston, 1555–1638. *Suffolk in the XVIIth. Century. The Breviary of Suffolk by Robert Reyce, 1618.* Edited by Lord Francis Hervey. 1902. See *Topographers of Suffolk.*

Rushbrook Regs. (S.G.B.)
Rushbrook Parish Registers, 1567–1850. Edited by S.H.A.H. (Rev. Sydenham Hervey). *Suffolk Green Books.* 1903

MS Rylands [Corder MS 62]
Collection of *Suffolk Arms, Pedigrees from Candler, Letteringham Church notes, Sheriffs of Norfolk from 1837–1885, etc.* J. Paul Rylands, F.S.A. c. 1885

Lt. Saxham Regs. (S.G.B.)
Lt. Saxham Parish Registers, 1559–1850. Edited by S.H.A.H. (Rev. Sydenham Hervey). *Suffolk Green Books.* 1901

Scott-Giles.
Civic Heraldry of England and Wales. C. Wilfrid Scott-Giles, O.B.E., M.A. 1953

Sharpe.
The Ancient and Modern Nobility in Suffolk. Compiled by William Sharpe, herald painter, c. 1800. Transcript by Horace Whayman, F.R.S.A. (Ireland), printed in *E.A.N. & Q. VII.* many entries; Index in VI. 251–5

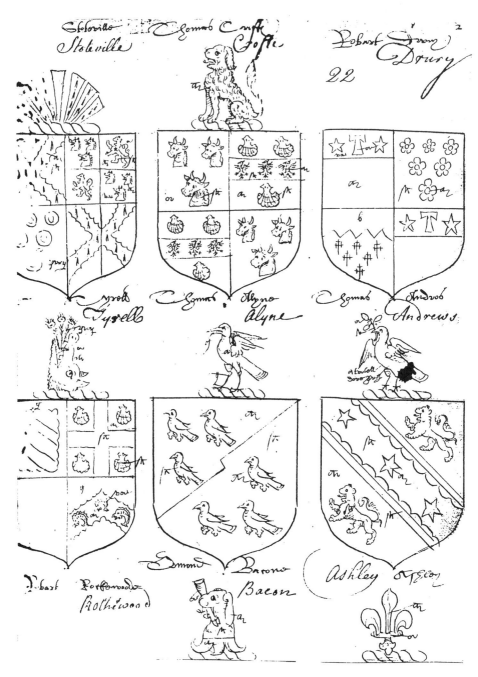

Philpot's Visitation [Corder MS 19] fo. 22 (upper part)

Shotley Regs. (S.G.B.)
Shotley Registers, 1571–1850 and *Shotley Parish Records.* Edited by S.H.A.H. (Rev. Sydenham Hervey). *Suffolk Green Books.* Two volumes. 1911–12

Shropshire Visit. 1623.
The Visitation of Shropshire . . . 1623. Edited by George Grazebrook, F.S.A. and John Paul Rylands, F.S.A. Harleian Society. Two volumes. 1889

Soc. of Ant. MS 378.
Society of Antiquaries MS 378. *Ordinary of Arms. Grants of Arms.* 18th Century MS Ordinary of Arms in trick and Transcripts of Grants dated 1521–1718. The Grants predominantly East Anglian

Somerset Visit. 1623.
The Visitation of the County of Somerset . . . 1623. Edited by Frederic Thomas Colby, D.D., F.S.A. Harleian Society. 1876

Sperling.
A Short History of the Borough of Sudbury in the County of Suffolk. C.F.D. Sperling, M.A. 1896

Stall Plates.
The Stall Plates of the Knights of the Order of the Garter 1348–1485. W.H. St. John Hope, M.A. 1901

Stutton.
Some Account of the Parish of Stutton, Suffolk. Frederick Arthur Crisp. 1881

Suckling.
The History and Antiquities of the County of Suffolk; with Genealogical and Architectural Notices of its several Towns and Villages. Rev. Alfred Suckling, LL. B. Two volumes. 1846 and 1848

Suff. Armorial Families.
Suffolk Armorial Families. MS collection of copies of Grants and Funeral Certificates, emblazoned. SRO Ipswich qS929.2

Suff. Green Books.
Suffolk Green Books. Edited by Rev. Sydenham Hervey (S.H.A.H.). See under Ickworth; Rushbrook; Saxham, Lt.; Shotley; West Stow; Whelnetham, Gt. & Lt.; Wordwell

Suff. Heraldic Brasses.
Suffolk Heraldic Brasses. T.M. Felgate. 1978

Surrey Visit. 1530.
The Visitations of the County of Surrey . . . 1530, 1572 and 1623. Edited by W. Bruce Bannerman, F.S.A. Scot. Harleian Society. 1899

Surrey Visit. 1662.
A Visitation of the County of Surrey, 1662–1668. Edited by Sir George J. Armytage, Bart., F.S.A. Harleian Society. 1910

Sussex Gen.
County Genealogies. Pedigrees of the

Families in the County of Sussex. William Berry [q.v.] 1830

Sussex Visits., 1530 & 1633–4.
The Visitations of the County of Sussex . . . 1530 and 1633–4. Edited by W. Bruce Bannerman, F.S.A. Harleian Society. 1905

Tanner.
Thomas Tanner, 1674–1735. Chancellor of Norwich Diocese 1701; Bishop of St. Asaph 1732; F.S.A. 1718. His MS Collections in the Bodleian Library include important material for East Anglia. See *Topographers of Suffolk.*

MS ex-Taylor Coll. [Corder MS 49]
Untitled. Arms in trick, many with Crests, collected from various MSS, including copies made by Glover of 'an Ancient Roll' and Taylor's own copy of a copy of Glover's Ordinary. Some printed Arms and bookplates pasted in. Inside the back cover is pasted a note in the hand and with the signature of William Flower, Norroy, see *Alphabet of Crests,* to his son-in-law, Robert Glover, Somerset Herald. The collection was made by Jno. B. Taylor, F.S.A. in about 1820

Taylor, Index. Mon.
Index Monasticus; the Abbeys, Monasteries, Alien Priories, Friaries etc . . . in the Diocese of Norwich. Richard Taylor. 1821

Thetford.
The History of the Town of Thetford, in the Counties of Norfolk and Suffolk. Thomas Martin, F.A.S., died 1771. This work published by Richard Gough, 1779. Gough and Martin see *Topographers of Suffolk.*

Thorington.
The Registers of the Parish of Thorington . . . and notices of the Bence Family. Rev. Thomas S. Hill, B.C.L., M.A. 1884

Timperley.
Timperley of Hintlesham, a study of a Suffolk Family. Sir Gerald H. Ryan, Bart. and Lilian J. Redstone. 1931

Topographers of Suffolk.
The Topographers of Suffolk, 1561–1935. Brief Biographies and Specimens of the Hands of Selected Suffolk Antiquaries. First edition 1976, fifth edition 1988. Edited by John Blatchly

Torlesse.
Some Account of Stoke by Nayland, Suffolk. Charles Martin Torlesse. 1877

Turner.
The Turner Family, of Mulbarton and Great Yarmouth, in Norfolk: 1547–1894. Harward Turner. 1895

Tyl.
William Tyllotson or Tillotson, died 1615. Curate at Capel 1590–8; Falkenham 1597; 'clericus' at St. Matthew's Ipswich 1601. Compiler of MS collections of Arms, Pedigrees and Church Notes, the latter now

Fitz-Williams   Sackford

Brook of Cheshire   Whichcot of Lincoln

aBrock

46

in the Library of the Society of Antiquaries, MS 4; compiled c. 1594, a transcript of extracts was made by Thomas William King, 1802–72; F.S.A., Rouge Dragon Pursuivant 1833, York Herald 1848 [Corder MS 07]. In 1610 he made a copy of Robert Cook's book called the 'Baron book', which he signed 'W^{mus} Tyllotson Scriptor' [Corder MS 10]. See *E.A.N. & Q. 1.7 & 17* and *IX. 57–8; Proc.S.I.A. VI. 225; XIX. 78–9* and *XXV. 295.* See also *Topographers of Suffolk.*

Tymms.
An Architectural and Historical Account of the Church of St. Mary, Bury St. Edmunds. Samuel Tymms, F.S.A. 1854

Visitation 1561 (MS G. 7) [Corder MS 01a, a photographic copy]
The Visitacon off Suffolke made by Wyllyam heruye . . . begon the XXiith daye of July an^o 1561 and the thred yere of Queene Elizabeth. Hervy's official Office Copy, with Arms and Crests in trick

Visitation 1561 (Iveagh Copy) [Corder MS 01b, a photographic copy]
The true visitacion [the rest torn away]. Copy of College of Arms MS G. 7 with Arms and Crests in trick. Formerly Phillipps MS 3803, later in the Iveagh Collection at Elveden Hall, it is now SR01 HD 1538/54. Both edited, from photocopies supplied by permission of the Chapter of the College of Arms, by Joan Corder, F.S.A. Harleian Society. Two volumes (New series. II. & III.) 1981 and 1984. See *Topographers of Suffolk.*

Visitation 1561 (ed. Howard).
The Visitation of Suffolke, 1561. Edited, with much additional material, by Joseph Jackson Howard, LL.D., F.S.A. Two volumes. 1866 and 1876

Visitation 1561 (ed. Metcalfe).
The Visitations of Suffolk made by Hervey, Clarenceux, 1561, Cooke, Clarenceux, 1577, and Raven, Richmond Herald, 1612 . . . with Additional Suffolk Pedigrees. Edited by Walter C. Metcalfe, F.S.A. 1882

Visitation 1664–8.
A Visitation of the County of Suffolk, begun Anno Dni. 1664 and finished . . . 1668, by Sir Edward Bysshe, K^t, Clarenceux King of Arms. Edited by W. Harry Rylands, F.S.A. 1910

Wagner.
Historic Heraldry of Britain. Anthony R. Wagner, F.S.A., Portcullis Pursuivant. 1939

Wall's Book.
Thomas Wall's Book of Crests. Written

1530. Edited by Oswald Barron, F.S.A. Printed in *The Ancestor, II. 178–90* and *12. 63–98.* 1904 and 1905. Copy, much enlarged, see *MS Alphabet of Crests.* [Corder MS 05]

Warner.
Sir Thomas Warner, Pioneer of the West Indies. Aucher Warner. 1933

Warren's Map.
Survey of the Borough of St. Edmund's Bury, in the County of Suffolk. Engraved by Thomas Warren. 1747

Warwick. Visit. 1619.
The Visitation of the County of Warwick in the Year 1619. Edited by John Fetherston, F.S.A. Harleian Society. 1877

Washbourne.
The Book of Family Crests. Henry Washbourne. Sixth edition. Two volumes. 1851

West Stow Reg.
West Stow Parish Register, 1558–1850. Edited by S.H.A.H. (Rev. Sydenham Hervey). *Suffolk Green Books.* 1903

Gt. Whelnetham.
Lt. Whelnetham.
Great Whelnetham Parish Registers, 1561–1850; Little Whelnetham Parish Registers, 1557–1850. Edited, in one volume, by S.H.A.H. (Rev. Sydenham Hervey). *Suffolk Green Books.* 1910

Wightman.
Records of the Wightman Family. Bryan I'anson. 1917

Withypoll.
The Family of Withypoll. With special reference to their Manor of Christchurch, Ipswich. G.C. Moore-Smith, Litt.D., F.B.A. Published by *Walthamstow Antiq. Soc., No. 34.* 1936

Worcs. Visitation, 1569.
The Visitation of the County of Worcester made in the year 1569. Edited by W.P.W. Phillimore, M.A., B.C.L. Harleian Society. 1888

Worcs. Visitation, 1634.
The Visitation of Worcestershire 1634. Edited by A.T. Butler, M.C., F.S.A., Windsor Herald. Harleian Society. 1938

Wordwell Reg.
Wordwell Parish Register, 1580–1850. Edited by S.H.A.H. (Rev. Sydenham Hervey). *Suffolk Green Books. 1903*

Wyncoll.
The Wyncolls of Suffolk and Essex. Col. C.E. Wyncoll. 1912

INDEX OF NAMES